D0176766

ENVIRONMENTAL ECONOMICS IN THEORY AND PRACTICE

Nick Hanley
University of Stirling

Jason F. Shogren
University of Wyoming

and

Ben White
University of Newcastle upon Tyne

New York   Oxford
OXFORD UNIVERSITY PRESS
1997

Oxford University Press

Oxford   New York
Athens   Auckland   Bangkok   Bogota   Bomba
Buenos Aires   Calcutta   Cape Town   Dar es Salaam
Delhi   Florence   Hong Kong   Istanbul   Karachi
Kuala Lumpur   Madras   Madrid   Melbourne
Mexico City   Nairobi   Paris   Singapore
Tapei   Tokyo   Toronto

and associated companies in
Berlin   Ibadan

Published by Oxford University Press, Inc.,
198 Madison Avenue, New York, New York 10016

Oxford is a registered trademark of Oxford University Press

Library of Congress Cataloging-in-Publication Data
Hanley, Nick.
Environmental economics : in theory and practice / Nick Hanley.
Jason F. Shogren, Ben White.
p.   cm.
Includes bibliographical references and index.
ISBN 0–19–521254–1 (alk. paper). — ISBN 0–19–521255–X (pbk. :
alk. paper)
1. Environmental economics.   I. Shogren, Jason F.   II. White, Ben
(Benedict)   III. Title.
HC79.E5H32923   1997
333.7—dc20   96–8717
                                                                    CIP

Printed in Great Britain

Contents

List of Figures   ix

List of Tables   xii

Introduction   xiii

Acknowledgements   xv

1 The Economy and the Environment:
   Two Parts of a Whole   1
1.1   Introduction   1
1.2   Interlinkages between the economy and the environment   2
1.3   The first two laws of thermodynamics   11
1.4   Conclusions   13
Technical note: game theory   14

2 Market Failure   22
2.1   Introduction   22
2.2   Incomplete markets   24
2.3   Externalities   29
2.4   Non-exclusion and the commons   37
2.5   Non-rivalry and public goods   42
2.6   Non-convexities   46
2.7   Asymmetric information   49
2.8   Concluding comments   56

3 Economic Incentives for Environmental Protection:
   An Overview   58
3.1   Introduction   58
3.2   Price rationing: charges and subsidies   61
3.3   Liability rules: non-compliance fees, bonds, and
            deposit refunds   79
3.4   Quantity rationing: marketable permits   87
3.5   Evaluative criteria   91
3.6   Practical conditions for use of economic incentives   95
3.7   Concluding remarks   97
Technical note: mathematical programming   98

4   Pollution Taxes for the Efficient Control of Pollution   106
4.1   Introduction   106
4.2   Efficiency properties of a tax on emissions   107
4.3   Problems with pollution taxes   115
4.4   Conclusions   128

5   Tradeable Pollution Permits   130
5.1   Introduction   130
5.2   The basic theory of tradeable pollution permits   130
5.3   Research issues in tradeable permit markets   139
5.4   Conclusions   155

6   Transboundary Pollution Problems   159
6.1   Introduction   159
6.2   Transboundary pollution as a problem of international
       externalities   163
6.3   Transboundary pollution and game theory   166
6.4   Conclusions   173

**7   An Introduction to the Economics of Natural
      Resource Exploitation   177**
7.1   Introduction   177
7.2   Elementary capital theory   179
7.3   The maximum principle of optimal control theory   182
7.4   The application of the maximum principle to specific
       fishery management problems   189
7.5   The discrete-time maximum principle and dynamic
       programming   202
7.6   Wiener processes, Itô's processes and stochastic calculus   206
7.7   Conclusions   214

8   Natural Resources: Types, Classification and Scarcity   216
8.1   Natural resource types and classification   216
8.2   Measuring resource scarcity   217
8.3   Conclusions   225

**9   An Economic Analysis of Non–renewable
      Natural Resources   227**
9.1   Introduction   227
9.2   Market structure and the exploitation of
       non-renewable resources   228

9.3   Production technology and extraction costs   248
9.4   Applying the theory   258
9.5   Government policy towards non-renewable
        resource taxation   264
9.6   Uncertainty and the rate of resource extraction   266
9.7   Summary   270

10 Renewable Resource Economics   **274**
10.1   Introduction   274
10.2   Population growth models   276
10.3   Static models of fishery exploitation in continuous time 281
10.4   Static economic models of fisheries   286
10.5   Comparative dynamic models of fishing   288
10.6   Fisheries policy   298
10.7   Applying the theory and the discrete-time model   303
10.8   Extending the theoretical model   308
10.9   Strategic behaviour in fishery management   313
10.10 Fishing under uncertainty   325
10.11 Summary   332

11 The Economics of Forestry Exploitation   **335**
11.1   Introduction   335
11.2   The principles of commercial forestry economics   336
11.3   Multi-use forestry and the socially optimal forest rotation 340
11.4   Forestry land use and agriculture   343
11.5   Forest policies   350
11.6   The optimal forest rotation under uncertainty   352
11.7   Summary   354

12 The Theory of Non-market Valuation   **356**
12.1   Introduction   356
12.2   Measures of economic value   357
12.3   Valuing risk and ex ante measures of value   368
12.4   Issues in non-market valuation   372
12.5   Concluding comments   381

**13 Methods for Valuing Environmental Costs
        and Benefits**   **383**
13.1   Introduction   383
13.2   Direct methods of valuation   384
13.3   Indirect methods of valuation   404
13.4   Summary   418

14   The Economics of Sustainable Development   425
14.1   Introduction   425
14.2   Possible sustainability rules   426
14.3   Indicators of sustainability   433
14.4   The Common–Perrings model of sustainable development   443

Index   451

List of Figures

1.1	Economy–environment interactions	3
1.2	Possible damage functions	4
1.3	Energy use to GDP ratios in four countries	9
T.1	Nash equilibrium	19
T.2	Stackleberg equilibrium	20
2.1	Socially optimal level of pollution	26
2.2	Alternative socially optimal levels of pollution	27
2.3	Socially and privately optimal level of pollution	30
2.4	Co-operative and non-co-operative self-protection	35
2.5	Total cost of co-operative and non-co-operative self-protection	36
2.6	Open access and the prisoners' dilemma	41
2.7	Co-ordination game	42
2.8	Pure public goods	46
2.9	Single-peaked net benefit curve	47
2.10	Non-convex marginal costs	47
2.11	Non-convexity and the optimal level of pollution	48
2.12	Multi-peaked net benefit curve	49
2.13	Environmental shirking	50
2.14	Moral hazard	52
2.15	Feasible insurance contracts given moral hazard	53
2.16	Quantity rationing of insurance	54
2.17	Adverse selection	55
3.1	Socially optimal level of pollution control	59
3.2	Privately and socially optimal levels of output	63
3.3	Charges given uncertainty	65
3.4	Optimal levels of output given ambient charge	70
3.5	Short and long run impacts of a pollution tax	74
3.6	Short and long run impacts of a pollution subsidy	75
3.7	Asymmetric information and an environmental subsidy	77
3.8	Subsidy paid ignoring information rents	78
3.9	Subsidy paid accounting for information rents	79
3.10	Quantity rationing under uncertainty	89
3.11	Mixed incentive system	91
4.1	Marginal abatement costs for a firm	109
4.2	An efficient tax on emissions	112
4.3	Savings under innovation with a pollution tax	119

ix

4.4	Savings under innovation, diffusion and regulatory response	120
4.5	Financial burden of a pollution tax	124
4.6	A possible time path for a stock pollutant	125
5.1	Firm's optimal response to a permit scheme	131
5.2	Supply and demand for permits	132
5.3	Permit revenues and expenditures	133
5.4	Innovation in permit markets	152
6.1	Non-co-operative and full co-operative outcomes	167
7.1	Logistic growth curve	181
7.2	A phase-plane diagram	193
7.3	Trajectory types	197
7.4	Phase-plane diagram showing stability analysis	198
7.5	Comparative dynamics and the steady-state solution	201
7.6	A dynamic programming problem	205
7.7	Fishery investment under uncertainty	213
8.1	Problems of defining 'reserves'	218
8.2	The mineralogical threshold	219
9.1	Comparative dynamics for costless extraction under competition and monopoly	233
9.2	Monopoly rent, current value	234
9.3	Monopoly rent, present value	235
9.4	Price path for the Nash–Cournot solution to the cartel problem	239
9.5	Quantity path for the Nash–Cournot solution to the cartel problem	240
9.6	Von Stackelberg equilibrium	242
9.7	Extraction costs	249
9.8	Time paths for the shadow price of a resource	257
10.1	The logistic growth curve	277
10.2	Growth curve showing depensation	278
10.3	A simple population cycle	279
10.4	Ricker curves	280
10.5	The effect of harvesting on population change	281
10.6	Equilibrium between fishing effort and the stock	283
10.7	Equilibrium between fishing effort and the catch	283
10.8	Equilibrium between fishing effort and the stock with critical depensation	283
10.9	Equilibrium between fishing effort and the catch with critical depensation	284
10.10	Static fishing equilibria	287
10.11	Equilibrium stock and the number of firms	294
10.12	Equilibrium shadow price against the number of firms	294

10.13   Phase-plane representation of the sole-ownership fishery
           with an endogenous price   297
10.14   Bioeconomic equilibrium in the harp seal population   306
10.15   Optimal harvest and investment   312
10.16   Pay-off sets   315
10.17   Pay-off possibility sets   316
10.18   Nash bargaining solution   317
10.19   Steady-state equilibria in a fish war   324
10.20   Stochastic stock recruitment   331
11.1   Tree growth function   336
11.2   Comparative statics for the Faustmann rotation   339
11.3   Grazing benefit function   342
11.4   Optimal Hartman rotation   343
11.5   The effect of a yield tax on the Faustmann rotation   351
12.1   Preferences, utility and consumer surplus   358
12.2   WTP for improved environmental services   361
12.3   WTP and WTA given perfect and imperfect
           substitutability   363
12.4   WTP and WTA measures of value, given an environment
           hazard   366
12.5   Value formation and preference learning   377
13.1   Hedonic price measures of value   412
14.1   Sustainability versus efficiency   433

List of Tables

4.1	Water quality levels and resource costs	110
4.2	Control costs for air pollution	118
4.3	Tax rates on greenhouse gases	123
4.4	Natural parameters for greenhouse gases	123
5.1	Abatement costs and emission reductions under different offset rules	141
5.2	Cost savings under sequential trading	149
7.1	Conditions for stability in systems of differential equations	196
8.1	World reserves, reserve bases and crustal abundances of selected minerals	220
9.1	Studies of non-renewable resource scarcity	255
9.2	Estimates for the output equation	262
10.1	The bionomic optimum	307
10.2	Pay-off matrix	314
13.1	Effects of more information on WTP to preserve heaths	397
13.2	Description of variables for analysis	410
13.3	Determinants of real consumer surplus per unit of use	411
13.4	Demand curve for broadleaved woods	415

Introduction

This book is aimed at final-year undergraduates in environmental and resource economics, graduate students and professionals. It provides a guide to the most important areas of natural resource and environmental economics: the economics of non-renewable and renewable resource extraction, the economics of pollution control, the application of cost–benefit analysis to the environment and the economics of sustainable development. However we cannot claim that all interesting areas of the subject are represented here. For example, the reader will find very little on distributional issues, on trade and the environment, or recycling and solid waste management. Reasons for omissions include the size and cost of the resultant volume. We have, instead, concentrated on those parts of theory which we find most interesting and have tried to show how this theory can be applied to real-world problems. Thus, for example, Chapter 12 considers the theory of environmental valuation, while Chapter 13 explains how valuation is actually done.

Throughout the book, results are presented in words, in figures and more formally using mathematical models. To aid this exposition, brief 'technical notes' inform readers about the Kuhn–Tucker conditions, game theory and linear programming. The book progresses through the laws of thermodynamics to an analysis of market failure. The economics of pollution control are then considered. Natural resources are the subject of the next section, and the book closes with an examination of environmental cost–benefit analysis and sustainable development.

All of the authors have been involved in teaching courses in environmental and natural resource economics to both undergraduates and graduates in Britain and North America, so we hope that some benefit has been gained from this experience which will in turn aid readers of this book. We have also sought to include material from areas of our own research, emphasising the beneficial links between teaching and research.

This book started life in 1991, and so has been a long time in the making. We would therefore first like to thank Stephen Rutt of the Macmillan Press for his patience and fortitude. Vic Adamowicz deserves a very big thank-you for reading over many draft chapters and providing comments: thanks, Vic. Nick Hanley also would like to thank many people for helpful comments on draft chapters, and for trying to explain the subject to him. In no particular order, these people include Mick Common, Charles Perrings, Jim Shortle, John Hartwick, David Pearce, Kerry Turner, Jack Pezzey,

Alistair Munro, John Haynes and Clive Spash. Thanks also to Paul Gill for the box sections in Chapter 14, David Parsisson for drawing Nick's diagrams on his Apple and Jenny Milne for compiling the contents pages. Finally, thanks to Fanny Missfeldt for co-authoring Chapter 6 with me. Jay Shogren would like to thank Tom Crocker, Bruce Forster, Todd Sandler and Joe Kenkuliet. Ben White would like to thank Tim Masters for reading parts of his section and Caroline Saunders for useful discussions on non-renewable resources, Caroline Faddy for secretarial assistance and his wife Jane for encouragement and support.

This book is dedicated to our families: Kate, Rose and Charlie; Deb, Riley and Maija; and Jane, Catherine and Steven.

Acknowledgements

The authors and publishers wish to thank the following for permission to use copyright material:

Academic Press, Inc. for Figure 4.4 from Scott Milliman and Raymond Prince (1989) 'Firm incentives to promote technical change in pollution control', *Journal of Environmental Economics and Management*, 17, pp. 245–65; and Figure 3.4 adapted from R. Cabe and J. Herriges (1992) 'The regulation of non-point sources of pollution under imperfect and asymmetric information', *Journal of Environmental Economics and Management*, 22, 134–46;

American Agricultural Economic Association for Tables 13.2 and 13.3 from V.K. Smith and W. Kauru (1990) 'Signals or noise? Explaining the variation in recreation benefit estimates', *American Journal of Agricultural Economics*, May, 419–33;

American Scientist for Figure 8.2 from B. Skinner (1976) 'A second iron-age?', *American Scientist*, 64, 258–269;

Kluwer Academic Publishers for Tables 4.3 and 4.4 from P. Michaelis (1992) 'Global warming: efficient policies in the case of multiple pollutants', *Environmental and Resource Economics*, 2, 61–78.

Every effort has been made to trace all the copyright-holders, but if any have been inadvertently overlooked the publishers will be pleased to make the necessary arrangement at the first opportunity.

■ *Chapter 1* ■

The Economy and the Environment: Two Parts of a Whole

1.1 Introduction
1.2 Interlinkages between the economy and the environment

1.3 The first two laws of thermodynamics
1.4 Conclusions
Technical note: game theory

■ *1.1* Introduction

The purpose of this chapter is to describe the ways in which the economy and the natural environment are interlinked. To an extent, these interlinkages are all-embracing; every economic action can have some effect on the environment, and every environmental change can have an impact on the economy. By 'the economy', we refer to the population of economic agents, the institutions they form (which include firms and governments) and the interlinkages between agents and institutions, such as markets. By 'environment', we mean the biosphere, the 'thin skin on the earth's surface on which life exists', to quote from Nisbet (1991), the atmosphere, the geosphere (that part of the earth lying below the biosphere) and all flora and fauna. Our definition of the environment thus includes life forms, energy and material resources (see Chapter 8), the stratosphere (high atmosphere) and troposphere (low atmosphere). These constituent parts of the environment interact with each other: an example is the effect of changes in biosphere composition on the composition of the atmosphere. (The effect of biological entities on their physical surroundings forms the basis of the Gaia hypothesis: see Lovelock, 1987.) Such interactions will be important throughout this book. Even more important from our perspective are the effects of human activity on the environment, and the consequences of these affects on human well-being.

As an example, consider the generation of electricity. In extracting fossil fuels to use as an energy source, we deplete the stock of such fuels in the geosphere. In burning these fuels to release their energy, we also release carbon dioxide (CO_2) and sulphur dioxide (SO_2), both of which may

1

produce undesirable environmental impacts that reduce human (and therefore economic) well-being. These particular effects are considered in detail in Chapter 6. As another example, agricultural support policies may have environmentally damaging effects which in turn rebound on human welfare. Thus, subsidizing cereal production in the European Community (EC) led to higher prices for such cereals, which are important inputs to the livestock sector. Two effects amongst many may be remarked on; higher output prices encouraged farming practices which contributed to soil erosion in both the USA and UK (Heimlich, 1991), while livestock farmers' demand for cheaper substitutes for feed resulted in the loss of rainforest in Thailand, as producers sought to increase cassava production for export to EC livestock farmers.

1.2 Interlinkages between the economy and the environment

The interlinkages between the economy and the environment are summarized in Figure 1.1. Here we simplify the economy into two sectors; production and consumption. Exchanges of goods, services and factors of production take place between these two sectors. The environment is shown here in two ways: as the three interlinked circles E_1, E_2 and E_3, and the all-encompassing boundary labelled E_4. The production sector extracts energy resources (such as oil) and material resources (such as iron ore) from the environment. These are transformed into outputs; some useful (goods and services supplied to consumers) and some which are waste products, such as SO_2. There is some recycling of resources within the production sector, shown by the loop R_1, and within the consumption sector, as shown by the loop R_2.

The environment's first role, then, is as a *supplier of resources*. Its second is as a *sink*, or receptor, for waste products. These wastes may result directly from production, as already mentioned, or from consumption: when an individual puts out their garbage, or when they drive to work, they are contributing to this form of waste. In some cases, wastes are biologically and/or chemically processed by the environment. For example, organic emissions to an estuary from a distillery are broken down by natural processes – the action of micro-organisms – into their chemical component parts. Whether this results in a harmful affect on the estuary depends on a number of factors, including the volume of waste relative to the volume of receiving water, the temperature of the water and its rate of replacement. That is to say the estuary has a limited *assimilative* capacity for the waste. As the level of organic input increases, the process of breaking it down will use up more and more of the oxygen dissolved in water, reducing the ability of

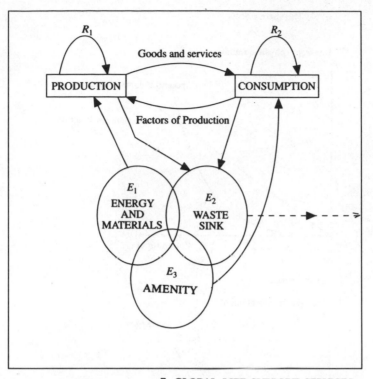

E_4 GLOBAL LIFE-SUPPORT SERVICES

Figure 1.1   *Economy–enviroment interactions*

the estuary to support fish. The notion of assimilative capacity has been criticised (see, for example, Nisbet, 1991), implying as it does that up to a fixed point emissions can occur with no deleterious impact. This is not strictly true in most cases, since what we have is a gradually increasing impact – although the rate of increase may exhibit abrupt changes due to 'threshold' effects. This is illustrated in Figure 1.2. However, the notion is useful in that it suggests that, up to a point, effects are not deemed important: only once the oxygen in the river drops below a critical level so that, for example, fish are no longer present, does the effect become 'significant' on some criteria.

For some inputs to the environment, there are no natural processes to transform them into harmless, or less harmful, substances. Such inputs, which are variously termed 'cumulative' and 'conservative' pollutants, include metals such as lead and cadmium, and man-made substances such as PCBs (polychlorinated biphenyls) and DDT (dichloro-diphenyl-trichloro-ethane). If, in our estuary example, PCBs are discharged into the water, then they will not be broken down by either chemical processes (oxidation) or through biological processes by micro-organisms (McLusky, 1989). Instead,

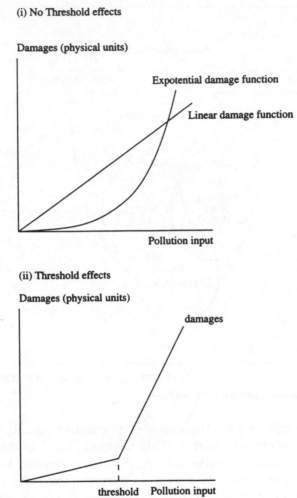

Figure 1.2 *Possible damage functions*

they will build up either in the mud at the bottom of the estuary, or in fish or invertebrates. This latter process is known as 'bioaccumulation'. For conservative pollutants a positive flow in a year F_t adds to the stock S_t^c. This is not true for degradable, assimilative wastes, where the stock in any time period S_t^a depends on current flows *less* that amount removed by biodegradation, or by chemical reactions in the case of gases such as methane.

For degradable pollutants, such as organic effluents from brewing or paper production, and methane, the stock in any time period t is given by:

$$S_t^a = F_t - A_t \tag{1.1}$$

where A is the amount assimilated in any period. For cumulative pollutants, the stock in any period t^* is:

$$S_{t^*}^c = \sum_{t_i}^{t=t^*} F_t \tag{1.2}$$

(where t_i is the historical date when emissions began) since assimilation is zero. For a given location, equation (1.2) may not accurately predict the stock of cumulative pollutants, since some transport of the pollutants is possible to another location, while sediments may build up over the stock pollutant and put it 'out of harm's reach': this has been the case with mercury discharges to the Forth Estuary.

With regard to equation (1.1), we should note that the amount assimilated in any period (A_t) may depend on the level of emissions in previous periods: emissions of either the pollutant whose stock is being modelled or another pollutant. As an example of the latter case, the hydroxyl radical in the atmosphere (OH) is responsible for breaking down methane, an important greenhouse gas. Methane (CH_4) is broken down in the atmosphere by the hydroxyl radical (OH) in the presence of nitrous oxides (NO) into water vapour, hydrogen and carbon monoxide. However, the amount of OH in the upper atmosphere is a function of the level of other pollutants, such as carbon monoxide (CO) and of hydroxyl production (which in turn depends partly on ozone levels in the lower atmosphere). The higher are CO levels, the lower, *ceteris paribus*, will be OH levels, and thus the less CH_4 will be broken down.

Box 1.1 *Uncertainty and the precautionary principle*

In many if not all cases of environmental management, there is some uncertainty over the effects of actions on the environment, and of the impact on humans of subsequent environmental changes. In some cases, the extent of this uncertainty is considerable. For example, while we know that carbon dioxide causes global warming, there is uncertainty as to the extent of warming caused by, say, a doubling of current CO_2 levels, and even more uncertainty about the physical effects this warming will have. Environmentalists will often argue that society should take action before such uncertainty is resolved, since the costs of not taking action may well be greater than the costs of preventative or anticipatory action taken now, especially when the absence of action today leads to irreversible undesirable environmental consequences (Taylor, 1991).

The policy stance of taking action before uncertainty about possible environmental damages is resolved has been referred to as the 'precautionary principle'. This was defined in the Declaration of the Third Ministerial Conference on the North Sea as: 'action to avoid potentially damaging impacts of substances that are persistent, toxic and liable to bioaccumulate even where there is no scientific evidence to prove a causal link between effects and emissions' (quoted in Haigh, 1993). Haigh (1993) argues that instances of the precautionary principle (PP hereafter) being applied include the Montreal Protocol on substances *likely* to damage the ozone layer, the North Sea conference decision to reduce polluting inputs to the North Sea by 50% by 1995 and the EC agreement to reduce CO_2 emissions. Indeed, the 1874 Alkali Act, often cited as one of the first pieces of environmental legislation in the UK, did not insist on *proof* that gases discharged from factories actually caused deleterious health effects, before they could be subject to control. More recently in the UK, the 1990 White Paper 'This Common Inheritance' states the PP as a first principle of environmental policy.

The PP, which can be extended to other areas of environmental management such as the conservation of fish stocks, would thus seem to be a widely accepted principle for wise environmental management. Indeed, it has also been argued to be an essential part of any sustainable development strategy, in the 1990 Bergen Declaration (signed by 84 countries as a follow-up to the Brundtland Commission report). However, two qualifications have emerged. First, the Rio summit adopted the PP to be applied by all countries, but only 'according to their capabilities', implying that the costs of actions under the PP should be considered, and might to deemed too great for some (poorer) countries. Second, the UK government, in the 1990 White Paper referred to above, stated that the PP should only be applied 'if the balance of likely costs and benefits justifies it' (paragraph 1.18). This second restriction is rather more severe, since to apply it would involve some estimates of the probabilities of different possible outcomes being known, that these outcomes could be physically described, and that they could be valued in monetary terms. But if this were so, then a more formal application of cost–benefit analysis could guide policy analysis: the PP would be incorporated in the treatment of risk (for example, by giving greater weight to the worst possible outcomes). Chapter 12 considers the treatment of risk and uncertainty in cost–benefit analysis in detail.

However, it should be noted that some have taken acceptance of the PP to mean that society should have as a firm objective the total elimination of activities where uncertain environmental damages are involved (Taylor, 1991). Examples of such bans do exist: for example, the banning of the disposal of radioactive wastes in the deep ocean, and the incineration of toxic wastes at sea. Alternatively, the PP could be taken to mean the minimisation of inputs of any effluents to any ecosystem. However, the economist might worry that the costs of either banning the disposal or minimising the input of effluents would be disproportionately large, and incur unnecessarily high opportunity costs for society. Such criticisms have been made by economists of, for example, expenditures on Environmental Protection Agency (EPA) mandated projects in the USA.

So far we have seen that the environment acts as a waste sink, as a partial recycling factory for human wastes from production or consumption and as a source of energy and material resources. The next role to be considered is that marked E_3 in Figure 1.1. The environment acts as a supplier of amenity, educational and spiritual values to society. For example, people in Europe may derive pleasure from the existence of wilderness areas in Northern Canada or in tropical moist forests ('rainforests'), while native peoples living in these areas attach spiritual and cultural values to them, and the flora and fauna therein. We need to make precise the sense in which such values 'count' for economists. The theory of environmental valuation is set out in detail in Chapter 12. For present purposes, the question can be addressed by asking what constitutes economic value within the currently dominant economic paradigm, which is neoclassical economics. Neoclassical economics judges economic value as being dependent on social well-being, measured in a particular way. Social well-being is seen as depending on the (possibly weighted) sum of individuals' levels of well-being. Individual well-being is measured by utility, thus social welfare is the sum of individual utilities. There is thus no separate 'collective' good. The weighting of individual utilities is implicit in the social welfare function: see Johansson (1991) for a discussion. Individuals derive utility from consuming goods and services (meals, holidays) and from the state of the natural environment. This is because individuals use the natural environment to 'produce' goods/services and because they are made happier by the mere existence of environmental assets such as wilderness areas and blue whales. Environmental systems are also clearly essential for peoples' continued existence, but we discuss this later. A representative individual will have preferences which could be represented in the following generalised way:

$$U_A = U(X_1, X_2 \ldots X_n; Q_1, Q_2 \ldots Q_m) \tag{1.3}$$

Where U_A is utility, $(X_1 \ldots X_n)$ are goods and services produced in the production sector, and $(Q_1 \ldots Q_m)$ are environmental assets. Q_1 could be local air quality, Q_2 local water quality and Q_m the stock of blue whales. The environment thus supplies utility directly to individual A via the vector of assets, and indirectly via its roles in the production of the vector of goods and services $(X_1 \ldots X_n)$. Clearly one result of an increase in the output of any element of the X vector will be a decrease in the quantity or quality of an element in the Q vector. For example, suppose X_1 is consumption of services provided by owning a car, but car production and operation cause decreases in air quality, Q_1. An increase in the consumption of 'car services' increases utility ($\partial U_A / \partial X_1$ is positive), but this increase in car use decreases air quality ($\delta Q_1 / \delta X_1 < 0$). This fall in air quality reduces utility in an amount ($\delta U^A / \delta Q_1 * \delta Q_1 / \delta X_1$). The net effect is thus ambiguous, depending on the relative strengths of these positive and negative changes.

What this simple example shows is that using the environment for one purpose (as a supplier of material resources) can reduce its ability to supply us with other services, such as the ability to breath clean air. This is why in Figure 1.1 the three circles E_1, E_2 and E_3 are shown as overlapping: there are conflicts in resource use. These conflicts would include the following:

- using a mountain region as a source of minerals means its amenity value is reduced;
- using a river as a waste-disposal unit means its amenity value is reduced and that we can no longer extract so many material resources (fish to eat) from it;
- felling a forest for its timber reduces the electricity-generating capacity of a dam, owing to soil erosion, and reduces amenity values since the forest's inhabitants (animal and human) are displaced or destroyed;
- preserving a wetland for its aesthetic qualities forgoes use of the drained land for agriculture.

The environment is thus a scarce resource, with many conflicting demands placed on it. We term the scarcity resulting from these conflicting demands *relative scarcity*, which in principle a correct set of (shadow) prices could solve. This we distinguish from *absolute scarcity*, whereby all demands on environmental services are simultaneously increasing (Daly, 1991). The major cause of absolute scarcity is economic growth: this implies an increasing demand for materials and energy, an increase in waste outputs (by the first law of thermodynamics, which is explained below) and increased demands for environmental quality as an input to recreational, educational and scientific activities. Yet if the amounts of environmental resources are fixed (limited assimilative capacity, limited supplies of minerals and so on) then absolute scarcity will increase as world economic growth occurs (but see Box 1.2).

It is apparent, therefore, that economics has a role to play, since much of economics is concerned with allocating source resources to conflicting demands. But it will also become clear that the *economic system*, primarily the market system, works very poorly in allocating environmental resources. The reasons for this failure are largely addressed in Chapter 2, but we can review the more important ones by saying that an imperfect specification of property rights results in a set of prices which send the wrong signals to producers, consumers and governments and that individual benefits of preserving our environment understate the collective benefits of preservation. Further, as Daly (1987) has argued, the price system may be unable to solve the problem of absolute scarcity, even with a correct set of relative prices in place. Such problems of 'scale' are only solvable, Daly believes, with quantity limits on resource use and on population.

Box 1.2 *Does rising output mean rising energy use?*

As economic growth occurs, energy and material demands per real dollar of output have tended to fall. For example, energy required per unit of real GDP in Denmark fell by 27% between 1979 and 1989 (World Resources Institute, 1992). In the UK, the ratio of primary energy use to GDP fell dramatically over the period 1950–90 (DTI, 1992). However, rising world population and an increased scale of economic activity would seem likely to produce a net increase in absolute scarcity over time. Moreover, recent work on energy saving and GDP growth by Robert Kaufman (1992) suggests that previous estimates of energy saving may be too high.

In Figure 1.3, energy use per unit of real GDP can be seen to have fallen for France, Germany, Japan and the UK over the last 40 years. This fall has traditionally been attributed to two factors: technological progress, which reduces the amounts of all inputs, energy inclusive, needed to produce one unit of output; and a real price effect, whereby rising real energy prices cause producers and consumers to substitute capital or labour for energy.

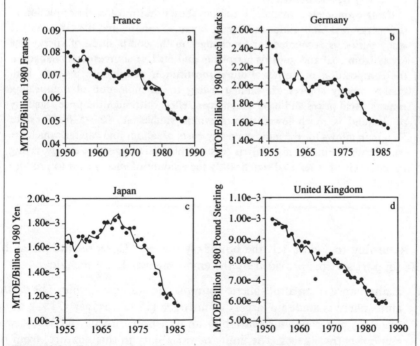

Figure 1.3 *Energy use to GDP ratios in four countries*
Note: Actual value for the energy real/GDP ratio (circles) and the value predicted by Kaufman's regression model (solid line).
Source: R.K. Kaufman (1992) 'A biophysical analysis of energy/real GDP ratios', *Ecological Economics*, 6(1), 35–56.

Kaufman notes, however, that there are other reasons why the energy/real GNP ratio may fall. First is a change in the composition of energy use. Different forms of energy (oil, coal, nuclear) are aggregated by converting them into heat units (kilocalories). However, the amount of work per unit of heat equivalent is not constant across energy sources, with some energy sources (higher quality) being able to do more work per kilocalorie than others (lower quality). Thus, if over time there is a transition from lower to higher quality energy sources – say, from coal to natural gas – then the energy/GDP ratio will fall. Second, a change in the mix of final demand can also change energy use per unit of GDP if energy-intensive commodities are replaced by less energy-intensive ones (where energy intensity is measured as kilocalories per dollar of output).

Kaufman also argues that traditional measures of energy substitution due to real price effects overestimate energy savings, since they ignore the energy component of the capital and labour used instead of energy. Evidence on this point has been gathered by other authors: for example, Pimentel *et al.* (1973) calculated that, while the amount of direct energy used to produce a bushel of corn in the US fell 15% between 1959 and 1970, total energy use per bushel actually rose by 3% once the energy content of other inputs (tractors, pesticides) was accounted for.

Using econometric analysis, Kaufman shows that most of the reduction in the energy/real GDP ratios in France, Japan, Germany and the UK over the study period is accounted for by changes in the composition of energy use (away from coal and towards petroleum and nuclear sources) and changes in the composition of output. Future substitution possibilities towards high quality energy sources are limited owing to an indication of diminishing returns. Real prices still have a significant effect, although the price elasticity of demand is much lower than previous studies at −0.045–0.389, since Kaufman allows for the indirect energy costs of labour and capital, which are considerable. Finally, his analysis 'casts doubts on claims that energy-saving technical changes reduced significantly the amount of energy used to produce output' (p. 52).

Returning to Figure 1.1, the boundary marked E_4 represents the global life-support services provided by the environment. These include:

- maintenance of an atmospheric composition suitable for life. The earth's atmosphere is made up largely of nitrogen (78%); oxygen (21%); argon (0.93%); water vapour (variable) and carbon dioxide (0.035%), with numerous trace gases. The limits of variability in this mixture, from the point of view of continued existence, are small;
- maintenance of temperature and climate. The naturally-occurring greenhouse effect warms the earth from its 'effective' mean temperature of −18°C to the current global average of 15°C. Changes in the

composition of the upper atmosphere can change this warming, as explained in Chapter 6.

• recycling of water and nutrients. Examples are the hydrological, carbon and oxygen cycles. Clearly, economic activity operates within this environment, and thus is shown as being encapsulated by it. The dashed line between E_2 and E_4 indicates that emissions can affect these global support services.

1.3 The first two laws of thermodynamics

Our last remaining task regarding Figure 1.1 is to ask whether the interlinkages portrayed are governed by any systematic physical processes or natural laws. We have already considered this to an extent in the discussion of assimilation. Now, however, we present two important physical laws, and discuss their relevance for the way we view the interrelationships shown. These laws are the first two laws of thermodynamics. Both laws hold true in strictly closed systems, systems with no external inputs. (More formally, a closed system is one which does not exchange matter or energy with its environment.)

The first law of thermodynamics states that matter, like energy, can neither be created nor be destroyed. This law, known also as the materials balance principle, implies that we can convert matter into energy, convert one form of energy into another form of energy and, in principle, convert energy into matter (although in nature this only happens inside nascent stars). However, a closed system cannot add to its stock of matter-energy. Clearly the earth is not a completely closed system, since we import energy from the sun, and occasionally matter, as meteorites. Kenneth Boulding has compared the earth to a spaceship: a spaceship partly powered by solar energy, with an initial, finite payload composed of terrestrial matter-energy. However, we only make use of a tiny fraction of the energy falling on the earth from the sun – about 1% is converted into chemical energy, an amount determined mainly by vegetative cover (the conversion process is known as photosynthesis, whereby carbon dioxide and water are combined, in the presence of sunlight, into carbohydrate and oxygen); whilst only a tiny proportion of total world energy production is accounted for by currently produced solar energy. The majority of world energy demand is met from the results of past solar energy, captured by photosynthesis and very gradually transformed into the fossil fuels: oil, natural gas and coal. Together, these three sources accounted for 94% of world energy production in 1991 (World Resources Institute, 1992).

However, the first law of thermodynamics has two important implications in addition to limits on matter-energy supply. The first is that, as more matter is extracted by the production process, more waste is generated which must eventually be returned to the environment, since the matter-energy content of the extracted material cannot be destroyed. Thus, if economic growth brings an increase in iron and aluminum extraction to satisfy increased demand, more iron ore waste, bauxite processing waste and scrap metal will eventually be returned to the environment. Economic growth which results in increased extraction of material and energy resources must produce an equivalent increase in residuals output. In this sense, 'consumption' is a rather inadequate description of what consumers do.

Secondly, the first law places limits on the degree to which resources can be substituted for each other in production. The degree of substitutability between inputs derived from the environment, man-made capital and human capital is a very important parameter in discussing 'limits to growth'. Christensen (1989) has argued that the first law places definite upper limits on this substitutability, and that neoclassical economics has ignored this fact because it has ignored the physical features of production. Christensen views the neoclassical notion of land, labor and capital as the primary inputs to production as a poor reflection of reality. He prefers to count all material and energy resources not produced by the economic system as primary factors. These primary factors are then combined with man-made capital and human capital to produce outputs, in endogenously determined structures (firms and markets). Output can only be increased by varying *all* of these inputs, or at least more than one at a time. From this perspective, the marginal products of neoclassical economics do not exist, being replaced by some sort of joint marginal products. Because man-made capital must be combined *with* primary inputs, the degree of substitutability between the two is very limited; that, is the elasticity of substitution is close to zero. We take this issue up again later on.

The second law of thermodynamics is also known as the entropy law, and will be familiar to many. There are a great many ways of stating this law, but for our purposes the following is useful: 'In a closed system, the use of matter-energy causes a one-way flow from low entropy resources to high entropy resources; from order to disorder. As an energy resource, for example, is used, the amount of work that energy can do is diminished.' The entropy law can also be stated as 'no process is possible where the sole result is the transfer of energy from a cooler to a hotter body' (Khalil, 1990). The alternative suggests what happens to energy when it is used. Consider a piece of coal. When the coal is burnt, the energy in it is released. We know from the first law that energy cannot be destroyed. We may be able to recapture some of the energy in a heat-exchanger, for this is where the energy 'goes': it dissipates as heat. This is due to the tendency towards equilibrium in thermodynamic systems, and thus a tendency for temperature differences, in our example, to be equalised. The major implication of the second law is that energy cannot be recycled in such a way that we get back *all* the capacity of the original energy source to do useful work, since the act of using the original low-entropy resource will result in some of its energy being lost as heat. If the earth is a closed system, with a limited stock of low entropy energy resources (fossil fuels), then that system is unsustainable, since economic activity inevitably degrades the energy resource so that, eventually, no capacity for useful work could remain.

The entropy law has an important implication for the recycling of matter, since production and consumption of matter can lead to its dissipation, and scarce matter or energy must be used up to recycle it. Biological and ecological systems are also constrained by the entropy law, particularly in terms of the proportion of energy which is passed between trophic layers. The earth is not, however, a closed system: we obtain energy directly from the sun, which we have a limited capacity to utilise. Thus, whilst the entropy law is very useful in understanding the limits of matter and energy recycling, it is not necessarily the harbinger of doom it once appeared to writers such as Georgescu-Roegen. Some economists (for example, Khalil, 1990) have disputed its applicability to the economic system (but see the reply by Lozada, 1991), whilst others have pointed to the possibility of technological progress offsetting the entropy process for material resources. Finally, we note that it seems more likely that the first law of thermodynamics, with its implications of increased residuals output, will be more likely to set a limit to growth (given the earth's limited capacity to assimilate these residuals) before the entropy constraint becomes binding and the world runs out of useful energy.

■ *1.4* Conclusions

The economy and the natural environment are linked to each other in four ways, with the environment supplying material and energy resource inputs, waste assimilative capacity, amenity, educational and spiritual values, and global life support services to the economic process. These interlinkages are dynamic, in that they are continually changing. The first and second laws of thermodynamics partially govern the interrelationships, although economists disagree on how important the two laws are in terms of their implications for future economic activity.

■ Technical note: game theory

For many problems in environmental economics, game theory provides a useful tool. Game theory is concerned with the strategic actions of different agents (firms, consumers, governments and so on), where these actions are in some way interlinked. For example, the interaction between firms in a permit market, or arguments between countries over cuts in carbon dioxide emissions can be represented as games. This note gives a brief review of those parts of game theory used in this book, in Chapters 6 and 10. Gibbons (1992), and Fudenberg and Tirole (1991) provide an excellent introduction to the field. We use Gibbons' notation in what follows.

Assume there are $i = 1 \ldots n$ agents who each can choose different strategies s_i from their sets of all possible strategies S_i : thus player 1 may choose s_1^* or s_1 from their strategy set S_1. Depending on their choice of strategy, and the choices of the other players, agents will receive payoffs of u_i, where $u_i = f(s_1 s_2, \ldots s_i \ldots s_n)$ so that u_i depends on the strategies chosen by all players. Games are usually categorised according to whether players all make their decisions simultaneously (static games) or sequentially (dynamic games); whether players know all the pay-off functions $u_i(\cdot)$ for all players or not (games of complete and incomplete information); and whether games are once-off or repeated. This note restricts itself to explaining three other pieces of terminology: dominated strategies, Nash equilibrium and leader–follower games.

To illustrate dominated strategies and Nash equilibrium, consider the following situation. Two countries (A and B) are bargaining over whether to cut sulphur dioxide emissions. Each country can make one of two decisions: to cut its emissions by a certain amount, or to make no cut. Because sulphur dioxide is a transboundary pollutant, A is affected by B's emissions, and vice versa. Each country knows what the pay-offs of each strategy will be, depending on what the other country does (so that this is a game of complete information). Think of these pay-offs as dependent on control costs net of avoided damages. Each country decides simultaneously what action to undertake. The game ('game 1') is set out below:

Game 1   *Pay-offs and strategies for emission reductions*

		Country B's actions	
		cut	not cut
Country A's actions	cut	(50, 50)	(−40, 60)
	not cut	(60, −40)	(−30, −30)

The pairs of numbers in parentheses indicate the pay-offs for each combination of actions, with A's pay-offs given first in each case. Negative numbers represent net losses to either country. Thus if A decides not to cut emissions, but B decides to cut, then A incurs no control costs and gets some benefits due to reductions in emissons originating from B: its pay-off is +60. But B will lose in net terms, since it does all the abatement, and receives no benefits from reduced deposition from A. B's payoff in this case is −40. Clearly the best outcome or most efficient solution from a social point of view is {cut, cut}, but how likely is this to occur? In this case, not likely at all. To see this, consider A's choices. If B cuts, the most profitable action for A is not to cut, since 60 is greater than 50. If B does not cut, A's best option is again not to cut, since a loss of 30 is less undesirable than a loss of 40. So no matter what B does, A will choose not to cut: we can say that the strategy 'not cut' strictly dominates the strategy 'cut'. Applying similar reasoning to B's decision, 'not cut' again strictly dominates 'cut'. Rational players should not play strictly dominated strategies, so the outcome of this one-shot game will be {not cut, not cut}, which is socially inefficient.

This game is an example of the 'prisoners' dilemma' type of game, where co-operation would yield an outcome preferred by both parties if they were able to negotiate before the start of the game and obtain binding commitments, but where simultaneously taken utility-maximising decisions yield worse outcomes than the co-operative solution. (Although, as Gibbons shows (p. 97), in an infinitely repeated 'prisoners' dilemma', co-operation may result: (the Folk theorem.)) Not all static, two-by-two games are prisonners' dilemmas. For example, in game 2, where the pay-offs have been slightly changed , the strategy 'cut' strictly dominates the strategy 'not cut' for both A and B, so here selfish behaviour will lead to the socially efficient outcome.

Game 2 *Alternative pay-offs for emission reductions*

		Country B's actions	
		cut	not cut
Country A's actions	cut	(70, 50)	(−20, 40)
	not cut	(60, −20)	(−30, −30)

Sometimes, however, games cannot be solved by this method, which is known as 'the elimination of strictly dominated strategies'. A different approach to solving for the outcome of such simple, static games is therefore necessary. The most widely used is that of deriving the Nash equilibrium for a game. Nash equilibrium as a concept is closely related to the elimination of strictly dominated strategies, but is a stronger notion of the solution to a game, in that it is more likely to produce a solution. By this we mean that any strategy choice that survives the elimination of dominated strategies is a Nash equilibrium, but that the reverse is not true. In fact, Nash's theorem states that in any finite game (that is, where the number of players and the number of possible strategies is less than infinite) at least one Nash equilibrium will exist. Note, however, that it may not be the only one, meaning that we must try to identify which is the 'best' of these equilibria in order to solve the game this way. A Nash equilibrium is informally defined as follows: if all players choose strategies that, for each player, correspond to their best action given the best actions of all other players, then that set of best strategies is a Nash equilibrium. At the Nash equilibrium, no player wants to change his predicted action, since that action is the best she can do given what everyone else has done.

Finding the Nash equilibrium of a game can be accomplished in a variety of ways. For game 1 above, one way is to start with player B, and find their best response to each action that A could take; then find the best response of A to each action B could take. Thus, in our example, B would say, 'Well, if A goes cut, I should not cut; but if A does not cut, then neither should I.' So, irrespective of A's decision, B will want not to cut. A would say, 'Well, if B goes cut, I would want not to cut; and if B does not cut, then neither will I ($-30 > -40$).' So the Nash equilibrium is {not cut, not cut}.

In fact, any strategy combination that is a Nash equilibrium will survive the elimination of strictly dominated strategies. But in the game below, we show that, while a Nash equilibrium exists, no solution can be found by the elimination of strictly dominated strategies. This game (game 3) shows the pay-offs to two pressure groups (the National Farmers Union and Friends of the Earth) when three strategies are available to them: support policy X, support policy Y, and oppose both X and Y by supporting neither. Here, the pay-offs are the utility the NFU and FOE get depending on which policy reform they support and the actions of their lobbying opponents.

Game 3   *Lobbying over policies*

		NFU action Policy X	Policy Y	Neither
FOE action	Policy X	(0, 8)	(8, 0)	(10, 6)
	Policy Y	(8, 0)	(0, 8)	(10, 6)
	Neither	(6, 10)	(6, 10)	(12, 12)

The Nash equilibrium is found as follows. Take FOE first. If the NFU support policy X, then FOE would want to support Y; if the NFU supports Y, FOE will want to support X, and if the NFU supports neither, then FOE will do the same. In the solution below these best actions for FOE are marked with a star; the same is done for the NFU. The cell with two stars is the Nash equilibrium and the (unique) solution to this game. But this solution could not be found by the elimination of strictly dominated strategies, since no strictly dominated strategies exist in this game. For example, FOE would choose X if the NFU choose Y; but would choose Y if the NFU chose X; and would choose neither if that was also the choice of the NFU. The outcome (12,12) or {neither, neither} is the unique Nash equilibrium in this case. However, as mentioned above, some games have more than one Nash equilibrium. For example, in game 4 where we return to pay-offs to two countries from emission reductions, both {cut, cut} and {not cut, not cut} are Nash equilibria. Obviously, each country would rather reach the former outcome, but this will only occur if country A can assure itself that country B will cut emissions if A also cuts. In this case, A can be sure of this (with complete information), since the outcome {cut, cut} is in a sense 'assured', since if A does decide to cut, B's best pay-off is to cut also. This is an example of an assurance game (Sandler, 1992). Gibbons gives an example of the derivation of a Nash equilibrium in a static problem of Garrett's 'Tragedy of the Commons': you will find this set out in Chapter 9.

Game 3 *Solution*

		NFU action Policy X	Policy Y	Neither
FOE action	Policy X	$(0, 8^*)$	$(8^*, 0)$	$(10, 6)$
	Policy Y	$(8^*, 0)$	$(0, 8^*)$	$(10, 6)$
	Neither	$(6, 0)$	$(6, 10)$	$(12^*, 12^*)$

Game 4 *An assurance game of emission reductions*

		Country B's actions cut	not cut
Country A's actions	cut	$(80, 80)$	$(-120, 0)$
	not cut	$(0, -120)$	$(0, 0)$

☐ *Sequential games*

Leader–follower games are an example of a sequential game, since not all parties make their moves at the same time. An example of such a game in the environmental economics literature is Hoel's paper (1989) on unilateral cuts in emissions of a global pollutant by one country. For example, if Norway goes ahead with a dramatic cut in its emissions of greenhouse gases, will other countries follow suit, or will they free ride? The best known economic example of such games is Stackleberg's (1934) model of a duopoly, where one firm (the leader) makes an output (or pricing) decision: the other firm observes this decision, and then makes its own. Here we run through the basic idea of a dynamic game, and then analyse Hoel's paper.

Sequential games have as their key feature that not all players make their moves simultaneously, and they may be solved through the process of 'backwards induction'. The simplest of these games involve situations where all stages of the game are known to all players (perfect information), who also know each others' pay-off functions (complete information). Backwards induction works as follows. Consider the following two-stage game. First, a monopoly union sets a wage w. Next, a firm decides how many workers to employ at this wage. The pay-off to the firm (its profits) depend on revenues (R), which in turn depend on the number of workers it hires (L); and on its wage bill, wL. The firm maximises profits subject to the wage demand of the union; the solution to this problem gives a 'reaction curve' $L^*(w)$, where L^* is the best level of L for any level of w. But the union can solve this problem too. It thus makes a decision about what wage to claim in period 1 by maximising its pay-off function u, where $u = u(w, L^*(w))$. Thus the strategy choice in the first period depends on the choice in the second period: this is backwards induction. It is possible to find Nash equilibria in dynamic games by this method: these equilibria are termed 'sub-game perfect' if they imply Nash equilibria at each stage of the game (that is, at each 'play'). This in turn implies, as Gibbons shows, an absence of unbelievable threats or promises from any player at any stage.

Hoel first considers a static game similar to the example at the beginning of this note. Two countries are affected by a global pollutant. In each country, the benefits of pollution control are $B_i = B_i(X1 + X2)$, where $X1$ and $X2$ represent emission reductions in countries 1 and 2; and the costs of pollution control are $C_i = C_i(X_i)$. Note that for country i, its benefits depend on emission reductions by both countries (since the pollutant is a global one), but that its control costs depend only on its own level of emissions reduction. We assume that, with respect to X_i, the first derivatives of $B_i(\cdot)$ are positive, but the second derivatives negative (that is, $B' > 0$ but $B'' < 0$) and that $C', C'' > 0$ (that is, marginal control costs are increasing). In a static game with no co-operation, each country solves the problem:

MAX: $B_1(X1 + X2) - C_1(X1)$

which gives as a necessary condition:

$B'_1(X1 + X2) = C'_1(X1)$

This gives the best choice of emission reductions from country 1 as a function of country 2's emission reduction: a reaction function, which we can call $R_1 (X2)$. Similarly, $R_2 (X1)$ would give country 2's best response to any level of $X1$. These functions are shown below in Figure T.1. Taking country one, it may be seen that its optimal level of emission reduction falls as $X2$ increases, since it benefits from these reductions by country 2, and since marginal benefits are decreasing whilst its own marginal control costs are increasing. The point where the two reaction functions cross (v, in Figure T.1) is in fact a (static) Nash equilibrium, since it shows a coincidence of best moves by each party. If the two reaction funtions do not cross (for example, if they are parallel to each other), then there will be no Nash equilibrium in this game, whilst non-linear reaction functions admit the possibility of multiple Nash equilibria.

But what if country 1 (Norway, say) acts unselfishly? Hoel shows the outcome by including an extra term in country 1's net benefit (pay-off) function, namely $h(\cdot)$. It becomes:

$$\Pi = B_1(X1 + X2) - C_1(X1) + h(X1 + X2)\ldots h > 0$$

Here, $h(\cdot)$ shows the additional benefit gained by country 1, which can be thought of as an altruistic benefit. If country 1's net benefit is now maximised, and a new reaction function ($R\#_1 (X2)$) derived, it will lie to the right of $R_1 (X2)$ and the new Nash equilibrium will change to v'.

This unselfishness can also be modelled as a sequential, leader–follower game. Let country 1 be the leader and country 2 the follower in the next period. The solution to the Stackleberg game can be found by backwards induction: finding country 2's optimum response to country 1's move. Hoel shows that this will involve country 1's optimal emissions being lower, the higher is h, with country 2's emissions rising, the greater the reduction by country 1. He also shows that total emissions will fall. Figure T.2 shows this

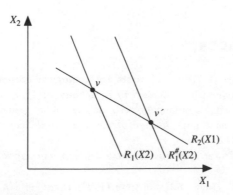

Figure T.1 *Nash equilibrium*

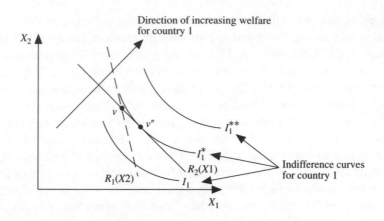

Figure T.2   *Stackleberg equilibrium*

result for $X1$ and $X2$ graphically. The response function of country 2 is again $R_2 (X1)$: remember that country 2 acts selfishly. Also shown are indifference curves for country 1. Along each indifference curve (I_1), net benefits for country 1 are constant. Country 1 can anticipate country 2's response to any level of $X1$, since this is given by $R_2 (X1)$. Country 1 wants to maximise its net benefits subject to this best response by country 2; this is the same as saying that country 1 wants to be on the highest indifference curve which is just tangent to country 2's response curve, which is at point v''. This has country 1 making higher emissions cuts (and country 2 making lower emissions cuts) than the original simultaneous move Nash equilibrium at v, where both countries behave selfishly.

Hoel goes on to show that circumstances can exist whereby unilateral, unselfish action can actually increase total emissions, but we leave the reader to study Hoel's paper to investigate this result.

■ References

Christensen, P.P. (1989) 'Historical roots for ecological economics – biophysical versus allocative approaches', *Ecological Economics*, 1(1), 17–37.

Daly, H.E. (1987) 'The economic growth debate. What some economists have learned but many have not', *Journal of Environmental Economics and Management*, 14(4), 323–337.

Daly, H.E. (1991) 'Towards an environmental macroeconomics', *Land Economics*, 67, 255–9.

DTI (Department of Trade and Industry) (1992) *Digest of UK Energy Statistics*, London: HMSO.

Fudenberg, D. and J. Tirole T (1991) *Game Theory*, Cambridge, MA: MIT Press.

Gibbons, R. (1992) *A Primer in Game Theory*, New York: Harvester Wheatsheaf.

Haigh, N. (1993) 'The precautionary principle in British environmental policy', mimeo, London: Institute of Environmental Policy.

Heimlich, R.E. (1991) 'Soil erosion and conservation policies in the United States', in N. Hanley (ed.), *Farming and Countryside, an economic analysis of external costs and benefits*, Oxford: CAB International.

Hoel, M. (1989) 'Global environmental problems: the effects of unilateral actions taken by one country', discussion paper 89/11, Department of Economics, University of Oslo.

Johansson, P.O. (1991) *An Introduction to Modern Welfare Economics*, Cambridge: Cambridge University Press.

Lovelock, J. (1987) *Gaia: A New Look at Life on Earth*, New York: Oxford University Press.

Kaufman, R.K. (1992) 'A biological analysis of energy/real GDP ratio: implications for substitution and technical change', *Ecological Economics*, 6(1), 35–57.

Khalil, E.L. (1990) 'Entropy law and exhaustion of natural resources : is Nicholas Georgescu-Roegen's paradigm defensible?', *Ecological Economics*, 2(2), 163–179.

Lozada, G.A. (1991) 'A defence of Nicholas Georgescu-Roegen's paradigm'. *Ecological Economics*, 3(2), 157–61.

McLusky, D. (1989) *The Estuarine Ecosystem*, Glasgow: Blackie.

Pimental, D., L. Hurd, A. Belotti, M. Foster, I. Okra, O. Scholes and R. Whitman (1973) 'Food production and the world energy crisis', *Science*, 182, 443–9.

Nisbet, E.G. (1991) *Leaving Eden – To protect and manage the earth*, Cambridge: Cambridge University Press.

Sandler, T. (1992) 'After the cold war: secure the global commons', *Challenge*, July–August, 16–23.

Taylor, R.E. (1991) 'The precautionary principle and the prevention of pollution'. *Ecos*, 12(4), 41–45.

World Resources Institute (1992) *A Guide to the Global Environment*, Oxford: Oxford University Press.

■ *Chapter 2* ■

Market Failure

2.1 Introduction

2.2 Incomplete markets

2.3 Externalities

2.4 Non-exclusion and the commons

2.5 Non-rivalry and public goods

2.6 Non-convexities

2.7 Asymmetric information

2.8 Concluding comments

■ *2.1* Introduction

A market is an exchange institution that serves society by organising economic activity. Markets use prices to communicate the wants and limits of a diffuse and diverse society so as to bring about co-ordinated economic decisions in the most efficient manner. The power of a perfectly functioning market rests in its decentralised process of decision making and exchange; no omnipotent central planner is needed to allocate resources. Rather, prices ration resources to those who value them the most and, in doing so, individuals are swept along by Adam Smith's invisible hand to achieve what is best for society as a collective. Optimal private decisions based on mutually advantageous exchange lead to optimal social outcomes.

But for environmental assets, markets can fail if prices do not communicate society's desires and constraints accurately. Prices often understate the full range of services provided by an asset, or simply do not exist to send a signal to the market-place about the value of the asset. Market failure occurs when private decisions based on these prices, or lack of them, do not generate an efficient allocation of resources. Inefficiency implies that resources could be reallocated to make at least one person better off without making anyone else worse off. A wedge is driven between what individuals want privately and what society wants as a collective.

As an example of market failure, consider habitat destruction and the threat to biodiversity in Madagascar. Madagascar is one of the ecologically richest, but economically poorest, countries in the world. As resource managers and policy makers became more aware of the importance of biodiversity to support and maintain human life locally and globally, international agencies dubbed Madagascar as a prime spot to conserve biodiversity – the totality of genes, species, populations and ecosystems. Biologists estimate that 150 000 of the 200 000 species on the island are unique to Madagascar, the fourth largest island in the world: 98 per cent of the palm species, 93 per cent of primates, 80 per cent of flowering plants, 95 per cent of reptiles, 99 per cent of frogs, 97 per cent of tenrec and 89 per cent of carnivores (USAID, 1992).

There are also over 12 million human inhabitants on Madagascar (50 per cent under 15 years of age), with a population density of 17.5 people/km^2 and a growth rate of 3 per cent per year. Agriculture employs over 85 per cent of the population, with over 70 per cent of farmers engaged in production on two-thirds of the cultivated land. As the locals try to increase or maintain their per capita income of about US$200 a year, habitat destruction through deforestation has increased rapidly over the last few decades. Deforestation is occurring at an estimated rate of 200 000 ha/yr, with nearly 80 per cent of the original forest cover already gone. The economic cost of environmental degradation has been estimated at US$100–290 million (5–15 per cent of GDP) – 75 per cent derived from deforestation.

The factors leading to habitat destruction and the loss of biodiversity originate in several sources of market failure. First, habitat destruction arises from public ownership of large areas of land with open access property right regimes and limited government capacity to manage the land. These economic incentives encourage the overexploitation of wildlife, timber, grazing lands and crop lands. Second, land tenure is often insecure since the locals in remote rural areas have little or no influence over the national laws, policies, social changes and economic forces. Lack of secure land tenure provides little incentive to maintain the habitat necessary for biodiversity conservation. The local residents have little incentive to conserve if they are unsure their kin will have access to the same land.

At the most basic level, the threat to biodiversity exists because many of the services provided are non-rival and non-excludable. A service is non-rival in that, one person's use does not reduce another's use, and it is non-exclusive in that it is extremely costly to exclude anyone from consuming the service. As a result of these characteristics, biodiversity in and of itself has no value reflected by market prices. In contrast, the commodity resources of the habitat (for example, chemicals, minerals, timber, game) are valued on the market, and the supply and demand reflect the relative scarcity of these goods. Therefore, there is pressure to harvest the commodity goods at the expense of biodiversity. This lack of a complete market implies that the unintended effects of private economic decisions can create biodiversity loss, to a socially inefficient level.

This chapter explores the relationship between markets and market failure for environmental assets. We first briefly define the theoretically ideal benchmark for an efficient allocation of resources – the perfectly competitive market where private decisions lead to a social optimum. We then consider how this perfect market benchmark misfires by examining six cases of market failure – incomplete markets, externalities, non-exclusion, non-rival consumption, non-convexities and asymmetric information. We define these terms as we go along, introducing each type of market failure sequentially (though all are related to a certain degree). Note that we do not discuss another common form of market failure, non-competitive behaviour such as monopoly power, that is often not associated with environmental assets.

■ 2.2 Incomplete markets

Ledyard (1987, p. 185) notes that 'the best way to understand market failure is to first understand market success'. The market system is considered successful when a set of competitive markets generates an efficient allocation of resources between and within economies. Efficiency is defined as Pareto optimality – the impossibility of reallocating resources to make one person in the economy better off without making someone else worse off. If consumers and producers are rational such that they maximise their private net benefits, a set of markets where each person has the opportunity to exchange every good with every other person will generate a socially optimal allocation of resources.

The theorems of welfare economics summarise the major benefits of markets on social welfare, of which the first fundamental theorem is of most concern for market failure. The first theorem says that if: (1) a complete set of markets with well-defined property rights exists such that buyers and sellers can exchange assets freely for all potential transactions and contingencies; (2) consumers and producers behave competitively by maximising benefits and minimising costs; (3) market prices are known by all consumers and firms; and (4) transaction costs are zero so that charging prices does not consume resources; then the allocation of resources will be a Pareto optimum. A market failure occurs when the conclusions of this theorem do not hold, and the allocation of resources is inefficient (Bator, 1958).

A key requirement to avoid a market failure is that markets are complete – enough markets exist to cover each and every possible transaction or contingency so that resources can move to their highest valued use (condition 1). Markets will be complete when traders can costlessly create a well-defined property rights system such that a market will exist to cover any exchange necessary. This well-defined property rights system represents a set of entitlements that define the owner's privileges and obligations for use of a resource or asset and have the following general characteristics:

(a)   *Comprehensively assigned.* All assets or resources must be either privately or collectively owned, and all entitlements must be known and enforced effectively.

(b) *Exclusive*. All benefits and costs from use of a resource should accrue to the owner, and only to the owner, either directly or by sale to others. This applies to resources that are owned in common as well as to resources for which private property rights have been assigned.

(c) *Transferable*. All property rights must be transferable from one owner to another in a voluntary exchange. Transferability provides the owner with an incentive to conserve the resource beyond the time he or she expects to make use of it.

(d) *Secure*. Property rights to natural resources should be secure from involuntary seizure or encroachment by other individuals, firms or the government. The owner has an incentive to improve and preserve a resource while it is in his or her control rather than exploit the assets.

But most market failures with environmental assets can be linked, in one way or another, to incomplete markets. Markets are incomplete because of the failure or inability of institutions to establish well-defined property rights. For example, many people own land and are able to take action when damage is done to it, but they do not generally own the rivers or the air, through which significant amounts of pollution travel. The lack of clear and well-defined property rights for clean air thus makes it difficult for a market to exist such that people who live downwind from a coal-fired power plant can halt the harm that the plant does to them or to successfully demand a fee, equivalent to the costs they bear, from the operator of the upwind plant. The plant operator does not bear the downwind costs, so he ignores them. With incomplete markets, he lacks any economic incentive to control emissions or to switch to less polluting practices. Similarly, there may be no legal or institutional basis that allows the downstream users of polluted river water to receive compensation from upstream farmers whose sediments, pesticides or fertilisers impose downstream costs in the form of contaminated drinking water, poor fishing or reduced recreational opportunities.

This inability or unwillingness to assign property rights such that a complete set of markets can be created has provided the rationale for governments to intervene as an advocate of proper management of environmental resources. But Coase (1960) pointed out that if the assumption of zero transaction costs (condition 4) is maintained, the set of markets can be expanded beyond normal private goods to include many non-market assets as long as institutional constraints to assigning well-defined property rights are removed. The so-called Coase theorem posits that disputing parties will work out a private agreement that is Pareto efficient, regardless of the party to whom unilateral property rights to the non-market asset are assigned initially. As long as these legal entitlements can be freely exchanged, government intervention is relegated to designating and enforcing well-defined property rights.

Consider an example to illustrate the Coase theorem. Suppose there are two parties, Riley and Ole, who disagree about the optimal level of pollution in the Cloquet river. Riley produces pulp and paper, and discharges the waste water back into the Cloquet River. Ole lives downstream and uses the river for his rafting and kayaking business. While both have rights to the water, Riley's emissions reduce the profitability of Ole's rafting and kayaking business. Figure 2.1 shows the marginal cost (MC) to Ole from the pollution, and the marginal benefit (MB) to Riley from the pollution. The socially optimal level of pollution, x^*, is where MB equals MC. But with markets being incomplete, there is no opportunity for the parties to trade for alternative levels of water quality even though both Riley and Ole could be better off with the trade.

The Coase theorem works as follows. First suppose that a neutral third party creates a legal bargaining framework by assigning the property rights to clean water to Ole. The marginal cost curve in Figure 2.1 represents Ole's supply of clean water, while the marginal benefit curve represents Riley's demand for clean water. Given Ole has the rights, Riley would compensate Ole by the amount C^* for each unit of pollution. If Ole demands a higher level of compensation, $C > C^*$, then there will be a surplus of clean water as Riley will not demand as much as Ole wants to supply. If Ole asks for a lower level of compensation, $C < C^*$, there will be a shortage as Riley's demand exceeds Ole's supply. The surplus forces compensation down, while the shortage forces the level up until the market clears at the compensation level C^*: the demand for clean water equals the supply at the socially optimal level of pollution, x^*.

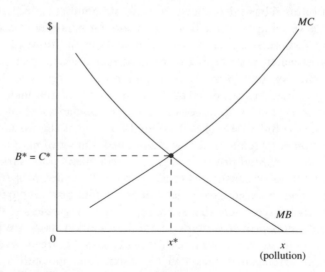

Figure 2.1 *Socially optimal level of pollution*

Now suppose that the neutral third party assigns the property rights to pollute to Riley. The marginal cost (*MC*) curve presented in Figure 2.1 now represents Ole's demand for pollution control, while the marginal benefit (*MB*) curve represents Riley's supply of pollution control. Given Riley has the right to pollute, Ole can offer a bribe to Riley of the amount B^* for each unit of pollution control. If Riley demands a higher bribe, $B > B^*$, there will be a surplus of pollution control as Ole will demand as much pollution control as Riley is willing to supply. If Riley asks for a lower bribe, $B < B^*$, there will be a shortage of pollution control as Ole will demand more than supplied. The bribe B^* clears the market: the demand for pollution control equals the supply at the socially optimal level of pollution, x^*.

Theoretically, the Coase theorem works: regardless of the initial assignment of property rights, the optimal per unit bribe equals the optimal per unit compensation, $B^* = C^*$, at the socially optimal level of pollution, x^*.

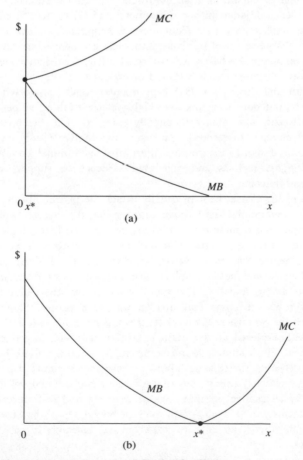

Figure 2.2 *Alternative socially optimal levels of pollution*

The market achieves the optimal level of pollution. Figure 2.2 further shows that, depending on the relative magnitude of the *MB* and *MC* curves, the optimal level of pollution may well be zero (high marginal costs) or equal to the private optimum where marginal benefits equal zero (low marginal costs).

Box 2.1   *Experimental evaluations of the Coase theorem*

Beginning with the seminal work of Hoffman and Spitzer (1982), the robustness of the Coase theorem has been tested in several labouratory experiments. Hoffman and Spitzer argued that the Coase theorem depended on a set of seven key assumptions: (1) zero transaction costs, (2) two agents to each bargain, (3) perfect knowledge of each other's well-defined profit or utility functions, (4) competitive markets for legal entitlements, (5) a costless court system to uphold all legal contracts, (6) profit-maximising producers and expected utility-maximising consumers, and (7) no wealth effects. Two behaviour implications arise from these assumptions: a *weak* behavioural outcome – bargainers will reach a Pareto efficient agreement, and a *strong* behavioural outcome – bargainers will reach a Pareto efficient agreement with a rationally self-interested distribution of expected wealth.

Hoffman and Spitzer's (1982) experimental results supported the *weak* behavioural outcome; bargains were highly efficient (about 90 per cent), but expected wealth was often split equally rather than in the predicted self-interested manner. In response, Harrison and McKee (1985) modified the experimental design to incorporate alternative institutional arrangements of property rights regimes and generated evidence to support the *strong* behavioural outcome.

Critics of the Coase theorem usually attack the plausibility of one of the seven key assumptions listed above, arguing that the theorem will probably not be robust when these restrictions are relaxed. To better understand the limits of the theorem, a series of boundary experiments have been designed and implemented that relax one or two assumptions. Hoffman and Spitzer (1982, 1986) showed that incomplete information did not reduce the efficiency of the bargaining, and they also found evidence that the Coase theorem is relatively robust in cases that involve up to 38 people. Shogren (1992) considered the case where the pay-off stream is uncertain, while Shogren and Kask (1992) explored an uncertain pay-off stream with imperfect contract enforcement. Both studies found some support for the *weak* behavioural outcome. Overall, the existing laboratory evidence suggests that the Coase theorem is relatively robust, but that efficiency and rational self-interest are affected by alternative presumptions of certainty and institutional features such as incentives and loyalty. Exploring the boundaries of the Coase theorem remains an important area of experimental research in environmental economics.

The basic complaint with the Coase theorem is that it is a tautology: the assumptions of two bargainers with zero transaction costs implies that an efficient agreement will be signed given the two agents have no incentive to quit bargaining until an efficient resource allocation is achieved. But if numerous parties are involved in the dispute, the large numbers should make bargaining too costly and complex (Baumol, 1972). Box 2.1 discusses laboratory experiments designed to test the robustness of the Coase theorem given alternative assumptions on the bargaining environment.

But Coase (1988) argues he has been misunderstood. He did not champion a zero transactions costs world; rather he argued that the institutional constraints on defining property rights are immaterial to economics from an efficiency standpoint only when transaction costs are zero. Since this world does not exist, efficiency is affected by the assignment of property rights. Coase (1988, p. 15) states that 'What my argument does suggest is the need to introduce positive transactions costs explicitly into economic analysis so that we can study the world that does exist.' This is the world of incomplete markets, and is pervasive in many different forms throughout the economy. We now consider the concept of the externality as a result of incomplete markets, but note in passing that market failure is not entirely to blame for incomplete markets: institutional constraints created by government can create financial obstacles to the effective creation of a market. Such government failure is beyond the scope of our present discussion (see Anderson and Leal, 1991).

■ *2.3* Externalities

The externality is the classic special case of incomplete markets for an environmental asset (Arrow, 1969). If the consumption or production activities of one individual or firm affect another person's utility or firm's production function so that the conditions of a Pareto optimal resource allocation are violated, an externality exists. Note that this external effect does not work through a market price, but rather through its impact on the production of utility or profit. The set of markets is incomplete in that there is no exchange institution where the person pays for the external benefits or pays a price for imposing the external costs. Riley and Ole's dispute about pollution in the Cloquet river is an example of a negative externality. Riley's disposal action has a direct negative impact on Ole's production of safe, enjoyable rafting and kayaking. If transaction costs are too great, so that the market for clean water or pollution control is non-existent, a wedge is driven between the private and socially optimal allocation of resources. Figure 2.3 shows the private optimum, x', and the social optimum, x^*, level of pollution for the Riley and Ole example, given markets are incomplete.

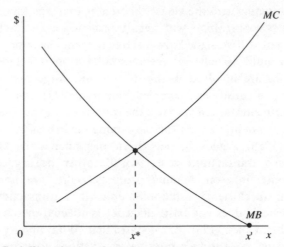

Figure 2.3 *Socially and privately optimal level of pollution*

Consider a simple representation of the externality in the Riley and Ole example. Given that Riley selects a privately optimal level of pollution, x, let his net profits, π^R, be written as

$$\pi^R = \pi^r - c(x)$$

where π^r is the profits before emission abatement, and $c(x) \geq 0$ is the cost of abatement such that costs decrease with increased pollution, $c'(x) \equiv dc/dx < 0$, where marginal abatement costs equal zero, $c'(x') = 0$, at a threshold level of pollution, x'. Therefore Riley's marginal benefit from increased pollution equals $-c'(x)$.

Let Ole's net profits, π^O, given he is damaged by Riley's pollution, be written as

$$\pi^O = \pi^o - D(x)$$

where π^o is Ole's profits given no pollution, and $D(x)$ is the monetary equivalent of the damage suffered where damages increase with increased pollution, $D'(x) \equiv dD/dx > 0$. Ole's marginal cost of increased pollution is therefore equal to $D'(x)$.

The socially optimal level of pollution is determined by taking account of Riley's impact on Ole. The social optimum requires that Riley's marginal benefit be balanced against Ole's marginal costs, $-c'(x) = D'(x)$, represented by x^* in Figure 2.3. If Riley ignores his negative impact on Ole, he will continue to pollute until his marginal benefits from pollution are zero, $-c'(x) = 0$; that is, Riley will pollute until he no longer receives any benefit. Riley's optimal level of pollution is represented by x' in Figure 2.3. Since $x' > x^*$, the market has failed to allocate resources efficiently: too much pollution is released into the Cloquet river. See Baumol and Oates (1988) for a general equilibrium representation of the efficiency impacts of an externality on a market system.

The cause and effect of the above externality was clear: Riley's emissions affected Ole's production of a service. However, cause and effect is often not as direct as economists assume. Rather the actions of one person can affect an ecosystem at one point which then reverberates through the ecosystem, ultimately affecting another person in a completely unexpected manner or at an unanticipated point. The pesticide DDT was banned not so much because it directly killed birds but rather because DDT thinned the shells of bird eggs to levels at which the embryo could not survive, a completely unpredicted cause and effect relationship. Citizens of Kern County, California around the turn of the century killed nearly all the natural predators in the area to protect domestic animals and children. Unfortunately, the ultimate effect was the largest rodent infestation experienced in the United States, with rodents invading the villages and farms, wiping out crops and causing untold mental stress.

Crocker and Tschirhart (1993) develop a general equilibrium model to show how these misunderstood ecosystem externalities reverberate through both economic and ecological systems. We present the basic version of their model for the Kern County example, and advise the interested reader to consult their detailed model for additional implications of ecosystem externalities.

Suppose there are three species that are linked: grain, which is consumed by rodents, which are consumed by predators such as owls, foxes and coyotes. Individual consumers are only affected by the grain for bread making and predator species; rodents do not directly affect their allocation of resources. How these rodents indirectly affect the allocation, however, will prove to be the missing link behind the ecosystem externality.

The Pareto optimal level of effort on making bread from the grain versus the elimination of the predators is determined as follows. Suppose a consumer's utility function is represented by

$$u = u(b, p, l) \tag{2.1}$$

where b is the level of bread consumed, p is the level of predators, and l is the amount of leisure. Assume increased bread and leisure increase utility, $u_b \equiv \partial u / \partial b > 0$, and $u_l \equiv \partial u / \partial l > 0$, while more predators decrease utility, $u_p \equiv \partial u / \partial p < 0$.

The link between predator removal and bread production works in three steps. First, the consumer gives up L_p units of leisure to eliminated the predator such that

$$p = p(L_p) \tag{2.2}$$

where $p' \equiv dp/dL_p < 0$. Second, grain is produced by

$$g = g(L_g, p) \tag{2.3}$$

where L_g is the labour units to produce grain, $g_1 \equiv \partial g/\partial L_g > 0$. Note that grain production also depends on the predator such that $g_2 \equiv \partial g/\partial p \neq 0$. This is the ecosystem externality, and we do not assume a negative or positive effect at this point. Third, the production of bread is represented by

$$b = b(g, L_b) \tag{2.4}$$

where L_b is the labour devoted to bread production, $b_1 \equiv \partial b/\partial g > 0$ and $b_2 \equiv \partial b/\partial L_b > 0$. Also note the total amount of available labour is

$$L = L_b + L_g + L_p + l$$

such that available leisure is given by

$$l = L - [L_b + L_g + L_p] \tag{2.5}$$

The Pareto optimal allocation of resources is determined by substituting equations (2.2) to (2.5) into the consumer's utility (2.1) so that

$$u(b(g(L_g, p(L_p)), L_b), p(L_p), L - [L_g + L_b + L_p]) \tag{2.6}$$

Solving for the optimal level of labour employed yields the first-order conditions for an interior solution

$$L_g: \quad u_b b_1 g_l = 0 \tag{2.7}$$

$$L_b: \quad u_b b_2 - u_i = 0 \tag{2.8}$$

$$L_p: \quad u_b b_1 g_2 p' + u_p p' - u_l = 0 \tag{2.9}$$

Rearranging and manipulating the conditions yields the following Pareto optimal allocation of labour:

$$\frac{u_p}{u_b} = \frac{b_2 - b_1 g_2 p'}{p'} \tag{2.10}$$

where the left-hand side of the equation represents the marginal rate of substitution between bread production and predator removal, and the right-hand side is the marginal rate of transformation between bread and predator removal.

The private or competitive equilibrium is determined as follows. Let k and w represent the price of bread and labour where all production of bread occurs in one firm (for simplicity). The firm's profits is given by

$$\pi = kb(\cdot) - w(L_g + L_b) \tag{2.11}$$

The firm selects the level of labour on bread and grain production to maximise (2.11) and the consumer selects the level of labour on grain production and predator removal and leisure to maximise (2.1) subject to the budget constraint $kb(\cdot) - w(L - l - L_p)$ yielding the condition

$$\frac{u_p}{u_p} = \frac{b_2}{p'} \tag{2.12}$$

Comparing condition (2.12) with condition (2.10) reveals that the private optimum does not accord with the Pareto optimal allocation of resources. The ecosystem externality term is missing from the private solution. Now in general the sign of the ecosystem externality term will depend on the precise linkages within the ecosystem. The empirical evidence in Kern County suggests that there was a negative impact of removing the predators, implying that the private optimum results in too few resources devoted to bread production and too many resources devoted to predator removal. The consumer ignores the negative impact that predator removal has on grain production. The ecosystem externality stresses that the economist must strive beyond his or her normal bounds to try to understand the biological and physical cause–effect relationships that are not always obvious and anticipated in standard cost–benefit analysis.

Another interesting aspect of the externality is the idea that environmental risks can be transferred through time and space by choice of pollution abatement strategy. The concept of the *transferable externality* implies that the individual protects himself from the external damages by simply transferring an environmental risk through space to another location or through time to another generation. The consequences of self-protection from pollution are not limited to the self-protected, but rather are passed on to others. The transferable externality differs from the traditional view of the pollution externality in that transferability is motivated by intentional behaviours, not by the simple, unintentional residuals of production. Agents select an abatement technology that transfers a risk, thereby creating conflict that induces strategic behaviour between people, firms or countries.

From a materials balance perspective, most environmental programmes do not reduce environmental problems since they do not reduce the mass of materials used. While continuing to allow waste masses to flow into the environment, the programmes simply transfer these masses through time and across space. Future generations and other jurisdictions then suffer the damages. For example, in the United States, the midwestern industrial states have reduced regional air pollution problems by building tall stacks at emitter sites. Prevailing weather patterns then transport increased proportions of regional emissions to the northeastern states and to eastern Canada. The midwestern states have reduced their damages by adopting abatement technologies which increase air pollution damages elsewhere. Other examples include agriculture where pollution from other sources encourages land, fertiliser and pesticide substitutions, which produce pollution that affects others. Intensive use of pesticides accelerates the development of immune insect strains with which future human generations must contend. In addition, some governments forbid the storage of toxins within their jurisdictions, thereby causing the toxins to be stored or dumped elsewhere.

The Des Moines, Iowa water works provides a good example of a transferable externality. The water works built the world's largest nitrates removal facility to clean nitrates from the city's Des Moines river drinking water supply. In 1991, nitrates at the water works intake exceeded 10 ppm for 29 days, prompting a legally imposed nitrate alert. Nitrate pollution, it is feared, promotes stomach cancer and methaemoglobinaemin (the blue baby syndrome). The removal facility simply transfers this risk, however, in that once removed, the nitrates are to be dumped back in the Des Moines river to pose threats downstream. L.D. McMullen, manager of the water works, notes that 'Unfortunately, the nitrate is not salable so we will just take it out of the water temporarily. We put it back into the water and someone has to worry about it downstream.'

Conflict is the inevitable consequence of the transferable externality as individuals purposely try to make others worse off to make themselves better off. The non-co-operative, unilateral use of self-protecting technologies creates environmental conflicts that add another layer of inefficiency to the market system – over investment in pollution abatement. Consider a simple model to illustrate the impact of the transferable externality.

Suppose Riley and Ole now have the ability to select an abatement technology that transfers the risk from a hazard from themselves to the other player. Riley and Ole select a level of self-protection, s^R and s^O, to minimise the sum of the damages from the hazard and the cost of the protection. Riley's cost minimisation problem is written as

$$C^R(s^R, s^O) = D^R(s^R, s^O) + \varphi^R(s^R) \tag{2.13}$$

while Ole's problem is

$$C^O(s^R, s^O) = D^O(s^R, s^O) + \varphi^O(s^O) \tag{2.14}$$

where Riley's damages decrease with an increase in his own self-protection, $D_R^R \equiv \partial D^R / \partial s^R < 0$, but increase with an increase in Ole's protection, $D_O^R \equiv \partial D^R / \partial s^O > 0$. Ole's damages are similar: they decrease with own protection, $D_O^O \equiv \partial D^O / \partial s^O < 0$, and increase with Riley's effort, $D_R^O \equiv \partial D^O / \partial s^R > 0$. Costs of protection increase with increased effort, $\varphi_O^O \equiv \partial \varphi^O / \partial s^O > 0$ and $\varphi_R^R \equiv \partial \varphi^R / \partial s^R > 0$.

If the players do not co-ordinate their self-protection efforts, Riley and Ole independently and simultaneously select their optimal level of self-protection to minimise their private costs, $C^R(s^R, s^O)$ and $C^O(s^R, s^O)$, ignoring the impact on the other player. Assuming a minimum exists, these actions yield the non-co-operative first-order conditions

$$-D_R^R = \varphi_R^R \tag{2.15}$$

and

$$-D_O^O = \varphi_O^O \tag{2.16}$$

These non-co-operative conditions imply that each player selects the level of self-protection that equates his marginal benefits, $-D_i^i$ $(i = R, O)$, with his marginal cost, φ_i^i $(i = R, O)$.

Now suppose both players decide to co-ordinate their actions. The co-operative level of self-protection by both players is determined by minimising the sum of both costs, $C^T = C^R(s^R, s^O) + C^O(s^R, s^O)$, yielding the co-operative first-order conditions of

$$-D_R^R = \varphi_R^R + D_R^O \tag{2.17}$$

and

$$-D_O^O = \varphi_O^O + D_O^R \tag{2.18}$$

Now these co-operative conditions imply that both players select the level of self-protection that equates their marginal benefits, $-D_i^i$ $(i = R, O)$, with two marginal costs: their private costs, φ_i^i $(i = R, O)$ and the external cost they impose on the other player, D_i^j $(i - R, O; j = R, O; j \neq i)$. Figure 2.4 shows

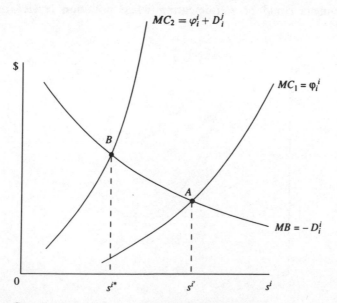

Figure 2.4 *Co-operative and non-co-operative self-protection*

that, if one accounts for the external cost, each player should cut back on their level of self-protection as the non-co-operative level exceeds the co-operative level, point *A* versus point *B*. Figure 2.5 shows that the co-operative solution $(s^* = s^{R^*} + s^{O^*})$ minimises the joint cost while the non-co-operative solution $(s' = s^{R'} + s^{O'})$ implies that costs are excessive – too much abatement with transferable externalities, point *C* versus point *D*. One can show this by substituting the non-co-operative solution (equations (2.15) and (2.16)) for self-protection into the co-operative equations (2.15) and (2.16), thereby yielding the positively sloped external marginal cost. This implies that the non-co-operative solution is on the right-hand-side of the minimum point on the total cost curve, point *D* (see Shogren and Crocker, 1991).

Environmental polices that allow unilateral transfers of pollution rather than encouraging co-operative resolutions will result in excessive expenditures on self-protection. Without public limits to individuals' non-co-operative self-protection activities, environmental abatement efforts are too expensive. Policy strategies that encourage self-protection need to be reconsidered since such strategies intensify the inefficiencies.

The framework presented above can be extend in numerous ways to show that transferability will prompt too much self-protection from recipients who have an elastic damage function. Limited empirical evidence supports the existence of an elastic damage function for environmental aesthetics when pollution levels are low and an inelastic damage function when pollution levels are high. Therefore non-co-operative environmental improvements could be self-defeating when pollution levels are already

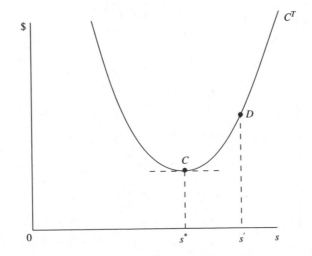

low. Aggregate expenditures on protection may then outweigh the environmental benefits. In contrast, some pollutants, such as ambient carbon monoxide, exhibit inelastic damages at low levels and elastic damages at high levels. It follows that accurate assessments of the benefits of policies to reduce environmental hazards require precise and accurate knowledge of the responsiveness of damages to non-co-operative forms of self-protection. Damage function elasticities are likely to be hazard-specific and activity-specific, as well as concentration- or level-specific.

■ *2.4* **Non-exclusion and the commons**

Another case where the market may fail to allocate resources efficiently is when it is impossible or at least very costly to deny access to an environmental asset. If your consumption of an asset rivals my consumption but we both have legal access to the asset, we both have an incentive to capture as many of the benefits that the asset provides as soon as possible before the other person captures them. In such cases we may overuse the asset relative to what is best for society. When overuse occurs as the result of non-exclusion the market has failed to signal the true scarcity of the asset. While the potential problems associated with non-exclusion implied by such open access property rights have long been recognised, the issue was popularised by Hardin's (1968) article entitled 'The Tragedy of the Commons'. Before we continue, a few definitions are in order: 'commons' refers to the environmental asset itself; 'common property resource' or 'common pool resource' refers to a property right regime that allows for some collective body to devise schemes to exclude others, thereby allowing the capture of future benefit streams to a collective set of users; and 'open access' implies there is no ownership of the asset in the sense that 'everybody's property is nobody's property' (see Gordon, 1954, p. 124). Box 2.2 presents a historical case of property rights and resource use in Scotland.

Box 2.2 *Property rights and the efficiency of resource use: a Scottish history lesson*

The management of the Scottish Highlands over the last thousand years offers an interesting example of problems associated with alternative property rights regimes, and an illustration of how misleading the phrase 'tragedy of the commons' can be (Hardin, 1968). The Scottish Highlands are characterised by relatively high rainfall, low temperatures and poor soils. Until the Act of Union with England at the end of the sixteenth century, however, the majority of the Scottish population was resident there, settling in the glens (valleys) and surviving on hunting, the growing of oats and bere (a type of barley) and fishing. From early times, the system of land ownership was a complex one. The Highlands were divided up amongst separate clans (from the Gaelic meaning 'children'). Land was owned by all members of the clan, but control was often exercised by the clan chief. Until about the mid-eighteenth century, land was managed on a 'runrig' system. This seems to have had an equitable use of land (as opposed to an efficient use of land) as its major objective. The more fertile areas around villages were divided into narrow strips. The productivity of land varied greatly across these strips, but each individual was given a turn at growing crops on the best land. This set up serious disincentive problems: there was little reward for hauling rocks off your strip of land this year, since next year someone else would get to farm it. The system was also very inefficient, since your farming area for a year could consist of strips at opposite ends of the glen. Indications are that output was sufficient, however, to keep the population above starvation levels (Grant, 1965).

This all changed after the Act of Union, and as a consequence of the aftermath of the unsuccessful Jacobite uprising in 1745 (led by Bonnie Prince Charlie). To minimise the likelihood of a similar uprising recurring, the English government destroyed as much of the old clan system as it could. This included the banning of the wearing of tartan and the speaking of Gaelic, for example. Many powers of the clan chiefs, such as the power to enforce the law and adjudicate in legal disputes, were removed. The clan chiefs responded by effectively privatising the clan lands, taking them into their ownership. Increasingly, a cash economy developed out of the former barter system, with tenants having to pay money rents for their holdings, which became concentrated on poor land as the landowners sought to increase their incomes. To do this, they turned to a number of ventures, including sheep (which led to the wholesale clearance of people from the glens, and their partly subsidised emigration to North America and Australia) and kelp gathering. Tenure rules again prevented the efficient use of land, for tenants could be evicted at the end of each year. Any improvements made to a tenant's land resulted in rises in real rents, as landlords used their monopoly power to extract all the profits.

This situation persisted into the mid-1800s, when a Royal Commission of enquiry found the conditions of most of the rural poor in the Highlands to be desperate. Pressure from Scottish MPs, and accompanying riots in places such as Skye, led eventually to the Crofting Reform Act of 1883. This set up the system of land holding that largely exists today in the 'crofting counties' of the Highlands (Argyll, Ross-shire, Caithness and Sutherland). A 'croft' is legally defined as a parcel of land below a certain maximum size. The crofter (who farms the croft) was given lifetime security of tenure, with the right to pass on the croft to one of his children. Any improvements made in the value of the croft can be realised by the crofter (who is *not* the landowner, but essentially a tenant) if the croft is transferred to another crofter. Transfers are supervised by the Crofting Commission, a government body.

The incentives for improvement being made to crofting land were thus substantially increased, but, given the small size of the crofts, access to grazing land was essential. This was provided for by a system of common grazing on the hillsides and mountainsides. This might sound like the classic Hardin open access problem of overgrazing on common land. In this case, however, the commons are not open access resources: only registered crofters may graze their livestock there. What is more, the maximum number of cattle and sheep that may be put on the hill by any one crofter is set by a crofter council which exists for each small geographic grouping of crofts (known as a 'township'). A community thus enforces its own code of practices on the management of a common access (but not common property, since the land is not actually owned by the crofters, but by other individuals who, for example, own the deer stalking rights too), with strict limits on the number of animals each individual can put on the hill. While this might and indeed has led to ecological overgrazing, due partly to the nature of agricultural policy in the sheep and beef sectors, it is not an example of the simplistic overuse portrayed by Hardin.

Fishing grounds are the best know example of a potential open access resource. Given that more fish caught by one party implies less fish for all others, all fishermen or women have an incentive to increase their fishing effort beyond the point where the market price for the fish equals the marginal cost of harvesting. Effort is expended to the level where market price equals the average cost of production. The scarcity value of the resource is ignored. The potential result is overfishing and a depletion of the stock to a level that cannot sustain itself. A recent example is the 1992 declaration of a moratorium on fishing endangered species such as cod and flounder off Canada's Grand Banks in the North Atlantic, once one of the richest fishing grounds. The moratorium has put nearly 30 000 Newfoundlanders out of work, and has stirred up a conflict between Canada and Spain, whose fleets continue to fish just off Canada's 200-mile limit.

The Black Sea is another example of a commons that has been severely affected by the unco-ordinated economic activity of numerous countries. The Black Sea coast is a common resource of six countries – Bulgaria, Georgia, Romania, the Russian Republic, Turkey and Ukraine – and also serves as a common receptacle for a drainage basin five times the area of the sea itself encompassing 16 countries (the six cited above, plus Austria, Bielorussia, Croatia, the Czech Republic, Germany, Moldova, Poland, Serbia, Slovakia and Slovenia) and 165 million people.

The inability to exclude agents from using or dumping waste into the commons has had a detrimental impact on the structure and functioning of the coastal marine ecosystem of the Black Sea (see Gomoiu, 1992; Mee,

1994). The main culprit is the increasing quantity of nutrients (inorganic and organic) flowing into the sea, causing marine eutrophication – overfertilisation of the sea. For example, the Danube currently introduces approximately 60 000 tons of total phosphorous per year, and about 340 000 tons of total inorganic nitrogen per year, about one-half from agricultural sources and half from industrial and domestic sources. In addition, numerous coastal communities directly discharge their sewage and waste into the sea. This increased nutrient load causes overfertilisation of the sea, leading directly to increased global quantities of phytoplankton and the occasional algae bloom. The effects of marine eutrophication include (1) a gradual shallowing of the euphotic zone – the surface layer where light is sufficient for net biological production; (2) disturbances in the oxygen content of the sea water, creating the appearance of hypoxic and anoxic conditions, leading to massive fish kill – a single occurrence of anoxia in 1991 eliminated an estimated 50 per cent of the remaining benthic fish; (3) increased quantities of dissolved and particulate organic matter in sea water and sediment two to three times greater than in the 1960s; (4) mass mortality of benthic organisms such as fish, molluscs and crustaceans, reducing filter-feeding populations and actually increasing the nutrient content of the sea; (5) a modification of the base of the marine food chain encouraging the development of nanoplankton; and (6) major structural modifications of fish and mammal populations in the Black Sea – drastic reductions, for example, in the stocks of sturgeon, turbot, mackerel and the dolphin. Only six of 26 species of commercial fish of the 1960s remain in significant quantities to harvest.

Chemical and microbiological pollution has also contributed to the decline in the fisheries. While data are sketchy, monitoring data from the 1989 Bucharest Declaration suggests that the Danube itself discharges 1000 tons of chromium, 900 tons of copper, nearly 60 tons of mercury, 4500 tons of lead, 6000 tons of zinc and 50 000 tons of oil. There are also inflows of synthetic organic contaminants such as DDT and other pesticides, heavy metals, radionuclides from Chernobyl, microbial pathogens such as cholera, dumping and toxic waste from the 16 official dump sites in the western Black Sea, and oil pollution from shipping and offshore exploration.

Figure 2.6 illustrates the incentives to overharvest an open access fishery. Suppose Riley and Ole both fish on Big Lake. Riley and Ole have a choice: they can either co-operate with each other by limiting their fishing fleet to one ship per day, or they can act non-co-operatively by sending out three ships every day. If they co-operate and send out only one ship they can each earn net profits of 30 (box A in Figure 2.6). But if Riley sends out three ships while Ole only sends out one, Riley can increase his net profits to 40 by capturing a disproportionate share of the rents. Ole would only earn net profits of 10 (box B). Since net profits of 40 exceeds 30, Riley has an

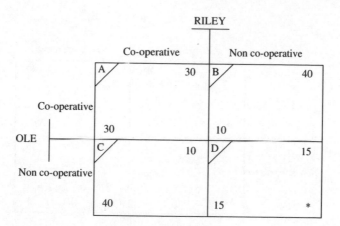

Figure 2.6 *Open access and the prisoners' dilemma*

incentive to cheat and send out three ships. Ole has the same incentive: if Riley co-operates and Ole does not, Ole can earn net profits of 40 while Riley only earns 10 (box C). If both fall for this incentive to act non-co-operatively by sending out three ships, they overfish Big Lake and their net profits fall to 15 each (box D). The end result is that both fisherman only earn total net profits of 30 (15 + 15), while the social optimum is total net profits of 60 (30 + 30) when both co-operate.

Technically, the choice of non-co-operation is the dominant strategy for each player. A dominant strategy gives a player a greater pay-off regardless of the other player's actions. In our example, the non-co-operative strategy dominates the co-operative one since 40 > 30 and 15 > 10. This outcome is called a Nash equilibrium. A Nash equilibrium exists if neither player will unilaterally change his strategy since a unilateral action would leave a player worse off without a reciprocal move by the other player. Our example of both players falling into the non-co-operative solution is the classic 'prisoners' dilemma' game: each prisoner has an incentive to betray his fellow partner in crime to secure a milder punishment for himself even though all are better off if they just keep their mouths shut (also see Ostrom, 1990).

Not all non-excludable resources are defined by the prisoners' dilemma game where the players are doomed to exist in a downward spiral of misallocated resources. Commons can also be represented by the game presented in Figure 2.7 – a co-ordination game. In this co-ordination game, there are two Nash equilibria, one where both players act non-co-operatively as before and the other where both co-operate. Each outcome is a Nash equilibrium since neither has a unilateral incentive to deviate from

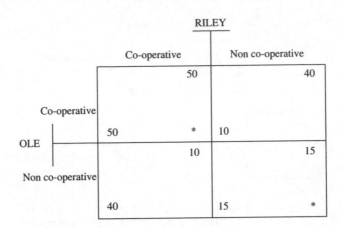

Figure 2.7   *Co-ordination game*

the strategy. Co-operation is a Nash equilibrium since a player receives 50 if both co-operate and only 40 if he unilaterally cheats. Non-co-operation is still a Nash equilibrium because a player receives 15 if he cheats and only 10 if he co-operates while the other player does not. Obviously, both players would prefer the co-operative Nash equilibrium since the pay-offs are the greatest, 50 each; society also prefers the co-operative outcome since the joint profits are the greatest: $100 = 50 + 50$.

Though there is no guarantee that the players will co-ordinate their strategies in such a way that they achieve the preferred co-operative solution, Ostrom (1990) documents several examples of actual common property resources where a group of players achieve a co-operative outcome. These groups establish self-governing common property regimes without strict private property rules or government intervention. Successful self-co-ordination of strategies in actual common property regimes appears to depend, among other things, on the information and transaction costs of achieving a credible commitment to the collective, active rules to self-monitor and sanction violators, and the presence of boundary rules that define who can appropriate resources from the commons. Market failure need not always occur with commons, but usually some boundary rule to exclude others is required.

■ 2.5 Non-rivalry and public goods

An environmental asset is considered a pure public good if its consumption is non-rival and non-excludable. A pure public good is available to all and one person's consumption does not reduce another person's consumption (Samuelson, 1954, 1955). Non-rivalry implies that the marginal social cost of supplying the good to an additional individual is zero. Therefore it is not Pareto efficient to set prices that will exclude anyone who derives positive marginal benefits from the public good – a market failure exists since a private firm cannot profit by providing a pure public good for free as dictated by Pareto efficiency.

In addition, since everyone benefits from the services provided by a pure public good and no one can be excluded from these benefits, these is a fear that people will 'free ride'. A free rider is someone who conceals his or her preferences for the good in order to enjoy the benefits without paying for them. Free-riding thus implies that the market will provide less of the public good than is socially desired, thereby misallocating resources away from the environmental asset to private goods where the conditions of rivalry and exclusive use hold (see Olson, 1965).

An example of a public good is a tropical forest that provides public goods to the local economy, given its capacity to manage water flow, soil erosion and nutrient recycling. The forest also provides public goods to the global economy, given the non-rival benefits of biodiversity, ecosystem linkages and carbon sequestration (see Myers, 1992, pp. 261–6). Wetlands also act as a local public good by buffering the economy from natural and man-made shocks by adjusting to fluctuating water levels from tides, precipitation and run-off, by providing water purification and habitat services. An ecosystem, in general, provides public services, given its ability to underpin and buffer the market economy against the external shocks of production and consumption activities. Note that there are also public goods that reduce utility or profits, such as pollution or noise. The loss suffered by one person from the pollution of air, for example, does not reduce the loss suffered by another. These public 'bads' will be oversupplied by the market.

To illustrate the market failure associated with a pure public good, now suppose that Riley and Ole voluntarily contribute to the provision of a public good. This public good could be abatement effort to reduce emissions that are feared to reduce the ozone layer or increase global warming. The aggregate level of the public good is represented by $Q = q^R + q^O$, where q^R and q^O represent Riley and Ole's respective private contributions. Given non-rivalry and non-exclusion, both Riley and Ole benefit from the aggregate level of the public good, Q. This is the 'summation' representation of a public good. See Cornes and Sandler (1986) for a discussion of alternative representations of how public goods can be supplied to the collective.

Let the utility function of each contributor be written as

$$u^i(z^i, Q) \qquad i = R, O$$

where z^i represents a private good. A person's utility increases as the consumption of the private good and the public good increases

$$u_z^i \equiv \partial u^i / \partial z^i > 0$$

and

$$u_Q^i \equiv \partial u^i / \partial Q > 0 \qquad i = R, O$$

Both Riley and Ole select their privately optimal levels of the private good and public good given a budget constraint

$$M = z^i + cq^i \qquad i = R, O$$

where M is a person's monetary income and c is the per unit cost of providing the public good. Assume for simplicity that the price of the private good, z^i, equals unity.

Riley will select a level of the private and public goods to maximise his utility subject to his budget constraint

$$\underset{z^R, q^R}{\text{Max}} \, [u^R(z^R, Q) | M = z^R + cq^R; Q = q^R + q^O]$$

We can simplify the presentation of Riley's problem by substituting the budget constraint into his utility function given $z^R = M - cq^R$,

$$\underset{q^R}{\text{Max}} \, [u^R(M - cq^R, q^R + q^O)]$$

Riley now selects his optimal contribution to the public good yielding

$$c = \frac{u_Q^R}{u_z^R}$$

or

$$c = MRS_{Qz}^R$$

These equations say that the per unit cost of the public good, c, equals the marginal benefits from the public good, in terms of the private good, that is, the marginal cost equals the marginal rate of substitution between the public and private good, $u_Q^R / u_z^R = MRS_{Qz}^R$.

Ole makes a similar decision to determine his optimal level of contributions to the public good,

$$\underset{q^O}{\text{Max}} \, [u^O(M - cq^O, q^R + q^O)]$$

such that Ole's optimal level is determined by

$$c = \frac{u_Q^O}{u_z^O}$$

or

$$c = MRS_{Qz}^{O}$$

Ole balances the marginal cost of his contribution with the marginal benefit from the public good, in terms of the private good.

As we can see, both Riley and Ole make their contribution decisions without concern for the way their contribution affects the other person. Turning to the question of the socially optimal allocation of resources for the public good, we have to consider how Riley's contribution affects Ole and vice versa. We determine the efficient level of the aggregate public good by selecting the levels of q^R and q^O to maximise one person's utility, say Riley, subject to the constraint that Ole achieves a utility level of v,

$$\underset{q^R, q^R}{\text{Max}} \, [u^R(M - cq^R, q^R + q^O)|v = u^O(M - cq^O, (q^R + q^O)]$$

yielding

$$q^R: -u_z^R c + u_Q^R - \lambda u_Q^O = 0 \tag{2.19}$$

and

$$q^O: u_Q^R - \lambda[-\lambda u_z^O c + u_Q^O] = 0 \tag{2.20}$$

where λ represents the Lagrangian multiplier that represents the shadow price of the constraint. Solving for λ in equation (2.19) and substituting it into equation (2.20) yields the condition for optimal provision of the public good

$$c = \frac{u_Q^R}{u_z^R} + \frac{u_Q^O}{u_z^O}$$

or

$$c = MRS_{Qz}^{R} + MRS_{Qz}^{R}$$

The efficient level of the public good says that the aggregate marginal benefit for the public good, in terms of the private good, should equal its marginal cost. The intuition behind the aggregate marginal benefits rests in the assumptions of non-rival and non-excludable consumption – the benefits of the public good are all inclusive. The source of the inefficiency with the private provision of the public good derives from Riley ignoring his impact on Ole and vice versa. Therefore neither person accounts for the extra benefit passed on to the other as each increases his contribution to the supply of the public good.

Figure 2.8 illustrates the socially optimal level of the public good for Riley and Ole. Let RR' and OO' represent Riley and Ole's demand curves for the public good assuming a given distribution of income. Let MC represent the marginal cost of providing the public good. If Q' is supplied, Riley's

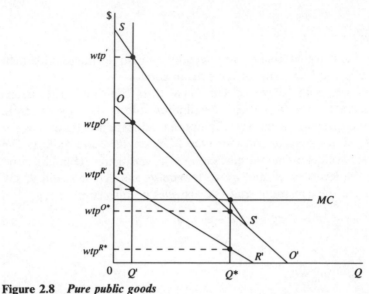

Figure 2.8   *Pure public goods*

marginal willingness to pay is wtp^R, and Ole's marginal willingness to pay is wtp^O for a total demand of $wtp' = wtp^R + wtp^O$. Because there are no rivalries with the public good, marginal social value is the vertical summation of the two persons' marginal values, such that summing the marginal private values at every level of the public good would yield line SS'. The optimal level of the public good, Q^*, is where the marginal social value equals the marginal cost. At this optimal level, each person would pay a personalised price: Riley would pay wtp^{R^*} and Ole would pay wtp^{O^*}. Actually revealing these personalised prices for pure public goods, however, is difficult in practice, as we will see in the chapters on non-market valuation (Chapters 12 and 13).

■ *2.6* Non-convexities

Up to this point we have assumed that the marginal benefit and cost functions associated with increased pollution have been well-behaved: marginal benefits are decreasing, while marginal costs are increasing (recall Figure 2.1). These well-behaved curves guarantee that, if an equilibrium level of pollution exists, it is unique. Therefore, if a set of complete markets exist for clean water or pollution control, the market will send the correct signal about the socially optimal level of pollution. Figure 2.9 shows that the net benefit curve is 'single-peaked', implying that there is one efficient level of pollution.

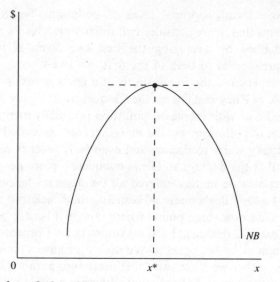

Figure 2.9   *Single-peaked net benefit curve*

But for many physical systems the marginal benefit or cost curve need not be so well-behaved. For example, marginal costs may at first increase with increased pollution but then may actually decrease or go to zero as the physical system is so badly damaged that there are simply no more costs as pollution increases. This is a non-convexity and it implies that there may be

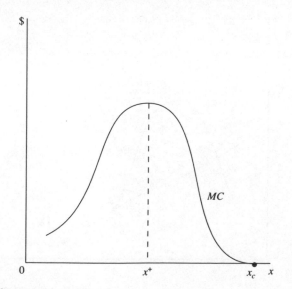

Figure 2.10   *Non-convex marginal costs*

more than one locally optimal level of pollution. Technically, a non-convexity means that, if we consider two different levels of a good or bad, a third level defined by averaging the first two levels is inferior in the individual's preferences to both of the first two levels.

To better understand the implications of a non-convexity, let us go back to the example of Riley and Ole on the Cloquet river. Figure 2.10 shows that Ole's marginal cost with increased pollution is initially increasing. But at a threshold level of pollution, x^+, the marginal cost associated with increased pollution actually starts to decline and eventually reaches zero at level, x_c. This implies that the damage to Ole is complete – more pollution does not raise his costs because he has suffered all the damages he can.

Figure 2.11 adds Riley's marginal benefits curve back into the picture. We see that there are now three points where marginal benefit equals marginal cost: points A and C represent local maximums of net benefits, while point B is a local minimum of net benefits. We no longer have a 'single-peaked' net benefit curve, rather we have two local maximum points where one of the points is the overall or global optimum. Whether point A with a low level of pollution or point C with a high level of pollution is the global maximum depends on the relative magnitude of the two hatched areas marked D and E. Area D represents the net marginal costs of increasing pollution to point C, while area E is the net marginal benefits of moving to point C. If the net marginal costs exceed the net marginal benefits of increasing pollution to point C (area D > area E), point A is the global maximum; otherwise point C is the global maximum and the socially optimal level of pollution is where

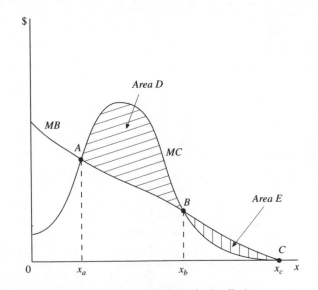

Figure 2.11   *Non-convexity and the optimal level of pollution*

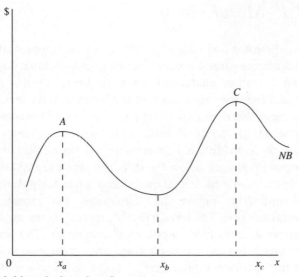

Figure 2.12   *Multi-peaked net benefit curve*

MB equals zero. Figure 2.12 shows the multi-peaked net benefit curve where the higher level of pollution is the global optimum. With a non-convexity, even if a set of complete markets exists, the market price might not send a correct signal as the local maximum point *A* may be selected rather than the global maximum of point *C*. Alternatively, if the net marginal benefits exceed the net marginal costs (area *E* > area *D*), the global optimum is the lower level of pollution, point *A*.

■ *2.7* **Asymmetric information**

Market failure can occur when one person in a transaction does not have full information about either the actions or the 'type' of the second person. 'Type' can imply the unknown quality of a good or the hidden characteristics of an agent such as inherent intelligence. For example, asymmetric information exists when an insuree knows more about his level of precautionary behaviour than the insurer, or a seller knows more about the quality of a product than a buyer. Without complete information, markets will be incomplete and can fail to allocate resources efficiently (also see Stiglitz, 1994). The two types of asymmetric information problems are referred to as moral hazard and adverse selection. The *moral hazard* or incentive problem arises when the actions of one person are unobservable to a second person. The *adverse selection* problem exists when one person cannot identify the type or character of the second person. We consider each in turn.

□ 2.7.1 Moral hazard

Moral hazard creates two related problems for environmental assets. First, when the regulators cannot monitor actions, an individual has an incentive to shirk on pollution abatement since he bears all the costs of such abatement and receives only a share of the benefits. Environmental shirking is likely to occur when an individual pays the costs of abatement but only receives a share of the total benefits to society. Ignoring transferable externalities, the individual has an economic incentive to reduce his or her effort to control pollution below the standard set by regulators, resulting in too few resources devoted to abatement, and too much pollution relative to the social optimum. Figure 2.13 illustrates the incentive effects of environmental shirking. The top curve, *BB*, represents the aggregate benefits to society from a firm's level of pollution abatement. The lower curve, *bb*, shows the firm's benefit from its own abatement action. The cost of abatement to the firm is represented by curve *cc*. Now society prefers that the firm invest in abatement level, s^*, since that is where marginal social benefits equal marginal costs. But, since the firm only receives a fraction of the total benefits generated but must suffer all the cost, it will set its abatement level at s'. Since $s^* > s'$ the market has not allocated enough resources to abatement.

Second, when the private market cannot monitor actions, an insurer will withdraw from the pollution liability market because the provision of insurance will also affect the individual's incentives to take precautions.

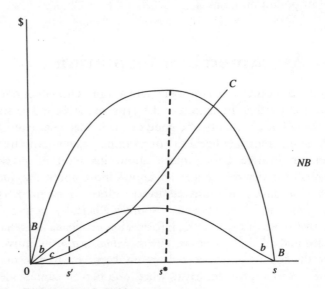

Figure 2.13   *Environmental shirking*

Given that accidental spills or storage of pollution can create potential financial liabilities (for example, clean-up costs or medical expenses), a firm would like to pay to pass these risks on to a less risk-averse agent such as an insurer. But since there is a trade-off between risk bearing and incentives, the market for pollution liability insurance will be incomplete as insurers attempt to reduce the information rents of the better-informed individual. The market will produce an inefficient allocation of risk.

We use the analytical framework of Arnott and Stiglitz (1988) to illustrate the inefficient risk-bearing problem associated with moral hazard. Consider a representative individual who confronts two mutually exclusive and jointly exhaustive states of nature. Let $U_0 \equiv U(w - \beta)$ represent the utility received under the good state of nature where w represents monetary wealth and β is the insurance premium paid by the individual. Assume $U_0' > 0$ and $U_0'' < 0$, where primes denote relevant derivatives. Let $U_1 \equiv U(w - D + \alpha)$ represent the utility received under the bad state of nature where D is the monetary damages suffered and α is the insurance payment net of the premium. Assume $U_1' > 0$ and $U_1'' < 0$.

Let p^i be the probability that the good state occurs, and $(1 - p^i)$ be the probability that the bad state is realised. Assume the individual can influence these likelihoods by his self-protection, s^i, where $i = H, L$ represent high (H) and low (L) levels of self-protection, such that $s^H > s^L$ and $p^H > p^L$. Examples of self-protection include voluntary restraint on the development of a forest or the reduction in draining and tiling wetlands. For this simple model we assume the two levels of self-protection are fixed, and are separable from and measurable in utility terms.

Let the individual's expected utility, V^H and V^L, given the high and low levels of self-protection, be written as

$$V^H \equiv (1 - p^H)U(w - \beta) + p^H U(w - D + \alpha) - s^H \tag{2.21}$$

and

$$V^L \equiv (1 - p^L)U(w - \beta) + p^L U(w - D + \alpha) - s^L \tag{2.22}$$

Figure 2.14 shows the individual's indifference curves in premium-net pay-off space for the high effort self-protection. The slope or marginal rate of substitution between α and β is given by

$$\left.\frac{d\beta}{d\alpha}\right|_{V^i} = \frac{p^i}{(1 - p^i)}\frac{U_1'}{U_0'} > 0 \qquad i = H, L$$

The curvature of the indifference curves, reflecting the individual's aversion to risk, is

$$\left.\frac{d^2\beta}{d\alpha^2}\right|_{V^i} = -\frac{p^i}{(1 - p^i)}\frac{U_1'}{U_0'}\left[\frac{U_1''}{U_1'} + \frac{p^i}{(1 - p^i)}\frac{U_0''}{U_0'}\right] < 0 \qquad i = H, L$$

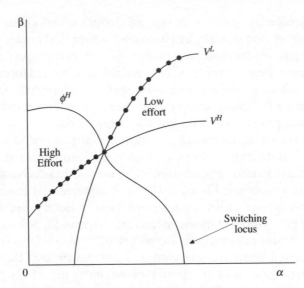

Figure 2.14   *Moral hazard (Arnott and Stiglitz, 1988)*

Note that at any point in $\alpha - \beta$ space the slope of the high effort indifference curve is flatter than the slope of the low effort indifference curve

$$\frac{d\beta}{d\alpha}\bigg|_{V^H} = \frac{p^H}{(1-p^H)}\frac{U_1'}{U_0'} < \frac{p^L}{(1-p^L)}\frac{U_1'}{U_0'} = \frac{d\beta}{d\alpha}\bigg|_{V^L} \tag{2.23}$$

This is because high effort decreases the probability of an accident and consequently requires a larger increase in payout to compensate for a given increase in the premium, holding the level of utility constant.

Manipulating equations (2.21) and (2.22), we see that the comparative levels of expected utility depend on the relative magnitudes of the benefits $(U_0 - U_1)$ and costs $([s^H - s^L]/(p^H - p^L)]$ of self-protection

$$V^H \gtreqless V^L \quad \text{as} \quad U_0 - U_1 \gtreqless \frac{s^H - s^L}{p^H - p^L} = \phi^{HL} \tag{2.24}$$

The expected utility of high effort equals the expected utility of low effort if the difference in utility between the good and bad states, $(U_0 - U_1)$, equals the difference in effort, $(s^H - s^L)$, divided by the difference in the likelihood of realising the good state $(p^H - p^L)$. For a given level of wealth, if the person believes that his or her self-protection causes a trivial reduction in the likelihood of damages, it is likely that $V^L > V^H$. Alternatively, if the individual perceives that his or her self-protection has a significant impact on the likelihood of a good state, the opposite holds: $V^H > V^L$.

In Figure 2.14, the point where expected utilities are equal, $V^H = V^L$, represents a switching point between low and high self-protection. At low levels of insurance, individuals choose high effort, while at high levels the individual picks low effort. The individual switches effort levels to increase his or her expected utility. The downward-sloping line, ϕ^{HL}, represents the entire switching line between low and high self-protection. Below the switching line high effort is used, above the line low effort is used. Therefore the individual's complete indifference curve is determined by the individual selecting the highest level of utility given the level of insurance offered, $\max\{V^H, V^L\}$: the scallop-shaped utility curve marked with dots in Figure 2.14 represents the individual's indifference curve in premium and net pay-offs space; that is, the indifference curve is non-convex.

Figure 2.15 shows that the set of feasible contracts between the insurer and insuree is also non-convex. A feasible contract is one where the insurer's profit is non-negative, $\pi \geq 0$. The shape of the outer boundary of the set of feasible contracts is represented by the two zero profit loci for high and low effort. For high effort, the zero profit locus is

$$\beta(1 - p^H) - \alpha p^H = 0$$

This locus is a ray from the origin with slope $p^H/(1 - p^H)$. The insurer earns zero profits when the price of insurance – the ratio of the premium to the net pay-offs – equals the ratio of the probability of an accident to the probability of no accident $\beta/\alpha - p^H/(1 - p^H)$. For low effort, the probability of an accident is higher and therefore the insurer needs a higher price to break even, as shown in Figure 2.15. The hatched lines represents the set of feasible contracts for the low and high self-protection; this set is also non-convex.

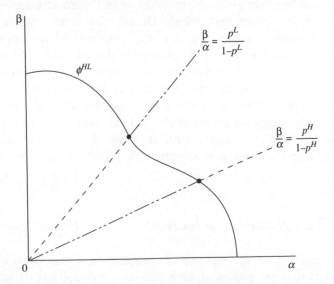

Figure 2.15 *Feasible insurance contracts given moral hazard*

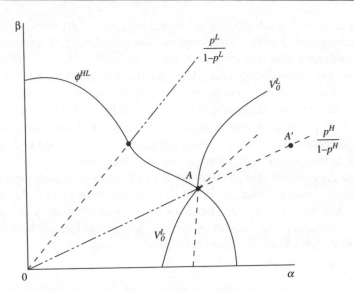

Figure 2.16   *Quantity rationing of insurance*

Finally, Figure 2.16 shows that the competitive equilibrium with moral hazard implies the quantity rationing of insurance. Assuming the case where the insurer can observe all insurance purchases by the individual and can therefore restrict the quantity of insurance sold, the equilibrium is characterised by an exclusive contract where the insuree buys all his insurance from one insurer. Let V_0^H and V_0^L represent the individual's non-convex utility function given effort. Point A in Figure 2.16 represents one exclusive contract given high effort. Though this is an optimal contract (marginal benefits = marginal costs), the contract is not feasible. The contract is not feasible since at this low price the insuree would like to buy more insurance because his private marginal benefit exceeds the costs. But if the insurer actually supplies more insurance at this price, the individual will switch to the low effort level (point A') and the contract would imply negative profits. Negative profits imply that the contract is not feasible, and there will be quantity rationing with an excess demand, that is, a market failure. Quantity rationing is common in pollution liability – insurance markets.

☐ *2.7.2   Adverse selection*

Adverse selection may well be a problem for the development of ecoproducts that are produced with practices that are less harmful to the environment. Sustainable production of products from tropical forests, for example, is a commonly promoted alternative to clear cutting activities. The problem with ecoproducts is that, while they may be of perceived higher quality to some consumers given the production process, these products may also be more expensive as the result of the lack of scale economies and the fact that the environment is not subsidising its production. Now if the buyer cannot distinguish the ecoproduct from the same product produced form standard practices, he will have no incentive to pay the extra premium. If the high quality, high price producers do not think that consumers will pay the premium then they will withdraw from the market. This process will continue until the market for the ecoproduct collapses.

Figure 2.17 shows a uniform distribution of quality, θ_i, for products with different quality as defined by perceived 'eco-friendly' practices. Higher quality products are assumed to generate higher prices. Now if a consumer cannot identify the quality, he or she has no incentive to pay any more than the average price, $E\theta$. Why should he or she pay more than average when he or she cannot distinguish high quality from low quality products? If all consumers behave this way, the producers with a quality above the average, $\theta_i > E\theta$, have no incentive to sell their product because they will earn a profit lower than their opportunity cost. When the above average producers leave the market, the distribution of goods is truncated at the mean, $E\theta$.

But this is not the end of the story. Now, if consumers realise that the above average producers have left the market, the new average quality is at $E\theta'$. Again consumers should not pay more than this new average quality

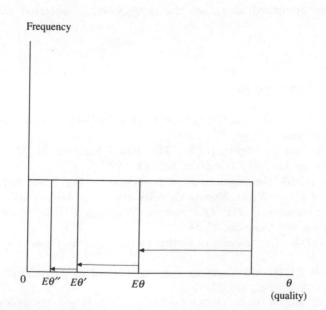

Figure 2.17 *Adverse selection*

level. However, those producers left in the market whose quality exceeds $E\theta'$ will now leave the market since they cannot receive enough revenue to cover their opportunity cost, and the market will be truncated again at the lower quality $E\theta'$. This behaviour will continue until either only the lowest quality producers are left in the market or the market collapses altogether. Unless there can be some acceptable warranty to verify production practices, the market for ecoproducts will be inefficient owing to the problem of adverse selection.

■ 2.8 Concluding comments

Markets serve society by efficiently organising economic activity. But there are constraints to the effectiveness of market allocation of many environmental assets and risks. Prices do not exist or they understate the value of an asset. Market failure implies that decentralised decisions based on these prices, or lack of them, do not generate an efficient allocation of resources. This chapter has explored the six most prominent cases of market failure for environmental assets – incomplete markets, externalities, non-exclusion, non-rival consumption, non-convexities and asymmetric information. How society will reduce these forms of failure through privatisation, collective action or government intervention is the fundamental debate in public economics. Chapters 3, 4 and 5 explore how economic incentives can be and have been employed to reduce the inefficiencies associated with market failure.

■ References

Anderson, T. and D. Leal (1991) *Free Market Environmentalism*, Boulder, Col.: Westview Press.

Arnott, R. and J. Stiglitz (1988) 'The Basic Analytics of Moral Hazard', *Scandinavian Journal of Economics*, 88, 383–413.

Arrow, K. (1969) 'The Organization of Economic Activity: Issues Pertinent to the Choice of Market Versus Nonmarket Allocation', *The Analysis and Evaluation of Public Expenditures: The PPB System*, Washington, D.C.: Joint Economic Committee, 91st Congress, 47–64.

Bator, F. (1958). 'The Anatomy of Market Failure', *Quarterly Journal of Economics*, 72, 351–79.

Baumol, W. (1972) 'On Taxation and the Control of Externalities', *American Economic Review*, 62, 307–22.

Baumol, W. and W. Oates (1988) *The Theory of Environmental Policy*, 2nd edn, Cambridge: Cambridge University Press.

Coase, R. (1960) 'The Problem of Social Cost', *Journal of Law and Economics*, 3, 1–44.

Coase, R. (1988) *The Firm, the Market and the Law*, Chicago: University of Chicago Press.

Cornes, R. and T. Sandler (1986) *The Theory of Externalities, Public Goods and Club Goods*, Cambridge: Cambridge University Press.

Crocker, T. and J. Tschirhart (1993) 'Ecosystems, Externalities, and Economies', *Environmental and Resource Economics*, 2, 551–68.

Gomoiu, M.-T. (1992) 'Marine Eutrophication Syndrome in the North-western Part of the Black Sea', *Science of the Total Environment* (Supplement), 683–91.

Gordon, S. (1954) 'The Economic Theory of a Common Property Resource: The Fishery', *Journal of Political Economy*, 62, 124–42.

Grant, I.F. (1965) *Highland Folk Ways*, London: Routledge & Kegan Paul.

Hardin, G. (1968) 'The Tragedy of the Commons', *Science*, 162, 1243–8.

Harrison, G. and M. McKee (1985) 'Experimental Evaluation of the Coase Theorem', *Journal of Law and Economics*, 28, 653–70.

Hoffman, E. and M. Spitzer (1982) 'The Coase Theorem: Some Experimental Tests', *Journal of Law and Economics*, 25, 73–98.

Hoffman, E. and M. Spitzer (1986) 'Experimental Tests of the Coase Theorem with Large Bargaining Groups', *Journal of Legal Studies*, 15, 149–71.

Ledyard, J. (1987) 'Market Failure', in J. Eatwell, M. Milgate and P. Newman (eds), *Allocation, Information, and Markets*, New York: W.W. Norton.

Mee, L. (1994) 'Management and Protection of the Black Sea Environment: An International Approach', Black Sea Environmental Programme – Global Environmental Facility, Istanbul.

Myers, N. (1992) *The Primary Source*, New York: W.W. Norton.

Olson, M. (1965) *The Logic of Collective Action*, Cambridge: Harvard University Press.

Ostrom, E. (1990) *Governing the Commons*, Cambridge: Cambridge University Press.

Samuelson, P. (1954) 'The Pure Theory of Public Expenditure', *Review of Economics and Statistics*, 36, 387–9.

Samuelson, P. (1955) 'A Diagrammatic Exposition of a Theory of Public Expenditure', *Review of Economics and Statistics*, 37, 350–56.

Shogren, J. (1992) 'An Experiment on Coasian Bargaining over Ex Ante Lotteries and Ex Post Rewards', *Journal of Economic Behavior and Organization*, 17, 153–69.

Shogren, J. and T. Crocker (1991) 'Noncooperative and Cooperative Protection from Transferable and Filterable Externalities', *Environment and Resource Economics*, 1, 195–214.

Shogren, J. and S. Kask (1992) 'Exploring the Boundaries of the Coase Theorem: Efficiency and Rationality given Imperfect Contract Enforcement', *Economics Letters*, 39, 155–61.

Stiglitz, J. (1994) *Whither Socialism?*, Cambridge, Mass.: MIT Press.

USAID (United States Agency for International Development) (1992) *Background Notes on Madagascar*, Washington, D.C.

■ *Chapter 3* ■

Economic Incentives for Environmental Protection: An Overview

3.1 Introduction

3.2 Price rationing: charges and subsidies

3.3 Liability rules: non-compliance fees, bonds and deposit refunds

3.4 Quantity rationing: marketable permits

3.5 Evaluative criteria

3.6 Practical conditions for use of economic incentives

3.7 Concluding remarks

Technical note: mathematical programming

■ *3.1* Introduction

Despite legal standards on the socially acceptable ambient concentration level of a pollutant, a producer has an incentive to shirk on pollution control. Since a producer's profits come from a market price that generally does not reflect society's preferences for environmental protection, the producer has no economic incentive to supply the level of pollution control society wants. If the market is not sending the correct signal to the producer about the socially optimal level of pollution control (see Chapter 2), a regulator has three general management tools she can turn to – technological restrictions such as mandated abatement methods, co-operative institutions that share information between regulators, polluters and victims, and economic incentives that increase the cost of shirking on pollution control.

This chapter explores the use of the third tool – economic incentives. Incentive systems have been promoted by economists for decades as a cost-effective alternative to technological restrictions and other forms of inflexible command-and-control environmental regulations. The idea behind economic incentives is to raise the cost of environmental shirking while allowing the producer the flexibility to find the least-cost pollution control strategy himself. By increasing the cost of shirking, the producer has a private incentive to provide the socially optimal level of pollution control. This chapter looks at some important overall issues in the use of incentives.

58

Chapters 4 and 5 look at two incentives (pollution taxes and marketable permits) in more detail.

Economic incentives can be grouped into three broad categories: price rationing, quantity rationing and liability rules. Price rationing increases the costs of shirking by setting a charge, tax or subsidy on producer behaviour or products. Emission or effluent charges are the most commonly discussed form of price rationing. Quantity rationing as an economic incentive sets the acceptable level of pollution by allocating marketable permits that provide an incentive to producers with low pollution control costs to reduce pollution and sell their excess permits to producers with high control costs. Liability rules set up a socially acceptable benchmark of behaviour such that, if a producer violates this benchmark, he suffers some financial consequence. Noncompliance fees, deposit-refund schemes and performance bonds represent alternative liability rules.

Theoretically, an economic incentive is used to alter a producer's pollution control strategy. Figure 3.1 shows the marginal cost (MC) and marginal benefit (MB) of pollution control. Marginal cost is positively sloped to reflect the reality that the control costs increase at an increasing rate – each incremental unit of pollution control costs more and more to achieve the next incremental level of environmental quality. Marginal benefit is negatively sloped to capture the belief that the benefits of control increase at a decreasing rate – each incremental unit of control provides fewer and fewer incremental benefits to society. The socially optimal level of control is where the marginal cost equals the marginal benefits of control (point A). If a

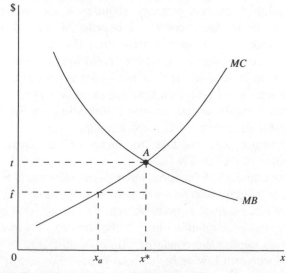

Figure 3.1 *Socially optimal level of pollution control*

market price does not reflect these social marginal benefits, the producer has no incentive to invest in this optimal level of control since he would earn greater profits by setting the level of pollution control at zero. In principle, the regulator can attempt to change the producer's behaviour by imposing an emissions charge of $t = MB = MC$. Now the producer can either invest in pollution control or pay the charge, t, for each unit of emissions. Since the tax exceeds the marginal control costs, $t > MC$, up to point A, the producer finds it more profitable to invest in control than to pay the charge. This charge provides the incentive for the producer to increase his level of control until his privately optimal level of control equals the social optimum, $MC = MB$. Such optimal taxes are known as Pigovian taxes.

To date, however, the majority of economic incentives actually used in the United States, Europe and Asia have not been used to change behaviour; rather they have been used to raise revenues for the general budget or some earmarked environmental fund. The incentives are typically set too low to induce producers to increase pollution control to the socially optimal level. Figure 3.1 shows the impact of setting the charge too low. If $\hat{t} < t$, the producer will now invest in a suboptimal level of control, $x_a < x$. Note that two-thirds of the 100 or more economic incentives used in the OECD countries have been used to raise revenue rather than change behaviour (O'Conner, 1993; Klarer, 1994; OECD, 1994, p. 177).

The divergence between the theory and reality of the use of economic incentives for environmental protection is driven by several factors, one of the most important being the lack of information required to implement successfully an incentive to achieve some social optimum. For both point and non-point sources of pollution, setting an incentive to alter a producer's pollution control strategy requires a significant amount of information on the marginal costs and benefits of control, including the environmental fate and transport systems and the value of life and limb. Recall that a point source is where pollution originates from one identifiable source or 'end-of-pipe'; a non-point source is where there are many, diffuse sources of pollution that are extremely costly to identify or monitor. Often a producer has private information on his own costs of pollution control or choice of control strategies and, if the regulator is uninformed, the producer can take advantage of this asymmetry to gain additional profits (Crocker, 1984).

As we proceed through the chapter, asymmetric information in the form of moral hazard or adverse selection will play an important role in the design and success of the economic incentive scheme. Recall that moral hazard exists when a regulator cannot observe the actions of a producer, while adverse selection implies the regulator cannot identify the producer's type, that is, a producer with low or high control costs. For example, non-point source pollution implies numerous, diffuse sources of emissions making it nearly impossible to monitor behaviour perfectly and enforce a pollution control level acceptable to society (see Shortle and Dunn, 1986; Russell & Shogren, 1993). Given this inability to monitor action, moral hazard implies that the producer has an incentive to shirk on pollution control since the expected costs of shirking are low. Unless the regulator can overcome this barrier of asymmetric information, the end result is too little pollution control and too much pollution. As a consequence, the regulator may have to give up some efficiency gains with an economic incentive scheme to reduce the information rents associated with moral hazard or adverse selection. A mixed system of economic incentives and technological restrictions is more likely to be considered by the regulator (see Lewis, 1996).

3.2 Price rationing: charges and subsidies

☐ 3.2.1 Emission charges

In principle, emission charges are fees levied on the discharge of pollutants into air or water, or onto the soil, or on the generation of noise. These charges are designed to reduce the quantity or improve the quality of pollution by making polluters pay at least part of the costs of the harm they do to the environment. Following Pigou, economists often favour emission charges over other options because, in principle, by charging for every unit of pollution released into the environment they induce firms to lower their emissions to the point where the incremental cost of pollution control equals the emission charges they must otherwise pay. Because pollution control costs typically differ among producers, those with lower control costs will tend to reduce their emission levels further than will higher cost polluters. Emission charges give producers an incentive to develop and adopt newer and better pollution control technologies as a means of bringing down the charges they must pay. To the degree that individual polluters use pollution control strategies which represent least cost solutions, the aggregate costs of pollution control should be minimised.

Emission charges are used in nearly all developed countries for some forms of point source pollution. Charges are normally applied to encourage water, waste and noise pollution control. In Europe, environmental protection agencies appear to believe that emission charges are effective when applied to water pollution but not for air quality control purposes. Factors such as the acceptability of charges to water users and the relative ability to identify sources of water pollution may explain why emission charges are used more frequently for water than for air pollution control. Note, however, that these charges are rarely, if ever, set at incentive levels that will change behaviour.

Waste is another pollutant where emission charges are widely applied. Since municipal and industrial wastes have to be treated before they are dumped, emission charges on waste take the form of waste treatment charges. Waste-related emission charges tend to vary as a function of the cost of waste treatment. Country experience with the use of emission charges for waste pollution control is also varied. While European countries and the United States all apply emission charges on municipal and industrial wastes, the available evidence suggests that they are successful in raising revenue, but unsuccessful in changing behaviour. The Dutch Manure Surplus charge appears to be an exception. The manure charge is based on the phosphate content above and beyond the amount farmers are allowed to put on their land, and appears to be more effective in increasing pollution control.

We can illustrate the basic idea behind the emission charge with a simple model of a profit-maximizing producer whose output generates emissions that pose some hazard to human or environmental health. Let the producer select a level of output, q, to maximise his or her net profits, $\pi = pq - c(q)$, where p is the fixed market price of q and $c(q)$ is the cost function associated with producing q. Assume costs increase at an increasing rate, $c' \equiv dc/dq > 0$ and $c'' \equiv d^2c/dq^2 > 0$. The producer's profit-maximizing problem is written as

$$\underset{q}{\text{Max}} \, [pq - c(q)] \tag{3.1}$$

The producer selects an optimal level of output, q^*, to maximise net profits by equating the marginal benefit of an extra unit of output, p, to the marginal cost, c',

$$MB \equiv p = c' \equiv MC \tag{3.2}$$

Figure 3.2 shows the private optimal level of production.

The production of q also emits a pollutant feared to damage human and environmental health. Let the total level of emissions of the pollutant be represented by a linear relationship, $\alpha = \beta q$, where β is a fixed emission coefficient, that is, as production increases, emissions increase at the constant rate of β. Let $D(\alpha)$ represent the monetary damages associated with the level of emissions. Assume that, as emissions increase, damages increase at a decreasing rate, $D' \equiv dD/d\alpha > 0$ and $D'' \equiv d^2D/d\alpha^2 < 0$.

Now if the firm was to incorporate the external damages to human and environmental health, the producer's problem is written as

$$\underset{q}{\text{Max}} \, [pq - c(q) - D(\beta q)] \tag{3.3}$$

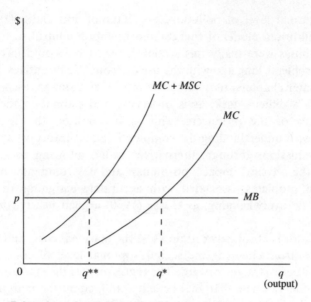

Figure 3.2 *Privately and socially optimal levels of output*

The producer now selects an optimal level of output, q^{**}, to maximise net profits by equating the marginal benefit, p, to the private marginal cost, c', and the marginal social cost, $\beta D'$,

$$MB \equiv p = c' + \beta D' \equiv MC + MSC \tag{3.4}$$

The producer accounts for the external damage by reducing the level of output. Figure 3.2 shows that, if we include the marginal social cost in the producer's decision, his or her optimal response is to decrease output until the marginal benefit equals the sum of the private and social marginal costs.

The question then becomes: how does society get the producer to internalise the marginal social cost into his decision making? One way is for the regulator to set an emission charge equal to the marginal social damages caused by the emissions associated with production:

$$t = \beta D' \tag{3.5}$$

Now the producer's problem is written as

$$\underset{q}{\text{Max}} \, [pq - C(q) - tq] \tag{3.6}$$

such that the producer chooses a level of q to maximise profits

$$p = c' + t \tag{3.7}$$

and since $t = \beta D'$, equation (3.7) is identical to equation (3.4) – the producer has internalised the external damages that his emissions have imposed on others – the producer's private optimum matches up with society's optimal level of pollution. See Baumol and Oates (1988) for a general equilibrium model of charges and pollution control.

Now if things were really this straightforward we would have resolved pollution problems long ago with the use of economic incentives. But, as we will see in later chapters, measuring the monetary damages associated with emissions is a difficult task, as is observing and estimating the pollution control costs of the producers. This is in addition to the difficulties associated with understanding the complex fate-and-transport systems that move the emissions through alternative media, allowing us to quantify accurately the physical impacts on human and environmental health. The information problems associated with accurately assigning an emissions charge can be overwhelming, as Coase (1960) argued nearly four decades ago.

If a regulator is absolutely certain as to the marginal costs and benefits of pollution control, achieving the socially optimal level of control with an emission charge is straightforward. The regulator sets the emission charge, t, equal to the level where marginal benefits, MB, equal the marginal cost of control, MC, $t = MB = MC$, as we saw in Figure 3.1. Given this charge, a producer would compare the charge to his marginal cost of control. If $t > MC$, the producer will invest in pollution control since it is cheaper than paying the emission charge per unit of emissions. The producer will continue to control pollution until $t = MC = MB$. At this level, the producer's private choice of pollution control will match the regulator's socially optimal level of control.

But if the regulator is uncertain about the marginal cost or benefit of pollution control, Weitzman (1974) has shown that the effectiveness of price rationing with an emission charge will depend on the slopes of the cost and benefit curves and how far expectations deviate from reality. The slopes represent how the marginal costs and benefits change given an increase in pollution control: a flat slope implies costs and benefits do not change much, while a steep slope implies the opposite. Suppose that the regulator knows the marginal benefits of control, but is uncertain about the marginal costs. The effectiveness of the emissions charge will depend on the slope of the marginal benefits curve. If marginal benefits are constant across alternative levels of pollution control, the uncertainty about marginal control costs does not matter – the social optimum can be achieved regardless of the realised cost. Figure 3.3a illustrates the horizontal MB curve representing the constant marginal benefits. The curve EMC represents the regulator's expectation, or best guess, about the producer's marginal control cost. Point A represents the expected social optimum, $x^* = x_E$, at which the marginal benefits equal the expected marginal costs, $MB = EMC$. The regulator sets the charge at $t = MB = EMC$, then waits to see if the realised cost deviates from his expectations.

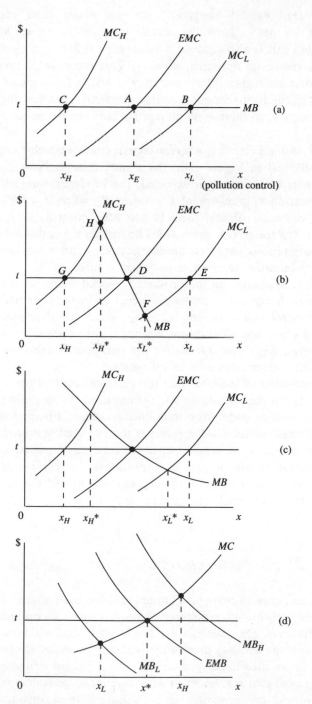

Figure 3.3   *Charges given uncertainty*

Suppose the realised marginal costs are lower than expected, as represented by MC_L. Now the social optimum is where $MB = MC_L$ (point B), but this is also equal to the charge, $t = MB = MC_L$: the private optimum is the social optimum, $x^* = x_L$. This result holds even if actual marginal costs are higher than expected, $t = MB = MC_H$ (point C), where $x^* = x_L$. The uniform emission charge perfectly matches the marginal benefit of control, so there is no divergence between the social and private optima.

However, in the polar case where marginal control benefits are extremely steep, as reflected in Figure 3.3b, the results change. Now if the actual marginal costs are lower than expected, the producer supplies too much pollution control, $x_L > x_L^*$ (point E v. point F), where $t = MC_L > MB$. If the actual costs are higher, there is too little control, $x_H < x_H^*$, where $t = MC_H > MB$ (point G v. point H). The further the realised costs deviate from the expectations, the worse the charge does – either providing too little or too much incentive to invest in pollution control.

Figure 3.3c illustrates an intermediately sloped marginal benefit curve. The emission charge still provides an incentive to over- or underinvest in pollution control, $x_H^* > x_H$ and $x_L^* < x_L$, given the divergence between realised and actual costs, but the inefficiency is not as severe as in the case of the extremely steep slope. The flatter the marginal benefits curve the less severe the divergence of costs is on efficiency.

If we reverse the situation so that the marginal control costs are known with certainty but the benefits are not, the emission charge again provides an incentive to over- or underinvest in pollution control. Figure 3.3d shows an intermediate case where EMB represents the expected marginal benefits of pollution control. If the actual benefits exceed the expected benefits, the emission charge results in too little pollution control $t = MC < MB_H$, $x_H > x^*$. The opposite occurs if the expectations exceed the actual benefit, $t = MC > MB_L$: too much pollution control, $x^* > x_L$.

☐ ## 3.2.2 *Ambient charge*

In general, an emission charge is a limited tool for many sources of pollution owing to the information requirements needed to set an optimal charge to change behaviour. Emission charges are likely to be inefficient because of moral hazard: the inability to monitor perfectly producer efforts to control pollution. In an attempt to reduce the moral hazard problem, Segerson (1988) suggested that regulators could design a charge system based on the overall ambient concentration of a pollutant in a region. Following Holmström's (1982) work on incentive structures for labour, Segerson introduced an ambient charge scheme that combines penalties and rewards for exceeding or beating a specific level of total ambient concentrations. The ambient charge scheme has two parts: a per unit charge or subsidy based on the deviation from some ambient standard and a lump sum penalty for not achieving the standard. The per unit charge or subsidy depends on the magnitude of the deviation from the standard, while the lump sum penalty is independent of the magnitude of deviation. The liability of each polluter depends on the aggregate emissions from the entire group of polluters, not just his own level of emissions, since these emissions are unobservable to the regulator. This creates a bubble of total ambient concentration that the entire group of producers must satisfy. If the total ambient concentration of a pollutant is found to exceed the standard, each polluter pays the full incremental social costs of the excessive ambient concentrations. Supposing the incremental damages cost society $1000, each polluter would then be required to pay the full $1000 rather than a share of the damages. The regulator therefore collects $n \cdot (\$1000)$ in total rather than $(\$1000)/n$, where n is the total number of polluters. Therefore the system is not budget balancing – more money is collected in charges from the polluters than society suffered in damages. The regulator can set the charge/subsidy and penalty in several different combinations to achieve the desired goal of reduced pollutant use. The major advantage of the ambient charge system is that it does not require continual monitoring of emissions.

Let us reconsider our model of the producer to see how the ambient charge system is constructed. Assume there are now several producers, $i = 1, 2, \ldots, n$, who are generating some output, q_i, that can be sold at a fixed price, p, and can be produced at a cost, $c_i(q_i)$, where costs increase with increased output, $c_i' \equiv dc_i/dq_i > 0$. As before, a producer's problem, absent any incentive scheme, is to select a level of output to maximise net profits

$$\underset{q_i}{\text{Max}} \ [pq_i - c_i(q_i)] \tag{3.8}$$

Producer i selects the privately optimal level of output, q_i^*, where the marginal benefits equal the marginal costs of production

$$p = c_i' \tag{3.9}$$

Again the production of q_i generates emissions. Let $\alpha_i = \beta_i q_i$ represent the emission level of output q_i given the fixed emission coefficient, β_i. However, suppose the regulator cannot directly monitor how producer i's emissions are transported into a central collection point such as a lake or river. The best the regulator can do is measure the total ambient concentration of the pollutant – the regulator cannot identify which producer contributed the most or the least to the total ambient concentration, given there is a random factor, ε, that affects the transport of emissions through the alternative environmental media. The random factor could be rainfall or soil conditions or wind. Let the ambient concentration of the pollutant be written as

$$\varphi = \varphi(\alpha; \varepsilon),$$

where $\alpha = (\alpha_1, \alpha_2, \ldots, \alpha_n)$. Assume the level of ambient concentration increases with increased emissions, $\varphi' \equiv \partial\varphi/\partial\alpha > 0$.

The ambient charge scheme is implemented by comparing actual ambient levels of the pollutant to a specific ambient standard. The standard is the cut-off beyond which ambient concentrations are perceived to increase the risk to an unacceptable level. Let $\bar{\varphi}$ be the specific ambient standard such that, if the observed ambient level exceeds this cut-off, $\varphi > \bar{\varphi}$, the producers will be penalised; if the level is less than or equal to the cut-off, $\varphi \le \bar{\varphi}$, the producers may receive a subsidy. Let $F(\bar{\varphi}, \alpha)$ represent the likelihood of the ambient concentration not exceeding the cut-off. The ambient charge is written as

$$T_i(\varphi) = \begin{cases} t_i(\varphi - \bar{\varphi}) + k_i & \text{if } \varphi > \bar{\varphi} \\ t_i(\varphi - \bar{\varphi}) & \text{if } \varphi \le \bar{\varphi} \end{cases}$$

where t_i is the variable charge to producer i and k_i is a fixed penalty imposed on producer i when the ambient cut-off is exceeded. This fixed penalty provides extra incentive to keep the ambient level of the pollutant below the cut-off level.

The level of the ambient charge depends on the perceived benefits of reduced pollution. Suppose the regulator knows the social benefit of decreasing the level of ambient concentrations, $B(\varphi(\alpha; \varepsilon) - \varphi(0; \varepsilon))$, where these benefits decrease with increased ambient concentrations, $B' \equiv (dB/d\varphi)(\partial\varphi/\partial\alpha) < 0$. The regulator selects the level of output to maximise

$$\underset{q_i}{\text{Max}} \; [pq_i - c_i(q_i) + E[B(\varphi(\alpha; \varepsilon) - \varphi(0; \varepsilon))]]$$

The optimal level of output, q_i^{**}, from the regulator's viewpoint is where the marginal benefits equal the marginal private costs and the expected marginal social costs defined in terms of lost benefits, $E[B']\beta_i$.

$$p = c_i' - E[B']\beta_i \tag{3.10}$$

The ambient charge is designed to provide an incentive for the producer to select this socially optimal level of output. The producer's revised problem is to select a level of output, given that the ambient charge is included in his net profit calculations

$$\underset{q_i}{\text{Max}} \; [pq_i - c_i(q_i) - E[T_i(\varphi(\alpha; \varepsilon))]]$$

where $E[T_i(\varphi(\alpha; \varepsilon))] = t_i E[\varphi(\alpha; \varepsilon)] - t_i\bar{\varphi} + k_i(1 - F(\bar{\varphi}, \alpha))$. Let E represent the expectation of the random factor, ε; that is, $E[T_i(\cdot)]$ is the expected ambient charge given that, say, weather is uncertain. The producer selects q_i such that marginal benefits equal the marginal private cost and the expected marginal cost of ambient charge

$$p = c_i' + t_i E[\varphi']\beta_i - k_i(\partial F/\partial \alpha_i)\beta_i \tag{3.11}$$

where $\partial \phi/\partial \alpha_i < 0$: increased emissions decrease the likelihood of observed ambient concentrations being lower than the cut-off standard. Comparing equation (3.11) with equation (3.10), we can see that there are several ways the regulator can set the ambient charge to achieve the desired level of production. The regulator could set the fixed penalty equal to zero and set the tax equal to the ratio of expected marginal benefits over the marginal contribution to ambient concentrations of increased production; set the tax equal to zero and set the fixed penalty equal to the ratio of expected marginal benefits over the marginal likelihood of exceeding the cut-off standard; or the tax could be set at an arbitrary level and the fixed penalty could be set equal to the ratio of the sum of expected marginal benefits and the tax-weight marginal contribution to ambient concentrations over the marginal likelihood of exceeding the cut-off standard:

(a) $k_i = 0$ and $t_i = -E[B']/E[\varphi']$
(b) $t_i = 0$ and $k_i = E[B']/(\partial F/\partial \alpha_i)$
(c) t_i set arbitrary and $k_i = (E[B'] + t_i E[\varphi'])/(\partial F/\partial \alpha_i)$

All three forms of the ambient charge give the producer an incentive to select the level of output that the regulator wants. Since each producer pays the full marginal damage of the total level of ambient pollution, there is no incentive to free-ride on the other producer's actions. Given that the regulator collects a tax on marginal damages from all producers, however, the implication is that the scheme is not budget balancing.

But, as with the case of the emission charge, Cabe and Herriges (1992) argue that the disadvantage of the ambient charge is the remaining information requirements needed to set the appropriate levels of the tax/subsidy and penalty. The ambient charge would require collecting site-specific data on the complex fate and transport systems associated with pollutant leaching, run-off and volatilisation, and the polluter's and regulator's prior beliefs about this transport system. Without this, the ambient charge will be misspecified and will not achieve its desired goal of achieving a socially optimal level of pollution.

Figure 3.4 illustrates the information problem with the ambient charge for pollutant control. The horizontal axis represents the level of production, q, that influences ambient concentration levels; the top vertical axis represents the net benefit to society that depends on production and emissions, B, while the bottom axis represents the level of the ambient charge, t. The socially optimal level of production is where the net social benefits are maximised,

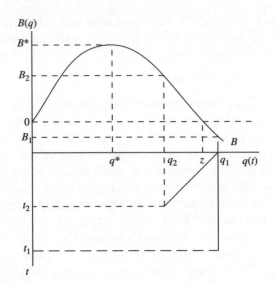

Figure 3.4   *Optimal levels of output drive given ambient charge (adapted from Cabe and Herriges, 1992)*

B^*, at production level q^*. Points to the left of q^* represent too little production from society's viewpoint, while points to the right imply too much production. Suppose that when the producer acts to maximise his own profits ignoring any social costs, he selects a privately optimal level of production, say at q_1.

If the producer does not perceive that his actions have any impact on pollution, he believes that his tax burden is independent of his production level and is determined by the solid vertical line in the lower half of Figure 3.4. The production level remains at q_1 and the producer stays in business as long as the ambient charge does not exceed some economic threshold, $t \leq t_1$. If the charge exceeds this threshold, $t > t_1$ the producer shuts down and leaves the industry because his profits are negative, i.e., $B_1 < 0$. In this case the ambient charge is a discrete policy tool – the producer either does what he would normally do without the charge ($t \leq t_1$) or he is completely shuts down ($t > t_1$). The reason is that the producer's beliefs influence the perceived impact of the charge. If the producer does not believe that his actions have a direct impact on the level of ambient concentrations, the ambient charge does not change his behaviour. The regulator will choose to continue production and pollution if $q < Z$ since $B > 0$; otherwise he will shut the producer down if $q > Z$, since net social welfare is negative, i.e., $B < 0$.

The information problems with ambient charges exist any time the producer's subjective beliefs about the relationship between production and pollution are small relative to the objective beliefs or the regulator's belief. Figure 3.4 shows that, if the producer believes their is some relationship between his tax burden and his level of production, the level of production will change little given an increase in the charge. The level of production is still beyond the social optimal level, q^*. Again the charge, t_2, can be set high enough to shut the producer down, but that will depend on the level of q_2 relative to Z. In the case illustrated in Figure 3.4, the regulator would want the producer to stay in operation, even though the production level is more than is socially optimal since net social benefits are positive, $B_2 > 0$. Given the regulator's ability or inability to determine and alter the producer's belief about the fate and transport system, quantity rationing in the form of traditional emission standards or technology restrictions may be the more attractive policy tool relative to the ambient charge.

☐ 3.2.3 Product charges

Given the information problems associated with the theoretically first-best schemes such as the emission and ambient charges, the regulator's alternative form of price rationing is product charges – an indirect attempt to influence behaviour by putting a charge directly on the product or input that is perceived to be causing the problem. Product charges are fees or taxes levied on outputs or inputs that are potentially hazardous to humans or the environment when used in production, or when they or the containers that carry them become waste matter. By increasing the cost of hazardous materials, product charges encourage producers and consumers to substitute more environmentally safe products or inputs. Product charges promote a life-cycle approach to pollutant control by focusing attention on potential environmental costs at each stage of the product cycle: production, use and disposal. In principle, product charges can be used to exercise control at any point in the pollutant product cycle. In addition, these charges may also be levied on input characteristics, such as the persistence of a pollutant. Product charges have many variations and are applied extensively.

The Netherlands uses a product charge with its general fuel charge in the form of a surtax on oil excise duties. Its rationale is that, while many of the individual inputs to a production process may not be environmentally friendly, the administrative cost of applying charges to a set of inputs such as pollutants would be too high. A tax on the energy required to process a set of inputs offers a straightforward alternative that may be also administratively efficient. Experience in western European countries suggests that product charges applied to identifiable intermediate or finished products are more difficult to use than when they are applied to inputs or post-consumption wastes. Nevertheless, some European countries have instituted product charges on a limited range of products. Norway and Sweden, for example, apply product charges to batteries, fertilisers and pesticides, while Italy levies a tax on plastic bags which is paid by manufactures and importers. Norway places a flat surcharge of 13 per cent on wholesale pesticide prices. Between 1986 and 1992, Sweden imposed a 20 per cent charge on the price of pesticides. The administrative efficiency of product charges has been found to be high, mainly because they can be incorporated into existing tax systems.

A common feature of almost all reported product charges, however, is their apparent lack of impact on the behaviour of producers (OECD, 1994). There is little evidence of product charges leading to significantly reduced use of target inputs or final products. The evidence suggests that product charges have been set at relatively low levels, so that it is more cost effective for producers and consumers to pay these charges than to seek alternative inputs or finished products, or to vary their practices with respect to waste disposal. While product charges may never induce desired behavioural changes, they appear to help regulators finance policies and programmes to deal with the environmental problems of the target products (see Russell, 1992).

☐ *3.2.4 Subsidies*

Subsidies are forms of financial assistance offered to a producer by regulators. Subsidies can be used as an incentive to encourage pollution control or to mitigate the economic impact of regulations by helping firms meet compliance costs. Subsidies normally take the form of grants, loans and tax allowances. Subsidies are widely applied in many countries, and are usually funded by environmental charges rather than from general tax revenues.

France provides loans to industry to control water pollution. Italy provides subsidies for solid waste recycling and recuperation, favouring industries which commit themselves to altering manufacturing processes. The Netherlands has a financial assistance programme that provides incentive to industries to promote compliance with regulation and promote technology research and the introduction of pollution control equipment. The German subsidy system assists small producers which could experience cash flow problems because of sudden additional capital requirements for pollution control, and to speed up the implementation of environmental programmes. Sweden used subsidies to reduce pesticide loadings by providing funds to test the efficacy of pesticide spraying equipment, to provide pest forecasts and warning services, to supply financial assistance and technical advice on organic farming, to increase training of applicators and to increase the level of research and technical training on low-dose sulphonylureas herbicides. The United States subsidised the construction of municipal water treatment plants and has spent billions helping farmers pay the costs of soil conservation and preventing erosion-induced losses of soil productivity.

Suppose that our producer receives a subsidy for selecting an output level that is below some fixed output level set by the regulator to achieve a specific level of ambient concentrations. Let the subsidy equal $S = \gamma(\bar{q} - q)$, where $\gamma = D'\beta$ represents the marginal social cost of producing q. If $q = \bar{q}$, the producer receives no subsidy, $S = 0$. If the producer shuts down operations, $q = 0$, he gets the full subsidy $S = \gamma\bar{q}$.

The producer's problem with the subsidy is written as

$$\underset{q}{\text{Max}} \ [pq - c(q) + \gamma(\bar{q} - q)]$$

The producer selects a level of output to maximise net profits where the marginal benefit, p, equals the marginal private cost, c', and the marginal opportunity cost of lost subsidy, γ,

$$p = c' + \gamma$$

Every unit of output results in a lost unit of the subsidy, γ. Therefore the producer has the incentive to reduce his output to the socially desired level, the same as in the case of the emission charge.

However, there is a difference between a subsidy and a charge viewed from a long-run perspective that considers entry and exit of producers into and from the industry. Without entry and exit, a subsidy and a charge lead to symmetric results, but with entry and exit the aggregate impacts differ – the charge reduces aggregate pollution, while the subsidy increases aggregate pollution. To see how charges and subsidies differ consider Figures 3.5 and 3.6. We first define the producer behaviour given the charge. Figure 3.5 shows the case of the charge with entry and exit. Figure 3.5a represents the behaviour of a representative producer, while Figure 3.5b represents the industry. Given the average cost curve and marginal cost curve without the tax are written as

$$AC = c(q)/q \quad \text{and} \quad MC = c'$$

the producer operates at output level q^* where his economic profits equal zero. We assume a perfectly competitive market so the producer does not earn positive economic profits. Recall that economic profits include the opportunity cost of the next best alternative, implying the producer earns the market rate of return, no more or no less. Positive economic profits imply the producer is earning more than the going market rate of return, while negative economic profits imply the producer is not covering his

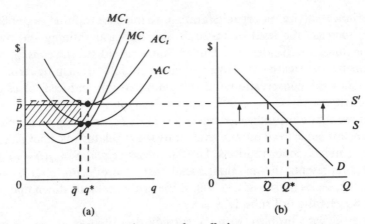

Figure 3.5 *Short and long run impacts of a pollution tax*

opportunity cost and should invest his resources elsewhere. Given perfect competition, this implies a perfectly elastic aggregate supply curve, as shown in Figure 3.5b and the market price, $\bar{p}$. Assuming the aggregate demand curve for the industry is downward sloping, the aggregate level of output is set at Q^*, where Q^* equals the sum of all the output, q^*, from every producer in the industry.

If the regulator now imposes a charge, as in equation (3.5), the average and marginal cost curves are rewritten as

$$AC_t = \frac{c(q)}{q} + t$$

$$MC_t = c' + t$$

Figure 3.5a shows that the charge results in a parallel shift up of both average and marginal cost. If the market price stays at $\bar{p}$, the producer operates where marginal benefit, $\bar{p}$, equals the new marginal cost, MC_t, and he will produce at $\bar{q}$ thereby making negative economic profit, $\pi < 0$. The hatched area in Figure 3.5a represents the negative profits. These negative profits will force some producers to leave the industry, thereby shifting back the aggregate supply curve, S to S' as shown in Figure 3.5b. The supply curve will shift back until a new market price is reached, $\bar{\bar{p}}$, such that the remaining producers are once again making zero economic profits, given the charge. This results in a decrease in the aggregate level of output to $\tilde{Q}$ from Q^*, thereby reducing the level of aggregate pollution. Note that the producers that remained in the industry are producing again at q^*, but because there are fewer producers, aggregate output and pollution are reduced. The charge achieved the desired long-term objective: a reduction in aggregate pollution.

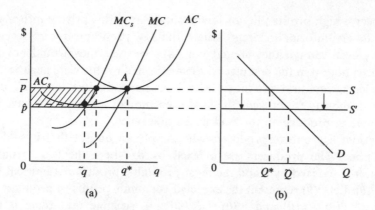

Figure 3.6 *Short and long run impacts of a pollution subsidy*

Now consider the subsidy scheme. With the subsidy, the average and marginal cost curves now are rewritten as

$$AC_s = \frac{c(q)}{q} + \frac{\varphi \bar{q}}{q} - \gamma$$

$$MC_s = c' + \gamma$$

Note that, while the effect of a subsidy on marginal cost is the same as the charge ($t = \gamma = D'\beta$); the effect on average cost is different. Instead of a parallel shift up in average costs as with the charge, the subsidy causes average cost to shift down and to the left. Figure 3.6a shows the impact of a subsidy on the individual producer. Again, if the producer initially was earning zero economic profits (point A), the subsidy will now cause him to reduce output to $\tilde{q}$ and earn positive economic profits, given that the market price stays at $\bar{p}$, as shown by the hatched area in Figure 3.6a. However, these positive profits will attract new producers to enter the industry, thereby shifting the aggregate supply curve out, resulting in a lower market price, $\hat{p}$, and a higher level of aggregate output, an increase to $\tilde{Q}$ from Q^* (Figure 3.6b). Now, even though each producer is generating less output, $\hat{q}$, and less individual pollution, there are more producers in the industry, so aggregate pollution actually increases. With unrestricted entry, the subsidy attracts more producers who produce less individual pollution but end up increasing aggregate pollution. The charge and subsidy schemes no longer lead to symmetric results in the long run, given free entry into and exit from the industry.

Lewis (1994) provides another useful example of the way a subsidy can be inefficient even if the regulator can measure perfectly the monetary damages to human and environmental health. A subsidy scheme can lend to inefficiencies if the polluter has private information about the profitability of his production of output. If the regulator does not know the type of producer – high profitability or low profitability – this private information leads to an 'information rent' where the low-profit producers receive a subsidy even though they should not have because they would not have produced output in the first place if their expected profits were negative. For example, agricultural producers who own unproductive land still could receive a subsidy to set aside the land even though it would not have been profitable to produce on the land in the first place.

Consider a group of producers who supply an output that is sold at a fixed price. The producers are indexed by θ, where the least profitable producer is indexed by $\underline{\theta}$ and the most profitable producer is indexed by $\bar{\theta}$, $\theta \in [\underline{\theta}, \bar{\theta}]$. Let $\pi(\theta)$ represent the expected economic profits of producer type θ, where $\pi(\bar{\theta}) > \pi(\underline{\theta})$ and $\pi'(\theta) \equiv d\pi/d\theta > 0$. Assume that there is some producer type, $\tilde{\theta}$, that has zero economic profits, $\pi(\tilde{\theta}) = 0$, where $\underline{\theta} < \tilde{\theta} < \bar{\theta}$. We presume the regulator does not know the profitability of any specific producer, but does know the distribution of producer types in the economy. For simplicity, assume the distribution of types is uniform: that is, there is an equal likelihood for each producer type.

Each producer emits a pollutant that imposes an external cost on society. Let $w > 0$ represent the social cost generated by each producer who operates in the economy. The net social surplus from production is $\pi(\theta) - w$. The socially optimal size of the industry is where the net social surplus is zero (there are no more gains from trade): $\pi(\hat{\theta}) - w = 0$, where $\hat{\theta}$ is the threshold producer type that separates those producers who should stay in business from those who should not, given that social costs are accounted for.

Figure 3.7 shows that if we ignore social costs, the size of the industry is the set of producers with positive expected profits, $\pi(\theta) \geq 0$, which are all the producers of types $\tilde{\theta}$ to $\bar{\theta}$. Those producer types between $\underline{\theta}$ and $\tilde{\theta}$ have negative expected profits, $\pi(\theta) < 0$, and will not enter the industry. If we accounted for the social costs, $\pi(\theta) - w$, the size of the industry should decline to the producers where $\pi(\theta) - w > 0$, which are the types between and $\hat{\theta}$ and $\bar{\theta}$. The industry should eliminate the producer types between $\tilde{\theta}$ and $\hat{\theta}$ where the net expected profits are negative, $\pi(\theta) - w < 0$. If these producer types between $\tilde{\theta}$ and $\hat{\theta}$ leave the industry, pollution will be reduced to the socially optimal level.

The producer types between $\tilde{\theta}$ and $\hat{\theta}$, however, need an incentive to leave the industry. They are not going to leave on their own since their private expected profits are positive. The regulator needs to provide an incentive to the producers to leave. Let this incentive be in the form of a subsidy equal to the unit social cost, w. Producers who receive the subsidy will halt production and leave the industry. Now only those producers with profits that exceed or equal the social cost (types $\hat{\theta}$ and $\bar{\theta}$) will enter the market, thereby resulting in the efficient allocation of resources.

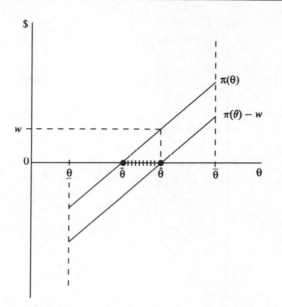

Figure 3.7 *Asymmetric information and an environmental subsidy (adapted from Lewis, 1994)*

But there is a potential financing problem with this subsidy scheme, given the regulator's inability to determine a producer's type. If the regulator is subject to a balanced-budget requirement such that the subsidy must be paid for from a tax on the benefits received by society for less pollution (that is, no deficit), the regulator cannot use the subsidy to reduce pollution to the socially acceptable level without violating the balanced-budget constraint. The reason is that, since the regulator cannot determine the producer types, he cannot identify which producers would not have entered production in the absence of the subsidy: that is, those producer types where $\pi(\theta) < 0$, types between $\underline{\theta}$ and $\tilde{\theta}$. These producer types are entitled to the subsidy since the regulator cannot discriminate between producers, therefore the regulator will have to pay out more in subsidies than he receives in taxes equalling the gains in environmental quality. The low-profitability producers have an information rent that they can exploit.

Figure 3.8 shows the divergence between the total subsidy paid out and the total benefits received, given the exit of low-profit producers. The regulator's subsidy would need to be paid to all producer types $\underline{\theta}$ to $\hat{\theta}$ who have negative expected net profits, $\pi(\theta) - w < 0$. The total subsidy would equal w times the number of producers between $\underline{\theta}$ and $\hat{\theta}$. This is area $A + B$ in Figure 3.8. The total benefit to society from this subsidy, however, is only area B: the group of producer types $\tilde{\theta}$ to $\hat{\theta}$ that would have operated without the subsidy but would have exited with the subsidy, $\pi(\theta) - w < 0 < \pi(\theta)$.

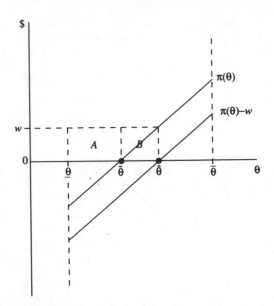

Figure 3.8 *Subsidy paid ignoring information rents*

Therefore, by setting the subsidy to reflect accurately the social costs of pollution, the regulator cannot balance his budget and efficiently allocate resources.

The regulator can get around this problem by relaxing the budget-balancing requirement or by offering a subsidy that does not perfectly capture the level of social damages. Figure 3.9 shows what happens if the regulator offers a lower subsidy, $\hat{w} < w$, to the producers. Now fewer firms leave the industry, so the benefits of improved environmental quality are smaller, areas $B + C$, but the total subsidy outlay is smaller as well, areas $B + A$. The lower subsidy attempts to curtail the information rent of the privately informed producers. If area A equals area C, the subsidies paid out equal the benefits gained, and the budget is balanced. The point to gain from this example is that, even if the regulator could accurately set a subsidy to reflect true social cost of pollution, producers with private information on profitability can exploit the incentive system to their own benefit, thereby leading to inefficient resource allocations. Therefore the regulator would not set the subsidy, or a tax for that matter, at the level of marginal social damages, but rather at a level that balances the costs of the information rents with the gains in environmental quality. This again implies that economic instruments alone may not be sufficient to achieve the socially desired level of environmental quality. A mixed system of incentives and technological restrictions or quantity constraints may be more appropriate (see Crocker, 1984; Laffont, 1994).

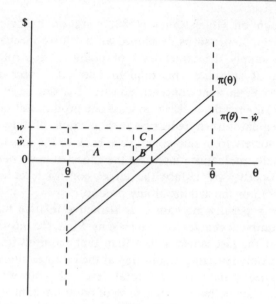

Figure 3.9 *Subsidy paid accounting for information rents*

3.3 Liability rules: non-compliance fees, bonds and deposit-refunds

Liability rules are set in such a way that there is an incentive for a producer to follow some prescribed mandate, technological restriction or acceptable behaviour. Liability rules can be set so that the producer pays a bond in advance and is reimbursed if there is no harm committed or pays a non-compliance fee after the harm has occurred. Liability rules attempt to reduce the level of shirking on environmental pollution control by raising the costs of misbehaviour. One important liability rule concerns the non-compliance fee: a producer is fined if his actions lead to a level of pollution that exceeds some set standard. But given the moral hazard problems associated with many types of pollution, identifying the exact culprit may not be that straightforward since ambient concentrations cannot be perfectly assigned to the responsible producer.

☐ 3.3.1 Non-compliance fees

Xepapadeas (1991) recognised the possibility of moral hazard, proposing a theoretically plausible incentive scheme with questionable political appeal.

Drawing again on Holmström's (1982) work on behavioural incentives within the firm, Xepapadeas developed an incentive mechanism to induce polluters to supply the target level of pollution control. Relying on a combination of subsidies and random fines, the mechanism works as follows. If total ambient concentration exceeds the target standard at a common site, the regulator selects at least one producer at random and fines him. The regulator then redistributes a portion of this fine minus the damages to society from non-compliance back to the other producers. The random penalty mechanism increases the expected costs of shirking and, if designed properly, will induce the target control level without actually having to monitor the actions of any producer.

The random penalty mechanism is attractive relative to the systems of emission or ambient charges for two reasons. First, the information required to implement the mechanism is less than that required for the charges or subsidies. By only requiring monitoring at the receptor site, the random fine mechanism needs data on the total level of ambient concentration; knowledge of each polluter's actual level of pollution control is unnecessary. In contrast, the charge approaches require data on the actual control efforts of each and every producer, information attainable at a significant cost. Second, the mechanism is budget balancing, and does not require additional revenues beyond the welfare gains generated by abatement. This contrasts with the charges where each producer incurs the full marginal damage associate with the target level of pollution, resulting in a multiple of damage costs collected or distributed when taxes or subsidies are used.

Herriges *et al.* (1994) demonstrate that the random penalty scheme will work only if all the producers are risk-averse. The reason is that the balance budget requirement creates an interdependence among the producers – one producer's loss is another producer's gain. A producer's incentive depends both on his own expected penalty and on the expected penalty suffered by the other producers, since he could potentially receive a share of their penalty to keep the budget balanced. Therefore, by increasing the magnitude of the penalty, the regulator is increasing both the costs and benefits of shirking. Increasing the penalty given balanced budgeting simply increases the variability of a producer's profits from shirking. If the producers are risk-neutral, the increased variability does not influence their tendency to shirk since they receive the full marginal benefit of shirking and only pay a fraction of the marginal cost. The expected rewards from shirking will still exceed the rewards from compliance. But if the producers are risk-averse, they are more afraid about losing profits than they are happy about receiving profits. This serves to magnify the perceived consequences of being caught shirking. And if producers are sufficiently risk-averse, they will magnify the fraction of marginal costs enough to offset the full marginal benefits of shirking. Consequently, the expected rewards from compliance will now exceed the expected rewards from shirking and the random penalty scheme will have achieved its objective – private decisions match social objectives.

Consider how the random penalty scheme works. Suppose we have our group of producers, $i = 1, 2, \ldots, n$, who now must select a level of pollution control, x_i. The regulator wants each producer to select the socially optimal level of control, x_i^{**}, but given the inability to monitor the control of each producer she constructs the following random penalty scheme. Let $\bar{\varphi}$ represent the critical threshold of the ambient level of the pollutant. If the observed ambient concentration does not exceed this cut-off, $\varphi \leq \bar{\varphi}$, then each producer will receive a subsidy, b_i, in the form of a share, ϕ_i, of the social benefit, $B(a(x))$, where $x = (x_1, x_2, \ldots, x_n)$.

But if the observed ambient level exceeds the cut-off, $\varphi > \bar{\varphi}$, the producer faces two possible outcomes – he will be randomly selected and fined, F_i, with probability, σ_i, or another producer will be selected and fined with likelihood ($\sigma_j, j \neq i$) and the remaining producers will receive the subsidy plus some share of the fine minus the damages to society from non-compliance. The random penalty scheme increases the cost of shirking on control effort, and is summarised below

$$
S_i(x) = \begin{cases} b_i - \phi_i B(a(x)) & \varphi < \bar{\varphi} \\ -F_i & \varphi > \bar{\varphi} \text{ with probability } \sigma_i \\ b_i + \phi_{ij}[b_j + F_j + \Gamma(a(x))] & \varphi > \bar{\varphi} \text{ with probability } \sigma_j, j \neq i \end{cases}
$$

where $\phi_{ij} \equiv \phi_i / \sum_{k \neq j} \phi_k$ denotes the share of producer j's penalty that is allocated to producer i, and $\Gamma(a(x)) \equiv B(a(x)) - \bar{B}$ represents the change in social benefits from the level targeted by the regulator, with $\Gamma(a(x)) < 0$ for $\varphi > \bar{\varphi}$.

Given this incentive scheme the risk-averse producer must select a level of abatement to maximise his expected utility received from profits, $\pi_i = \pi_i^0 - c_i(x_i) + S_i(x)$, where π_i^0 represents fixed profits from a given output. The producer's level of expected utility from complying with the socially optimal level of control, provided all other producers comply, is represented by

$$
EU(\pi_i(x_i^{**}, x_{-i}^{**})) = U(\pi_i^0 - c_i(x_i^{**}) + b_i)
$$

where $x_{-i}^{**} = (x_1^{**}, x_2^{**}, \ldots, x_{i-1}^{**}, x_{i+1}^{**}, \ldots, x_n^{**})$. Now if the producer decides to shirk, x_i^*, given that he believes all the other producers will comply, x_{-i}^{**}, his expected utility from cheating on abatement is

$$
EU(\pi_i(x_i^*, x_{-i}^{**})) = \sigma_i U(\pi_i^0 - c_i(x_i^*) - F_i)
$$

$$
+ \sum_{j \neq i} \sigma_j U(\pi_i^0 - c_i(x_i^*) + b_i + \phi_{ij}[b_j + F_j + \Gamma(a(x))])
$$

The incentive system of subsidies and random penalties will yield the socially optimal level of pollution control if the expected utility from shirking is less than the expected utility from complying with the optimal level of pollution control,

$$\Omega_i \equiv EU(\pi_i(x_i^*, x_{-i}^{**})) - EU(\pi_i(x_i^{**}, x_{-i}^{**})) < 0$$

Herriges *et al.* (1994) show that simultaneously increasing the fines for all producers increases the variability of the expected profits from shirking. Therefore, if all producer's are risk-averse, the expected utility losses of being caught and fined exceed the utility gains from cheating and not being caught, $\Omega_i < 0$. A set of risk-neutral producers will not be affected by the increased variability since they capture the full marginal benefit from shirking but suffer only a fraction of the marginal cost. But with risk aversion, this fraction of marginal costs is magnified by the producers' fear of losing wealth, and the net rewards from shirking relative to compliance become negative.

Govindasamy *et al.* (1994) identify an alternative incentive scheme that attempts to bridge the information requirements of the ambient charge and the potential political unattractiveness of the random penalty scheme – the environmental rank-order tournament. The environmental tournament would use readily available information on input use or pollution control effort to construct an ordinal ranking of the set of producers. An advantage of the tournament is that the ordinal ranking of producers by some proxy of actual pollution control provides information that is typically less costly to obtain than the cardinal rankings required by ambient charges, and it attempts to rank producers by actions rather than a random assignment of blame required by the random penalty scheme. In the case of nitrate pollution, for example, a regulator would monitor, say, surface water contamination for the entire area, rank producers according to their input use or pollution control effort, and then penalise one or more of the lowest ranking producers if the ambient concentrations for the area exceed the prescribed standard. Alternatively, the regulator might reward the highest ranking producers if the ambient concentration was better than the prescribed standard. Rewards or penalties depend on the relative rank of the producers, not on the absolute level of pollution emissions. In addition, the environmental tournament does not require information on common disturbances such as weather effects. A regulator who cannot observe a common shock will do no worse than a regulator who can observe the shock. A regulator who can administer an emissions or ambient charge can reduce costs by using a tournament structure that requires less information. The disadvantage to the non-point tournament is that, if the information used to construct the ordinal ranking is biased as the result of a heterogeneous fate-and-transport system, the tournament may send incorrect signals to the polluters and the wrong producers will be punished or rewarded.

Suppose the regulator wants to set up an environmental rank-order tournament between two producers ($i = 1, 2$). A producer's actual level of pollution control, x_i, cannot be perfectly observed by the regulator. Rather the regulator can observe a proxy variable, z_i, for pollution control that is constructed from one or more observable actions such as technology choice. We assume the relation between the actual control, x_i, and the proxy measure, z_i, takes the form

$$x_i = f(z_i) + \varepsilon_i \qquad (3.12)$$

where $f(z_i)$ represents the transformation of effort to pollution control, with $f'(z_i) \equiv df/dz_i > 0$, and ε_i is a random factor that could include weather events or unknown characteristics of the producer.

The regulator sets up a tournament with a fixed-reward scheme such that the winner's reward equals R, while the loser's reward is r, $R > r$. The regulator ranks the two producers on the basis of their observable proxy measures of pollution control, and determines the winner and loser. To maintain a balanced budget, the regulator sets the total rewards equal to the economic value of the socially optimal level of pollution control, $R + r = Vx^{**}$, where V is the per unit social benefit of control and $x^{**} = x_1^{**} + x_2^{**}$ is the socially optimal level of control.

Operating within the fixed-reward tournament system, the risk-neutral producer i selects a level of effort, z_i, to maximise his expected profits, given the cost of effort, $c_i(z_i)$

$$E\pi_i = \pi_i^0 + \sigma_i(x_1, x_2)[R - c_i(z_i)] + (1 - \sigma_i(x_1, x_2))[r - c_i(z_i)] \qquad i = 1, 2 \qquad (3.13)$$

where π_i^0 represents profits without any expenditures on pollution control, and $\sigma_i(x_1, x_2)$ is the likelihood of producer i winning the large reward, R,

$$\sigma_i(x_1, x_2) = \text{Probability } (x_i > x_j)$$

Assume that the likelihood of producer i winning R increases as his actual abatement increases or as producer j's abatement decreases, $\partial\sigma_i/\partial x_i > 0$ and $\partial\sigma_i/\partial x_j < 0$.

Substituting equation (3.12) into (3.13), producer i's problem of selecting a level of proxied pollution control to maximise expected profits yields

$$(R - r)(\partial\sigma_i/\partial x_i)(f'(z_i)) = c_i'(z_i) \qquad i = 1, 2 \qquad (3.14)$$

The marginal benefits of increased control are represented by the left-hand side of equation (3.14): $(R - r)$ is the spread between the large and small reward, $(\partial\sigma_i/\partial x_i)$ is the increased likelihood of winning the large reward and $f'(z_i)$ is the marginal increase in actual control given that effort increases.

The marginal costs are represented by the right-hand side of equation (3.14), $c_i'(z_i) \equiv dc_i/dz_i > 0$.

Now if the regulator sets the spread of the rewards equal to the per unit social benefit divided by the marginal likelihood of winning the large reward,

$$(R - r) = V/(\partial\sigma_i/\partial x_i) \tag{3.15}$$

the producers will have an incentive to select the socially optimal level of pollution control, z_i^{**}. To see this, substitute equation (3.15) into equation (3.14) which yields

$$Vf'(z_i^{**}) = c_i'(z_i^{**}) \qquad i = 1, 2$$

The producer equated his marginal private cost of pollution control to the marginal social benefit ($Vf'(z_i^{**})$) of control. The tournament scheme rewards producers for increasing their control effort to the socially optimal level.

☐ 3.3.2 Deposit refund systems

Under deposit refund systems purchasers of potentially polluting products pay a surcharge, which is refunded to them when they return the product or its container to an approved centre for recycling or proper disposal. This instrument rewards good environmental behaviour. Deposit refund systems have been in place worldwide for many years to control the disposal of beverage containers. India, Syria, Lebanon, Egypt, Cyprus, Australia, Canada, France, Germany, Switzerland and the USA, among others, all have deposit refund systems for particular kinds of beverage containers. These systems can also help to prevent the release of toxic substances into the environment from the disposal of batteries, the incineration of plastics or residuals from pesticide containers. Denmark, Finland, Norway and Sweden all have studies under way to implement such systems for other articles such as batteries with a high content of mercury and cadmium. Well functioning deposit refund systems may also stimulate the emergence of markets in safe waste disposal. Such systems pay people to look for opportunities to return waste back into the economy. If some people throw cans out, other people have incentives to find and return them. From an economic point of view, deposit refund systems are efficient. They provide economic benefits for good environmental behaviour and impose costs for bad behaviour. These systems also are efficient from an administrative point of view because, once the deposit is paid, no further significant involvement by authorities is needed (see Bohm, 1981, for the definitive study).

☐ 3.3.3 Performance bonds

A performance bond is a direct mechanism argued to induce socially desirable incentives in a producer (see Bohm and Russell, 1985). With a performance bond, a producer posts a bond before operations begin, forfeiting the bond if his activities cause environmental harm or if he pollutes in excess of acceptable levels. The bond increases the costs of shirking, thereby reducing the incentive for malfeasance. Performance bonds are less common than non-compliance fees and are applied primarily in cases of clear-cut environmental damage, for example with surface mining. The administrative efficiency of non-compliance fees is low because of the high proportion of cases that must be settled in court.

Bonds can reduce the incentive to shirk. With perfect monitoring, the value of the bond should equal or exceed the value of damages. With imperfect monitoring, the value of the bond should reflect both the damages and the probability of detection and damage. Any combination of the detection probability and magnitude of the bond should yield the desired result. Therefore, since the regulator expends real resources monitoring behaviour, but collecting the bond does not, the regulator's most efficient strategy is to set the detection probability as low as possible while setting the bond as high as possible. This is the classic economic solution to shirking. A regulator that requires a producer to post a bond imposes an actual cost for environmental shirking. The producer must take this cost into account when deciding whether or not to shirk, recognizing that any identified violation may result in the loss of the bond. The producer internalises his impact on social welfare, and will try to provide more of the effort that the regulator desires. There is an increased incentive to provide a socially optimal level of pollution control or safety precautions, given the positive cost for shirking.

Perrings (1989) identifies several benefits of environmental bonds. Value registration would require an explicit registration of the potential damages that pollutants could cause to environmental resources. By requiring that producers post bonds, the cost of the environmental damage will be registered, and therefore open to public debate and scrutiny. Value registration can act as a benchmark with which to guide the environmental costs of future innovative activities. Forcing the producer to post a bond shifts the burden of proof to the producer from society. Instead of taking the producer to court to prove the producer was liable for damages, now the producer must prove that no environmental effects occurred to avoid forfeiting the bond.

The value of the bond is determined by the potential environmental impact of the producer's actions. If a producer shows that the cost of environmental damages of an activity is less than the cost of their posted bond, the value of the bond can be reduced. Therefore the firm has an incentive to invest resources in R&D to discover the true value of environmental damage or increase the use of inputs that are more benign to the environment. Perrings (1989) has also suggested that, once the bond is posted, the interest income generated by the firm could be used for further research into the damaging effects of production.

But bonds are rarely used in environmental policy. Shogren *et al.* (1993) identify three key limitations to environmental bonds: moral hazard, liquidity constraints and legal restrictions on contracting. The first limit to bonding is the fear of regulator moral hazard. In this case, moral hazard exists when the actions of the regulator are unobservable by the producer. If the regulator is interested in maximizing his own private welfare rather than social welfare, there is a chance that the government will label the producer as a shirker, thereby confiscating the value of the bond. When the regulator is the sole seller of bonds, the producer has no choice but to post the bond or not go into business in that country. The regulator has an incentive to capture the producer's bond by arguing that the producer has shirked, regardless of whether he has or not. The producer will then be left with the option of challenging the regulator, reposting the bond or starting a new business. Given that legal action is costly, the producer may search for new opportunities. A producer who wants to do business in a foreign country will face the risk that the government will unjustifiably take the bond. Appeals to third parties may be ineffective given the lack of an effective international court. Unless there is an impartial third party, the producer will have no incentive to post a bond to a regulator whose trustworthiness is uncertain.

The second major factor limiting the use of bonds is liquidity constraints. Liquidity constraints exist when a producer is forced to post a bond ex ante, but he cannot acquire the capital necessary for the bond. When a large bond is required, the producer may have insufficient liquid assets to deposit in advance. If the producer cannot post the bond, the project may be dropped, even though from the social welfare viewpoint the proposal may be beneficial. A possible solution is for insurance markets to spread the risk of the firm defaulting on borrowed assets used to post the bond. The size of bonds needed for environmental issues, however, suggests that insurance markets will bear a significantly higher risk of a major multi-million dollar claim. The cost of a policy backing an environmental bond will be significant, increasing the possibility of default on the loan.

Third, imperfect contract enforcement can affect bond performance for a variety of reasons, including performance excuses, formation defences (e.g. duress, bargaining power, and unconscionability), illegalities and the inability of the enforcer to do the job. Suppose a producer has its performance bond confiscated because of some perceived non-compliance with pollution control. The producer may argue that the breach was caused by an act of God which was not explicitly identified in the contract. Alternatively, the producer may argue that there was some form of imperfection in the procedures to define the contract such as unilateral or mutual mistake, misrepresentation or unconscionability (for example, threats, bargaining incompetence and asymmetric information).

When should a producer post an environmental bond? Shogren *et al.* (1993) identify seven conditions under which bonds may work for environmental problems: well-understood costs of environmental damages, observable producer actions (that is, no moral hazard), few agents to administer, fixed time horizons for remittance issues, well-defined outcomes and their likelihood of occurrence, no irreversible effects and a relatively small bond value. Many forms of pollution, such as non-point sources, do not satisfy these conditions: the long-term health costs are still debated, the actions of the producers are unobservable, there are numerous agents to monitor, the time horizon associated with environmental contamination and other impacts on ecosystem functions is ambiguous, the states of nature are still being identified, and liquidity constraints may pinch the ability to post the value of the bond.

3.4 Quantity rationing: marketable permits

Crocker (1966) and Dales (1968) introduced the idea of quantity rationing through marketable permits. Marketable permits specify a predetermined total level of emissions or emission concentrations within a specified region. Permits equal to the permissible total emissions are distributed among producers in the region. The permits can be traded among plants of a single producer as well as among producers. Producers that keep their emissions levels below their allotted permit level can sell or lease their surplus permits to other producers or use them to offset emissions in other parts of their own facilities. To ensure that such permits serve their purpose as incentives to change pollution control to socially desired levels, total emission levels within a given region are limited so that the permits are valuable to producers. This scarcity value creates an incentive to trade to permits. The USA makes limited use of marketable permits for pollution control (see Box 5.1). Probably the most important permit systems are those developed and implemented at the state level to comply with federal ambient air quality standards enacted by the US Congress's Clean Air Act.

The main feature of quantity rationing with marketable permits is the shift to producers from regulators as regards the design and location of pollution control strategies. Evidence from the USA suggests that permits have not achieved significantly more reductions in emissions than standard regulatory systems, but that the unit costs of reductions are themselves reduced (Hahn, 1989). The evidence is ambiguous as to whether marketable permits have stimulated any more innovation in pollution control technology than the command-and-control technological restrictions. Marketable permits have proved to be administratively cumbersome. Their application has been hindered by debates about baseline emission levels, the need for government approval at all stages of policy formulation, and the process in which producers must engage as they exchange proposals for carrying out a permit trade. In addition, the permit trading process has technical, financial and legal dimensions which have to be addressed before each trade in permits occurs.

Regulators must have sufficient knowledge to design the market. This includes knowing how to establish the time frame of the permits, such as weekly or monthly; knowing the kinds of information required to allocate permits efficiently and fairly; knowing how monitoring data will be obtained and tested; and knowing what the inspection schedule should be. The producers also need knowledge on these topics if they are to make good decisions about buying or selling permits. Marketable permits need a legal structure to define the property rights to trade permits and to ensure that these rights are well defined and enforceable. The nature of the permits and the terms of exchange have to be carefully specified; these issues are taken up in more detail in Chapter 5.

Hahn and Noll (1990) identify several criteria that a marketable permit system should satisfy to function efficiently. First, the number of permits should be limited and well-defined so as to give them a value that can be accurately estimated. Second, permits should be freely tradeable with limited restrictions on the scope of trading, thereby guaranteeing that those producers who value the permits the most will be able to buy or keep them. Third, permits must be storable to maintain their usefulness in times of thin buying and selling. Fourth, the trading of permits should not be expensive as the result of transaction costs, thereby opening up entry into the market and promoting efficiency. Fifth, penalties for violating a permit must be greater than the permit price to give incentive for producers to play within the rules of the market. Sixth, permits should only be expropriated in extreme circumstance to maintain the stability of the market. Finally, producers must be allowed to keep any profits they earn from the trade of permits.

If the regulator knows the marginal costs and benefits of pollution control with certainty, the level of marketable permits can be set so that they lead to a socially optimal reduction in emissions. The number of permits would be set at the control level where marginal benefits equal marginal cost, as in Figure 3.1. Given that the permits can be freely traded, supply and demand would set the permit market price equal to where marginal costs equal marginal benefits of control, $m = MB = MC$. Note that with complete certainty the permit market price would equal the optimal emission charge, $m = t = MB = MC$.

But now suppose control costs are uncertain. Figure 3.10 shows the effectiveness of a marketable permit system given the three cases of marginal benefits considered earlier in section 3.3.1 – flat, extremely steep and intermediate slope. In the case where the slope of the marginal benefits curve is flat (Figure 3.10a), the emission charge works poorly. The regulator sets the number of marketable permits, the emission charge x_m, at the level

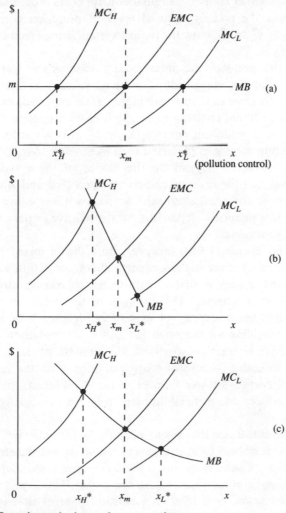

Figure 3.10 *Quantity rationing under uncertainty*

where marginal benefits, MB, equal the expected marginal costs, EMC. Now if realised marginal costs are lower than expected, $MC_L < EMC$, the permit scheme provides too little pollution control, $x_m < x_L^*$. The permit scheme cannot adjust to the lower realised costs if the number of permits is fixed, thereby leading to an inefficiently low level of control. Alternatively, if realised costs exceed expectations, $MC_H > EMC$, too much pollution control is used, $x_m > x_H^*$. Again the quantity of permits does not adjust to the realised control costs. In the case of a flat marginal benefits curve, an emission charge system appears preferable to the marketable permit system.

At the other extreme, if the slope of marginal benefit curve is very steep, the marketable permit system performs well. Figure 3.10b shows that, regardless of whether realised marginal control costs exceed or are less than expected costs, the socially optimal level of pollution control is nearly achieved, $x_m \cong x_L^* \cong x_H^*$. Now the permit system is preferred to the emission charge scheme.

Figure 3.10c presents the intermediate case where permits lead to inefficiencies, but the magnitude is reduced relative to the flat marginal benefit curve. In general, if costs are higher than expected, the permits lead to too much pollution control, $x_m > x_H^*$; if costs are lower than expected, there is too little pollution control, $x_m < x_L^*$. In this case, it is unclear whether a permit scheme is preferred to the emission charge. The preferred scheme will ultimately depend on the slopes of the marginal cost and benefits curves and the divergence between expected and actual costs and benefits. One can construct alternative scenarios where either the charge or permit scheme is preferred, depending on the relative slopes of the marginal benefits and cost curves.

Roberts and Spence (1976), however, note that a mixed permit–charge system can be more effective than either a charge or permit alone. The idea with the mixed system is that it combines the relative strengths of the charge and permit schemes. The strength of the permit system is that it protects against the possibility of extremely high levels of environmental damage by providing an incentive for too much pollution control when control costs are higher than expected; the strength of the charge is that it provides an incentive to control more pollution than the permits require when control costs are lower than expected. Combined, the two schemes give the producer more flexibility to respond to changes in market conditions.

Figure 3.11 illustrates the mixed permit–charge scheme. The regulator uses the mixed scheme to approximate the marginal benefit function by setting a charge, t, subsidy, s, and a level of permits, x_m. Suppose that the realised marginal control costs, MC_H, are higher than expected. The mixed scheme would result in a level of pollution control that is higher than optimal, $x_H^{mx} > x_H^*$, but not as high as if the permit system were operating

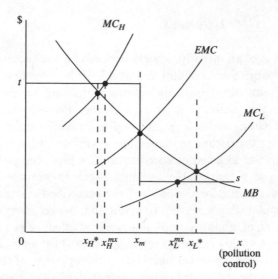

Figure 3.11 *Mixed incentive system*

alone, $x_m > x_H^{mx} > x_H^*$. If the realised marginal control costs, MC_L, are lower than expected, the mixed system results in too little control, $x_L^{mx} < x_L^*$, but more than if the permit system operated alone, $x_m < x_L^{mx} < x_L^*$. The charges work to dampen the inefficiencies associated with large deviations between actual and expected marginal costs. If the costs fall within the range $t > m > s$, the private optimum equals the social optimum. Ideally, the mixed system would have numerous levels in this step function such that it more closely approximates the marginal benefit curve. By breaking down the steps the scheme begins to approach a theoretically feasible but difficult to construct variable charge scheme that would allow the regulator to achieve the social optimum with a decentralised system.

■ 3.5 Evaluative criteria

Judgements about the usefulness and practicality of the economic incentives we have discussed can be based on the extent to which they meet four criteria: effectiveness, efficiency, equity and flexibility. Regardless of theoretical appeal, an incentive scheme will fail if it is ineffective in reducing pollution damage, unacceptably inefficient in accomplishing these goals, violates social norms of equity or lacks the flexibility to change with shifting economic, technological and environmental conditions.

☐ 3.5.1 Effectiveness

The effectiveness of an incentive system depends on the success in achieving the regulator's objective in pollution control. If the objective is to secure a given level of emissions, quantity rationing through marketable permits appears to be the preferred incentive scheme. Permits establish a fixed quantity of emissions within a specific region, and offer more predictability and control over the decline in emissions. Therefore, if the risks associated with small increases in emissions are assessed as high, the prudent strategy would be to use a marketable permit system to narrow the potential difference between actual emissions and the prescribed emission standard.

But if the regulator's objective is to maintain more certainty over the costs of pollution control, quantity rationing is not as effective as price rationing through a charge scheme. Charges set a specific cost for emissions, however, the level of pollution control is uncertain – the opposite of the marketable permit system. If the regulator believes there is significant uncertainty about the control costs and the risks change slowly as emissions increase, the strategy may be to use a charge system that offers more predictability in costs and accept the variability in the level of pollution control. This is especially true if the charge is not set sufficiently high to motivate producers to increase their pollution control. Producers may simply pay the charge and not reduce emissions.

Effectiveness debates are usually based on theory, not experience, since no incentive system has been used enough to make detailed statements of support for or against. It is unclear that the effectiveness advantage of emission charges would be realised in connection with practical applications of this instrument. The use of incentives within market economies has produced little evidence that any system stimulates innovative behaviour in pollution control technology. Given that most charges are not sufficiently high to motivate producers to change their behaviour, regulators could consider increasing emission charges and reducing allowable emission levels to increase pollution control.

☐ 3.5.2 Efficiency

Efficiency is desirable in that it implies that the regulator's objectives are achieved at the lowest possible cost. In principle, quantity rationing with marketable permits and price rationing with emission charges are equally efficient. In practice, however, the efficiency of the two systems can differ significantly, depending on the characteristics and source of the pollution. The critical issue is the cost of monitoring and enforcement. An emission charge requires continuous data on the quantities of emissions from sources to be controlled. Regulators must also have the administrative capacity to use the data to set appropriate charges and to collect them. Regulators using marketable permit systems, in contrast, need to establish the trading and organisation rules of the permit market, must monitor the trades among producers and must determine that the producers selling permits reduce their emissions appropriately. With a large number of producers, continuous monitoring and enforcement requirements can be expensive. But if there are not enough producers, there may not be enough competition in permits, and the market will be inefficient.

Again the lack of long-term experience with these incentive systems makes judgements about their relative efficiency speculative. The US experience provides some evidence that there are more cost savings with marketable permits than with emission charges. In developing and transition economies, however, the restricted technical and administrative capacity in regulatory agencies, the shortage of financial resources, and limited institutional and administrative resources to monitor and enforce emission controls strengthen the case for price rationing with product charges, over quantity rationing through marketable permits. Price rationing probably would not require the establishment of new administrative systems since most countries already have institutions for taxing relevant commodities. Most countries will need to create new institutional apparatus to implement and manage a quantity rationing system of marketable permits.

☐ *3.5.3 Equity*

Economic incentives can influence the distribution of costs and benefits among members of society. These distribution effects raise the issue of equity and fairness, both within and across generations. Regulators must identify the winners who capture the benefits of the cleaner environment and losers who bear the financial burden of a system. For example, a regulator can implicitly assign the rights to pollute by using either a charge or a subsidy. The popular 'polluter pays' principle used in Western Europe forces the producer to pay the control costs, the emissions charge or the compensation to any victims who are harmed by his emissions. The producer does not have the right to pollute, and must pay for his emissions or damage. Alternatively, the regulator could assign the producer the right to pollute, and it is up to society to provide a subsidy to increase his level of pollution control. In this way, the regulator attempts to keep the producer in operation, thereby protecting jobs and promoting economic growth. Equity and efficiency often conflict – protecting jobs of inefficient producers does not necessarily increase the size of the economic pie.

The producers' burden of an incentive system is the decrease in profits and in industry-wide competitiveness, both domestically and internationally. If a charge raises costs so that a producer is no longer competitive in national or world markets, profits fall and some producers will leave the industry or move to other countries. In the case of emission charges, some firms pollute less than others because of different local conditions or because of differences in the relative availability of low versus high-polluting inputs. If all are charged according to their emissions, producers in areas where they pay lower charges will have an advantage over firms in other areas. Location will also affect the amount of environmental damage caused by a given level of emission, so uniform emission charges, in some cases, may be perceived as inequitable.

Equity also involves the relative burden placed on consumers, businesses and workers. Understanding equity requires knowing how the costs of an incentive scheme can be shifted forward to consumers from producers through higher prices, or backward to workers through lower wages or lower prices paid for raw materials. The ease with which a producer can shift the cost burden depends on competitive conditions in input, labour and product markets. A large number of consumers with limited substitution opportunities and only a few producers suggests that the costs will be passed forward and consumers will face higher prices. But a few consumers with readily available substitutes buying from a large number of producers creates a case where each producer will have to accept lower profits or try to pass the costs to workers or suppliers. The burden of the incentive system will follow the path of least economic resistance.

☐ 3.5.4 Flexibility to achieve objectives

An economic incentive system should adapt to changes in markets, technology, knowledge and social, political and environmental conditions. Given the difficulty in achieving a social objective, the system should be sufficiently flexible to accommodate several iterations of use. For example, the flexibility in an emission charge depends on the ability of the regulator to respond to changes in emissions. If altering a charge requires several levels of authority, the change might be too late to be effective. Flexibility also requires that a charge system be indexed to inflation. In countries where prices inflate 50 to 1000 per cent every year a fixed emission charge would soon lose whatever effectiveness it has to reduce pollution or generate revenue. An inflation-indexed charge system will be more flexible than one in which the administering agency is required to obtain authority to adjust the charge each year (see Zylicz, 1994, for a discussion of indexation in the charge system in Poland).

A marketable permit system allows the price of the permits to be set by transactions among producers participating in the market. These prices adjust to changing economic, technological and inflationary conditions insofar as these changing conditions affect the decisions of participating producers and their emission rates. For example, if a new technology to reduce emissions is developed, the permit market will reflect this change through shifts in the supply and demand for permits. This will, in turn, affect permit prices. Because of these characteristics, marketable permit systems may prove more flexible in price than emission charges, but less flexible in the total level of emissions.

3.6 Practical conditions for use of economic incentives

Certain conditions are required before economic incentives can be used effectively to promote environmental protection. King *et al.* (1993) discuss a set of necessary conditions: an adequate information base and administrative capacity; a strong legal structure; competitive markets; administrative capacity; and political feasibility. Since conditions in developed, transition and developing economies differ significantly, no attempt is made to determine which alternatives are most useful. King *et al.* highlight questions regulators might want to consider before attempting to develop and apply any of the incentive systems we have discussed. We draw heavily from their discussion.

3.6.1 Information base and administrative capacity

Effective use of economic incentives requires information on the costs and benefits of alternative incentive systems and a recognition of the winners and losers; the technological and institutional opportunities and constraints in pollution control; and the substitution possibilities that would allow both the regulator and producers to assess potential trade-offs between pollution control and production processes. This information needs to be collected, stored and disseminated to provide an adequate knowledge base to implement an economic incentive scheme. Economic incentives are likely to be ineffective when the expected policy objectives are unclear or when the legal structure is not established through environmental legislation. Legislation must specify the chain of authority, the range and assignment of jurisdiction and the legal standing of the affected parties. Regulators also need to specify which indicators of improvement in environmental quality and human welfare will be used to judge success, which will provide a yardstick against which progress can be measured.

Regulators who want to achieve the socially optimal level of pollution control will be constrained by their own administrative capacity to implement the economic incentive system. Regulators need staff and funding to implement, monitor and enforce the system effectively, as producers need staff and funding to determine the consequences of the system for their operations. As a result, regulators will combine the efficiency gains of economic incentives with the strict standards of command-and-control to promote pollution control.

□ 3.6.2 Legal structure

The effective use of an economic incentive system requires the legal structure to define property rights clearly, provide the legislative authority to issue the incentives and specify who has legal standing and jurisdiction in the use of the system. An effective property rights scheme requires that the rights holder be able to transfer the rights, control access to the resource, receive all the benefits and bear all the costs associated with its management. Under this definition, ill-defined or conflicting property rights structures will not produce the set of access claims necessary to allow economic incentives to work effectively. In many developing and transition economies, property rights may be unfavourable for effective use of economic incentives. In particular, incentives based on private property may not be effective under conditions of open access, common property or centralised property systems. Under centralised property regimes the condition that the rights holder alone receives the benefits and bears the costs is often violated. Evidence from transition economies indicates that regulators operating under centralised property regimes often do not pay the costs of poor management. The tenure of regulators often depends more on their political connections than on their merits and, consequently, they do not always receive or send the correct sets of incentives and have lower incentives to manage pollution control efficiently.

□ 3.6.3 Competitive markets

Economic incentives will be more effective if competition plays a meaningful role in the economy and in the decisions of the regulators. Unless competitive markets exist, attempts to create a market for permits will be difficult. Economic incentives are most advantageous, relative to direct regulations, in markets where there are a large number of buyers and sellers. Credit, liability and insurance markets also play an important role in the use of economic incentives. Producers short of capital will find it difficult to post a performance bond unless they have access to credit markets. Without these markets, economic incentives that require cash outlays could give a competitive advantage to large producers over small or rural producers who cannot cross-subsidise the products that require more pollution control.

□ *3.6.4 Political feasibility*

While economists can promote economic incentives as a cost-effective tool to increase pollution control, it is the regulator who must face the winners and losers of any proposed incentive system. These winners and losers include other regulators, producers and individuals affected by the emissions and by organisations who represent the victims of pollution. The push and pull of these countervailing forces will determine the political feasibility of the proposed incentive system. For example, the random penalty scheme may not be politically feasible, given that a producer could be penalised even if he has complied with the socially optimal level of pollution but the group of producers has not. The performance bond will also raise political challenges owing to the thin capital and insurance markets associated with pollution control. Producers may claim the bonds will impose unnecessary hardships and will result in increased local unemployment, a factor sure to interest any politician up for re-election.

■ *3.7* **Concluding remarks**

This chapter has explored how economic incentives can be used to reduce the inefficiencies associated with market failure. Information constraints now dominate the majority of discussions on incentive design for environmental protection. The effectiveness of nearly all proposed incentive schemes depends on acquiring information on behavioural types or adjusting the optimal incentive to reduce potential information rents gathered by those being regulated. Better understanding these information-incentive tradeoffs is the future of environmental regulation, for all forms of economic incentives.

Technical note: mathematical programming

☐ *The Kuhn–Tucker conditions*

The aim of mathematical programming is to find the maximum (or minimum) of a function subject to weak inequality constraints. This note is a brief review of mathematical programming; a fuller discussion of this topic is found in Chiang (1984, ch. 21) and Beavis and Dobbs (1990, ch. 2). The general form of the problem is to

$$\text{maximise } f(x) \quad \text{subject to } g^i(x) \le b \quad x \ge 0 \quad i = 1, \ldots, m \tag{1}$$

A function $f(x)$ of a vector of choice variables x is maximised subject to a set of constraints, $g^i(x)$ in the form of weak inequalities. The elements of x must be non-negative. Here, maximisation problems are considered, but the methods described are equally applicable to minimisation problems.

Consider the following single variable problems where a non-linear objective function is maximised subject to a non-negativity constraint:

$$\text{maximise } f(x_1) \quad \text{subject to } x_1 \ge 0$$

The first stage in solving the problem is to form the Lagrangean composite function

$$L(x_1, \lambda_1) = f(x_1) - \lambda_1 x_1 \tag{2}$$

In Figure T.3(i), the maximum of the function lies at point a where the first derivative of the objective function is equal to zero, $f'(x_1) = 0$. Likewise, in Figure T.3(ii), the maximum is at b where $f'(x_1) = 0$. Point a is known as an interior solution, whilst point b is a boundary solution. In Figure T.3(iii), the

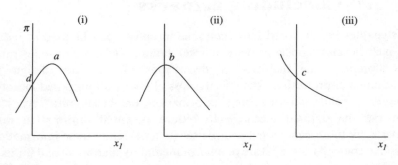

Figure T.3

maximum is at c, but the derivative, $f'(x_1) < 0$ and $x_1 = 0$. If, conversely, $f'(x_1) > 0$, a corner point solution would not be optimal: it would be possible to increase the value of the objective function, by increasing x_1 for instance at d in Figure T.3(i).

The three alternative conditions for a maximum, the Kuhn–Tucker (K–T) conditions are summarised in equations (3) and (4) (where subscripts represent partial derivatives):

$$L_{x_1} = f'(x_1) - \lambda_1 \leq 0; \qquad x_1 \geq 0; \qquad x_1 L_{x_1} = 0 \tag{3}$$

$$L_{\lambda_1} = x_1 \geq 0; \qquad\qquad \lambda_1 \geq 0; \qquad \lambda_1 L_{\lambda_1} = 0 \tag{4}$$

For instance from (3), at the maximum either $x_1 = 0$, as in Figure T.3(iii), or $f'(x_1) - \lambda_1 = 0$ as in Figure T.3(i) or both as in T.3(ii). The complementary slackness condition in the case of (4) implies that either the constraint is satisfied, that is $x_1 = 0$, or $x_1 > 0$ and $\lambda_1 = 0$.

In general, for n variable and m constraints, the Lagrangean function is

$$L = f(x_1, x_2, \ldots, x_n) + \sum_{i=1}^{m} \lambda[b_i - g^i(x_1, x_2, \ldots, x_n)] \tag{5}$$

The corresponding K–T conditions are:

$$L_{x_j} \leq 0; \qquad x_j \geq 0 \quad \text{and} \quad x_j L_{x_j} = 0; \qquad (j = 1, 2, \ldots, n)$$

$$L_{\lambda_i} \geq 0; \qquad \lambda_i \geq 0 \quad \text{and} \quad \lambda_i L_{\lambda_i} = 0; \qquad (i = 1, 2, \ldots, m)$$

☐ *Some complications*

The K–T conditions pick out possible optimal solutions. Unfortunately there are some problems where the K–T conditions do not identify the optimal solution. The approach used is to check that a problem *is* one for which the K–T conditions work: that is, identify solutions which may include a global optima. Problems which are not solved by the K–T conditions are identified by what are called *constraint qualifications*; these impose restrictions on the type of constraint functions which ensure that the K–T conditions are valid. If the problem fails the constraint qualifications it must be treated differently, see Beavis and Dobbs (1990, p.63) for an account.

The following non-linear programming problem is an example where the K–T conditions do not identify the optimal solution:

Maximise $\pi = x_1$; subject to $x_2 - (1 - x_1)^3 \leq 0$; $\qquad x_1, x_2 \geq 0$

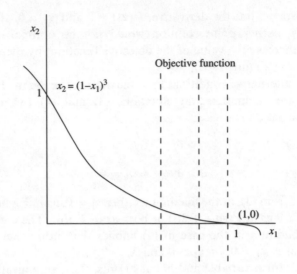

Figure T.4

From Figure T.4 the feasible region lies below the line $x_2 = (1 - x_1)^3$. The optimal solution is clearly $x_1 = 1$. Now consider the K–T conditions, the Lagrangean function is

$$L(x_1, x_2, \lambda_1) = x_1 + \lambda_1[-x_2 + (1 - x_1)^3]$$

The K–T conditions stipulate that the first derivative of the Lagrangean multiplier with respect to x_1 should be:

$$L_{x_1} = 1 - 3\lambda_1(1 - x_1)^2 \leq 0$$

However, at the optimal point $L_{x_1} = 1$. The solution occurs at a *cusp* where the constraint forms a sharp point with the non-negativity constraint on x_2.

Problems which contain cusps are identified by Slater's constraint qualification that: there exists a point $x^0 \geq 0$ such that $g^i(x^0) < b_i$. In other words, a non-negative point at which all inequality constraints are satisfied as strict inequalities. This excludes outward-pointing cusps such as the one encountered in Figure T.4. A more general form of the constraint qualification is found in Chiang (1984, p. 734).

☐ *Linear programming*

There are a set of mathematical programming problems, which include linear programming, for which the K–T conditions always identify global optimal solutions, if they exist. Finding the global optimum may involve searching among the set of solutions which satisfy the K–T conditions. Reliable computer software exists to mechanise this search, and these programming problems have been widely applied in natural resource and environmental economics.

For instance, a farmer wishes to maximise profit by producing two crops, wheat (x_1) and barley (x_2), subject to a land area of 100 units and a labour availability of 300 units. The profit rate per unit of wheat is £50 and of barley is £20, each crop uses 1 unit of land, wheat uses 3 units of labour and barley 2 units of labour. In the form of a mathematical programming problem, the farmer solves the following:

maximise $\quad \pi = 50x_1 + 40x_2$

subject to: $\quad x_1 + x_2 \leq 100; \quad 4x_1 + 2x_2 \leq 300; \quad x_1, x_2 \geq 0$

The Lagrangean for the problem is

$$L(x_1, x_2, \lambda_1, \lambda_2) = 50x_1 + 40x_2 + \lambda_1(100 - (x_1 + x_2)) + \lambda_2(150 - (4x_1 + 2x_2))$$

Applying the K–T necessary conditions gives

$$L_{x_1} = 50 - \lambda_1 - 4\lambda_2 \leq 0; \qquad x_1 \geq 0; \qquad x_1 L_{x_1} = 0 \qquad (6)$$

$$L_{x_2} = 40 - \lambda_1 - 2\lambda_2 \leq 0; \qquad x_2 \geq 0; \qquad x_2 L_{x_2} = 0 \qquad (7)$$

$$L_{\lambda_1} = -(x_1 + x_2) + 100 \geq 0; \qquad \lambda_1 \geq 0; \qquad \lambda_1 L_{\lambda_1} = 0 \qquad (8)$$

$$L_{\lambda_2} = -(4x_1 + 2x_2) + 150 \geq 0; \qquad \lambda_2 \geq 0; \qquad \lambda_2 L_{\lambda_2} = 0 \qquad (9)$$

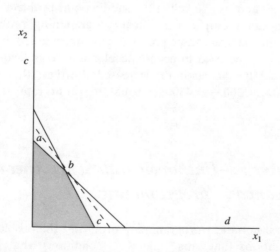

Figure T.5 *Solution to the primal LP problem*

It is then a matter of finding the optimal solution from among those points which satisfy the K–T conditions. Figure T.5 shows the three points which satisfy the K–T conditions, namely the vertices a, b and c. The solutions for x_1, x_2, λ_1 and λ_2 are given in Table T.1. These are derived by solving the K–T conditions at each vertex.

Table T.1   *Solutions to Problem 1 at vertices*

Vertex	x_1	x_2	λ_1	λ_2	π
a	0	100	0	50	4000
b	50	50	30	5	4500
c	75	0	0	20	3750

The optimal point is at b, which in this example is easily shown by the inclusion of the highest isoprofit line which is just feasible, that is, just touches the outside of the feasible region. The solutions a, b and c satisfy the necessary conditions for an optimum, but the global optimum at b solves the saddle point problem which is a sufficient condition for a solution x^* to be a global optimum

$$\max_{x} \min_{\lambda} L(x, \lambda) \quad \text{subject to } x \geq 0 \quad \lambda \geq 0$$

Where x^* and λ^* represent a global optimum if:

$$L(x, \lambda^*) \leq L(x^*, \lambda^*) \leq L(x^*, \lambda)$$

Returning to the example, it can be shown that the solution at b, $x_1 = 50$, $x_2 = 50$, $\lambda_1 = 30$ and $\lambda_2 = 5$ solves the saddle point problem.

The Lagrangean multipliers in linear programming problems can be interpreted as the marginal value product (sometimes called dual or shadow prices). These may be used in economic planning to indicate which fixed resources should be increased or decreased. Further, the total resource valuation, $100\lambda_1 + 300\lambda_2 = 4500$ is equal to profit rate at the optimal solution.

The Arrow–Enthoven sufficiency theorem: quasiconcave programming

In more general nonlinear programming problems, the problem is first one of finding solutions that satisfy the K–T conditions, that is, satisfy the necessary conditions; the second is that they satisfy some additional sufficiency conditions which check that a particular solution is indeed a global optimum. Arrow and Enthoven (1961) introduce a set of conditions which if they are satisfied ensure that a solution which satisfies the K–T conditions is both necessary and sufficient. Again consider the problem

maximise $f(x)$ subject to $g(x) \leq b$ $x \geq 0$

A solution x^* will be a global maximum of $f(x)$ if:

1. $f(x)$ is differentiable and quasiconcave for non-negative values of x. A quasiconcave function is one where if $f(x) \geq f(x^0)$ this implies $f(\lambda x + (1 - \lambda)x^0) \geq f(x^0)$ for all λ, $0 \leq \lambda \leq 1$.
2. $g(x)$, the constraint functions, are differentiable and quasiconvex for non-negative values of x. A quasiconvex function, $g(x)$ is one where $-g(x)$ is quasiconcave.
3. x^* satisfies the K–T conditions.
4. Plus any one of the following: (a) $f_j(x^*) < 0$ for at least one x_j; (b) $f_j(x^*) > 0$ for a variable x_j that can take a positive value without violating constraints; (c) all the second-order partial derivatives exist at the maximum point, x^*; (d) the function $f(x)$ is concave.

In addition, where the constraints are nonlinear the following constraint qualification test applies: (a) all constraint functions are differentiable and quasiconvex; (b) there exists a point x^0 in the non-negative orthant such that all the constraints are satisfied as strict inequalities, this tests for the existence of cusps; (c) one of the following is true: every constraint function is convex; the partial derivatives of every $g(x)$ are not all zero when evaluated for all x in the feasible region.

This implies that if (1), (2) and one of the conditions in (4) are satisfied, the K–T conditions are both necessary and sufficient for a global maximum. In economics much theory and applied work proceeds by assuming that these assumptions or even more restrictive ones hold.

☐ Summary

The account starts with the general conditions K–T conditions for a non-linear programming problem, then introduces constraint qualifications to identify problems where the K–T conditions do not identify the optimal solution. Linear programming represents problems where K–T conditions identify the global optimum, and for this reason they are widely used in applied economics. Arrow and Enthoven identified a more general set of restrictions on functions which means that the K–T conditions are both necessary and sufficient.

■ References

Arrow, K.J. and A.C. Enthoven (1961) 'Quasi-concave programming', *Econometrica*, 29, 779–800

Baumol, W. and W. Oates (1988) *The Theory of Environmental Policy*, 2nd edn, Cambridge: Cambridge University Press.

Beavis, B. and I.M. Dobbs (1990) *Optimization and Stability Theory for Economic Analysis*, Cambridge: Cambridge University Press.

Bohm, P. (1981) *Deposit-Refund Systems: Theory Application to Environmental, Conservation, and Consumer Policy*, Baltimore: Johns Hopkins University Press.

Bohm, P. and C. Russell (1985). 'Comparative Analysis of Alternative Policy Instruments', in A. Kneese and J. Sweeny (eds), *Handbook of Natural Resource and Energy Economics*, New York: Elsevier Publishers, 395–460.

Cabe, R. and J. Herriges (1992) 'The Regulation of Nonpoint Sources of Pollution Under Imperfect and Asymmetric Information', *Journal of Environmental Economics and Management*, 22, 134–146.

Chiang, A.C. (1984) *Fundamental Methods of Mathematical Economics*, 3rd edn, New York: McGraw-Hill.

Coase, R. (1960) 'The Problem of Social Cost', *Journal of Law and Economics*, 3, 1–44.

Crocker, T. (1966) 'The Structuring of Atmospheric Pollution Control Systems', in H. Wolozing (ed.), *The Economics of Air Pollution*, New York: W.W. Norton, 61–86.

Crocker, T. (1984) 'Scientific Truths and Policy Truths in Acid Deposition Research', *Economic Perspectives on Acid Deposition Control*, Boston: Butterworths, 65–79.

Dales, J. (1968) *Pollution, Property, and Prices*, Toronto: University of Toronto Press.

Govindasamy, R., J. Herriges and J. Shogren (1994) 'Nonpoint Tournaments', in C. Dosi and T. Tomasi (eds), *Nonpoint Source Pollution Regulation: Issues and Analysis*, Amsterdam: Kluwer Academic Publishers, 87–105.

Hahn, R. (1989) 'Economic Prescriptions for Environmental Problems: How the Patient Followed the Doctor's Orders', *Journal of Economic Perspectives*, 3, 95–114.

Hahn, R. and R. Noll (1990) 'Environmental Markets in the Year 2000', *Journal of Risk and Uncertainty*, 3, 351–367.

Herriges, J., R. Govindasamy and J. Shogren (1994) 'Budget-Balancing Incentive Mechanisms', *Journal of Environmental Economics and Management*, 27, 275–285.

Holmström, B. (1982) 'Moral Hazard in Teams', *Bell Journal of Economics*, 13, 324–340.

King, D., P. Crossen and J. Shogren (1993) 'Use of Economic Instruments for Environmental Protection in Developing Countries', *Economic Instruments for Environmental Management in Developing Countries*, OECD Document, 67–98.

Klarer, J., ed. (1994) *Use of Economic Instruments in Environmental Policy in Central and Eastern Europe*, Budapest: The Regional Environmental Center for Central and Eastern Europe.

Laffont, J.-J. (1994) 'Regulation of Pollution with Asymmetric Information', in C. Dosi and T. Tomasi (eds), *Nonpoint Source Pollution Regulation: Issues and Analysis*, Amsterdam: Kluwer Academic Publishers, 39–66.

Lewis, T. (1994) 'Instruments of Choice for Environmental Protection', University of Florida.

Lewis, T. (1996) 'Protecting the Environment when Costs and Benefits are Privately Known', *Rand Journal of Economics* (forthcoming).

O'Connor, D. (1993) 'The Use of Economic Instruments in Environmental Management: The Experience of East Asia', *Economic Instruments for Environmental Management in Developing Countries*, OECD Document, 33–43.

Organisation for Economic Co-operation and Development (1994) *Managing the Environment: The Role of Economic Instruments*, Paris: OECD.

Perrings, C. (1989) 'Environmental Bonds and Environmental Research in Innovative Activities', *Ecological Economics*, 1, 95–110.

Roberts, M. and M. Spence (1976) 'Effluent Charges and Licenses Under Uncertainty', *Journal of Public Economics*, 5, 193–208.

Russell, C. (1992) 'Monitoring and Enforcement of Pollution Control Laws in Europe and the United States', in R. Pethig (ed.), *Conflicts and Cooperation in Managing Environmental Resources*, Berlin: Springer-Verlag, 196–212.

Russell, C. and J. Shogren (1993) *Theory, Modeling and Experience in the Management of Nonpoint-Source Pollution*, Amsterdam: Kluwer Academic Publishers.

Segerson, K. (1988) 'Uncertainty and Incentives for Nonpoint Pollution Control', *Journal of Environmental Economics and Management*, 15, 87–98.

Shogren, J., J. Herriges and R. Govindasamy (1993) 'Limits to Environmental Bonds', *Ecological Economics*, 8, 109–133.

Shortle, J. and J. Dunn (1986) 'The Relative Efficiency of Agricultural Source Water Pollution Control Policies', *American Journal of Agricultural Economics*, 68, 668–677.

Weitzman, M. (1974) 'Price vs. Quantities', *Review of Economic Studies*, 41, 477–491.

Xepapadeas, A. (1991) 'Environmental Policy Under Imperfect Information: Incentives and Moral Hazard', *Journal of Environmental Economics and Management*, 20, 113–126.

Zylicz, T. (1994) 'Poland', in J. Klarer (ed.), *Use of Economic Instruments in Environmental Policy in Central and Eastern Europe*, Budapest: Regional Environmental Center for Central and Eastern Europe, 93–121.

■ *Chapter 4* ■

Pollution Taxes for the Efficient Control of Pollution

4.1 Introduction

4.2 Efficiency properties of
    a tax on emissions

4.3 Problems with pollution taxes

4.4 Conclusions

■ *4.1* Introduction

In this chapter, we will be considering some alternative policy options which could be used to attain a specified target for pollution reduction. This target will be assumed to be different from the optimal level of pollution which, as we argued in the previous chapter, is virtually impossible to identify. Targets instead will be assumed to have been set through the political process, using scientific inputs on likely damages, and economic inputs on both damage costs and control costs. Such targets are typically of two types. The first is a target reduction in emissions output, across a specified set of dischargers. Examples of such targets include the US government's target reduction of 40 per cent in SO_2 emissions from power stations, relative to 1980 emissions of 25.5 million tons. This target is to be achieved over two phases, phase one ending in January 1995, and phase 2 in January 2000 under the Clean Air Act Amendments of 1990. Another example of a load reduction target is the UK government's objective of a 50 per cent reduction in the discharge of certain water-borne pollutants (so-called 'Red List' substances) to the North Sea by 1995 (Hallett *et al.*, 1991).

The second type is a target improvement in ambient environmental quality. An example here is the range of target improvements in ambient water quality parameters adopted as 'environmental quality standards' by the Scottish River Purification Boards (RPBs). Thus an RPB may have an objective of increasing dissolved oxygen levels in an estuary up to 7 mg/l, through a policy of reducing discharges of substances exerting a biological oxygen demand (BOD) in the estuary.

For either type of target, an environmental control agency has a number of policy options open to it. These are (1) exhortation and persuasion; (2) quantitative and qualitative limits on discharges ('standards'); (3) taxes on polluting inputs; (4) taxes on emissions; (5) product taxes; (6) subsidies on pollution reduction; (7) a system of tradeable emission permits; (8) a system of tradeable input permits and (9) combinations of the preceding alternatives. Standards may themselves be characterised into two groups: *design standards*, whereby the regulator specifies the type of plant a firm or group of firms must use, and *performance standards*, where the regulator specifies the maximum quantity and minimum quality of a firm's emissions. The focus of this chapter is a comparison of tax and standards policies; in the next chapter we consider tradeable permit systems.

What criteria could the environmental quality agency adopt in order to choose amongst these alternatives? One obvious criterion which economists would suggest is efficiency, in terms of a desire to minimise the total control costs associated with achieving a given target. This is the focus of much of the proceeding argument, but it should be stressed that this is not the only criterion with which an agency could (or should) be concerned. Recent research in the UK (Hanley *et al.*, 1990) shows that the apparent fairness of a policy is likely to be important, in terms of how the total financial burden – the sum of control costs and transfer payments incurred – is spread across dischargers, and between dischargers and the public. The 'polluter pays' principle has been enshrined in OECD policy statements since the early 1970s (see Pezzey, 1988, for a full discussion) and embodies a notion that dischargers should certainly bare the control costs of achieving a given level of pollution, and perhaps in addition pay any residual damage costs.

In addition to apparent fairness, other criteria likely to be important are the degree of uncertainty attaching to the achievement of the environmental target through using any policy, and the political acceptability of the policy. This latter will depend partly on the three criteria of efficiency, fairness and uncertainty, but may have wider dimensions, such as a desire for local control, or the policy's compatability with a particular ethical system.

4.2 Efficiency properties of a tax on emissions

In order to present the most fundamental result in efficient pollution control (the Baumol and Oates least cost tax theorem), we shall initially assume that efficiency is the sole criterion used in deciding policy choice. This assumption will be relaxed once the basic result has been established and discussed. In deriving the result, a new piece of terminology is introduced: the notion of *abatement costs*, and in particular the *marginal abatement cost* function.

For a firm, an abatement cost function describes the cost of reducing the output of an emission. In general, firms have a number of options open to them to reduce emissions. First, they may reduce output of their product. So, if a coal-fired power station wishes to cut its output of waste gases, such as SO_2, it can reduce the number of hours that its furnaces run. Electricity output falls, but so does the output of SO_2. Second, a firm may change its production process. Thus the power station could switch to a combustion process that produces less waste gases per kwh of electricity, or else substitute lower-sulphur coal for its existing coal input. Finally, the power station can install a filter on the end of its chimney to remove SO_2 from the waste gas stream (a process known as flue gas desulphurisation). This 'end-of-pipe' technology is available for many production processes – paper mills, for instance, are able to install settlement ponds and centrefuges to reduce the sediment content of liquid effluent.

Our assumption will be that firms will always seek the lowest cost method of pollution control available to them. This may involve a combination of approaches – say input substitution up to a certain level of emission reduction, and then end-of-pipe treatment; or it may involve the use of two or all three approaches simultaneously. We shall assume also that, as a general principle, each firm is better informed about the most efficient manner for reducing its own emissions than is the regulator.

Empirical evidence (for example, Bergman, 1991) and theory both suggest that marginal abatement costs, defined as the change in the lowest cost way of reducing emissions for a change in emission reduction, are increasing in the level of emission reduction, as is shown in Figure 4.1.

In a free market system, with no government control on emissions and no altruism on the part of the firm (we also assume that emissions from the firm do no damage to that firm itself), the firm will locate at e_f, spending no money on emissions control. As emissions are reduced, abatement costs rise at an increasing rate. Specifying a continuously increasing MAC function is convenient analytically, since it implies that local and global cost-minimising solutions will coincide. Rowley *et al.* (1979) found that, for some discharges, economies of scale are present in emissions treatment. The implications of this are discussed in Box 4.1. For the remainder of this chapter, however, we will assume continuously increasing MAC functions.

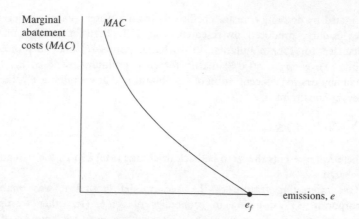

Figure 4.1 *Marginal abatement costs for a firm*

Box 4.1 *Pollution control in the Tees estuary*

During the 1970s, economists at the University of Newcastle-upon-Tyne, carried out the first UK study of pollution taxes for the control of water pollution (Rowley *et al.*, 1979). This study was commissioned by the UK government following the famous 'minority report' of the Royal Commission on Environmental Pollution, in order to see whether the theoretical cost-saving properties of pollution taxes over standards could be shown to exist in a simulation model. Rowley *et al.* studied a number of pollutants, including ammonia, organic compounds exerting a BOD and heavy metals. At the time of the study, the Tees estuary was classified as 'grossly polluted' by the regulatory agency, the Northumbria Water Authority, incapable of support-ing fish life and having an offensive smell and appearance. The major sources of pollution were point source industrial discharges and sewage treatment works (STWs), which jointly resulted in a zero level of DO in the middle reaches around Victoria Bridge.

The Newcastle team constructed a mathematical programming model of point source discharges on the Tees. This necessitated the collection of a large volume of data on pollution abatement technologies (in terms of their capacities and fixed and operating costs). The model involved the minimiza-tion of the sum of discounted abatement costs (D_{ki}) for abatement options k across $i = 1 \ldots n$ dischargers. These abatement costs depend on whether a particular technology is introduced ($X^t_{ki} = 1$) or not ($X^t_{ki} = 0$) in any particular time period t, where t represents three discrete time periods:

Minimize $\quad D = \sum_{i=1}^{n} \sum_{ki=1}^{mi} \sum_{t=3}^{9} D^t_{ki} X^t_{ki}$

This minimization occurs subject to some technical constraints on capacity utilization, and also constraints on water quality impacts. These latter were estimated by deriving transfer coefficients from a water quality model of the Tees estuary, produced by researchers at ICI. Transfer coefficients were calculated for four pollutants, 40 discharge points (i) and 40 monitoring points (j), giving a 40×40 matrix for each pollutant, denoted a_{ij}. If the maximum desired concentration of a pollutant p at any stretch is $\bar{C}_j^p$, then the relevant constraint is:

$$\sum_{i=1}^{n} a_{ji}^p (\bar{L}_i^p - Z_i^p) \leq \bar{C}_j^p$$

Where $\bar{L}_i$ represents the 'zero cutback discharge rate' and Z_i the reduction in discharge.

One interesting feature of the Tees model is that it was unable to incorporate STWs, owing to economies of scale. (In other words, the aggregate abatement cost function is not strictly convex.) Economies of scale are a problem in the approach used here, since any local optimum identified by a tax policy may not be a global optimum (see Rowley *et al.*, p. 73). In this case, STWs must be treated separately from industrial discharges (by, for example, allocating a particular amount of assimilative capacity to STWs before setting $\bar{C}_j$ above).

The Newcastle team used their model to compare the costs of meeting certain targets for DO and for other pollutants using tax rates which varied along the Tees according to the shadow prices calculated by the cost-minimization model. Example results are given below:

Table 4.1   *Water quality levels (ppm) and resource costs*

Water quality standard	DO	Ammonia	Cyanide	£ million
1	4.2	3.7	0.486	14.5
2	5.1	3.7	0.053	16.3

This yielded total tax revenues (transfer payments) of £12.6 million (standard 1) and £13.4 million (standard 3) in 1976 prices. The resource costs of the tax policy were slightly greater than the least-cost solution, owing to indivisibilities in pollution control (see also Hanley and Moffatt, 1993, on this point). The resource costs under the tax solution are much less than the costs of a spatially differentiated performance standard, where the regulation is aware of transfer coefficients but not of abatement costs; and cheaper still than a policy of uniform performance standards, where all firms are faced with the same required reduction:

	(£m) *Resource costs of performance standard*	
Water quality standard	*Spatially differentiated*	*Uniform*
1	£19.7 (DO = 4.1 mg/l)	£29.1 (DO = 6.4 mg/l)

> However, the Newcastle team noted that a system of perfectly differentiated taxes could be expensive to administer and could raise political objections on equity grounds. They thus considered a simpler zonal tax scheme (referred to as 'spatial weighted taxes'). These gave resource costs of £15.9 million to achieve water quality standard 1.

It is also to be expected that MAC functions will vary across sources, for a given pollutant. This means that some sources of, for example, BOD will find incremental reductions in BOD output (much) less expensive than others, owing to differences in plant location, age and design; different production processes (distilling, paper making, oil refining); differing levels of current emissions reduction; and differing levels of managerial knowledge and ability. For example, Hanley and Moffat (1993) found that MACs for direct discharges of BOD to the Forth Estuary in Scotland varied by as much as thirty-fold.

The observation that MACs vary across sources is a key insight into why the cost-minimising (that is, most efficient) means of securing target reduction in emissions will involve different amounts of emission reduction across sources. Assume for the present that a uniformly-mixed pollutant, such as a volatile organic compound (VOC) is the object of control. This means that the target reduction in emissions is independent of the source of emission, since a tonne less of discharge from any source in the control area is equally effective in meeting a pollution reduction target as the same reduction from any other source. It would seem sensible, in this situation, for high abatement cost sources to reduce emissions by less than low abatement cost sources. In fact, a necessary condition for an efficient solution in this case is that abatement costs, at the margin, are equalised across all sources. This is proved formally below, but the intuition is clear enough: if at the current allocation of emission reduction responsibility source A can achieve a one-unit cut in VOCs at a cost of £100/unit, and source B faces a cost of £500/unit at the margin, then a unit of emission reduction responsibility can be reallocated from B to A for a net saving of (£500 − £100) or £400. These cost savings will remain possible so long as MACs are not equal.

This is demonstrated in Figure 4.2, where emissions from two sources with varying MACs, source A (low cost) and source B (high cost) are shown. For convenience, both MAC functions are shown as originating at the same point. A performance standard designed to achieve the target emission level of $[\frac{1}{2}(e_A^f + e_B^f)]$ might set a maximum limit on each firm emissions of $\bar{e}$ (a 'uniform standard'). (Not all performance standards are uniform. Consents issued for water pollution control in the UK are examples of non-uniform

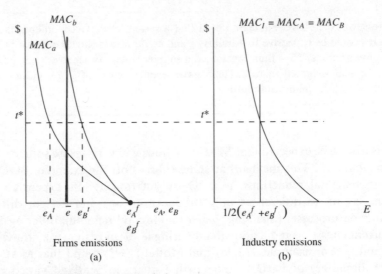

Figure 4.2   *An efficient tax on emissions*

performance standards.) However, this results in firm B having a higher MAC at $\bar{e}$ than firm A – efficiency is thus not achieved, in this case.

Baumol and Oates (1971) showed that an efficient outcome could be achieved by setting a tax on emissions such as t^*. As shown in Figure 4.2(b), t^* is calculated as the MAC (MAC_I) of the industry (here, firm A plus B) at the target level of emissions. Faced with t^*, each firm, as shown in Figure 4.2(a), equates the tax rate with its MAC schedule by varying its level of emissions. This is its cost-minimising reaction. For firm A, emitting more than e'_A is inefficient, since the marginal benefits of reducing emissions (avoided tax payments on the marginal unit, t^*) exceed the marginal costs, as shown by MAC_A. Similarly, cutting emissions below e'_A is inefficient, as the marginal costs exceed the marginal benefits. Note that, through self-interest alone, the desirable pattern of emission reduction has been achieved, since firm B (the high abatement cost source) has reduced emissions by less, relative to its 'no intervention' level of e^f_B, and we have the result that $MAC_A = t^* = MAC_B$. To state the theorem as Baumol and Oates put it: 'A tax rate set at a level that achieves the desired reduction in the total emission of pollutants will satisfy the necessary conditions for the minimisation of the programme's cost to society' (Baumol and Oates, 1988). One important caveat to state here is that it is the resource costs to society that we seek to minimise: the solution to this problem will only coincide with firms' reactions to a tax if the costs that firms face in controlling pollution are identical to social costs – it rules out, for example, the case where pollution reduction processes actually increase emissions of a second pollutant at no cost to the discharger. In this case, private resource cost minimisation will not coincide with social resource cost minimisation, since the marginal private costs of inputs will not equal their marginal social costs, unless all pollutants are subject to Baumol and Oates-type taxes. We should also stress that the present analysis relates solely to a uniformly mixed pollutant: allowing for non-uniform mixing complicates the tax policy option, as will be discussed later.

Formal proofs of the efficiency properties of a tax on emissions have been provided by Baumol and Oates, and by Fisher (1980). Our proof of the theorem is adapted from Fisher. Suppose there is some uniformly mixed pollutant, defined at any point in time as a flow E_t. Total emissions are given by the sum of individual discharges across all sources k, e_k:

$$E_t = \sum_k e_{kt} \tag{4.1}$$

Dropping the time subscript form henceforth, firms produce output y_k using inputs r_{ik} (so that input r_{1k} is the amount of input 1 used by firm k), according to a production function $y_k = f_k(r_{ik} \ldots r_{nk})$. Firms can make use of end-of-pipe technology (v_k) to reduce polluting emissions, which can also be cut by reducing output, so that there is an emissions function $b_k(y_k, v_k) = e_k$. The cost of a unit of abatement technology is given as p_v, the price of inputs (assumed exogenous to the firm) is p_i. The social planners' problem is to:

minimise $\displaystyle\sum_i \sum_k p_i r_{ik} + \sum_k p_v v_k$ $\tag{4.2}$

subject to: $f^k(r_{ik} \ldots r_{nk}) = y_k^*$ $\tag{4.3}$

and $\quad b^k(y_k^*, v_k) = e_k$ $\tag{4.4}$

and $\quad \displaystyle\sum_k e_k \leq E^*$ $\tag{4.5}$

and $\quad e_k, y_k \geq 0, \quad \text{for all } k = 1 \ldots k.$ $\tag{4.6}$

The planner thus seeks to minimise the sum of input costs (the first term in equation 4.2) and pollution abatement costs (the second term in 4.2), subject to production being equal to some specified level for each firm (y_k^*), given equation (4.3), the emissions production function (4.4) and a constraint on the maximum permitted level of emissions (4.5). Non-negativity constraints on emissions and output are also specified. Substituting for the actual level of emissions ($\sum_k e_k$) using the emissions production function, and forming the Lagrangian, we have:

$$L = \sum_i \sum_k p_i r_{ik} + \sum_k p_v v_k + \sum_k \lambda_k [y_k^* - f^k(\cdot)] + \mu \left[\sum_k b^k(\cdot) - E^* \right] \tag{4.7}$$

where λ_k and μ are Lagrangean multipliers. The first-order conditions for a minimum of (4.7) with respect to input use r_i and pollution abatement v_k are:

$$\partial L/\partial r_i = p_i - \lambda_k \, \partial f^k/\partial r_i = 0 \quad \text{all } i, k \tag{4.8a}$$

$$\partial L/\partial v = p_v + \mu \, \partial b^k/\partial v = 0 \quad \text{all } k \tag{4.8b}$$

These conditions say that inputs, and pollution abatement, should be employed up to the point where their prices are equal to the value of their marginal products.

Let us suppose that the planner decides to achieve the target emission level E^* by setting a per unit tax on emissions of t^*. Clearly, this must be of a particular value to achieve E^*, given firms' abatement costs – from the earlier graphical analysis, it is known that t^* will equal aggregate MACs at E^*. Taking the problem faced by a representative, cost-minimising firm facing an emissions tax set at t^*, firm k will want to:

$$\text{minimise} \sum_i p_i r_{ik} + p_v v_k + t_k^* e_k \tag{4.9}$$

subject to equations (4.3), (4.4) and (4.6). Again, substituting for e_k using the emissions production function $b^k(\cdot)$ and forming the Lagrangean:

$$L^k = \sum_i p_i r_{ik} + p_v v_k + t_k^* b^k(\cdot) + \beta^k[y_k^* - f^k(\cdot)] \tag{4.10}$$

Differentiating L^k with respect to input and abatement use and assuming no boundary solutions, the first-order conditions for a minimum are:

$$p_i - \beta^k \, \partial f^k/dr_i = 0 \quad \text{all } i \tag{4.11a}$$

and

$$p_v + t_k^* \, \partial b^k/\partial v_k = 0. \tag{4.11b}$$

Comparing equations (4.11) with equations (4.8), it can be seen that the firm's optimum will coincide with the social optimum if:

1. input prices faced by the firm p_i and the pollution abatement price p_v correspond to their competitive levels: that is, the firm has no price-setting power in the input or pollution abatement markets (we also require $\beta^k = \lambda^k$ for all k, but, as Fisher points out, this is time by definition in equilibrium, if conditions (1) and (2) are met);
2. the tax rate t_k^* is equal to μ, the shadow price of pollution reduction in the social planners' problem. Note that this is just what was said above: the least-cost tax is equal to the marginal (shadow) cost of abatement at the target level of emissions, E^*. This can be seen more clearly if the second condition in (4.11) is rearranged, giving

$t^* = -p_v/b_v^k$ (where $b_v^k \equiv \partial b^k/\partial v_k$), since the expression $(-p_v/b_v^k)$ is the marginal abatement cost for firm k. Note that this also implies, for a given t^*, that MACs across all firms must be equal under the cost-minimising solution, which is the conclusion we reached earlier by an intuitive route.

What if the control authority does not know the MAC functions for all discharges it wishes to regulate? Then it must guess the correct tax rate. If the agency guesses too low, too little pollution abatement will result, and the tax rate must be raised. If the agency guesses too high, then too much abatement occurs, and the agency must cut the tax. This iterative process may in fact impose costs on firms and prevent them from minimising abatement costs if they become locked into inappropriate pollution control technology (Walker and Storey, 1977). A continually changing tax rate also increases uncertainty, which at the macro level has a depressing influence on the level of investment.

■ *4.3* **Problems with pollution taxes**

□ *4.3.1 Non-uniformly mixed pollutants*

For many potentially polluting substances, ambient concentrations at a given monitoring point are dependent not just on the total amount of emissions (E in the preceding model), but also on their spatial location. A good example is dissolved oxygen (DO) levels at a particular point j in a river. For given flow and temperature conditions, the DO level will be a function of both the total amount of BOD discharges upstream of point j, *and* their location. This is because 2000 kg/day of BOD discharged one mile upriver of point j will have a bigger impact on the DO level than the same quantity discharged five miles upriver since, in this latter case, natural degration and reaeration proesses will have had longer to 'work' on the effluent than in the former case. This spatial relationship is also true for many air pollutants: acid deposition (from SO_2, NO_x and ammonia discharges) in a particular forest will depend on prevailing wind directions and distance from major discharge points. Indeed, this fact creates many problems of international pollution policy co-ordination, which are addressed in Chapter 6.

What are the implications for the Baumol and Oates theorem of a non-uniformly mixed pollutant? Basically, that a single tax rate will no longer be efficient, since the tax rate should vary across sources according to their marginal impacts on ambient air or water quality levels. Suppose that the ambient level of pollution at any monitoring point j, a_j, is a weighted function of emissions from all sources:

$$a_j = \sum_k d_{jk}e_k \tag{4.12}$$

The d_{jk} coefficients are often referred to as 'transfer coefficients' and form a $(K \times J)$ matrix, where there are $k = 1 \ldots K$ sources and J $(j = 1 \ldots J)$ monitoring points. Any particular transfer coefficient, such as d_{11}, shows the impact of discharges from source 1 on water quality (for example) at monitoring point 1. These d_{jk} terms will vary, for a river or estuary, according to the time of year and consequent variations in temperature and flow rate. They are often measured under worse case conditions (known as dry weather flow, DWF). For an air shed, transfer coefficients may be calculated as an average across all windspeed/direction conditions recorded in some time period. In all cases, the transfer coefficient matrix is generated from some model of the environmental system of interest: a river, the air shed over a city. An excellent account of such a process is given in O'Neil *et al.* (1983).

For non-uniformly mixed pollutants, the control agency's target might be specified as seeking to reduce ambient concentrations to some target ambient level (such as 7 mg/l of DO under DWF conditions). This can be written as:

$$\sum_k d_{jk}e_k \leq a_j^* \tag{4.13}$$

where a_j^* is the ambient target at each monitoring point. Assuming this to be the same for all j, this can be simplified to a^*. The planners' problem is now to minimise (4.2) subject to (4.3), (4.4), (4.6) and (4.13). The Lagrangean becomes:

$$L = \sum_i \sum_k p_i r_{ik} + \sum_k p_v v_k + \sum_k \lambda_k [y_k^* - f^k(\cdot)] + \mu \left(\sum_k d_{jk}[b^k(\cdot)] - a^* \right)$$

Solving for the first-order conditions with respect to r and v, and comparing these with the decisions of firms faced with a pollution tax, it is possible to show that, in order to achieve an efficient solution, each firm must face a different tax rate t_k^*, which is determined by that firm's degradation of environmental quality at each monitoring point (given by the transfer coefficients) and the ambient target itself. Shadow prices of improving ambient quality at any monitoring point j, μ_j, are positive so long as emission reductions are necessary to meet the ambient target and where, after the imposition of the tax policy, the ambient standard is met exactly. In the language of linear programming (see p. 100), shadow prices are 'dual' values and exist only for constraints which are binding in the optimal solution. Since firms can have different transfer coefficients for different monitoring points, it might be desirable to calculate tax rates on the basis of transfer coefficients for the most polluted monitoring point, or the monitoring point where economic measures of pollution damage are highest. The alternative, as Tietenberg (1973) first proved, is to have separate tax rates for each monitoring point, which are then adjusted for each firm according to its transfer coefficient relating to that point. Firms would thus face a different tax bill for each monitoring point they face, with the firm's total tax bill being the sum of taxes paid at each monitoring point. Thus a unique shadow price or tax rate μ_j exists at each monitoring point j, and firm k pays a tax equal to $[d_{jk}\mu_j]$ for emissions affecting point j. The total tax paid by the firm would be $[\sum_{j=1}^{J} d_{jk}\mu_j]$ per unit of emissions.

Box 4.2 *Pollution taxes and air quality*

In a 1983 paper in the *Journal of Environmental Economics and Management*, Seskin *et al.* examine the costs of meeting a target improvement in ambient levels of nitrogen dioxide (NO_2) in Chicago. They compare a uniform standards regime with pollution taxes, using a mathematical model of air quality to estimate transfer coefficients between emission sources and 600 receptor (monitoring) points. Dischargers fell into nine source categories, inlcuding power stations, municipal incinerators and industrial boilers. Each policy option was compared to a 'no control' baseline, under which 36 receptors were found to be in violation of the NO_2 standard. Engineering data were used to estimate marginal abatement cost functions for discharge sources, and a type of programming model (known as integer programming) used to simulate the least-cost outcome.

The control strategies modelled were:

1 a state implementation plan (SIP) strategy, whereby uniform design standards were imposed on similar categories of sources;
2 a uniform emissions tax, set at a rate high enough to ensure that those sources having the largest effect on ambient air quality per unit of discharge were controlled sufficiently to meet the target improvement; and
3 an emission tax differentiated by source category.

Given that NO_2 is a non-uniformly mixed pollutant, none of these strategies could replicate the least-cost solution, which enables the target to be met at all points for an annualised total abatement cost of $9 million. This is because the least-cost solution requires all sources to face a unique tax rate, that is, that there is a perfectly differentiated tax system. Simulation results are given below.

Table 4.2   Control costs for air pollution

Policy	Number of sources controlled	Area-wide reduction in emission (%)	Annual control costs ($m)
Least cost	100	3	9
SIP	472	21	130
Uniform tax	534	84	305
Source category tax	472	18	66

As may be seen, the uniform tax rate has to be set so high (high enough to sufficiently restrict emissions from the most damaging source) that this policy has a higher resource cost than the command and control option of the SIP. The uniform tax rate also gives the biggest reduction in area emissions, since this high tax rate produces too much abatement from less damaging sources (note that *all* policies in the table achieve the ambient target level of air quality).

A source category charge, however, is more efficient than either a SIP or a uniform charge, with tax rates varying between $15 800 (per year per pound of NO_x per hour) for industrial coal-fired boilers to $13 500 for industrial process units. None of these three policies, however, achieves the least cost solution, which would require, as noted already, a perfectly differentiated tax scheme.

As Tietenberg (1974) first pointed out, 'forcing upwind and downwind polluters to pay the same tax will produce the desired concentration (reduction), but at a cost which exceeds the minimum cost means of achieving that concentration' (Tietenberg, 1974, p. 464). Tietenberg goes on to point out that a perfectly differentiated tax system, with each polluter facing a unique, location-determined tax rate, would be 'administratively difficult at best and politically infeasible at worst', so that a compromise, such as a zonal tax system where tax rates vary across zones but not within zones might be preferred. Empirical evidence on this point was provided by Seskin *et al.* (1983) – see Box 4.1.

One important advantage of pollution taxes over design or performance standards concerns dynamic cost-savings (OECD, 1989). Suppose a firm could adopt a production process which had lower marginal abatement costs (MAC_{NEW}, in Figure 4.3) associated with it, relative to the firm's existing technology (MAC_{OLD}). Installing this cleaner technology incurs a cost, but benefits acrue in terms of abatement cost savings. These benefits can be shown to be greater under a tax than under a uniform standard. Under the uniform standard $\bar{e}$, the firm saves total abatement costs of area (xze^f) by switching. Under a tax set at t^1, the firm would find it cost-effective

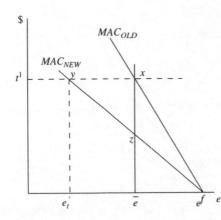

Figure 4.3 *Savings under innovation with a pollution tax (Milliman and Prince, 1984)*

to reduce its emissions from $\bar{e}$ to e_t^1 if it switched to the new technology. The firm, under the old technology, incurred control costs of $(\bar{e}xe^f)$ and tax charges of $(ot^1x\bar{e})$. With MAC_{NEW}, control costs are $(e_t^1ye^f)$ and tax payments total $(ot^1ye_t^1)$. This produces net savings under the new technology of area (yxe^f), which exceeds the savings under the uniform standard $\bar{e}$ *and* results in lower emissions. A tax system, relative to a standard, would thus, over time, result in a progressive reduction in both abatement costs and emission levels.

More recently, Milliman and Prince (1989) have shown that emission taxes provide higher incentives for firms to innovate cleaner technologies, for the diffusion of these technologies, and for pressure on regulators to then adjust environmental controls, than emission subsidies, certain forms of tradeable permits or uniform standards. These three stages in dynamic adjustment are shown in Figure 4.4, which is taken from Milliman and Prince (1989) (note that the horizontal axis shows emission reductions, rather than emissions). Innovation, the process considered in the preceding paragraph, shifts the *industry* marginal abatement cost curve to MAC_2 from MAC_1. This produces savings equal to area (E_M, A, B). Diffusion of this cleaner technology produces a further fall in the industry MAC curve to MAC_3, and a further cost saving of (E_M, B, C). This changes the optimal level of emissions control to E^{**}, which, if the agency recognises this, further increases benefit by area (CAD).

While tradeable permits, emission taxes and emission subsidies offer identical advantages over uniform standards in terms of incentives to promote innovation (the case we discussed in Figure 4.2), once diffusion and agency response incentives are considered, emission taxes emerge as the policy instrument most likely to maximise welfare gains.

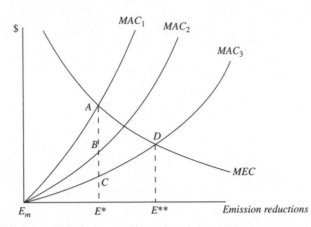

Figure 4.4 *Savings under innovation, diffusion and regulatory response (Milliman and Prince, 1984)*

Summarising, the message from both Figures 4.2 and 4.3 is clear: uniform regulation, the type of pollution policy most commonly practised by control agencies, results in lower incentives for cost reductions in pollution control than market mechanisms. Uniform regulation (and, indeed, non-uniform regulation where standards vary across firms) thus reduces the speed of innovation in pollution control. The encouragement to reduce costs provided by market mechanisms has been referred to as 'over the long haul, perhaps the most important criterion on which to judge environmental policies' (Kneese and Schultze, 1978).

We now turn to a listing of some further problems with tax policies for the achievement of pollution reduction targets. Firstly, the pollution control agency must set the tax rate (or vector of rates for a non-uniformly mixed pollutant). To get this exactly correct requires full information on abatement costs and transfer coefficients. As Baumol and Oates originally agreed, agencies could iterate onto the correct tax rate (for a uniformly mixed pollutant) by setting a best-guess rate and then observing the consequent reduction in emissions. If this was too great, the tax rate should be reduced; if too little, then the tax rate should be increased. However, this neglects three problems: (1) setting an initially incorrect tax rate can lock firms into incorrect investments in pollution control equipment, preventing them from minimizing costs (Walker and Storey, 1977); (2) setting an initial rate too low may result in irreversible, or reversible but serious, damage to the water body/air shed in question; and (3) the aggregate MAC function is not stable through time. It will be changing in real terms owing to fluctuations in energy costs, input costs and product prices, and also in nominal terms as the result of inflation. Getting the tax rate correct may thus be an impossible task.

A second problem concerns the issue of new entrants to a region. Suppose the major pollution problem in an estuary is emissions from oil refining. If new refineries are established in the area, then the aggregate MAC function will shift to the right, implying that, unless the tax rate is increased, aggregate emissions will increase. This is really just another aspect of the problem discussed in the preceding paragraph.

Box 4.3 *Taxes on multiple pollutants*

In a number of important cases of pollution problems, an undesirable environmental effect is brought about by a number of pollutants, which jointly produce the effect. Perhaps the best example is global warming, where the effect (an decrease in reradiation of solar energy, leading to an increase in global mean temperature) is caused by a number of gases, the so-called 'greenhouse gases': carbon dioxide (CO_2), methane (CH_4), nitrous oxide (N_2O) and chlorofluorocarbons (CFC11 and CFC12). The increased accumulation of these gases is, according to many global models, producing an increase in global mean temperature (see, for example, Cline, 1992; Rosenberg *et al.*, 1989). A comprehensive account of economic analysis of the greenhouse effect is provided by Cline (1992).

Michaelis (1992) considers this problem, from the point of view of how to design a tax system. The important question here is the level of efficient relative tax rates for the four main greenhouse gases (GHGs). Michaelis also considers the dynamics of this problem, in that there is a finite assimilative capacity in each time period for GHGs, but also a constraint on the total stock if undesirable warming is to be avoided.

Let us denote the four GHGs $G_1 \ldots G_4$, uncontrolled, baseline emissions $\hat{e}_i(t)$ in period t, and pollution abatement as $V_i(t)$. Baseline emissions grow at an exogenous rate g_i due to economic growth. Thus actual emissions e_i are given by:

$$e_i(t) = \hat{e}_i(0)(1 + g_i)^t - v_i(t) \tag{1}$$

Natural degradation occurs for each greenhouse gas at a constant rate $q_i (0 \le q_i \le 1)$. The change in the stock s_i between two periods is thus:

$$s_i(t + 1) - s_i(t) = e_i(t + 1) - q_i(s_i(t)) \tag{2}$$

Assuming for simplicity that the initial stock of each GHG is zero, the current stock in any period t^* is given as:

$$s_i(t^*) = \sum_{t=1}^{t^*} (1 - q_i)^{t^* - t} e_i(t) \tag{3}$$

Each pollutant has a different contribution to the overall stock S (that is, to global warming potential), which is represented by a parameter α; For the stock S of GHGs this means:

$$S(t) = \sum_{i=1}^{n} \alpha_i s_i(t) \tag{4}$$

An absolute constraint on total GHG stock S^0 is specified, with the requirement that $S_t \leq S^0$ for all $t = 1 \ldots T$. Lastly, there are abatement cost functions $C_i(V_i(t))$ for each GHG, which are assumed to have 'conventional' forms, so that both first and second derivatives are positive.

Setting up the Lagrangean for this problem (that is, minimizing total discounted abatement costs) and differentiating reveals that an efficient solution requires, for any pair of GHGs i and j:

$$\frac{C_i'(v_i(t))}{C_i'(v_j(t))} = \frac{\alpha_i}{\alpha_j} \left[\frac{1 - q_i}{1 - q_j} \right]^{(T-t)} \tag{5}$$

so that relative marginal abatement costs $(c_i'[v_i(t)]/c_j'[v_j(t)])$ are equal to the ratio of warming potential, taking into account relative rates of natural degradation. Thus higher tax rates will be imposed on GHGs with higher α and lower q values. For any two adjacent time periods $\{t, t+1\}$, a further requirement is that:

$$C_i'[V_i(t+1)] = \frac{1+r}{1-q_i} C_i'[V_i(t)] \tag{6}$$

where r is the social rate of discount. The pollution taxes needed to achieve the efficient solution satisfy the following properties:

$$\frac{P_i(t)}{P_j(t)} = \frac{\alpha_i}{\alpha_j} \left[\frac{1 + q_i}{1 - q_j} \right]^{(T-t)} \tag{7}$$

and

$$P_i(t+1) = \left(\frac{1+r}{1-q_i} \right) P_i(t) \tag{8}$$

Equation (7) tells us that relative tax rates between pollutants i and j depend on their relative damage and dispersion coefficients, following the logic behind equation (5). Equation (8) says that taxes on a given pollutant must grow at the discount rate, adjusted for the decay rate (see equation (5)). Michaelis shows that absolute tax rates depend on the initial stock of GHGs, the time period over which the model is run (T), the level of abatement costs and the initial period level of emission.

In Table 4.3, some simulation results from the Michaelis model are presented. These results can be understood by considering equations (7) and (8), and the 'natural parameters' α_i and q_i, which are given in Table 4.4. As may be seen, relative to CO_2, CFCs have the highest impact per molecule on overall warming potential (the largest α coefficients). This means tax rates on CFCs will be relatively high amongst the GHGs. Comparing the taxes on methane and CO_2, we see that, if only warming potential was considered, methane would have a tax 58 times higher than CO_2. However, because methane degrades more quickly than CO_2 (its atmospheric lifetime is only 10 years, compared with a 120 year lifetime for CO_2), the tax rate in period 1 is only just over ten times higher for methane relative to CO_2. Taxes on all GHGs rise over time as scarce overall assimilative capacity is used up.

Table 4.3 *Tax rates on greenhouse gases*

	CO_2	CH_4	N_2O	*CFC 11*	*CFC 12*
$t = 1$	50.4	508	10 631	169 433	291 023
$t = 2$	52.4	584	11 131	179 171	305 001
$t = 3$	55.0	671	11 653	189 470	319 651
$t = 4$	57.7	772	12 200	200 360	335 004
$t = 5$	60.5	887	12 773	211 877	351 094
$t = 6$	63.4	1 019	13 373	224 055	367 958
$t = 7$	66.5	1 172	14 001	236 934	385 631
$t = 8$	69.7	1 347	14 659	250 552	404 153
$t = 9$	73.1	1 548	15 347	264 954	423 357
$t = 10$	76.7	1 779	16 068	280 183	443 909
$t = 11$	80.4	2 045	16 822	296 287	465 230
$t = 12$	84.3	2 350	17 612	313 318	487 576
$t = 13$	88.5	2 701	18 439	331 327	510 994
$t - 14$	92.8	3 105	19 305	350 317	535 538
$t = 15$	97.3	3 569	20 211	370 510	561 260
$t = 16$	102.0	4 102	21 160	391 806	588 218
$t = 17$	107.0	4 714	22 154	414 326	616 471
$t = 18$	112.2	5 418	23 194	438 141	646 080
$t = 19$	117.7	6 228	24 283	463 325	677 112
$t = 20$	123.4	7 158	25 423	489 956	709 634

Notes: For a social discount rate $(r) = 4$ per cent and $T = 20$.
Source: Michaelis (1992).

Table 4.4 *Natural parameters for greenhouse gases*

	CO_2	CH_4	N_2O	*CFC 11*	*CFC 12*
Warming potential, α_i	1	58	206	3970	5750
Atmospheric lifetime, c_i	120	10	150	60	130
Degradation rate, q_i	0.0083	0.0952	0.0066	0.0165	0.0077

Note: q_i estimated as $q_i = 1 - e^{-(1/ci)}$.
Source: Michaelis (1992).

Finally, pollution taxes can be objected to on equity and uncertainty grounds. In terms of equity, John Pezzey (1988) has argued that pollution taxes can overpenalise firms in terms of what is conventionally understood about the polluter pays principle (PPP). In Figure 4.5, a single polluter on a river is shown, in terms of the MAC schedule, and a marginal damage cost (MDC) schedule, which relates the amount of emissions to the monetary value of environmental damages caused by these emissions. If MDC were known, then an (optimal) tax of t^* could be set, realising emissions of e^* if the firm is a cost minimiser which is fully informed as to its MAC schedule.

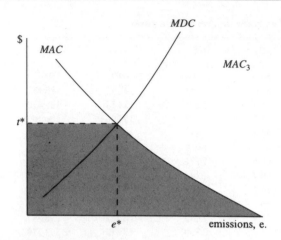

Figure 4.5   *Financial burden of a pollution tax*
Note: The shaded area equates to the financial burden

However, the total financial burden to the firm (the shaded area, being the sum of abatement costs and tax payments) exceeds what Pezzey calls the conventional PPP *and* the 'extended PPP'. The conventional PPP is interpreted as meaning that firms should pay their own control costs up to the socially desired level of control (e^*). The extended PPP adds to this burden the value of damages done by this socially desired level of emissions, the area under MDC up to e^*. That the financial burden to the firm under the tax of t^* exceeds both these amounts might be judged to be unfair. The size of transfer payments implied by a pollution tax policy has been argued to have been a major barrier to the acceptance of pollution taxes in the OECD. However, in principle this obstacle is surmountable at the aggregate level, since transfers could be returned to industry as lump sum payments (for example, as capital grants for investment in pollution control).

In terms of the uncertainty criterion, we note that a pollution tax such as t^* will only achieve the desired outcome (e^* in this case) if (1) all polluters are cost minimizers; (2) all are well informed about their MAC schedules; and (3) no untaxed emissions are possible. Point (1) is important since, unless dischargers wish to minimise costs, they will not behave in the manner suggested by the models presented earlier in this chapter. Firms might emit at levels where $MAC > t$. Whilst the assumption of cost minimisation seems reasonable for single owner, partnership and equity-financed companies irrespective of market structure (an important point), it may not describe nationalised companies and municiple treatment works. Point (2) is important since firms cannot make optimal cost-minimizing adjustments to emission levels if they do not know their MAC functions. Finally, if firms can cheat, and escape paying taxes on emissions, then again the target reduction in pollution will not be achieved. The question of enforcement is taken up in detail at the end of this chapter. For now, the conclusion is that if either of conditions (1), (2) or (3) holds, a tax system cannot guarantee a particular level of emissions reduction.

Box 4.4 *Stock pollutants*

Stock pollutants are defined as pollutants which accumulate through time with continued emissions, and where there may be some natural rate of decay of the pollutant over time. The economics of stock pollutant control was first investigated by Plourde (1972). One important resource affected by stock pollutants is groundwater. In the USA, many groundwater supplies are contaminated, often by pollutants of an agricultural origin, with the Soil Conservation Service reporting in 1987 that 42 states suffered groundwater pollution from agricultural sources. Conrad and Olson (1992) report a study of groundwater contamination by the stock pollutant aldicarb in the Long Island region of New York. Aldicarb is implicated in a number of health problems and had been banned from use on Long Island in 1979, when over 2000 wells (where groundwater is extracted) were found to have aldicarb levels in excess of the state upper recommended limit of 7 micrograms per litre.

Conrad and Olson use the following equation to describe aldicarb build-up in groundwater:

$$Z_{t+1} = (1 - \gamma)Z_t + \alpha NS_{t-\tau}$$

where Z_t is the pesticide concentration in groundwater in time t, γ is the rate of degradation of pesticide in groundwater, α is a scaling parameter, N is the number of hectares under cultivation, S is the amount of pesticide applied per year, and τ is the number of years it takes aldicarb to reach the aquifer. In Figure 4.6, we replicate Conrad and Olson's Figure 1, where they show a

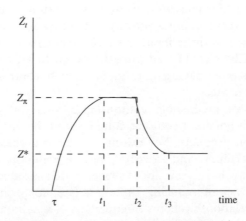

Figure 4.6 *A possible time path for a stock pollutant*

possible time path for Z, up to some equilibrium level Z_π, where inputs to the groundwater equal natural degradation. This equilibrium is given by:

$$Z_\pi = \frac{\alpha}{\gamma} NS_\pi$$

where $S\pi$ is the profit-maximising level of application per year. If this equilibrium exceeds the maximum desired level, shown as Z^* in the figure, then the government must intervene. Conrad and Olson solve for the marginal value of economic damages implied by this standard theoretically, and then estimate it for aldicarb on Long Island. They found that, given the very swift passage of aldicarb from the top of the soil surface to groundwater (less than a year in this case) and an estimated half-life for aldicarb of 8.378 years, the implied marginal social value of damages was $4172 per part per billion[2] in water). This implies a maximum application rate of 0.295 kg/hectare, which is, according to the authors, a level one-tenth of that actually recommended that farmers apply on pest control grounds. This case would seem to be one of forgoing agricultural activity of a particular type (potato growing) in order to achieve public health benefits.

So far in this chapter the discussion has been entirely in terms of a tax on emissions. However, the Baumol and Oates theorem can be extended either to a tax on inputs or to a tax on outputs, rather than an emissions tax. With regard to inputs, Common (1977) showed that, so long as the 'pollution production function' relating inputs to emissions was known, a desired reduction in emissions could be achieved at least cost with a tax on inputs. Input taxes are very important for the control of non-point pollutants where the monitoring of emissions is either difficult or impossible. But input taxes could also be utilised for point source emissions, an example being taxes on the sulphur content of coal as a means of reducing SO_2 emissions from power stations. Input taxes may involve problems where an input substitution occurs as a result of an input tax, and where the substitute input has adverse environmental effects. For example, taxing CFCs could lead firms to switch to HCFCs, which have been argued to be more damaging to global climate control, per molecule, than CFCs, as coolants.

Finally, if a stable, predictable relationship between output of a product and emissions of a pollutant could be found, then a Baumol and Oates tax could be levied on products. For example, a tax on wheat might reduce use of nitrogen fertilizer, and so reduce nitrate pollution. However, such empirical work as has been done suggests that product taxes are a relatively costly way of reducing pollution (see, for example, England, 1986), while the relationship between emissions of a pollutant and product prices may be difficult to estimate.

Box 4.5 *Implications of a carbon tax for the Netherlands*

In order to reduce the threat of global warming, many economists have recommended the imposition of a carbon tax, since carbon dioxide is one of the principal 'greenhouse gases'. Indeed, some countries (Norway, for example) have already introduced carbon taxes. Such a tax might be levied on fossil fuels in terms of their carbon content. Bovenberg (1993) has discussed the implications of such a tax for the economy of the Netherlands. Bovenberg begins his analysis by noting several of the advantages of such a tax; besides the least-cost and innovation-inducing aspects discussed in this chapter, these include a desirable impact on the structure of industry (firms are discouraged from entering carbon-intensive industries by the higher tax rates facing firms in these industries), and the 'double dividend' (Pearce, 1991). This double dividend refers to the large amounts of revenue that would be raised by a carbon tax, as a result of the inelastic demand for fossil fuels. This revenue could replace revenue gained from distortionary taxes elsewhere in the economy, such as on labour. Labour taxes are especially high in the Netherlands, where participation in the labour force is low.

However, a carbon tax introduced *unilaterally* by the Netherlands has disadvantages too. First, suppose that the tax is imposed on firms in the energy-intensive sectors. Since the Netherlands is a small, open economy, these firms now suffer a competitive disadvantage relative to their competitors in EC countries not imposing such a tax. Under EC law, the Netherlands is not allowed to refund these taxes to exporting firms, nor is it allowed to impose carbon taxes on imports from other EC countries. Production of energy-intensive goods thus transfers out of the Netherlands and into countries not imposing the tax, with the long-run transfer exceeding the short-run transfer, since in the long run capital may relocate. The net effect on global carbon dioxide emissions is uncertain, since the shift in production of energy intensive goods abroad may lead to higher emissions if production in these countries uses higher carbon-content fuels than are used in the Netherlands (for example, coal instead of natural gas). The 'knock-on' effects on the Dutch economy will of course exceed the loss in production from the energy-intensive goods sector, since many suppliers will lose their business. This leads to a further loss in output, as the economy adjusts towards a new equilibrium.

Bovenberg argues that this 'down side' of a unilaterally imposed carbon tax is due to the second-best situation that the Netherlands faces, namely that other countries do not act to internalise their externalities at the same time by also imposing a carbon tax. Given this circumstance (and as the section on game theory in Chapter 6 and in the technical note on pp. 14–17 shows, co-operation is not at all guaranteed), the Dutch might use a second-best policy option; namely to use subsidies instead of the tax. Subsidies are usually criticised as leading to an increase in the number of firms in a polluting sector, and for being in conflict with the 'polluter pays' principle. However, in the case of unilateral action, they may be the best option available. The subsidy in question is a payment to firms to reduce their emissions of carbon dioxide. This avoids the competitive disadvantaging of firms producing energy-intensive goods, while achieving the reduction in CO_2 emissions. However, whilst the financial burden of paying the subsidy bill is spread across the economy, this may still impose sizeable efficiency losses elsewhere in the economy in cases where the existing level of distortionary taxes is high: exactly the situation facing the Netherlands. Subsidies could also be argued by other EC countries and by non-EC countries party to GATT (such as the USA) to constitute unfair trade practices. Bovenberg's conclusion is that, in the absence of international co-operation, a mixture of taxes, subsidies, regulation and voluntary agreements with industry is likely to be the best way ahead.

■ *4.4* Conclusions

Pollution taxes have long been advocated by environmental economists as an efficient means of controlling pollution. The case in favour of pollution taxes over design or performance standards has been made in terms of their efficiency advantages, both static and dynamic. In many simulation studies, such as that discussed in Box 4.2, standards have been shown to result in 'overcontrol', with respect to a particular target for a reduction in pollution. We might note that this overcontrol itself confers benefits, measured by the increase in welfare due to a further decrease in pollution. The implicit assumption is exceeded by the extra abatement costs (although for an argument to the contrary, see Oates *et al.*, 1989).

■ References

Baumol, W. and W. Oates (1971) 'The use of standards and prices for the protection of the environment', *Swedish Journal of Economics*, 73, 42–54.

Baumol, W. and W. Oates (1988) *The Theory of Environmental Policy*, 2nd edn, Cambridge: Cambridge University Press.

Bergman, L. (1991) 'General equilibrium effects of environmental policy: A CGE modelling approach', *Environmental and Resource Economics*, 1(1), 43–63.

Bovenberg, A (1993) 'Policy instruments for curbing carbon dioxide emissions: the case of the Netherlands', *Environmental and Resource Economics*, 3(3), 233–44.

Cline, W. (1992) 'Scientific basis for the greenhouse effect', *Economic Journal*, 101, 904–19.

Common, M. (1977) 'A note on the use of taxes to control pollution', *Scandinavian Journal of Economics*, 79, 345–349.

Conrad, J.M. and L.J. Olson (1992) 'The economics of a stock pollutant: aldicarb on Long Island', *Environmental and Resource Economics*, 2(3), 245–58.

England, R.A. (1986) 'Reducing the nitrogen input on arable farms', *Journal of Agricultural Economics and Management*, Jan., 13–25.

Fisher, A. (1980) *Environmental and Resource Economics*, Cambridge: Cambridge University Press.

Hallett, S., N. Hanley, I. Moffat and K. Taylor-Duncan, (1991) 'UK water pollution control: a review of legislation and practice', *European Environment*, 1, 7–14.

Hanley, N. and I. Moffatt (1993) 'Controlling water pollution using market mechanisms: a simulation approach'. In R.K Turner (ed.), *Sustainable Environmental Economics and Management*, London: Belhaven Press.

Hanley, N. and I. Moffatt and S. Hallet (1990) 'Why is more notice not taken of economists' prescriptions for the control of pollution?', *Environment and Planning A*, 22, 1421–39.

Kneese, A.V. and C.L. Shultze (1978) *Pollution Prices and Public Policy*, Washington D.C.: Brookings Institute.

Michaelis, P. (1992). 'Global warming: efficient policies in the case of multiple pollutants', *Environmental and Resource Economics*, 2, 61–78.

Milliman, S.R. and R. Prince (1989) 'Firm incentives to promote technological change in pollution control', *Journal of Environmental Economics and Management*, 17, 247–65.

Oates, W.E., P.R. Portney and A.M. McGartland (1989) 'The net benefits of incentive-based regulation: A case study of environmental standards', *Environmental Standard Setting*, 79(5) 1233–42.

OECD (1989) *Economic Instruments for Environmental Protection*, Paris: OECD.

O'Neil, W., M. David, C. Moore and E. Joeres (1983) 'Transferable discharge permits and economic efficiency: the Fox river', *Journal of Environmental Economics and Management*, 10, 346–55.

Pearce D.W. (1991) 'The role of carbon taxes in adjusting to global warming', *Economic Journal*, 101, 938–48.

Pezzey, J. (1988) 'Market mechanisms of pollution control', in R.K Turner (ed.), *Sustainable Environmental Management: Principles and Practice*, London: Belhaven Press.

Plourde, C.G. (1972) 'A model of waste accumulation and disposal', *Canadian Journal of Economics*, 5, 119–25.

Rosenberg, N., W. Easterling, P. Crosson and J. Darmstadler (1989) *Greenhouse Warming: Adaption and Abatement*, Washington, DC: Resources for the Future.

Rowley, C., B. Beavis, C. McCabe and D. Storey (1979) *A Study of Effluent Discharges to the Tees*, London: Department of the Environment.

Seskin, E.P., R.J. Anderson and R.O. Reid (1983) 'An empirical analysis of economic strategies for controlling air pollution', *Journal of Environmental Economics and Management*, 10, 112–24.

Tietenberg, T.H. (1973) 'Controlling pollution by price and standard systems: A general equilibrium analysis', *Swedish Journal of Economics*, 75, 193–203.

Tietenberg, T.H. (1974) 'On taxation and the control of externalities: comment', *American Economic Review*, 64, 462–6

Walker, M. and D. Storey (1977) 'The standards and prices approach to pollution control: problems of iteration', *Scandinavian Journal of Economics*, 79, 99–109.

■ Chapter 5 ■

Tradeable Pollution Permits

5.1 Introduction
5.2 The basic theory of tradeable
    pollution permits

5.3 Research issues in
    tradeable permit markets
5.4 Conclusions

■ 5.1 Introduction

In Chapter 4 we looked at pollution taxes as a potentially least-cost means of achieving a desired reduction in pollution. In this chapter an alternative approach is considered, that of tradeable pollution permits (TPPs). This idea, which originated with Crocker (1966) and Dales (1968), has gained much popularity recently with environmental economists. However, as we will see, TPPs have their own set of problems. In this chapter the basic theory of TPPs is first set out, for uniformly and non-uniformly mixed pollutants. We then consider some current research issues in the area of TPPs. A concluding section examines the use of TPPs in practice, and we also ask why more use has not been made of economic instruments including both TPPs and the pollution taxes described in Chapter 4.

■ 5.2 The basic theory of tradeable pollution permits

□ 5.2.1 Uniformly mixed pollutants

From Chapter 2, we know that the major economic explanation for pollution is an absence of a sufficient set of private property rights in environmental resources. The main idea behind TPPs is to allocate such rights, and make them tradeable. This results in a market for the right to pollute developing and consequently a market price for this right. Under certain conditions, this price provides the correct incentive for dischargers to arrange emission levels such that a cost-minimizing solution is reached. For a uniformly mixed pollutant, we know from Chapter 4 that this involves an

130

equality of MACs across polluters. Let us see how this works out, considering first the simplest case, namely an assimilative, point-source, uniformly mixed pollutant: for example, carbon dioxide emissions from power stations. All that the control agency is concerned to achieve is a specified reduction in total emissions, irrespective of the locations of dischargers. Suppose current emissions from a region are 200 000 tonnes per year, and that the target reduction is 100 000 tonnes, leaving 100 000 tonnes of continuing emissions. The agency issues 100 000 permits, each one of which allows the holder to emit one tonne per year of CO_2. Discharges are illegal without sufficient permits to cover them.

These permits may be issued in two ways: (1) by giving them away, perhaps pro rata with existing emissions (this process is known as 'grandfathering'), and (2) by auctioning them. Firms are then allowed to trade these permits. We expect firms with relatively high MACs to be buyers, and firm with low MACs to be sellers, assuming the initial allocation *not* to conform to the least-cost one. This is shown in Figure 5.1, where the horizontal axis measures both emissions and permits held by the firm. Before any intervention by the agency, the firm is at e_f, controlling no emissions. Suppose a TPP system of control is now introduced, and market price for permits of p^* is established. The firm will choose to hold e^* permits, since for any holding below this level, MACs lie above the permit price (it is cheaper to buy permits than to reduce emissions), but if the firm initially holds more than e^* (and thus can emit to the right of e^*), it will choose to sell, since the price it can get (p^*) exceeds the marginal cost of making permits available for sale by reducing emissions. A firm with higher costs of controlling pollution will wish to hold more permits given a permit price of p^*.

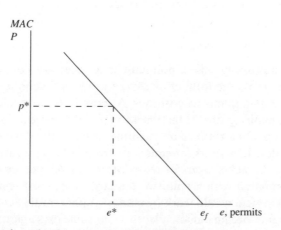

Figure 5.1 *Firm's optimal response to a permit scheme*

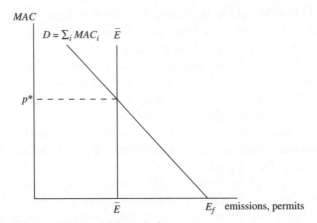

Figure 5.2 *Supply and demand for permits*

Where does p^* come from? It is the equilibrium price in the permit market, as is shown in Figure 5.2. The agency issues a fixed number of permits, $\bar{E}$ (100 000 in this case). We know that each firm compares its MAC schedule with the permit price to decide how many permits to hold. If prices fall, the firm will hold more permits and control fewer emissions. The MAC curve for a firm is thus its demand curve for permits, and so the aggregation of MAC curves across $i = 1 \ldots n$ firms in the control region ($\sum_i MAC_i$) is the regional demand for permits. If the authority increases or decreases the supply of permits then, given a particular demand curve, the market-clearing permit price will fall or rise, respectively.

The intuition behind the least-cost property of TPPs should now be clear. In Figure 5.1, the firm equates the permit price with its MAC schedule, so that for firm 1, say, we get $MAC_1 = p^*$. Another firm, 2, will make the same adjustment to its emission levels in the face of p^*, and if all n firms do the same, then we get:

$$MAC_1 = MAC_2 = \cdots MAC_n = p^*$$

which for a uniformly mixed pollutant is a necessary condition for cost-minimisation across the total of dischargers. These reactions by firms move them to their cost-minimising positions. Alternatively, we could view TPPs as a way of maximising the reduction in emissions subject to a given total expenditure on abatement. For example, Kling (1993) calculates that a system of tradeable permits for emissions from light-duty cars and trucks in California could achieve an increase of up to 65 per cent in emission reduction compared with a uniform standard on exhaust emissions. In this case, the TPP system would work by manufacturers trading emission permits internally (higher design emission levels from some cars against lower design levels from others) or by their trading with other car/van manufacturers.

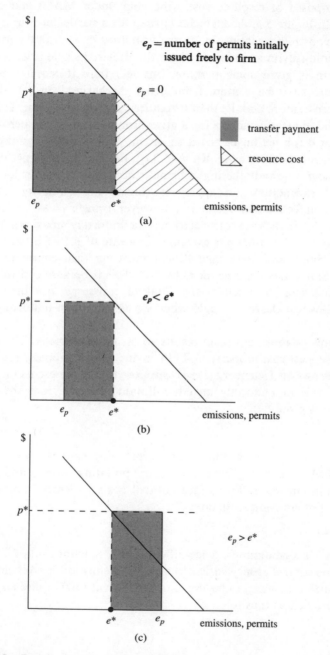

Figure 5.3 *Permit revenues and expenditures*

As with the tax scheme, the total financial burden to any individual firm will be composed of resource costs (the sum under MAC) and transfer payments. In Figure 5.3, the financial burden for a particular firm is shown under three possible scenarios. In (a), the firm must pay for all the permits it wishes to hold (say in an auction, where the declared single price is p^*). In (b), the firm is given some permits, but less than it requires for cost minimisation, so it buys more from other dischargers. In (c), the firm initially receives more permits than it requires, and so sells some. It may be seen that the transfer payments for a given firm depend on the permit price and whether it is a net buyer or net seller (in all three cases, resource costs (that is, control costs) are as shown in (5.3a)). For the industry, net transfers are zero under a 'grandfathering' scheme, since revenue from sales cancels out permit expenditures in aggregate (unless the authority levies an administration fee). Under an auction, however, transfers leave the industry *en bloc*. Finally, in the case considered here (a uniformly mixed pollutant), it should be obvious that permits exchange at a rate of 1:1. If Bloggs sell 100 permits to Smith and Sons, then Bloggs must cut their emissions by 100 units, and Smith may increase theirs by 100. This is because control, as has already been said, is aimed at the total of emissions, not their spatial location. This will clearly not hold when we consider non-uniformly mixed pollutants.

Let us now establish our main results so far more formally. The original proof of the least-cost property of TPPs is due to Montgomery (1972), but our proof draws on Tietenberg (1984). Suppose that A represents the level of carbon dioxide (a uniformly mixed pollutant) emitted from the control region, and is given by:

$$A = \alpha + \sum (e_{fi} - x_i) \tag{5.1}$$

where α is emissions from other sources including natural sources, e_{fi} are 'uncontrolled' emissions from $i = 1 \dots n$ polluting firms, and x_i are reductions in emissions. Firms face control costs C_i which depend solely on the level of emission reduction:

$$C_i = C_i(x_i) \tag{5.2}$$

where $C_i(x_i)$ is a continuous, twice-differentiable function, with $C' > 0$ and $C'' > 0$. The control agency wishes to hold total emissions at or below some level $\bar{A}$, which is assumed to be less than the current total of discharges. The agency's problem is thus to:

$$\underset{(x)}{\text{Min}} \sum_i C_i(x_i) \tag{5.3}$$

subject to:

$$\alpha + \sum (e_{fi} - x_i) \leq \bar{A} \tag{5.4}$$

and

$$x_i \geq 0 \tag{5.5}$$

Constraint (5.4) says that the sum of background emissions plus firm emissions net of reductions must be no greater than the desired maximum amount. The solution to this problem can be gained from employing the Kuhn–Tucker method discussed in the technical note on pp. 98–9 Forming the Lagrangean:

$$L = \sum C_i(x_i) + \lambda(\bar{A} - \alpha - \sum (e_{fi} - x_i)) = 0$$

Differentiating with respect to x_i yields the Kuhn–Tucker conditions for an optimum:

$$\delta C_i(x_i)/\delta x_i - \lambda \geq 0 \qquad i - 1 \ldots n$$

Or, using simpler notation,

$$C_i'(X_i) - \lambda \geq 0 \tag{5.6a}$$

and

$$x_i[C_i'(x_i) - \lambda] = 0 \qquad i = 1 \ldots n \tag{5.6b}$$

$$\alpha + \sum (e_{fi} - x_i) \leq \bar{A} \tag{5.6c}$$

$$\lambda[\alpha + \sum (e_{fi} - x_i) - \bar{A}] = 0 \tag{5.6d}$$

$$x_i \geq 0; \quad \lambda \geq 0 \qquad i = 1 \ldots n \tag{5.6e}$$

From the above we can see that λ is the shadow price of the pollution constraint, the same result we got in Chapter 4, which is only positive if the pollution constraint (equation 5.4) is binding. All firms' MACs (given as $C_i'(X_i)$) must be equal to this value, although some sources may have control costs that are too high for them to enter into the least-cost solution (so that, for this source, we would have $x = 0$).

For a permit market to achieve this outcome, we need to issue a permit supply of $\bar{E} = \sum (e_{fi} - x_i)$, since this is the permitted level of emissions. Permits will then trade at a 1:1 rate between dischargers. This is known as an *emissions permit system* (EPS) (Tietenberg, 1984). Suppose each firm is given as initial allocation of e_i^o permits, where $\sum e_i^o = \bar{E}$, and that a price of P is initially (arbitrarily) set for permits. The representative firm's problem is now to:

$$\underset{x_i}{\text{Min}} \ C_i(x_i) + p(e_{fi} - x_i - e_i^o) \tag{5.7}$$

The solution to this problem implies:

$$C'_i(X_i) - p \geq 0 \tag{5.8a}$$

$$x_i[C'_i(x_i) - p] = 0 \tag{5.8b}$$

$$x_i \geq 0 \tag{5.8c}$$

Comparing these equations with (5.6a–5.6e) we can see that the least cost solution will be replicated if the price p is equal to λ, which it will be if the permit market is competitive (see Montgomery, 1972).

Box 5.1   *US environmental policy and tradeable permits*

The USA has made more use of tradeable permits for the control of pollution than any other country. (For a detailed review of US environmental policy, see Tietenberg, 1992, or Portney, 1990).) An important step in air quality control policy was the establishment of national ambient air quality standards under the 1970 Clean Air Act. These national standards were established for the major air pollutants such as sulphur dioxide and ozone, set at both 'primary' and 'secondary' levels, and for less common but more toxic pollutants such as benzene. This Act placed a responsibility on states to implement action plans to attain these national targets, under state implementation plans (SIPs), to be approved by the EPA (Environmental Protection Agency). In each SIP, firms were required to meet certain maximum emission levels for regulated pollutants (that is, control by performance standards rather than design standards).

As Tietenberg notes (1992), by the mid-1970s it was clear that many states would not achieve the national air quality targets within the timetable originally set. Congress thus empowered the EPA to refuse permission for new pollution sources to set up in so-called 'non-attainment areas' where national pollution standards had not been met. However, this produced a conflict between the goals of environmental policy and economic growth, since many non-attainment states were typified by a predominance of heavy, declining industries (such as steel manufacture). The first use of TPPs in the USA was therefore a response to a desire to minimise these conflicts (Andrews, 1984). Moreover, the 'grandfathered' TPP system introduced avoided the income effects which, according to Nelson (1987) had prevented the adoption of a pollution tax system despite strong lobbying by the EPA.

Thus in 1977 the offset system was introduced. This allowed new sources to set up in non-attainment areas so long as they could offset their resulting emissions against a reduction in emissions by an existing source. Existing sources, by reducing their emissions below the maximum allowed by law, may qualify for an 'emission reduction credit'. For such credits to be granted, the emission reduction must be permanent, enforceable and quantifiable (Tietenberg, 1992). These credits can then be sold to another firm. In the offset policy, a new source in a non-attainment area must buy enough credits to cover about 120 per cent of their planned emission. Total emissions thus fall as a result of trade.

Other elements of this emissions trading system were introduced in later years. In 1979, a 'bubble' policy was introduced, whereby an existing source could offset its control responsibility by buying emission reduction credits from another source; alternatively, one firm with multiple emission points on a single site (many smoke stacks, for instance) could trade off more than legally required emission reductions at one point against less than required reductions at another point. Additional variants of the emissions trading system are netting and banking . In the former case, existing sources seeking to expand can avoid stringent new standards by reducing emissions elsewhere on site; in the latter, emission reduction credits can be saved either for future use by that source, or for future sale.

The success of the emissions trading scheme has been reviewed by a number of authors (Liroff, 1986; Hahn, 1989a; Tietenberg, 1990). A consensus view might be that, whilst the scheme has resulted in substancial cost savings to some participants, the level of trading has been less than expected. Hahn quotes a figure of \$435 million for the savings produced by some 129 bubble trades relative to the no-trade situation. For the off-set system, around 200 trades are reported, with cost savings 'in the hundreds of millions of dollars'. That fewer trades have occurred than expected may be due to a large number of causes; these are investigated at the general level in section 5.3.1. However, Tietenberg (1990, 1992) has placed much stress on the high transactions costs of carrying out trades and a lack of information between potential traders; while US tax law also mitigated against external trades.

In 1990, Congress passed additional Clean Air Act Amendments which introduced a rather different TPP system for the control of sulphur dioxide emissions from large point sources (primarily power stations). The impetus for this measure came from Bush campaign promises to take action on acid rain, and from support for the idea of TPPs to achieve this from the Environmental Defense Fund and members of the President's Council of Economic Advisors. The system is intended to bring about a 50 per cent reduction in the total emissions of SO_2 from such sources. Most permits were 'grandfathered' (a great deal of time was spent in arguments over this allocation, both across regions and industry groups), although a small proportion were retained by the EPA for allocation to new sources, and for auction at the Chicago Board of Trade. Auction rules involve permits being exchanged on the basis that sellers with the lowest asking (selling) price will be matched with buyers with the highest buying (offer) price, with the seller with the lowest asking price amongst all sellers being 'paired off' first. Casson (1993) shows that this design will result in a downward pressure on permit prices below the competitive level, and a consequently inefficient allocation of permits.

Sulphur permits are denominated in annual tons of emissions, and can be banked. Auction prices have so far been in the range of \$131–\$450/ton, with environmental groups paying the highest price to retire permits and so cut total emissions. While many trades have occurred, most have been internal rather than external, and high monitoring costs may have eroded the cost savings of the scheme. But large cost savings have still resulted, estimated by the General Accounting Office at $2 billion per year (*Financial Times*, 1.3.95). This cost saving is partly due to the phenomenon whereby the existence of trading possibilities has reduced prices of scrubbers, while fuel switching is also allowed.

Barriers to the greater success of the acid rain trading programme include the need for firms to meet local air quality standards; requirements by some states that sources carry out pollution abatement to protect local jobs; and the requirements of some states that permit trades must be preceded by environmental impact analyses. Finally, it should be noted that whilst SO_2 is a non-uniformly mixed pollutant, trades are permitted at a 1:1 rate across sources, irrespective of geographic location. This may lead to localised pollution problems (such as continued acidification of lakes in the Adirondack Mountains, New York) depending on the regional pattern of trade.

☐ 5.2.2 *Non-uniformly mixed pollutants*

So far, it has been assumed that the pollutant of interest is uniformly mixed. Many pollutants, however, are non-uniformly mixed: for example, organic wastes discharged to a watercourse, and sulphur dioxide discharged to the air. In this case, the control agency is interested in both the amount of discharges and their spatial distribution, since these two factors combine to determine the effect of the pollutant on ambient air or water quality at monitoring points. As will be recalled from Chapter 4, transfer coefficients can be estimated which relate discharges at any point i to ambient air/water quality at some other point j. Admitting non-uniformly mixed pollutants changes the nature of the cost-minimisation problem, by changing the pollution constraint. Ambient pollution concentration at any point j is given by:

$$A_j = \alpha_j + \sum d_{ij}(e_{fi} - x_i) \tag{5.9}$$

where α_j is pollution from other sources arriving at point j; and the d_{ij} terms are the transfer coefficients. The problem now is to:

$$\text{Min} \sum C_i(x_i)$$

subject to:

$$\alpha_j + \sum d_{ij}(e_{fi} - x_i) \leq \bar{A}_j$$

where $\bar{A}_j$ are the maximum allowable pollutant concentrations at each point j. Assuming for simplicity that all sources do some controlling (that is, that $x_i > 0$, $\forall i$), then the Kuhn–Tucker condition of interest is:

$$C'_i(x_i) - \sum d_{ij}\lambda_j = 0 \tag{5.10}$$

so that each source's MAC is equal to the weighted average of the shadow cost of emissions reductions needed to hit the targets. Put another way, there is now a shadow price (λ_j) at each monitoring point, so that we have got away from the simple 'equalize MACs' rule that was relevant in the uniform mixing case. This system of permits is known as an *ambient permit system*.

5.3 Research issues in tradeable permit markets

In this section we will be looking at a number of current research issues in the area of TPPs. The purpose of this is to highlight some of the problems which researchers have identified with the basic theory set out in the previous section, and to suggest some possible approaches to the solution to these problems. These problems divide into those concerned with the operation of the market and those associated with extensions to the basic model.

5.3.1 Problems associated with the market itself

Trading rules and the design of permit systems

In the preceding section, two designs of permit system were mentioned: an emissions permit system (EPS) and the ambient permits system (APS). Under the former, permits are denominated in units of pollutant emitted (one permit permits one tonne of BOD, for example). Trades of permits between firms take place at a one-for-one rate. In other words, if source A sells one permit, it must reduce its emissions by the amount of emission covered by the permit. When source B buys this permit, it can increase its emissions by the same amount. Total emissions therefore do not increase. The EPS is a simple system, and for a uniformly mixed pollutant may work well. For non-uniformly mixed pollutants, however, trades under an EPS could result in violations of ambient quality targets, since if source B is located in a more sensitive part of, say, a river, then its increase of x tonnes of emissions will do more damage than is avoided by A reducing its emissions by x tonnes.

To get around this problem, the APS was proposed. However, this has the problem that it is a very complicated market. Permits are denominated in units of damage at receptors. There is a separate market in permits at each receptor, and firms must trade in as many markets as their emissions affect receptors. For a pollutant such as sulphur dioxide, this could be a very large number of markets. Transaction costs would therefore be relatively high, whilst the number of traders in each market would be relatively low, giving rise to potential problems of imperfect competition (see below). What is more, total emissions can rise as a result of trading. If firm A sells permits which permit a reduction of 1 mg/l in dissolved oxygen at receptor point z, and if B's emissions have a relatively small impact on dissolved oxygen at point z, then B can increase its emissions by more than A reduces its own. Cost savings under the APS are to an extent realised by allowing a degradation of air or water quality down to the target level at receptors where, pre-trade, air/water quality is better than the target. An APS may also result in an increase in the long-range transport of pollutants (Atkinson and Tietenberg, 1987).

To get around the problems of both EPS and APS alternatives, economists have proposed a number of different trading rules. All basically work on the principle of permits being denominated in units of emissions (one permit per tonne of BOD), but with rules governing trades in permits to stop the violation of ambient quality targets. The three best known of these trading rules systems are the pollution offset, the non-degradation offset and the modified pollution offset. The pollution offset system (Krupnick *et al.*, 1983) works by imposing a rule on trades that they may not violate the ambient quality target at any receptor point. However, this is consistent with worsening ambient quality up to the target level and an increase in total emissions. The non-degradation offset imposes the additional constraint that total emissions may not increase as a result of trades (Atkinson and Tietenberg, 1982). Finally, the modified offset (McGartland and Oates, 1985) allows trades so long as neither the pre-trade quality level nor the target level, whichever is the stricter (cleanest) is not violated. As Atkinson and Tietenberg (1987) point out, there is no general conclusion which can be drawn as to the relative cost-effectiveness of the modified and non-degradation offset systems (they rule out the simple offset system as being incompatible with environmental quality objectives). Comparisons must instead be made on a case-by-case basis. In their empirical analysis, they find the following for models of two US cities (St Louis and Cleveland) for the control of suplhur oxides (Cleveland) and particulate emissions (St Louis). In each case, the two offset systems are compared with the theoretically obtainable least-cost solution (which in this case would result from a perfect implementation of an APS) and with the command-and-control alternative of uniform design standards (denoted SIP, for state implementation plan). (SIPs were prepared by all US states in response to the Clean Air Act). Simulation results are set out in Table 5.1.

Table 5.1 *Abatement costs and emission reductions under different offset rules*

Policy	Total control costs, Cleveland ($/year)	Emission reductions, Cleveland (g/sec)	Total control costs, St. Louis ($/day)	Emission reductions, St Louis (tons/day)
Least cost	7.19 million	1328	82	13.49
SIP	11.18 million	1391	2314	23.50
Non-degradation offset	7.415 million	1391	116	23.50
Modified pollution offset	9.71 million	1440	190	22.24

Box 5.2 *Pollution permits in the Forth estuary*

The Forth estuary is a multi-use water body in Central Scotland. Current uses include industrial and municipal waste discharge, use of cooling water by power stations and recreation, while the estuary is also an important wildlife habitat. Water pollution control currently operates by means of performance standards ('consents') issued and monitored by the Forth River Purification Board. Consents, which may vary across different firms discharging the same pollutant, are set with regard to the environmental quality standards (EQS) the Board has established for most pollutants. For dissolved oxygen (DO), the EQS is 4.5mg/l, being the minimum level needed to support salmonid fish such as trout and salmon. The major source of the biological oxygen demand that depletes DO is industrial discharges to the estuary, accounting for over 80 per cent of total loading.

During conditions of low flow and high temperature in the estuary, the actual DO level frequently falls below the EQS, thus endangering salmonids. Hanley and Moffatt (1993) report the results of a simulation analysis which compared uniform regulation, the current consent system and a hypothetical system of TPPs for the estuary, all designed to reduce the biological oxygen demand on the estuary.

Two sets of results were reported. In the first, a series of reductions in total BOD loading were simulated under (a) uniform standards and (b) a perfectly competitive permit market where all gains from trade are realised. Results were as follows:

Target reduction per cent	Actual reduction (kg BOD/day)	Resource costs under uniform standards (£/year)	Resource costs with a TPP market (£/year)
10	6499	1 340 560	275 455
25	15 497	7 835 448	692 365
50	37 379	16 128 660	3 075 989

As may be seen, very large savings in resource costs are potentially available under a TPP system in this case. This is due to the large variation in marginal abatement costs across the dischargers modelled.

However, such total reductions in BOD loading are more than is needed to remove the DO sag in the estuary. Using a water quality model of the estuary, a matrix of transfer coefficients was calculated. This was then added to the economic model, and two policy scenarios were compared, both of which increased DO to at least 4.5 mg/l under worst-case conditions in the estuary (that is, lowest flow and highest temperature). These policies were, first, the current consent system, using the Board's own plan for getting rid of the sag (this policy was termed 'flexible regulation', since only those dischargers with the highest transfer coefficients were to be targets of the Board under this alternative) and, second, a TPP system using a trading rule to ensure there was no violation of the EQS at any point along the estuary. Results were as follows:

Policy	Cost per year
Flexible regulation	£1 182 600
TPP	£1 016 840

As may be seen, only very small efficiency gains result from the TPP scheme. This is because the flexible regulation plan, by chance, was aimed, not only those sources with the highest transfer coefficients, but also at those with the lowest abatement costs. However, as Hanley and Moffatt point out, this relative equality of outcomes is only true in a static sense. As was pointed out in Chapter 4, market mechanisms such as TPPs provide superior incentives to performance standards for cost savings over time (see also section 5.3.2).

Hanley and Moffatt also report on the distributional effects of the TPP schemes considered, and note that the assumption of a perfectly competitive market is unlikely to describe the trading conditions in a TPP market for BOD if actually introduced. This is because only a small number of firms (seven at

> most) would be involved in the market whilst, owing to the size of their discharges, two firms would hold a powerful influence over the market price. Simulations showed that trade between these two firms would account for about 80 per cent of total trades in the market.

Imperfectly competitive permit markets

In the formal models in section 5.2 we made the assumption that the permit markets being studied were perfectly competitive, in that each individual firm had no control over the market price. This seems a reasonable assumption where a large number of similarly sized traders operate in a market. However, if only a few firms are present, or if one of these firms is large enough to influence the permit price through its own buying and selling behaviour, then the least-cost property of TPPs may not hold. Why should a firm seek to influence the permit price? In order to minimise the sum of control costs *plus* net expenditures on permit purchases. Consider a firm which holds a relatively large stock of permits. This firm can earn revenues by selling permits; the costs it incurs in freeing-up permits for sale are given by its MAC. Clearly, the firm would like to receive as high a price for each permit as it can, if it has monopoly market power, then by restricting the number of permits sold on the market it can push up the price. The extent to which a firm will choose to engage in such behaviour clearly depends on the price elasticity of demand for permits and the slope of the firm's MAC schedule, since the latter determines the price of freeing up permits for sale, whilst the former (which in turn depends on other firms' MAC schedules) dictates the degree to which the permit price will rise as the number of permits offered for sale decreases. (For a formal analysis of the behaviour of a firm with market power, see Hahn, 1984, or Misiolek and Elder, 1989.)

Alternatively, with monopsonistic power in the market, by buying fewer permits the firm can reduce the price it must pay for those permits it does purchase. Again, the cost of this price-setting behaviour is given by the firm's MAC schedule, the slope of which will influence the degree to which the firm engages in such behaviour.

Summarizing the above, we may say that in the monopoly case the market power firm spends too little on abatement, as it sells fewer permits than it would do in the competitive outcome. Other firms spend too much on abatement. In the monopsony case, the market power firm spends too much on abatement and buys too few permits relative to the competitive case. There is no empirical evidence from actual permit markets of the effects of price-setting behaviour in these pure forms, although many studies have pointed out the potential for such uncompetitive outcomes to emerge. For example, O'Neil *et al.* (1983) found that only 10 traders would be involved on the Fox river in Wisconsin; whilst Eheart *et al.* (1980) found that only two sources would control 80 per cent of all permits sold for phosphorus discharges into Lake Michigan. Some simulation results do, however, exist. Maloney and Yandle (1984) modelled price-setting behaviour through the establishment of cartels. For monopoly power, the increases in total control costs over the competitive base line were at most 41 per cent (with 90 per cent of the sources owned by the monopolist); for monopsony power, the greatest increase in total abatement costs was only 8 per cent, again at a 90 per cent holding for the monopsonist. However, even in the worst monopoly case, the (uncompetitive) permit market still achieved a 66 per cent saving over the command-and-control outcome. Hahn (1984) considers a permit market for particulate sulphates in the Los Angeles region, a market in which earlier work by the author had shown that one source (a power station) could be responsible for over 50 per cent of 'controllable emissions'. In this case, the market clearing permit price varies from $3200/ton with monopsony, to the competitive price of $3900, to a price of $21 000/ton with full monopoly power. The extent to which total abatement costs increase when one firm is a price setter depends on the initial permit allocation to the market power firm: as its initial allocation increases (and so that to the price-taking firms decreases), total control costs rise as the market power firm chooses to hold on to more permits.

Finally in this section, Misiolek and Elder (1989) have considered another motivation for uncompetitive behaviour besides that discussed above (which they term 'cost-minimising manipulation'). Firms may also seek to raise the permit price so as to increase the total costs faced by their rivals in an industry, or to make entry less attractive for potential rivals. This may occur when actual or potential rivals must purchase permits in the same market as that of the firm wishing to take exclusionary action. Misiolek and Elder argue that such exclusionary action is most likely to be taken by large firms with relatively low MACs, to exclude smaller potential or actual entrants with higher MACs. They show that exclusionary action can increase both short-run and long-run profits for a firm. In a sense, exclusionary behaviour counteracts cost-minimising manipulation: we have seen above that the latter can lead to a firm with monopsony power buying too few permits; yet exclusionary behaviour will cause it to wish to buy too many permits. The two effects might thus cancel out. For a monopolist however, whose cost-minimising manipulation involves selling fewer permits than in the competitive case, the effect of exclusionary manipulation is to worsen the distortion.

However, Munro *et al.* (1995) have argued that if firms in a permit market can practise perfect price discrimination, then market power cannot be used as an argument for the level of cost-saving trades being reduced. Perfect price discrimination is feasible where there are few sellers and few buyers; this might well describe many instances where a TPP might be introduced (see, for example, Box 5.2). If sellers can extract the maximum willingness to pay from each potential buyer, then there is no incentive for the seller to restrict supplies of permits. Where firms perceive gains from trades, net of transactions costs, then they will strike bargains, subject to the institutional rules concerning permit trades (see above).

Box 5.3 *Non-point pollution and TPPs*

Non-point pollution enters the environment from many, diffuse sources. Examples of such pollution include soil erosion, pesticides run-off and nitrate leaching from farmland. Non-point pollutants, because they do not enter the ecosystem from a single, easily identified point (such as a chimney) have the feature that the measurement of actual emissions is very difficult. Thus, controls must be aimed either at estimated emissions or at the production processes that lead to non-point pollution occurring. To take the example of nitrate pollution, the application of organic and inorganic fertilisers to farmland results in some of these nitrates leaching or running off into surface water and groundwater. This results in possible threats to human health if water is used for drinking and/or in an environmental problem known as eutrophication. Here, an excessive level of nutrients (such as nitrates) in a water body leads to excessive growth of algae. This reduces water quality, since the algae reduce dissolved oxygen levels in the water as they rot down, while some are directly poisonous (see Hanley, 1990).

Measuring actual emissions (leaching, run-off) of nitrates is very difficult. Thus a tax on actual emissions, or a TPP market in actual emissions, is impractical. Instead, a tax or TPP market in nitrate inputs or in estimated emissions could be established. Similarly, the command-and-control approach to non-point pollution could involve setting mandatory limits on the amount of nitrates which may be applied to farmland. Common (1977) first showed that the Baumol and Oates theorem held for input taxes just as it does for taxes on emissions, provided that the exact relationship between inputs and pollution outputs was known. Both theoretical and empirical work on non-point pollution has since carried on apace (for a recent survey, see Shogren and Russell, 1993).

In this Box, we briefly consider the use of TPPs to control nitrate pollution. Early work in this area was carried out by Taylor (1975). More recently, Moxey and White (1994) modelled the use of TPPs for the River Tyne catchment in Northern England. Estimates of nitrate emissions from different land types and cropping patterns were obtained from the EPIC model developed by the USDA. These were then linked into an aggregate linear programming (LP) model of farming in the catchment. Nitrate emissions were related to nitrate concentrations in river water using data from the Institute of Hydrology. Moxey and White then calculated the reductions in farm profits of increasingly strict required reductions in ambient nitrate concentrations under two policies: a TPP market in estimated emissions and a TPP market in nitrate input. Since the objective of policy is to control nitrate concentrations rather than nitrate inputs, the expectation is that the former policy will be more efficient than the latter (since there is no simple proportionality between nitrate use and nitrate concentrations owing to variations in transfer coefficients). Results showed that this was so:

Percentage abatement	Profit reduction under estimated emission TPPs (per cent)	Profit reduction under input TPPs (per cent)
10	1.34	2.74
20	6.33	9.31
30	17.75	23.55
40	38.95	46.14

It is also apparent that abatement costs rise sharply with the target reduction in ambient concentration. However, a TPP system based on estimated emissions would be much more difficult (costly) to administer than a system based on input use, since for every farm estimated emissions must be predicted. In addition, legal challenges to court cases brought on the basis of estimated emission seem very likely (English, 1993). A system based on input use might then be preferable, although where the degree of variation in transfer coefficients is great this could cause major regional income re-distribution. A compromise has recently been suggested by Pan and Hodge (1994), whereby permits would be denominated in terms of land use (for example, growing wheat on land of a particular class). The amount of permits necessary to authorise a particular land use on a particular soil type would be calculated by the regulator on the basis of estimated emissions, but once this had been done the regulator would not need to repeat the calculation every time a trade took place, since all that must be monitored is land use and permit holding. Pan and Hodge show that, whilst such a TPP system is less efficient than an economic instrument (in their case, a perfectly differentiated tax) based on estimated emissions, the cost penalty is not great, while the savings in transactions costs might be substantial.

Auctions

Given that one way of instituting a TPP system is to initially auction off the stock of permits, economists have been interested in the effects on resource allocation and income distribution of different types of auctions. One point already made in this chapter is that an auction will imply an additional financial cost to firms, namely the payments they initially make for their permits. These transfer payments leave the industry *en bloc*, unlike what happens with 'grandfathering', which decreases the political attractiveness of auctions. Lyon (1982) has calculated that, for point source dischargers of phosphates to Lake Michigan, the total financial burden on firms (abatement costs plus permit purchases) was approximately three times the sum of abatement costs alone. Lyon goes on to consider two alternative designs for an auction system. The first is the simplest design, a single price auction, whereby firms submit sealed bids for permits. Permits are then sold to the highest bidder for 'a price that could represent either the lowest accepted bid or highest rejected bid' (page 18). This mechanism is known to encourage strategic behaviour in that, if bidders believe that their bid could be the marginal bid, they benefit from understating their true WTP. The second alternative is an incentive-compatible 'Groves mechanism', whereby the highest bidders win the permits, but where a discharger's own bid never affects the price it pays. The Groves mechanism used by Lyon is an adaptation of the Vickrey second price auction (whereby the highest bidder pays the price bid by the second-highest bidder), due to Green and Laffont (1977). Lyon finds that total transfer payments under the incentive-compatible auction are lower than under the single price auction by some 16 per cent.

More recently, Casson (1993) has considered the rules to be used by the US Environmental Protection Agency (EPA) in their auction of permits to discharge sulphur dioxide from power stations, under the permit trading system set up by the 1990 amendments to the US Clean Air Act. This set targets of a 10 million ton reduction in sulphur emissions from 1980 levels of 25.5 million tons, by the year 2000. ('Clean air Act amendements; summary materials', US EPA, November 1990). Permits are denominated as one ton of SO_2 per year, and are fully tradeable at a one-for-one rate. Casson finds that EPA auction rules will encourage firms to understate their maximum WTP for permits, thus resulting in an inefficient level of permit purchases.

Sequencing of trades

Many authors (for example, Tietenberg, 1992) have argued that the US EPA's Emissions Trading System has resulted in many fewer trades than had been expected (the Emissions Trading System is discussed in Box 5.1). One possible explanation lies with a comparison between the way the trading process has been modelled in simulation analysis and how trading actually occurs. Most simulation studies (such as Krupnick, 1986) assume that trading happens in a multilateral, simultaneous, fully informed manner, since this is the implication of representing the least-cost outcome from a mathematical programming model, which is achieved without violating ambient standards, as the trading outcome. However, actual trades are bilateral, sequential and often take place without traders being fully informed as to the minimum compensation demanded (supply price) and maximum WTP (willingness to pay) (demand price) of potential trading partners. Atkinson and Tietenberg (1991) consider the implications for the number of trades and the level of cost saving of this difference. In sequential trading under EPA rules, *each* trade is restricted from (a) violating ambient standards and (b) allowing an increase in emissions. This is much more restrictive than requiring the *total* of trades to meet these conditions.

Atkinson and Tietenberg modelled a number of trading scenarios, using data from the St Louis area in the USA. In each case, their programme solves the standard problem:

$$\operatorname*{Min}_{x_j} TC = \sum_j \beta_j X_j^2$$

subject to $\quad Ax \geq b$

$$0 \leq x \leq x^*$$

where TC is regional control costs, X is tons of controlled emissions for the $j = 1 \ldots n$ sources, A is a matrix of transfer coefficients, x is a vector of actual emission reductions, b a vector of required improvements in ambient quality and x^* a vector of maximum available levels of emission reductions. Four scenarios were modelled which impose gradually more restrictive outcomes on the trading process. They were:

1. Simultaneous, full information: no increase in total emissions allowed.
2. Sequential, full information: first, a matrix M of possible cost savings from each pair-wise trade was identified. The biggest cost–saving trade was allowed, and the emission vector updated. These two traders were then eliminated before M was recalculated, and the next pair chosen. This process continued until all cost–saving trades were exhausted.
3. Partial information (a). The matrix M is not known. The firm with the lowest cost is chosen as first seller, then the best trading partner identified. These two firms are then eliminated and the process is repeated.
4. Partial information (b). The matrix M is not known. A firm is selected randomly as the first seller and its best trading partner identified. The elimination process then continues as in (3).

In all cases, the percentage of cost savings associated with the least cost solution were calculated. Results were as shown in Table 5.2, for two air quality standards, a primary standard and a stricter secondary standard.

Table 5.2   *Cost savings under sequential trading*

Scenario	Percentage of least-cost savings under primary standard	Percentage of least-cost savings under secondary standard
Simultaneous trading, full information	91	66
Sequential trading, full information	88	50
Partial information (a)	13	39
Partial Information (b)	48	25

As may be seen, fully-informed but sequential trading incurs a large cost penalty over the hypothetical least-cost solution; this penalty is greater the stricter is the target environmental improvement. Under full information, the best trades (those which save most resources) proceed first; but under partial information 'early sub-optimal trades reduce future opportunities (for cost-saving) considerably' (Atkinson and Tietenberg, 1991, p. 27). While the partial information outcomes are probably too pessimistic, since they ignore firms' abilities to find the best bargains going, they do point out the desirability of increasing information flows in the permit market: it is possible that the EPA could help here, by increasing the amount of information available to potential traders. The sequential scenario shows, more importantly, that not all of the cost savings available in the (hypothetical) least-cost outcome will be realised, given the way trading actually occurs.

Sequencing of trades has also been studied by Klaasen and Førsund (K & F) (1993). K & F model the potential market for sulphur dioxide credits in Europe. They note that in the cost-minimising solution to the standard problem for a non-uniformly mixed pollutant (see equation 5.10) the following holds:

$$\frac{c_i}{c_s} = \frac{\sum a_{ij}\lambda_j}{\sum a_{sj}\lambda_j} = v$$

where $c_i(c_s)$ is the marginal abatement cost for source $i(s)$, the a_{ij} terms are the transfer coefficients for emissions from sources i and s affecting j receptors, and the λ terms are the shadow prices for all j binding receptors so affected. This defines an 'exchange rate', v, for trades between the two sources, which may then trade in one market. K & F show that, if all sources trade at this rate, then the least-cost solution will not be reached, although they suggest that the rule is more practical than the offset systems discussed above, since it is based on the ratio of marginal costs in the least-cost solution, which ratios for all possible trading partners could be declared by the control agency in advance of the commencement of trading. They then simulate the operation of this mechanism using the RAINS model, a model of European acid emission and deposition covering 38 emission regions and 547 receptor sites. Trading is specified as a sequential, bilateral process, in a similar manner to Atkinson and Tietenberg's 'sequential trades, full information' scenario, with the differences that here trades are constrained by the exchange rates, v, and by estimates of the transactions costs of making trades, and that no constraint is placed on total emissions. K & F find that sequential trading with exchange rates does not achieve the least-cost solution (total abatement costs are 44 000 million DM as opposed to 31 200 million DM in the least-cost solution), but still achieves a 30 per cent reduction in abatement costs compared with a uniform emission reduction requirement. Target maximum deposition loads are met in all cases.

Other possible explanations for the low level of trading have been suggested (Munro *et al.*, 1995). These include:

1. principle–agent problems: environmental managers in large firms may personally benefit more from large scale waste treatment operations than from permit trading, even if the latter increases a firm's profits;
2. uncertainty over permit tenure: if firm A believes that its allocation of permits in the next round will depend on how many it holds at the end of the current round, it may be less willing to sell permits. Munro *et al.* (1995) found that, in a survey of firms involved in a potential TPP market in the Forth estuary, hoarding was most likely in a system where permit allocations in allocation rounds after the initial round were based on firms' holdings of permits at the end of (as opposed to at the beginning of) the trading period;
3. firms may be unwilling to sell permits to firms with which they are in product market competition. However, Munro *et al.* (1995) found no evidence of such (intended) behaviour in their survey of firms on the Forth estuary;
4. transactions costs may be very high in permit markets (especially if complicated trading rules apply), thus reducing the net gains from trading.

Hanley, *et al.* (1990) also discuss barriers to trade in permit markets.

☐ *5.3.2 Extensions to the basic model*

Innovation and TPPs

A number of authors have argued that TPP systems offer superior incentives to firms to engage in long-term reductions of emissions by investing in cleaner technologies, relative to the incentives available under a design or performance standard. The 'case in favour' for this argument has been put by Milliman and Prince (1989) (see Chapter 4) and by Downing and White (1986). (See Milliman and Prince, 1989, for a more complete summary of the literature on innovation.) Figure 5.4 gives the simplest proof of the argument. Suppose MC_1 represents MACs under an old, dirty technology, and MC_2 represents MACs under the cleaner technology (assume there is no effect on fixed costs). Suppose that the firm faces a performance standard equal to $q1$. Then, by adopting the clean technology, it would save the area (abc). Under marketable permits, where the permit price is p, the firm chooses to emit the emission level $q1$ under the old technology, but if it invests in the clean technology it will increase its emissions reductions to $q2$. In doing this, it incurs extra control costs of $(q1, c, d, q2)$ but sells permits with value $(q1, b, d, q2)$ as well as earning the reduction in control costs of (abc) on emission reductions $(0 - q1)$. The firm thus saves more under the TPP system than under a performance standard and, for a given cost of making the investment, is more likely to invest in the cleaner technology. However, we should note two caveats to this argument. First, Milliman and Prince show that, under an auctioned TPP system, cost savings will be greater than under a 'grandfathered' TPP. They reach this conclusion after considering the whole process of innovation (inventing the cleaner technology, 'CT'), facilitating the diffusion of CT across the industry and pressuring regulators to make any subsequently desirable adjustments in pollution control law (as MACs fall, a higher degree of pollution control becomes optimal). However, 'grandfathered' permits still give a greater incentive to innovate in CT than performance standards. This finding has been challenged by Malueg (1989), who claims that, for a firm which is a buyer of permits both before and after the innovation, the incentive to invest in CT is lower under ('grandfathered') permits than under performance standards.

Multiple pollutants

An interesting problem in environmental economics arises where several pollutants all contribute to a particular environmental problem. Examples include acid deposition, which is caused by SO_2, NO_x and NH_3, and fish mortality in rivers, which may be caused by a whole cocktail of pollutants. When the pollutants interact linearly, then no major revisions to the theories presented so far occur. For example, if M is an index of fish mortality, and two pollutants A and B are chiefly responsible for this, a linear interaction would be:

$$M = \alpha_1 + \alpha_2 A + \alpha_3 B$$

where $\alpha_1 \ldots \alpha_3$ are constants. However, if synergisms exist between these pollutants, then such a linear relationship may not hold. A synergism occurs when A and B acting together have a greater effect on an environmental quality indicator than the sum of A and B acting alone. Examples are effects on human health when sulphur dioxide and particulates levels are both increased, and the effects of cyanide on fish in the presence of other heavy metals. This case was originally studied by Beavis and Walker (1979).

Concerning TPPs, Hahn (1989b) has shown that, for linear damage functions such as that above, and multiple pollutants, trading across firms could still result in the least cost outcome, so long as permits were traded off at a rate equal to their relative contributions to the environmental quality indicator (this is really just an extension of the APS). Recently, however, Zylicz (1993) has shown that when the pollutants react synergistically, so that the damage function is non-linear, permit trading cannot replicate the least cost outcome. This is also true of a system of least-cost taxes. If the damage function is quadratic, then the least-cost property of the TPP market can in principle be 'rescued' by levying firm-specific taxes in addition to the permit system; these taxes depend for each firm on the level of emissions for that firm and their interactions with emissions from other firms (although this clearly raises the administration costs of the TPP scheme). For other non-linear forms, however, the tax fix does not work and neither the TPP market nor a system of taxes can achieve the least-cost outcome. Zylicz proves this by comparing the first order conditions for the cost minimisation problem with those facing a representative firm when the permit price is set equal to the shadow cost of the pollution constraint; the two sets of conditions are shown to differ in this case

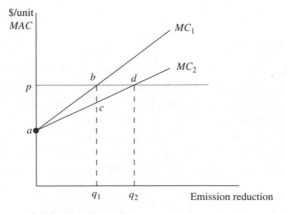

Figure 5.4   *Innovation in permit markets*

Box 5.4 *Why is more use not made of economic instruments for the control of pollution?*

A conclusion which might be drawn from both the theoretical and empirical studies reported in this chapter and Chapter 4 is that economic instruments, such as taxes and TPPs, offer the possibility of considerable efficiency gains over 'command-and-control' approaches such as design and performance standards. However, as several recent surveys of actual pollution control policy in the OECD have shown, governments have made relatively little use of economic instruments as yet (Opschoor and Vos, 1989). The few examples which are usually cited are: the emissions trading system in the USA for the control of certain air pollutants (see Box 5.1), and water pollution charging schemes in the Netherlands and Germany. In Germany, performance standards regulate the maximum discharge which firms and municipal treatment works are allowed to make into controlled waters. However, firms also pay a fee per unit of pollution discharged. The pollutants covered by the scheme are chemical oxygen demand, phosphorus, nitrogen, organic halogens, heavy metals and substances toxic to fish (Royal Commission on Environmental Pollution, 1992). Charge rates vary according to the nature of the pollutant. Firms and local authorities can save on charge payments by emitting less than the maximum permitted. Funds raised by the scheme are used to pay for administration/monitoring costs, with the balance made available as investment grants for new pollution abatement plant. A report by ERL in 1990 suggested that the charge had resulted in 'significant reductions in pollution ... especially from sewage treatment works'. (ibid., p. 149).

A similar system operates in the Netherlands, where significant improvements in water quality have also been linked to the introduction of these charges. However, while both the Dutch and German schemes offer flexibility to firms in deciding how much below their emission ceiling to go, neither might be termed 'pure' economic instruments, since charge rates are not set so high as to yield the desired level of control if regulations were not also in place. Opschoor and Vos distinguish between incentive charges, which are set high enough to give firms some incentive to reduce emissions (in the sense that the charge exceeds marginal abatement costs at the current level of emission) and revenue-raising charges, where charges are set so low that no such incentive exists. Instead, revenue-raising charges exist in order to raise revenue, usually to help meet the administrative and monitoring costs of the regulatory system (as with the French water pollution charge scheme, and payments for water pollution consents in England and Scotland). Opschoor and Vos found that most pollution charges existing in the OECD were revenue-raising rather than being set at incentive levels. Revenue-raising charges may, however, have a beneficial effect on water quality; in Germany, the charge rate in 1992 was DM50/unit of pollution compared to an estimate of average abatement costs of DM150/unit of pollution in North Rhine Westphalia, for example (RCEP, 1992).

Why, then, has so little use been made of economic instruments? This question has been investigated by several authors (Hahn, 1989a; Cumberland, 1990; Hanley *et al.*, 1990), investigating four possible reasons. The first of these is ignorance on the part of policy-makers. Beckerman (1975) suggested that the reason economic instruments were not used was that policy makers were unaware of their potential. However, this is no longer true in the OECD. The UK government, for example, has recently published a document supporting the concept of economic instruments (Department of the Environment, 1993); Hanley *et al.* (1990) found in a survey of policy makers and regulators that at least a superficial knowledge of economic instruments was almost universally present in the UK, while economic instruments have been debated in the USA since the early 1970s (Nelson, 1987).

Second is practical problems. These include the use of either spatially differentiated taxes or complex trading rules for non-uniformly mixed pollutants; interactions between regulated pollutants, stochastic influences on pollution emissions and resultant concentrations; and the way the regulator could reduce the supply of permits (or the level of pollution that a given supply permits) before the end of the permits' expiry dates. For many water pollutants in many physical settings, the potential number of traders in a TPP scheme is very small; whilst the financial transfers implicit in pure pollution tax schemes mitigate against their political acceptability.

A third possible reason is institutional problems. This is perhaps the most important category. The logic behind a preference for economic instruments is that regulators prefer more cost-effective policies to less cost-effective ones. Yet Hanley *et al.* found that cost-effectiveness was ranked very low by regulators in a list of policy objectives. Some regulators stated that their principal objective was the elimination of pollution regardless of costs imposed; lack of uncertainty over the outcome of policy, and apparent fairness of the policy were also highly ranked. Efficiency was only given as a principal objective by 23 per cent of the regulators surveyed. A second institutional problem is connected with the ethical implications of economic instruments. Kelman (1981) has argued that pollution taxes, by putting a price on the right to pollute, somehow debase the notion of environmental quality: his survey of the US environmental lobby found that 68 per cent of those questioned took this view of pollution taxes (interestingly, the same survey found that 85 per cent of industrialists were opposed to pollution taxes, on the grounds that these increased the financial burden on firms relative to those imposed by the regulatory system). Tradeable permits could also be thought of as 'rights to pollute' and thus also subject to ethical opposition from environmental groups.

Finally, both pollution taxes and TPPs are significant changes in pollution control policy. Consequently, resistance can be expected from those with a vested interest in the preservation of the existing system, while bureaucracies in general may resist wholesale changes in policy. It is interesting in this regard that the best examples of economic instruments in the OECD were all introduced to the legislation in a gradual process, rather than as a dramatic change. In Germany, for example, charge levels were gradually increased over the first four years of the scheme, and are planned to increase biannually until 1999.

As environmental standards become stricter, it is likely that the cost savings offered by economic instruments will become more attractive to policy-makers. However, the lesson from the last 20 years is that most changes come gradually, that cost-savings can be over-estimated by eager economists, and that lobby groups will seek to retain regulation which is relatively favourable to their own interests.

■ *5.4* **Conclusions**

Tradeable permits have become established as the principal alternative to taxes as an efficient mechanism for pollution control. Early simulation studies suggested that very large savings were available to regulators if a TPP system were introduced in place of a design or performance standard-based system. What is more, TPPs are more attractive than taxes in some respects: notably that the agency does not need to know the MAC schedules of firms in order to arrive at the target level of emissions. TPPs are also guaranteed not to exceed the target level of emissions (in the simple uniform mixing case anyway), so long as firms are honest; whilst 'grandfathered' TPPs avoid the large transfer payments associated with a tax. For non-uniformly mixed pollutants, trading rules seem to offer an alternative to a differentiated tax scheme. Finally, TPPs are, in a sense, a less dramatic change in the manner of pollution regulation than taxes, compared with the currently dominant means of regulation (performance standards) and thus may be easier to introduce into practice.

However, it is now clear, from both theory and from the evidence of actual TPP markets, that the cost-saving potential of permits implied by early studies was exaggerated. This is due to the institutional design of actual permit markets (principally the specified trading rules), problems associated with market power and information flows. What is more, permit markets must be designed with great care in cases where multiple pollutants are involved. Yet most environmental economists would argue that TPPs are in many cases likely to be less expensive in aggregate abatement cost terms than design or performance standards, even if many areas of TPP theory remain to be worked out. It seems likely that more and more TPP markets will be introduced worldwide, if only at a slower rate than some economists might wish.

■ References

Andrews, R. (1984) 'Economics and environmental decisions', in V.K. Smith (ed.), *Environmental Policy under Reagan's Executive Order*, Chapel Hill, NC: University of North Carolina Press.

Atkinson, S. and T. Tietenberg (1982) 'The empirical properties of two classes of designs for transferable discharge markets', *Journal of Environmental Economics and Management*, 9, 101–21.

Atkinson, S. and T. Tietenberg (1987) 'Economic implications of emissions trading rules', *Canadian Journal of Economics*, 20, 370–86.

Atkinson, S. and T. Tietenberg (1991) 'Market failure in incentive based regulation: the case of emissions trading', *Journal of Environmental Economics and Management*, 21, 17–31.

Beavis, B. and M. Walker (1979) 'Interactive pollutants and joint abatement costs', *Journal of Environmental Economics and Management*, 6, 275–86.

Beckerman, W. (1975) *Pricing for Pollution*, London: Institute for Economic Affairs.

Casson, T. (1993) 'Seller incentive properties of the EPA's emission trading auction', *Journal of Environmental Economics and Management*, 25, 177–95.

Common, M. (1977) 'A note on the use of taxes to control pollution', *Scandinavian Journal of Economics*, 79, 345–9.

Crocker, T. (1966) 'Structuring of atmospheric pollution control systems', in H. Wolozin (ed.), *The Economics of Air Pollution*, New York: W.W. Norton.

Cumberland, J. (1990) 'Public choice and the improvement of policy instruments for environmental management', *Ecological Economics*, 2(2), 149–62.

Dales, J.H. (1968) *Pollution, Property and Prices*, Toronto: University of Toronto Press.

Department of the Environment (1993) *Making Markets Work for the Enviornment*, London: HMSO.

Downing, P.B. and L.J. White (1986) 'Innovation in pollution control', *Journal of Environmental Economics and Management*, 13, 18–29.

Eheart, J., E. Joeres and M. David (1980) 'Distribution methods for transferable discharge permits', *Water Resources Research*, 16, 833–43.

English, R. (1993) 'No fault liability: the Cambridge water case', *Journal of Planning and Environmental Law*, May, 409–16.

Green, J. and J.-J. Laffont, (1977) 'Characterization of a satisfactory mechanism for the revelation of preferences for public goods', *Econometrica*, 45, 427–38.

Hahn, R. (1984) 'Market power and transferable property rights', *Quarterly Journal of Economics*, 99, 753–65.

Hahn, R. (1989a) 'Economic prescriptions for environmental problems', *Journal of Economic Perspectives*, 3, 95–114.

Hahn, R. (1989b) 'A new approach to the design of regulation in the presence of multiple objectives', *Journal of Environmental Economics and Management*, 17, 195–211.

Hanley, N. (1990) 'The economics of nitrate pollution', *European Review of Agricultural Economics*, 17, 129–51.

Hanley, N. and I. Moffatt (1993) 'Efficiency and distributional aspects of market mechanisms for the control of pollution', *Scottish Journal of Political Economy*, 40(1) 69–87.

Hanley, N., I. Moffatt and S. Hallett (1990) 'Why is more notice not taken of economists' prescriptions for the control of pollution?', *Environment and Planning A*, 22, 1421–39.

Kelman, S. (1981) 'Economists and the environmental policy muddle', *Public Interest*, 64, 106–23.

Klaasen, G. and F. Førsund (1993) 'Emission trading in Europe with an exchange rate', paper to the fourth annual conference of EAERE, France, June.

Kling, C. (1993) 'Environmental benefits from marketable discharge permits', mimeo, Department of Agricultural Economics, University of California, Davis.

Krupnick, A. (1986) 'Costs of alternative policies for the control of nitrogen dioxide in Baltimore', *Journal of Environmental Economics and Management*, 13, 189–97.

Krupnick, A., W. Oates and E. Van der Verg (1983) 'On the design of a market for air pollution permits', *Journal of Environmental Economics and Management*, 10, 233–47.

Liroff, R. (1986) *Reforming Air Pollution Policy: the Toil and Trouble of the EPA's Bubble*, Washington, D.C.: Conservation Foundation.

Lyon, R. (1982) 'Auctions and alternative procedures for allocating pollution rights', *Land Economics*, 58, 16–32.

Maloney, M. and B. Yandle (1984) 'Estimation of the cost of air pollution regulation', *Journal of Environmental Economics and Management*, 11, 244–63.

Malueg, D.A. (1989) 'Emission credit trading and the incentive to adopt new pollution abatement technology', *Journal of Environmental Economics and Management*, 16, 52–7.

McGartland, A. and W. Oates (1985) 'Marketable permits for the prevention of environmental deterioration', *Journal of Environmental Economics and Management*, 12, 207–28.

Milliman, S. and R. Prince (1989) 'Firm incentives to promote technological change in pollution control', *Journal of Environmental Economics and Management*, 17, 247–65.

Misiolek, W. and H. Elder (1989) 'Exclusionary manipulation of markets for pollution rights', *Journal of Environmental Economics and Management*, 16, 156–66.

Montgomery, W. (1972) 'Markets in licences and efficient pollution control programmes', *Journal of Economic Theory*, 5, 395–418.

Moxey, A. and B. White (1994) 'Efficient compliance with agricultural nitrate pollution standards', *Journal of Agricultural Economics*, 45(1), 27–37.

Munro, A. N. Hanley, R. Faichney and J. Shortle (1995) 'Notes on impediments to trade in markets for pollution permits', *Discussion Papers in Ecological Economics*, no. 95/1, University of Stirling.

Nelson, R. (1987) 'The economics profession and the making of public policy', *Journal of Economic Literature*, 25, 49–87.

O'Neil, W., M. David, C. Moore and E. Joeres (1983) 'Transferable discharge permits and economic efficiency: the Fox river', *Journal of Environmental Economics and Management*, 10, 346–55.

Opschoor, J. and H. Vos (eds) (1989) *Economic Instruments for Environmental Protection*, Paris: OECD.

Pan, J.H. and I. Hodge (1994) 'Land use permits as an alternative to fertilizer and leaching taxes for the control of nitrate pollution', *Journal of Agricultural Economics*, 45(1), 102–12.

Portney, P. (1990) *Public Policies for Environmental Protection*, Washington, DC: Resources for the Future.

Royal Commission on Environmental Pollution (1992) *Sixteenth Report: Freshwater Quality*, London: HMSO.

Shogren, J. and C. Russell (1993) *Theory, Modelling and Experience in the Management of Non Point-Source Pollution*, Boston: Kluwer.

Taylor, C. (1975) 'A regional market for rights in fertilizer use', *Journal of Environmental Economics and Management*, 2, 7–17.

Tietenberg, T. (1984) 'Marketable emission permits in principle and practice', DP123, Washington D.C.: Resources for the Future.

Tietenberg, T. (1990) 'Economic instruments for environmental protection', *Oxford Review of Economic Policy*, 6(1), 17–33.

Tietenberg, T. (1992) *Environmental and Natural Resource Economics*, New York: Harper-Collins.

Zylicz, T. (1993) 'Improving the environment through permit trading: the limits of the market approach', *Beijer Discussion Papers*, no. 23, Stockholm: Beijer Institute.

■ *Chapter 6* ■

Transboundary Pollution Problems

6.1 Introduction
6.2 Transboundary pollution as a problem of international externalities

6.3 Transboundary pollution and game theory
6.4 Conclusions

■ *6.1* Introduction

Many of the best-known instances of pollution involve the actions of more than one country. Obvious examples include acid rain, global warming, pollution of the North Sea and damage to the stratospheric ozone layer. This chapter, which was co-written with Fanny Missfeldt, describes some of the important issues emerging from economic analysis of these problems. In some cases, this involves making use of concepts from game theory, as set out in the technical note on pp. 14–20. In Chapter 10 a more detailed example of transboundary pollution is given regarding an international fishing conflict.

Two important features of transboundary pollution problems are the uniformity of the damage function and the extent of mixing of the pollutant (concepts which were both introduced in Chapter 4).

☐ *6.1.1 The uniformity of damages*

Whether the focus is on acid rain, global warming or pollution of the North Sea, different countries suffer different damages per unit of pollution output. This is due to physical factors and economic factors. To take acid rain as an example, physical factors influence the degree of damage once deposition has occurred (see Box 6.2). Acid rain causes more damage per unit deposition on more acidic soils than on less acidic soils. Soils vary in their acidity owing to the nature of underlying rocks. Soils based on granite, for example, are relatively acid. This means that they have a poor buffering

159

capacity to cope with acid deposition, so that physical damages such as fish deaths in lakes and streams show up sooner. Much of Eastern Canada (including large parts of Ontario and Quebec) has poor buffering capacity owing to acid soils. Pollution of the North Sea by nutrients such as nitrates also exhibits non-uniform damages: countries such as Denmark suffer more from algal growth due to nutrient enrichment (a phenomenon known as eutrophication, which has adverse effects on fishing) than does the UK, because of the deeper coastal waters around the UK. Economic factors are also important, though. This may be because the valuation of environmental quality varies across countries, or may result from variations in the structure of economic activity. A country which depends greatly on a sector which is more sensitive to, say, an increase in average temperatures or a fall in rainfall due to global warming will record a higher economic impact per unit of physical impact than a country facing the same physical impacts which is less dependent on sensitive sectors (Nordhaus, 1991a). An example is developing countries which depend largely upon agricultural commodities and forestry.

Box 6.1   *Global warming*

The greenhouse effect refers to the phenomenon whereby carbon dioxide and other gases trap long-wave infra-red radiation (heat) in the atmosphere, thereby warming the earth. It is an entirely natural phenomenon: without the effect, the average temperature on earth would be 33 degrees C lower than at present. The infra-red radiation emitted by the earth can be trapped by atmospheric carbon dioxide (CO_2), nitrous oxide (N_2O), chlorofluorocarbons (CFCs), methane (CH_4), ozone (O_3), and other gases. The concentration of these greenhouse gases (GHGs) in the atmosphere reduces the re-radiation of heat into space. The operation of this mechanism has become a pollution problem because of the rate at which anthropogenic emissions of infra-red trapping gases have increased, creating a larger stock in the atmosphere.

Major sources of CO_2 are the combustion of fossil fuels, such as oil, coal and gas; CO_2 is also produced naturally by decay. Major natural sinks for CO_2 exist, where the gas is locked up. These include the world's oceans and peat bogs. The concentration of CO_2 in the upper atmosphere has risen from roughly 280 parts per million (ppm) in 1880 to 355 ppm today (IPCC, 1992). The principal cause of this increase has been the combustion of fossil fuels. Major sources of N_2O are the combustion of fossil fuels and the production of fertilisers. CFCs are produced as propellants, refrigerants and foam expanders, and are used in air conditioning systems. Methane is produced from sewage treatment, livestock wastes and landfill sites.

The four major greenhouse gases vary in terms of their lifetimes in the atmosphere before they are broken down (CO_2: 500 years; N_2O: 150 years; CFCs: 75–110 years; and methane: 9–13 years (IPCC, 1992)). They also vary in terms of the 'radiative forcing' that each induces – as set out in Chapter 4 – and in their current contribution to the level of warming potential.

In terms of the physical results of the greenhouse effect, these are subject to a wide range of predictions. Current 'mainstream' predictions show a rise in global climate of between 1.5 to 4.5 degrees C by the next century for a doubling of CO_2 (Jamieson, 1988); and a rise in sea level of between 0.6–3.5 m by 2100 (Titus, 1989). Regional effects are much less certain but seem to involve some regions becoming much drier and some wetter. An increase in global temperatures is now thought inescapable, in that, due to the long residence time of some GHGs in the upper atmosphere, we have already committed the earth to a further warming of between 0.3 to 1.9 degrees C as a result of past emissions (Ciborowski, 1989).

A large literature has now emerged over the economics of the greenhouse effect. This is summarised in Cline (1992) and, from an explicitly cost-benefit analysis point of view, in Hanley and Spash (1993) and Spash and Hanley (1994). This literature has concentrated on estimating the abatement costs involved in reaching certain reduction targets for CO_2, and on the damage costs of global warming. In most of these cases, a doubling of CO_2 over the current atmospheric concentration is assumed.

☐ 6.1.2 The uniformity of mixing

Mixing uniformity refers to the extent to which each unit of emissions from different countries contributes to overall pollution potential. Physical factors determining the transport of pollutants and their eventual deposition are one important source of non-uniform mixing. Acid rain is a good example here: because of prevailing westerly winds, much of the UK's production of acid rain precursors (sulphur dioxide, nitrogen dioxide) is deposited in Scandinavia. Much US production of these gases is deposited in Canada. The UK therefore contributes more to pollution potential in Scandinavia than it does to pollution potential in southern England per unit of SO_2 produced (some UK SO_2 gets deposited in upland regions of North Wales, Scotland and north-west England). Global warming, on the other hand, is usually thought of as a problem of uniformly mixed pollutants. However, this is an assumption which is taken to simplify matters, because the precise origins and potential effects of global warming are subject to substantial (scientific) uncertainties (see Box 6.1). Depletion of the ozone layer is similar, in that no matter whether CFCs originate from China or Canada, a similar depletion of ozone occurs (assuming all other factors are equal). Damages from ozone layer thinning are non-uniform, however, since some countries (such as New Zealand) are more likely to suffer damage from unfiltered UV rays than others further away from the poles (see Box 6.3).

Box 6.2   *Acid deposition*

The gases sulphur dioxide (SO_2), oxides of nitrogen (NO_x) and ammonia (NH_3) are all causes of acid deposition. Acid deposition can occur in dry form, and as acid snow, fog, mist or rain. Dry deposition occurs close to the point of discharge, but wet deposition, as acid rain for example, can occur thousands of kilometres away from its source of discharge. In the northern hemisphere, acid deposition (acid rain for brevity, from now on) is a major source of environmental degradation. This degradation impacts on human health (OECD, 1981), agricultural and forest crops (Baker *et al.*, 1986), freshwater ecosystems (Adriano and Johnson, 1989), fish populations (Muniz and Levestad, 1980; Harriman, 1984) and building materials (Webb *et al.*, 1990).

In the United Kingdom a major cause for concern has been damage to the biodiversity of vulnerable mountain areas where some of the most natural and least disturbed sites important for nature conservation occur (Fry and Cooke, 1987) and which are important spawning waters for the Atlantic salmon (*Salmo salar*) and brown trout (*Salmo trutta*). Affected areas are characterised by high deposition levels, acidic geology (implying a low buffering capacity) and shallow, organic-rich soils with only a limited capacity for neutralising acid inputs (Wright *et al.*, 1993). Undesirable effects on aquatic systems have also been recorded in Scandinavia, parts of Canada, parts of Ireland, and the North-Eastern United States. Effects on forestry are more disputed, although excessive inputs of nitrogen from acid rain seem to exacerbate deficiencies of other nutrients and thus harm trees. Acid rain also causes direct harm to the leaves/needles of some trees, such as red spruce (MacKenzie and El Ashry, 1988). Recent estimates suggest that total European damage costs due to forest damages are around $23 billion per year (in 1987 $s) (IIASA, 1990), although given scientific uncertainty, much caution should be attached to such figures. An excellent summary of the scientific literature is given in Adriano and Johnson (1989) and EPA (1985).

Major sources of acid rain precursors are fossil fuel combustion and farming. In the Netherlands, ammonia emissions from intensive farming are thought to be a major cause of acidification (van Ierland, 1989). Worldwide, stationary sources such as power stations and industrial boilers are responsible for about 35 per cent of human-caused NO_x emissions and nearly all of human-caused SO_2 emissions (WRI, 1993). Control options include reductions in fossil fuel use, fuel switching to less sulphur-intensive fuels, and end-of-pipe pollution control. End-of-pipe controls such as flue gas desulphurisation units are currently being installed in much of Europe, due to the EEC's Large Plant Combustion Directive, whereby all member states have agreed to reduce SO_2 emissions by 60 per cent of 1980 levels by 2003, and NO_x emissions by 30 per cent.

Most economic work on acid rain can be divided into two categories. First, there is a large body of work looking at the costs of reducing acid rain precursors, especially SO_2. Examples include Welsh (1988), Atkinson (1983) and Wiersma (1991). Mäler's 'acid rain game' (see main text) is another example, as is van Ierland (1989). Both of these studies use a meterological model of acid rain transport across Europe known as EMEP. Second, a smaller body of work exists estimating the damage costs of acid rain, principally to fisheries (e.g. Navrud, 1989), but also to biodiversity losses more generally (Ecotec, 1993; Macmillan, Hanley and Buckland, 1994).

6.2 Transboundary pollution as a problem of international externalities

Transboundary pollution is best characterised as a problem of international externalities, which arises from to a lack of property rights in the global commons. These commons include the atmosphere, oceans, global biodiversity reserves and important terrestrial ecosystems, such as tropical rainforests. Because ownership of the air is absent, nation states are free to pollute their neighbours. However, a crucial distinction between national and international externality problems is that, whilst for the former a government exists which can internalise these externalities by, for instance, levying pollution taxes, this is not the case with the global commons. No supranational government exists which has complete authority to internalise externalities. While the European Union can officially require member nations to abide by EU pollution directives by enacting them in environmental law, in practice enactment of these directives by member states is very uneven; the EU cannot in any case order non-member states to, say, introduce a carbon tax to reduce global warming. Canada cannot compel the USA to introduce taxes on US SO_2 emissions, while the United Nations cannot compel Brazil to protect its rainforests, from which global public goods are supplied.

International externalities thus involve the decrease in welfare of one country owing to the actions of another. The 'victim' in this case cannot gain compensation as a right, although some international agreements do at least recognise the need to safeguard against international environmental spillovers. The OECD declaration on the environment from the 1972 Stockholm conference stated that 'states have...the responsibility to ensure that activities do not cause damage to the environment of other states'. Attention has in fact been given to the question as to when it might be desirable for victims to actually compensate polluters, as we shall see shortly.

Given the lack of a competent international authority to internalise international environmental spillovers, voluntary international agreements are necessary to safeguard the global commons. Examples of such agreements are given in Box 6.4. However, an obvious difficulty with any such agreement, such as an international agreement for all nations to cut CO_2 emissions by a given percentage, is the free-rider problem. Given the public good nature of the benefits of reducing global warming (their non-excludability), for example, country A has a strong incentive not to sign such an agreement, since as long as some countries reduce CO_2 outputs, country A gets a benefit (avoided global warming damages) despite not spending resources on cutting its own CO_2 emissions. What is more, some other country B may actually benefit from global warming: it will certainly have no incentive to agree to a cut in its emissions (this kind of problem is encountered in the acid rain game described in section 6.3).

However, free-riding will reduce world welfare if it means that pareto superior outcomes to the status quo are not forthcoming. Suppose that, under a possible world agreement on cuts in CO_2, country C loses $50 million, even though net gains worldwide are positive and exceed this amount. Country C could be compensated for its losses and would thus agree to the reduction programme, with a consequent improvement in world welfare (in the language of cost–benefit analysis, the gainers can compensate the loser and still be better off). Similarly, Brazil could offer to forgo income from felling its rainforest if countries who derive utility from the preservation of the rainforest compensate Brazil for these losses. Disregarding the question of whether compensation can be made in principle for environmental losses (but see Hanley and Spash, 1993, ch. 8), key problems are how to enforce such 'side-payments' in such a way that country C can be sure that, if it undertakes the programme, compensation will actually be paid; whether within a country those agents who make losses if their government agrees to an international programme are compensated for their individual losses; and how to decide which countries should make what compensation payments.

Such problems (at the inter-country level) are usually expressed in terms of game theory, with reference to co-operative and non co-operative solutions. Clearly free-riding is also an obstacle to such side-payment agreements: UK citizens would benefit from the preservation of Brazilian rainforest, but the UK might not agree to make side-payments on the grounds that, so long as some other countries make such payments, the UK makes gains (some rainforest is preserved) at no cost, even though world welfare could be higher if the UK 'bought' rainforest (assuming that the marginal WTP (willingness to pay) in the UK for preservation exceeds the marginal cost of preserving rainforest: the rainforest supply price (Ruitenbeck, 1992)).

Box 6.3 *The stratospheric ozone layer*

High above the earth's surface a relatively thin layer of the gas ozone (O_3) performs a vital function. If the earth's atmosphere were compressed to a pressure of 1000 millibar the atmosphere would be 5 miles thick. Of this, the ozone layer would only account for some 3 mm. This is how ozone levels are now measured: in Dobson units (Nisbet, 1991). Ozone is formed naturally in the upper atmosphere when oxygen molecules are struck by ultra-violet light from the sun. Ozone absorbs ultra-violet (UV) light, and is continually being broken down (into oxygen) and recreated in natural equilibrium. Ozone also acts as a greenhouse gas. Since the early 1970s, it has been known that chloroflourocarbons (CFCs) can break down ozone. The process is a complicated one. CFCs contain chlorine atoms. These can attach themselves to oxygen atoms in ozone, forming oxygen and chlorine monoxide, the presence of the latter being one test for ozone thinning. One chlorine atom can break down 100 000 molecules of O_3 in this way. As the concentration of ozone falls, so does the temperature of the stratosphere. This leads to the formation of ice clouds which greatly speed up the O_3 degradation process, by providing a surface for reactions to take place which allow chlorine atoms to be separated from their constituent molecules, and thus become available for ozone destruction. In this sense, the ozone hole 'feeds on itself' (Nisbet, 1991).

In the mid-1980s, a large hole in the ozone layer over the Antarctic was noticed by a UK survey team. The air above the Antarctic is very cold, and at certain times of the year ice clouds are common. This means ozone degradation can occur rapidly. In October 1987 ozone abundance fell to half its average level, a fall well outside the normal range of fluctuation. Data published in the journal *Nature* two years earlier had already shown a steady fall in ozone levels over the period 1956–1984 (Farman *et al.*, 1985). In 1989, a hole of similar proportions to the 1987 hole was recorded in Antarctica, whilst a smaller hole was found over the (warmer) Arctic in 1990. Ozone depletion has the greatest potential impact in the southern hemisphere due to the cold Antarctic air, with impacts decreasing as one moves away from the south pole; but the upper northern hemisphere has also been recently affected. In 1991, a 3 per cent reduction in the ozone layer over the US was recorded, which resulted in a 6 per cent increase in UV incidence. This was predicted to result in an extra 12 million cancer cases in the US over the next 50 years (WRI, 1993; WMO/UNEP, 1991). In 1991 there was also a 60 per cent loss in ozone over Antarctica during September.

What are the costs of stratospheric ozone thinning? Most studies have looked at increased incidence of skin cancers (including potentially fatal melanomas), suppression of immune systems and increases in eye cataracts (Mintzis, 1986) . UNEP have estimated that a 10 per cent drop in ozone levels can produce a 26 per cent rise in non-melanoma skin cancers (Australia has already recorded a three-fold rise in incidence of this disease). Dickie, Gerking and Agee (1991) report a study estimating WTP for the reduction of risks of skin cancer due to increased UV radiation. Adults in California and Wyoming were sampled to self-assess their perceived risk of skin cancer; and then asked their maximum WTP for a new sun cream which would guard against getting skin cancer for one year. Results showed that respondents had a lifetime valuation for a reduction of 1 per cent in the perceived risk of getting skin cancer of between $5.64 and $1.67 depending on the age of respondents and on the discount rate. This indicates total US benefits of reducing UV exposure such that skin cancer risks fall by 1 per cent of $300–$800 million.

High doses of UV rays can also damage crops, especially soybeans. Potentially the greatest long-term impacts, however, involve damage to krill stocks, which play a vital role in marine food chains.

Some studies (e.g. Nordhaus, 1991b) have also studied the costs of reducing CFC emissions. The main problem here is that cutting new production of CFCs will not be sufficient to cut emissions in the short term, since CFCs are stored in air conditioning units, refrigerators and blown foam. If households face too low an incentive to recycle these CFCs, then releases will occur. Most cost estimates for long-term CFC control rest on substitutions to more costly alternatives, but many of these alternatives involve environmental costs too: freons, for example, also deplete ozone.

6.3 Transboundary pollution and game theory

As mentioned above, game theory is a fruitful environment in which to explore problems of international co-operation relating to environmental spillovers. In particular, since Mäler (1989) presented a first attempt to capture empirically the transboundary problems related to acid rain in a game theory set-up, an increasing number of papers have investigated the use of game theory for this purpose. In the following sub-section, Mäler's 1989 paper, 'The acid rain game', is summarised, since it contains many of the important features in this field. We also discuss other aspects of applications of game theory to environmental spillovers, including the notion of countries trading off rewards from one set of negotiations against those from another. A comprehensive survey of game theory applications to transboundary pollution problems is given in Missfeldt (1995).

Many games are set up in terms of optimality, where it is assumed that both the marginal benefits and marginal costs of pollution control are known. This is clearly a strong assumption, especially with respect to the benefits of pollution control (see Chapters 12 and 13). If this assumption is made, then it is possible to identify the full co-operation solution as the best possible outcome in terms of world welfare. This is where the sum of the costs of pollution abatement and pollution damages is minimised worldwide. As pollution damage reductions are usually assumed to be pure public goods, this outcome is given where the sum of marginal damage costs

$$\sum_{j=1}^{J} MDC_j = MAC_j \qquad \forall j = 1 \ldots J$$

across all j countries is equal to the marginal abatement costs of each country (the Samuelson condition). This is shown graphically in Figure 6.1, which is adapted from Barrett (1994). Assuming linear marginal abatement and cost functions, the cooperative outcome is at point Q_c, where each country sets its own MAC (MAC_j) equal to the global marginal benefits of abatement, given by global (avoided) marginal damages, MDC.

However, as noted above, this condition may involve some countries being worse off than under the status quo. The full cooperative solution is thus not an equilibrium (in the absence of side-payments), since country j can increase its welfare by not cooperating. Purely selfish behaviour by each country leads to a Nash equilibrium (see technical note on pp. 14–17), whereby each country sets its own MAC and MDC equal. This is that country's best response to the optimal selfish choices of all other countries:

$$MDC_j = MAC_j \qquad \forall j = 1 \ldots J$$

The transboundary damage will be captured through the MDC. This produces a pareto inferior solution to the full cooperation outcome, shown in Figure 6.1 as Q_n, where each country sets its own marginal damages equal to marginal abatement costs. As will be seen, $Q_n < Q_c$.

In general, various equilibria might exist which make each country at least as well off, and possibly better off, than under the Nash equilibrium. Such

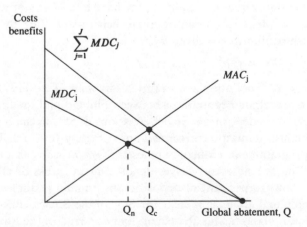

Figure 6.1 *Non-co-operative and full co-operative outcomes*

solutions can result from binding offers of side-payments, as discussed in the previous section. Many possible sets of side-payments exist, redistributing the rewards of full or partial co-operation from gainers to losers. Some attention has been given to what a rule for making side-payments should look like (that is, how side-payments should be decided). Two possibilities discussed by Barrett (1992) are distributions based on a country's population, or on the extent to which each country co-operates. Two other solutions are often analysed in this optimality framework. These are (1) a pareto dominant outcome, whereby the sum of abatement and damage costs is minimised subject to the condition that no country is made worse off than under cooperation; and (2) the formation of coalitions. Both these concepts may be viewed as unstable, however, as in the absence of additional punishments or inducements, countries still have an incentive to free-ride. Finally, as was mentioned in the technical note on p. 19, the effects of unilateral action by a country can be investigated.

If damage costs are not assumed to be known, then attention turns to cost-effective solutions. Rather than looking at the trade-offs between reduced damage and increased costs from abatement policies, here costs are traded off against an absolute pollution limit. In this case, the full co-operative solution involves minimising total abatement costs across all countries subject to a pollution constraint (such as critical loads not being exceeded for acid deposition). The optimal rule of choice in this case becomes

$$\sum_{j=1}^{J} MAC_j = 0 \qquad \text{s.t. } P \leq P^* \qquad \forall j = 1 \ldots J$$

where P^* represents the pollution limit and P the actual amount of pollution. This plan, however, may involve some countries in making losses relative to the status quo, especially if they have low MACs or high transfer coefficients. Countries can again improve their own welfare by free-riding, and the Nash equilibrium is given where:

$$MAC_j = 0 \qquad \text{s.t. } P_j \leq P_j^* \qquad \forall j = 1 \ldots J$$

again subject to a pollution constraint. Tahvonen *et al.* (1993) take this approach to modelling negotiations between Finland and the former Soviet Union on acid rain deposition. Soviet emissions of SO_2 in the border region outweigh Finnish domestic emissions approximately fourfold. Finland has pursued a programme of reducing domestic SO_2 emissions as a result of the fact that all of its land area receives depositions in excess of critical loads. Since only about 20 per cent of deposition in Finland is domestic-sourced, and since marginal abatement costs for SO_2 in the Soviet Union are much lower than in Finland (as no abatement had occurred in the Soviet Union), then cost-saving gains from co-operation seemed possible.

A non-co-operative solution occurs where each country minimises its own abatement costs subject to meeting a domestic maximum deposition vector (defined by critical load) and to the emissions of the other country. A co-operative solution is where the sum of abatement costs across both countries is minimised subject to these environmental constraints. Tahvonen *et al.* simulate both of these strategies empirically, using data on abatement costs, deposition targets and transfer coefficients from a meterological model. They also simulate a 1987 agreement between Finland and the Soviet Union, whereby each agreed to reduce emissions by 50 per cent. The authors' computations show that Finland gains but the Soviet Union loses in the full co-operation outcome. If the Soviet Union cheats on this outcome but Finland does not, then the former saves money whilst deposition targets are violated in the latter. Interestingly, the 50 per cent agreement also gives incentives to cheat, as each country does better in the Nash equilibrium (no co-operation). If a higher level of emission reduction is required in the agreement (80 per cent), then Finland loses whilst the Soviet Union gains, relative to full co-operation. But in no case does co-operation give sizeable efficiency gains. Tahvonen *et al.* attribute this to the relatively small transfer coefficients between the two countries. In a reformulation of the problem's environmental constraints, larger gains from co-operation arise, in that Finland cannot meet its own deposition targets unless the Soviet Union co-operates. This co-operation costs the latter country money, so side payments from Finland to the Soviet Union will be needed.

Game theory also suggests how incentives to free ride on international agreements can be reduced. (Here we ignore problems of monitoring compliance with international agreements. Remote sensing technology has made such monitoring less difficult than previously.) As mentioned above, side-payments can become an instrument for increasing the incentive to join an agreement. Barrett (1992) and Whalley (1991) suggest a means other than side payments. Parties could be made to co-operate by linking negotiations on transboundary environmental spill-overs to negotiations on, for example, trade barriers. Thus China could be persuaded to sign up to an international agreement to cut CFC production by the offer of favourable trade deals with the West. Folmer *et al.* (1993) and Folmer and Mouche (1993) have formalised the idea of linking negotiations through the concept of 'interconnected games', which incorporates the idea that countries can condition their actions in the environmental area to outcomes previously observed in, say, the trade area and vice versa. They have shown that interconnection may be a means to overcome a 'prisoners' dilemma' type of situation and to induce co-operation. The linking of negotiations on different issues (including international environmental spillovers) thus may constitute an alternative to the use of side-payments to achieve greater co-operation, and thus higher world welfare.

Finally, the dimension of time is crucial in this context. In particular, there are two aspects of time which are important. On the one hand, incorporating time will affect the strategies of the countries involved and, on the other hand, stocks of pollutants, which accumulate over time, can be considered. The first aspect relates to the fact that decisions of countries today affect other countries' decisions tomorrow. For example, international contracts have to be designed so that the signatories will not have an incentive to breach them afterwards. This problem is generally referred to as 'postcontractual risk'. Mohr (1991) shows in a theoretical model that the incorporation of high enough sanctions along with side payments can in fact help to overcome this problem. He underlines, however, that evidence from international debt relations suggests that sanctions only pose a very limited threat in international relations. Others (see, for example, Cesar, 1994, for a thorough discussion of dynamic issues related to global warming) have explicitly chosen dynamic game theory models ('differential games') in order to take account of the structural time dependence of pollutants (as with the building up of pollution 'stocks') and/or to show how pollution abatement schemes would have to evolve over time in order to make a contract acceptable to all parties.

Box 6.4   *International environmental agreements*

This box section summarises two international agreements covering problems of transboundary environmental spill-overs. Although as the main text makes clear there are major problems in the negotiation of such treaties, some limited success has been recorded.

☐ *The Montreal Protocol*

Perhaps the best-known international treaty on transboundary pollution is the Montreal Protocol on CFC production, ratified by 156 nations in March 1996. The Protocol committed signatories to freeze production of five CFCs at 1986 levels and cut total CFC production by 50 per cent by the year 2000, in response to (then) new evidence of damage to the stratospheric ozone layer. Developing countries were allowed to increase CFC use for 10 years, however, whilst enforcement of the Protocol was left to signatories (although trade sanctions were included as possible enforcement measures). China and India, nations who were looking to CFCs as useful materials in their development plans, refused to sign the Protocol, since they (presumably) believed that their losses from signing would be too great. The Protocol did not cover carbon tetrachloride, a substance which also depletes ozone. One study of the effectiveness of the Protocol assumed that without the agreement, 'group 1' CFCs would have increased 100 per cent over 1986 levels by 2009, but that with the agreement the predicted change varied from a 20 per cent increase to a 45 per cent decrease from 1986 levels (Office of Technology Assessment, 1989).

In 1989, EC environment ministers agreed to a stricter target of a total phase-out of CFCs by 2000, whilst the Clean Air Act Amendments of 1990 in the US banned CFC production from 2000 onwards (Smith, 1992). The most interesting development, however, occurred in London in 1990, where the initial signatories to the Protocol, plus 35 new signatories, signed a new agreement. This called for the total phase-out of halons, carbon tetrachloride and CFCs by 2000, and of methyl chloroform by 2005 (Tietenberg, 1994). The signatories also offered a side-payment of $240 million to India, China and other developing nations if they would also sign. In 1992 in Copenhagen, a further amendment to the Protocol advanced the phase-out of CFCs and carbon tetrachloride to January 1996 (Department of the Environment, 1992).

☐ *The Global Environment Facility*

The Global Environment Facility (GEF) was established in 1991 by the World Bank, the United Nations Development Programme and the United Nations Environment Programme, to provide help for developing countries to deal with climate change, threats to biodiversity and water pollution. The GEF is thus an example of countries paying other countries to supply global public goods such as biodiversity preservation. The GEF was relaunched at the 1992 Earth Summit in Rio, with the promise of $2 billion from the developed countries. Funding was to be split across donor countries in line with their shares in the International Development Association, the 'soft' loans division of the World Bank. The two largest contributors are the US ($430 million) and Japan ($400 million). As of 30 June, 1993, the GEF had approved projects for a total of over $700 million in 63 countries.

☐ *6.3.1 Mäler's acid rain game*

In 1989, Mäler published one of the first applications of game theory to transboundary pollution problems. His paper is concerned with acid deposition in Europe, and presents one of the first empirical results in the field of game theory applications to transboundary pollution problems. Even though the results are quite limited owing to substantial uncertainties, they are nonetheless very interesting. A total of 27 countries are included in the model. The distribution of deposition within each country is ignored. Transfer coefficients, a_{ij} are used to represent the transport of emissions from country j to country i. There is thus a 27×27 matrix of transfer coefficients **A**, derived from the Norwegian EMEP (European Monitoring and Evaluation Programme) model of SO_2 movements across Europe. Each country i has a continuous, piece-wise linear cost function C_i (E_i), where E represents emissions. Reductions in E mean increases in C. Steady-state deposition in each country is given by:

$$\mathbf{Q} = \mathbf{AE}$$

where E is a vector of emissions and Q a vector of national deposition rates. Finally, a damage function D_i (Q_i) is specified, although, as Mäler admits, this function is subject to high levels of uncertainty: he assumes that each country is in a Nash equilibrium as the status quo, so that the marginal abatement cost divided by the transfer coefficient relating deposition in country i to emissions from that country can be used as the marginal damage cost (see Mäler, 1989, p. 240). Thus the implicit assumption is made that pollution by acid rain is already internalised at the national level. As the damage cost functions are assumed to be linear, this marginal damage cost is a constant in each country.

Mäler then computes the full co-operation outcome, where side-payments are assumed to be possible. This results in a 40 per cent reduction in emissions over baseline (1984) levels, and total net benefits for all 27 countries of DM6248 million. However, several countries lose in this solution: Finland, Italy, Spain and the UK. The UK suffers the biggest loss, and abates by the maximum amount allowed in the model. This result is due to the large influence of UK emissions on damages in the rest of Europe (see section 6.1). Norway and Sweden do very little emission reduction because of their low transfer coefficients and high *MAC*s.

However, if side-payments are not possible then the full co-operation solution will not occur. Mäler thus simulates a Pareto dominating outcome, where no country is worse off than under the status quo (Nash equilibrium), but some are better off. This gives smaller total European net benefits than full co-operation of DM5892 million, and a smaller total emission reduction of 37 per cent. The UK has a net gain of zero in this case. However, the UK has no incentive to agree to such a programme as it could do better by minimizing its own total costs. The Pareto dominating outcome is also therefore not an equilibrium. Finally, Mäler considers possible coalitions of countries as an outcome. He finds empirically that a coalition of all countries who do not lose in net terms in the full co-operation scenario could gain DM6002 million in net benefits, whilst some countries outside the coalition (Italy, the UK) do much better by behaving selfishly than by joining the coalition.

Mäler (1991) suggests an extension of the acid rain game to a dynamic framework. This not only makes it possible to incorporate the accumulation of sulphur in surface water, groundwater and soil, which constitutes a dynamic process, but also changes the strategic situation of the negotiating parties: from general game theory it is known that the incentive to free-ride on other players' abatement efforts will diminish as the time horizon of the game goes to infinity (the so-called 'Folk Theorem').

■ *6.4* Conclusions

The literature on the application of game theory to international environmental problems has developed quite dramatically in recent years. However, empirical evaluation in this area is still in its infancy. More progress will largely depend on developments in environmental sciences, especially where the transport of pollutants, their impacts on the environment and the estimation of critical loads are concerned. Many of the issues touched on in this brief chapter need much more investigation: these include the interpretation of the Nash equilibrium as the status quo (see Fankhauser and Kverndokk, 1992), incentives for countries to agree to make side-payments (the enforcement of co-operative solutions) and differential games. However, game theory has been shown to be a very useful tool with which to look at international environmental spillovers. In particular we have seen how co-operation is very likely to be necessary in order to best solve transboundary pollution problems, yet negotiating such agreements is very difficult unless either side-payments or interconnected games can be used.

■ References

Adriano, D.C. and A.H. Johnson (eds) (1989) *Acidic Precipitation (Vol. 2): Biological and Ecological Effects*, New York: Springer-Verlag.

Atkinson, S. (1983) 'Marketable pollution permits and acid rain externalities', *Canadian Journal of Economics*, 16, 704–22.

Baker, C.K., J.J. Colls, A.E. Fullwood and G.G.R. Seaton (1986) 'Depression of growth and yield in winter barley exposed to sulphur dioxide in the field', *New Phytologist*, 104, 233–41.

Barrett, S. (1992) 'Strategies for environmental protection', CSERGE working paper PA92-03, University of London.

Barrett, S. (1994) 'Self-enforcing international agreements', *Oxford Economic Papers*, 46, 878–94.

Cesar, H.S.J. (1994) 'Control and Game Models for the Greenhouse Effect: Economic Essays on the Comedy and Tragedy of the Commons'. PhD thesis (Lecture Notes in Economics and Mathematical Systems nr. 416), Heidelberg: Springer-Verlag.

Ciborowski, P. (1989) 'Sources, sinks, trends and opportunities' in D. Abrahamson (ed.), *The Challenge of Global Warming*, Washington, DC: Island.

Cline, W. (1992) *The Economics of Global Warming*, Washington, DC: Institute for International Economics.

Department of the Environment (DoE) (1992) Press release, 25/11/92.

Dickie M. S. Gerking and M. Agee (1991) 'Health benefits of PMP control' in H. Opschoor and D. Pearce (eds), *Persistent Pollutants: Economics and Policy*, Dordrecht: Kluwer.

Ecotec (1993) *A Cost-Benefit Analysis of Reduced Acid Deposition: UK Natural and Semi-Natural Systems*, Working Paper 5, Birmingham, UK: Ecotec.

EPA (Environmental Protection Agency) (1985) *The Acidic Deposition Phenomenon and its Effect*, Washington, DC: US EPA.

Fankhauser, S. and S. Kverndokk (1992) 'The global warming game: simulations of a CO_2 reduction agreement', CSERGE discussion paper WP92-10, University of London.

Farman, J. B. Gardiner and J. Shanklin (1985) 'Large losses of total ozone in Antarctica' *Nature*, 343, 207–10.

Folmer, H. and P. v Mouche (1993) 'Interconnected games and international environmental problems. II', Wageningen: Landbouwuniversiteit.

Folmer, H., P. v Mouche and S. Ragland (1993) 'Interconnected games and international environmental problems', *Environmental and Resource Economics*, 3(4), 313–36.

Fry, G.L.A. and A.S. Cooke (1987) *Acid Deposition and Its Implications for Nature Conservation in Britain*, Focus on Nature Conservation 7, Peterborough: Nature Conservancy Council.

Graham, G. (1994) 'Hopes of global green fund', *Financial Times*, 14 March.

Hanley, N. and C. Spash (1993) *Cost–Benefit Analysis and the Environment*, Aldershot: Edward Elgar.

Harriman, R., B.R.S. Morrison, L.A. Caines, P. Collen and A. W. Watt (1987) 'Long term changes in fish populations of acid streams and lochs in Galloway, South-West Scotland', *Water, Soil and Air Pollution*, 32, 89–112.

IIASA (International Institute for Applied Systems Analysis) (1990) 'The price of pollution: acid and the forests of Europe', *Options*, September.

IPCC (International Panel on Climate Change) (1992) *Climate Change: The Supplementary Report to the IPCC Scientific Assessment*, Cambridge: Cambridge UP.

Jamieson, D. (1988) *Managing the Future: Public Policy, Scientific Uncertainty and Global Warming*, Working Paper, Dept. of Philosophy, University of Colorado.

MacKenzie, J. and M. El Ashry (1988) *Ill Winds: Air Pollution's Toll on Trees and Crops*, Washington: World Resources Institute.

Macmillan, D., N. Hanley and S. Buckland (1994) 'Valuing biodiversity losses due to acid deposition: a contingent valuation study of uncertain environmental gains', paper presented to the European Association of Environmental and Resource Economists conference, Dublin.

Mäler, K.-G. (1989) 'The acid rain game', in H. Folmer and E. van Ierland (eds), *Valuation and Policy Making in Environmental Economics*, Amsterdam: Elsevier–North Holland.

Mäler, K.-G. (1991) 'Global Warming: Economic Policy in the Face of Positive and Negative Spillovers', in H. Siebert (ed.), *Environmental Scarcity*, Kiel: Institut für Weltwirtschaft.

Mintzis, M. (1986) 'Skin cancer: the price for a depleted ozone layer', *EPA Journal*, 12, 7–9.

Missfeldt, F. (1995) 'The Economics of Transboundary Pollution: A Review', *Discussion Papers in Ecological Economics*, 95/3, University of Stirling.

Mohr, E. (1991) 'Global Warming: Economic Policy in the Face of Positive and Negative Spillovers' in H. Siebert (ed.), *Environmental Scarcity*, Kiel: Institut für Weltwirtschaft.

Muniz, I.P. and H. Leivestad (1980) 'Acidification – effects on freshwater fish', in D. Drablos and A.Tollan (eds), *Ecological Impacts of Acid Precipitation*, Oslo: SNSF, pp. 84–92.

Navrud, S. (1989) 'Estimating social benefits of environmental improvements from reduced acid depositions: a contingent valuation survey', in H. Folmer and E. van Ierland (eds), *Valuation Methods and Policy Making in Environmental Economics*, Studies in Environmental Science 36, Amsterdam: Elsevier.

Nisbet, E. (1991) *Leaving Eden: To Protect and Manage the Earth*, Cambridge: Cambridge UP.

Nordhaus, W. (1991a) 'A sketch of the economics of the greenhouse effect', *American Economic Review*, 81(2), 146–50.

Nordhaus, W. (1991b) 'To slow or not to slow: the economics of the greenhouse effect', *Economic Journal*, 101, 920–38.

OECD (1981) *The Costs and Benefits of Sulphur Oxide Control*, Paris: OECD.

Office of Technology Assessment (1989) 'An analysis of the Montreal protocol' in D. Abrahamson (ed.), *The Challenge of Global Warming*, Washington, DC: Island.

Ruitenbeek, H. (1992) 'The rainforest supply price: a tool for evaluating rainforest conservation expenditures' *Ecological Economics*, 6(1), 57–78.

Smith, Z. (1992) *The Environmental Policy Paradox*, New Jersey: Prentice Hall.

Spash, C. and N. Hanley (1994) 'Cost-benefit analysis and the greenhouse effect', Discussion papers in Ecological Economics 94/6, University of Stirling.

Tahvonen, O., V. Kaitala and M. Pohjola (1993) 'A Finnish–Soviet acid rain game: non-cooperative equilibria, cost efficiency and sulphur agreements', *Journal of Environmental Economics and Management*, 24, 87–99.

Tietenberg, T. (1994) *Environmental Economics and Policy*, New York: HarperCollins.

Titus, J. (1989) 'The cause and effects of sea level rise', in D. Abrahamson (ed.), *The Challenge of Global Warming*, Washington, DC: Island.

Van Ierland, E. (1989) 'Cost-benefit analysis and acidification in Europe', mimeo, Wageningen Agricultural University, Netherlands.

Webb, A.H., R.J. Bawden, A.K. Busby and J.N. Hopkins (1990) 'Studies on the effects of air pollution on limestone degradation in Great Britain', in *Acidic Deposition: Its nature and impacts*, The Royal Society of Edinburgh Conference Abstracts.

Welsh, H. (1988) 'A cost comparison for alternative sources for sulphur dioxide control', *Energy Economics*, October, 287–97.

Whalley, J. (1991) 'The interface between environmental and trade policies' *The Economic Journal*, 101 (March), 180–89.

Wiersma, D. (1991) 'Static and dynamic efficiency of pollution control strategies', *Environmental and Resource Economics*, 1, 63–82.

WMO/UNEP (World Meterological Organisation/United Nations Environment Programme) (1991) *Scientific Assessment of Stratospheric Ozone 1991*, WMO.

WRI (World Resources Institute) (1993) *Toward Sustainable Development: World Resources 1992–3*, New York: Oxford University Press.

Wright, R.F., R. Cosby, R. Ferrier, A. Jenkins and R. Harriman (1993) 'Regional surveys in 1979 and 1988 and evaluation of the MAGIC model', *Journal of Hydrology*, 2, 112–27.

■ *Chapter 7* ■

An Introduction to the Economics of Natural Resource Exploitation

7.1 Introduction
7.2 Elementary capital theory
7.3 The maximum principal of optimal control theory
7.4 The application of the maximum principle to specific fishery management problems

7.5 The discrete-time maximum principle and dynamic programming
7.6 Wiener processes, Itô's processes and stochastic calculus
7.7 Summary

■ *7.1* Introduction

This chapter introduces the economics of natural resource exploitation. The natural resources considered in this book are a diverse and complex group of factors of production, they include renewable resources such as fish populations and forests and non-renewable resources such as oil reserves and mineral deposits. In particular we analyse the rate at which a 'rational' firm should exploit such resources through time. This approach leads to normative issues about how society *should* exploit a resource efficiently and also to hypotheses of how firms *actually* behave.

The stock of a resource, in terms of the population of fish in a lake or the number of barrels of oil remaining in an oil field, measures the state of a natural resource. Renewable resource stocks are those, like fish, which grow through reproduction; non-renewable resources, such as oil, are available in fixed quantities. Harvesting or extraction is the rate of stock depletion during a particular time period. These attributes of natural resource exploitation have much in common with man-made capital goods; that is, produced means of production. Just as growth increases and harvesting depletes the stock of a natural resource, so depreciation decreases and investment increases the stock of man-made capital.

It is reasonable to suppose that the economics of natural resources has a basis in the economics of capital. Indeed, natural resource stocks might be viewed as capital goods with a set of specific characteristics which relate, in

177

the case of renewable resources, to biological growth and, in the case of non-renewable resources, to the existence of a finite stock and the characteristics of reserves held within geological structures.

Dorfman's defines capital theory as 'the economics of time. Its task is to explain if, and why, a lasting instrument of production can be expected to contribute more to the value of output during its lifetime than it costs to produce or acquire... it deduces both normative and descriptive conclusions about the time-path of the accumulation of capital by economic units and entire economies' (Dorfman, 1969, p. 817). Similarly, Bliss (1975) says: 'What we must capture in our theory to have it encompass capital is this intertemporal aspect of production and consumption. In this view, time is the essence of capital' (p. 4). Both authors emphasise the existence of capital through time as the attribute which distinguishes capital from other factors of production. The modern economic analysis of natural resource problems is considered by most authors to commence with the article by Hotelling (1931) which identifies the need for an intertemporal approach to exhaustible resource economics: 'the static equilibrium type of economic theory is plainly inadequate for an industry in which the indefinite maintenance of a steady state is a physical impossibility' (p. 139). In his seminal contribution to the analysis of renewable natural resources, Clark asserts: 'Recognizing the capital-theoretic nature of resource stocks is essential to a clear understanding of resource economics. From this viewpoint resource management simply becomes a special problem in capital theory, although it is an especially interesting and difficult problem' (Clark, 1990, p. 68).

Dorfman and Bliss make a strong case for adopting a comparative dynamic approach to the economics of capital accumulation; Hotelling argues for a comparative dynamic approach to the analysis of non-renewable resource problems and Clark considers natural resource stocks as capital. A comparative dynamic approach is different to the more familiar comparative static approach of intermediate microeconomics (see, for example, Varian, 1984). Comparative statics analysis assesses how the equilibrium values of the endogenous variables change with changes in exogenous variables. A comparative dynamic analysis considers how the whole *time path* of endogenous variables changes in response to changes in exogenous variables. However, a comparative static equilibrium may emerge in a comparative dynamic analysis as a special case: in renewable resources a steady state may be reached where the rate of biological growth equals the harvest rate.

This chapter approaches natural resource economics as a branch of applied capital theory, requiring an analytical framework which is dynamic and sufficiently general to approximate the geophysical, biological and economic elements of resource management problems. Unfortunately, this generality comes at a cost of increased complexity: the specification of a dynamic equilibrium is not as clear-cut as a static equilibrium. The key issue posed for the individual resource-extracting firm and for society as a whole is one of how much of a natural resource should be exploited now and how much left for the future. This has much in common with the trade-off encountered when a firm chooses between profit now or a capital investment which generates a stream of profits in the future.

The analysis in this chapter proceeds towards a general framework for natural resource analysis in three stages. In the first, the ideas are introduced by the simplest model of intertemporal equilibrium between two capital assets. This is applied to simple renewable and non-renewable resource problems. We then consider a dynamic multi-period model and derive the conditions for optimal resource exploitation through the maximum principle of optimal control theory. The next section extends the analysis to consider dynamic programming, which is equivalent to optimal control theory, but is a useful approach to real-world management problems. The final section extends the analysis to include uncertainty using a stochastic control framework.

The natural resource chapters in this book adopt, as far as possible, a common approach to resource economics. The perspective is predominantly one of normative microeconomics which considers which factors *should* affect the decisions of individual firms to extract a natural resource. The approach uses mathematical models extensively, but, to make some important concepts more accessible, we refer to specific natural resources, make use of specific functional forms for growth, cost and demand equations and use numerical examples. The more diligent reader is referred to the original sources for more rigorous treatments and mathematical proofs. This chapter sets out the mathematical tools required for the analysis of natural resources. It has a pivotal role in this part of the book and is an essential precursor to the chapters which follow.

■ 7.2 Elementary capital theory

□ 7.2.1 Introduction

Consider a durable asset, say a machine. Let v_t be the rent for its services during a period t and μ_t its price at the start of the period. Prices are measured relative to a numeraire asset, which is an investment, yielding a rate of return r_t. (For instance, this might be a bond or a deposit account or even another machine.) The rate of return is the opportunity cost of funds tied up in the machine. In equilibrium the firm is indifferent between holding the numeraire asset or holding machines. Since $1/\mu_t$ machines can be bought with a unit of numeraire asset each of which yields a rent v_{t+1} in period $t+1$ and can be sold for μ_{t+1}, in equilibrium the total return from buying machines $(v_{t+1} + \mu_{t+1})/\mu_t$ equals the total return from holding the numeraire asset

$$\frac{(v_{t+1} + \mu_{t+1})}{\mu_t} = 1 + r_{t+1} \tag{7.1}$$

Out of equilibrium the opportunity exists for making pure profits by arbitrage: either borrowing the numeraire to buy the durable asset or selling the durable asset and loaning out the proceeds. The *own rate of return* on the durable asset is the rental income divided by the price of the asset; this gives the rent in terms of the number of machines that rent will purchase. If the rate of return using the two accounting systems in terms of machines and in terms of numeraire asset is different, this can only be accounted for by a change in price. This leads to restating (7.1) as

$$v_{t+1} = r_{t+1}\mu_t - (\mu_{t+1} - \mu_t) \tag{7.2}$$

that is, a difference between the interest rates must be accounted for by a change in the price of the asset. If $v_{t+1} < r_{t+1}\mu_t$, the value of capital is appreciating, $\mu_{t+1} > \mu_t$. Conversely, if $v_{t+1} > r_{t+1}\mu_t$ the value of capital is depreciating, $\mu_{t+1} < \mu_t$. Equation (7.1) can be expressed in its more convenient continuous time form:

$$v(t) = r(t)\mu(t) - \dot{\mu}(t) \tag{7.3}$$

where $\dot{\mu}(t)$ is the time derivative for $\mu(t)$ and is the increase or decrease in the price of capital. In capital theory (7.3) is the short-run equation of yield (Dixit, 1976, p. 39) or the *arbitrage equation* (Dasgupta and Heal, 1979, pp. 105–7) which is the preferred term here. This equation can now be used to define equilibria in natural resource stocks.

☐ 7.2.2 Non-renewable natural resources

In the case of a non-renewable natural resource, which can be extracted costlessly, the stock is said to be sterile: that is, unlike the case of a machine, no benefit derives directly from holding the stock and the rental value is zero, $v(t) = 0$. Thus the own rate of return on the stock is zero. On this basis (7.3) is:

$$r(t) = \frac{\dot{\mu}(t)}{\mu(t)} \tag{7.4}$$

An equilibrium, where the firm is indifferent between holding the numeraire asset and the exhaustible natural resource, can only occur if the price of the asset appreciates, $\dot{\mu}(t) > 0$ at the own rate of return of the numeraire asset. This fundamental result is called Hotelling's rule and it defines the optimal extraction of non-renewable resources. Another way of considering Hotelling's rule is to imagine a firm precommiting itself to supply a resource over a number of time periods. The forward price agreed for each period would have to satisfy Hotelling's rule; that is, rise at least at the rate of return of the numeraire asset; otherwise the firm would be better off extracting the whole resource in the initial period and investing the proceeds in the numeraire asset.

□ 7.2.3 Renewable natural resources

The difference between non-renewable and renewable resources is that a renewable stock grows by reproduction. Before applying the arbitrage equation to renewable resources it is necessary to describe a growth function. In continuous time the stock grows according to the function

$$\dot{x}(t) = g(x(t), q(t), t) \tag{7.5}$$

where $x(t)$ is the stock and $q(t)$ is the rate of harvest. The logistic growth function, illustrated in Figure 7.1, is widely used in empirical analysis. (The logistic growth function and other growth functions are discussed in more detail in Chapter 10.) It has the characteristic that, at low stock rates, the rate of growth is low, it peaks at $\bar{x}$ and then declines towards zero as the ecosystem reaches its maximum carrying capacity $\tilde{x}$; that is for $0 < x < \tilde{x}$, $g_x > 0$ and $g_{xx} < 0$. (Subscripts are used here and elsewhere to indicate partial derivatives.)

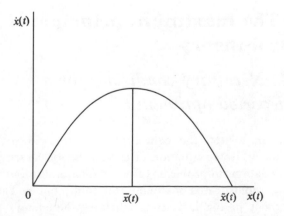

Figure 7.1 *Logistic growth curve*

At equilibrium the firm is indifferent between holding the last unit of natural resource and the amount of numeraire asset it would purchase. For our purposes here, assume an equilibrium has been reached where the growth in each period equals the harvest; that is $\dot{x} = g(x^*, q^*) = 0$. This is called a *steady-state* equilibrium. The total value of the stock over an infinite time horizon at a constant price with no harvest costs is:

$$W = \int_0^\infty pg(x^*, q^*)e^{-rt}\,dt = \frac{pg(x^*, q^*)}{r} \tag{7.6}$$

where r is the discount rate. (The integral (sum) of a convergent geometric progression over an infinite number of periods is given as $\int_0^\infty e^{-rt}\,dt = 1/r$. The term e^{-rt} is the continuous time discount factor.) Differentiating with respect to the stock gives the shadow price of stock:

$$\frac{dW}{dx^*} = \mu e^{-rt} = \frac{pg_x}{r} = \lambda \tag{7.7}$$

This defines the present-value shadow price of stock and its current-value equivalent $\lambda = \mu e^{-rt}$.

Equation (7.7) defines the condition for an equilibrium steady state

$$pg_x e^{rt} = \mu r \tag{7.8}$$

This is comparable with equation (7.3); $pg_x e^{rt}$ is the rent and the μ term is zero as the stock is assumed to be constant. The term g_x is of great importance: it indicates how the rate of stock growth changes with respect to the stock and it therefore represents the return on retaining the marginal unit of stock. It should be noted that in market equilibrium the market price of fish should equal the shadow price $p = \mu e^{-rt} = \lambda$ and $g_x = r$. Thus g_x is the own rate of return on the stock.

▌ 7.3 The maximum principle of optimal control theory

☐ 7.3.1 Necessary conditions for a multi-period optimum

The last section related the equilibrium solution to natural resource problems to the arbitrage equation of capital theory. Describing comparative dynamic solutions to problems of optimal natural resource exploitation requires more sophisticated mathematical tools, but is based upon the principles set out in the last section, namely Hotelling's rule for non-renewable resources and for renewable resources, that the marginal growth rate equals the discount rate. (The account given here is a brief intuitive account of the maximum principle. Readers who want a rigorous proof should refer to Beavis and Dobbs (1990, ch. 7) and those who require a longer introduction should refer to Chiang (1992). This section is based upon the approach adopted by Dorfman (1969).)

The aim is to establish necessary conditions for optimal resource extraction. To make the account more concrete, imagine a firm which owns a fishery. The firm possesses an initial stock of fish x_0 and wishes to maximise profits over a time interval which runs continuously from $t = 0$ to $t = T$. The population grows according to the function $\dot{x} = g(x(t), q(t), t)$ and profit is a function of fishing effort $q(t)$, the stock $x(t)$ and a discount factor e^{-rt}. Harvesting is costless. At each instant through time the profit function is $\pi(q(t), x(t), t) e^{-rt}$. Thus the total discounted profit derived by the firm over the time interval is as shown in equation (7.9). (In what follows the time argument will often be omitted; thus x is equivalent to $x(t)$. Where the subscript is used, as in x_0 or generally, x_t, this indicates the value of x at a given point in time.)

$$W(x_0, \mathbf{q}) = \int_0^T \pi(q, x, t) e^{-rt} \, dt \tag{7.9}$$

This is the sum of profit at each instant discounted to the initial date, starting with stock x_0 using the vector of harvest decisions, $\mathbf{q}$. The firm can choose the time path for the harvest rate, but the stock is determined by the initial stock, the growth function and previous harvest decisions. Finding an optimal solution to this problem appears formidable as it involves finding a vector of optimal harvest rates. Informally speaking, the approach to solving this problem is to reduce it to one of finding a solution to q at each point in time which takes account of the marginal value or shadow price of the stock harvested.

To this end we generalise (7.9) to start at an arbitrary date t, stock x_t using the vector, $\mathbf{q}$ until the end point T:

$$W(x_t, \mathbf{q}, t) = \int_t^T \pi[q, x, \tau] \, d\tau \tag{7.10}$$

where τ is the variable of integration. The expression has been simplified by incorporating the discount factor in the profit function. Now divide $W(\cdot)$ into two parts; profit earnt during an initial period of duration Δ and profit from the remaining time, $t + \Delta$ to T:

$$W(x_0, \mathbf{q}, t) = \pi[q_t, x_t, t]\Delta + \int_{t+\Delta}^T \pi[q, x, \tau] \, d\tau \tag{7.11}$$

or, more concisely,

$$W(x_0, \mathbf{q}, t) = \pi[q_t, x, t]\Delta + W(x_{t+\Delta}, \mathbf{q}, t + \Delta) \tag{7.12}$$

The value from an optimal choice of **q** is given by J:

$$J(x_t, t) = \text{maximum } W(x_t, \mathbf{q}, t) \tag{7.13}$$

Note that **q** has been maximised out of $J(\cdot)$. $J(\cdot)$ gives the maximum value derived by proceeding from x_t at time t to the end of the planning horizon. Rewrite (7.13) as the profit during the current period plus all future periods:

$$J(x_t, t) = \text{maximum } \{\pi[q_t, x_t, t]\Delta + J(x_{t+\Delta}, t + \Delta)\} \tag{7.14}$$

Differentiate (7.14) with respect to the decision variable q_t and set equal to zero. (This is a necessary condition which only identifies a maximum when other conditions hold, but for our purposes here we assume that the first derivative with respect to q_t is indeed at a maximum when the partial derivative is zero. Assume $\pi(\cdot)$ and $J(\cdot)$ are continuous, twice differentiable and concave.) This gives

$$\Delta \frac{\partial \pi}{\partial q_t} = -\frac{\partial J(x_{t+\Delta}, t + \Delta)}{\partial q_t} \tag{7.15}$$

For an optimal harvest, the marginal profit in the initial period equals the marginal reduction in the total profit over the remaining periods or the shadow price.

The second term in (7.15) is expanded by noting that $J(\cdot)$ does not involve q_t explicitly; however, by the chain rule

$$\frac{\partial J(x_{t+\Delta}, t + \Delta)}{\partial q_t} = \frac{\partial J(x_{t+\Delta}, t + \Delta)}{\partial x_{t+\Delta}} \frac{\partial x_{t+\Delta}}{\partial q_t} \tag{7.16}$$

To clarify this expression, define the costate variable as

$$\lambda(t) = \frac{\partial J(x_t, t)}{\partial x_t} \tag{7.17}$$

where $\lambda(t)$ is the marginal value of stock; it is equivalent to λ in (7.7).

By definition,

$$x(t + \Delta) = x(t) + \Delta \dot{x}(t) \tag{7.18}$$

that is, the amount of stock at $t + \Delta$ is equal to amount of stock at t plus the rate of change of stock multiplied by the duration of the interval. Recalling that stock growth is $\dot{x} = g(x, q, t)$, (7.16) can be restated as:

$$\frac{\partial J(x_{t+\Delta}, t + \Delta)}{\partial q_t} = \lambda(t + \Delta)\Delta \frac{\partial g}{\partial q} \tag{7.19}$$

Equivalently to (7.18)

$$\lambda(t + \Delta) = \lambda_t + \Delta \dot{\lambda}_t$$

inserting this result into (7.19) and cancelling out the common factor Δ gives

$$\frac{\partial \pi}{\partial q_t} + \lambda_t \frac{\partial g}{\partial q} + \dot{\lambda}_t \Delta \frac{\partial g}{\partial x_t} = 0 \tag{7.20}$$

if Δ approaches zero then the third term becomes negligibly small compared to the other two. This gives the necessary condition that

$$\frac{\partial \pi}{\partial q_t} = -\lambda_t \frac{\partial g}{\partial q} \tag{7.21}$$

This is the continuous time version of (7.15) and it has the same intuitive interpretation, that the marginal profit equals the marginal value of stock. It remains to establish how the shadow price of stock, λ changes through time. If we differentiate (7.14) with respect to x and simplify, the resulting expression gives the costate condition:

$$-\dot{\lambda} = \frac{\partial \pi}{\partial x} + \lambda \frac{\partial g}{\partial x} \tag{7.22}$$

The term on the left-hand side, $\dot{\lambda}$, gives the rate at which the present value of the shadow price changes. Equation (7.22) is a more general form of the arbitrage equation (7.3) which ensures that, given the shadow price λ, the firm is indifferent between holding the last unit of stock or selling the stock and investing in the numeraire asset. This condition is termed 'portfolio balance' by Neher (1990, p. 26) as it represents the firm's equilibrium between holding the natural resource stock and the numeraire asset.

The correspondence between (7.3) and (7.22) can be demonstrated by converting (7.3) to a present-value form by substituting $\mu = \lambda e^{rt}$. Thus (7.3) becomes $v(t) = r\lambda e^{rt} - (\dot{\lambda} e^{rt} + r\lambda e^{rt})$ or, after simplification, $v(t) e^{-rt} = -\dot{\lambda}$. Thus the right-hand side of (7.22) gives the present-value of the stock rent. This has two components a current profit component, $\partial \pi / \partial x$ and stock growth component $\lambda(\partial g / \partial x)$.

The necessary conditions can be represented more succinctly by introducing the Hamiltonian function, $H(\cdot)$.

$$H[q, x, \lambda, t] = \pi[q, x, t] + \lambda g(x, q, t) \tag{7.23}$$

This function is equal to the profit plus the change in the stock valued by its shadow price. The Hamiltonian allows a convenient representation of the necessary conditions which comprise the maximum principle: first differentiate $H(\cdot)$ with respect to q

$$\frac{\partial H}{\partial q} = 0 \tag{7.24}$$

which is condition (7.21), where the Hamiltonian is maximised with respect to q. In addition, (7.22) is given as

$$\frac{\partial H}{\partial x} = -\dot{\lambda} \tag{7.25}$$

the costate condition.

The two necessary conditions and the equation of motion, $\dot{x} = g(x, q, t)$ define a system of differential equations which, if they satisfy sufficiency conditions, define an optimal solution. However, two further conditions are required; these concern the starting-point and end-point of the time path for the state variable and are called *transversality conditions*, discussed in the next sub-section.

The reader may be curious as to how control theory relates to static constrained optimisation and the usual approach of maximising a Lagrangean composite function. This is straightforward once it is recognised that the Lagrangean multiplier or costate variable ensures that the equation of motion is satisfied. Thus the maximum value function as defined in (7.13) is:

$$J(x(0), 0) = \text{maximum} \int_0^T \{\pi[q, x, t] + \lambda[g(x, q, t) - \dot{x}]\} \, dt \tag{7.26}$$

that is, the maximum value over the planning horizon is the integral of the profit plus a constraint on stock. The next step is to integrate the term, $\lambda \dot{x}$, by parts (see Chiang, 1984, p. 445)

$$\int_0^T \lambda \dot{x} \, dt = -\int_0^T \dot{\lambda} x \, dt - \lambda(0)x_0 + \lambda(T)x_T$$

substituting this result into (7.26) and redefining the first two terms as the Hamiltonian

$$J(x(0), 0) = \text{maximum} \int_0^T \{H[q, x, \lambda, t] + \dot{\lambda}x\} \, dt + \lambda(0)x_0 - \lambda(T)x_T \tag{7.27}$$

It is left to the reader to confirm that differentiating (7.27) with respect to q and x results in the necessary conditions (7.24) and (7.25). In fact the Hamiltonian is little more than a device for remembering the necessary conditions for maximising the Lagrangean (7.26) without having to write it down explicitly. The Lagrangean (7.26) is used extensively in the literature – see, for instance, Kamien and Schwartz (1990) – as an approach for deriving necessary conditions for control problems with a range of different transversality conditions and constraints on the control variable. We now turn to consider transversality conditions.

☐ 7.3.2 *Transversality conditions*

The detailed specification of all the starting-point and end-point conditions encountered in optimal control problems would require more space than is available here. Leonard and Van Long (1992, pp. 221–62) devote a whole chapter to the subject and identify 12 such conditions. The account here is confined to transversality conditions which are relevant in the analysis of most renewable and non-renewable resource problems.

There are three essential attributes of transversality conditions; the first specifies constraints on the state variable, the second is whether the terminal time is fixed or free and the third concerns the presence of a 'scrap-value' function which places a value on the stock at the terminal time. In this sub-section we confine attention to end-point conditions and make the assumption that the initial time and initial stock are fixed.

First assume that the terminal time is fixed and, end-point conditions on the stock correspond with conditions upon the costate variable at the end of the planning horizon, $\lambda(T)$. If the stock is unconstrained, it has a zero value at the end of the planning horizon:

$$\lambda(T) = 0$$

By definition this is true: if the costate variable had a positive value this implies profit would be increased by further exploiting the stock. This is also the case with an infinite time horizon, as the discount factor ensures the present value of stock declines asymptotically to zero as $\lim t \to \infty$; thus $\lambda(\infty) = 0$. This form of transversality condition is widely used in theoretical models.

Second if the constraint upon the stock is as a weak inequality, that is, $x(T) \geq x_T$, the above is modified as a Kuhn–Tucker condition, (see the technical note on pp. 98–103). We require that

$$\lambda(T) \geq 0 \quad \text{and} \quad [x(T) - x_T]\lambda(T) = 0$$

that is, either the constraint is binding and the stock equals the constraint, x_T, or the costate variable at the end of the planning horizon is zero.

Thirdly where a scrap value exists, $B(x(T))$, the costate value equals the marginal scrap value of stock

$$\lambda(T) = \frac{\partial B}{\partial x(T)}$$

The first transversality condition applies to renewable resource problems where it is reasonable to assume in theoretical models that the terminal time can be fixed at infinity. This eliminates the transversality condition and allows the solution to reach a steady state. In applied analysis the use of 'scrap value' functions may be appropriate if, for instance, a firm who rents a resource, say a fishery is paid compensation based on the estimated stock size when the lease expires. This tends to complicate the comparative dynamic analysis as the transversality condition affects the optimal stock trajectory.

Non-renewable resource problems require a different form of transversality condition. The terminal time, when the resource is no longer extracted, is always finite, but it is also undetermined; that is, the terminal time is free. The transversality condition can be derived from first principles from (7.27). If there is a free choice over T, then it will be chosen to maximise the value function, thus if we differentiate (7.27) with respect to T and set equal to zero:

$$J(x(0), 0) = \mathrm{H}[\tilde{q}(T), \tilde{x}(T), \lambda(T), T] + \dot{\lambda}(T)\tilde{x}(T)$$

$$+ \int_0^T \left\{ (\mathrm{H}_x + \dot{\lambda}) \frac{d\tilde{x}}{dT} + \mathrm{H}_q \frac{d\tilde{q}}{dT} \right\} dt - \frac{d\lambda(T)}{dT} x_T = 0$$

The notation is simplified by setting q and x to their optimal values $\tilde{q}$ and $\tilde{x}$. The third term on the right-hand side in braces includes the maximum principle conditions which at the optimal solution must be zero, so the integral is zero. Further, $\dot{\lambda}(T)\tilde{x}(T) = [d\lambda(T)/dT]x_T$ by definition, thus the transversality condition for a free terminal time becomes:

$$\mathrm{H}[\tilde{q}(T), \tilde{x}(T), \lambda(T), T] = \pi[\tilde{q}(T), \tilde{x}(T), T] + \lambda(T)g(\tilde{x}(T), \tilde{q}(T), T) = 0$$

For instance, in the case of a non-renewable resource problem $g(x(t), q(t), t) = -q$; thus the terminal time is where $\pi[q(T), x(T), T] = \lambda(T)q(T)$; that is, the profit in the last period equals the marginal value of stock extracted. In other words, the Hamiltonian at the terminal time equals zero.

☐ 7.3.3 *The current-value Hamiltonian*

The economic analysis of comparative dynamic problems employs two forms of Hamiltonian: the present-value Hamiltonian given in (7.23), where the profit is discounted, and the current-value Hamiltonian where the profit and the shadow price are measured as their current value. The relationship between the two forms is given by

$$H \equiv \mathrm{H} e^{rt}$$

the current-value Hamiltonian, H is identically equal to the present-value Hamiltonian, H, compounded. In an expanded form

$$H(x, q, t) \equiv f(x, q, t) + \mu g(x, q, t) \equiv \mathrm{H}(x, q, t) e^{rt} \equiv [f(x, q, t) e^{-rt} + \lambda g(x, q, t)] e^{rt}$$

where $\mu = \lambda e^{rt}$. Recall that the maximum principle requires that the present-value Hamiltonian is maximised in each period. Thus the value of q which maximises $\mathrm{H}(\cdot)$ also maximises $H(\cdot)$ as the term e^{rt} is a constant for any given time period. Thus the first-order condition is:

$$H_q = 0$$

The costate condition involves the time derivative of λ. To derive an expression for this note

$$\mu = \lambda e^{rt}$$

thus by the product rule

$$\dot{\lambda} = \dot{\mu} e^{-rt} - r\mu e^{-rt}$$

Further

$$-H_x e^{-rt} = -H_x$$

thus the costate condition in terms of the current-value Hamiltonian is:

$$\dot{\mu} - r\mu = -H_x$$

The two forms of the Hamiltonian are used interchangeably in this book, depending on which gives the clearer representation of a particular problem. However, it is necessary to be clear which form is being used as the costate condition is different.

7.4 The application of the maximum principle to specific fishery management problems

The purpose of this section is to introduce some of the mathematical concepts required in later chapters in the context of two simple fishery models. Fishery problems are chosen to make the account more accessible. The important lessons in this section concern the application of optimal control theory and not the specific implications for fishery economics, which is the subject of Chapter 10.

The solutions to optimal resource exploitation problems presented in this section are termed 'open-loop control'. They represent once-and-for-all solutions to dynamic optimisation problems which are as if the firm decides in the initial period what to do for all future periods and sticks to that plan. This type of decision making is appropriate for most of the decision making problems posed here and in later resource chapters, but not all. There is a growing literature on the use of closed-loop or feedback optimal control; this is where the decision a firm takes at a point during the time interval is contingent upon the state variables which describe the system. This type of decision making is of particular importance when a strategic interaction exists between a small number of firms; in this case, the decision taken may depend upon what other firms are observed to do and there is no clear rule for saying exactly what they *are* going to do at the beginning of the time interval. Examples of closed-loop control are considered briefly in Chapters 9 and 10. This chapter is exclusively concerned with open-loop control.

☐ 7.4.1 *A linear fishery problem*

In this example a firm owns a fishery, can catch fish at zero cost and sells the fish in a competitive market at a fixed price p. The firm aims to maximise profit over an infinite time interval. The objective function is to

$$\text{maximise}_q \quad \int_0^\infty pq\,e^{-rt}\,dt$$

$$\text{subject to} \quad \dot{x} = g(x, q, t) \qquad x(0) = x_0$$

(The format maximise$_q$, means maximise with respect to q.) The Hamiltonian function (see 7.23) for the problem is as follows. (From here on the time subscript, (t) will be omitted to clarify the exposition. It should be assumed that the variables, x, q and λ all have time subscripts. In some instances a value at a specific time period is referred to; for instance, $x(0)$ refers to the initial stock. These should be clear from the context.)

$$H(x, q, \lambda, t) = pq\,e^{-rt} + \lambda g(x, q, t)$$

Differentiating this with respect to q and setting equal to zero,

$$pe^{-rt} + \lambda g_q = 0$$

and the costate condition is

$$\dot{\lambda} = -\lambda g_x \tag{7.28}$$

Assuming a logistic growth function

$$g(x, q, t) = ax + bx^2 - q \qquad a > 0; \quad b < 0$$

these conditions become, when the specific functional forms are included,

$$pe^{-rt} = \lambda \tag{7.29}$$

and

$$\dot{\lambda} = -\lambda(a + 2bx) \tag{7.30}$$

The procedure now is to eliminate the costate variable and define a steady-state solution.

To this end, differentiate (7.29) with respect to time

$$\dot{\lambda} = -rp\,e^{-rt}$$

equate with the (7.30) and eliminate λ using (7.29) to define a steady-state equilibrium

$$r = (a + 2bx) = g_x$$

This is a specific form of the arbitrage equation for renewable resources (7.8). It is worth noting the step above where the derivative of the Hamiltonian with respect to the control variable, q, is then differentiated with respect to time to give an expression for λ. This is almost invariably the trick required to eliminate the costate variable.

The problem is a *linear control problem*, as the Hamiltonian function is linear in the control variable, q. In equilibrium, the growth is harvested; thus $g(x^*, q^*) = 0$. If the stock is out of equilibrium, nothing is harvested when $x < x^*$ and the maximum is harvested $q = q_{max}$ when $x > x^*$, until the equilibrium is established. This is called 'bang-bang' control. These conditions are summarised by defining a switching function:

$$s(t) = p e^{-rt} - \lambda = H_q$$

if $s(t) = 0$ then $q = q^*$, if $s(t) > 0$ then $q = q_{max}$ and if $s(t) < 0$ then $q = 0$.

☐ 7.4.2 A non-linear fishery problem

The linear control problem is a special case of optimal control which is characterised by a bang-bang solution. In our next model (Clark, 1990, p. 97) the firm is a monopoly. The growth function is a continuous-time logistic and the demand function is linear. The firm aims to maximise its profit subject to the stock; there is no constraint on the catch in a period and catching fish is costless. Mathematically the problem is

$$\text{maximise}_q \quad \int_0^\infty R(q) e^{-rt} dt \tag{7.31}$$

$$\text{subject to} \quad \dot{x} = g(x, q, t) \qquad x(0) = x_0$$

where q is the harvest rate at time t, x is the stock, $R(\cdot)$ is a revenue function and $g(\cdot)$ is a logistic growth function of the form

$$g(x, q, t) = ax + bx^2 - q \qquad a > 0; \quad b < 0$$

The revenue function can be written as

$$R(q) = f(q)q$$

where $f(\cdot)$ is the inverse demand function.

First define the Hamiltonian (see (7.23))

$$H(x, q, \lambda, t) = R(q) e^{-rt} + \lambda g(x, q, t)$$

differentiate with respect to q and set equal to zero (see (7.24))

$$R'(q)e^{-rt} + \lambda g_q = 0 \qquad (7.32)$$

and the complementary costate condition is (see (7.25))

$$-\dot{\lambda} = \lambda g_x \qquad (7.33)$$

The costate variable is not of direct interest, so (7.32) and (7.33) are used to eliminate it. In the same series of manipulations, the time variable is also eliminated so that results can be expressed independently of time.

First write (7.32) explicitly for the logistic growth function

$$R'(q)e^{-rt} - \lambda = 0 \qquad (7.34)$$

and note that this implies that harvest continues until the marginal profit equals the marginal value of stock, λ. Differentiate (7.34) with respect to time

$$\dot{\lambda} = -rR'(q)e^{-rt} + R''(q)\dot{q}e^{-rt}$$

factor out $R'(q)e^{-rt}$

$$\dot{\lambda} = R'(q)e^{-rt}\left[-r + \frac{R''(q)}{R'(q)}\dot{q}\right]$$

replace $R'(q)e^{-rt}$ with λ from (7.34) and $\dot{\lambda}$ with $-\lambda g_x$ from (7.33) to give

$$-\lambda g_x = \lambda\left[-r + \frac{R''(q)}{R'(q)}\dot{q}\right]$$

Cancel λ and rearrange

$$\dot{q} = (r - g_x)\frac{R'(q)}{R''(q)} \qquad (7.35)$$

This implies that $\dot{q} = 0$ when $g_x = r$, which is a form of the arbitrage equation given in (7.8). The system of differential equations is completed by the growth equation

$$\dot{x} = g(x, q) = ax + bx^2 - q \qquad (7.36)$$

This is the required result: it represents the problem as two autonomous differential equations, (7.35) and the equation of motion (7.36). (Autonomous differential equations are independent of time.) These equations are used, first, to find the optimal harvest rate given initial conditions (x_0, q_0), second to determine a steady-state solution to the problem (x^*, q^*) where $\dot{q} = 0$ and $\dot{x} = 0$ and third, to assess the stability of the steady state. A steady-state solution may be viewed as the comparative static solution to the dynamic problem where the stock and the harvest rate are constant and no incentive exists to adjust them.

☐ 7.4.3 Phase-plane diagram

A phase-plane diagram represents the solution of dynamic problems such as that described by (7.35) and (7.36). The diagram is presented with the decision variable q on the vertical axis and the state variable, x on the horizontal axis. Two *isoclines* are drawn which join points where the differential equation has the same value: here the isoclines $\dot{q} = 0$ and $\dot{x} = 0$ are of particular interest as they cross at a steady-state solution to the system.

The $\dot{x} = 0$ isocline is derived from (7.35); it joins points where the harvest equals the growth rate

$$ax + bx^2 = q$$

The $\dot{q} = 0$ isocline is where the change in the growth rate with respect to the stock, g_x, equals the interest rate, this is seen from the term in the brackets on the right-hand side of (7.35). This point is independent of the harvest rate and thus is a vertical line. It is noteworthy that the equilibrium is only at the point of the maximum sustainable yield, $\bar{x}$, when the interest rate is zero. Figure 7.2 is the phase-plane diagram which represents the steady-state solution.

☐ 7.4.4 Stability

When a steady-state equilibrium to a dynamic system has been identified, it is important to assess if the solution is stable when subjected to slight perturbations to the steady state: does the system diverge from the

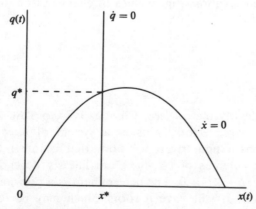

Figure 7.2 *Phase-plane diagram*

equilibrium or return to it rapidly when perturbed? This gives a qualitative understanding of whether or not the system converges upon the steady state and if it is sensitive to slight perturbations of the stock and harvest rate. The stability of a renewable resource exploitation problem may be of importance in policy making: a system which is prone to instability, which may lead to the destruction of the resource, must be managed more carefully than one which is inherently stable. In practice this is a complex issue. The ecological literature, notably Holling (1973) indicates that an ecosystem may be unstable but resilient; this is where the populations fluctuate but do not collapse irreversibly. In other words the basic linkages within the ecosystem remain intact. By contrast an ecosystem may be stable but lack resilience to environmental perturbations.

Take the dynamic system described above by the differential equations (7.35) and (7.36). These equations can be written as

$$\dot{q} = v(x, q) \qquad \dot{x} = \xi(x, q) \tag{7.37}$$

The steady state is where $v(x^*, q^*) = \xi(x^*, q^*) = 0$. If the functions, $v(\cdot)$ and $\xi(\cdot)$ are smooth the system of differential equations can be approximated by the first-order Taylor series expansion:

$$\dot{q} \cong v_q(x - x^*) + v_x(q - q^*) \qquad \dot{x} \cong \xi_q(x - x^*) + \xi_x(q - q^*) \tag{7.38}$$

where the partial derivatives are evaluated at (x^*, q^*).

As a Jacobian matrix the partial derivatives are given by

$$B = \begin{bmatrix} v_q & v_x \\ \xi_q & \xi_x \end{bmatrix}$$

Stability is indicated by the eigenvalues of the matrix of partial derivatives, at the steady-state solution. Eigenvalues or characteristic roots φ solve

$$B\gamma = \varphi\gamma \tag{7.39}$$

or

$$(B - \varphi I)\gamma = 0 \tag{7.40}$$

where I is an identity matrix (see, Chiang, 1984, p. 326). Box 7.1 revises eigenvalues and eigenvectors. This is a system of n equations and n unknowns. It has a non–trivial solution (that is, other than $\gamma = 0$), if and only if the columns of $(B - \varphi I)$ are linearly dependent; that is, if the determinant $|B - \varphi I| = 0$. The determinant is a polynomial expression to the nth degree. It will have n roots which may be real or complex numbers.

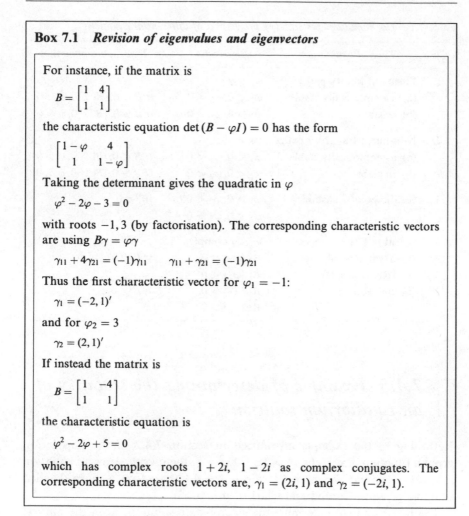

Box 7.1 *Revision of eigenvalues and eigenvectors*

For instance, if the matrix is

$$B = \begin{bmatrix} 1 & 4 \\ 1 & 1 \end{bmatrix}$$

the characteristic equation $\det(B - \varphi I) = 0$ has the form

$$\begin{bmatrix} 1 - \varphi & 4 \\ 1 & 1 - \varphi \end{bmatrix}$$

Taking the determinant gives the quadratic in φ

$$\varphi^2 - 2\varphi - 3 = 0$$

with roots $-1, 3$ (by factorisation). The corresponding characteristic vectors are using $B\gamma = \varphi\gamma$

$$\gamma_{11} + 4\gamma_{21} = (-1)\gamma_{11} \qquad \gamma_{11} + \gamma_{21} = (-1)\gamma_{21}$$

Thus the first characteristic vector for $\varphi_1 = -1$:

$$\gamma_1 = (-2, 1)'$$

and for $\varphi_2 = 3$

$$\gamma_2 = (2, 1)'$$

If instead the matrix is

$$B = \begin{bmatrix} 1 & -4 \\ 1 & 1 \end{bmatrix}$$

the characteristic equation is

$$\varphi^2 - 2\varphi + 5 = 0$$

which has complex roots $1 + 2i$, $1 - 2i$ as complex conjugates. The corresponding characteristic vectors are, $\gamma_1 = (2i, 1)$ and $\gamma_2 = (-2i, 1)$.

Consider the case of a $2 \times 2 B$ matrix:

$$|B - \varphi I| = \begin{vmatrix} v_q - \varphi & v_x \\ \xi_q & \xi_x - \varphi \end{vmatrix} = \varphi^2 - \text{tr } B\varphi + |B| = 0 \tag{7.41}$$

where the trace of the matrix, $\text{tr } B = v_q + \xi_x$.

Defining $\phi = (\text{tr } B)^2 - 4|B|$, the roots are

$$\varphi = (\text{tr } B \pm \phi^{\frac{1}{2}})/2$$

Eigenvalues are real if $\phi > 0$ and complex if $\phi < 0$. The terms of (7.41) identify the type of solution and whether or not it is stable. These are summarised in Table 7.1 and the different forms of trajectory are illustrated in the phase-plane diagrams in Figure 7.3; see Beavis and Dobbs (1990, p. 157) for a more detailed account.

Table 7.1   *The conditions for stability in systems of differential equations*

Case	Type of equilibrium	Eigenvalues	Trace, determinant, ϕ
1.	Linear trajectory paths	$\varphi_1 = \varphi_2$	
	(a) asymptotically stable	$\varphi_1 < 0, \varphi_2 < 0$	$\operatorname{tr} B < 0, |B| > 0, \phi = 0$
	(b) unstable	$\varphi_1 > 0, \varphi_2 > 0$	$\operatorname{tr} B > 0, |B| > 0, \phi = 0$
2.	Non-linear trajectory paths	$\varphi_1 \neq \varphi_2$	
	(a) asymptotically stable	$\varphi_1 < 0, \varphi_2 < 0$	$\operatorname{tr} B < 0, |B| > 0, \phi > 0$
	(b) unstable	$\varphi_1 < 0, \varphi_2 < 0$	$\operatorname{tr} B > 0, |B| > 0, \phi > 0$
3.	Saddle points, unstable	$\varphi_1 > 0, \varphi_2 < 0$ or $\varphi_1 < 0, \varphi_2 > 0$	$|B| < 0$
4.	Spiral points	φ_1, φ_2 complex	
	(a) asymptotically stable (Re: real part)	$\operatorname{Re}(\varphi_1) < 0,$ $\operatorname{Re}(\varphi_2) < 0$	$\operatorname{tr} B < 0, \phi < 0$
	(b) unstable	$\operatorname{Re}(\varphi_1) > 0,$ $\operatorname{Re}(\varphi_2) > 0$	$\operatorname{tr} B > 0, \phi < 0$

7.4.5 *Example of determining the stability of an equilibrium solution*

Returning to the example introduced in section 7.4.2, if the population growth function is $\dot{x} = g(x, q) = 1x - 1x^2 - q$, the inverse demand equation is $p = 1 - 1q$, and the discount rate is $r = 0.1$ (based on a more detailed example given in Conrad and Clark, 1987, p. 55).

The first step is to determine the steady-state solution, from the harvest differential equation this is found where $g_x = r$; that is, $1 - 2x = 0.1$, so $x^* = 0.45$. This is then substituted into the growth equation to give the growth rate, so that in a steady state the harvest rate equals the growth rate; thus $q^* = 0.2475$.

The second step is to assess the nature of this steady-state solution using the conditions in Table 7.1. Ideally, it would be preferable to determine the qualitative nature of the steady state from the derivatives of functions $v(\cdot)$ and $\xi(\cdot)$. However, the precise nature of a solution may be ambiguous on the basis of the analytical derivatives alone. If this is the case, the nature of the solution can only be assessed for specific numerical solutions or parameter values. We return to this point later in this section.

Proceed by defining the matrix B as in section 7.4.4, by evaluating the derivative at the steady-state solution (x^*, q^*), then find the determinant,

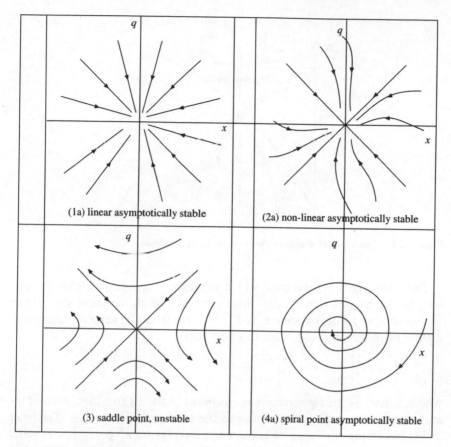

Figure 7.3 *Trajectory types*

trace and eigenvalues of B. The following gives the matrix of derivatives evaluated at the steady-state solution:

$$\begin{bmatrix} v_q & v_x \\ \xi_q & \xi_x \end{bmatrix} = \begin{bmatrix} 0 & -0.504 \\ -1 & 0.1 \end{bmatrix}$$

The eigenvalues $\varphi_1 = -0.662$ and $\varphi_2 = 0.762$ indicate, from Table 7.1, that the steady-state solution is a saddle point. It is represented by the phase-plane diagram (Figure 7.4) which is a geometric analysis of the behaviour of the dynamic system. The phase-plane diagram is constructed by identifying the isoclines, $\dot{x} = 0$ and $\dot{q} = 0$, which divide the space into regions where the trajectories move in a particular direction. There are also special trajectories – called separatrices – which converge upon the steady-state solution as $t \to \infty$; they represent solutions where the stock and the harvest rate reach the steady-state solution.

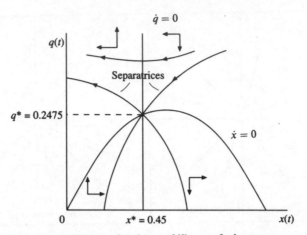

Figure 7.4   *Phase-plane diagram showing stability analysis*

The convergent separatrices, which represent the optimal solution, can only be determined numerically. First approximate the solution around the steady state as a linear system as in (7.38); then from the solution to a linear system of differential equations this becomes:

$$\begin{bmatrix} q - q^* \\ x - x^* \end{bmatrix} = c_1 \begin{bmatrix} \gamma_{11} \\ \gamma_{21} \end{bmatrix} e^{\varphi_1 t} + c_2 \begin{bmatrix} \gamma_{12} \\ \gamma_{22} \end{bmatrix} e^{\varphi_2 t}$$

where γ_1 and γ_2 the eigenvectors correspond to the eigenvalues, φ_1, and φ_2 and constants, c_1 and c_2. Returning to the example, $\varphi_1 < 0 < \varphi_2$. The term $e^{\varphi_2 t}$ is increasing with time, thus for x to converge on x^* parameter c_2 must equal zero. Thus for the initial value of the separatrices the relationship holds

$$q(0) = c_1 \gamma_{11} + q^* \tag{7.42}$$

$$x(0) = c_1 \gamma_{21} + x^* \tag{7.43}$$

This is the condition that the initial values of the stable separatrices are proportional to the eigenvector associated with the negative eigenvalue (see Beavis and Dobbs, 1990, p. 159, for a proof). With reference to our example, if we choose a point close to the steady state for $x(0)$, for instance $x(0) = 0.40$, it is possible to determine $q(0)$. The eigenvector is derived as:

$$\begin{bmatrix} 0 - \varphi & -0.504 \\ -1 & 0.1 - \varphi_1 \end{bmatrix} \begin{bmatrix} \gamma_{11} \\ \gamma_{21} \end{bmatrix} = 0$$

that is, $\gamma_1 = (0.762, 1)$. The eigenvector is normalised so as to make the largest element equal one. Eigenvector γ_1 determines the convergent separatrices and an initial value for the harvest is derived by solving

(7.43) for $c_1 = -0.05$ and then (7.42) to give $q(0) = 0.2094$. The term γ_{11} gives the slope of the separatrix as it approaches the equilibrium. This is confirmed by

$$\frac{(q^* - q_0)}{(x^* - x_0)} = \frac{c_1\gamma_{11}}{c_1\gamma_{21}} = \frac{(0.2475 - 0.2094)}{(0.45 - 0.40)} = 0.762$$

It should be noted that this trajectory is a linear approximation of a non-linear trajectory and the accuracy of the approximation declines as points are chosen further away from the equilibrium value. However, once an initial point on the convergent separatrix away from the equilibrium has been determined, it is possible to solve the original differential equations backwards to trace out the remainder of the trajectory. The equations are reversed by changing the signs of (7.35) and (7.36) and solving numerically.

This approach to assessing stability is acceptable in applied problems where parameter values are known; it is more restrictive where only the form of the functions is known. Reconsider the Jacobian matrix with the signs of the partial derivatives next to it:

$$B = \begin{bmatrix} v_q & v_x \\ \xi_q & \xi_x \end{bmatrix} \begin{bmatrix} 0 & - \\ -1 & + \end{bmatrix}$$

For instance, the derivative of the differential equation for the harvest rate, v_x, changes negatively with respect to the stock and the partial derivative with respect to the harvest rate is zero. From this it is possible to sign the determinant $|B| < 0$, and the trace $\text{tr}(B) > 0$. Thus $\phi = (\text{tr}(B)^2 - 4|B| > 0$ and the eigenvalues are real and of opposite signs, which indicates a saddle point solution. In more detail we have

$$\varphi_1 = (\text{tr}(B) + \phi^{\frac{1}{2}})/2$$

which is clearly positive,

$$\varphi_2 = (\text{tr}(B) - \phi^{\frac{1}{2}})/2$$

which in full is

$$\varphi_2 = \xi_x - (\xi_x^2 - 4v_x)^{\frac{1}{2}}$$

and, as $v_x < 0$ and $(\xi_x^2 - 4v_x)^{\frac{1}{2}} > \xi_x$, is negative. This confirms that the steady state is indeed a saddle point.

☐ 7.4.6 Sufficiency conditions

It is usual in static optimisation problems to check that the solution identified by the necessary conditions is indeed a maximum or a minimum.

The approach adopted for dynamic problems is more restrictive in that the check is on the form of the original functions to see if the maximum principle conditions are both *necessary* and *sufficient*. This is directly analogous to the Arrow–Enthoven sufficiency theorem discussed in the technical note on pp. 98–103 which runs through a 'health check' on the functions in the problem which ensures that the Kuhn–Tucker conditions are both necessary and sufficient.

Here we discuss the more general Arrow sufficiency conditions. See Chiang (1992, pp. 217–19) for a more detailed discussion and Kamien and Schwartz (1971) for a proof. The test of sufficiency is applied to the fishery problem. Given values of x, λ, and t, the value of q which maximises the Hamiltonian function is a function of these variables:

$$\tilde{q} = \theta(x, \lambda, t)$$

When this value is substituted into the Hamiltonian we have

$$\tilde{H}(x, \lambda, t) = R(\tilde{q}) e^{-rt} + \lambda g(x, \tilde{q}, t)$$

where q has been maximised out of the function. Arrow's theorem states that, if the maximum principle conditions are to be both necessary and sufficient the maximised Hamiltonian must be concave in x for any given λ.

Using the functional forms given in the fishery example we maximise the Hamiltonian with respect to q by taking the first derivative and setting equal to zero; thus

$$\tilde{H}_q = [a - 2bq] e^{-rt} - \lambda = 0$$

and thus

$$\tilde{q} = \theta(\lambda, t) = \frac{1}{2b} [a - \lambda e^{rt}]$$

Here $\tilde{q}$ is independent of x. This allows q to be eliminated from the maximised Hamiltonian:

$$\tilde{H}(x, \lambda, t) = R(\theta(\lambda, t)) e^{-rt} + \lambda g(x, \theta(\lambda, t), t)$$

It is now a matter of showing that this function is concave in x. This is achieved by checking that the second derivative of the maximised Hamiltonian with respect to x is non-positive:

$$\frac{\partial^2 \tilde{H}}{\partial x^2} = \lambda 2b$$

As $\lambda \geqslant 0$; that is, the shadow price of stock is non-negative and $b < 0$, the condition for concavity is satisfied and a solution which satisfies the maximum principle necessary conditions is both necessary and sufficient.

□ 7.4.7 Comparative dynamics

The introduction to this chapter distinguishes between comparative statics and comparative dynamics. However, it is possible to lose sight of this idea among the details related to identifying the steady state and checking its stability. The form of comparative dynamic analysis depends upon a particular context. Take the fishery problem if the analysis concerns the sensitivity of the solution to a change in the discount rate, an exogenous variable. One approach would be to focus on the steady state and show how that changes with respect to r. (Caputo, 1990, views this as a comparative static analysis, as it concerns only a single point on the time path.) It is immediately apparent that the stock declines as r increases. The comparative dynamic approach analyses the time path of a solution which is initially out of equilibrium. Analysing the comparative dynamics of a time path instead of a steady state is much more problematic. Heuristically it is possible to use the phase diagram to compare the time paths under two levels of the discount rate r. More general methods for comparative dynamics have been proposed by Oniki (1973) and applied to non-renewable resources by Caputo (1990). An understanding of the whole time path of extraction is of more importance in non-renewable resource economics where the rate of extraction tends to change over the whole time path. In the analysis of renewable resource problems it is often appropriate just to identify the steady state and its local stability.

This point is illustrated by the analysis of a change in the discount rate r given in Figure 7.5. If the discount rate increases from r_1 to r_2, the steady state switches from (x_1^*, q_1^*) to a lower stock and harvest rate, (x_2^*, q_2^*). Corresponding to the steady-state solution are four optimal trajectories

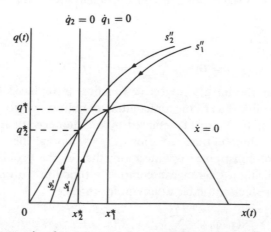

Figure 7.5 *Comparative dynamics and the steady-state solution*

s_1', s_2', s_1'' and s_2'' and they represent the comparative dynamic solutions to the problem when the stock is either greater than or less than the steady-state stock.

7.5 The discrete-time maximum principle and dynamic programming

This section covers two topics which extend the scope of the continuous-time optimal control model. Many natural resource problems are not readily described in continuous time. Data on the output of non-renewable and renewable resources are recorded at discrete-time intervals. Further, some renewable resources are only harvested during discrete short seasons which might be viewed as a single harvesting event. These attributes of natural resources make it difficult to employ a continuous-time format: a continuous-time format might be appropriate for developing theoretical models, but a discrete-time model is often more suitable for applications of the theory.

Here discrete-time dynamic optimisation is considered from two standpoints. First we describe the discrete-time maximum principle and then introduce dynamic programming as a method of determining numerical solutions to complex real-world problems. For a more detailed discussion, see Conrad and Clark (1987).

☐ 7.5.1 The discrete-time maximum principle

Consider the following discrete-time dynamic optimisation problem and compare this with the continuous-time problem given in (7.31).

$$\text{maximise}_{q_t} \quad \sum_{t=0}^{T} \pi(x_t, q_t, t)$$

$$\text{subject to} \quad x_{t+1} - x_t = G(x_t, q_t) \qquad x_0 = c \qquad t = 0, \dots, T$$

First note that the integral objective function is replaced by the sum of discounted profits. Next, the differential equation which represents the change in the state variable is replaced by a difference equation, $G(\cdot)$. The form of the discrete-time solution draws upon the more familiar mathematics of constrained optimisation; that is, the problem is stated as one of maximising a Lagrangean composite function with a constraint on the amount of stock available at any point in time:

$$L(x_t, q_t, t) = \sum_{t=0}^{T} \pi(x_t, q_t, t) + \sum_{t=0}^{T} \lambda_t (x_t + G(x_t, q_t) - x_{t+1})$$

Differentiating the Lagrangean with respect to q_t, x_t and λ_t yields the first-order conditions:

$$\pi_{q_t} + \lambda_t G_{q_t} = 0 \tag{7.44}$$

$$\pi_{x_t} + \lambda_t - \lambda_{t-1} + G_{x_t} = 0 \tag{7.45}$$

$$x_t + G(x_t, q_t) - x_{t+1} = 0 \tag{7.46}$$

These give the maximum principle conditions where (7.44) is equivalent to the first order derivative of the Hamiltonian with respect to the control variable (7.24), (7.45) is the costate condition (7.25) and (7.46) is the equation of motion (7.36). These first-order conditions may be restated more succinctly by defining the discrete-time Hamiltonian:

$$H(x_t, q_t, t) = \pi(x_t, q_t, t) + \lambda_t G(x_t, q_t)$$

equation (7.44) is

$$H_{q_t} = 0$$

and equation (7.45)

$$\lambda_t - \lambda_{t-1} = -H_{x_t}$$

gives the costate condition.

☐ 7.5.2 *Dynamic programming*

The maximum principle of optimal control theory provides necessary conditions for deriving optimal time paths for continuous-time and discrete-time dynamic problems. However, analytical solutions to such problems are not always available. Dynamic programming is an equivalent approach to solving dynamic problems which is more amenable to empirical analysis. In fact, as optimal control theory is the main tool of theoretical analysis in natural resource problems, dynamic programming – as its analogous numerical method – has become a key tool in applied work, especially where problems are best described in discrete-time units. The technique is also capable of representing discontinuous functions, irreversibility and uncertainty. We discuss these aspects of dynamic programming (DP) later.

Consider a discrete-time renewable resource management problem.

$$\text{maximise}_{q_t} \quad \sum_{t=0}^{T} \pi(x_t, q_t, t) \tag{7.47a}$$

subject to $\quad x_{t+1} - x_t = G(x_t, q_t) \tag{7.47b}$

$$x_t \in X, \quad t = 0, 1, \ldots, T \tag{7.47c}$$

$$x_0 = c \tag{7.47d}$$

where x is a set of predetermined state variables. Define an index, n, which indicates the number of periods which remain to the end of the time interval which ends at T; a maximum value function, $J_n(x)$, gives the maximum total value of the objective function when n periods remain. Thus

$$J_n(x_{T-(n-1)}) = \max \sum_{t=T-(n-1)}^{T} \pi(x_t, q_t, t)$$

gives the maximum profit derived from starting at $x_{T-(n-1)}$ and harvesting optimally until the end of the planning horizon.

For $n = 1$, the maximum value function is

$$J_1(x_T) = \max \pi(x_T, q_T, T)$$

this solves a static optimisation problem for the value of stock at the end of the planning horizon. Moving back one period, $n = 2$

$$J_2(x_{T-1}) = \max [\pi(x_{T-1}, q_{T-1}, T-1) + J_1(G(x_{T-1}, q_{T-1}) + x_{T-1})]$$

that is, the optimal value for $T - 1$ is the profit generated during $T - 1$ plus the maximum profit which can be generated by the resulting state, given by the growth function, $G(x_{T-1}, q_{T-1}) + x_{T-1})$. For $n = 3$

$$J_3(x) = \max [\pi(x_{T-2}, q_{T-2}, T-2) + J_2(G(x_{T-2}, q_{T-2}) + x_{T-2})]$$

and so on, until $n = T$. In general

$$J_n(x_{T-(n-1)}) = \max [\pi(x_{T-(n-1)}, q_{T-(n-1)}, T-(n-1))$$

$$+ J_{n-1}(G(x_{T-(n-1)}, q_{T-(n-1)}) + x_{T-(n-1)}))]$$

An optimal policy has the property that, whatever the initial state and decision are, the remaining decisions must constitute an optimal policy with regard to the state resulting from the first decision (Bellman, 1957, p. 83).

7.5.3 An example of dynamic programming applied to fishery management

For example, a fish harvest problem has a duration of three periods, commencing at $t = 0$ with an initial stock fixed at x_{02} and the final stock is fixed at x_{31}. This imposes a transversality condition. The first subscript refers to the time period, t, the second to the fixed stock level, i. At the end of period one, $t = 1$ and period two, $t = 2$, the stock can assume one of three preset values: $x_{t1} = 0.5$, $x_{t2} = 1$ and $x_{t3} = 1.5$. Figure 7.6. represents the problem: the three discrete state levels are on the vertical axis and time on the horizontal axis; the solid lines between the state nodes represent harvest

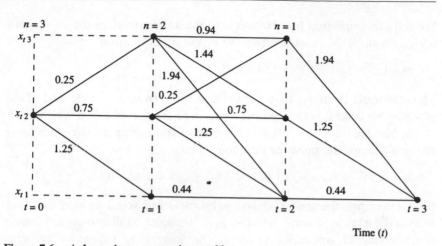

Figure 7.6 *A dynamic programming problem*

decisions, with the profit rates indicated above the harvest lines. DP involves iterating backwards through a 'mesh' of preset state variable levels to determine the optimal solution.

The optimal harvest is found iteratively by moving backwards from the end of the planning horizon to the initial stock. To see how this works, consider the problem where the objective function is

$$\text{maximise}_{q_t} \quad \sum_t \pi_t = pq_t$$

where $p = 1$ is the price per tonne of stock and q_t is the harvest rate. For simplicity, discounting is ignored. Profit maximisation is constrained by the initial stock $x_{02} = 1$, the transversality condition that there must be 0.5 units of stock at the end of the time interval, $x_T = 0.5$. The growth function is

$$x_{t+1} - x_t = G(x_t, q_t) = x_t - 0.25x_t^2 - q_t \tag{7.48}$$

Iterations are constructed by solving (7.48) for q_t. Recall that the values for the state variable are fixed. Starting at $n = 1$, calculate the profit derived from moving from x_{21} to x_{31}, x_{22} to x_{31} and x_{23} to x_{31}. At this stage there is only one possible harvest decision for each level of the state variable. For instance, the profit derived from proceeding from x_{23} to x_{31} is

$$q_2 = -x_{31} - 0.25x_{23}^2 + 2x_{23} = 1.9375$$

Moving back in time, it is a matter of finding the best routes to each of the levels of x at $n = 1$, but using the results already estimated at $n = 1$. Taking x_{13} as an example, compare the routes from x_{13} to x_{23}, x_{13} to x_{22} and x_{13} to x_{21}:

$$J_2(x_{13}) = \max \left[\pi(x_{13}, q_1, 1) + J_1(G(x_{13}, q_1) + x_{13}) \right]$$

We solve this equation by iteration over the different values for q_1, namely, 0.94, 1.44 and 1.94. This involves the following evaluation:

$$0.94 + 1.94 > 1.44 + 1.25 > 1.94 + 0.44$$

Thus the route from x_{13} to x_{21} is the best route from x_{13} to the end of the planning horizon: it is the optimal solution to the sub-problem which starts at x_{13}. Moving back to $t = 0$, it is a matter of comparing the decisions using the results from the previous iterations. Thus

$$0.25 + (0.94 + 1.94) > 0.75 + (0.25 + 1.94) > 1.25 + (0.44 + 0.44)$$

In this example, the global optimal solution is to harvest so that the stock follows the path $x_{02} \rightarrow x_{13} \rightarrow x_{23} \rightarrow x_{31}$. This solution illustrates a common characteristic of optimal trajectories for finite time renewable resource harvesting problems; that is, that the stock is initially built up but is then reduced as the end of the planning horizon approachs. This example also illustrates the importance of the transversality condition in determining the optimal trajectory.

The limitations of *DP* lie in the computational burden of iterating through the levels of the state variable. This becomes onerous when there is more than one state variable and has become known as the 'curse of dimensionality'.

In comparing the two approaches to dynamic optimisation it is appropriate to view them as complementary. On the one hand, optimal control theory provides intuitive necessary conditions and a framework for analysing the stability of the steady-state solution. However, finding an explicit solution is far from straightforward and involves solving non–linear differential equations numerically or using a linear approximation to determine the optimal trajectory for any given initial condition. On the other, *DP* is equivalent to control theory (see Kamien and Schwartz, 1981, p. 238), but requires a computer program which can calculate the optimal solution by backward induction (Kennedy, 1986). The other advantage of *DP* is that transversality conditions, weak inequality constraints on state variables and decision variables can be handled implicitly by restricting the set of predetermined state variable levels, X.

7.6 Wiener processes, Itô's processes and stochastic calculus

We now consider how uncertainty can be introduced into dynamic models of resource exploitation. The importance of this subject is undisputed; most resource exploitation problems involve a degree of uncertainty. In non-renewable resources uncertainty exists about future costs and prices and future reserve levels. In renewable resource economics market variables such as price and the total harvest are uncertain and the resource stock responds stochastically to changes in environmental conditions. The presence of uncertainty in the absence of perfect contingent markets, that is, futures markets or insurance markets, affects firms' decisions. This is the case where firms shows risk aversion and take decisions which reduce their exposure to risk; it is also the case when a firm is risk-neutral and aims to maximise the expected profit. This is in contrast to the usual assumption in economics that, if a firm is risk-neutral, decisions are based upon expected prices, output and costs and their objective of maximising profits simply becomes one of maximising expected profits (see Hey, 1979; Hirshleifer and Riley, 1992, for a review).

This sub-section establishes a theoretical framework for analysing the comparative dynamics of uncertain resource exploitation problems. In common with other contributions in the literature, it must do this within a restricted mathematical framework. To this end, we establish, at an intuitive level, some of the important results of stochastic calculus. In the next sub-section these are applied to a simple example. (Those requiring a more detailed account of this subject should refer to Dixit and Pindyck, 1994, for an excellent introduction, and Malliaris and Brock, 1982, for a more rigorous account.)

☐ 7.6.1 *Mathematical introduction*

This section is mathematically more difficult than previous sections and might be treated as optional. The starting-point is the Wiener process, $z(t)$, which is a continuous-time stochastic process and is the continuous-time equivalent of a random walk (Dixit and Pindyck, 1994). Define $\varepsilon(t)$ with the characteristics that $\varepsilon(t)$ is normally distributed with an expected value of zero and variance of 1, for each t; for any two time periods the covariance between $\varepsilon(t)$ is zero. Thus $\varepsilon(t)$ has the same normal distribution for all t and values of $\varepsilon(t)$ are statistically independent. The stochastic process, $z(t)$, is related to $\varepsilon(t)$ and t as follows:

$$\Delta z = \varepsilon(t)\sqrt{\Delta t} \tag{7.49}$$

This implies that z changes over some finite interval according to

$$z(s + T) - z(s) = \sum_{i=1}^{n} \varepsilon_i \sqrt{\Delta t}$$

As the ε_i's are independent with mean 0 and variance $n\Delta t = T$, the variance of a Wiener process grows linearly with the time interval into the future. This result requires further clarification. Using the expectation operator, $E[\cdot]$ the variance of $z(t)$ is

$$\text{var}\,[\Delta z(t)] = E[\{\Delta z(t) - E[\Delta z(t)]\}^2]$$

but $E[\Delta z(t)] = 0$; thus this simplifies to:

$$\text{var}\,[\Delta z(t)] = E[\Delta z(t)^2]$$

Substituting in (7.49) for $\Delta z(t)$

$$\text{var}\,[\Delta z(t)] = E[(\varepsilon(t)\sqrt{\Delta t})^2]$$

and passing expectations through the expression gives

$$\text{var}\,[\Delta z(t)] = \Delta t E[\varepsilon(t)^2]$$

By noting that $\text{var}\,[\varepsilon(t)] = E[\varepsilon(t)^2] = 1$ we have our required result:

$$\text{var}\,[\Delta z(t)] = \Delta t$$

We can now tidy up some of the notation. By allowing the discrete-time change to tend to zero $\Delta t \to 0$ (7.49) becomes:

$$dz = \varepsilon\sqrt{dt} \tag{7.50}$$

this equation defines the Wiener process, z; that is, if this equation could be integrated it would equal z. It is assumed that at an initial point $t = 0$ the value of z is zero, but as t increases the uncertainty about z increases. The fundamental attribute of the process is $dz^2 = dt$. This can be shown:

$$\text{var}\,[z(t)] = \int_0^t dt = t$$

$$dz^2 = (\varepsilon\sqrt{dt})^2 = \varepsilon^2\,dt$$

The expected value of dz^2 is

$$E[dz^2] = E[\varepsilon^2\,dt] = E[\varepsilon^2]\,dt = dt$$

This is the case as $\text{var}\,[\varepsilon] = E[\varepsilon^2] = 1$. Thus the variance of dz^2 is

$$\text{var}\,[dz^2] = E[(dz^2 - E[dz])^2] = E[(\varepsilon^2\,dt - dt)^2] = dt^2 E[\varepsilon^4 - 2\varepsilon^2 + 1]$$

But dt^2 is zero, thus the variance of dz^2 is zero. If the variance is zero, $dz^2 = E[dz^2] = dt$ with certainty.

The basic Wiener process is used for other more general stochastic processes which have expected values other than zero and variance other than t. The Brownian motion x is described by the stochastic differential equation

$$dx = \alpha x\,dt + \beta x\,dz$$

where dz is defined by (7.50) and α and β are constants. The process x is a Wiener process with drift α and variance β^2. The expected value of dx is $\alpha\,dt$. The instantaneous standard deviation of the change in x is β. The variance at a point in time t periods ahead is $\text{var}[x(t)] = \beta^2 t$.

The Wiener process is also the basis of more general stochastic differential equations called Itô's processes, of the form:

$$dx = \mu(x, t)\,dt + \sigma(x, t)\,dz \tag{7.51}$$

In this case the constant mean is replaced by $\mu(x, t)$ and the constant standard deviation by $\sigma(x, t)$. These functions have the same interpretation, except that now the mean and variance of dx may increase as a function of x. A Wiener process is a specific form of Itô process.

It is also possible to have Itô processes for more than one variable

$$dx = \mu_x(x, y, t)\,dt + \sigma_x(x, y, t)\,dz_x$$

$$dy = \mu_y(x, y, t)\,dt + \sigma_y(x, y, t)\,dz_y$$

The variables ε_x and ε_y may be correlated with each other; that is, $\text{cov}[\varepsilon_x, \varepsilon_y]$ need not be zero. Since the variance and the standard deviation of ε_x and ε_y all equal 1, the correlation coefficient between x and y is $\text{cov}[\varepsilon_x, \varepsilon_y] = \rho_{xy}$.

The next step is to specify how a stochastic differential equation can be converted into a more manageable form. This involves Itô's lemma, which is the fundamental theorem of stochastic calculus. Itô's lemma is most readily understood as a Taylor series expansion. If we wish to find the total differential of a function $F(x, t)$ where x follows an Itô process, the form in normal calculus is

$$dF = F_x\,dx + F_t\,dt$$

but it is also possible by Taylor's theorem to include further terms:

$$dF = F_x\,dx + F_t\,dt + \tfrac{1}{2}F_{xx}(dx)^2 + \tfrac{1}{6}F_{xxx}(dx)^3$$

In ordinary calculus higher order terms all vanish at the limit when dx becomes infinitesimally small, as $dx > (dx)^2, (dx)^3$. To see if this is the case in stochastic calculus, substitute in (7.51) for dx and $(dx)^2$

$$(dx)^2 = \mu(x, t)^2 (dt)^2 + 2\mu(x, t)\sigma(x, t)\varepsilon(dt)^{3/2} + \sigma(x, t)^2\,dt$$

The terms $(dt)^2$ and $(dt)^{3/2}$ vanish as dt vanishes to zero and $(dx)^2 = \sigma(x, t)^2\,dt$. It can easily be shown that the term $(dx)^3$ is zero. Hence Itô's lemma gives the differential dF as

$$dF = F_x\,dx + F_t\,dt + \tfrac{1}{2}F_{xx}(dx)^2 \tag{7.52}$$

or equivalently by substituting for dx

$$dF = [F_t + \mu(x, t)F_x + \tfrac{1}{2}\sigma(x, t)F_{xx}]\,dt + \sigma(x, t)F_x\,dz$$

Where there are i Itô's processes we have in general:

$$dF = F_t\, dt + \sum_i F_i\, dx_i + \frac{1}{2}\sum_i \sum_j F_{ij}\, dx_i\, dx_j \qquad (7.53)$$

Let us consider an example of the application of Itô's lemma. The example is a geometric Brownian motion where $F(x) = \log x$. It follows that $F_t = 0$, $F_x = 1/x$ and $F_{xx} = -1/x^2$. From (7.52)

$$dF = (1/x)\, dx - (1/2x^2)(dx)^2$$

$$= \mu\, dt + \sigma\, dz - \tfrac{1}{2}\sigma^2\, dt$$

$$= (\mu - \tfrac{1}{2}\sigma^2)\, dt + \sigma\, dz$$

Hence over a finite time interval T, the change in $\log x$ is normally distributed with mean $(\mu - \tfrac{1}{2}\sigma^2)T$ and the variance $\sigma^2 T$. To translate this into an economic example, if x is the price of an asset, it says that future returns are lognormally distributed with a standard deviation which grows with the square of the holding period.

☐ 7.6.2 *Example of applying Itô's lemma to natural resource economics*

Itô's stochastic calculus has a role in theoretical economics where it allows us to derive comparative static and comparative dynamic results under uncertainty. It has been employed to examine the effects of uncertainty upon optimal resource extraction. The issue is: does the existence of uncertainty affect the rate of resource exploitation? As we will see in later chapters, this is a complex issue and is only partially addressed by this form of analysis.

In this sub-section we approach the application of Itô's lemma through a very simple problem which is concerned with irreversible investment in natural resource exploitation. The example is based upon examples given in Dixit and Pindyck (1994, ch. 5). This illustrates an important attribute of such problems, that a value exists in delaying taking an investment decision until more information becomes available. The specific example is one where a firm owns a fishery, but is yet to invest in a boat to catch the fish. Owing to price variability, the value of investing in the boat is uncertain and can be represented by a geometric Brownian motion:

$$dV = \alpha V\, dt + \sigma V\, dz \qquad (7.54)$$

This implies that the current value of the project is known and future values are lognormally distributed with mean $(\alpha - \tfrac{1}{2}\sigma^2)t$ and variance $\sigma^2 t$. The value of the investment opportunity is:

$$J(V) = \max E[(V_T - I)e^{-rT}]$$

that is, the expected value of investment, $E[V_T]$ less the known cost of investment, I. The time of investment, T, is not known.

Before turning to analyse this problem directly, let us consider the deterministic case where $\sigma = 0$; thus (7.54) can be solved directly $V(t) = V_0 e^{\alpha t}$, where $V_0 = V(0)$. Thus

$$J(V) = (Ve^{\alpha T} - I)e^{-rT} \tag{7.55}$$

In the case where $0 < \alpha < r$, then $J(V) > 0$ even if currently $V < I$, as eventually V will exceed I owing to the drift term α. Even if $V > I$, so long as it is not too much greater it may still pay to wait as, through time, the cost of investment falls by a factor e^{-rT}, while the pay-off is reduced by a smaller factor, $e^{-(r-\alpha)T}$.

The first-order condition for maximising $J(V)$ is:

$$J_T = -(r - \alpha)Ve^{-(r-\alpha)T} + rIe^{-rT} = 0$$

which implies the firm should invest immediately if the critical value V^* is exceeded

$$V^* = \frac{r}{r - \alpha}I > I$$

or wait until

$$T^* = \frac{1}{\alpha} \log\left[\frac{rI}{(r - \alpha)V}\right]$$

time periods have passed. Substituting this into (7.55) yields the result that, when $V \leq V^*$,

$$J(V) = \frac{\alpha I}{(r - \alpha)}\left[\frac{(r - \alpha)V}{rI}\right]^{r/\alpha}$$

gives the value of waiting to invest.

Returning now to the stochastic problem, the firm will retain the fishery, even when it is not being exploited, when the current rate of return on its value is equal to its expected rate of capital appreciation:

$$rJ\,dt = E[dJ] \tag{7.56}$$

That is, over the interval dt, the total expected return on the investment opportunity, $rJ\,dt$, equals the expected capital appreciation, $E[dJ]$. We can expand $E[dJ]$ by Itô's lemma:

$$dJ = J'(V)\,dV + \tfrac{1}{2}J''(V)(dV)^2$$

Substituting (7.54) for dV,

$$E[dJ] = \alpha V J'(V)\, dt + \tfrac{1}{2}\sigma^2 V^2 (dV)^2 J''(V)\, dt$$

making this substitution and dividing through by dt, (7.56) becomes

$$\tfrac{1}{2}\sigma^2 V^2 (dV)^2 J''(V) + \alpha V J'(V) - rJ = 0 \tag{7.57}$$

which is Bellman's equation. In addition, this equation must satisfy three boundary conditions:

$$J(0) = 0 \tag{7.58}$$

this implies that if $V = 0$ then it stays at zero and the fishery has zero value. The next boundary condition is *value matching*:

$$J(V^*) = V^* - I \tag{7.59}$$

that is, when the firm invests the value received is the net pay-off. The *smooth pasting* condition ensures that the firm cannot increase profit by delaying investment when the critical value is reached:

$$J'(V^*) = 1 \tag{7.60}$$

The problem faced by the firm is one of determining V^*, that is the value of the investment; this a 'free boundary ' point problem, that is, one where the terminal time is not known.

The solution to the second-order differential equation (7.57) proceeds heuristically: in other words, guess what the functional form of $J(V)$ is and assess by substitution if it is correct. Dixit and Pindyck (1994) show that the following solution is indeed correct:

$$J(V) = A V^\beta \tag{7.61}$$

Thus if (7.61) is substituted into (7.57) we have

$$\tfrac{1}{2}\sigma^2 \beta(\beta - 1) + \alpha\beta - r = 0 \tag{7.62}$$

which has two roots, one positive and one negative. For economic reasons only the positive root is relevant; in particular, if $\beta < 0$, then boundary condition (7.58) is not satisfied. More formally, the general solution to (7.57) is $J(V) = A_1 V^{\beta_1} + A_2 V^{\beta_2}$. The boundary condition (7.58) implies $A_2 = 0$, as $\beta_1 > 0$ and $\beta_2 < 0$, $A_2 V^{\beta_2} \to \infty$ when $V \to 0$.

From the boundary condtions (7.59) and (7.60) we obtain the important result that

$$V^* = \frac{\beta}{(\beta - 1)} I$$

Thus if the parameter β is greater than one, which is ensured by assumptions for the parameter values, then uncertainty and irreversibility drive a wedge, $\beta/(\beta - 1)$ between the value of the fishery and the cost of investing in boats.

We next consider how this changes with the level of uncertainty. Here, uncertainty is measured by the standard deviation σ. From the solution to the quadratic (7.62) for β in terms of α and σ, we find that $\partial\beta/\partial\sigma < 0$ and, as a result, $\beta/(\beta - 1)$ increases. Thus, as uncertainty increases, so does the size of the 'wedge' between I and V^*.

Consider the following example, where $r = 0.10$, $\alpha = 0.06$ and $I = 1$. Consider two cases: in the first, the firm is certain about the expected future value of the fishery; in the second, the variance is $\sigma = 0.2$. In both cases if $V < V^*$ it pays to delay investment until the value of the fishery has increased to some critical level; increased uncertainty implies that the firm is only willing to invest when the value of the fishery exceeds a still higher critical value. In Figure 7.7, as the variance increases, it shifts the critical value to the right, from 2.5 to 3.225.

This result has implications for the economics of natural resources where firms face irreversible investment opportunities. This is the case with specialist fishing equipment where equipment has a low salvage value. It may also expain the decision to invest in oil exploration and extraction, where oil prices have to rise above a certain critical level before a firm invests. Once investment in specific oil exploration and extraction capital has taken place these costs are sunk.

Dixit and Pindyck (1994) extend the same model described here to explain *hysteresis* effects, where firms require the price to rise above the point where the cost of investment equals the net present value (NPV) of that investment before investing. Once the firm has made the investment and its investment costs are sunk costs with a low or zero salvage value, it may remain in the

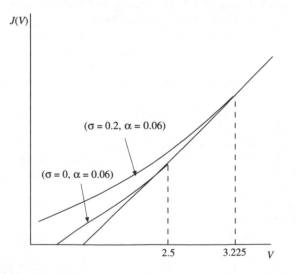

Figure 7.7   *Fishery investment under uncertainty*

market until the price falls below the point where the investment cost equals the NPV. Thus hysteresis describes a situation where a firm does not respond, by either investing or disinvesting, to price fluctuations within a critical price band. This form of model is of particular importance in oil and mineral extraction where a large proportion of investment costs are irreversible.

■ 7.7 Summary

This chapter has introduced the tools of natural resource economics. It commenced with an account of the similarities between the economics of natural resource extraction and capital theory. This model was extended to the multi-period case through the maximum principle of optimal control theory in continuous and discrete time. We then considered dynamic programming which is analogous to optimal control theory, but is an approach to finding numerical solutions to a wider range of discrete-time natural resource problems. The final section introduced the analysis of the effect of uncertainty in models of resource exploitation. In Chapters, 9, 10 and 11 these tools will be used as the basis for developing theoretical and applied models of natural resource exploitation.

■ References

Beavis, B. and I.M. Dobbs (1990) *Optimization and Stability Theory for Economic Analysis*, Cambridge: Cambridge University Press.

Bellman, R.E. (1957) *Dynamic Programming*, Princeton: Princeton University Press.

Bliss, C.J. (1975) *Capital Theory and the Distribution of Income*, New York: Elsevier.

Caputo, M.R. (1990) 'A Qualitative Characterization of the Competitive Non-renewable Resource Extracting Firm', Journal of Environmental Economics and Management, 18, 206–26.

Chiang, A.C. (1984) *Fundamental Methods of Mathematical Economics*, 3rd edn, New York: McGraw-Hill.

Chiang, A.C. (1992) *Elements of Dynamic Optimization*, New York: McGraw-Hill.

Clark, C.W. (1990) *Mathematical Bioeconomics*, 2nd edn, Chichester: Wiley.

Conrad, J.M. and C.W. Clark (1987) *Natural Resource Economics*, Cambridge: Cambridge University Press.

Dasgupta, P.S. and G.M. Heal (1979) *Economic Theory and Exhaustible Resources*, Cambridge: Cambridge University Press.

Dixit, A.K. (1976) *The Theory of Equilibrium Growth*, Oxford: Oxford University Press.

Dixit, A.K. and R.S. Pindyck (1994) *Investment under Uncertainty*, Princeton: Princeton University Press.

Dorfman, R. (1969) 'An Economic Interpretation of Optimal Control Theory', *American Economic Review*, 59, 817–31.

Hey, J.D. (1979) *Uncertainty in Microeconomics*, New York: New York University Press.

Hirshleifer, J. and J.G. Riley (1992) *The Analytics of Uncertainty and Information*, Cambridge: Cambridge University Press.

Holling, C.S. (1973) 'Resilience and Stability of Ecological Systems', *Annual Review of Ecology and Systematics*, 4, 1–23.

Hotelling, H. (1931) 'The Economics of Exhaustible Resources', *Journal of Political Economy*, 39, 137–75.

Kamien, M.I. and N.L. Schwartz (1971) 'Sufficient Conditions in Optimal Control Theory', *Journal of Economic Theory*, 3, 207–14.

Kamien, M.I. and N.L. Schwartz (1990) *Dynamic Optimization: The Calculus of Variations and Optimal Control in Economics and Management*, 2nd edn, Amsterdam: North-Holland.

Kennedy, J.O.S. (1986) *Dynamic Programming: Applications to Agriculture and Natural Resources*, London: Elsevier Applied Science.

Leonard, D. and N. Van Long (1992) *Optimal Control Theory and Static Optimization in Economics*, Cambridge: Cambridge University Press.

Malliaris, A.G. and W.A. Brock (1982) *Stochastic Methods in Economics and Finance*, New York: North-Holland.

Neher, P.A. (1990) *Natural Resource Economics: Conservation and Exploitation*, Cambridge: Cambridge University Press.

Oniki, H. (1973) 'Comparative Dynamics (Sensitivity Analysis) in Optimal Control Theory', *Journal of Economic Theory*, 6, 265–83.

Varian, H.R. (1984) *Microeconomic Analysis*, New York: W.W. Norton.

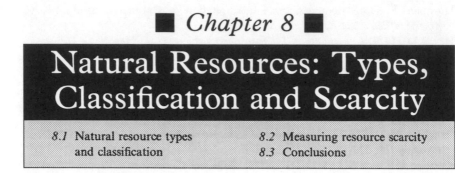

■ *Chapter 8* ■

Natural Resources: Types, Classification and Scarcity

8.1 Natural resource types
and classification

8.2 Measuring resource scarcity

8.3 Conclusions

The term 'resources' covers a multitude of meanings and it is necessary to be very precise about its use in what follows. We also discuss various measures of resource scarcity, introducing some which will be important in Chapters 9 to 11.

■ *8.1* Natural resource types and classification

In Chapter 1, a distinction was made between 'material' and 'energy' resources. This distinction relates to the conventional end-uses of these resources, in that material (or mineral) resources are utilised as part of the physical constituency of commodities (iron ore, converted into steel, in car bodies; aluminium in saucepans; copper in pipes; and cobalt in jet engines). (A mineral is defined as a solid crystalline chemical element or compound in fixed composition. A mineroid is a mineral which occurs in non-solid form. Rocks are aggregates of one or more minerals. A mineral deposit is an accumulation of a specific mineral.) Energy resources, on the other hand, are converted into heat and other forms of energy. Thus the chemical energy in natural gas is converted into heat energy when gas is burnt in domestic central heating boilers. Clearly, some resources are used both as material and as energy sources; oil is the prime example here, being used for propulsion in internal combustion engines and to make plastics. Conversion of material resources into useable forms also requires inputs of energy resources (for smelting and for mining). Material resources may be further divided into metallic and non-metallic materials, the latter including soils, water and sand. There are some 88 minerals occurring on earth. Of these, only 12 make up 99 per cent of the earth's crust: the most common of these are silicon (27 per cent), aluminium (8 per cent) and iron (6 per cent).

One obvious distinction between resource types is in terms of their potential for natural growth. Clearly a forest, which may be used as both a material and an energy resource, is different to a deposit of iron ore, in that the former exhibits a natural rate of growth, whilst the latter does not. It is usual, then, to distinguish between 'renewable' and 'non-renewable' resources, with the former classification reserved for those resources exhibiting a positive natural rate of growth. This is a clearer distinction than the classification into 'exhaustible' and 'non-exhaustible' resources, since even a renewable resource can be exhausted (by continuing to harvest in excess of the natural rate of growth, for example), and a non-renewable resource may not be exhausted if it becomes uneconomic to extract the last reserves.

■ *8.2* **Measuring resource scarcity**

□ *8.2.1* *Some basics*

One of the most common questions in debates over the use of natural resources is 'are we running out of resources?' Clearly, for any non-renewable resource (in this sub-section, we concentrate on non-renewable resources), a positive rate of extraction means that the physical stock of the resource is reduced in size. However, (1) there are major problems in defining what this physical stock should represent; (2) the economic measure of the size of the reserve of this material is not the same as the physical size of the reserves; (3) the value of the economic reserve will change over time; and (4) there are alternative measures for the *scarcity* of this economic reserve, which may well give different answers to the above question.

To anticipate some of this discussion, consider Figure 8.1, which is adapted from Zwartendyk (1973). The two axes show the influence of physical and economic parameters. As the ratio of the price of the resource to its marginal extraction cost falls, then clearly extracting the resource today becomes less attractive: the term 'economic reserves' is often used to describe that portion of a deposit (or collection of deposits) which it is profitable to extract, given current prices and costs. Costs, as will be seen in Chapter 9, depend partly on the state of technology, and on cumulative extraction: clearly these costs will be changing over time. Prices will also change, in response to the decisions of extractors over extraction rates (which might depend, for example, on the agreement reached by a cartel of producers, such as OPEC), demand for the material and government intervention on prices (the setting of price ceilings and floors). Thus the dashed horizontal line in Figure 8.1 will move up and down over time,

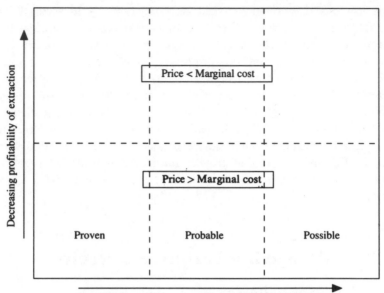

Figure 8.1   *Problems of defining 'reserves'*
Source: Adaped from Zwartendyk (1973).

changing the measured level of 'economic reserves' as it does so. For example, the minimum concentration of copper in a copper deposit required for profitable extraction fell from 3 per cent in the 1800s to 0.5 per cent in the mid-1960s with technological progress, which at constant real prices would result in the size of the economic reserve increasing over time.

There is also uncertainty over the actual amount of a resource in a given geographic area. For example, it is not known with certainty how much oil lies under the North Sea. Some oil deposits have been found and are in production, others have been found and are not in production. Other deposits are thought to exist, given the nature of the surrounding geology. But the total size of deposit may be greater than this. However, even with respect to defining the physical size of a deposit, or of all deposits for a particular material, difficulties arise. For example, should all amounts of copper be counted, irrespective of their concentration, or of the form in which they are present?

Several writers (such as Harris and Skinner, 1982; Anderson, 1985) have argued that a crucial concept here is that of the 'mineralogical threshold'. Below this threshold, minerals occur as silicates, in that they are chemically bonded to silica. The total amount of a mineral which exists on earth is known as its 'crustal abundance', also referred to as the resource base.

However, only a small fraction (roughly 3 per cent on average) of the crustal abundance of most minerals exists in non-silicate form, as oxides, sulphides or carbonates. For some minerals, very few deposits exist which are in non-silicate form. Skinner (1976) calls these minerals 'geochemically scarce'. To take the example of lead, its average concentration in the earth's crust is 0.001 per cent, but extraction currently takes place in ore deposits where lead is found in concentrations of between 2 and 20 per cent. Once these ore deposits have been worked out, then vastly more energy will be required to extract lead from its silicate form, where it is trapped by 'atomic substitution'. This extraction would also produce large quantities of geochemically abundant minerals as a by-product. Geochemically scarce minerals include copper, lead, mercury and gold (Anderson, 1985). For geochemically abundant minerals, such as iron, the energy required to extract the mineral increases smoothly as the purity of the ore declines, as Figure 8.2 shows; for geologically scarce minerals, energy use jumps at the mineralogical threshold. A prediction from the mineralogical threshold model is that geochemically abundant minerals will be substituted for geochemically scarce minerals as the threshold is approached.

Table 8.1 gives recent estimates of world economic reserves, the reserve base and crustal abundance, for a range of materials.

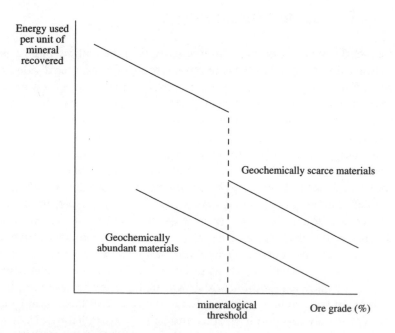

Figure 8.2 *The mineralogical threshold*
Source: Skinner (1976).

Table 8.1   *World reserves, reserve bases and crustal abundances of selected materials*

Material	Economic reserves[1] (000 metric tonnes)	Reserve base[2] (000 metric tonnes)	Crustal abundance (million tonnes)
Aluminium	21 800 000	24 500 000	$1\,990\,000 \times 10^6$
Iron	151 000 000	229 000 000	$1\,392\,000 \times 10^6$
Copper	321 000	549 000	$1\,510 \times 10^6$
Lead	70 000	120 000	290×10^6
Mercury	130	240	2.1×10^6
Zinc	144 000	295 000	$2\,250 \times 10^6$

Notes
1   Defined in the data source (WRI, 1992) as 'those deposits whose quantity and grade have been determined by samples and measurements and which can be profitably recovered at the time of the assessment. Changes in geologic information, technology, costs of extraction and production, and prices of mined product can affect the reserve'.
2   Defined as 'the portion of the mineral resource that meets grade, thickness, quality and depth criteria defined by current mining and production processes'. It includes measured and indicated reserves, and does not take account of profitability of extraction (WRI, 1992).
Sources: World Resources Institute (WRI) (1992); Anderson (1985).

☐   *8.2.2   A bad measure*

A frequently-cited measure of resource scarcity is the lifetime of a resource. This is usually expressed as the economic reserve of a resource divided by its current annual consumption rate, with perhaps an allowance for a predicted growth in this rate over time. Fisher (1980) quotes (but does not endorse!) a measure of 45 years for copper in 1974: in other words, a prediction that by the year 2019 the world will run out of copper. The most immediate problem here is clearly that, if we instead divided the reserve base by annual consumption, we would arrive at a much larger figure, one that allows for higher-cost deposits being brought on line as prices rise; but which measure is correct? The answer is neither. As a resource gets scarcer, its price will, other things equal, tend to rise. This will reduce consumption (by substitution, for example) and increase production (suppliers move along their marginal cost curves). These changes will, of course, change the lifetime measure. What is more, as prices rise producers will be encouraged to engage in more exploration, which will increase the reserve base if finds are made. In fact, lifetime measures for many resources have been found to be approximately constant over time, and have been argued by Fisher to say more about firms' attitudes to holding inventories of minerals than about scarcity.

☐ 8.2.3 *Unit cost measures*

Some of the earliest arguments in natural resources economics about scarcity centred around the costs of extraction. Ricardo, Mill and Jevons all pointed out that cumulative extraction could result in increasing unit costs. For example, as a mine is depleted, miners have to travel further and further underground to recover coal, causing labour costs per unit of output to rise; as a country mines its copper, it has to move onto less and less pure grades of ore. Ricardo considered the use of agricultural land: as demand increased for food, production would move onto less and less productive land (note the key assumption made by Ricardo: that the best quality farm land would be the first to be cultivated). As production moved onto worse land, this expansion at the extensive margin would require food prices to rise sufficiently to cover the higher costs of production (higher because marginal land is less productive). This creates scarcity rents on good land, since all farmers now receive the higher price. The increase in rents on good land also encourages farmers to apply more capital and labour inputs to this land. At both the intensive and extensive margin, therefore, capital and labour inputs per unit output increase over time, given a constant state of technology.

Cumulative production increases average costs, which costs are therefore an indicator (a 'Ricardian' indicator) of scarcity. In the 1960s, Barnett and Morse (1963) studied trends in average costs over the time period 1870–1957 for a variety of primary products. With one exception (forestry), they found that an index of real unit (capital plus labour) costs had declined over the period, indicating decreasing scarcity: real capital-plus-labour inputs declined by 54 per cent for the farm sector, 78 per cent for the minerals sector and 55 per cent for the total extractive sector. Barnett and Morse's work was repeated by Johnson *et al.* (1980), who found that, if anything, the rate of decline in unit costs had increased over the period 1958–70.

Are these results proof that these materials were becoming less scarce over this time period? Unfortunately, many problems exist with this unit cost measure. First, technological progress has undoubtedly reduced unit costs over this time period (see Norgaard, 1975, for empirical evidence from the oil sector). This will also have the effect of increasing the size of economic reserves. Second, the unit cost hypothesis relies on the assumption that firms will always deplete the lowest cost deposit first; yet to know which deposit is the lowest cost implies a perfect knowledge of the characteristics of all deposits, some of which are yet to be discovered! Norgaard (1990) has termed this the 'Mayflower problem': 'if the pilgrims knew where the best places for an agricultural colony were, they would not have gone to Plymouth Rock...Many generations passed before American agriculture shifted from the relatively poor soils of the east coast to the more productive mid-west.'

Third, whilst unit capital and labour costs may have been falling, this might be due to substitution of some other input for capital and labour. The obvious missing input here is energy. Hall *et al.* (1986) recomputed Barnett and Morse's figures for the coal and petroleum sectors, including energy use with capital and labour use: they found that, whilst the Barnett and Morse data showed a 35 per cent decline in unit costs for the petroleum sector, including energy use changed this to a 10 per cent *increase*. Fourth, unit costs are a poor predictor of future scarcity, since they are based entirely on past experience, and are not 'forward looking': technological advances could increase future economic reserves even if, historically, unit costs have risen.

☐ *8.2.4 Real prices*

Prices are well-established in conventional microeconomics as indicators of scarcity. For natural resources, a rising real price has been argued by many to be a potentially good measure of increasing scarcity (for example, Fisher, 1980). This will be so when prices signal all future and current opportunity costs of using up a unit of a non-renewable resource today. In simple versions of the Hotelling model, the price of a resource rises at the rate of interest along an optimal depletion time path, until it is equal to the price of the 'backstop resource': its closest substitute. (Note that for some resources, few substitutes exist for their current uses. For example, there are few substitutes for titanium in the production of jet engines, for cobalt in the production of cemented carbides in machine tools, or for germanium in the production of infra-red optics: Deadman and Turner, 1988.) Several empirical studies have looked at price data. Herfindahl (1959) studied copper prices, but the earliest comprehensive study was by Barnett and Morse (1963). They found that, for most primary products, real prices had remained approximately constant from 1870 to 1957. More recently, Slade (1982) suggested that the time path of prices might follow a U shape, as an initial decline in prices due to technological progress was eventually overcome by the tendency for increasing cumulative production to increase costs, and by the desire of resource extractors to see rents rising at the real rate of interest. Slade found that a U shape fitted the price series of 12 materials better than a linear form, indicating that for aluminium, for example, real prices started to rise in the 1960s.

Hall and Hall (1984) also analysed the problem of scarcity, making the observation that what empirical measure one chose depended on the type of scarcity one wished to measure. They identify the following possibilities:

- Malthusian Stock Scarcity: where a resource is fixed in size, and where the unit costs of extraction in period t do not vary with the rate of extraction in period t;
- Malthusian Flow Scarcity: where a resource is fixed in size, but unit costs in period t are increasing in extraction in period t;
- Ricardian Stock Scarcity, where for all practical purposes the stock is not limited in size, but where unit costs rise with cumulative extraction over all periods up to t;
- Ricardian Flow Scarcity, which is Ricardian Stock Scarcity with extraction costs in period t dependent on both cumulative extraction up to period t and the rate of extraction in period t.

For Ricardian Flow Scarcity, the appropriate scarcity measure is argued to be unit costs; for all the other measures, real prices are preferred. Hall and Hall measure both unit costs and real prices for 12 non-renewable and four renewable resources. They include a dummy variable in their price trend equation to try to allow for the influence of the formation of OPEC on materials prices in the 1970s. A crude summary of their results is that scarcity as measured by real prices increased in the 1970s, having declined in the 1960s, although in many cases the relationship between price and time was insignificant. This picture is by and large repeated for unit costs. Finally, Anderson and Moazzami (1989) repeated Slade's analysis, using a somewhat different econometric technique. They found strong evidence of increasing scarcity for some materials (such as coal and copper), but only weak evidence of increasing scarcity for others (such as aluminium and iron).

However, a number of criticisms can be levelled at the use of real prices as scarcity measures. First, the influence of producer cartels on prices of primary products can be great, and yet not reflect scarcity changes. For example, the large oil price increases produced by OPEC in 1974 and 1979 were more to do with a voluntary reduction in supply to increase oil revenues than an increase in scarcity. Other commodities (such as tin) have been similarly affected. Second, governments intervene in resource markets, imposing price controls which distort price signals. An example here is actions by the UK government in the 1970s and 1980s to keep gas prices high, in order to reduce a loss in sales by the nationalised electricity companies (gas is a substitute for electricity in domestic heating and cooking). Tietenberg (1992) documents distortions caused by the imposition of maximum prices (price ceilings) by the US government for natural gas. Third, natural resource prices do not measure social opportunity costs, partly because producers are not forced to pay for the environmental damages caused by the extraction and processing of these resources. For example, oil prices could be argued to be too low since not all of the external costs associated with oil drilling and refining are imposed on producers; a similar statement could be made for aluminium extraction (via bauxite mining) and processing. Natural resource prices therefore do not measure one element of social opportunity costs, namely the environmental benefits forgone in their production. Finally, the appropriate deflator to select for calculating the real price series is not obvious: should an input price or product price deflator be chosen? Hall and Hall (1984) present results for three different deflators.

☐ 8.2.5 *Economic rent*

In Chapter 7, a formal argument was presented over the optimal depletion rate of a non-renewable resource. One result from this analysis is that, in some cases, an efficient depletion path involves resource rents rising at the rate of interest. The intuition behind this is clear: if resource rents represent the rate of return on 'holding' a non-renewable resource deposit, then this should be equal at the margin to the return on holding any other kind of asset, such as a savings bond. Rent is defined as (price-marginal extraction cost). Rising rents are thus an indicator of scarcity. However, some problems exist with this measure. First, empirical data are scarce. Economic rents are the difference between price and marginal extraction costs, but are not the same as accounting profits. Neither firms nor governments are in the habit of recording these data. Empirical economists have thus often relied on proxy measures, such as exploration costs. The argument here is that rational firms will spend no more on exploration than the expected net benefits (that is, the expected future rents) to be thus gained. Devarajan and Fisher (1980) measured average exploration costs for oil in the USA over the period 1946–1971 and found them to be rising, an indicator of increasing scarcity despite the fact that no such trend exists in oil prices over that period. Yet, as expected prices are a component of expected rents, the criticisms of the real price measure given in the previous section also apply to the rent measure.

Second, the use of rent as a scarcity measure assumes that firms are following optimal depletion plans (Faber and Proops, 1993). Yet there is very little evidence that this is so in reality (see Chapter 9, section 4). What is more, to be able to follow the optimal depletion plan, firms need to be fully informed about future prices and extraction costs: a rather more extreme version of the Mayflower problem (although it is certainly possible to define a best depletion programme under conditions of uncertainty). Optimal depletion programmes will also be affected by interest rate movements, so that changes in rent will pick up these macroeconomic effects too.

While rent is perhaps the best scarcity indicator from a theory point of view (after all, it shows that gap between what society is willing to pay for one more unit of the resource and the cost of extracting that unit), it suffers from empirical drawbacks. Indeed, it is quite possible for the rent on a resource to *decrease* even though its physical abundance is falling: as Conrad and Clark (1987) point out, 'if an abundant resource can substitute for a resource that is becoming physically scarce, that resource may no longer be viewed as scarce from an economic perspective... there is a strong indication that [the rent] for copper has fallen and from an economic viewpoint it is now more abundant' (p. 131). Whether this is a 'problem' depends on whether one views the economic or the geological perspective as more important.

■ *8.3* Conclusions

We have seen in this chapter how resources are classified. The principal divisions are between energy and material resources, and renewable and non-renewable resources. Whether or not a mineral is geochemically scarce has also been argued to be of some importance.

With respect to indicators of resource scarcity, it is important to distinguish between economic and physical measures. The lifetime of a resource tells us little of use. The most commonly used alternatives are unit costs, real prices and rents, but none is free from problems. Norgaard and Howarth (1989) have commented that unless resource allocators are well informed about scarcity, none of these measures means very much; and that if resource allocators were so informed, the easiest way to find out whether resources were becoming scarcer would be simply to ask resource allocators: 'Quite simply, if the conditions necessary for the economic analysis of scarcity existed, there would be little reason to undertake economic analyses of scarcity' (Norgaard and Howarth, 1989, p. 11).

■ References

Anderson, F. (1985) *Natural Resources in Canada*, Toronto: Methuen.

Anderson, F. and B. Moazzami (1989) 'Resource scarcity re-examined', discussion paper 11-89, Lakehead University, Ontario.

Barnett, H.J. and C. Morse (1963) *Scarcity and Growth: The Economics of Natural Resource Scarcity*, Baltimore: Johns Hopkins Press.

Conrad, J. and C. Clark (1987) *Natural Resource Economics: Notes and Problems*, Cambridge: Cambridge University Press.

Deadman, D. and R.K. Turner (1988) 'Resource conservation, sustainability and technical change', in R.K. Turner (ed.), *Sustainable Environmental Management*. London: Belhaven.

Devarjan, S. and A. Fisher (1980) 'Exploration and scarcity', *Working Papers in Economic Theory*, IP-290, Berkeley: University of California.

Faber, M. and J. Proops (1993) 'Natural resource rents, economic dynamics and structural change', *Ecological Economics*, 8(1), 17–44.

Fisher, A.C. (1980) *Resource and Environmental Economics*, Cambridge: Cambridge University Press.

Hall, D. and J. Hall (1984) 'Concepts and measures of natural resource scarcity with a summary of recent trends', *Journal of Environmental Economics and Management*, 11, 363–79.

Hall, D., C. Cleveland and R. Kaufmann (1986) *Energy and Resource Quality: the Ecology of the Economic Process*, New York: John Wiley.

Harris, D. and B. Skinner (1982) 'The assessment of long-term supplies of minerals', in V.K. Smith and J. Krutilla (eds), *Explorations in Natural Resource Economics*, Baltimore: Johns Hopkins Press.

Hefindahl, O. (1959) *Copper Costs and Prices, 1870–1957*, Baltimore: Johns Hopkins Press.

Johnson, M., F. Bell and J. Bennett (1980) 'Natural resource scarcity: empirical evidence and public policy', *Journal of Environmental Economics and Management*, 7, 256–71.

Norgaard, R. (1975) 'Resource scarcity and new technology in US petroleum development', *Natural Resources Journal*, 15, 265–82.

Norgaard, R. (1990) 'Economic indicators of resource scarcity: a critical essay', *Journal of Environmental Economics and Management*, 19, 19–25.

Norgaard, R. and R. Howarth (1989) 'The scarcity of resource economics', mimeo, Energy and Resources Programme, University of California, Berkeley.

Skinner, B. (1976) 'A Second Iron Age?', *American Scientist*, 64, 258–69.

Slade, M. (1982) 'Trends in natural resource commodity prices: an analysis of the time domain', *Journal of Environmental Economics and Management*, 9, 122–37.

Tietenberg, T. (1992) *Environmental and Natural Resource Economics*, New York: Harper-Collins.

World Resources Institute (1992) *World Resources*, Oxford: Oxford University Press.

Zwartendyk, J. (1973) 'Mineral wealth: how should it be expressed?', *Canadian Mining Journal*, April, 44–52.

■ *Chapter 9* ■

An Economic Analysis of Non-Renewable Natural Resources

9.1 Introduction
9.2 Market structure and the exploitation of non-renewable resources
9.3 Production technology and extraction costs
9.4 Applying the theory

9.5 Government policy towards non-renewable resource taxation
9.6 Uncertainty and the rate of resource extraction
9.7 Summary

■ *9.1* Introduction

Non-renewable resources are those which are available in fixed quantities. Examples include metal ores, oil and coal. In some texts such resources are referred to as exhaustible resources. However, this is misleading when there is resource exploration and the marginal cost of finding additional reserves and extracting known reserves increases as the resource is depleted. The key issues in the economics of non-renewable natural resources are, first, the rate at which a rational firm exploits the resource, second, the price path of the resource and how it changes through time; and third, the life-cycle of the resource, that is, how quickly it is economically exhausted. It is the fact of inevitable economic exhaustion which sets the economics of non-renewable resources apart from conventional capital theory.

This chapter applies the comparative dynamic approach developed in Chapter 7 to progressively more sophisticated and realistic models of non-renewable resource firms. The next section considers a simple version of Hotelling's model and assesses the importance of market structure in determining the rate of resource extraction. The two extremes of perfect competition and monopoly are evaluated, then imperfect competition, in the form of cartels and oligopolisitc firms, is assessed. The third section extends the basic model to include forms of extraction cost and exploration cost function. Section 4 illustrates how Hotelling's model can be tested econometrically and offers a critique of the theory. Section 5 discusses taxation policy for non-renewable resource industries and assesses the effect of taxation on the rate of extraction. Section 6 analyses the effect of uncertainty on the rate of resource extraction.

9.2 Market structure and the exploitation of non-renewable resources

The emergence in the early 1970s of OPEC, a cartel in the oil market, led economists to analyse the effects of market structure upon the rate of non-renewable resource extraction. The issue is whether different forms of imperfectly competitive market structure exhaust a resource more or less rapidly than a competitive market. The extraction rate of a competitive market is socially optimal and provides a benchmark against which the extraction paths of other market structures can be compared.

This section is concerned with the comparative dynamics of non-renewable resource extraction. To draw clear-cut conclusions it is often necessary to make the following strong assumptions. A firm has perfect foresight of its own production plan and the plans of all other firms. The industry demand curve is known, thus all future prices are known: that is, firms hold rational expectations in the sense that they take account of all relevant information and understand how the market works. Perhaps the way to view decision making is as if the firm decides what its output will be over the planning period before the resource is exhausted, and then signs a binding contract at the beginning of the period to follow the plan. This is an open-loop equilibrium, as defined in section 7.4.

There is a price level at which the demand for the natural resource is zero owing to the presence of a 'backstop technology' which offers a perfect substitute for the natural resource, but at a higher cost. There are two forms of the backstop technology. First, it might be a high-cost invention which is held in abeyance until the price of the resource is high enough to make its production viable; second, it may be an alternative source of the natural resource which is available in virtually limitless quantities, but is more costly to extract. For instance, there are large quantities of oil in shale reserves in North America, but, these remain unexploited owing to relatively high extraction costs.

9.2.1 A competitive market structure and socially optimal extraction

In this section the rate of extraction of a competitive industry is analysed. To simplify the account extraction costs are assumed to be zero. In a competitive industry there are a large number of small firms, all of whom are price takers. For a firm to be indifferent between extracting the resource in the current period and a future period the price must rise at the discount rate, which is Hotelling's rule, introduced in section 7.2.1. The total stock declines at the rate of aggregate extraction and there exists some time when the industry's stock is exhausted, T_c. The optimal extraction path for the firms and the industry can be found without recourse to the maximum principle.

By assumption, the individual mine owner is indifferent between $p^c(0)$ at $t = 0$ and $p^c(0) e^{rt}$ at time t. It also follows that as the resource is exhausted extraction ceases and demand for the resource is zero, that is, $q^c(T_c) = 0$. For this to occur, the price at T_c must reach a level where demand is zero, $d(p^c(T_c)) = 0$. In other words, the price equals the backstop price, $p^c(T_c) = p^b$. By these assumptions, the initial resource price is related to the final resource price by

$$p^c(0) = f(q^c(T_c)) e^{-rT_c} = f(0) e^{-rT_c} = p^b e^{-rT_c}$$

that is, the initial price $p^c(0)$ equals the backstop price, p^b discounted from $t = T_c$ to $t = 0$, where $f(\cdot)$ is the inverse demand function. Conversely, the price in any period during the time interval $[0, T_c]$ is the initial price compounded. Using the result above we have

$$p^c(t) = p^b e^{-rT_c} e^{rt} = p^b e^{r(t-T_c)}$$

Determining the price and extraction paths depends upon finding T_c. The present value of total profit, $p^c(0)x_0$, is strictly increasing in x_0, thus it must be optimal to extract all the stock. The time when the resource is exhausted, T_c, is found by equating the integral of extraction to the initial stock.

$$S^c(p^b, r, T_c) = \int_0^{T_c} q^c(t) \, dt = \int_0^{T_c} d[p^b e^{r(t-T_c)}] \, dt = x_0 \tag{9.1}$$

that is the sum of the quantity extracted over the time interval $[0, T_c]$ must equal the initial stock.

The results derived are for an industry comprising a large number of firms acting to maximise profit. This can be compared with the social optimum where a planner determines the extraction path which maximises the present value of a welfare measure such as consumer surplus net of total resource costs. In the example chosen here, costs are assumed to be zero, so the problem reduces to one of maximising consumer surplus.

Consumer surplus is defined as the area under the inverse demand curve,

$$u(q) = \int_0^q f(w)\, dw$$

and the social planner's objective function is to maximise the present value of consumer surplus over the life of the resource,

$$\text{maximise}_q \quad \int_0^{T_c} u(q)\, e^{-rt}\, dt$$

subject to $\quad x(0) = x_0; \quad \dot{x} = -q$

The current-value Hamiltonian for the planner's problem is:

$$H = u(q) - \mu q$$

the first-order conditions are

$$u'(q) - \mu = 0$$

and the costate condition

$$\dot{\mu} - r\mu = -\frac{\partial H}{\partial x} = 0$$

Note that $u'(q) = p$. Substituting this for μ and rearranging the costate condition yields

$$r = \frac{\dot{p}}{p}$$

which is Hotelling's rule. Thus the social planner chooses the same extraction path as the competitive industry so long as r equals the social rate of time preference.

☐ 9.2.2 Monopoly

The economics of monopoly extraction is arguably more clear-cut than that of the competitive industry; there is no need to make assumptions about how much firms expect other firms to extract or for firms to form rational expectations of all future prices. Instead, the market price is endogenous to the monopoly firm.

The monopoly's optimal control problem is:

$$\text{maximise}_{q^m} \quad \int_0^{T_m} f(q^m) q^m\, e^{-rt}\, dt$$

subject to $\quad x(0) = x_0; \quad \dot{x} = -q^m$

As in section 7.3.3, we specify a current-value Hamiltonian

$$H(q^m, \mu) = f(q^m)q^m - \mu q^m$$

where μ is the costate variable which gives the marginal current value of a unit of stock. The first order conditions are

$$\frac{\partial H}{\partial q^m} = f(q^m) + f'(q^m)q^m - \mu = 0 \tag{9.2}$$

which can be simplified by defining a revenue function, $R(q) = f(q)q$

$$R'(q^m) = \mu$$

The costate condition is

$$\dot{\mu} - r\mu = -\frac{\partial H}{\partial x} = 0 \tag{9.3}$$

If (9.2) is differentiated with respect to time, equated with (9.3) and $R'(q^m)$ is substituted for μ

$$\frac{\dot{R}'(q^m)}{R'(q^m)} = r \tag{9.4}$$

This is Hotelling's rule for the monopoly firm. It states that the rate of change in the marginal revenue on the last unit conserved must equal the rate of return on a numeraire asset. In other words, this is the monopoly firm's portfolio equilibrium where they are indifferent between holding the marginal unit of resource stock and its equivalent value as the numeraire asset.

The implication of these results is that the monopoly equates the present value of the marginal revenue across the life of the resource; in effect the monopoly operates a form of perfect price discrimination through time. Initially, it supplies at a relatively low price on the less elastic segment of the demand curve; just before depletion it supplies at a point where the elasticity is high. The 'markets' are separated by time but also by the fact that the price rises at less than the discount rate, so no incentive exists for the speculative storage and resale of resource stocks by traders.

From (9.4) it follows that the value of stock over time must be related by $\mu(t) = \mu(0) e^{rt}$ and specifically that $\mu(T_m) = \mu(0) e^{rT_m}$ where T_m is the time when the monopoly firm exhausts its stock. As $q(T_m) = 0$, (9.2) is

$$f(0) - \mu(T_m) = 0$$

recall that demand is zero at the backstop price, p^b, thus $\mu(T_m) = p^b$. By the fact that μ must increase by the discount rate, $\mu(0) = p^b e^{-rT_m}$, thus for the time interval $[0, T_m]$

$$\mu(t) = \mu(0) e^{rt} = (p^b e^{-rT_m}) e^{rt} = p^b e^{r(t-T_m)} \tag{9.5}$$

Equating (9.2) with (9.5)

$$f(q^m) + f'(q^m)q^m = p^b e^{r(t-T_m)} \tag{9.6}$$

the solution of the problem lies in solving (9.6) for q^m and integrating the resulting expression to determine the time taken to extract the initial stock. General solutions to (9.6) are not straightforward. It follows that the initial rate of extraction over the time interval $[0, T_m]$ increases with the discount rate and declines with p^b. We return to this problem in the next section, where a linear demand function is assumed.

☐ 9.2.3 *Competitive and monopoly extraction with a linear demand curve*

This section derives optimal extraction paths for competitive and monopoly industries based on a linear demand curve. Results exist for generalised demand functions (Stiglitz and Dasgupta, 1982); however these are not discussed in any detail here. The demand curve is

$$q = d(p) = \frac{p^b}{\beta} - \frac{1}{\beta} p \qquad \beta > 0 \tag{9.7}$$

where p^b is the backstop price, and β is the slope of the inverse demand function, thus:

$$p = f(q) = p^b - \beta q$$

when $q = 0$, $p = p^b$. Substituting this function into (9.1) to obtain a solution for T_c:

$$\int_0^{T_c} \frac{p^b}{\beta} (1 - e^{r(t-T_c)}) \, dt = p^b T_c - \frac{p^b(1 - e^{-rT_c})}{r} = \beta x_0 \tag{9.8}$$

which can be solved numerically for T_c using Newton's method. Once T_c is determined the price path is $p(t) = p^b e^{r(t-T_c)}$; thus by Hotelling's rule $p(t) = p(0) e^{rt}$ and the extraction path is derived from the demand function (9.7).

Now consider the monopoly case. After some rearranging, (9.6) for a linear demand function becomes

$$q^m = \frac{p^b}{2\beta} (1 - e^{r(t-T_m)})$$

introducing the resource exhaustion constraint and integrating

$$\int_0^{T_m} \frac{p^b}{2\beta} (1 - e^{r(t-T_m)}) \, dt = p^b T_m - \frac{p^b(1 - e^{-rT_m})}{r} = 2\beta x_0 \tag{9.9}$$

This can be compared with the corresponding condition for the competitive industry (9.8), the result that $T_m > T_c$ emerges immediately as $T - (1 - e^{-rT})/r$ is increasing in T.

The comparative dynamics are presented in a four quadrant diagram, Figure 9.1. The price path is shown in the south-west quadrant, the extraction path in the north-east quadrant and the demand curve in the north-west quadrant. Initially, the competitive industry extracts more rapidly than the monopoly, but then less rapidly as the price increases towards the backstop price, p^b, shown in the south-west quadrant. The initial price of the monopoly firm is higher than that of the competitive

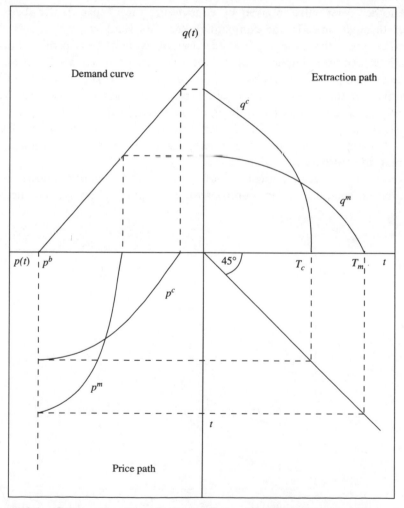

Figure 9.1 *Comparative dynamics for costless extraction under competition and monopoly*

industry. It then increases more gradually towards the backstop price. The rate of price increase for the monopoly is less than the discount rate. If this is not the case, opportunities exist for the resource to be purchased by speculators, stored and sold at a later date, thus reducing monopoly profits.

The comparative dynamics of changes in the exogenous variables, the discount rate r, the backstop price p^b, and the initial stock x_0 are considered in two stages: first, in terms of how this affects the time when the resource exhausts from (9.9) and then how this changes the price path from (9.6). For instance, increasing the discount rate reduces T_m, increases the rate of extraction during the early phase of extraction and increases the rate of price increase.

Another perspective is given by considering the change in the shadow price through time. In the competitive case the shadow price equals the resource price, that is $p^c = \mu^c$, as the present value of total profits simply equals $p^c(0)x_0$; this implies that the total resource rent equals the present value of total profits, that is by definition $p^c(0)x_0 = \mu^c(0)x_0$. In other words, if firms rent the resource at its equilibrium rent, their profit is zero. The monopoly case is somewhat different. The current value of profit per unit of stock is p^m, but the rent per unit of stock is given by (9.6) $p^m + f'(q^m)q^m = \mu^m$. Thus the monopoly profit over the equilibrium amount of rent paid is $f'(q^m)q^m$.

Returning to our numerical example, once the price path is known, it is possible to solve for the monopoly rent μ^m. Figure 9.2 shows the current

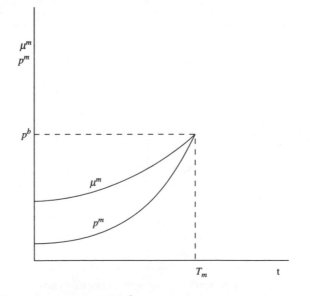

Figure 9.2 *Monopoly rent, current value*

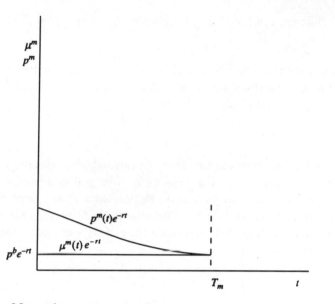

Figure 9.3 *Monopoly rent, present value*

value of prices and marginal rents, Figure 9.3 the present value. Note that the present value of rent, $\lambda^m = \mu^m(t)\,e^{-rt}$, is constant as the discounted value of the backstop and the present value of profits is highest when $t = 0$.

☐ 9.2.4 *Constant elasticity demand curve*

The results derived in the previous section for the linear demand curve are representative of a class of demand curves where the demand elasticity declines with respect to the quantity demanded. If instead we assume a constant elasticity demand function, Stiglitz (1976, p. 656) shows that the extraction and price paths for a competitive industry and monopoly are identical.

This can be shown by considering the monopoly firm's problem. The inverse demand curve is $p = q^{\beta-1}$ and revenue $pq = q^{\beta-1}q = q^{\beta}$. The present-value Hamiltonian for the problem is

$$H(q, \lambda) = q^{\beta}\,e^{-rt} - \lambda q$$

Differentiating with respect to q and substituting in p gives

$$\beta p\,e^{-rt} - \lambda = 0$$

and then differentiating with respect to time by the product rule gives

$$\dot{\lambda} = \dot{p}\beta e^{-rt} - pr\beta e^{-rt}$$

By noting that the costate condition is $\dot{\lambda} = 0$, that is, the present value of marginal revenue is equal across all time periods, divide through by βe^{-rt} and rearrange for the result

$$\frac{\dot{p}}{p} = r$$

That is, the price increases at the discount rate, which is Hotelling's rule for the competitive firm. Thus the monopoly firm and competitive industry pursue the same extraction path and exhaust stock at the same time for a constant elasticity demand curve. The monopoly firm can only engage in intertemporal price discrimination when the elasticity is a declining function of the quantity demanded.

□ 9.2.5 *Imperfect competition*

We turn now to the important case of more general imperfect competition where the market structure lies between the extremes of monopoly and competition. Imperfect competition is of particular importance in natural resource markets where access to the resource is a necessary prerequisite to entering the market: this restricts entry to natural resource markets and has provided an incentive for firms to establish dominant positions in a market. Recent history has shown the impact and importance of market power in natural resource markets through the emerging power and strategic importance of OPEC during the 1970s and early 1980s and international cartel agreements in other natural resources, including copper and bauxite. In recent years the importance of cartels has declined, but many natural resource markets are dominated by small numbers of large multinational and state controlled companies. There remains the possibility that cartels will periodically re-emerge as important market structures. This section will first be concerned with the cartelisation of a resource and then be extended to a more general model of oligopolistic competition.

The non-renewable resource cartel

The firms in the market are divided into two groups: an atomistic competitive fringe which behaves as firms in a competitive industry and an alliance of firms operating as a cartel. The competitive fringe constrains the monopoly power of the cartel. The extent to which this is possible depends upon the stocks held by the cartel and its extraction costs relative to those of the fringe. There has been much debate in the economic literature concerning three issues. First, does the market attain a Nash–Cournot equilibrium or a von Stackleberg equilibrium where the cartel is the market leader? Second, is the equilibrium dynamically inconsistent; that is, does an incentive exist for the cartel to make promises about their supply schedule which they will subsequently wish to break? And third, is the cartel itself stable or does an incentive exist for the individual firms within the cartel to renege on their original agreement? These are complex issues and we approach them by considering the Nash–Cournot solution proposed by Salant (1976) and then the more complex von Stackleberg equilibrium proposed by Newberry (1981)and further developed by Groot *et al.* (1992) and Karp and Newberry (1993).

In common with the practice of most other authors, the analysis is presented by recourse to a linear demand function with a backstop price and a constant marginal cost. Costs are introduced here to give an element of realism; it is usual to assume that the cartel has a lower marginal cost than the fringe. Hotelling's rule for a competitive firm is modified in the presence of cost so that

$$\frac{\dfrac{d(p-c)}{dt}}{p-c} = r$$

that is, that the percentage increase in p less the constant marginal cost, c equals the discount rate. Resource extraction with costs is discussed in more detail in section 9.3.

These restrictive assumptions about cost and demand functions have been found to be necessary to derive *any* results for this market structure. The problem with analysing this form of market structure is that extraction may take place in a number of phases; for instance, when the cartel has a relatively low marginal cost the cartel enters the market at a price below the fringe's marginal cost, the fringe waits until the price rises above its marginal cost level and then starts to extract and ultimately exhausts its reserves when the backstop price is reached. The resulting discontinuous form of price, quantity and shadow price trajectory makes the direct application of the maximum principle difficult. Moreover, open-loop control theory may actually be dynamically inconsistent: although the maximum principle defines an optimal solution, incentives exist for the cartel to change the optimal solution at a later date; in other words the cartel may only stick to its original supply schedule if it signs a binding contract in the initial period. The likelihood of such contracts being honoured is questioned by Newberry (1981): 'international contracts, can only be enforced by mutual self-interest and not by appeal to higher authority, then agents may subsequently wish to depart from the plan derived from the maximum principle. In short, in these cases the plan ceases to be credible, and hence ceases to characterise the rational expectations equilibrium' (p. 617).

The structure of the model is outlined with reference to the control theory format used by Groot *et al.* (1992). The superscript f refers to the fringe, d the cartel. The competitive fringe

$$\text{maximises}_{q^f} \quad \int_0^T e^{-rt}(p - c^f)q^f\, dt$$

$$\text{subject to} \quad x^f(0) = x_0^f; \quad \dot{x} = -q^f$$

$$x_0^f \geq 0 \qquad q^f(t) \geq 0$$

The non-negativity constraints on the stock and and the rate of extraction lead to a solution specified as Kuhn–Tucker conditions. In this problem these constraints are emphasised as it is usual for the fringe to harvest nothing for periods during the planning horizon. See the technical note on pp. 98–103 for details on Kuhn–Tucker conditions. The Hamiltonian for the problem is

$$H^f(q^f, x^f, t) = e^{-rt}(p - c^f)q^f - \lambda^f q^f \tag{9.10}$$

and the first-order derivative with respect to q^f is:

$$H_{q^f}^f = e^{-rt}(p - c^f) - \lambda^f \leq 0$$

with the complementary slackness condition, $q^f H_{q^f}^f = 0$. This implies that the fringe only extracts when the marginal profit rate exceeds the marginal value of *in situ* stock. That (9.10) includes the price as a parameter implies the fringe adopts a Nash–Cournot strategy which assumes the price and therefore the rate of extraction of the cartel is given to the fringe. The problem of the cartel is more difficult in that its behaviour affects the rate at which the fringe extracts and the time when the fringe exhausts its stock. The Nash–Cournot cartel faces the problem:

$$\text{maximises}_{q^d} \quad \int_0^T e^{-rt}(p^b - \beta(q^f + q^d) - c^d)q^d\, dt$$

$$\text{subject to} \quad x^d(0) = x_0^d; \quad \dot{x} = -q^d$$

$$x_0^d \geq 0 \qquad q^d(t) \geq 0$$

That is, the cartel maximises its profit but assumes that the fringe's output is fixed. This formulation is modified for the von Stackleberg equilibrium as follows:

$$\text{maximises}_{q^d, q^f} \quad \int_0^T e^{-rt}(p^b - \beta(q^f + q^d) - c^d)q^d \, dt$$

subject to
$$x^d(0) = x_0^d; \qquad \dot{x} = -q^d$$

$$x_0^d \geq 0; \qquad q^d(t) \geq 0$$

$$x^f(0) = x_0^f; \qquad \dot{x} = -q^f$$

$$x_0^f \geq 0; \qquad q^f(t) \geq 0$$

$$e^{-rt}(p^b - \beta(q^f + q^d) - c^f) - \lambda^f \leq 0; \qquad q^f H_{q^f}^f = 0$$

In this case the cartel chooses not only its own extraction trajectory but the fringe's as well, subject to the first-order conditions for the fringe. We consider the Nash–Cournot and von Stackleberg equilibria in turn.

Nash–Cournot equilibrium

The cartel maximises its own profit by taking as given the sales of the fringe. The cartel chooses a price path to maximise its discounted profits, the fringe takes the price path as given and chooses an extraction path to maximise its profit. A situation where each actor maximises benefits, given the optimal choice of the other agents, is a Nash–Cournot equilibrium.

Consider Figures 9.4 and 9.5. Resource exploitation can be divided into two phases. During the first phase the price, from Figure 9.4, less the

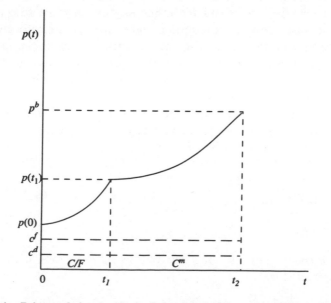

Figure 9.4 *Price path for the Nash–Cournot solution to the cartel problem*

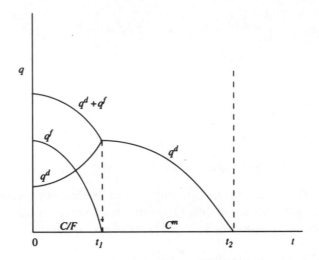

Figure 9.5   *Quantity path for the Nash–Cournot solution to the cartel problem*

marginal cost for the fringe rises at the discount rate and the market is supplied by both the cartel and the fringe (C/F in Figures 9.4 and 9.5); the cartel's marginal revenue less the cartel's marginal cost rises at the discount rate. At the end of the first phase, $t = t_1$, the fringe exhausts its stock and the cartel is free to operate as a monopoly (C^m in Figures 9.4 and 9.5) and its marginal revenue less marginal cost rises at the discount rate until the price reaches the backstop price and the monopoly exhausts its reserves. The solution is a Nash–Cournot equilibrium and is also dynamically consistent in the sense that no incentive exists for the cartel or the fringe to deviate from its original extraction plan. Further no arbitrage opportunities exist for speculators to buy the resource and sell it at a later date as the price increases at or below the discount rate.

The Nash–Cournot equilibrium is not easily determined analytically, but can be solved by dynamic programming or other numerical methods. For instance, if the price is given by ($\beta = 1$):

$$p = p^b - q$$

the price over the first period is

$$p = e^{-r(t_1 - t)}(p(t_1) - c^f) + c^f \tag{9.11}$$

That is, the net margin must increase by the discount rate, it follows the quantity extracted is

$$q^f + q^d = p^b - \{e^{-r(t_1 - t)}(p(t_1) - c^f) + c^f\} \tag{9.12}$$

Exhaustion occurs when the fringe and the cartel exhaust their stock. For the fringe we have

$$x_0^f = \int_0^{t_1} q^f \, dt \tag{9.13}$$

and the cartel exhausts its reserves over two phases

$$x_0^d = \int_0^{t_1} q^d \, dt + \int_{t_1}^{t_2} q^d \, dt \tag{9.14}$$

In addition the condition for the cartel's net marginal revenue is:

$$p - 2q^d - q^f - c^d = (p^b - c^d) e^{-r(t_2 - t)}$$

That is, the net marginal revenue increases by the discount rate over the whole life of the resource. The unknowns in this problem are t_1, t_2, $p(0)$, $p(t)$, $q^f(t)$, $q^c(t)$, which exceed the number of equations which define the problem. It is for this reason that some authors, notably Newberry (1981) and Ulph (1982) resort to 'diagrammatic' solutions of these problems rather than analytical ones. A prediction of these models is that cartelisation increases the profit of the fringe by a greater proportion than that of the cartel. This is as a result of the slope of the price path and the fact that the fringe's extraction occurs exclusively in the first phase when the present value of the price is highest.

Von Stackelberg leader–follower equilibrium

In this case, instead of passively assuming that the fringe's output is fixed, the cartel manipulates the behaviour of the fringe to increase its profits. In turn the fringe assumes that the cartel's output is fixed. As Groot *et al.* (1992) show, the exact solution depends upon the relative costs of the fringe and the cartel and their initial stocks. In the most usual case, where the cartel has a relatively large stock and a lower marginal cost, a solution involves four phases: the first where the cartel sells at the competitive price; a second where the cartel sells as a monopoly; a third where the fringe exhausts its reserves; and a fourth where the cartel sells as a monopoly and exhausts its stock when the price reaches the backstop price.

Consider Figure 9.6. the optimal solution is found where the cartel sells at the competitive price p^c up to t_1, then at the monopoly price p^m between t_1 and t_2; the fringe exhausts its stock between t_2 and t_3 and finally the cartel operates as a monopoly from t_3 to t_4. The price path depends upon a binding contract or open-loop control solution where all the decisions are taken in the initial period. However, an incentive exists for the cartel to break its agreement during period t_2 and t_3 and to supply at the higher competitive price. Further if the price step at t_2 is anticipated by traders, supplies will be purchased during $t = 0$ to $t = t_2$, stored and sold during t_2 to t_3, thus smoothing out the optimal price path and reducing the cartel's profit.

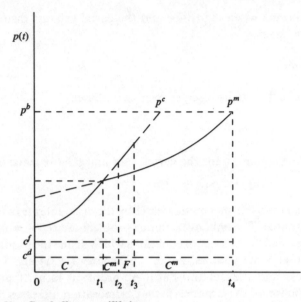

Figure 9.6   *Von Stackelberg equilibrium*

This type of pattern of resource pricing emerges over a number of different assumptions regarding stocks price and costs and calls into question the von Stackelberg equilibrium as a valid equilibrium, first because there is no incentive for the cartel to stick to its extraction schedule, second because the fringe has no incentive to accept what the cartel announces as its proposed pattern of extraction, and third because the price structure may be undermined by arbitrage if the extracted resource can be stored cheaply. Some estimates of the monopoly power of cartels are given in Box 9.1.

Box 9.1   *Gains to producers from the cartelisation of exhaustible resources*

It is argued that the reason for OPEC's formation and success as a cartel is the gains derived from forming a cartel in the world oil market. Indeed, a case has been made Eckbo (1975) that successful cartels are in markets where monopoly profits are greatest. These profits are necessary to compensate for the costs associated with cartelisation itself in terms of frequent political negotiations, price and supply monitoring in world markets and cartel administration.

Pindyck (1978b) analyses dynamic econometric models of the petroleum, copper and bauxite markets to assess the gains from forming cartels. The gains from cartelisation are measured by taking reserve levels and estimated supply and demand relationships, assuming that producers are profit maximisers and measuring the increase in discounted profits under cartelisation.

The results indicate the following conclusions.

Oil OPEC accounted for about 66 per cent of non-communist world oil production. The gains from cartelisation in the oil market over a competitive market are between a 50 per cent and a 100 per cent increase in profits. The incentives for maintaining the cartel are considerable.

Bauxite The bauxite market is run by the IBA (International Bauxite Association) which includes seven countries which account for 74 per cent of non-communist bauxite production. In the long term cartelisation results in a 60 per cent to 500 per cent increase in profits over a competitive market.

Copper The copper market is dominated by CIPEC (International Council of Copper Exporting Countries) which includes four countries and accounts for 32 per cent of non-Communist world copper production. The gain from cartelisation is 8 per cent to 30 per cent above the competitive market profits.

Over a range of assumptions about the discount rate there are considerable gains from cartelisation in the cases of petroleum and bauxite. This is due to the high market share held by the cartel and slow rate of short-term demand adjustments: the demand and supply of petroleum and bauxite adjust only slowly to changes in price. In contrast the relatively small gains to cartelisation in the the copper market are due to the small market share of the copper cartel and the short-term responsiveness of the secondary copper markets to price which acts to eliminate monopoly profits.

Cartel stability

There has been a tendency for natural resource cartels to break up when the price of the commodity is low and supply restraint can become a target for political pressure to maintain government revenue from taxes on resource extraction. The stability of the cartel depends upon long-run benefits weighed against the short-run benefits of breaking a cartel agreement and also the way the additional profits due to the cartel are divided amongst its members. Members of OPEC honoured their supply quotas during periods of high oil prices but exceeded quotas when the oil price fell in the late 1980s, at which time the quota system was suspended and OPEC no longer operated as as cartel.

Both the Nash–Cournot cartel and the von Stackelberg cartels are inherently unstable as a firm in the cartel can increase its profits by shifting its extraction from the later monopoly phase to the earlier competitive phase. A firm benefits to a greater extent from this activity if it goes undetected and the remaining firms in the cartel comply with the agreement. However, if a large number of firms cheat on the agreement the market reverts to being competitive or, more typically, oligopolistic.

We consider this form of market structure next. Cartels can only be sustained if the benefits can be distributed in a way which keeps the cartel stable and eliminates strong incentives for individual countries to abandon the cartel and join the fringe. Successful cartels often depend upon one major supplier who recognises the long-term benefits of cartelisation, but can also credibly threaten other producers with massive oversupply and price collapse if they do not abide by agreements. Saudi Arabia assumed this role within OPEC and was largely responsible for the initially successful operation of supply quotas. See Gilbert (1987) for a general review of commodity agreements.

9.2.6 Oligopolistic non-renewable resource extraction

The previous section considered non-renewable resource markets which comprise a single cartel with a competitive fringe. However, an alternative analysis could be based upon oligopolistic competition where a few firms dominate a market without forming a cartel. Non-renewable resource markets are often characterised by a small number of countries holding significant reserves of a mineral. Such markets may alternate between cartelised and oligopolistic market structures as collusive alliances are formed and then revoked.

Loury (1986), develops a model of the oil market as an oligopolistic market structure. Two models of the oil market have emerged: one which analyses the market as a cartel, the other as a more general oligopolistic market structure. Loury's model may be viewed as a generalisation of Salant's (1976) model of a Nash–Cournot equilibrium in a cartelised oil market. It allows for a range of market structures from monopoly at one extreme to competition at the other, with intermediate oligopolistic market structures in between.

The firms possess an initial stock $x_{i0}(i = 1, 2, \ldots, n)$. The extraction rate of the firm is q_i. The total extraction from all firms is q. Additional assumptions that are required to ensure a Nash–Cournot equilibrium are that the total industry revenue, $R(q) = p(q)q$, is concave in q and that the elasticity of demand η is decreasing in q. This last assumption ensures that imperfectly competitive firms earn more profits than competitive ones. This point is made by Polasky (1992, p. 219)

> Imperfectly competitive producers earn more than competitive producers by acting as price discriminators over time. Since price is low and quantity is high in initial time periods, elasticity is low relative to later periods.

Intertemporal price discrimination requires setting higher prices in earlier periods and lower prices in later periods relative to a non-price discriminating intertemporal allocation. If [the] assumption [that the demand elasticity is decreasing in q] is violated, intertemporal price discrimination is impossible and the market outcome will be competitive regardless of market structure.

This point has already been alluded to in sections 9.2.2 and 9.2.4.

Assume that the marginal extraction costs are constant and identical for all firms. The firm's problem is to choose an open-loop strategy q_i, when all other firms choose open-loop strategies $q_{\sim i} = \{q_i, q_2, \ldots, q_{i-1}, q_{i+1}, \ldots, q_n\}$ where $q_{\sim i}$ is the supply of all firms except q_i

$$\pi_i(q_i, q_{\sim i}) = \int_0^T e^{-rt}[p(q) - c]q_i \, dt$$

A Nash equilibrium in open-loop strategies is a set of feasible strategies $\{q_1^*, q_2^*, \ldots, q_N^*\}$ such that for all i $\pi_i(q_i^*, q_{\sim i}^*) \geq \pi_i(q_i, q_{\sim i}^*)$ for all feasible strategies. The necessary and sufficient conditions for an optimal extraction path are:

$$e^{-rt}\{p'(q^*)q_i^* + p(q^*) - c\} = \lambda_i \qquad \text{if } q_i^* > 0$$

$$e^{-rt}\{p'(q^*)q_i^* + p(q^*) - c\} \leq \lambda_i \qquad \text{if } q_i^* = 0$$

and the costate condition:

$$\dot{\lambda} = 0$$

Thus if $q_i^* > 0$ the discounted marginal profit is equal across the planning period, which is Hotelling's rule.

Loury proves three propositions; first, if the initial stock of one firm is greater than another's $x_{i0} > x_{j0}$ then $\lambda_i > \lambda_j$. Intuitively, this implies that a large firm places a lower shadow price on reserves. So from the necessary conditions above, the firm with a relatively large reserve supplies a larger amount yielding a lower marginal profit than a firm with a smaller reserve. Second, firms with large reserves extract a smaller proportion of their reserves in each period than a firm with smaller reserves. Third, an increase in the marginal extraction costs for a firm causes the firm to extract its reserves more slowly relative to its rivals. These results have implications for the rate at which an industry extracts its resource: the larger the firms are in a natural resource industry, the more gradual is the rate of resource extraction. Box 9.2 presents econometric evidence in support of Loury's results. We now demonstrate this point by recourse to a linear demand curve.

Oligopolistic extraction with a linear demand curve

First assume the duopoly case where the firms produce perfect substitutes and assume that the output of the other firm is given and known in any period. Further assume that each firm holds half the stock and that exhaustion of each firm's stock is simultaneous. Extraction is costless. The demand curve

$$p = f(q_1, q_2) = p^b - \beta(q_1 + q_2)$$

is similar to that for the cartel except that there are two separate, identical firms. The problem for each firm is to

$$\text{maximise}_{q_i} \quad \int_0^{T_i} f(q_1, q_2) q_i \, e^{-rt} \, dt$$

subject to $\quad x_i(0) = \tfrac{1}{2} x_0; \quad \dot{x}_i = -q_i \quad i = 1, 2$

As the firms are identical it is possible to analyse this problem for just one of the firms. The current-value Hamiltonian for firm 1 is

$$H(q_1, q_2, \mu_1) = f(q_1, q_2) q_1 - \mu_1 q_1$$

differentiating with respect to q_1 gives

$$f_{q_1} q_1 + f(q_1, q_2) = \mu_1 \tag{9.15}$$

and the costate condition is

$$\dot{\mu}_1 - r\mu_1 = -\frac{\partial H}{\partial x_1} = 0$$

In common with the monopoly problem the marginal revenue in the last period is

$$p^b = \mu_1(T_1)$$

by the portfolio equilibrium condition, that the marginal revenue of each firm must rise at the discount rate, from (9.15) we have

$$p - \beta q_1 = p^b e^{-r(T_1 - t)}$$

or substituting in the inverse demand function for p

$$p^b - \beta(q_1 + q_2) - \beta q_1 = p^b e^{-r(T_1 - t)}$$

If we make the strong assumption that the oligopolies follow cournot policies and each supplies an identical share of the market, thus $q_1 = q_2$, $\mu_1 = \mu_2, = \mu$ and $T_1 = T_2 = T_o$ it follows that

$$q_1 = \frac{p^b}{3\beta} \left(1 - e^{-r(T_1 - t)}\right)$$

By the constraint of stock exhaustion for the firm

$$\int_0^{T_o} q_1 \, dt = \int_0^{T_o} \frac{p^b}{3\beta} (1 - e^{r(t-T_o)}) \, dt = \frac{p^b}{3\beta} \left[T_o - \frac{(1 - e^{-rT_o})}{r} \right] = \frac{x_0}{2}$$

for the industry it follows that

$$p^b \left[T_o - \frac{(1 - e^{-rT_o})}{r} \right] = \frac{3\beta x_0}{2}$$

This implies, as would be expected, that the duopoly resource industry exhausts its reserves more rapidly than the monopoly firm, see (9.9), but less rapidly than the competitive industry, see (9.8). To generalise to other oligopolistic structures with identical firms

$$p^b \left[T_o - \frac{(1 - e^{-rT_o})}{r} \right] = \frac{(1 + N)\beta x_0}{N}$$

where N is the number of firms in the industry, as N increases the solution approximates the solution for the competitive industry given in (9.8).

If the assumption that the firms are identical is relaxed and firms have different resource stocks, the result would be consistent with Loury's predictions, but would be difficult to analyse due to firms with small resource stocks exhausting before firms with larger stocks. This is similar to the analysis of the cartel problem (section 9.2.5) where the marginal revenue path has a number of phases and may converge on the monopoly extraction path as firms with smaller reserves exhaust their stock and only a few larger firms remain in production, see Polasky (1992) for an example.

Box 9.2   *Testing Loury's Theory of Oligopolistic Oil Extraction*

Loury (1986) provides a set of propositions concerning the oligopolistic extraction of oil. Polasky (1992) develops an econometric framework for testing these propositions. In a general form extraction by producer i at time t can be written as a function of reserves and extraction costs:

$$q_i = f(x_i, c_i)$$

If Loury's propositions are correct, then $f_x > 0$, $f_{xx} < 0$ and $f_c < 0$. The functional form used to test these propositions is:

$$\ln(q_i) = \ln(\alpha) + \beta_1 \ln(x_i) + \beta_2 \ln(w_i) + \beta_3 \ln(d_i) + \beta_4 s_i + \varepsilon_i$$

where w_i is production per well by producer i in year t, d_i is the average well depth drilled by producer i, s_i is the percentage of off-shore production for producer i and α and the β's are parameters. Estimates of this equation using data from 69 oil producing countries over the period 1970–89 yielded the results:

$$\ln(q_i) = 3.0671^* + 0.1571^* \ln(x_i) + 0.74^* \ln(w_i) - 0.025 \ln(d_i) + 0.0066^* s_i + \varepsilon_i$$

(*denotes significance at the 5 per cent level) $R^2 = 0.95$

The estimate for the parameter β_1 is positive but less than one; this implies that $f_x > 0$ and $f_{xx} < 0$. Therefore the estimate is consistent with the theory: the rate of extraction increases with reserves, but at a declining rate. The remaining variables are proxies for marginal extraction costs, in which case a high production per well, a low average depth drilled and a low percentage of off-shore production would all be associated with lower marginal costs. The estimated parameters, with the exception of the one on off-shore production, are consistent with Loury's propositions.

9.3 Production technology and extraction costs

The previous section examined the implications of market structure upon the market price, the rate of extraction and the time of resource exhaustion. Clearly, the models presented are not entirely realistic as they assume production is either costless or at a constant marginal cost. This section considers the impact on the extraction path of non-linear cost functions of two forms: first, as a function of extraction costs and, second, as a function of cumulative resource depletion. Cost functions represent how production technology impinges upon the economics of resource extraction. A careful consideration of the nature of cost functions is important in studies of natural resource extraction as the production process, which is largely determined by the form of geological structures, is often quite different from manufacturing or agricultural production.

9.3.1 A competitive industry with a non-linear extraction cost

Here we consider the problem of the individual firm as the starting-point and then consider how price and the rate of extraction evolves for the industry as a whole. The firm's problem is to

$$\text{maximise}_q \quad \int_0^T (pq - c(x, q))\, e^{-rt}\, dt$$

$$\text{subject to} \quad x(0) = x_0; \quad \dot{x} = -q$$

Costs are a function both of the quantity extracted and of the remaining stock; the assumptions concerning the cost function are $c_{qq} > 0$ and $c_x < 0$. That is, the marginal cost is increasing in terms of the quantity extracted and the cost decreases as a function of the resource stock remaining. This can be thought of in terms of a mine: increasing output at a point in time increases the marginal cost, while depleting the stock, by moving to reserves further from the minehead, increases overall cost levels. This is represented in Figure 9.7, where average costs are given by $c(x_1, q)/q$ and $c(x_2, q)/q$, where $x_1 > x_2$, and marginal costs $c_q|x_1$ and $c_q|x_2$.

The first-order conditions for optimal extraction are derived from the current-value Hamiltonian

$$H(q, \mu, t) = pq - c(x, q) - \mu q \tag{9.16}$$

The first-order conditions are

$$p(t) - c_q - \mu = 0 \tag{9.17}$$

$$\dot{\mu} = r\mu + c_x \tag{9.18}$$

The costate condition (9.18) includes the cost term c_x; this includes in the value of the stock the change in costs with respect to the stock. That is, stock has a value in terms of making extraction cheaper. Differentiating (9.17) with respect to time, equating with (9.18) and then substituting for μ from (9.17):

$$\frac{\frac{d}{dt}(p - c_q)}{(p - c_q)} - \frac{c_x}{(p - c_q)} = r \tag{9.19}$$

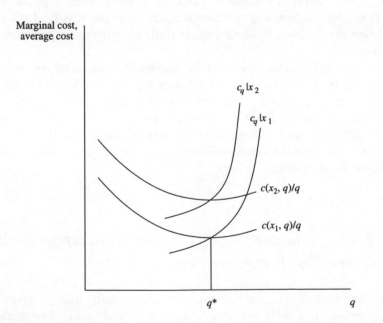

Figure 9.7 *Extraction costs*

which is the modified version of Hotelling's rule. The transversality condition that $H(T) = 0$ for a free terminal time problem, implies that

$$\mu(T) = p(T) - \frac{c(x(T), q(T))}{q(T)}$$

From (9.17) it also follows that

$$\mu(T) = p(T) - c_q$$

Thus after substituting

$$c_q = \frac{c(x(T), q(T))}{q(T)} \tag{9.20}$$

that is, the output at T is where the marginal cost curve crosses the average cost curve at $q(T) = q^*$, see Figure 9.7. The marginal value or shadow price of stock, μ, drives a wedge between the price and the marginal cost; from (9.17) it follows that the way the shadow price changes through time depends upon the cost function. We return to this issue later in this section.

Despite the simplification represented by the above equation and even if it is possible to solve the marginal cost function for q, solving for the optimal extraction path over N firms remains a formidable problem. It may be possible to proceed by assuming all the firms have identical costs and stocks – but this is a very strong assumption. An alternative assumption might be a market for resource stock at a rental rate, $\mu_i(t)$ which is determined by the firm with the lowest costs; however, it is far from clear that reserves of natural resource such as coal, bauxite and oil are tradeable in this way.

The empirical studies discussed in section 9.4 side-step the issue of aggregating from N firms up to the industry supply, demand and extraction path by modelling either a single firm or a representative firm facing a given price. It is also assumed that the resource market ensures that the resource rent equilibrates across firms and chooses a single 'satisfactory' cost function which can be estimated from data for either a single firm or aggregate industry data.

9.3.2 The costs of extracting a heterogeneous reserve with exploration

Thus far there has been an implicit assumption that reserves are homogeneous. For most resources this is a simplification. For instance, the pressure in oil fields declines as extraction proceeds and eventually gas may be pumped into the reservoir to force out the last reserves. In mines the first reserves extracted are of the highest grade and close to the surface. Once these are exhausted, mining is moved to progressively deeper deposits or more remote areas where extraction is more costly.

The most influential model of joint exploration extraction process is due to Pindyck (1978). He assumes that the competitive firm maximises the following problem:

$$\text{maximise}_{q,w} = \int_0^\infty [pq - c_1(x)q - c_2(w)] e^{-rt} \, dt$$

subject to $\quad \dot{x} = y - q \qquad y = \omega(w, Y) \qquad x(0) = x_0$

The average extraction cost function, $c_1(x)$, is a function of proven reserves, but marginal cost is constant in q. Thus as reserves are depleted the marginal extraction cost increases. In addition the discovery cost function $c_2(w)$ is convex in the exploration effort w; this decision variable through a discovery production function, $\omega(w, Y)$, determines the rate of discovery of new reserve y; it is increasing with exploration effort but decreasing in cumulative discoveries, Y. Discovering reserves has two effects: it delays exhaustion and reduces extraction costs. An interesting prediction of the Pindyck model is that the price path may be U-shaped. Initially the price decreases as discoveries are made cheaply early in the life of the resource and the marginal cost falls; price then increases as discoveries become more expensive and the marginal cost increases.

Solow and Wan (1976) developed an alternative model to represent the progressive increase in costs as the reserve is depleted. Their model assumes constant returns to scale and constant unit extraction costs for a deposit; however, extraction costs increase with cumulative extraction. Define the deposit-cost profile, $F(c, t)$, as the fraction of resource reserves at t with a unit extraction cost less than c, and let $F(c, 0) = F(0)$. It is shown by Solow and Wan that it is optimal to extract from the lowest-cost deposit first, the 'cheapest-first' rule. The initial deposit-cost profile specifies the aggregate extraction cost function for the industry. Let $c(x)$ be the minimum cost of extracting a unit from the remaining deposits. Thus the total cost is $c(x)q$, that is the rate of extraction multiplied by the aggregate unit extraction cost function. The cost per unit at a particular stock is given by:

$$c(x) = F^{-1}\left(1 - \frac{x}{x_0}\right) \tag{9.21}$$

where F^{-1} is an inverse function.

Equation (9.21) is readily illustrated by a simple example. If there is an initial stock of 100 units and the cost increases linearly from a zero extraction cost up to a maximum extraction cost of £10 per unit,

$F(c) = 0.1c$; that is, if $c = 0$ the proportion of the deposit with a cost below zero is zero, if $c = 10$, the proportion of the stock with an extraction cost less than 10 is 1. The inverse function relates this proportion to the cost and is simply $c(\gamma) = F^{-1}(\gamma) = 10\gamma$ where $\gamma = (1 - x/x_0)$ is the proportion of the initial deposit remaining. Unit extraction cost as a function of the remaining deposit are found by $c(x) = 10(1 - x/x_0)$. For instance, if 50 units of stock remain, $c(50) = 10 \cdot 0.5 = 5$.

The unit extraction cost function does not allow for the possibility of exploration and discovery of new deposits. In the development of non-renewable resource stocks the discovery rate is critical in determining the rate of extraction and the price path of the resource. In their paper, Swierzbinski and Mendelsohn (1989) extend Solow and Wan's aggregation procedure to an industry where new deposits are discovered by a random search. Their assumptions are, first, that there are constant returns to scale in both extraction and exploration and that individual firms are risk-neutral. Thus the model is specified in terms of the cost of locating and extracting units of resource. Within each field there is a constant search or exploration cost d for each unit discovered. This cost differs between fields but is known prior to any exploration, as is the total resource in each field. By paying d, a prospector identifies the location of a unit of resource and learns the cost of extracting it. The identification of units of resource does not tell the prospector where other units are.

Exploration separates the resource into two stocks. As before, x is the located reserve and s the unlocated reserve. It is optimal for a profit-maximising prospector to explore fields with the lowest extraction cost first. In common with extraction costs, the exploration cost function $d(s)$ is the minimum cost of identifying a unit of resource in the remaining unexplored field. The total exploration cost is $y\,d(s)$ where y, a second decision variable, is the discovery rate; thus $\dot{s} = -y$. As the cumulative discovery increases, so does the cost of discovering an additional unit, $d'(s) < 0$.

As in the no-discovery case, owners extract first from identified deposits with the lowest extraction costs. Thus extraction exhausts reserves and newly discovered deposits with extraction costs less than $c(x, s)$ first. The function $c(\cdot)$ is decreasing in both x and s. The cumulative extraction is

$$x_0 + s_0 - x - s = (x_0 + s_0 - s)F(c(x, s))$$

that is, the proportion of the total stock, which includes cumulative discoveries $(s_0 - s)$ with a cost less than $c(x, s)$. Equating these two expressions for cumulative extraction yields the analogue of (9.21):

$$c(x, s) = F^{-1}\left(1 - \frac{x}{(x_0 + s_0 - s)}\right)$$

The total extraction rate is $yF(c(x,s), t) + q$, where $F(c(x,s), t)$ represents the proportion of new discoveries which have a cost lower than $c(x, s)$. The stock changes by

$$\dot{x} = y[1 - F(c(x,s))] - q$$

The total extraction cost of newly-discovered low-cost deposits is

$$y \int_{c_0}^{c(x,s)} cF'(c) \, dc$$

where c_0 is the minimum cost for the initial deposit-cost profile, $F(c)$. This expression indicates the cost of extracting new deposits whose extraction costs are less than $c(x, s)$.

The cost function for the case where exploration and discovery occurs can be used to define a maximisation problem for a welfare (consumer surplus) maximising planner; as we show in section 9.2.1, this coincides with the optimal extraction schedule for a competitive resource industry. Let the benefit function equal the consumers surplus:

$$B(q) = \int_0^q f(w) \, dw$$

where $f(\cdot)$ is the inverse demand function. The planner's problem is to

$$\text{maximise}_{q,y} \int_0^T e^{-rt} \left\{ B(yF(c(x,s)) + q) - y \int_{c_0}^{c(x,s)} cF'(c) \, dc - c(x,s)q - y \, d(s) \right\} dt$$

subject to $\dot{s} = -y; \quad \dot{x} = y[1 - F(c(x,s))] - q; \quad s(0) = s_0; \quad x(0) = x_0; \quad q, y \geq 0$

The current-value Hamiltonian for the problem is:

$$H(x, s, q, y, \mu, \tau) = B(yF(c(x,s)) + q) - y \int_{c_0}^{c(x,s)} cF'(c) \, dc - c(x,s)q - y \, d(s)$$
$$+ \mu(y[1 - F(c(x,s))] - q) - \tau y$$

where μ is the marginal value of a unit of stock and τ is the marginal value of undiscovered stock. Taking the partial derivatives of $H(\cdot)$ with respect to q

$$H_q = f(yF(c(x,s)) + q) - c(x,s) - \mu$$

and y

$$H_y = F(c(x,s))f(yF(c(x,s)) + q) - \int_{c_0}^{c(x,s)} cF'(c) \, dc - d(s) + (1 - F(c(x,s)))\mu - \tau$$

The Kuhn–Tucker necessary conditions for q and y are $H_q \leq 0$ with $qH_q = 0$ and $H_y \leq 0$ with $yH_y = 0$. The costate conditions are

$$\dot{\mu} = r\mu + qc_q - yF'(c(x,s))c_x H_q$$

and

$$\dot{\tau} = r\tau + y\,d'(s) + qc_s - yF'(c(x,s))c_sH_q$$

Taking the time derivative of H_q and substituting for $\dot{x}$, $\dot{s}$ and $\dot{\mu}$ in the usual way, if $q > 0$ and $y = 0$:

$$\dot{p} = r[p - c(x,s)] \qquad (9.22)$$

which is a version of Hotelling's rule. If $y > 0$ then $H_y = 0$. Taking the time derivative of H_y, substituting for $\dot{x}$, $\dot{s}$, $\dot{\mu}$ and $\dot{\tau}$:

$$\dot{p} = r\left(p - \frac{1}{F(c(x,s))}\left[\int_{c_0}^{c(x,s)} cF'(c)\,dc + d(s)\right]\right) \qquad (9.23)$$

If both $q > 0$ and $y > 0$ then (9.22) and (9.23) must be satisfied simultaneously, which implies:

$$c(x,s) = \frac{1}{F(c(x,s))}\left[\int_{c_0}^{c(x,s)} cF'(c)\,dc + d(s)\right] \qquad (9.24)$$

that is, the marginal cost of extracting a unit from previously identified reserves equals the marginal cost of identifying and extracting a unit from a new deposit. If (9.23) is not satisfied then either $y = 0$ or $q = 0$. If this is the case then the planner's solution involves an initial adjustment period of bang-bang control for x and s until (9.23) is satisfied. Equations (9.23) and (9.24) lead to the important conclusion that, over the life of the resource, the price is strictly increasing; this is in contrast to the conclusion from Pindyck's model that there may be an initial period when the price is decreasing. However, this is a complex empirical and theoretical issue to which we return in the next section.

☐ 9.3.3 Measures of resource scarcity

One of the most controversial theoretical and empirical issues related to non-renewable resource economics concerns the nature and measurement of resource scarcity. There is now a consensus (Farzin, 1992) that the price of the extracted resource should exceed the marginal extraction cost to reflect the opportunity cost of the resource. But there is no general agreement over how the shadow price of the resource should change through time or how it should relate to other measures of resource scarcity, namely, the marginal extraction cost and the price.

The evidence from empirical studies is one where a number of contra-dictory results emerge. The results of some influential papers are summarised in Table 9.1.

Table 9.1 *Studies of non-renewable resource scarcity*

Authors	Resources	Period	Price	Extraction cost	Shadow price
Barnett and Morse (1963)	Range	1870–1957	constant	<0	
Nordhaus (1974)	11 minerals and fuels	1900–1970	<0		
Slade (1982)	11 metals and fuels	1870–1978	U-shaped	<0	>0
Halvorsen and Smith (1984	Canadian metal	1956–1974	>0		<0
Halvorsen and Smith (1991)	Canadian metal	1956–1974	>0		>0
Devarajan and Fisher (1982)	Crude Oil	1946–1971	constant		<0

These studies indicate that the conclusions drawn concerning the time path of price, extraction cost and the shadow price may depend critically upon the assumptions made in developing the model. Farzin (1995) makes the point that 'the existing (empirical) insights derive from highly unrealistic assumptions such as a fixed stock of the resource, constant marginal extraction costs, no depletion cost effect and, perhaps most importantly, no technological change' (p. 106).

Farzin (1992) presents a more general model of natural resource extraction as a means of explaining the divergence amongst empirical results. In particular, assumptions concerning the extraction cost function, which represents production technology, are critical. The cost function is given as $c(q, X, z)$ where X is the cumulative extraction up to time t. This differs from the usual definition of the state variable as the resource stock remaining and avoids the need to know the initial stock x_0. Clearly if the initial stock is known $X = x_0 - x = \int_0^t q\, d\tau$. The variable z represents an index of the state of technology. The assumptions concerning the cost curve are $c_q > 0$, $c_X > 0$, $c_z < 0$ and also that $c_{qq} > 0$ diminishing returns to extraction, $c_{Xq} = c_{qX} > 0$, the depletion effect and the technology effect $c_{qz} < 0$. In other words, the cost curve is convex in q and X. This ensures an optimal solution and, in the absence of technical change, that a finite amount of resource will be extracted. This form of the model differs from earlier models insofar as the initial stock is not fixed and there is no need to explicitly assume a backstop price.

The firm's maximisation problem is

$$\text{maximise}_q \quad \int_0^\infty e^{-rt}[pq - c(q, X, z)]\, dt$$

subject to $\dot{X} = q; \quad X(0) = 0$

The current-value Hamiltonian is

$$H = pq - c(q, X, z) + \chi q$$

where the costate variable is now defined as the marginal external cost of an increase in the cumulative extraction instead of the usual shadow price of resource. However, the shadow price is related to χ simply as $\mu = -\chi$ and to make the analysis more accessible we will use the two costate variables interchangeably; we also hold technology constant. The necessary conditions for an optimum are:

$$p - c_q + \chi = 0 \tag{9.25}$$

$$\dot{\chi} - r\chi = c_X \tag{9.26}$$

and the transversality condition

$$\lim_{t \to \infty} e^{-rt}\chi = 0$$

that is, as the duration of extraction approaches infinity, the present value of the shadow price of stock approaches zero.

Solving the costate condition (9.26) illustrates how the cost function determines χ as the discounted sum of incremental costs over the life of the resource, assuming $\dot{z} = 0$

$$\mu = -\chi = \int_t^\infty e^{-r(\tau - t)} c_X\, d\tau = \int_t^\infty e^{-r\tau} c_X\, d\tau / e^{-rt} \tag{9.27}$$

The rule of resource depletion is found in the usual way by differentiating (9.25) with respect to time; substituting into (9.26) to give a version of (9.19)

$$\frac{\dot{\mu}}{\mu} = r - \frac{c_X}{\displaystyle\int_t^\infty e^{-r(\tau - t)} c_X\, d\tau} \tag{9.28}$$

This states that in equilibrium the shadow price increases at the discount rate less the percentage ratio of the discounted current incremental cost c_X to the present value of all future increases in incremental costs. Farzin (1992) makes the point that the right-hand side of this rule may be either positive or negative: it depends upon the exact form of the cost function. To analyse this in more detail, we assess the value of μ as $t \to \infty$ from (9.27) using L'Hopital's rule:

$$\lim_{t \to \infty} \mu = \lim_{t \to \infty} \int_t^\infty e^{-r\tau} c_X\, d\tau / e^{-rt} = \frac{1}{r} \lim_{t \to \infty} c_X \tag{9.29}$$

and when the stock is no longer exploited, $\lim_{t\to\infty} c_X = c_X(0, \bar{X})$ where $\bar{X}$ represents the maximum economic cumulative extraction. This then implies that the shadow price (9.28) converges to a constant as $t \to \infty$ and, consequently, from (9.25) that the price converges to a constant:

$$\lim_{t\to\infty} p = \bar{p} = c_q(0, \bar{X}) = \frac{1}{r} \lim_{t\to\infty} c_X(0, \bar{X})$$

The price as extraction ceases, $\bar{p}$, may be interpreted, where appropriate, as a backstop price.

Now that these results have been established, we focus upon the time path of the scarcity rent. On substituting (9.27) into (9.26) and integrating by parts:

$$\dot{\mu} = \int_t^\infty e^{-r(\tau - t)} \frac{d}{d\tau} c_X \, d\tau$$

where, noting that $q = \dot{X}$,

$$\frac{d}{d\tau} c_X = c_{Xq}\dot{q} + c_{XX}q + c_{Xz}\dot{z}$$

This is the key result as it indicates that the shadow price can be increasing or decreasing monotonically, remain constant or change non-monitonically over time. As q, the change in technology, $\dot{z}$, c_{Xq}, c_{XX} and c_{Xz} are all positive by assumption, the direction of the time path is largely determined by $\dot{q}$. Figure 9.8 illustrates the different time paths for μ. More detail is given in

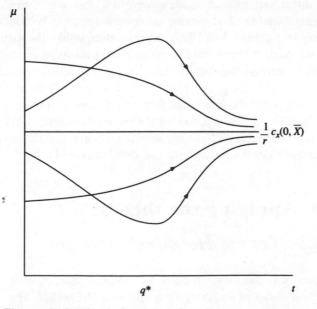

Figure 9.8 *Time paths for the shadow price of a resource*

Farzin (1992). All time paths converge to a constant shadow price, but the scarcity rent may take a number of different time paths.

These results have implications for the analysis of measures of scarcity. The relationship between the three measures of scarcity, from (9.25)

$$\dot{p} = \frac{d}{dt} c_q + \dot{\mu}$$

need not necessarily point in the same direction; for instance, the price may be rising while the shadow price and marginal extraction costs are falling. The range of theoretical possibilities detailed by Farzin (1995) has been borne out by the empirical analysis which has produced conflicting results.

The original model includes a technological change term. Technological change has an important effect on the costs of resource extraction. Farzin (1995) considers two types of technological change – extraction-biased, which reduces extraction costs $c_{qz} < 0$, depletion-biased, which reduces the marginal depletion cost $c_{Xz} < 0$ and neutral technological change which increases both by the same proportion. A complete description of the effects of these forms of technological change is complex, so we pick out the main results. Extraction-biased technological change leads to an increase in the rate that the shadow price increases, so it tends to make the resource economically scarcer. In contrast, depletion-based technological change reduces the rate of increase in resource scarcity and thus reduces scarcity. The effects of neutral technological change are ambiguous.

Fisher (1979) states that an ideal measure of scarcity 'should summarise the sacrifices, direct and indirect, made to obtain a unit of resource'. Economic theory suggests that the best measure of resource scarcity is its shadow price. The analysis by Farzin (1992, 1995) indicates that, unlike the assumptions of Hotelling's model, it is not always the case that resource scarcity increases monotonically through time or that the resource price and marginal extraction cost stand as a reliable proxy for the shadow price. The implication for empirical work is that the functional forms used to estimate cost functions for firms should be flexible enough to identify the true time path of the underlying shadow price. Examples of studies which estimate flexible cost functions include Pesaran (1990) and Lasserre and Ouellette (1991).

■ 9.4 Applying the theory

□ 9.4.1 Testing Hotelling's theorem

This chapter has described models of optimal extraction of increasing complexity in terms of industry structure and the technology of resource extraction and exploration. However, there remains an empirical question as to whether Hotelling's rule adequately represents extraction behaviour by firms owning reserves of natural resources. This is closely linked with the discussion in the previous section concerning appropriate measures of resource scarcity. Modelling the extraction decisions of non-renewable resource firms is a formidable undertaking. Deterministic theoretical models must be modified so that they can be applied to stochastic markets where the assumption that producers form rational expectations cannot be taken for granted. Data on extraction rates, costs and prices must be modified to fit into the theoretical framework and assumptions made about the shadow price of the resource.

Pesaran (1990) outlines an approach to modelling non-renewable resource extraction. First, empirical models should be consistent with the theory and represent dynamic optimisation problems. Second, attention must be given to the way in which firms form expectations; for instance, are they formed adaptively or rationally? Thirdly, models should take explicit account of the geological characteristics of the problem, such as the pressure dynamic found in an oil field or variations in ore quality in a mineral deposit.

His article presents an econometric analysis of oil exploration and extraction on the UK continental shelf. The exploration and development of oil resources in the North Sea commenced in 1964 on a modest scale, but by the mid-1970s increased rapidly with the discovery of two new oil-fields at Forties and Brent and the stimulus of the oil price shock in 1973/4 which brought a fourfold increase in the price of oil. Following the discovery of substantial oil reserves in the early 1970s, oil production commenced in 1975 and rose to 230.69 million barrels in the fourth quarter of 1986. The analysis is concerned with the period once production has become established.

The model is based upon the assumptions that producers are risk neutral and determine the extraction in each period, q_t, and exploration, w_t, on the basis of the discounted future stream of profits conditional on the information set Ω_{t-1} available in the previous period. That is,

$$\text{maximise}_{q_t, w_t} \quad E\left\{ \sum_{t=0}^{\infty} \rho^t \pi_t \mid \Omega_{t-1}) \right\}$$

where $\rho = 1/(1 + r)$ is the discrete-time discount factor and π_t is producer profit defined as

$$\pi_t = p_t q_t - c(q_t, x_{t-1}) - d_t w_t$$

where p_t is the price at the well-head, the cost of development and extraction at t, $c(q_t, x_{t-1})$, is a convex function which varies positively with the rate of extraction, q_t, and negatively with the level of proven reserves, that is, $c_q > 0, c_{qq} > 0, c_x < 0, c_{xx} < 0$. Exploration costs d_t give the cost per unit of exploration effort, w_t, measured as the number of wells drilled.

The constraints in the problem include the fact that the stock is given by:

$$x_t - x_{t-1} = y_t + e_t - q_t$$

That is, the change in stock equals discoveries y_t less revisions/extensions e_t less extraction. The determination of y_t is based upon the observed nature of the discovery process in petroleum exploration. There are two assumptions: first, the reservoir size is lognormally distributed; second, the exploratory process is a matter of sampling without replacement in proportion to the reservoir size. On this basis the discovery function is

$$y_t = \Phi(w_t, W_{t-1})v_t$$

where W_t represents the level of cumulative exploratory effort defined as $W_t = W_{t-1} + w_t$. The term v_t is the unpredictable component of discovery: it has an expected value of 1. The discovery function is expected to satisfy the following conditions. First, $\Phi_w > 0$, that is, marginal discovery as a function of exploration effort is positive. Second, $\Phi_{WW} < 0$, which implies a diminishing marginal productivity of exploration effort. Third, $\Phi_{W_{t-1}} < 0$ for $W_t \geq W_m$ which reflects the 'discovery decline phenomenon', where, beyond some threshold level W_m, the rate of discovery begins to decline even when the rate of exploratory effort is maintained. Finally, as the cumulative discoveries increase, the probability of additional discoveries declines to zero, $W_{t-1} \rightarrow \infty \lim \Phi(w_t, W_{t-1}) = 0$.

The firm's optimisation problem can be defined by maximising the expected value of the Hamiltonian function in each period

$$H_t = \pi_t + \mu_t(y_t + e_t - q_t - x_t + x_{t-1}) + \tau_t(W_t - W_{t-1} - w_t)$$

with respect to the decision variables q_t and w_t. The multipliers, μ_t and τ_t are the shadow price of reserves in the ground and the net value of the marginal product of reserve discovery. The first-order conditions are as follows

$$E_{t-1}[\mu_t] = E_{t-1}[p_t] - E_{t-1}\left[\frac{\partial c_t}{\partial q_t}\right] \tag{9.30}$$

$$E_{t-1}[\mu_t] = \rho\left(E_{t-1}[\mu_{t+1}] - E_{t-1}\left[\frac{\partial c_{t+1}}{\partial x_t}\right]\right) \tag{9.31}$$

$$E_{t-1}[\tau_t] = E_{t-1}\left[\mu_t \frac{\partial y_t}{\partial w_t}\right] - E_{t-1}[d_t] \tag{9.32}$$

$$E_{t-1}[\tau_t] = \rho\left(E_{t-1}[\tau_{t+1}] - E_{t-1}\left[\mu_{t+1} \frac{\partial y_{t+1}}{\partial W_t}\right]\right) \tag{9.33}$$

Equation (9.30) gives the expected shadow price of oil in the ground as the difference between the expected well-head price and the expected marginal extraction cost. Condition (9.31) is the arbitrage equation. If the second term on the right-hand side equal to zero this is Hotelling's rule and requires that the net marginal profit increases at the discount rate. Equations (9.32) and (9.33) give the necessary conditions for exploratory effort; $E_{t-1}[\tau_t]$ in (9.32) is the expected net return to exploratory effort as the difference between the value of additional discoveries and the expected unit cost of exploration. Equation (9.33) is an arbitrage relationship which states that the current net return to exploration should equal the discounted value of the net return to exploration minus the discounted expected change in the value of the marginal product of exploration due to the cumulative effect of exploration. These equations represent a set of non-linear stochastic equations; the next stage is to simplify them into a form that provides the basis for econometric estimation.

The output equation is constructed as follows. Since the resource rent μ_t and the net benefit to exploration τ_t are unobservable they need to be eliminated from equations (9.30) to (9.33). To this end (9.30) can be rewritten as:

$$E_{t-1}[\mu_{t+1}] = E_{t-1}[p_{t+1}] - E_{t-1}\left[\frac{\partial c_{t+1}}{\partial q_{t+1}}\right]$$

substituting this into (9.31) and using (9.30) to eliminate $E_{t-1}(\mu_t)$

$$E_{t-1}\left[\frac{\partial c_t}{\partial q_t}\right] = E_{t-1}(p_t - \rho p_{t+1}) + \rho E_{t-1}\left(\frac{\partial c_{t+1}}{\partial q_{t+1}} + \frac{\partial c_{t+1}}{\partial x_t}\right) \tag{9.34}$$

This equation does not depend on the the shadow prices and can be estimated. Assume that the cost function is of the translog form:

$$C(q_t, x_{t-1}) = \alpha_0 + \alpha_1 q_t + \frac{1}{2}\left(\alpha_2 + \frac{\alpha_3}{x_{t-1}}\right)q_t^2 + \varepsilon_t q_t \tag{9.35}$$

where ε_t represents random shocks to marginal extraction cost. The pressure dynamics of petroleum reserves implies that α_3 is positive; that is, marginal costs increase as the reserve is depleted. The parameters are expected to satisfy

$$E_{t-1}\left[\frac{\partial c_t}{\partial q_t}\right] = \alpha_1 + \left(\alpha_2 + \frac{\alpha_3}{x_{t-1}}\right)q_t > 0$$

and

$$E_{t-1}\left[\frac{\partial^2 c_t}{\partial q_t^2}\right] = \alpha_2 + \frac{\alpha_3}{x_{t-1}} > 0$$

These conditions ensure that for a given level of initial reserves the cost function is convex and the expected marginal cost of extraction is positive.

Under (9.35), (9.34) can be solved for the optimal or desired level of extraction:

$$q_t^* = [-(1-\rho)\alpha_1/\alpha_2]z_{t-1} + \alpha_2^{-1}z_{t-1}E_{t-1}(p_t - \rho p_{t+1}) + \rho z_{t-1}E_{t-1}(q_{t+1})$$

$$+ \rho\gamma z_{t-1}E_{t-1}(h_{t+1}) \tag{9.36}$$

where $z_t = x_t/(x_t + \gamma)$, $\gamma = \alpha_3/\alpha_2$ and $h_t = (q_t/x_{t-1}) - \frac{1}{2}(q_t/x_{t-1})^2$.

The requirement that pressure within the oil reservoir is maintained implies a partial adjustment formulation as the rate of extraction can only be adjusted gradually towards the desired level. Thus, $q_t - q_{t-1} = \phi(q_t^* - q_{t-1})$, $0 \leq \phi \leq 1$.

Price expectation may be formed under the rational expectation hypothesis (REH) where expectations are derived from solving the economic model explicitly. From (9.30) and (9.31) it follows that:

$$E_{t-1}(p - \rho p_{t+1}) = p_t - \rho p_{t+1} + \varepsilon_{pt}$$

Alternatively, price expectations may be formed as a weighted average of past price levels, the adaptive expectation hypothesis (AEH) in this case:

$$\bar{p}_t(\theta) = E_{t-1}(p_t) = (1-\theta)\sum_{i=1}^{\infty} \theta^{i-1}p_{t-i}$$

The estimates of parameters of the model are given in Table 9.2

Table 9.2 *Estimates for the output equation*

Parameter	REH model	AEH model
ϕ	0.567	0.371
	(0.113)	(0.228)
ρ	0.989	1.044
	(0.020)	(0.084)
δ_2	−0.613	−0.011
	(0.192)	(0.061)
δ_3	6832.5	457.1
	(1850.4)	(352.9)
θ	—	0.96
$\bar{R}^2$	0.97	0.97

Source: Based on Pesaran (1990). (Standard errors are given in parentheses.)

Superficially, at least, the results give support to the REH model; the partial adjustment parameter ϕ is between zero and one, the discount rate implied by $\rho = (1/(1+r))$ is 1 per cent, which is acceptable, but this is quite low for an industry subject to uncertainty about future prices and costs. The parameter in the cost function, δ_2 and δ_3 are consistent with prior expectations. The parameter δ_3 confirms the existence of an inverse relationship between extraction costs and reserves. In contrast, the AEH equation has none of the cost function parameters significant and the estimate of ρ implies a negative discount rate. However, the 'better' REH equation implies a marginal cost level which is greater than would be expected and implies a negative shadow price. This leads to the rejection of the model by Pesaran in favour of a simpler equation:

$$q_t = 0.712q_{t-1} + 5.552z_{t-1}\tilde{p}_t(\theta) + \varepsilon_t$$

This includes an adaptive expectation component $\tilde{p}(\theta)$. The short-run and long-run price elasticities of supply from this model are 0.31 and 1.07, respectively.

Pesaran's paper illustrates the problems of applying the theoretical models of resource extraction to real data. It also highlights the difficulties faced by firms when their production and market environment is uncertain. Maximising expected profits may be an inappropriate and unattainable objective for such firms, especially when they may be unclear about the probabilities which attach to all the possible outcomes.

☐ 9.4.2 A review of other studies

The article by Pesaran provides an insight into the problems of applying Hotelling's rule to real-world resource extraction problems. This paper lends some support for Hotelling's rule, but this is qualified by the rejection of the rational expectations hypothesis in favour of an adaptive expectations model: Hotelling's rule requires that firms possess perfect foresight. This paper is one of a number which have attempted to test Hotelling's rule and its extensions. The ambiguity of this body of empirical evidence has called into question the validity of the theory, see for instance Eagan (1987). The theory is criticised for the strong assumptions it makes about the firm's ability to anticipate the future by forming expectations rationally and then, effectively, sign a binding contract to supply according to a fixed schedule. The view that these assumptions are unrealistic is supported by econometric studies which reject Hotelling's rule, although, as we saw from Pesaran's article developing econometric models of natural resource markets is complicated by the difficulties associated with estimating theoretically consistent non-linear dynamic models.

Agbeyegbe (1989) shows that a range of metal prices do not increase at the rate of interest but are related to the change in interest rates; this concurs with an earlier study by Heal and Barrow (1980). In a detailed study of an individual firm engaged in mining lead, Farrow (1985) shows that the behaviour of the firm is inconsistent with a form of the Hotelling rule. He considers a misspecification in the basic Hotelling model of the costs incurred in mining operations. Halvorsen and Smith (1991) strongly reject Hotelling's rule and indicate that price uncertainty may effect producer decisions. Miller and Upton (1985) adopt a somewhat different approach and consider changes in the market value of reserves instead of the price of the extracted resource. Their study lends support to Hotelling's rule.

This leads to the question of where economists are to turn next. In his paper, Pesaran adopts a simpler model of the formation of price expectations and firm decision making and achieves a reasonable statistical representation of the change in the rate of extraction and the shadow price of reserves. Considering more general models of firm behaviour may provide one approach to establishing descriptive models of resource firms. As a normative model of how firms should behave, the Hotelling model remains of value, but needs to be extended to include the way in which firms form price expectations and assimilate new information about resource extraction costs and market prices. The approach to testing Hotelling's rule econometrically has much in common with that of measuring resource scarcity. Possibly the most significant difficulty lies in representing the technology of resource extraction and exploration. In particular, technological factors may make firms relatively insensitive to changes in market prices once the fixed investment to exploit a reserve has been made.

9.5 Government policy towards non-renewable resource taxation

The central importance of extractive natural resources in the economies of developed and developing countries has led to specific government policies towards natural resource industries. These include: the formation of nationalised industries; joint ventures with multinational firms; schemes for selling; the rights to search for reserves of natural resources and special tax schemes which capture some of the economic rent generated by the exploitation of natural resources. The concern of economists has been the effect which tax schemes have in distorting the pattern of competitive resource extraction.

The most widely applied form of taxation is a severance tax levied on the value of extracted output. The impact of this tax can be shown for the more realistic case where extraction costs increase as the stock is depleted. The firm's problem is to

$$\text{maximise}_q \quad \int_0^T [(1 - \tau)pq - c(q, x)]\, e^{-rt}\, dt$$

where τ is the tax rate and the price is given, the current-value Hamiltonian for the problem is:

$$H = (1 - \tau)pq - c(q, x) - \mu q$$

and the transversality condition requires that as $T \to \infty$ then

$$\mu(T)x(T) = 0$$

That is, either the shadow price is zero or the stock is exhausted at the point when the exploitation ceases. As the stock is depleted costs rise, $c_x > 0$; this reduces the shadow price to zero at T. At this point the Hamiltonian is:

$$(1 - \tau)p = c(q(T), x(T))/q(T)$$

and by the first derivative of the Hamiltonian with respect to q:

$$(1 - \tau)p = c_q$$

at T the price net of tax must equal marginal cost and average cost. Note that the higher is the tax rate the lower is the cost at which this occurs. As the cost curve is strictly increasing in x, this implies that the abandoned shock increases with the tax rate. In mining terms an increase in the tax rate increases the 'cut-off' ore grade, the grade of ore at which mining ceases. In this way, a severance tax reduces the total production from a given reserve.

The severance tax can be compared with a marginal tax on profits, v; in this case the firm aims to:

$$\text{maximise}_q \quad \int_0^T [pq - c(q, x)](1 - v)\, e^{-rt}\, dt$$

as the taxation term, $(1 - v)$, can be factored out of the integral,

$$\text{maximise}_q \quad (1 - v)\int_0^T [pq - c(q, x)]\, e^{-rt}\, dt$$

and is a constant, this form of taxation is not distortionary, but as Neher (1990, p. 323) indicates, it may be difficult to administer as firms overstate costs and understate revenues. It also reduces the incentives for firms to explore for new reserves.

This section discusses two forms of taxation applied to non-renewable resource firms. The reader is referred to Deacon (1993) for an account of the impact of taxation within the US petroleum sector; to Krautkraemer (1990) for a discussion of more complex cut-off grade issues; and to Conrad and Hool (1981) for a general review of different forms of taxation.

▉ 9.6 Uncertainty and the rate of resource extraction

☐ 9.6.1 Introduction

The firm engaged in exploiting a non-renewable resources is uncertain about most aspects of production planning. The degree of uncertainty faced by such firms may be higher than is normally encountered owing to the inherent instability in world commodity markets, the dependence of production on geological structures and the tendency for catastrophic market changes due to war or the activities of other countries and firms. In this section the aim is to attempt to characterise the various forms of uncertainty.

The impact of uncertainty depends upon the attitudes of firms towards risk. If producers are risk-averse then they will take extraction decisions which attempt to reduce the level of risk; but if they are risk-neutral they base their decisions exclusively upon the expected monetary value of a decision. This is a difficult issue, especially where the firms involved are multinationals and attributing a particular attitude towards risk to an organisation is highly questionable – such firms may by operating in a number of sectors, be able to offset risk faced in one sector against risks faced in another, or may be able to use futures and options contracts to insure against price risks. For instance, if a firm both extracts oil and produces plastics from oil, profits from oil extraction may be reduced by an oil price fall, but profits from the production of plastic will be increased by a reduction in raw material costs.

In his review, Fisher (1981) identifies three sources of demand uncertainty. In the first case the level of demand uncertainty increases with the time into the future considered. That is, demand is non-stationary and the variance associated with future demand levels is increasing. In this situation a risk-averse firm would bring extraction decisions forward; a risk-neutral firm would be guided entirely by the expected demand function. This form of uncertainty has been studied in more detail by Koopmans (1974) and Weinstein and Zeckhauser (1975).

The second form of uncertainty identified by Fisher might be termed 'stationary demand uncertainty', where demand varies randomly from period to period but the distribution of price levels remains constant; thus price variation is not increasing through time. The variations of revenue, on the other hand, depend upon the quantity extracted during a period: the variance increases directly with the quantity extracted. In this situation, the extraction rate of the risk-neutral firm is unaffected, but the risk-averse firm will aim to spread the extraction rate more evenly over the planning horizon, which results in an increase in extraction rates in future periods. This is a portfolio diversification effect in that the firm avoids harvesting large quantities in a 'freak' low price year. The third form of demand uncertainty can be described as uncertainty over the backstop technology, that is, uncertainty about when demand for the resource will fall to zero following the development of a new product. This tends to increase the rate of extraction in the current period and reduce the rate of extraction in future periods for which there is a possibility that the stock will be worthless. This problem is analysed in detail by Lewis (1977).

Another form of uncertainty is uncertainty about the resource size. This problem has been characterised as one of eating a cake of unknown size. In this situation the risk-averse firm will deplete more gradually to reduce the probability of the resource being exhausted at any given time. This problem has been analysed by Loury (1978).

☐ 9.6.2 *A more detailed analysis of uncertainty*

This sub-section, which includes more difficult mathematics than other sections in this chapter and may be treated as optional, focuses upon demand and resource reserve uncertainty in the model of uncertain non-renewable resource markets developed by Pindyck (1980). Demand uncertainty involves the demand function shifting continuously through time according to a random process. Current demand is known exactly; the variance of future demand increases with time. Reserve uncertainty is modelled by assuming that variable reserves shift up or down according to a stochastic process. Thus a firm may find over time that more or less of the reserve is available than was expected, although the firm is certain about the current reserve level. The present sub-section applies the principles of stochastic calculus devloped in section 7.6.

The market demand curve is given by:

$$p = p(q, t) = \psi(t)f(q)$$

where $f(\cdot)$ is an inverse demand function and $\psi(t)$ a stochastic process of the form

$$\frac{d\psi}{\psi} = \alpha \, dt + \sigma_1 \, dz_1 = \alpha \, dt + \sigma_1 \varepsilon_1 \sqrt{dt} \tag{9.37}$$

that is, the proportional change in ψ is given by an Itô process (see section 7.6). Equation (9.37) implies that uncertainty about demand increases with the time horizon.

Reserves fluctuate randomly over time according to the stochastic process:

$$dx = -q\,dt + \sigma_2\,dz_2 = -q\,dt + \sigma_2\varepsilon_2\sqrt{dt} \tag{9.38}$$

where q is the rate of extraction. The effective reserve is a random variable given by:

$$x = \int_0^T q(t)\,dt = x_0 + \sigma_2\int_0^T dz_2$$

the sum of extractions over the time interval $[0, T]$. However, because effective reserves and demand are uncertain, the end of the planning horizon T is also uncertain. Further, it is assumed that the stochastic processes driving demand and reserves are independent, thus, $E[\varepsilon_1\varepsilon_2] = 0$ for all t.

The problem facing the competitive firm is one of stochastic optimisation. Firms must determine the rate of production over time so that the expected value of discounted profits is maximised. At the beginning of the planning horizon when $t = 0$, the problem is:

$$\text{maximise}_q \quad E_0\int_0^T [\psi f(q) - c(x)]q\,e^{-rt}\,dt = E_0\int_0^T \pi(t)\,dt$$

The solution for this problem requires the application of stochastic dynamic programming and Itô's lemma to derive analytical results. First, define the optimal value function:

$$J(\psi, x, t) = \text{maximum } E_0\int_t^T \pi(\tau)\,d\tau$$

The fundamental equation of optimality is

$$\text{maximum}\,[\pi(t) + (1/dt)E_t\,dJ] = 0 \tag{9.39}$$

this equation merits further discussion. The terms are the profit generated at time t plus the change in expected future profits with respect to time. The term $(1/dt)E_t\,dJ$ relates to stochastic calculus and it applies an expectation operator to dJ before taking the time derivative. Itô's lemma is applied to evaluate the term dJ

$$dJ = J_t dt + J_\psi\,d\psi + J_x\,dx + \tfrac{1}{2}J_{\psi\psi}(d\psi)^2 + \tfrac{1}{2}J_{xx}(dx)^2$$

substituting in for $d\psi$ and dx from (9.37) and (9.38) yields

$$dJ = J_t\,dt + J_\psi(\alpha\,dt + \sigma_1\,dz_1)\psi + J_x(-q\,dt + \sigma_2\,dz_2) + \tfrac{1}{2}J_{\psi\psi}(\alpha\,dt + \sigma_1\,dz_1)^2$$

$$+ \tfrac{1}{2}J_{xx}(-q\,dt + \sigma_2\,dz_2)^2$$

now by recalling that $dt^2 = 0$, $dt\,dz = 0$, $E[dz] = 0$ and $dz\,dz = dt$, if we take expectations of the above and divide through by dt we obtain the required expression for $(1/dt)E_t\,dJ$:

$$(1/dt)E_t\,dJ = J_t + \alpha\psi J_\psi - qJ_x + \tfrac{1}{2}\sigma_1^2\psi^2 J_{\psi\psi} + \tfrac{1}{2}\sigma_2^2 J_{xx}$$

We can now write (9.39) as:

$$\text{maximise}_q \quad [\pi(t) + J_t + \alpha\psi J_\psi - qJ_x + \tfrac{1}{2}\sigma_1^2\psi^2 J_{\psi\psi} + \tfrac{1}{2}\sigma_2^2 J_{xx}] = 0 \tag{9.40}$$

(9.40) is linear in q, which implies a bang-bang control where q is either at its maximum value or zero. Market clearing implies $\pi = J_x q$ where J_x is the shadow price of the resource as it gives the increase in the maximum value due to an increase in x. The derivative of (9.40) with respect to q is

$$\frac{\partial\pi}{\partial q} = J_x \tag{9.41}$$

Taking the derivative of (9.40) with respect to x and setting equal to 0 for a maximum gives:

$$\frac{\partial\pi}{\partial x} + (1/dt)E_t\,d(J_x) = 0 \tag{9.42}$$

By the stochastic differential operator both sides of (9.41) can be differentiated with respect to time:

$$(1/dt)E_t d(\partial\pi/\partial q) = (1/dt)E_t d(J_x)$$

This equation and (9.42) can be be combined to eliminate J:

$$(1/dt)E_t d(\partial\pi/\partial q) = -\frac{\partial\pi}{\partial x} \tag{9.43}$$

This states that the expected change in the marginal profit rate at any time is equal to the reduction in increase in costs due to a reduction in the stock. Equation (9.43) can now be used to derive the the expected price dynamics:

$$\frac{\partial\pi}{\partial q} = (p - c(x))e^{-rt}$$

Substitute this into (9.43) and divide through by e^{-rt}

$$-r(p - c(x)) + (1/dt)E_t(dp) - (1/dt)E_t(dc(x)) = -\frac{\partial\pi}{\partial x}e^{rt} = qc'(x) \tag{9.44}$$

The term $dc(x)$ is given by Itô's lemma:

$$dc(x) = c'(x)\,dx + \tfrac{1}{2}c''(x)(dx)^2$$

Substituting into (9.44) using $E_t(dx) = -q\,dt$ and $E_t[(dx)^2] = \sigma_2^2\,dt$ yields:

$$(1/dt)E_t(dp) = r(p - c(x)) + \tfrac{1}{2}\sigma_2^2 c''(x)$$

and this is the result that we require. It shows that the expected rate of change of the competitive price only differs from the certain case ($\dot{p} = r(p - c(x))$) when $c(x)$ is non-linear. For instance, in the usual case where $c''(x) > 0$ if random increases and decreases in reserves balance each other out. This will increase production costs as a unit fall in x will increase costs more than a unit rise in x. This means that prices start lower but rise more rapidly than is the case of a known reserve and demand, implying that the firm will extract more rapidly and abandon the resource earlier.

■ 9.7 Summary

This chapter considers three aspects of non-renewable resource economics: first, the effect of market structure on the rate of resource extraction which shows that the average rate of extraction declines relative to the level of concentration in the industry: a competitive industry extracts rapidly and a monopoly slowly. Section 9.2 also evaluates the effect of the cartelisation on natural resource markets. Cartels have been important in natural resource markets, but they have also been unstable, so that market structures tend to change through time.

Section 9.3 considers production technology through the cost curve. Extraction costs are affected by the rate of extraction, but also by the level of stock. It has been found that, as the level of stock declines the marginal cost of extraction increases; thus the discovery of new deposits by active exploration has a value not only through the new stock itself but also because of the reduction in the level of costs. Section 9.4 considers how the theory is applied. It is apparent that the stochastic nature of real markets and the lack of data on the shadow price of stock have led to numerous difficulties in testing Hotelling's rule. Most, but not all, of these studies have either been equivocal towards Hotelling's rule and its extensions or have rejected the theory. However, Hotelling's rule may still provide a useful normative model for firms and policy makers.

Section 9.6 considers the effect of uncertainty on the decisions taken by firms and how the presence of uncertainty tends to accelerate the rate of resource when compared with the deterministic case. The study of stochastic dynamic systems remains a difficult area in economics and thus conclusions concerning the behaviour of actual firms are tentative. However in the model analysed in detail through stochastic calculus the conclusion is that the presence of stock and demand uncertainty leads to an increased rate of extraction in the current period compared to the deterministic case.

■ References

Agbeyegbe, T.D. (1989) 'Interest Rates and Metal Price Movements: Further Evidence', *Journal of Environmental Economics and Management*, 16, 184–92.

Barnett, H.J. and C. Morse (1963) *Scarcity and Growth : The Economics of Natural Resource Availability*, Baltimore: Johns Hopkins University Press.

Conrad, R.F. and B. Hool (1981) 'Resource Taxation with Heterogeneous Quality and Endogenous Reserves', *Journal of Public Economics*, 16, 17–33.

Deacon, R.T. (1993) 'Taxation Depletion and Welfare: A Simulation Study of the U.S. Petroleum Resource'. *Journal of Environmental Economics and Management*, 24, 159–87.

Devarajan, S. and A.C. Fisher (1982) 'Exploration and Scarcity', *Journal of Political Economy*, 90, 1279–90.

Eagan, V. (1987) 'The optimal depletion of the theory of exhaustible resources', *Journal of Post Keynesian Economics*, 9, 565–71.

Eckbo, P.L. (1975) OPEC and the Experience of Some Non-Petroleum International Cartels', MIT Energy Laboratory Report.

Farrow, S. (1985) 'Testing the Efficiency of Extraction from a Resource Stock', *Journal of Political Economy*, 93, 452–87.

Farzin, Y.H. (1992) 'The Time Path of Scarcity Rent in the Theory of Exhaustible Resources', *Economic Journal*, 102, 813–30.

Farzin, Y.H. (1995) 'Technological Change and the Dynamics of Resource Scarcity Measures', *Journal of Environmental Economics and Management*, 29, 105–120.

Fisher, A.C. (1979) 'Measures of Natural Resource Scarcity', in K.V. Smith (ed.), *Scarcity and Growth Reconsidered*, Baltimore: Johns Hopkins University Press.

Fisher, A.C. (1981) *Resource and Environmental Economics*, Cambridge: Cambridge University Press.

Gilbert, C.L. (1987) 'International Commodity Agreements: Design and Performance', *World Development*, 15, 591–616.

Groot, F, C. Withagen and A. De Zeeuw (1992) 'Note on the Open-loop von Stackleberg Equilibrium in the Cartel Versus Fringe Model', *Economic Journal*, 102, 1478–84.

Hall, D.C. and J.V. Hall (1984) 'Concepts and Measures of Natural Resource Scarcity', *Journal of Environmental Economics and Management*, 11, 363–79.

Halvorsen, R. and T.R. Smith (1984) 'On Measuring Natural Resource Scarcity', *Journal of Political Economy*, 92, 954–64.

Halvorsen, R. and T.R. Smith (1991) 'A Test of the Theory of Exhaustible Resources', *The Quarterly Journal of Economics*, 123–40.

Heal, G.M. and M.M. Barrow (1980) 'The Relationship Between Interest Rates and Metal Price Movements', *Review of Economic Studies*, 48, 161–81.

Karp, L. and D.M.G Newberry (1993) 'Intertemporal Consistency Issues in Depletable Resources', in A.V. Kneese and J.L. Sweeny (eds), *Handbook of Natural Resource and Energy Economics*, Vol. III, Amsterdam: Elsevier.

Koopmans, T.C. (1974) 'Proof of the Case where Discounting Advances Doomsday', *Review of Economic Studies Symposium on the Economics of Exhaustible Resources*, 117–20.

Krautkraemer, J.A. (1990) 'Taxation, Ore Quality, and the Depletion of a Heterogeneous Deposit of a Nonrenewable Resource', *Journal of Environmental Economics and Management*, 18, 120–35.

Lasserre, P. and P. Ouellette (1991) 'The Measurement of Productivity and Scarcity Rents: the Case of Asbestos in Canada', *Journal of Econometrics*, 48(3), 287–312.

Lewis, T.R. (1977) 'Attitudes Toward Risk and the Optimal Extraction of an Exhaustible Resource', *Journal of Environmental Economics and Management*, 4, 111–19.

Loury, G.C. (1978) 'The Optimal Exploitation of an Unknown Reserve', *Review of Economic Studies*, 45, 621–36.

Loury, G.C (1986) 'A Theory of "Oil"igopoly: Cournot Equilibrium in Exhaustible Resource Markets with Fixed Supplies', *International Economic Review*, 27, 285–301.

Miller, M.H. and C.W. Upton (1985) 'A Test of the Hotelling Valuation Principle', *Journal of Political Economy*, 93, 1–25.

Newberry, D.M.G. (1981) 'Oil Prices, Cartels, and the Problem of Dynamic Inconsistency', *The Economic Journal*, 91, 617–46.

Nordhaus, W.D. (1973) 'The allocation of energy resources', *Brooking Papers in Economic Activity*, 3, 529–70

Nordhaus, W.D. (1974) 'Resource as a Constraint on Growth', *American Economic Review*, 64, 22–6.

Neher, P.A. (1990) *Natural Resource Economics: Conservation and Exploitation*, Cambridge: Cambridge University Press.

Pesaran, M.H. (1990) 'An Econometric Analysis of Exploration and Extraction of Oil in the U.K. Continental Shelf', *Economic Journal*, 100, 367–90.

Polasky, S. (1992) 'Do Oil Producers Act as "Oil"igopolists?', *Journal of Environmental Economics and Management*, 23, 216–47.

Pindyck, R.S. (1978a) 'The Optimal Exploration and Production of Nonrenewable Resources', *Journal of Political Economy*, 86, 841–61.

Pindyck, R.S. (1978b) 'Gains to Producers from Cartelization of Exhaustible Resources', *Review of Economics and Statistics*, 60, 238–51.

Pindyck, R.S. (1980) 'Uncertainty and Exhaustible Resource Markets', *Journal of Political Economy*, 88, 1203–25.

Salant, S.W. (1976) 'Exhaustible Resources and Industrial Structure: A Nash–Cournot Approach to the World Oil Market', *Journal of Political Economy*, 84, 1079–93.

Slade, M.E. (1982) 'Trends in Natural-resource Commodity Prices: An Analysis in the Time Domain', *Journal of Environmental Economics and Management*, 9, 122–37.

Solow, R. and F. Wan (1976) 'Extraction costs in the theory of exhaustible resources', *Bell Journal of Economics*, 359–70.

Stiglitz, J.E. (1976) 'Monopoly and the Rate of Extraction of Exhaustible Resources', *American Economic Review*, 66, 655–61.

Stiglitz, J.E. and P. Dasgupta (1982) 'Market Structure and Resource Depletion: A Contribution to the Theory of Intertemporal Monopolistic Competition', *Journal of Economic Theory*, 28, 128–64.

Swierzbinski, J.E. and R. Mendelsohn (1989) 'Exploration and Exhaustible Resources: The Microfoundations of Aggregate Models', *International Economic Review*, 30, 175–86.

Ulph, A. (1982) 'Modelling Partially Cartelized Markets for Exhaustible Resources', in W. Eichhorn *et al.* (eds), *Economics of Natural Resource*, Würzburg: Physica Verlag.

Weinstein, M.C and R.J. Zeckhauser (1975) 'The Optimal Consumption of Depletable Natural Resources', *Quarterly Journal of Economics*, 89, 371–92.

■ *Chapter 10* ■

Renewable Resource Economics

10.1 Introduction
10.2 Population growth models
10.3 Static models of fishery
    exploitation in continuous
    time
10.4 Static economic models
    of fisheries
10.5 Comparative dynamic
    models of fishing

10.6 Fisheries policy
10.7 Applying the theory
    and the discrete-time model
10.8 Extending the theoretical
    model
10.9 Strategic behaviour in fishery
    management
10.10 Fishing under uncertainty
10.11 Summary

■ *10.1* Introduction

Renewable natural resources are those capable of self-reproduction. In this chapter the primary concern is with fishery management, although the theory has been extended to other exploited animal and plant populations. The economic analysis of renewable resources differs from that of non-renewable resources in two ways. First, it is not concerned with the finite availability of the resource and the time when a resource industry ceases to exist: a renewable resource can remain productive indefinitely, although it may be driven to extinction if it is overexploited. Second, the issue of market structure and the potential for cartelisation is not a prominent feature of renewable resource literature: market power is prone to being competed away by the close sub-stitutability between one fish stock and another. Instead, the focus is upon the nature of the fishery production function and how fishing effort in the form of labour and capital interacts with the fish stock. The other central issue in fishery economics is the open-access nature of resource stocks and policy measures used to protect the resource from economic overexploitation.

The chapter develops a capital-theoretic approach to renewable resource economics. However, the complexity of this subject requires a gradual development of the necessary analytical tools. Section 2 considers growth functions for biological populations, first in continuous time and then in discrete time. The potential confusion engendered in adopting two model structures is justified: continuous-time models have been used extensively in the development of the theory and discrete-time models in applications of the theory. Further, fisheries, unlike most non-renewable resources, show production cycles and seasonality which occur at discrete-time intervals. In fact, the continuous-time model is often used for analytical convenience in developing general principles, rather than as a realistic representation of a particular fish population. Section 3 introduces static models of fishery exploitation. Section 4 considers a static model of optimal fishery exploitation. Section 5 introduces a dynamic model of fishery exploitation where the rate of catch can change through time. It is a trait of the economic analysis of renewable resource problems that the economic conditions for efficient resource exploitation can only be developed by suppressing the complexity of fish population growth. It is notable that the population growth models applied by fisheries biologists (see Beverton and Holt, 1957) are much more complex than the approximations employed by economists. (However, see Clark, 1990, for an analysis of more complex fishery problems.)

Section 6 takes the dynamic model developed in section 5 to explore aspects of fishery policy. The aim of fishery policy, according to the economic orthodoxy, is to persuade rational fishermen to pursue fishing rates which collectively ensure a socially optimal catch in perpetuity. In theory this involves setting taxes on the catch or catch quotas so that producers behave *as if* they value the stock at its socially optimal shadow price. In practice this is difficult, if not impossible, to achieve, given the problems of measuring fishery stocks and regulating a large number of fishermen.

Section 7 returns to the discrete-time model, reviews the discrete-time maximum principle and dynamic programming and then proceeds to discuss the application of the theory to the econometric estimation of models of renewable resources. Section 8 considers the problem of asset fixity where a significant difference exists between the purchase price and second-hand price for fishing equipment, which leads to patterns of boom and bust in fisheries. Section 9 adopts a different theoretical framework to consider the strategic interaction of two countries as they compete for a common access fishery resource. This topic has become nicknamed 'fish wars'. Finally, section 10 considers the impact of uncertainty over the rate of stock growth upon the rate of fishery exploitation. This is approached for both the continuous-time and discrete-time model. This subject is left until last, not because it is unimportant – which is not the case – but because it is analytically difficult and the results are inconclusive.

■ *10.2* **Population growth models**

□ *10.2.1 Stock growth in continuous time*

Models of fishery exploitation must include a representation of the biological growth process. Most economic studies employ relatively simple functional forms to represent the relationship between the population size and the rate of growth. For instance, if a population has a birth rate, b, and a mortality rate, m, which are proportional to the population size, $\gamma = b - m$, then instantaneous growth can be represented by

$$\frac{dx}{dt} = \gamma x$$

Integrating this equation yields $x(t) = x(0) e^{\gamma t}$ and two solutions are possible: if γ is positive the population grows exponentially to infinity, if γ is negative it declines exponentially towards zero.

However, the extremes of an infinite population and extinction are not realistic. Typically, there is some mechanism which reduces the rate of growth as the food and space available for each individual decline. This implies that the growth rate should depend upon the size of the population; as the population increases above some level, the rate of growth declines. Thus the growth equation can be generalised to give:

$$\frac{dx}{dt} = \gamma(x)x \tag{10.1}$$

where $\gamma(x)$ is a decreasing function of x, the population shows *compensation* or negative feedback which reduces the growth of the population as its level increases.

The most widely used form is $\gamma(x) = \gamma(1 - x/K)$ where γ is the intrinsic growth rate and K is the environmental carrying capacity. The growth rate is γ when the population is zero, and is zero when the population is K. Substituting this expression into (10.1) gives the logistic growth function

$$\frac{dx}{dt} = g(x) = \gamma\left(1 - \frac{x}{K}\right)x \tag{10.2}$$

The carrying capacity, K, represents a stable equilibrium where, over time, the population returns to K. This implies that, if $0 < x < K$, the growth rate is positive, $\dot{x} > 0$, and negative if $x > K$, $\dot{x} < 0$: that is, the growth function is concave as $\gamma_{xx} < 0$. This can be appreciated from (10.2) where the expression in the brackets becomes negative when $x > K$. Equation (10.2) can be integrated over time to give

$$x(t) = \frac{K}{1 + c e^{-rt}} \quad \text{where} \quad c = \frac{K - x_0}{x_0}$$

The relationship between the level of stock and stock growth is shown in Figure 10.1.

The upper diagram gives the growth rate, the lower shows how the population changes through time and converges asymptotically to the carrying capacity K. If the population rises above K then growth is negative and the population declines to K. The value of K depends on environmental characteristics such as the food supply.

The standard logistic curve shows *pure compensation*; that is, the proportional growth rate, $\dot{x}/x$ is a decreasing function of x. If instead the proportional growth rate is an increasing function over a range of values for x it is said to show *depensation*; further, if it has the property that the growth rate is negative for population levels close to zero, it is said to show *critical depensation*, which is discussed later in this section. The growth curve in Figure 10.2 shows depensation, $g_{xx} > 0$, for $0 < x < K^*$ and compensation, $g_{xx} < 0$ for stock $x > K^*$.

Although a number of functional forms can be used to represent the relationship between the growth and the population, most are generalisations of the basic logistic form. For instance the modified logistic

$$\dot{x} = \gamma x^\alpha \left(1 - \frac{x}{K}\right) \qquad \alpha > 0$$

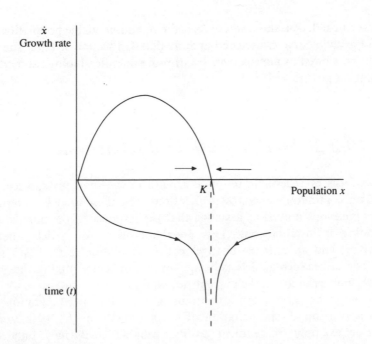

Figure 10.1 *The logistic growth curve*

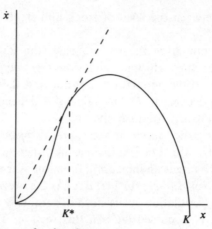

Figure 10.2 *Growth curve showing depensation*

shows pure compensation if $\alpha < 1$ but the maximum growth is skewed towards low stock levels; if $\alpha = 1$ it is the standard logistic curve and if $\alpha > 1$, it shows depensation at low stock levels. The growth function

$$\dot{x} = \gamma x \left(\frac{x}{K_0} - 1 \right)\left(1 - \frac{x}{K} \right)$$

shows critical depensation, where K_0 is the minimum viable population. This type of growth curve is discussed in more detail in section 3. These functions should be viewed as approximations of more complex biological models of population growth.

☐ *10.2.2 Stock growth in discrete time*

The analysis of renewable resource growth in the previous sub-section is based on continuous-time growth functions. For these models to represent real populations it must be assumed that the response of the population to harvesting is instantaneous. This does not allow for a delay between harvesting and an ultimate change in the population level. Clark (1990, p. 197) describes such models as being 'without memory'; that is, the growth rate depends entirely on the current population.

For a number of reasons a continuous-time differential equation, even as an approximate representation of stock growth, might be inappropriate. For example, recruitment to the fishable stock may only occur several years after the current generation of mature adults spawns. Fish stocks may also be subject to seasonal availability and stock estimates and statistics on the level of fishing effort may only be measured at discrete-time intervals.

Growth in discrete time can be represented by first-order non-linear difference equations of the form

$$x_{t+1} = G(x_t)$$

that is, the population at time $t + 1$ is a function of the population level in the previous time period. The time period is selected to represent the cycles observed by a species; for instance, the time unit may be a year, thus the present population is determined by the population a year ago.

The simplest form of discrete-time growth model is the stock recruitment model, which is outlined in Figure 10.3. In this model, the parent stock, x_t, gives birth to a number of young, y_t which in turn provide recruits, w_t. Some of these recruits are harvested, but others 'escape' to form the parent population in the next period: the parent stock is often called the 'escapement'. The model assumes that none of the parent stock survive to add to the harvestable stock and that harvesting occurs just prior to reproduction.

In the absence of harvesting, an equilibrium population occurs where the parent population equals the rate of recruitment. Thus the population is constant or self-sustaining. However, the behaviour of non-linear difference equations can be unexpected when the parent population is initially out of equilibrium.

To explore this further, consider the *Ricker curves* (Ricker, 1954) which have been used to represent, among other fish populations, the population

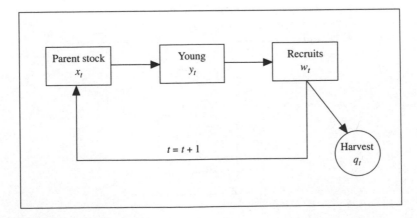

Figure 10.3 *A simple population cycle*

of Pacific salmon. In general, Ricker curves are given by the difference equation

$$y_{t+1} = G(x_t) = x_t \, e^{\gamma(1-x_t)}$$

Following Clark (1990, p. 202) three forms of the Ricker curve are drawn in Figure 10.4. In the first, Figure 10.4a, $0 < \gamma \le 2$, a stable equilibrium, exists at K; that is, if the population is perturbed away from the equilibrium it returns to it. In the second case, there exists a number of critical values for γ, $2 \le \gamma < 2.6924$, for which the population shows stable, limit-cycle oscillations, where $\gamma^* = 2.6924$ is a *critical value* for the non-linear difference equation. For instance, when $\gamma = 2$ the population shows a two-period cycle (see Figure 10.4b), when $\gamma = 2.6$ it shows a four-period cycle (see Figure 10.4c). In the third case, $\gamma > \gamma^*$ the equation shows cyclical behaviour for some starting values, but for others may show chaotic behaviour, where the population neither converges nor cycles, but exhibits apparently random fluctuations (see May, 1974, p. 645).

It is difficult to make generalisations about the behaviour of non-linear difference equations. However, if $G(x_t)$ is continuous and differentiable, with an equilibrium K, then the equilibrium is stable if $-1 < G'(K) < 1$ and unstable if $G'(K) > 1$ or $G'(K) < -1$ (see Clark, 1990, p. 202, for a discussion and a proof of this theorem).

(a)

(b)

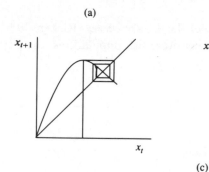

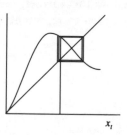

(c)

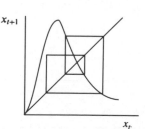

Figure 10.4 *Ricker curves*

10.3 Static models of fishery exploitation in continuous time

The combination of man-made capital, labour and fish stocks define a fishery production function. The harvest rate, $q(t)$, changes the population:

$$\dot{x} = g(x) - q(t)$$

For instance, if the harvest rate is constant $q(t) = q$ and the growth curve is a logistic, this leads to the two equilibrium points, x_1 and x_2 in Figure 10.5.

The equilibrium which results depends upon the initial stock. If the stock is above x_2, harvesting reduces the stock until the harvest equals stock growth. If the stock is above x_1, the growth rate exceeds the harvest and the population increases up to x_2. If the stock is less than x_1, then harvesting reduces the stock. It follows that x_2 is a stable equilibrium and x_1 an unstable equilibrium. The harvest level q_{msy} represents the maximum sustainable yield and is defined by, $q_{msy} = \text{maximum}\ \{g(x)\}$. In the case of the logistic growth curve this occurs at $x = K/2$.

Fishing effort measures the capital, energy and labour devoted to fishing during a particular time period. For instance, it might be measured by the number of standardised vessels operating in a fishery during a particular day. The number of fish caught is, in general, stock-dependent. This reflects the fact that the more fish there are, the easier they are to locate and catch. It is also necessary to distinguish between the effort of an individual fishing firm and the fishing effort of all the firms operating in a fishery.

For the individual firm the production function is

$$q_i = q_i(b_i, l_i, x)$$

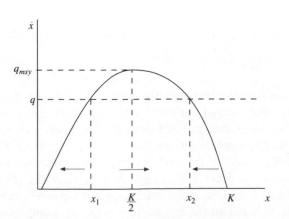

Figure 10.5 *The effect of harvesting on population change*

where b is the capital input and l is the labour input (the model is simplified to include just labour and capital). For the industry the output is:

$$q = \sum_i q_i = q(B, L, x)$$

Notice that the stock term is identical in both production functions; that is, by depleting the stock, a firm imposes an externality on the other firms in the industry.

The resources devoted to fishing are termed collectively the 'fishing effort'. In one of the original models of fishery economics, Schaefer (1954) assumes that the harvest is proportional to the stock level

$$\frac{q}{E} = \theta x$$

that is, the catch per unit of effort is a constant proportion θ of the stock. This is usually written as

$$q = \theta E x$$

For the logistic growth function, for instance, we define an equilibrium between yield and effort

$$\dot{x} = g(x) - \theta E x = \gamma x \left(1 - \frac{x}{K}\right) - \theta E x$$

Bionomic equilibrium, that is both biological and economic equilibrium, occurs where the catch equals the growth rate

$$\gamma x \left(1 - \frac{x}{K}\right) - \theta E x = 0$$

This gives a unique equilibrium catch at each level of effort. For instance, for a constant level of effort, E_1,

$$x_1 = K \left(1 - \frac{\theta E_1}{\gamma}\right)$$

This leads to an equilibrium level of stock x_1. If we define the catch as

$$q_1 = \theta E_1 x_1 = q(E_1) = \theta K E_1 \left(1 - \frac{\theta E_1}{\gamma}\right) \tag{10.3}$$

this gives the relationship between the harvest and the level of effort. The stock level has been solved for its equilibrium level and substituted out. Figure 10.6 shows equilibrium catch rates and stock levels for three different levels of effort. The catch increases as effort increases from E_1 to E_{msy}. If effort exceeds E_{msy}, say E_2, this reduces both the equilibrium catch and the equilibrium stock. In general, if E exceeds E_{msy} both the stock and catch decline. Figure 10.7 shows this relationship as one between fishing effort and the catch. This is based on the equilibrium between fishing effort, the stock and the catch defined in (10.3).

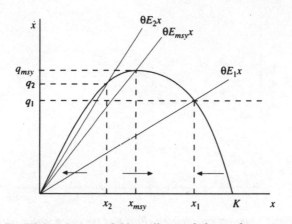

Figure 10.6 *Equilibrium between fishing effort and the stock*

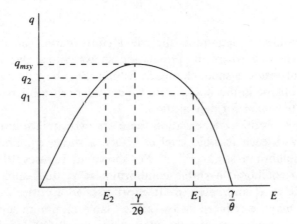

Figure 10.7 *Equilibrium between fishing effort and the catch*

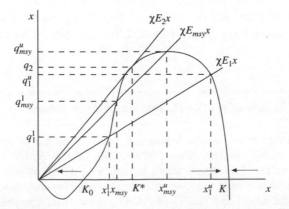

Figure 10.8 *Equilibrium between fishing effort and the stock with critical depensation*

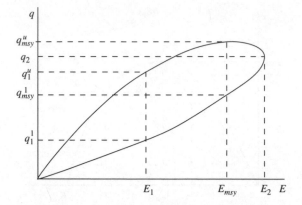

Figure 10.9   *Equilibrium between fishing effort and the catch with critical depensation*

It is possible to determine the yield–effort curve for most growth functions. The case where the population shows critical depensation is of particular interest as a small change in fishing effort beyond a critical point leads to a collapse in the stock. Here we consider critical depensation. The principles are similar for depensation.

In the case of critical depensation there are two equilibrium stock levels associated with each feasible level of effort: a stable equilibrium and an unstable equilibrium stock. Effort E_1, shown in Figures 10.8 and 10.9, permits two equilibria: a stable equilibrium at x_1^u and catch q_1^u, and an unstable one at x_1^l and catch q_1^l. If effort rises to a critical level, E_2, the population may be reduced below some viable minimum level, K_0. This characterises populations like the blue whale Small (1971) whose rate of reproduction is reduced significantly at low population levels. The implication of this is that, once the population falls below K_0, a policy aimed at conservation will be ineffective. Box 10.1 gives an example of how yield effort curves have been estimated for the North American lobster fishery.

Box 10.1   *Models of the North American lobster fishery*

The North American Lobster fishery has been the subject of a number of economic studies, notably Bell (1972), Hall (1977), Smith (1980) and Townsend (1986). These applications provide an example of how the theory can be applied to predict the level of landings. They also describes alternative models of the fishery and Townsend (1986) comments on how the biologist's approach to modelling populations may differ from the economist's.

The model by Bell (1972) provides an application of the Schaeffer yield–effort model. The total catch, q_t, in the fishery during a time period is given by the Cobb–Douglas relationship (see equation (10.3)):

$$q_t = \theta E_t x_t \tag{1}$$

where θ is the catchability constant, E_t is the aggregate fishing effort, x_t is the stock. This form of the fishery production function precludes externalities in production within a time period. The catch is proportional to effort, thus the marginal product of additional boats is constant. If stock growth follows a logistic growth function:

$$\dot{x} = \gamma(K - x_t)x_t - q_t \tag{2}$$

In equilibrium, where $\dot{x} = 0$, equation (1) can be rearranged to give x_t in terms of E_t and q_t and substituted into (2) to the Schaeffer yield–effort function:

$$q_t = \theta K E_t - (\theta^2/\gamma)E_t^2 \tag{3}$$

The curve is a quadratic function which is symmetric about the point of maximum sustainable effort, E_{msy}. Equation (3) is non-linear in the effort variable. To overcome this, Bell divides through by E_t to give the linear estimation equation:

$$s_t = \theta K - (\theta^2/\gamma)E_t + bF + u_t$$

where $s_t = q_t/E_t$; that is, the catch rate per unit of effort. He also includes a mean seawater temperature variable in degrees Fahrenheit, F and an error term u_t. The estimated equation is:

$$\hat{s}_t = -48.4 - 0.000024^* E_t + 2.13^* F_t \tag{4}$$

(* denotes significance at the 5 per cent level.)

This form of the model is criticised by Hall (1977). In particular, the constant term in (4) is negative, which is not permissible as the parameters γ and θ must be positive. In his alternative formulation, Hall makes the carrying capacity a function of the sea temperature

$$K = b_0 + b_1 F_t$$

thus

$$s_t = \theta b_0 - (\theta^2/\gamma)E_t + \theta b_1 F + u_t$$

This allows a reinterpretation of Bell's equation as the constant term can now be negative.

Smith (1980) provides an alternative model which relaxes some of the restrictions associated with Bell's model. First, the constant marginal product Cobb–Douglas production function is replaced by one which allows a diminishing marginal product. Second, the assumption of a steady state is relaxed, there is an interaction between the growth rate and the catch and the production function includes a stochastic error term. The stock in discrete time is given by

$$x_t = x_{t-1} + \Delta x_{t-1} - q_{t-1} + u_t \tag{5}$$

That is, the stock equals the previous stock, plus growth, Δx_{t-1} less the harvest, where

$$\Delta x_t = \gamma(K - x_t)x_t \tag{6}$$

The production function is

$$q_t = \theta E_t^\beta x_t \tag{7}$$

where $0 < \beta < 1$. After substituting (5) for Δx_t and (7) for x_t the non-linear estimating equation is:

$$[q_t/q_{t-1}][E_{t-1}/E_t]^\beta - 1 = \gamma K - [\gamma q_{t-1}/\theta E_{t-1}]^\beta - \theta E_{t-1}^\beta + v_t$$

where

$$v_t = u_t[\theta E_{t-1}^\beta/q_{t-1}]$$

The estimated value of $\beta = 0.3961$ is significantly less than 1, thus Bell's assumption of a constant return to effort is not justified.

In his paper Townsend (1986) criticises both these models on the basis of their out of sample predictions. He then proceeds to describe a more complex, biological model based on models developed by Beverton and Holt (1957) where the population is subdivided into cohorts of lobsters of different ages. This model gives more accurate forecasts than the simpler models described above based on the Schaeffer model. The fishery economist must make a choice between simplistic tractable models such as the Schaeffer model and the potential for more accurate predictions offered by more sophisticated 'biological' models.

10.4 Static economic models of fisheries

Hitherto the discussion has described the technological aspects of fishery exploitation. This account is analogous to a description of a production function in production economics: the relationships are technical and have no economic content. Now, under some highly restrictive assumptions, we introduce prices and costs and determine the static equilibrium of an *open-access* fishery. The model is due to Gordon (1954).

Assume a constant price, p, for harvested biomass and a constant cost, c, per unit of fishing effort. From the yield curve, $q(E)$ define the economic rent, the sum of profits across all the firms in the industry as:

$$\pi = pq(E) - cE$$

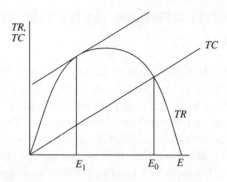

Figure 10.10 *Static fishing equilibria*

The term $pq(E)$ is total revenue (TR) and cE is total cost (TC). Where the fishery is open-access, firms enter the industry until the economic rent is zero, that is where total revenue equals total cost. In other words, excess profits induce more firms to enter until positive profits are competed away. This solution is represented in Figure 10.10, where E_0 represents an open-access equilibrium. It is argued that a level of fishing above E_0 would result in at least some fishermen making losses and, as a result, resources shift out of the fishery. If, instead, effort is below E_0, then fishermen earn profits and additional resources are attracted to fishing. Recall that costs in economics are always interpreted as the opportunity cost of the resource. A problem associated with many fishing communities is that the opportunity cost of labour and capital devoted to the fishing effort are typically low, since few alternative employment opportunities exist for the labour and capital employed in fishing. Thus resources may be locked into fishing at high levels of effort which are damaging to the sustainability of fish stocks.

The equilibrium in open-access fisheries represents *economic overfishing* where more resources than is socially optimal are devoted to the fishing effort. Further the fishery may also show *biological overfishing* where the harvest is below the maximum sustainable yield. In extreme cases this may lead to the fish population being reduced to such low levels that its exploitation is no longer viable. If instead the fishery was owned by a single firm, the firm would use effort E_1 to maximise profits. This is equivalent to the theory of the firm equilibrium where marginal cost equals marginal revenue, that is, $pq'(E) = c$, if the marginal cost is assumed to be constant. Note that in the absence of externalities, and assuming all input and output prices equal their socially optimal levels, then E_1 is also a social optimum which maximises the net benefits of the fishery.

▌ 10.5 Comparative dynamic models of fishing

Gordon's model neglects the dynamics of the economic and biological processes that govern a fishery. In the context of the fishery, comparative dynamics is concerned with the time path of the stock, how it is affected by market structure, policy measures and stock stability. This section considers a number of comparative dynamic fishery models of increasing complexity. The first is of a sole-ownership fishery where the fish are sold to a competitive market; the next is a modification of this model where the fish are sold monopolistically. The sole-ownership model is realistic for inland fisheries, but it is unrealistic for many marine fisheries. However, it does define the social optimum and as such provides a benchmark toward which fisheries policies might be directed. The monopoly model shows the effect of imperfect competition in fishery markets. The model is then further developed to include a cost function and is used to analyse fisheries policies and the issue of property rights. It also incorporates the Schaeffer and Gordon models as a special case.

☐ 10.5.1 Sole ownership of a competitive fishery and the social optimum

The key assumption for this model is that fish can be harvested costlessly. The owner of the fishery's objective function is to maximise discounted profits given a fixed price, p, a stock growth function and a harvest constraint:

$$\text{maximise}_q \quad \int_0^T pq\, e^{-rt}\, dt \tag{10.4}$$

$$\text{subject to} \quad \dot{x} = g(x) - q \qquad x(0) = x_0 \qquad 0 \le q \le q_m$$

where q_m is the maximum harvest level. The Hamiltonian for the problem is

$$H(x, q, \lambda, t) = pq\, e^{-rt} + \lambda(g(x) - q) \tag{10.5}$$

the first-order conditions for a maximum are

$$\lambda = p\, e^{-rt} \tag{10.6}$$

and the costate condition

$$\dot{\lambda} = -\lambda g'(x) \tag{10.7}$$

Differentiating (10.6) with respect to time, equating with (10.7) and substituting (10.6) for λ yields

$$rp\,e^{-rt} = p\,e^{-rt}g'(x)$$

which on cancelling $p\,e^{-rt}$ gives the result

$$g'(x) = r \tag{10.8}$$

That is, in equilibrium the marginal growth rate with respect to stock is equal to the discount rate. If we multiply both sides by p and rearrange

$$\frac{pg'(x)}{p} = r \tag{10.9}$$

this is equivalent to equation (7.8), where the rate of return on the last pound invested in the fish stock just equals the opportunity cost of that money, the rate of return on a numeraire asset, r.

In equilibrium the harvest rate equals the growth rate. If the initial stock is above equilibrium, the producer harvests up to their maximum capacity until the equilibrium stock is established. Conversely, if the initial stock is below equilibrium the producer harvests nothing until equilibrium is established. This describes a most rapid approach path to the equilibrium solution. The equilibrium holds when the planning horizon is relatively long, even infinitely long. However, if the length of ownership of the resource is of short duration, there is a tendency for the optimal harvest rate to approach the equilibrium and then increase as the end of the planning horizon approaches. The exact time path for the harvest rate depends upon the end-point conditions (see section 7.3.2). The equilibrium is also socially optimal if r is the social rate of time preference.

☐ *10.5.2 Monopoly fishery*

This problem has already been introduced in section 7.4.2 as an example of a non-linear control problem. It is re-introduced here so that the effects of imperfect competition can be analysed. Fishing monopolies are not common, but a degree of imperfect competition tends to be observed in the fish-processing sector, which in turn provides the incentives for fishermen to achieve a particular harvest level.

The problem is

$$\text{maximise}_q \quad \int_0^\infty R(q)\,e^{-rt} \tag{10.10}$$

$$\text{subject to} \quad \dot{x} = g(x, q) \qquad x(0) = x_0$$

The revenue function can be written as

$$R(q) = f(q)q$$

where $f(\cdot)$ is the inverse demand function.

First define the Hamiltonian (see (7.23))

$$H = R(q)e^{-rt} + \lambda(g(x) - q) \tag{10.11}$$

and then differentiate with respect to q and set equal to zero. This gives

$$R'(q)e^{-rt} - \lambda = 0 \tag{10.12}$$

and the complementary costate condition

$$-\dot{\lambda} = \lambda g_x \tag{10.13}$$

The costate variable is not of direct interest, thus (10.12) and (10.13) are used to eliminate it. In the same series of manipulations the time variable is also eliminated so that results can be expressed independently of time as a function of q and x.

First, differentiate (10.12) with respect to time to give

$$\dot{\lambda} = -rR'(q)e^{-rt} + R''(q)\dot{q}e^{-rt} \tag{10.14}$$

The factor out $R'(q)e^{-rt}$ to give

$$\dot{\lambda} = R'(q)e^{-rt}\left[-r + \frac{R''(q)}{R'(q)}\dot{q}\right]$$

Note that $R'(q)e^{-rt}$ can be replaced by λ from (10.12) and $\dot{\lambda}$ from (10.13) to give

$$\lambda g_x = \lambda\left[-r + \frac{R''(q)}{R'(q)}\dot{q}\right]$$

Finally cancel λ and rearrange, giving

$$\dot{q} = (r - g_x)\frac{R'(q)}{R''(q)} \tag{10.15}$$

thus $\dot{q} = 0$ when $g_x = r$.

This is the required result: it represents the problem as two autonomous differential equations. Although there is no guarantee that these equations can be solved analytically they allow us to assess the optimal harvest rate given initial conditions (x_0, q_0) and a steady-state solution to the problem (x^*, q^*) where $\dot{q} = 0$ and $\dot{x} = 0$. The steady-state solution may be viewed as the comparative static solution to the dynamic problem.

The equilibrium solution to the competitive problem (10.9) is identical to that of the monopoly (10.15). However, if the initial stock is away from the equilibrium, the monopoly moves to the equilibrium point more gradually along the separatrices shown in Figure 7.3 (see Clark, 1990, p. 100, for a more detailed discussion). This implies that, out of equilibrium, the monopoly firm may harvest either too little, where $x_0 > x^*$, or too much, when $x_0 < x^*$, compared with the socially optimal harvest.

10.5.3 The competitive fishery and the social optimum with costs

The previous sub-section established some basic results for the case where fishing effort is costless, but clearly this is unrealistic and we now extend the model to include the cost of fishing effort. The value of this model is in defining a more realistic social optimum which can be used as a benchmark against which an open-access fishery can be compared and towards which policies to regulate an open-access fishery can be directed.

A key role of fishery economics is in defining policies capable of overcoming the economic inefficiency of an open-access fishery. If there are a large number of firms then they are inclined to take account of their own direct costs but not the cost they impose upon other users of the resource. No value is placed on conserving the resource because there is no guarantee that an individual firm benefits from showing restraint. The task of fishery management, from an economic perspective, is one of compelling firms to take account of the socially optimal shadow price for stock.

Consider a fishery in which a fixed number of N firms exploit the fish stock. (This section is based on Arnason (1990), who relaxes the assumption of identical firms and considers firms of varying sizes with different cost structures.) The firms' production functions are a generalised form of the Schaeffer model. For convenience it is assumed that all firms are identical:

$$q(E_i, x) \qquad i = 1, 2, \ldots, N$$

The function $q(\cdot)$ is twice continuously differentiable and jointly concave in E_i and x. The harvest cost functions are

$$c(E_i) \qquad i = 1, 2, \ldots, N$$

and are assumed to be twice continuously differentiable and convex in effort, E_i. In this case effort stands as a proxy for the amount of labour and capital employed in fishing. The problem for the fishery manager is to maximize the present value of the profits of all firms in the industry:

$$\text{Maximize}_{E_i} \quad \int_0^\infty N\pi(E_i, x, p)\, e^{-rt}\, dt$$

subject to $\quad \dot{x} = g(x) - Nq(E_i, x) \qquad x(0) = x_0$

The current-value Hamiltonian for the problem is

$$H = N[pq(E_i, x) - c(E_i)] + \mu(g(x) - Nq(E_i, x)) \tag{10.16}$$

The first-order conditions for each identical firm are to choose the level of effort, E for all firms so that

$$pq_E - c_E - \mu q_E = 0 \tag{10.17}$$

or

$$(p - \mu)q_E = c_E \tag{10.18}$$

where the net marginal benefit of effort comprises the marginal benefit of selling fish at the market price less the imputed shadow price of stock. The costate equation is:

$$\dot{\mu} = [r - g'(x)]\mu - (p - \mu)Nq_x \tag{10.19}$$

The equilibrium solution of these equations is found by setting the growth rate equal to the total harvest, $g(x) = Nq(E, x)$. In equilibrium the rate of return from the numeraire asset must equal the rate of return from the fishery. Substituting (10.18) for μ into (10.19) and setting $\dot{\mu} = 0$ gives

$$g'(x) + \frac{c_E q_x N}{pq_E - c_E} = r \tag{10.20}$$

From (10.20) the rate of return on holding the marginal unit of stock can be decomposed into two parts: the return from increased stock growth, $g'(x)$ and the return from reduced costs. This implies that the optimal level of stock is greater in the presence of costs than would be the case for zero costs: see (10.9). The shadow price of stock in equilibrium is from (10.19)

$$\mu = \frac{pq_x N}{r + q_x N - g'(x)}$$

The problem faced by the individual firm who shares the fishery is different to the extent that they are only concerned with private costs and benefits. Arnason (1990) argues that if a firm is rational this will include a valuation of the stock; however, this valuation will vary inversely with the number of firms operating in the fishery and is only identical to the socially optimal valuation when there is sole ownership. (This represents a generalisation to the usual assumption in fisheries economics of two extreme cases of open access and sole ownership.) The firm's problem is to

$$\text{maximise}_{E_i} \quad \int_0^\infty \pi(E_i, x, p) e^{-rt} \, dt$$

$$\text{subject to} \quad \dot{x} = g(x) - Nq(E_i, x) \qquad x(0) = x_0$$

The stock constraint includes the fishing effort of *all* firms. The current-value Hamiltonian for the problem is

$$H = pq(E_i, x) - c(E_i) + \eta(g(x) - Nq(E_i, x))$$

where η represents the valuation of the stock to the individual firm. The first-order conditions are

$$(p - \eta)q_{E_i} = c_{E_i} \tag{10.21}$$

which is identical to (10.18) with η substituted in the place of μ. The costate condition is

$$\dot{\eta} = [r - g'(x)]\eta - (p - \eta N)q_x \tag{10.22}$$

In equilibrium the rate of return for the firm is:

$$g'(x) + \frac{c_E q_x N}{pq_E - c_E} = r$$

and is identical to that for the socially optimal catch; however, the equilibrium marginal stock valuation is different:

$$\eta = \frac{pq_x}{r + q_x N - g(x)} \tag{10.23}$$

The marginal valuation of stock is only equal to the socially optimal valuation when $N = 1$, that is $\mu = \eta$, otherwise $\mu > \eta$ for given x and E. The equilibrium for the firm may be characterised as a Nash–Cournot equilibrium where each firm correctly predicts the catch of the other firms and then chooses their own optimal harvest level accordingly.

The implications of this model can be explored for the specific case of identical, symmetrical firms, the cost function $TC = cE$, the Schaeffer function for effort, $q = \theta Ex$ and a logistic growth function. First it is possible to identify two extreme equilibrium outcomes: the stock and growth under open-access and the socially optimal stock and growth. The open-access equilibrium is found by setting $\eta = 0$, thus from (10.21) $p\theta x = c$. If $p = 1$, $\theta = 0.2$ and $c = 1$, the stock is 5 units. The growth function is $g(x) = x - 0.01x^2$ which has a maximum sustainable yield of 50 units.

The social optimum is found by solving (10.20) for the level of effort, E, substituting the equilibrium condition that $g(x) = \theta Ex$ for E and solving for x. The socially optimal stock is much higher than the open-access stock at 48.02 units, with a discount rate $r = 0.1$. These represent two extremes, one where a single manager controls the stock and the outcome is identical to sole ownership, and open access which is where an infinite number of firms have access to the stock. Intermediate cases may also be envisaged, where the number of identical firms who have access to the stock, perhaps through fishing licences, is progressively increased. This comparative static result is

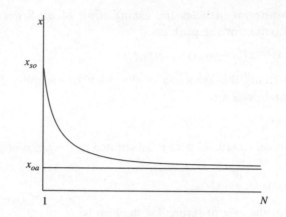

Figure 10.11   *Equilibrium stock and the number of firms*

derived by solving the firms' equilibrium E and substituting the equilibrium condition $g(x) = N\theta Ex$, where each firm's effort is identical and N is the total number of firms and then solving for x. It is also possible to solve (10.23) for η.

From Figure 10.11 we note that, as the number of firms increases, the equilibrium stock declines asymptotically towards the open-access equilibrium. Two extreme cases are identified, sole ownership stock, x_{so}, and shadow price, η_{so}, and open-access stock, x_{oa}, and shadow price, η_{oa}. Similarly, as the number of firms increases the shadow price of the resource to the firms declines to zero. By definition, in an open-access fishery the marginal value of stock is zero (Figure 10.12). The example indicates the outcome in a fishery with and without a socially optimal policy. According

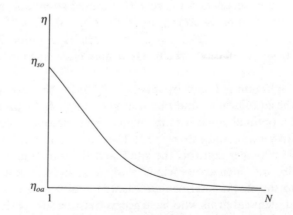

Figure 10.12   *Equilibrium shadow price against the number of firms*

to this model the solution moves further from the socially optimal stock as the number of firms increases. However, if the firms take account of the socially optimal value of stock this is not a problem and the solution is independent of the number of firms who have access to the fishery.

10.5.4 *Fishery exploitation with endogenous prices*

In the models described so far in this chapter the assumption is made that the price of fish is constant. The justifications for this assumption are that the fishery firms tend to be small relative to the industry and have no market power – they are price takers. Further if the analysis of the exploitation of a fishery is primarily concerned with finding the steady state, then this solution also implies *ceteris paribus* a constant price. In this sub-section the fishery model is extended to include the assumption that the price adjusts to the quantity harvested and that firms are able to anticipate that prices will change through time. Extending the fisheries model to include an endogenous price allows a direct comparison between models of renewables resources and those of non-renewable resources developed in Chapter 9. It should be recalled that a key assumption of models of non-renewable resource extraction is that the price changes through time in accordance with Hotelling's rule and that firms anticipate these changes with perfect foresight.

The model employed here is similar to that presented in the last sub-section, with the exception that all firms are sole owners of their fishing stock. Under this assumption the competitive optimum and the social optimum are identical. The purpose of this assumption is to suppress the need for explicit aggregation from the firm to the industry. One further crucial assumption is that the demand curve $d(p)$ is downward sloping. In common with Hotelling's rule (section 9.2), firms have the ability to forecast prices exactly on the basis that they know the demand curve, other firms' cost curves and the stock. The equilibrium is in essence a rational expectations equilibrium. Berck (1981) provides a more detailed technical account of the assumptions which underlie the model; here we have recourse to a specific function form to give an intuitive account of the equilibrium.

The firm solves the following problem

$$\text{maximize}_q \quad \int_0^\infty (pq - c(x)q)\, e^{-rt}\, dt$$

subject to $\quad \dot{x} = g(x) - q \qquad x(0) = x_0$

where q is given by the Schaeffer equation, $q = \theta Ex$. It should be noted that this form of catch technology implies a particular form of cost function $c(x)q = (c/\theta x)q$. That is, the cost per unit caught is a declining function of the stock, $0 < \theta < 1$. This is the equivalent of the dual relationship between production and cost functions in production economics.

The present-value Hamiltonian for the problem is:

$$H = (pq - c(x)q)e^{-rt} + \lambda(g(x) - q)$$

The usual first-order condition is

$$(p - c(x))e^{-rt} = \lambda \tag{10.24}$$

and the costate condition

$$\dot{\lambda} = -H_x = c'(x)qe^{-rt} - \lambda g'(x) \tag{10.25}$$

Differentiate (10.24) with respect to time

$$\dot{\lambda} = \frac{d((p - c(x))e^{-rt})}{dt} = \dot{p}e^{-rt} - rpe^{-rt} - c'(x)\dot{x}e^{-rt} + rc(x)e^{-rt} \tag{10.26}$$

This differential equation is highlighted: the usual assumption in fisheries models is that the term $\dot{p} = 0$, that is the price is constant. Here the assumption is that the price may change through time, although it will be constant if the fishery reaches a steady state.

Equating (10.25) with (10.26) and simplifying

$$\dot{p} = (r - g'(x))(p - c(x)) + c'(x)g(x) \tag{10.27}$$

yields the required result. This result is more general than that given by (10.20); for instance, if $\dot{p} = 0$ it becomes:

$$g'(x) - \frac{c'(x)g(x)}{(p - c(x))} = r$$

which is equivalent to (10.20) with the exception that the harvest, q, instead of the effort, E, is the decision variable. If the cost function and growth function are zero, (10.27) is Hotelling's rule for the price of a non-renewable resource. This relationship links the economics of renewable and non-renewable resources and shows Hotelling's rule as a special case. Returning now to the interpretation of (10.27), restate as:

$$\frac{\dot{p} - c'(x)\dot{x}}{(p - c(x))} - \frac{c'(x)q}{(p - c(x))} = (r - g'(x))$$

This can be interpreted in a similar way to (9.19); that is, the price net of the marginal cost rises (or falls) at the discount rate adjusted for stock growth and the proportional change in cost $c'(x)q/(p - c(x))$.

The implications of this model can be assessed using a phase-plane diagram based on the logistic growth function, $g(x) = 1x - 1x^2$, and the

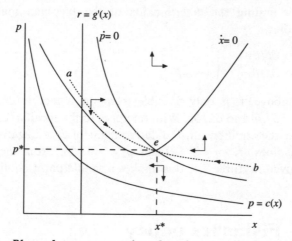

Figure 10.13 *Phase-plane representation of a sole-ownership fishery with an
endogenous price*

lincar demand curve $d(p) = 1 - 0.07p$, $c(x) = 0.5q/0.3x$, and $r = 0.1$. The
aggregate stock function in equilibrium is given by:

$$\dot{x} = g(x) - d(p) \tag{10.28}$$

Equilibrium is determined by the intersection of the isocline where $\dot{x} = 0$
and $\dot{p} = 0$. This is represented in Figure 10.13.

The price isocline is given by (10.27) and the stock isocline by (10.28).
Equilibrium occurs where these isoclines cross at e. At levels of stock
which are out of equilibrium, the industry determines an initial price which
lies on the convergent separatrices ae and eb. It follows that, where the
stock is low, the price is initially above the equilibrium and declines as
stock increases. The form of the $\dot{x} = 0$ isocline depends on the form of the
growth function, $g(x)$.

Other elements of Figure 10.13 are the $p = c(x)$ curve, which represents
the minimum price at each stock level for the fishery to be viable, and the
$r = g'(x)$ line, which indicates the conventional fishery equilibrium and is the
point at which the $\dot{p} = 0$ isocline tends to infinity: the equilibrium will be to
the right of this point.

The numerical solution to the problem is $x^* = 0.542$, $p^* = 10.74$,
$q^* = 0.2482$. These can be compared with the solution to constant cost
fishery problem represented in Figure 7.4. In that problem, price is not a
determinant of the equilibrium. The final stage is to consider the nature of
the solution. Figure 10.13 represents a saddle point. However, this can only

be verified by finding the determinants of the Jacobian matrix at the equilibrium point,

$$B = \begin{bmatrix} \partial\dot{p}/\partial p & \partial\dot{p}/\partial x \\ \partial\dot{x}/\partial p & \partial\dot{x}/\partial x \end{bmatrix} = \begin{bmatrix} + & +/- \\ + & +/- \end{bmatrix}$$

As indicated above, it is only possible from the algebraic derivatives to definitely sign $\partial\dot{p}/\partial p$ and $\partial\dot{x}/\partial p$. With reference to the specific functions and parameters, at the equilibrium, the determinant of B is negative (-1.711) and the eigenvalues are $\varphi_1 = 2.579$ and $\varphi_2 = -0.663$. From the conditions for stability given in Table 7.1, this implies a saddle point equilibrium.

■ *10.6* Fisheries policy

The model developed in the last section identifies the optimal harvest rate. The problem faced by the fisheries manager is how to transmit incentives to producers so that the socially optimal harvest and stock are maintained. The choice of policy instrument depends upon their economic efficiency, their informational feasibility and their costs of administration and enforcement. The problems associated with fishery management have much in common with the problems of policies for environmental control. In the case of fisheries the externality comes through the additional costs imposed by firms on one another through the stock effect.

> The fundamental externality of common-property fisheries derives from the resource base itself. The resource stock is a factor in each firm's production function. Thus by their harvesting activity the firms impose a production diseconomy on each other. The result is a tendency towards excessive fishing effort and over exploitation of the resource. (Arnason, 1990, p. 631)

That is, firms do not give the socially optimal valuation of the stock and, in the case of an open-access fishery, place a zero valuation on future stock. Thus the fishery management problem is one of compelling producers to take account of the socially optimal shadow price for stock. In other words producers should behave as if they had to rent the stock at the socially optimal shadow price.

> The concept of resource rents was employed by Gordon in his seminal paper on the fisheries problem in 1954. Since then the problem of common-property fisheries has generally been seen as one of dissipation of resource rents and the objective of fisheries management the restoration of these rents. (Arnason, 1990, p. 645)

□ 10.6.1 Taxes

The use of a tax which is equal to the the the shadow price of an externality is a well established principle of welfare economics (Pigou, 1946). In an open-access fishery the marginal condition (see (10.18)) is

$$c_i'(E_i) = pq_E$$

that is, the marginal cost of effort is equated with the marginal revenue of effort. In the socially optimal fishery we have instead the marginal condition

$$c_i'(E_i) = (p - \mu)q_E$$

The two solutions are identical if the shadow price is replaced by an identical tax per unit of landed fish, that is, $\mu = \tau$. The corresponding condition becomes:

$$c_i'(E_i) = (p - \tau)q_E \tag{10.29}$$

This approach to fishery management is appealing in that it leaves operational decisions, such as how much to catch, under the control of individual fishermen. Despite this advantage, it is typically opposed by fishermen who suffer the income effect of the tax and some of the less efficient fishermen may be eliminated from the industry. A second difficulty is that a tax policy requires the management authority to know the cost structure of each firm as well as the biological characteristics of the fish population. The tax would have to be recalculated as fishing technology, stock estimates and the number of firms in the fishery change. For these reasons taxes on fish harvests are rarely used as a policy for fishery management.

□ 10.6.2 Individual transferable quota system

Catch quotas stipulate the maximum catch of each fishing firm at a point in time, where the quota period is infinitesimally small. Assume the fishery management agency makes a total quota, Q, available which, given current information about the fishery, aims to achieve the socially optimal solution. The catch quotas are homogeneous and perfectly divisible and can be traded at an equilibrium market price of s.

The fishery firm now faces the constrained optimisation problem

$$\text{maximise}_{q_i} \quad \pi_i(x, q_i) = pq_i - c_i(q_i, x)$$

$$\text{subject to} \quad q_i \leq Q_i$$

If quota is freely tradeable, it is possible to incorporate it in the producer's objective function as a cost, that is, producers adjust their holding of quota optimally by either buying or selling; thus

$$\pi_i(x, q_i) = pq_i - c_i(q_i, x) - sq_i$$

where the last term on the right-hand side represents the opportunity cost of holding quota and no incentive exists for a producer to hold surplus quota. Differentiating with respect to q_i,

$$c_{q_i} = (p - s)q_E$$

From this relationship it is possible to derive a demand for quota function, for instance for the Schaeffer model

$$q_i = \frac{c_i}{\theta x^2(p - s)}$$

the total demand function for N identical firms is

$$\sum_i q_i = N\frac{c}{\theta x^2(p - s)} = Q$$

By manipulating the quota, Q, the quota authority can achieve any desired quota price s. They can also force the fishery to pursue the socially optimal policy by maintaining the quota level so the price is $s = \mu$. In this respect quota is equivalent to an optimal tax.

Objections to such a quota system are in terms of their distributional implications. Taxes accrue to the fishery management authority while the benefits of quotas accrue to the firms who receive them. Other problems concern the monitoring and enforcement of quotas, the costs of which may render a quota system inoperable. Finally, there is the problem of the amount of information required to allocate quota optimally which, as in the case of optimal taxation, requires that the authority has detailed information about both firm's costs and the biology of the exploited population. Alternatively, tradeable quotas can achieve a reduction in the level of effort at a minimum cost, since the most efficient producers buy quota from the least efficient, who leave the industry.

☐ *10.6.3 Other policies*

A wide range of other policy instruments have been employed in fishery management. These are treated separately here as they are not motivated by strictly economic criteria. Limited entry to a fishery is a policy whereby the number of vessels in the fishery is restricted by licensing. If the number of vessels in a fishery is reduced this leads to an immediate reduction in effort; however, each vessel still exerts a level of effort

$$c'_i(E_i) = pq_E$$

which is greater than the optimal effort even if only the socially optimal number of vessels are licensed. In the longer term, the fishermen will have an incentive to upgrade their equipment (Fraser, 1978) thus leading the fishery back to its original level of overfishing.

Non-allocated total catch quotas restrict the access to the fishery with the aim of achieving a target level of stock; that is, the fishery is only open for a restricted period and the catch is restricted to some maximum level. This means that fishermen compete for a share of a fixed catch. This tends to lead to overinvestment in fishing effort even though the survival of the fishery is ensured. See Clark (1990, p. 261) for a fuller account of the way this policy was applied to the Pacific halibut fishery; such a policy also operates in the European Union.

Box 10.2 *A critique of 'traditional' bioeconomic theory*

Wilson (1982) provides a critique of the traditional theory of fishery economics (which constitutes the subject matter of this chapter) and the policy prescriptions which derive from it. The key elements in his critique are that the assumptions of the traditional model are unrealistic in the way fish populations are represented, in the assumptions concerning fisherman behaviour and in the disregard for transaction and informational costs associated with fisheries policies.

Unlike the stable single-species systems of accepted bioeconomic theory, fisheries tend to be highly variable, multi-species systems with biological and social dynamics that are imperfectly understood and parameters which are difficult to measure. As a result these fishery systems present difficult problems in public policy making under conditions of uncertainty. (Wilson, 1982, p. 417)

Accepted economic theory of fisheries is based on the observation that market processes provide at best an imperfect collective mechanism for the conservation of fisheries resources. The theory argues that the impairment of the market result is due solely to the absence of well-defined property rights or a mechanism for simulating their effects ... This conclusion is not wrong *per se*, but it is misleading in that it tends to direct analysis away from a consideration of many reasonable and economical non-property rights policy alternatives. Property rights are not the only social rules that are capable of altering economic behaviour; depending on the circumstances, they may very well be more costly and less beneficial than other less extensive sets of behavioural rules. (Ibid., p. 418)

In Wilson's analysis institutions have not emerged spontaneously to counter overfishing problems, owing to the infrequent occurrence of the problem in many fisheries and the complex nature of the resource. Overfishing is of two types: short-term overfishing which reduces the efficiency of the fishing fleet, and age of capture overfishing where fishermen catch progressively younger fish as the stock is depleted. The assumptions concerning the biology of the fishery are not well known; this is due to the interaction of a large number of species. In turn, the availability of fish is subject to wide variations and there is little evidence for simple links between current and future population sizes. Fish have a patchy spatial distribution and for this reason a large component of fishing cost is the cost of acquiring information about the location of fish. Fishermen adapt to this situation by switching between species as they become harder to catch. However, this adaptive switching behaviour of fishermen increases their efficiency as they can operate at capacity for a larger part of the year.

The factors considered lead Wilson to the conclusion that

In general, accepted economic theory on the management of fisheries presents a simplified picture of the fishery and also one that represents an extreme set of conditions. In every instance, the consideration of 'complicating factors' – multiple species, variability, patchiness, search and information costs – tends to lead to the conclusion that the social costs of unregulated fishing (although still positive) are less than might otherwise be expected on the basis of accepted theory. At the same time these complicating factors indicate higher social costs associated with the attempt to regulate. These two effects tend to limit the range of economically feasible management options and appear to create a strong preference for simple systems of management rules. This does not mean that regulation is not necessary, but that its objectives and specific forms are likely to be very different from those of the traditional economic view. (Ibid., p. 433)

Wilson's paper presents valid criticisms of the traditional theory. The question raised is how models should be modified to account for these shortcomings. It was perhaps the case in the past that models were created which were easy to solve analytically. Models which include more complex assumptions about fisherman behaviour, multi-species fisheries and uncertainty are analytically intractable. Possibly a change in emphasis might be envisaged where complex simulation models are developed to represent the population dynamics of multi-species fisheries and their interaction with the level of fishing effort without attempting to determine an elusive optimal policy. The simulation model could be used to assess the impact on the fishery of a discrete number of alternative policy scenarios.

10.7 Applying the theory and the discrete-time model

☐ 10.7.1 *Discrete-time maximum principle*

In Chapter 7 we established that there is a discrete-time analogue for the maximum principle and that discrete-time problems may also be solved by dynamic programming. This approach is illustrated here with reference to stock-recruitment models. The owner of the fishery aims to maximise discounted profit

$$\sum_{t=0}^{\infty} \pi(y_t, q_t)\rho^t$$

where $\pi(\cdot)$ is profit as a function of the harvest q_t and the recruitment rate, y_t, and ρ^t is the discrete-time discount rate, $1/(1+r)^t$. The state equation is

$$y_{t+1} - y_t = G(y_t - q_t) - y_t$$

The present-value Hamiltonian is

$$\text{II}(y_t, q_t, t) = \pi(y_t, q_t)\rho^t + \lambda_t(G(y_t - q_t) - y_t)$$

Differentiating with respect to q_t,

$$H_q = \rho^t \pi_q - \lambda_t G'(y_t - q_t) = 0 \tag{10.30}$$

Rearranging in terms of λ_t

$$\lambda_t = \rho^t \frac{\pi_{q_t}}{G'(y_t - q_t)}$$

and it follows immediately that this expression can be lagged

$$\lambda_{t-1} = \rho^{t-1} \frac{\pi_{q_{t-1}}}{G'(y_{t-1} - q_{t-1})}$$

In equilibrium $y = y_t = y_{t-1}$ and $q = q_t = q_{t-1}$, thus

$$\lambda_t - \lambda_{t-1} = (\rho^t - \rho^{t-1}) \frac{\pi_q}{G'(y - q)} \tag{10.31}$$

The costate condition is

$$\lambda_t - \lambda_{t-1} = -H_{y_t} = -\rho^{t-1}\pi_{y_t} - \rho^{t-1}\pi_q(1 - 1/G'(y_t - q_t)) \tag{10.32}$$

Equating (10.31) with (10.32) we obtain the equilibrium condition:

$$G'(y - q) \frac{\pi_y + \pi_q}{\pi_q} = \frac{1}{\rho} = 1 + r \tag{10.33}$$

In the specific case where harvest costs depend upon the number of stock recruits remaining, the profit rate will decline during the fishing season as the recruits are harvested. Thus

$$\pi(y_t, q_t) = \int_{y_t - q_t}^{y_t} [p - c(z)] \, dz \qquad (10.34)$$

that is, the profit is summed for the season, from the level of recruitment to the level of recruitment less that harvest. To simplify this definite integral we define a function:

$$\phi(y_t) = \int_{y_\infty}^{y_t} [p - c(z)] \, dz$$

Where $p - c(y_\infty) = 0$, on this basis, (10.34) can be rewritten as

$$\pi(y_t, q_t) = \phi(y_t) - \phi(y_t - q_t)$$

or equivalently in terms of escapement, $x_t = y_t - q_t$, in equilibrium

$$\omega(x) = \phi(G(x)) - \phi(x)$$

Substituting this into (10.33) yields

$$G'(x) \frac{p - c(G(x))}{p - c(x)} = 1 + r$$

This is the discrete-time equivalent of the equilibrium condition for a fishery given as (10.23) for the continuous-time model. The rate of return on the fishery is equated with $1 + r$ as the function $G(\cdot)$ relates to the stock level and not its growth rate, as is the case with the continuous-time growth function $g(\cdot)$.

10.7.2 Applying the discrete-time fishery model: a bioeconomic model of the North West Atlantic harp seal

Canadian harp seal pups are hunted for their pelts. They have been the subject of a bitter dispute between hunters and animal rights groups who wish to see seal hunting banned on humanitarian and 'ecological' grounds. Political pressure led to a ban on seal products by the European Community in 1982 which reduced the price of pelts and put an end to commercial hunting. The paper by Conrad and Bjørndal (1991) analyses the history of harp seal exploitation from 1952 to 1977. While this is no longer a heavily exploited resource, this paper gives an insight into how such populations are modelled and managed.

The harp seal reproduces in three colonies: on the pack ice off Newfoundland, Jan Mayen Island and the White Sea. Pregnant females whelp in late February and March. Newborn pups are covered in long white fur and are called 'whitecoats'. After 18 days the foetal hair is replaced by a spotted juvenile coat, when mottled pups are called 'beaters'. Immature animals born in the previous season are called 'bedlamers'. All these immature animals were hunted by small vessels from Newfoundland ports. Hunting took place during the whelping period and the later moulting period.

Population dynamics are assumed to be governed by the following difference equations:

$$w_{t+1} = \gamma x_t (1 - x_t/K) \tag{10.35}$$

$$x_{t+1} = (1 - m_0)(w_t - q_t) + (1 - m)(x_t - y_t) \tag{10.36}$$

where pup production, w_t is a logistic, γ is the intrinsic rate of pup production, m_0 the first-year mortality of pups, and m the mortality of seals of greater than one year old, q_t is the harvest of pups, y_t the harvest of seals and x_t the stock of seals. The model is a simple representation of the growth of the population. In effect it includes two cohorts, pups and seals older than one year. Equilibrium relationships are derived by setting $x_{t+1} = x_t$, solving (10.36) for $\tilde{x}$ and substituting into (10.35) to determine the equilibrium $\tilde{w}$. With a zero harvest $q_t = y_t = 0$, the equilibrium number of seals and pups are:

$$\tilde{x} = \frac{K[\gamma(1 - m_0) - m]}{\gamma(1 - m_0)}$$

$$\tilde{w} = \frac{Km[\gamma(1 - m_0) - m]}{\gamma(1 - m_0)^2}$$

This equilibrium is shown in Figure 10.14 as the point where the number of pups recruited to the seal population offsets the mortality of seals. A sufficient condition for stability is that the eigenvalues of the linearised system of equations (10.35) and (10.36) evaluated at $(\tilde{x}, \tilde{w})$ are less than one in absolute terms.

The harvestible surplus s, is maximised at $\tilde{x}/2$; this is the difference between the number of pups produced and the number recruited to the seal population given by:

$$s = \gamma x(1 - x/K) - mx/(1 - m_0)$$

Model parameters are estimated from biological studies and simulation. Simulation results using data on actual harvesting from the model indicate that over the period 1952 to 1977 the population initially declined and then increased from 1972 onwards as a result of the imposition of quotas by the Canadian government.

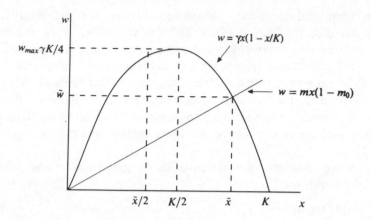

Figure 10.14   *Bioeconomic equilibrium in the harp seal population*

The socially optimal hunting problem is an application of the discrete-time maximum principle. Mathematically, the problem is to

$$\text{maximise}_{q_t, y_t} \sum_{t=0}^{\infty} \rho^t \pi(q_t, y_t)$$

subject to $w_{t+1} = \gamma x_t (1 - x_t/K)$ $x_{t+1} = (1 - m_0)(w_t - q_t) + (1 - m)(x_t - y_t)$

The problem contains two state variables, the number of pups and the number of seals, and two corresponding control variables, the pup harvest and the seal harvest. The Lagrangean composite function for the problem is;

$$L = \sum_{t=0}^{\infty} \rho^t \{ \pi(q_t, y_t) + \rho \lambda_{t+1} (\gamma x_t (1 - x_t/K) - w_{t+1})$$

$$+ \rho \mu_{t+1} ((1 - m_0)(w_t - q_t) + (1 - m)(x_t - y_t) - x_{t+1}) \}$$

The first-order conditions are:

$$\pi_q = (1 - m_0)\rho\mu_{t+1}$$

$$\pi_y = (1 - m)\rho\mu_{t+1}$$

$$\lambda_t = (1 - m_0)\rho\mu_{t+1}$$

and

$$\mu_t = \rho\lambda_{t+1}\gamma(1 - 2x_t/K) + (1 - m)\rho\mu_{t+1} \tag{10.37}$$

The objective function is given as producer profit:

$$\pi(q_t, y_t) = p_w q_t + p_s y_t - c_w(q_t) - c_s(y_t)$$

If costs are of the quadratic form

$$c_w(q_t) = q_t(a_0 + a_1 q_t)$$

and

$$c_s(y_t) = y_t(b_0 + b_1 y_t)$$

the objective function is a separable quadratic function where the producer surplus derived from harvesting pups and seals is added together.

The system of equations (10.35), (10.36) and (10.37) can be solved for optimal steady-state values for x, w, q and y. The results are presented in Table 10.1 for two discount rates.

Table 10.1 *The bionomic optimum*

	r	
	0.02	*0.1*
x^*	1 388 587	765 645
w^*	364 527	248 217
y^*	47 062	36 009
q^*	173 976	131 144
π^*	\$1 287 284	\$1 382 508
π^*/r	\$64 391 190	\$13 825 080

The value of producer surplus is presented in two ways: the annual value π^* and the value of the resource in perpetuity, π^*/r. It is notable that this value is highly sensitive to the discount rate: the total present value of the resource is reduced by approximately 79 per cent as the discount rate goes from 2 per cent to 10 per cent. As expected, the size of the optimal stock is lower at the higher discount rate.

This table gives an indication of the net value lost owing to the discontinuation of commercial seal hunting in 1982 when the European Community banned imports. It also suggests that the original concerns about the extinction of the population were largely unfounded. As the population returns to its unharvested steady state of 3 062 581 seals. Conflicts may arise as commercial fishing stocks are depleted. Hunting has largely been discontinued because of the price collapse brought about by the EC ban on pelt imports. In the future however, there remains an issue of how the seals should be managed as their populations expand and they start to reduce fish stocks significantly.

□ 10.7.3 *Dynamic programming*

In this section, dynamic programming is presented as an alternative, but equivalent, approach to the maximum principle for solving discrete-time problems over a finite time horizon, such as that introduced in section 10.7.1

$$\text{maximise}_q \quad \sum_{t=0}^{T} \pi(y_t, q_t)\rho^t$$

$$\text{subject to} \quad y_{t+1} = G(y_t - q_t)$$

and the constraint

$$(y_t, q_t) \in U \quad \forall t$$

that is, there is a finite number of values for y_t and q_t which are elements of the closed set U. The maximisation problem involves solving Bellman's equation:

$$J(y, t) = \text{maximise}_q \left[\pi(y_t, q_t)\rho^t + J(G(y_t, q), t + 1) \right]$$

Despite appearing in a different format, this equation is equivalent to the maximum principle. The first term on the right-hand side is the current profit rate, the second term gives the present-value of profits generated over the remainder of the planning horizon. Differentiating with respect to q_t yields:

$$\pi_{q_t}\rho^{t-1} - J_{x_t}G'(y_t - q_t) = 0$$

Noting that by definition, $J_{x_t} = \lambda_t$, that is the first derivative of the maximum value function with respect to the number of recruits is equal to the costate variable, this is the derivative given in (10.30) and its interpretation is identical to that found in section 10.7.1.

■ **10.8 Extending the theoretical model**

□ 10.8.1 *Optimal investment in renewable resource harvesting*

Thus far, the problem associated with open-access fisheries and the need for corrective policy measures have been assumed to arise because of free entry to the fishery. New entrants enter the fishery as soon as positive rents are earnt by the incumbent fishermen. This may be the case for some inshore fisheries where relatively inexpensive boats are adequate. However, most deep sea fisheries require expensive specialist equipment which may cost millions of dollars to purchase.

Clark *et al.* (1979) address the issue of capital investment in the fishery and make the assumption that investment is irreversible. This is reflected by the second-hand price or scrap price of boats being much less than the purchase price *as soon as* the boat is purchased. The model explores a common problem in many fisheries where resources can become 'trapped' in a fishery by their low opportunity cost, as scrap. In agricultural economics this is termed 'asset fixity'.

The model, which is for the sole owner of a fishery, includes two state variables, the stock of fish and the stock of capital. Fish harvesting is represented by the Schaeffer model,

$$\dot{x} = g(x) - \theta E x$$

where E is fishing effort. The capacity, K, determines the maximum fishing effort by $0 \leq E \leq K$. The capacity, K is a second-state variable and represents the capacity of fishing equipment. Capacity increases through investment, I, but there is no disinvestment in the fishery as we assume K has no value outside the fishery:

$$\dot{K} = -\delta K + I$$

where δ is the rate of depreciation. Investment incurs a fixed cost of c_f. To make the problem more tractable, fishing effort is a proportion ϕ of the capacity

$$E = \phi K$$

By substituting for effort, the problem is to

$$\text{maximise}_{\phi, I} \quad \int_0^\infty e^{-rt}\{(p\theta x - c_v)\phi K - c_f I\} \, dt$$

subject, to $\dot{x} = g(x) - \theta\phi Kx$ $x(0) = x_0$

$\dot{K} = -\delta K + I$ $K(0) = K_0$

$0 \leq \phi \leq 1$ $0 \leq I$

The Hamiltonian for the problem is

$$H = e^{-rt}\{(p\theta x - c_v)\phi K - c_f I\} + \lambda(g(x) - \theta\phi Kx) + \tau(-\delta K + I)$$

and is rearranged to separate out two switching functions (see section 7.4.1):

$$H = \{e^{-rt}(p\theta x - c_v)K + \lambda\theta Kx\}\phi + \{-e^{-rt}c_f + \tau\}I + \lambda g(x) - \tau\delta K \tag{10.38}$$

The problem is linear in the two control variables, the proportion of capacity employed in fishing, ϕ, and the rate of investment I. The solution to a linear control problem involves a combination of singular solutions and bang-bang control (see section 7.4.1 for a definition of these terms).

Clark *et al.* (1979) identify a number of solutions. In the original paper a further two cases were considered, one where both ϕ and I are singular, which can be shown to be inconsistent, and a second where $\phi = 0$, that is its lower limit, and I is singular; this is clearly not optimal: a firm will not invest in capacity when the current capacity is idle. Case 1 is where ϕ is singular; thus the switching function for ϕ equals zero.

$$H_\phi = e^{-rt}(p\theta x - c_v)K - \lambda\theta Kx = 0$$

which rearranges to give

$$\lambda = e^{-rt}\left(p - \frac{c_v}{\theta x}\right) \tag{10.39}$$

Differentiating this with respect to time gives

$$\dot{\lambda} = e^{-rt}\left\{-r\left(p - \frac{c_v}{\theta x}\right) + \frac{c_v}{\theta x^2}[g(x) - \theta\phi Kx]\right\}$$

The costate equation for x is

$$\dot{\lambda} = -H_x = -e^{-rt}p\theta\phi K + \lambda\theta\phi K - \lambda g'(x)$$

substitute (10.39) for λ to give

$$\dot{\lambda} = -H_x = -e^{-rt}\left\{p\theta\phi K - \left(p - \frac{c_v}{\theta x}\right)\theta\phi K + \left(p - \frac{c_v}{\theta x}\right)g'(x)\right\} \tag{10.40}$$

Equate the time derivative of (10.39) with (10.41) and simplify to give

$$g'(x) + \frac{c_v g(x)}{x(p\theta x - c_v)} = r \tag{10.41}$$

which is the basic formula for an equilibrium stock level. Denote the constant solution to (10.41) as x^*. This singular solution only depends upon the variable costs of fishing; as no investment is being made, $I = 0$, the solution is not affected by the cost of investment, c_f, which can be interpreted as a fixed cost. This represents a singular solution where $x = x^*$, $E = E^* = g(x^*)/\theta x^*$. The singular solution is transient as $I = 0$ and, through depreciation, the growth rate eventually exceeds the harvest rate $g(x^*) > \theta\phi Kx^*$, $\phi = 1$.

Case 2 is where I is singular and the maximum harvest level is maintained; thus $\phi = 1$, that is ϕ is set at its upper limit. This makes economic sense as investment will only be optimal when the present harvesting capital is used to capacity. A singular value for I implies that the second term in braces on the right-hand side of (10.38) is zero, thus:

$$H_I = -e^{-rt}c_f + \tau = 0$$

differentiating with respect to time,

$$\dot{\tau} = -re^{-rt}c_f \tag{10.42}$$

The costate equation for K, where τ is the shadow price of fishing capacity, is

$$\dot{\tau} = -H_K = -[e^{-rt}(p\theta x - c_v) - \lambda\theta x]\phi - \tau\delta \tag{10.43}$$

By noting that $\phi = 1$ and equating (10.42) with (10.43) gives

$$-re^{-rt}c_f = -[e^{-rt}(p\theta x - c_v) - \lambda\theta x] - e^{-rt}c_f\delta$$

Which on rearranging gives

$$\lambda = e^{-rt}\left\{p - \frac{c_v + (r + \delta)c_f}{\theta x}\right\}$$

Differentiating with respect to time, setting equal to (10.40) and defining $c_a = c_v + (\delta + r)c_f$ gives

$$g'(x) + \frac{c_a g(x)}{x(p\theta x - c_a)} = r \tag{10.44}$$

This is a version of the basic formula for the equilibrium stock and is similar to (10.41) except that the variable cost term is now replaced by total cost, c_a, which is variable cost plus the depreciation and interest forgone on the fixed cost expenditure $(\delta + r)c_f$. Equation (10.44) defines a second singular solution and long-run equilibrium, where $x = x^{**}$, $E = E^{**} = g(x^{**})/\theta x$ and as $\phi = 1$, $K^{**} = E^{**}$, $I^{**} = \delta K^{**}$. As $c_a > c_v$, it follows that $x^{**} > x^{*}$ from (10.44) and (10.41). The two singular solutions may be characterised as a short-run equilibrium, x^{*}, which only accounts for the variable costs of fishing effort, but allows the fishing capacity to decline, and a long-run equilibrium which takes account of both variable and fixed costs, x^{**}, and replaces the capacity as it depreciates.

The approach paths to the long-run equilibrium solutions are rather complex. The authors of the original paper (Clark *et al.*, 1979) indicate that they were found by guesswork, although they are shown to be optimal in the formal proof given in the original paper. The solution is given for two different initial sets of capacity and stock levels. The first represents an unexploited stock with no fishing capacity, the second is where the stock has been overexploited. Figure 10.15 represents the approach paths in state space where the diagram is subdivided by the switching curves, S_1 (given by $H_I = 0$) and S_2 (by $H_\phi = 0$) into three regions, R_1, R_2 and R_3. The regions are characterised by different values for the control variables; in R_1 where the stock is underexploited, the fishing capacity is increased immediately until it reaches the switching function S_1. In R_2 there is no investment, so capacity declines at the rate of depreciation, $I = 0$, but fishing effort is at its maximum level, $E = K$. In R_3, where the fishery may be viewed as over-exploited, both $I = 0$ and $E = 0$.

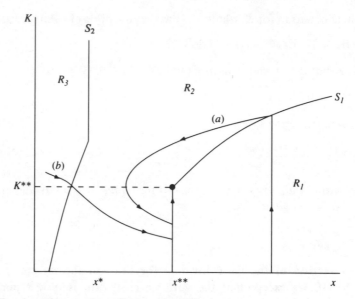

Source: Based on diagrams from Clark *et al.* (1979).
Figure 10.15   *Optimal harvest and investment*

First consider the unexploited stock, where the capacity is zero. The initial phase of exploitation is a pulse of investment which takes the fishery up to the switching function S_1 and into region R_2 along the path (a) where the maximum effort is employed, leading to progressive reduction of the resource stock and the capacity through depreciation. Eventually, depreciation reduces the capacity to such an extent that the maximum harvest rate is less than the growth rate and the stock starts to increase. However, no further investment takes place until $x = x^{**}$, which leads to another investment pulse which takes the fishery to the long-run equilibrium (K^{**}, x^{**}). The solution can be characterised as a boom-and-bust cycle where initially there is overinvestment in capacity and then a decline in the industry and an eventual recovery.

The situation where the initial capacity and stock are in region R_3 may be viewed as representing a resource which has been overexploited and is now being managed under a policy regime which mimics sole ownership. Since $x_0 < x^*$, $E = 0$ will initially be optimal. If $K < E^*$ a switch from $E = 0$ to $E = E_{max}$ occurs before the stock reaches x^*. This is indicated by the kink in the switching curve S_2. Once the stock has recovered sufficiently to move to the switching function and effort has switched to $E = K$, the stock gradually increases to $x = x^{**}$. At the same time the capacity declines by depreciation. When the stock equals x^{**}, there is a pulse of investment and the long-run equilibrium is attained.

Under both starting conditions the fishery reaches an equilibrium state which corresponds to the optimum sustained yield for which the cost function includes the full cost of fishing and not just the variable costs. However, during the cycle of fishery exploitation there are periods, in fact they might be quite long periods, where the fishery holds excess capacity and only attains the equilibrium by the gradual depreciation of the capacity; this overcapacity is shown to be optimal by the authors where the salvage value of capital is zero. The policy implications of this model are that fishing moratoria might be detrimental to a large number of fishing firms who are unable to transfer resources out of fishing effort in a particular fishery: thus the less readily transferable resources are, the more gradual a policy for reducing fishing effort would have to be to prevent large-scale bankruptcy among fishermen.

10.9 Strategic behaviour in fishery management

Fishery economics is concerned with the effect which property rights over a fishery have. It is usual, for analytical convenience, to identify two extremes, sole ownership and open access. The fishery policy problem may be characterised as one of finding a set of policy instruments which approximate the sole-ownership outcome in a fishery given the constraints of the necessary information being available for policy decisions and taking account of administration and policing costs. Policy aims to increase the welfare of a country by increasing the sustainable level of fish caught and thus increasing consumer surplus by selling more fish at a lower price. Where a single country has exclusive access to a fishery protected, say, by a 200 mile fishing exclusion zone, these policy objectives are clear-cut even if difficult to apply in practice. For many fisheries, including those which fall under European Community fisheries policies, more than one country has access to the fishery and a potential for conflict arises as each country attempts to maximise the benefits to their fishermen and consumers. This is also the case of fisheries in international waters where open access is still permitted, but a small number of large national fleets can be identified: for instance, the Australian tuna industry where the fish migrate between the Australian coastal zone and the off-shore region where Japanese trawlers have access to the fish (Klieve and MacAulay, 1993).

The existence of a situation where a small number of countries have access to a fishery led Levhari and Mirman (1980) to analyse such 'fish wars' as game-theoretic problems. Before describing their model in detail we consider a simple fishery game. (See Fudenburg and Tirole, 1991, for a more rigorous introduction to game theory. The technical note on pp. 14ff gives an introduction to game theory concepts.) There are two types of games that are relevant to fisheries management, non-cooperative games where player compete and cooperative games where there is a negotiated settlement. In the case considered, the two countries are the players and the strategies that they adopt include their fisheries policies, the pay-off is in terms of the welfare of their citizens. Consider the strategic form of such a game given in Table 10.2, where there are just two players, each with two strategies. The (conserve, conserve) strategy pair results in the sole-ownership outcome, the (deplete, deplete) strategy pair results in the open-access outcome. This is an example of the prisoners' dilemma described in the technical note on pp.14ff.

Table 10.2   *Pay-off matrix*

		Country B	
		Conserve	Deplete
Country A	Conserve	(10, 10)	(1, 12)
	Deplete	(12, 1)	(4, 4)

☐ *10.9.1   Non-cooperative games*

The Pareto optimal strategy is (conserve, conserve). However, this does not necessarily represent an equilibrium solution to this non-cooperative game. The equilibrium concept applied is due to Nash (1951). Here we will describe the *Nash equilibrium* for the two-person game given above, but it should be noted that it generalises to the case of an *N*-person game. The vector of strategies s^* is a Nash equilibrium if s^* is feasible, that is, $s^* \in S$; the pay-off is given by the function $u(\cdot)$,

$$u_1(s^*) \geq u_1(s_1, s_2^*) \quad \text{for any} \quad s_1 \in S_1$$

and

$$u_2(s^*) \geq u_2(s_1^*, s_2) \quad \text{for any} \quad s_2 \in S_2$$

The strategy combination s^* is a Nash equilibrium if each s_i^* is in the strategy set – it is available to the player, and no player can obtain a higher pay-off through the use of a different strategy given the strategy choices of the other player. On this basis (conserve, conserve) is not a Nash equilibrium as it would pay each player to switch to (deplete) if the other player conserved. The Pareto optimal outcome requires a different vector of strategies to the Nash equilibrium. The Nash equilibrium represents a *saddle point* where the strategy which maximises the minimum pay-off for both players coincides. If this is not the case, then a Nash equilibrium may exist in mixed strategies where each player plays their non-dominated strategies a certain proportion of the time; see the technical note on game theory, on pp. 14ff.

☐ 10.9.2 Cooperative solutions

As indicated, the cooperative solution to this game might be quite different. This is the case where the players sign a binding agreement before the game is played. We define a modified game with a pay-off region and a bargaining set. First it is helpful to assume that the pay-offs are in monetary terms so that there are no problems with transferring utility between countries. Second, the binding contract can specify that the strategies are used for a certain proportion of the time; this means that all convex combinations of the original strategies are feasible. Next assume that transfer payments can be made between the players. The original game is given in Figure 10.16.

The Pareto efficient set of solutions lies along the outside of the set of all possible pay-offs illustrated in Figure 10.17. Nash, however, thought that rational individuals would be more focused in determining a bargaining

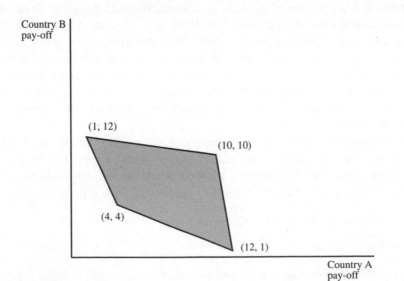

Figure 10.16 *Pay-off sets*

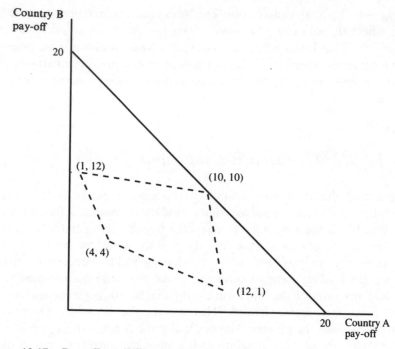

Figure 10.17 *Pay-off possibility sets*

solution. The existence of this solution depends upon three conditions being satisfied: first, the set of pay-offs is convex, second, the set is closed and bounded from above, and third, free disposal is allowed. A set is closed if it contains all its boundary points. A set is bounded above if there exists b such that $x \leq b$ for each x in X. Free disposal is an expedient condition which simplifies the set X by allowing a player to throw money away. In practice this never happens because rational individuals will always attempt to find a solution on the upper boundary of the set, so it is by way of a technicality; see Binmore (1992, p. 175).

A bargaining solution is a function $f(X, d)$ which is in the set X which gives the pay-off pair that a rational player would agree. The bargaining solution maximises the distance between what the players could receive if they disagreed, d, and their pay-off in agreement. It is a point s at which

$$\text{maximise}_{x_1, x_2} \quad (x_1 - d_1)(x_2 - d_2)$$

$$\text{subject to} \qquad x \in X \qquad x \leq d$$

is achieved. Returning to our example, each country can achieve a pay-off level of at least 4 in disagreement; thus any bargain will have to represent a higher pay-off if it is to be accepted by both countries.

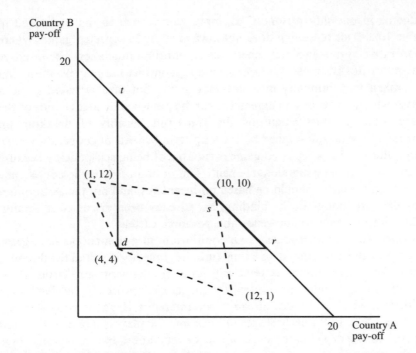

Figure 10.18 *Nash bargaining solution*

The upper boundary of the set has two points *t* and *r* which define a sub-set of rational outcomes of bargaining.

$s = \alpha r + \beta t$

where α and β measure the relative bargaining power of the players. If the players have equal bargaining powers, $\alpha = \beta = 0.5$, the solution is half-way between *t* and *r*. This is shown in Figure 10.18. In our example, if the countries have equal bargaining powers, the solution is (conserve, conserve) and each country achieves a pay-off of 10.

☐ 10.9.3 Dynamic games

The above example represents a one-shot game; that is, the game is played just once. Typically, fishery management problems involve the repeated strategic interaction of two countries, where the game is played over and over again. In this sub-section we focus on one result in dynamic games which is relevant here. We have seen that, in the absence of some means of engaging in pre-play bargaining, there is no guarantee of a beneficial outcome in one-shot prisoners' dilemma games such as that described in Table 10.2. This reasoning does not always apply in repeated games where cooperative agreements may emerge as equilibrium outcomes. The intuitive reason for this is simple. Without a binding contract pre-play promises can be broken with impunity in a one-shot game, but in a repeated game a player who goes against an agreement can be punished in later rounds of the game; thus in most situations the short-run benefits of breaking an agreement are far outweighed by the long-term benefits of cooperation. The implication is that a repeated game is capable of being self-policing because of the costs of breaking an agreement. The notion of dynamic consistency and that agreements should be based on incentives, and not the assumption that they are automatically binding, has already been discussed in section 9.2.5 with reference to non-renewable resource cartels.

Cooperation only emerges as an equilibrium in a non-cooperative game when the game continues over a long (infinite) time horizon and the discount factor for future returns is relatively large (Fudenberg and Tirole 1991, p. 110). In the finite time case the argument proceeds by backward induction, which is an idea already encountered in dynamic programming (section 7.5.3). In the early stages of the game the players might be deterred from choosing depletion because of fear of retaliation, but in the final stage of the game there is no possibility of later retaliation, so each player depletes. Moving back to the penultimate stage of the game, again there is no fear of retaliation as each player already knows that the other will deplete at the last stage. This argument is then repeated back to the beginning of the game. This outcome suggests that players do not behave sensibly even when they have the opportunity to move to a better long-term solution.

One strategy in this infinitely repeated prisoners' dilemma is to conserve until the other player depletes and then deplete thereafter. This is known as a trigger strategy. Any deviation from 'conserve' is punished by 'deplete'. However, if both players follow this strategy then no occasion for punishment will arise and players cooperate forever. We assume a discount factor of 25 per cent. The present value of co-operating is

$$PV_c = 10 + 10(0.75) + \cdots + 10(0.75)^{N-1} + 10(0.75)^N + 10(0.75)^{N+1} + \cdots$$

Can a player gain by deviating? If a country deviates by playing deplete it receives

$$PV_d = 10 + 10(0.75) + \cdots + 10(0.75)^{N-1} + 12(0.75)^N + 4(0.75)^{N+1} + 4(0.75)^{N+2}$$

as the other player always retaliates. If deviation was profitable then $PV_c - PV_d < 0$, but

$$PV_c - PV_d = (10 - 12)(0.75)^N + (10 - 4)(0.75)^{N+1} + (10 - 4)(0.75)^{N+2} + \cdots$$

$$= (0.75)^N[-2 + 6\{(0.75)^1 + (0.75)^2 + \cdots\}]$$

By the infinite sum of a geometric progression the term in the braces becomes

$$PV_c - PV_d = (0.75)^N \left\{ -2 + 6 \frac{0.75}{1 - 0.75} \right\} = (0.75)^N 16 > 0$$

It is thus unprofitable to deviate and the strategies of (conserve, conserve) are a Nash equilibrium for the repeated game. In conclusion, in some infinitely repeated games the cooperative solution of the one-shot game emerges as the non-cooperative equilibrium. This conclusion is of particular interest in the context of fisheries management as the exploitation of fisheries involves the repetition of fishing effort by the players. However, as we will see, the situation is complicated by the stock, which changes the constraints faced by the fishing industries through time. We are now ready to consider a more complex dynamic fishery game.

☐ *10.9.4 Fish wars*

International conflicts over fishing rights are a common occurrence. Possibly the most fiercely contested was the 'Cod War' of 1972 between Iceland and the United Kingdom. Such 'conflicts' on a smaller scale occur on numerous occasions, most notably among the member countries of the European Community, for instance the recent conflict between France and Spain over tuna fishing in the Bay of Biscay in 1994 and between the European Community and Canada over fishing off Greenland in 1995. These conflicts are not dissimilar to oligopolistic competition, where a small number of participants compete for a market. In the case of fisheries it is countries competing for a share of the stock in a fishery. Each of these problems contains a strategic element where the participants must take account of the actions of other participants. However, where the fishery problem differs from the simple oligopolistic competion problem is that the actions of the participants affect the fish population and thus the harvesting action of one country imposes an externality on other countries by increasing their costs of catching a given quantity of fish.

Levhari and Mirman (1980) develop a model of fish wars which uses discrete-time dynamic programming. The difference between the game described in this sub-section and the example given above is that the form of the game changes through time as the population of fish changes. It should be noted that such games usually have a large number of equilibria; it is only by making restrictive assumptions about the behaviour of the countries that it is possible to find a unique equilibrium.

The model assumes that access to the fishery is restricted to two countries. Each country aims to maximise the sum of the discounted utility of consumption over a planning horizon. The utility function is $u(c_i) = \log c_i$ for country i. The discount factor is $0 < \rho_i < 1$ and may be different for each country. Each country has a utility for the fish it catches in each period and thus an interest in the long-run effect of its present catch. However, each country takes the catch of the other country into account when deciding upon its own catch. Assume that each country behaves in a way which ensures a Nash equilibrium: that is, they maximise utility by taking the behaviour of the other country as given.

The fish stock is given by the following difference equation (this form of growth function is used here in preference to a discrete-time logistic or Ricker curves, discussed in section 10.2.2, to ensure that the equilibirum solution to the differential game is tractable):

$$x_{t+1} = x_t^\alpha \qquad 0 < \alpha < 1$$

and is normalised so that the steady-state fish population is where $x_{t+1} = x_t = 1$; this is represented in Figure 10.19.

The solution to the problem is developed in a number of stages. Let us first consider a two-period maximisation problem where the countries harvest during the first period and then share the remaining stock out equally in the second period. This rule for sharing the stock in the second period is a transversality condition. The objective function for Country 1 is thus

$$\text{maximise}_{c_1,c_2} \quad \{\log c_1 + \rho_1 \log \tfrac{1}{2}(x - c_1 - c_2)^\alpha\}$$

$$\text{subject to} \qquad 0 \leq c_1 \leq x - c_2$$

where $x - c_1 - c_2$ are the fish remaining at the the end of the first period which become $(x - c_1 - c_2)^\alpha$ in the next period. Equivalently, the objective function can be written as

$$\text{maximise}_{c_1,c_2} \{\log c_1 + \rho_1\alpha \log(x - c_1 - c_2) + \rho_1 \log \tfrac{1}{2}\}$$

which separates out the constant term $\rho_1 \log \tfrac{1}{2}$. The optimal value for c_1 is found by differentiating the objective function with respect to c_1 and setting equal to zero. Using the law of differentiating logs and, for the second term, the function of a function rule:

$$\frac{1}{c_1} - \frac{\rho_1\alpha}{x - c_1 - c_2} = 0$$

and simplifying,

$$(1 + \rho_1\alpha)c_1 + c_2 = x \tag{10.45}$$

This represents the reaction curve for Country 1 to the consumption of Country 2. By a similar argument the reaction curve for Country 2 is

$$c_1 + (1 + \rho_2\alpha)c_2 = x \tag{10.46}$$

The Nash equilibrium is given where the two reaction curves intersect, $\bar{c}_1$ and $\bar{c}_2$. These points are found by solving (10.45) and (10.46) simultaneously

$$\bar{c}_1 = \frac{\rho_1 \alpha x}{\rho_1 \rho_2 \alpha^2 + \rho_1 \alpha + \rho_2 \alpha}$$

$$\bar{c}_2 = \frac{\rho_2 \alpha x}{\rho_1 \rho_2 \alpha^2 + \rho_1 \alpha + \rho_2 \alpha}$$

the remaining stock is

$$x - \bar{c}_1 - \bar{c}_2 = \frac{\rho_1 \rho_2 \alpha^2 x}{\rho_1 \rho_2 \alpha^2 + \rho_1 \alpha + \rho_2 \alpha}$$

When the planning horizon extends to three periods, we assume that the solution given above over the last two periods holds. This is a dynamic programming approach where the last decision is taken as a static optimisation and the result is then 'carried back' and taken into account when the decision is made in the first period. The Nash equilibrium can be represented as:

$$\log \bar{c}_1 + \rho_1 \log \tfrac{1}{2} + \alpha \rho_1 \log (x - \bar{c}_1 - \bar{c}_2) = (1 + \alpha \rho_1) \log x + A_1 \tag{10.47}$$

where

$$A_1 = \log \frac{(\rho_2 \alpha)(\rho_1 \rho_2 \alpha^2)^{\rho_1 \alpha}}{(\rho_1 \rho_2 \alpha^2 + \rho_1 \alpha + \rho_2 \alpha)^{1 + \rho_1 \alpha}} + \rho_1 \log \tfrac{1}{2}$$

The term A_1 is a constant which gathers together all the terms which are independent of x. The objective function for the three-period problem is

$$\log c_1 + \alpha \rho_1 (1 + \alpha \rho_1) \log (x - c_1 - c_2) + A_1 \tag{10.48}$$

where the stock left after harvesting in the first period is substituted in for x on the right-hand side of (10.47). The country is free to choose c_1 so long as that choice is feasible and leads to an optimal solution across the whole planning horizon. Taking the derivative of (10.48) with respect to c_1 and setting equal to zero yields

$$(1 + \alpha \rho_1 + \alpha^2 \rho_1^2) c_1 + c_2 = x$$

and for country 2

$$c_1 + (1 + \alpha \rho_2 + \alpha^2 \rho_2^2) c_2 = x$$

Solving these equations simultaneously yields the Nash equilibrium for the three-period case. This can be extended to an infinite horizon case to give:

$$\bar{c}_1 = \frac{\rho_2 \alpha (1 - \rho_1 \alpha) x}{1 - (1 - \rho_1 \alpha)(1 - \rho_2 \alpha)} \tag{10.49}$$

$$\bar{c}_2 = \frac{\rho_1 \alpha (1 - \rho_2 \alpha) x}{1 - (1 - \rho_1 \alpha)(1 - \rho_2 \alpha)} \tag{10.50}$$

and

$$x - \bar{c}_1 - \bar{c}_2 = \frac{\rho_1 \rho_2 \alpha^2 x}{\rho_1 \alpha + \rho_2 \alpha - \rho_1 \rho_2 \alpha^2} \tag{10.51}$$

(In the original paper by Levhari and Mirman (1980) the derivations of the infinite horizon equilibria are more complex than is indicated here and involve the formula of infinite convergent geometric progressions.) Equations (10.49) and (10.50) represent consumption policies for Countries 1 and 2, respectively, where an infinite horizon is considered. Equation (10.51) represents both countries' investment in fish. It is important to note that these policies are applicable in each period and, because the planning horizon is infinite, do not depend upon the actual period considered.

The next step in the analysis is to determine the steady-state solution so that the outcome is independent of the period selected and the arbitrary starting values: this should now be a familiar approach to complex comparative dynamic problems.

The dynamic population equation is

$$x_{t+1} = [x_t - c_1(x_t) - c_2(x_t)]^\alpha \tag{10.52}$$

starting with the initial stock, x_0, (10.52) becomes from (10.51)

$$x_1 = [x_t - c_1(x_t) - c_2(x_t)]^\alpha = \left(\frac{\rho_1 \rho_2 \alpha^2}{\rho_1 \alpha + \rho_2 \alpha - \rho_1 \rho_2 \alpha^2} \right)^\alpha x_0^\alpha \tag{10.53}$$

then by repeated substitution for x_t into (10.52)

$$\lim_{t \to \infty} x_t = \left(\frac{\rho_1 \rho_2 \alpha^2}{\rho_1 \alpha + \rho_2 \alpha - \rho_1 \rho_2 \alpha^2} \right)^{\alpha/(1-\alpha)} = \bar{x} \tag{10.54}$$

the steady state for the fish population.

For example, if both countries have the same rate of time preference, $\rho_1 = \rho_2 = \rho$ then (10.54) is

$$\bar{x} = \left(\frac{\rho \alpha}{2 - \rho \alpha} \right)^{\alpha/(1-\alpha)} \tag{10.55}$$

This result can be compared with the steady-state stock if the two countries cooperate. In terms of the Nash bargaining solution (10.49) and (10.50) represent one possible disagreement point: that is, the worst outcome given the behavioural assumptions for the two countries.

☐ 10.9.5 Cooperation

The bargaining solution in this case represents a maximisation of the total utility between the two countries, and as this amounts to no more than a rescaling of the utility function, the problem is equivalent to a single country fisheries problem. Using the format introduced in section 10.7.1, we have in general

$$\text{maximise}_{c_t} \quad \sum_{t=0}^{\infty} u(c_t)\rho^t$$

subject to $\quad x_t - x_{t-1} = G(x_t - c_t) - x_{t-1} \qquad x_0 = k$

The Hamiltonian corresponding to this problem is

$$H_t = \rho^t u(c_t) + \lambda_t(G(x_t - c_t) - x_t)$$

By the discrete maximum principle we have

$$\frac{\partial H}{\partial c_t} = \rho^t u'(c_t) + \lambda_t G_c = 0 \tag{10.56}$$

and the costate condition:

$$\lambda_t - \lambda_{t-1} = -\frac{\partial H}{\partial x} = -\lambda_t(G_x - 1) \tag{10.57}$$

Solve (10.56) for λ_t and substitute into (10.57)

$$\lambda_t - \lambda_{t-1} = \frac{\rho^t u'(c_t)}{G_c}(G_x - 1)$$

Difference (10.56) to give an expression for $\lambda_t - \lambda_{t-1}$ and equate with (10.57)

$$\frac{\rho^t u'(c_t)}{G_c} - \frac{\rho^{t-1} u'(c_{t-1})}{G_{c_{t-1}}} = \frac{\rho^t u'(c_t)}{G_c}(G_x - 1) \tag{10.58}$$

At the steady-state population level, $c = c_t = c_{t-1}$ and $x = x_t = x_{t-1}$. Thus (10.58) simplifies by dividing by $u'(c_t)$ and ρ^t and multiplying by G_c to give:

$$G_x = \frac{1}{\rho} = 1 + r$$

which is the discrete-time analogue of the bionomic equilibrium. However, note that G_x refers to gross productivity of a unit of stock and not the net productivity represented in section 7.5.1. At this point it is convenient to reintroduce the specific growth function

$$\frac{\partial G}{\partial x_t} = \alpha(x_t - c)^{\alpha - 1}$$

Thus (10.55) is

$$\frac{\alpha(x_t - c)^{\alpha}}{x_t - c} = \frac{1}{\rho} \tag{10.59}$$

Also in equilibrium, by definition

$$x_t - x_{t-1} = G(x_t - c_t) - x_{t-1} = 0$$

thus

$$x_t = G(x_t - c)$$

substituting into (10.59) and rearranging

$$x_t - c = \alpha \rho x_t$$

that is the optimal $x_t - c$ term is $\alpha \rho x$. In a steady-state

$$x_t = (\alpha \rho x_t)^\alpha$$

and, on rearranging,

$$\hat{x} = \alpha \rho^{(\alpha/1-\alpha)}$$

It follows immediately that under cooperation the steady-state stock, $\hat{x}$ is larger the steady-state stock resulting from Nash equilibrium $\bar{x}$

$$\hat{x} = \alpha \rho^{(\alpha/1-\alpha)} > \bar{x} = \left(\frac{\rho \alpha}{2 - \rho \alpha}\right)^{\alpha/(1-\alpha)}$$

It also follows that the consumption is greater under cooperation. If we take the total consumption under Nash equilibrium, c_N, we have from equation (10.51):

$$c_N = 2\left(\frac{(1 - \alpha \rho)}{(2 - \alpha \rho)}\right)\bar{x} < (1 - \alpha \rho)\hat{x} = c_c$$

In short, where a fish war is fought, countries consume too many fish at low stock levels. On the other hand, if there is cooperation and a binding agreement, both the stock and the consumption level are increased. The solution is represented in Figure 10.19.

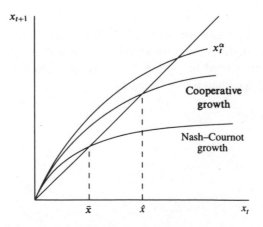

Figure 10.19   *Steady-state equilibria in a fish war*

■ *10.10* Fishing under uncertainty

☐ *10.10.1 Introduction*

Fishing firms and fishery managers operate in a highly uncertain environment. The fishing firm is uncertain about prices, costs and the harvest that their fishing efforts will yield. The fishery manager can only estimate what the fish stock is, how it will grow, and how it will respond to fishing. The sources of uncertainty in fishing relate to all aspects of the fish population: its size, concentration, response to environmental fluctuations and response to fishing effort. The policy relevance of this uncertainty is that the policy instruments, such as fishing quotas, should adapt in response to random fluctuations. This is sometimes not possible because the stock is unobservable (see Clark, 1985, for a review).

The literature on fishing under uncertainty is disparate. This sections reviews two aspects of it. Section 10.10.2 uses Itô's lemma to consider the problem of the fishery manager where the stock growth is uncertain. Section 10.10.3 considers a model for the sole-ownership firm using a simple stock recruitment model. Section 10.10.2 is concerned with theoretical issues relating to the impact of uncertainty on the harvest rate relative to the case of certainty; it is mathematically more difficult than other sections in the chapter and readers may wish to omit this section and consider the simpler discrete-time account given in section 10.10.3. Section 10.10.3 focuses on fishery management at the firm level and employs a more realistic model.

☐ *10.10.2 Fishing under uncertainty: an application of Itô's lemma*

The economic models of fishery exploitation discussed so far have assumed that all aspects of the resource exploitation problem are known with certainty. However, this is not the case. Amongst other sources of uncertainty, the owner of the fishery resource is uncertain about stock levels and how they will grow. The presence of this 'ecological' uncertainty (Pindyck, 1984) raises two main issues. First, how does uncertainty affect the value of the *in situ* stock, and second, how does it affect the rate of harvest? The model adopted by Pindyck is similar to that discussed in section 10.5.4, where the price of the resource is assumed to be endogenous.

The approach adopted here is that developed in section 7.6; that is, to employ Itô's stochastic calculus. Unfortunately, this framework is not capable of providing a complete representation of all forms of uncertainty that are important in the decisions taken by fishery firms. In particular it cannot be assumed that there is certainty about the size of the current fish stock.

The stochastic fishing problem for the i-th identical firm is where the expected profit at t is maximised

$$V^i(x) = \text{maximise}_q \, E_0 \int_0^\infty [p - c(x)]q^i \, e^{-rt} \, dt$$

subject to the stochastic growth equation,

$$dx = [g(x) - q^i] \, dt + \sigma(x) \, dz \tag{10.60}$$

This implies that the current stock is known, but the rate of growth is random. The fundamental equation of optimality is

$$rV^i \, dt = \text{maximum}_{q^i} \, \{[p - c(x)]q^i \, dt + E_t dV^i\} \tag{10.61}$$

This states the instantaneous return on the resource stock, $rV^i \, dt$, equals the optimal profit, $[p - c(x)]q^i \, dt$, plus the expected change in valuation. The stochastic variable, the future values of the stock, is confined to $E_t dV^i$. By Itô's lemma:

$$dV^i = V^i_x dx + \tfrac{1}{2} V^i_x (dx)^2$$

Noting that $q = nq^i$ and $E_t(dz) = 0$ gives

$$E \, dV^i = [g(x) - nq^i]V^i_x dt + \tfrac{1}{2} V^i_{xx}(dx)^2$$

and substituting (10.60) for dx gives

$$E \, dV^i = [g(x) - nq^i]V^i_x \, dt + \tfrac{1}{2}\sigma^2(x)V^i_{xx} \, dt$$

From this result the fundamental equation of optimality can be rewritten as

$$rV^i = \text{maximum}_{q^i} \, \{[p - c(x)]q^i + [g(x) - nq^i]V^i_x + \tfrac{1}{2}\sigma^2(x)V^i_{xx}\} \tag{10.62}$$

Note that this equation is linear in q^i, so maximisation implies

$$q^i = \begin{cases} q^i_{\max} & \text{if } p - c(x) > nV^i_x = \tilde{V}_x \\ 0 & \text{if } p - c(x) < nV^i_x = \tilde{V}_x \end{cases}$$

$\tilde{V} = nV^i$ is the value of the resource to all producers. The competitive equilibrium is identical to the socially optimal outcome. By assuming market clearing, the total catch is such that

$$\tilde{V}_x = p(q) - c(x)$$

or equivalently

$$q^*(x) = p^{-1}[V_x + c(x)] \tag{10.63}$$

which can be solved for the optimal output $q^*(x)$. The socially optimal solution is found by solving:

$$rV = \int_0^{q^*(x)} p(q)\,dq - c(x)q^*(x) + [g(x) - q^*(x)]V_x + \tfrac{1}{2}\sigma^2(x)V_{xx} \tag{10.64}$$

where the profit term is replaced by the sum of producer and consumer surplus as the area under the demand curve less total harvest costs. If (10.64) is differentiated with respect to x

$$rV_x = [p - c(x) - V_x]q_x^* - c'(x)q^* + g'(x)V_x$$

$$+ \sigma'(x)\sigma(x)V_{xx} + [g(x) - q^*]V_{xx} + \tfrac{1}{2}\sigma^2(x)V_{xxx} \tag{10.65}$$

the equilibrium condition ensures that the term in brackets on the right-hand side equals zero. Equation (10.65) can be simplified to

$$rV_x = - c'(x)q^* + g'(x)V_x + \sigma'(x)\alpha(x)V_{xx} + (1/dt)E_t d(V_x) \tag{10.66}$$

by replacing the last three terms by $(1/dt)E_t d(V_x)$. Equation (10.63) implies that

$$(1/dt)E_t d(V_x) = (1/dt)E_t d(p - c(x))$$

Now combining equations (10.63), (10.66) and (10.67) yields:

$$\frac{(1/dt)E_t d(p - c)}{p - c} + g'(x) - \frac{c'(x)q^*}{(p - c)} = r - \sigma'(x)\sigma(x)\frac{V_{xx}}{V_x} \tag{10.67}$$

This term requires careful interpretation. First note that it reduces to deterministic equilibrium, see section 10.5.3:

$$g'(x) - \frac{c'(x)q^*}{(p - c)} = r$$

if $(1/dt)E_t d(p - c) = 0$ and $\sigma(x) = 0$. The profit function is strictly concave, hence the term $(V_{xx}/V_x) < 0$. In turn, $\sigma'(x) > 0$; that is, the stock variance increases with the stock, overall $\sigma'(x)\sigma(x)(V_{xx}/V_x) < 0$, thus the right-hand side of (10.64) is increased by the presence of stock variance. This variance effect increases the expected rate of capital gain needed to hold the marginal unit of stock rather than harvest it. This has the effect of reducing the stock holding and implies that with uncertainty the equilibrium stock is lower than it would be under certainty.

However, there are other effects on the rent and extraction rate. First, because the growth function is concave, stochastic fluctuations reduce the expected growth, which increases stock scarcity, thereby increasing the stock rent and reducing the rate of extraction through equation (10.63). Second, because the cost function is convex, stochastic fluctuations in x increase expected extraction costs over time and reductions in costs due to positive deviations in the growth rate are outweighed by increases in costs due to negative deviations. This increases the incentive to extract, thereby reducing the expected amount of increased cost.

Overall the effect on the rate of extraction of the presence of stock growth uncertainty is indeterminate. To summarise: first, fluctuations in the value of stock, which are a function of the stock, provide an incentive to harvest more rapidly; second, cost fluctuations provide an incentive to harvest more rapidly; third, fluctuations in stock growth reduce the expected stock and increase stock scarcity and thus the rent, which leads to a reduction in the rate of harvest.

Pindyck applies the general model described above to solve for a sole-ownership fishery with a logistic growth function, $g(x) = \gamma x(1 - x/K)$, a constant elasticity demand function $q(p) = bp^{-\eta}$ and cost function $c(x) = cx^{-\omega}$ with the elasticity of demand, $\eta = 0.5$ and the elasticity of marginal cost, $\omega = 2$. (The choice of these specific functional forms for growth, demand and costs is motivated, primarily, by the desire to ensure mathematical tractability.) The stochastic component is introduced by $\sigma(x) = \sigma x$. The analysis proceeds in a similar way to section 7.6. Equation (10.64) is restated to include the function forms given. The solution for $V(x)$, the social value of the resource is found by guesswork, that is by finding an equation for $V(x)$ which satisfies (10.65). See section 7.6.2 for a simple example. It is then usual, for renewable resource problems, to determine the steady state. However, because the resource is stochastic the steady state cannot be described as a single value; instead the stock may converge to a stationary probability distribution. From this it is possible to derive the expected stock and expected harvest rate. This allows a comparison of the point steady state where the resource is deterministic with the expected stock and harvest rate under uncertainty.

Equation (10.64) becomes

$$rV(x) = -2b(V_x + c/x^2)^{1/2} + [\gamma x - (\gamma/K)x^2]V_x + \tfrac{1}{2}\sigma^2 x^2 V_{xx} \tag{10.68}$$

The solution to this equation has been found to be:

$$V(x) = -\phi/x - \phi\gamma/r$$

on substituting this into (10.68) and solving

$$\phi = \frac{2b^2 + 2b[b^2 + c(\gamma + r - \sigma^2)^2]^{1/2}}{(\gamma + r - \sigma^2)^2}$$

The shadow price of the stock is

$$V_x = \phi/x^2$$

and, substituting this into (10.63), the harvest is

$$q^*(x) = b(\phi + c)^{-1/2}x$$

We now turn to deriving the steady-state distribution. This is derived from a result based upon the *Kolmogrov forward equation*, which describes the evolution over time of the probability density function associated with a stochastic process (see Dixit and Pindyck, 1994, pp. 88–92, for a derivation). The distribution in the steady state, if it is not degenerate, equals:

$$f(x) = \frac{m}{\sigma^2(x)} \exp\left[2 \int^x \frac{(g(v) - q^*(v))}{\sigma^2(v)} \, dv\right] \qquad (10.69)$$

where $g(v)$ is the growth function, $q^*(v)$ the harvest function (10.63) and m is a constant chosen so $f(x)$ integrates to unity. When the specific functions are substituted into (10.69) and the integral evaluated this gives the steady-state distribution

$$f(x) = \left[\frac{(2\gamma/\sigma^2 K)^{2\theta/\sigma^2 - 1}}{\Gamma(2\theta/\sigma^2 - 1)}\right] x^{2\theta/\sigma^2 - 2} e^{-2\gamma x/\sigma^2 K} \qquad (10.70)$$

where

$$\theta = \gamma - b(\phi + c)^{-1/2}$$

The first term on the right-hand side of (10.70) is $m/\sigma^2(x)$ from (10.69), the gamma function, $\Gamma(\cdot)$ in the denominator ensures the distribution integrates to unity; the second term on the right-hand side is derived as the integral from (10.69). From this we observe that x follows a gamma distribution (see Arnold, 1990, p. 163).

From (10.70) we derive the expected stock

$$\bar{x} = K[1 - \sigma^2/2\gamma - b/\gamma(\phi + c)^{1/2}] \qquad (10.71)$$

and the harvest

$$\bar{q} = K[(1 - \sigma^2/2\gamma)b/(\phi + c)^{1/2} - b^2/r(\phi + c)]$$

The expected steady-state stock and the harvest are both falling with σ^2, $\partial \bar{x}/\partial \sigma^2 < 0$ and $\partial \bar{q}/\partial \sigma^2 < 0$. Pindyck explains this intuitively:

> Because the growth function $g(x)$ is concave, an increase in σ^2 increases the physical scarcity of the resource by reducing its expected growth rate, and this increases its rent. In this specific example, this increase in rent outweighs the decrease in rent associated with the convexity of $c(x)$ and that $\sigma'(x) = \sigma > 0$. (Pindyck, 1984, p. 297)

In this example for any stock the socially optimal harvest rate is reduced.

For a further illustration, consider the unexploited stock, from (10.70) if $c \to \infty$

$$\bar{x} = K(1 - \sigma^2/2\gamma]$$

it follows immediately that σ^2 reduces the steady-state stock; in fact, if $\sigma^2 \geq 2\gamma$, the probability distribution becomes degenerate and the population becomes extinct, $x(t) \to 0$ with certainty.

The analysis presented forms the basis for establishing quite general models of renewable resource exploitation. In his paper, Pindyck (1984) proceeds to show a range of different affects of uncertainty on optimal resource extraction: he also shows that these results depend critically upon the function forms specified; in other words, there remains some ambiguity as to whether increasing uncertainty increases, decreases or leaves unchanged the harvest rate. We now turn to a simpler discrete-time model of fishing under uncertainty, which may come closer to a model which is applicable to real-world problems in fishery management.

10.10.3 *Fishing under uncertainty: a discrete-time model*

Pindyck's continuous-time model of a stochastic fishery is difficult to solve for numerical problems. A number of authors have developed alternative discrete-time fishery models with a stochastic stock recruitment. The most widely applied is that of Reed (1979); this model is further analysed by Clark and Kirkwood (1986). The stochastic stock-recruitment equation is:

$$x_{t+1} = z_t G(s_t)$$

$$s_t = x_t - q_t$$

where x_t is the recruitment, s_t is the escapement and z_t is a random factor which is assumed to be independent and randomly distributed with the density function $f(z)$ and $E[\bar{z}] = 1$. The stochastic recruitment function is illustrated in Figure 10.20, where $z_{2t} > 1 > z_{1t} > 0$, and $G(s_t)$ represents the average recruitment. There are two sources of uncertainty over x_{t+1} in the model: first through the random multiplier, z_t, and second through the previous level of recruitment x_t. To simplify this, we assume that the recruitment x_t is known with certainty at the end of the period.

Over a finite planning horizon the problem for the sole owner of the fishery is to:

$$\text{maximise}_{q_t} \quad E\left[\sum_{t=0}^{\infty} \rho^t \bar{\pi} q_t\right]$$

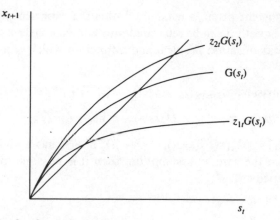

Figure 10.20 *Stochastic stock recruitment*

where $\bar{\pi}$ is the average profit rate during a period. This term is necessary as the profit rate declines as fishing reduces the level of escapement. The total profit is given as the integral:

$$\Pi(x_t, s_t) = \pi(x_t) - \pi(s_t) = \int_{s_t}^{x_t} \pi'(w)\, dw$$

where w is a variable of integration and $\pi'(w) = p - c(s_t)$. As $c'(s) > 0$, there exists some level of escapement at which it is no longer economic to fish, s_∞. At this point the marginal profit is zero $p - c(s_\infty) = 0$; this is the open-access level of escapement. An appropriate cost function would, for instance, be $c(s_t) = c/s_t$.

The fishery problem defined above can be solved by dynamic programming. The problem is solved for the last period, which represents a static optimisation problem.

$$J_0(x_T) = \text{maximise}_{0 \leq s_T \leq x_T} \Pi(x_T, s_T) = \text{maximise}_{0 \leq s_T \leq x_T} [\pi(x_T) - \pi(s_T)]$$

As the remaining stock is of no value it is optimal to harvest if the escapement is greater than the open-access level of escapement. The optimal escapement is:

$$s_T^* = \begin{cases} x_T & \text{if } x_T \leq s_\infty \\ s_\infty & \text{if } x_T > s_\infty \end{cases}$$

Thus, if it is optimal to do so, the owner harvests down to the level of zero net revenue, s_∞.

Now moving back one period, $t = T - 1$ and assuming that the stock is greater than the open-access escapement, $x_{T-1} > s_\infty$

$$J_1(x_{T-1}) = \text{maximum}_{0 \leq s_{T-1} \leq x_{T-1}} \{\Pi(x_{T-1}, s_{T-1}) + \rho E_z[J_0(zG(s_{T-1}))]\}$$

that is, the current profit is maximised plus the expected profit in the last period. This equation can be separated into known constants which play no part in the maximisation problem and a function which is to be maximised as follows:

$$J_1(x_{T-1}) = \text{maximum}_{0 \le s_{T-1} \le x_{T-1}} \{\pi(x_{T-1}) - \pi(s_{T-1}) + \rho E_z[\pi(zG(s_{T-1})) - \rho\pi(s_\infty)]\}$$

$$\text{maximum}_{0 \le s_{T-1} \le x_{T-1}} \{V(s_{T-1}) + \pi(x_{T-1}) - \rho\pi(s_\infty)\}$$

where $V(s_{T-1}) = \rho E_z[\pi(zG(s_{T-1}))] - \pi(s_{T-1})$. If $V(\cdot)$ has a unique maximum, which is often the case by assumption, then it is possible to determine the optimal escapement, s^*:

$$s^*(x) = \begin{cases} s^* & \text{if } x > s^* \\ x & \text{if } x \le s^* \end{cases} \tag{10.72}$$

It can be shown that identical problems exist for all time periods; thus (10.72) provides a general rule for all periods $t \le T - 1$. The solution is termed a 'most rapid approach path' where harvesting is switched on and off as the population level fluctuates above and below the optimal or target escapement.

The optimal escapement level can be solved from $V(s)$ by numerical integration to determine the expectation $\rho E_z[\pi(zG(s_{T-1}))]$. If $V(\cdot)$ is differentiable then at the maximum

$$V'(s) = \rho E_z[\pi'(zG(s))zG'(s)] - \pi'(s) = \rho E_z[z\pi'(zG(s))z]G'(s) - \pi'(s) = 0$$

On rearranging, this gives the stochastic equivalent of the familiar condition for an equilibrium optimal harvest,

$$G'(s)\frac{E_z[z\pi'(zG(s))]}{\pi'(s)} = \frac{1}{\rho}$$

This should be compared with the condition given in section 10.7.1, equation (10.33). The stochastic and deterministic models have identical harvest strategies; that is, the presence of uncertainty has no effect on the expected equilibrium harvest, although the actual harvest will be affected by the stochastic nature of the resource.

▪ 10.11 Summary

The economics of renewable resource exploitation concerns two attributes which set it apart from mainstream capital theory. The first is the nature of the production function where fishing effort in terms of the labour and capital devoted to fishing interact with a natural population to give a harvest rate. The second concerns the open-access status of many marine fisheries which can lead to market failure: that is, the absence of a market for rented stock at a socially optimal shadow price leads to the over exploitation of the fishery. The problems of ill-defined property rights over fisheries also give rise to conflicts between countries as they contest the right to catch fish. This leads to the analysis of 'fish wars' and a demonstration of the potential for co-operation. However, the evidence suggests that fisheries are often exploited sub-optimally because of a lack of information on complex multi-species fish stocks and their interaction with fishing effort.

■ References

Arnason, R. (1990) 'Minimum information management in fisheries', *Canadian Journal of Economics*, 23, 630–53.

Arnold, S.F (1990). *Mathematical Statistics*, New York: Prentice-Hall.

Bell, F.W. (1972) 'Technological externalities and common-property resources: An empirical study of the US northern lobster fishery', *Journal of Politics and Economics*, 80, 148–58.

Berck, P. (1981) 'Optimal Management of Renewable Resources with Growing Demand and Stock Externalities', *Journal of Environmental Economics and Management*, 8, 105–17.

Beverton, R.J.H. and S.J. Holt (1957) 'On the Dynamics of Exploited Fish Populations', *Fisheries Investigations Series*, 2(19), London: Ministry of Agriculture Fisheries and Food.

Binmore, K. (1992) *Fun and Games*, Lexington: Heath and Company.

Clark, C.W. (1985) *Bioeconomic Modelling and Fisheries Management*, New York: Wiley Interscience.

Clark, C.W. (1990) Mathematical Bioeconomics, 2nd edn, Chichester: Wiley Interscience.

Clark, C.W. and G.P. Kirkwood (1986) 'Optimal Harvesting of an Uncertain Resource Stock and the Value of Stock Surveys', *Journal of Environmental Economics and Management*, 13, 235–44.

Clark, C.W., F.H. Clarke and G.R. Munro, (1979) 'The optimal exploitation of renewable resource stocks: problems of irreversible investment', *Econometrica*, 47, 25–47.

Conrad, J.M. and T. Bjørndal (1991) 'A Bioeconomic Model of the Harp Seal in the Northwest Atlantic', *Land Economics*, 67, 158–71.

Dixit, A.K. and R.S. Pindyck (1994) *Investment under Uncertainty*, Princeton: Princeton University Press.

Fraser. G.A. (1978) 'License limitation in the British Columbia salmon fishery', in B.R. Rettig and J.J.C. Ginter (eds), *Limited Entry as a Fishery Management Tool*, Seattle: University of Washington Press.

Fudenberg, D. and J. Tirole (1991) *Game Theory*, Cambridge, Mass.: MIT Press.

Gordon, H.S. (1954) The economic theory of common property resources', *Journal of Political Economics*, 124–42

Hall, D.C. (1977) 'A note on natural production functions'. *Journal of Environmental Economics and Management*, 4, 258–64.

Klieve, H. and T.G. MacAulay (1993) 'A game theory analysis of management strategies for the southern bluefin tuna industry', *Australian Journal of Agricultural Economics*, 37, 17–32.

Levhari, D. and L.J. Mirman (1980) 'The great fish war: an example using a dynamic Cournot–Nash solution', *Bell Journal of Economics*, 11, 322–44.

May, R.M. (1974) 'Biological populations with nonoverlapping generations: stable points, stable cycles, and chaos', *Science*, 186, 645–7.

Nash, J.F. (1951) 'Noncooperative games', *Annals of Mathematics*, 54, 289–95.

Pigou, A.C. (1946) *The Economics of Welfare*, 4th edn, London: Macmillan.

Pindyck, R.S. (1984) 'Uncertainty in the Theory of Renewable Resource Markets', *Review of Economic Studies*, 51, 289–303.

Reed, W.J. (1979) 'Optimal escapement levels in stochastic and deterministic harvesting models', *Journal of Environmental Economics and Management*, 6, 350–63.

Ricker, W.E. (1954) 'Stock and recruitment', *Journal of Fisheries Research Board of Canada*, 11, 559–623.

Schaefer, M.B. (1954) 'Some aspects of the dynamics of populations important to the management of commercial marine fisheries', *Bulletin of the Inter-American Tropical Tuna Commission*, 1, 25–56.

Small, G. (1971) *The Blue Whale*, New York: Columbia University Press.

Smith, J.B. (1980) 'Replenishable resource management under uncertainty: A reexamination of the US northern fishery'. *Journal of Environmental Economics and Management*, 7, 209–19.

Townsend, R.E. (1986) 'A Critique of Models of the American Lobster Fishery', *Journal of Environmental Economics and Management*, 13, 277–91.

Wilson, J.A. (1982) 'The economical management of multispecies fisheries', *Land Economics*, 58, 417–34.

■ *Chapter 11* ■

The Economics of Forestry Exploitation

11.1 Introduction
11.2 The principles of commercial forestry economics
11.3 Multi-use forestry and the socially optimal forest rotation

11.4 Forestry land use and agriculture
11.5 Forest policies
11.6 The optimal forest rotation under uncertainty
11.7 Summary

■ *11.1* Introduction

Forests are considered as a separate natural resource in this book because they represent an unusual capital investment problem where a long time lag exists between the decision to invest in tree seedlings and the decision to harvest. At any point in time a forester may be simultaneously deciding to invest by replanting and to disinvest by clear-felling mature trees, which are the result of investment decisions taken some generations earlier.

Forests represent a complex economic resource. In addition to their timber value they are also valuable as an amenity resource, as a store of biodiversity, as a carbon store and in reducing the severity of floods. Where these non-timber values are significant, the socially optimal forest rotation between planting and harvesting may diverge from the private optimal rotation pursued by forest owners. Market intervention is required to induce forest owners to pursue socially optimal policies. Governments, including those in the UK and the USA, have nationalised a significant part of the national forest to ensure that the diverse objectives of forest management are, to some degree, achieved. Broadly this involves a trade-off between maximising profit from timber production and a range of non-timber values.

The tropical rainforests are an example of another form of forest management problem. They represent a valuable store of biodiversity, a store of carbon, reduce the frequency of local flooding and prevent soil erosion. Their value is widely recognised in the developed world, but the largest areas of rainforest are in some of the poorest countries of South America, Africa and Asia. Their destruction is irreversible and the local and global environmental damage due to their destruction may, in the long run, be catastrophic. Despite the obvious benefits of reducing deforestation, conservation policies are either non-existent because many tropical countries do not perceive a net benefit in preserving the rainforest or ineffective because peasant farmers and ranchers treat the forest as an open-access common.

This chapter considers these issues, first by considering the problems of managing forest as a timber crop. Section 3 analyses the impact of non-timber values on socially optimal forest rotations. Section 4 considers the relationship between forestry and agriculture as competing users of land and the economics of rainforest preservation both nationally and globally. Section 5 considers public policy towards forestry, especially in the form of taxation. Section 6 extends the model to incorporate the impact of uncertainty on the optimal forest rotation.

11.2 The principles of commercial forestry economics

The timber value of a tree is determined by the volume of saleable timber a tree can produce. The volume of timber in a uniform forest depends upon the age of the trees and is represented by the growth function $f(t)$. Saleable timber is only produced after the trees have reached a minimum age, t^*. The growth of trees may continue for many years although ultimately the volume of timber reaches a plateau and then declines as the trees decay and eventually die. A representative tree growth function is given in Figure 11.1 A forest rotation which starts with planting and finishes with clear-felling

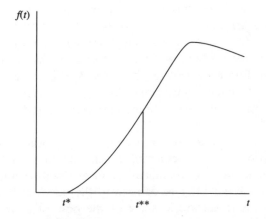

Figure 11.1   *Tree growth function*

varies from species to species, but may take 100 years for oak trees and as few as 40 years for sitka spruce. Forests may also be thinned at an earlier stage in their growth; this activity produces saleable timber and increases the growth rate of the remaining trees. The economics of this decision are not considered here.

The presence of a delay between the decision to plant and the production of timber sets forestry management apart as a distinct problem in capital theory. The decision variable is the time allowed to lapse between planting and felling and replanting. The aim of the forest owner is assumed to be the maximisation of the present value of profit from felling. The profit depends on the volume of timber. The volume of timber increases with time, $f'(t) > 0$, then when $t > t^{**}$ the rate of growth is declining, $f''(t) < 0$. The revenue is $pf(t)$ where p is a constant real price of timber per unit of volume net of harvest costs; planting costs are a constant, c. The current value of profit for a single rotation is $pf(T) - c$, where T is the age of trees when they are clear-felled. If the costs of planting are incurred at the start of the rotation and the revenue from clear-felling at the end with a discount rate r, the present-value of profit is:

$$\pi = e^{-rT}pf(T) - c$$

Differentiating with respect to T by the product rule and maximising, yields:

$$\frac{pf'(T)}{pf(T)} = r \tag{11.1}$$

This states that felling should be delayed until the return on the forest stand, the right-hand side of (11.1), equals the discount rate. In other words felling is delayed until the return $pf'(T)$, from the capital tied up in the forest stand; $pf(T)$ equals the rate of return those funds could earn elsewhere, r.

Equation (11.1) is the solution to a single-period forest rotation problem. If replanting is possible, the optimal rotation should take account of the delay in receiving profits from subsequent harvests. Assuming that all the other parameters remain unchanged, define a set of rotations $t_1 < t_2 <, \ldots, t_\infty$ when the forest is clear-felled and replanted. Commencing by planting at $t = 0$ on bare land, the objective function is

$$J = -c + e^{-rt_1}[pf(t_1) - c] + e^{-rt_2}[pf(t_2) - c] + \cdots + e^{-rt_\infty}[pf(t_\infty) - c] \tag{11.2}$$

If we recognise that the producer faces the same problem in each rotation, $t_i = iT$ where $i = 1, 2, \ldots, \infty$ and by the sum of a convergent geometric progression, (11.2) simplifies to

$$J = \sum_{i=1}^{\infty} e^{-r_i T}[pf(T) - c] - c = \frac{pf(T) - c}{e^{rT} - 1} - c \tag{11.3}$$

Differentiating with respect to T and setting equal to zero

$$\frac{pf'(T)}{pf(T) - c} = \frac{r}{1 - e^{-rT}} \tag{11.4}$$

This is Faustmann's formula, which can be interpreted more readily in the form:

$$pf'(T) = rpf(T) + r \frac{pf(T) - c}{e^{rT} - 1} \tag{11.5}$$

thus, in equilibrium, the rate of return on the forest stand, $pf'(T)$, should equal the interest that the net value of the forest generates if it were invested, plus the rate of return of investing the present value of all future rotations at the rate of interest, r. The term, $(pf(T) - c)/(e^{rT} - 1)$, is the site value, thus the second term in (11.5) is the opportunity cost of investment tied up in the trees and the site. Faustmann's formula is a key result in forestry economics and has a similar status to Hotelling's rule as a basis of normative and positive economic models of forest management.

Equation (11.4) can be subjected to comparative static analysis (see Bowes and Krutilla, 1985, p. 536). If the discount rate is increased, the term $r/(1 - e^{-rT})$ is strictly increasing. As $pf'(T)/(pf(T) - c)$ is strictly decreasing in T, by assumption, this implies that the length of the optimal rotation is reduced. The effects of changes in timber prices and harvesting and replanting cost can be considered jointly as the cost–price ratio. This is seen by rewriting the left-hand side of (11.4) as $f'(T)/(f(T) - c/p)$. *Ceteris paribus* the length of the rotation increases as replanting cost increases. This is because a cost increase reduces the value of the forest and thus increases the rate of return on the existing stand.

The comparative static analysis is presented in Figure 11.2. Here the right-hand side of (11.4) is plotted for $r = 0.2$ and $r = 0.05$. Forest growth is based on the logistic equation estimated by Swallow *et al.* (1990) for a pine forest,

$$f(T) = \frac{37.93}{(1 + e^{(6.1824 - 0.0801T)})} \tag{11.6}$$

where the maximum yield of the forest is 37.93 thousand board feet per hectare. The price net of harvesting cost is set equal to one, $p = 1$. Two forest return curves are drawn. When $c/p = 1$ the optimal rotation is 52 years at (i) when $r = 0.2$ and 75 years at (ii) when $r = 0.05$; If costs are increased so that $c/p = 5$ the length of the rotation is increased: at (iii), the rotation is 74 years and at (iv) 87 years. A change in price, induced by a shift in demand or supply parameters, has the opposite effect to a change in costs: that is, a price increase reduces the length of the optimal rotation, a price decrease extends it.

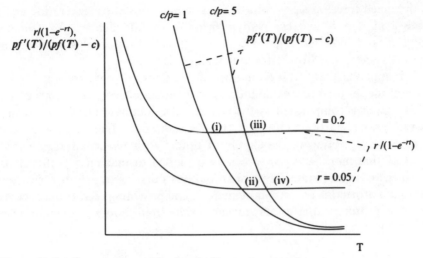

Figure 11.2 *Comparative statics for the Faustmann rotation*

The second-order conditions for a maximum are that the second derivative of (11.4) is negative. This implies that the marginal benefit of delaying felling cuts the marginal opportunity cost line from above.

11.2.1 Extensions of the model and market structure

Attempts to extend the Faustmann formula to more complex forest exploitation problems have been bedevilled by the mathematical complexities of dynamic optimisation problems with a delay between the decision to plant and felling. The state variable which is the age of the forest must reflect the fact that the age of different parts of a forest may vary. Crabbe and Long (1989) and Heaps (1984) establish a tractable model by imposing restrictions on the way that trees are harvested, notably that the oldest trees are always harvested first. However, if the felling and replanting cost are non-linear there is no reason why the age distribution of the forest should not change through time. At least, the forest may take a long time to reach a steady state if the initial distribution is different from the steady state distribution.

A small number of articles have attempted to assess the impact of market structure upon the rate of felling. Basic economics suggests that a monopoly firm would fell trees at a younger age than would a competitive firm as a means of reducing the supply and increasing the price of timber. This intuition is not supported by Crabbe and Long (1989) who conclude that, with a fixed forest area, a uniform forest and a constant regeneration cost, both a monopoly and competitive firms follow an identical Faustmann rotation and have the same output and prices. This conclusion depends upon a result proved by Mitra and Wan (1985).

It is apparent that forest economists are some way from agreeing upon a general model of forest exploitation for a monopolistic market structure. The analysis is complicated by the fact that the dominant owner of forestry in European countries and North America is the state. Even if a state holds a monopoly position in the supply of timber to a particular region it is unlikely that monopoly power will be exploited to maximise profits. It is often the case that state forest organisations pursue a range of objectives including protecting conservation interests and providing recreational access which may run counter to maximising profits from timber production as a monopolist.

11.3 Multi-use forestry and the socially optimal forest rotation

Standing natural forests may have non-timber values in addition to their value as a timber resource. Forests provide recreational areas, valued wildlife habitats, flood control, a store of carbon, agricultural grazing and a reservoir of biodiversity. Typically, but not exclusively, the non-timber value of a forest is at its greatest when the forest is well-established and at its lowest just after it has been clear-felled. The implication of this is that a socially optimal forest rotation will be longer than the private optimal rotation which only accounts for the timber value.

This problem is treated as a modified Faustmann formula following the analysis of Hartman (1976). The value of a forest over a single rotation starting with bare land is

$$w_1 = \int_0^T g(t)\,e^{-rt}\,dt + pf(T)\,e^{-rT} - c$$

where $g(t)$ is the flow of non-timber values from the forest as a function of its age, $pf(T)$ is the timber value at the end of the rotation net of harvesting costs and c is the cost of planting. On the basis that the forest is initially bare and is felled at regular intervals, the value of the forest over an infinite time horizon is:

$$w_\infty = w_1 + e^{-rT}w_2 + e^{-r2T}w_3 + e^{-r3T}w_4 + \cdots \tag{11.7}$$

The problem facing the forest manager is to choose the rotation length, T, to maximise (11.7). Equation (11.7) can be simplified as

$$J = \text{maximise}_T \, \frac{1}{1 - e^{-rT}} \left[\int_0^T g(t) \, e^{-rt} \, dt + pf(T) e^{-rT} - c \right] \tag{11.8}$$

by the sum of convergent geometric progressions.

Differentiating and setting equal to zero yields after some rearranging:

$$pf'(T) - rpf(T) + g(T) - rJ = 0 \tag{11.9}$$

where J can be interpreted as the value of the site when the socially optimal rotation is followed. This can be compared with the original Faustmann formula by putting (11.4) into the same format:

$$pf'(T) - rpf(T) - rJ = 0$$

Thus if $g(T) = 0$, the forest follows a Faustmann rotation. The benefits of delaying harvesting for a further infinitesimal time increment include the increase in the volume of timber and the flow of amenity, $g(T)$. Costs include interest forgone on selling timber in the current cycle, $rpf(T)$ and the interest cost of delaying timber and non-timber benefits from all future cycles, rJ.

The function $g(T)$ will vary from forest to forest. There is no reason to suppose that it might be monotonically increasing with the age of the stand; in fact it may be declining or constant. At one extreme, if the amenity value increases with age, it may be optimal never to harvest; at the other, if the amenity value is constant, it would be optimal to pursue a Faustmann rotation.

☐ 11.3.1 Multiple-use forest: an example

The National Forest in Western Montana provides cattle grazing in addition to timber production (Swallow *et al.*, 1990). When the forest is up to 12.5 years old the grazing value, measured in animal units per month, is increasing. But as the forest canopy closes the grazing value declines asymptotically to zero. The grazing benefit function, which is estimated by ordinary least squares, is given by

$$g(t) = \beta_0 t \, e^{-\beta_1 t} \tag{11.10}$$

where parameter values are $\beta_0 = 1.45$ and $\beta_1 = 0.08$. The peak grazing value is found by differentiating (11.10) with respect to t and setting equal to zero;

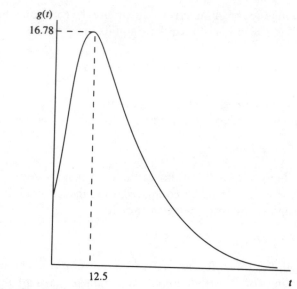

Figure 11.3   *Grazing benefit function*

from this $T_a = 1/\beta_1 = 12.5$ years. At this age the grazing benefit is \$16.78 per ha. Equation (11.10) is plotted in Figure 11.3.

The timber value of the forest is given by (11.8), the price per thousand board feet is \$120. The policy maker's problem is to maximise:

$$J = \text{maximise}_T \; \frac{1}{1 - e^{-rT}} \left[\int_0^T g(t) e^{-rt} \, dt + pf(T) e^{-rT} - c \right]$$

The first-order conditions for an optimal forest rotation are illustrated in Figure 11.4.

The first-order conditions, indicate a local optimum of \$355/ha at 26 years at T^* which is dominated by the grazing benefits of the forest land, the global maximum occurs at 73 years (T^{**}) and has a present value of \$366/ha. This compares with the Faustmann rotation of 76 years. The reduction in rotation length is due to the grazing benefits which arise at early stages of future rotations. The existence of non-convexities in the net present-value curve shows the importance of evaluating second-order conditions to check for a global optimum and may lead a myopic policy maker to choose the first point where the marginal opportunity cost (MOC) and marginal benefit of delay (MBD) curves cross. See Swallow *et al.* (1990) for a fuller discussion of the policy implications of non-convexities in the present-value function.

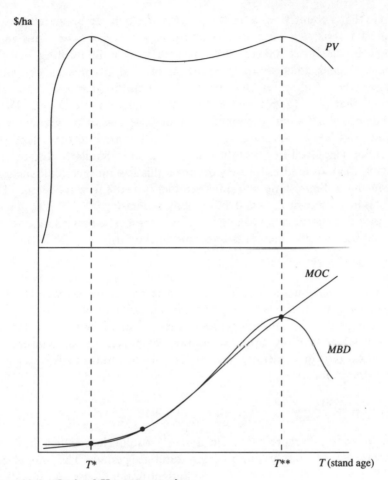

Figure 11.4   *Optimal Hartman rotation*

■ *11.4* Forestry land use and agriculture

□ *11.4.1 Managed forests*

The area of managed forest in a country depends upon the relative value of land in forestry compared with its alternative uses. In some regions land may only be suitable for forestry; in others it may also be used for agriculture. If the profitability of agriculture is increased then this may lead to a reduction in the area of forestry as farmers bid a higher price for land than do firms engaged in forestry. This sub-section presents a simple model of equilibrium between forestry and agricultural land use. The model assumes that a country has a fixed land area, $\bar{a}$ which can be shared between managed forests, $a = \gamma\bar{a}$ and agriculture $a_a = (1 - \gamma)\bar{a}$. The firms in the country are all price takers. Both sectors face a diminishing marginal product of land; thus, as the proportion of land devoted to agriculture increases the equilibrium rent paid by agriculture for the land $w(\gamma)$, deceases, that is, $w'(\gamma) > 0$ and $w''(\gamma) < 0$. Samuelson (1976) and Comolli (1981) employ a similar argument. This may be due to progressively less suitable land being used for agriculture or to the fixity of other factors of production employed in agriculture such as labour. Similarly, the carrying capacity, $K(\gamma)$, of land in forestry declines, this is a more specific means of introducing a diminishing marginal product into the forestry sector. Thus $f(T, \gamma)$ is increasing in $T, f_T > 0$, but strictly decreasing in $\gamma, f_\gamma < 0, f_{\gamma\gamma} < 0$. The price is a net price and includes harvesting costs, replanting costs are zero and the growth function is a logistic of the form:

$$f(T, \gamma) = K(\gamma)/(1 + e^{(b_0 + b_1 T)})$$

This allows the optimal rotation to be determined independently of the carrying capacity as the term $f_T/f(T, \gamma)$ is independent of K.

The competitive equilibrium between forestry and agriculture exists where the rate of return on the last hectare employed in agriculture, the agricultural rent in perpetuity, equals the rate of return on forestry given by Faustmann's formula

$$\frac{pf(T^*, \gamma^*)}{e^{rT^*} - 1} = \frac{w(1 - \gamma^*)}{r} \qquad 0 \leq \gamma \leq 1$$

where T^* and γ^* represent a steady-state equilibrium which implies a constant rate of supply during each discrete period. The model is a simplified account of the links between agricultural land use and forestry. It is, however, representative of the situation observed in the United Kingdom where forestry tends to be restricted to marginal agricultural areas, where agricultural incomes and thus rents are very low. The extension of forestry to less marginal areas has involved subsidising the costs of establishing forests. However, a component of these subsidies is often to compensate farmers for the loss of subsidies available for agricultural production. Thus they often contain a transfer payment element as well as a component which reflects the positive externalities associated with forests.

☐ *11.4.2 Natural forests*

The relationship between agriculture and forestry is a cause for concern in tropical regions where areas of tropical rainforest are replaced by agricultural land. In these situations, the forest is being mined as a non-renewable resource and there is no possibility of establishing a sustained Faustmann rotation in a complex multi-species tropical rainforest. The decision to harvest a forest rests primarily upon the timber value of the forest set against the value of an addition to the stock of agricultural land.

In their paper, Ehui *et al.* (1990) develop a theoretical model to represent the socially optimal rate of deforestation for a country's tropical rainforest. The aim of the country is to maximise utility as a function of the present value of the stream of profits derived from agriculture and forestry, subject to a fixed stock of forest and the stock of arable land. Formally the objective function is to

$$\text{maximise}_{q,y} \quad W = \int_0^\infty u[\pi(q, y, a)] e^{-rt} \, dt \tag{11.11}$$

subject to $\quad \pi(q, y, a, = B(a) + p_f a + (\bar{a} - a)p_a z(q, (\bar{a} - a), y) - p_y y$

$$\dot{a} = -q; \quad A = (a(0) - a)$$

$$a(0) = a_0$$

where q is the rate of deforestation in hectares, y is the quantity of purchased inputs used in crop production, a is the forest area, A is cumulative deforestation. Prices in the model include the price of forest products, p_f crop prices p_a and input prices p_y. The constraints are the profit from forestry and agriculture. Maximising W is equivalent to maximising social welfare, where in each period welfare is given by a quasi-concave utility function $u(\cdot)$. The profit function is split into the profit from crop land and the private and public benefits of the forest which are represented by a function $B(a)$. Agricultural revenues are given as a production function per hectare, multiplied by the crop price, p_a, and the area in agriculture $(\bar{a} - a)$ as the total area $\bar{a}$ less the forest area a. The production function $z(\cdot)$ gives crop yield as a function of the current rate of deforestation, the cumulative loss of forest area $(\bar{a} - a)$ and variable inputs, y.

The assumptions about the functions are as follows. The utility index is increasing in the aggregate benefits from forestry, $u_\pi > 0$, but marginal utility is diminishing $u_{\pi\pi} < 0$. The average agricultural yield function $z(\cdot)$ represents agricultural production technology and how it relates to conventional agricultural inputs and to the forest area. This function embodies the scientific evidence on the total effects of deforestation, and encompasses two effects. The rate of deforestation during the current period increases average yield through the plant nutrients released from forest ash, thus $z_q > 0$, but the marginal increase in average yield declines, $z_{qq} < 0$. Cumulative deforestation reduces the average yield as agriculture moves onto more marginal land, $z_A < 0$, and this decline occurs at an increasing rate, $z_{AA} < 0$. The assumption about the marginal product of purchased inputs is as expected, $z_y > 0$, but there is a diminishing marginal product, $z_{yy} < 0$. However, purchased inputs, in the form of fertiliser, substitute for plant nutrient in forest ash. This is represented by the cross partial derivative $z_{yq} < 0$. To simplify results $z_{aa} = 0$ and $z_{ay} = 0$. The forest benefit function represents the benefits from timber, biodiversity and carbon sequestration, $B'(a) > 0$ and $B''(a) \geq 0$. Thus the marginal benefit from the forest increase as the area shrinks.

The current-value Hamiltonian for this problem is

$$H = u[\pi(q, y, a)] - \mu q$$

differentiating with respect to q,

$$\mu = u_q = u_\pi(\bar{a} - a)p_a z_q \tag{11.12}$$

and y,

$$0 = u_y = u_\pi A(p_a z_y - p_y) \tag{11.13}$$

and a costate condition

$$\dot{\mu} - r\mu = -u_a = u_\pi[B'(a) + Ap_a z_a - p_a z + p_y y] \tag{11.14}$$

Differentiating (11.12) with respect to time, equating with (11.14), using (11.12) to eliminate μ and combining with (11.13) gives:

$$\dot{q} = -\frac{u_{yy}}{(u_{yy}u_{qq} - u_{qy}^2)}\left[-ru_q + \left\{u_a - q\left(u_a - \frac{u_{qy}}{u_{yy}}u_{ay}\right)\right\}\right] \tag{11.15}$$

The condition for concavity is that $(u_{yy}u_{qq} - u_{qy}^2) > 0$. Given that the first term on the right-hand side of (11.15) is unambiguously positive, by assumption, the sign on $\dot{q}$ is determined by the term in braces on the right-hand side of (11.15), specifically

$$\dot{q} \gtreqless 0 \quad \text{as} \quad r^{-1}\left[u_a - q\left(u_{qa} - \frac{u_{qy}}{u_{yy}}u_{ay}\right)\right] \gtreqless u_q$$

Intuitively, u_q is the marginal utility of deforestation, and a relatively high value for u_q indicates a large agricultural yield response from the deforestation during the current period. This implies that agriculture is still confined to relatively favourable land. The term in square brackets represents the 'conservation motive', since it gives the difference between the marginal utility of forest stock, u_a, and the interaction between the stock and the productivity of purchased inputs and the rate of deforestation. The interest rate in the denominator gives the value of this term over an infinite time horizon. Equation (11.15) allows a comparative dynamic analysis of the effect of the discount rate. It is apparent that $\dot{q}_r \leq 0$: that is the rate of deforestation starts out high and declines more rapidly through time as the discount rate increases.

The steady state occurs where the forest area is constant, and no incentive exists for further deforestation. In this case, $\dot{a} = \dot{q} = 0$ and $q = 0$. At the steady-state forest area, a^*, the following condition holds from (11.15):

$$\frac{u_a(q^*, a^*, y^*)}{r} = u_q(q^*, a^*, y^*)$$

that is, the present value of the stream of marginal utility derived from holding forestry is equal to the marginal utility of deforestation. The other condition is that optimal use of the variable agricultural input, y, ensures that:

$$z_y(q^*, a^*, y^*) = p_y/p_a$$

Two outcomes could arise: either the forest is preserved and an equilibrium is attained or the forest is mined to extinction. In the first case, $u_a(0, a^*, y^*)/r = u_q(0, a^*, y^*)$ and a is positive, thus the right-hand side is sufficient to ensure an equilibrium where some forest remains. In the second, $u_a(0, 0, y^*)/r \leq u_q(0, 0, y^*)$, that is the marginal returns from deforestation exceed or equal the conservation motive when the forest area is zero. The results of an econometric analysis based upon this model are presented in Box 11.1.

Box 11.1   *Deforestation in the Ivory Coast*

In Ehui *et al.* (1989) reported that the Ivory Coast is losing rain forest at the rate of 300 000 ha a year, and that of the original 16 million hectares of rainforest only 3.4 million hectares remain. The loss of forest is due mainly to encroachment by shifting cultivation which is driven by a rising population and a poor definition of property rights over forest land. Deforestation has led to soil erosion, a reduction in agricultural productivity and the siltation of waterways. Attempts by the government to define protected forest areas have been frustrated by the common property nature of much of the forest areas, since peasant farmers have virtually unrestricted access to forest areas for shifting cultivation.

In their paper the authors estimate an average agricultural yield function

$$z(t) = z((-)q, (+)y, (-)A)$$

where q is the rate of deforestation, y is level of agricultural inputs such as fertiliser and A is the cumulative deforestation. The signs in brackets indicate the effect which these variables have upon the agricultural yield; deforestation reduces agricultural yield by accelerating soil erosion and shifting agriculture to less suitable areas, agricultural inputs, such as fertiliser, can mitigate some of these effects and increase yields.

The steady-state level of forestry is where the forest is fixed and the agricultural yield is constant. The results of this analysis indicated that the area of forest was highly sensitive to the discount rate. At $r = 0.03$ (3 per cent) 5.4 million hectares of forest is optimal, at $r = 0.11$ (11 per cent) 2 million hectares is optimal. In a country subject to economic instability, high interest rates tend to be the norm; thus it is expected that the forest area will be further reduced.

The study takes no account of the value of the forest as a global reserve of biodiversity. The problem remains of how control over the forest use can be established and how the value placed on the forest can be used to establish incentives which lead to greater areas of preserved forest. However, it represents the problem of a poor country which must trade a wish to maintain its rainforest area for environmental reasons against population pressures which increase demand for agricultural land.

11.4.3 The global problem of rainforest destruction

The loss of rainforests has become recognised as an international environmental issue over the last 30 years and was a focus of negotiation at the Earth Summit in Rio in June 1992. The area of rainforest, which currently stands at a world total of 800 million hectares, is being depleted at the rate of 1.8 per cent per annum (Repetto, 1988). (This figure is an approximate estimate based upon satellite images.) At this rate of depletion most of the world's rainforest will be destroyed in 50 years' time unless policies are put into place to curb the rate of destruction. The motivation to preserve the rainforests can be divided into their global and local effects. Rainforests are home to over half the world's plants and animals, which have an existence value, but also have a value as a source of gene material which can be used to create new crops and drugs. Notably, approximately 25 per cent of the drugs sold in the USA are derived from tropical plants (Repetto, 1988). The rainforest also provides a store of carbon and thus reduces the amount of carbon dioxide (a greenhouse gas) in the environment. Locally, the rainforest protects watersheds from silting and reduces the rate of soil erosion.

The benefits of reducing the rate of rainforest destruction are clear. However, the issues involved in devising effective international policies are complex. Rainforests are largely located in poor countries who do not have the resources to benefit from the biodiversity of the rainforest. The effects of global warming are expected to have a greater impact upon developed countries which are located at higher latitudes. The tropical nations face problems of ill-defined property rights over the forest area which is treated by the peasant farmers and ranchers who account for 61 per cent of the total loss as open-access commons.

Among the developed nations there is no consensus on what constitutes an appropriate policy. This leads to free-riding as developed countries try to avoid the costs of an effective policy, or weak general agreements which are ineffective and cannot be monitored. Similarly, there are problems of reaching agreement among the tropical nations who face different environmental and political conditions.

To formalise some of these issues, Sandler (1993) develops a conceptual model of the benefits derived from rainforest preservation. The rainforest is viewed as providing private goods in the form of timber to developed countries (1) and to the tropical nations (2). Non-rival and non-excludable public goods can be divided into public goods restricted to the developed countries – these include existence and option values on the rainforest – and local public goods restricted to the tropical nations, which include reduced soil erosion, watershed protection and nutrient recycling. Global public goods are those of benefit to the whole world. They include carbon sequestration, biodiversity and the bequest value of a preserved rainforest.

The tropical rainforest produces public and private goods simultaneously as joint products. The problem faced by the two sets of nations can be formulated as follows. Each country aims to maximise:

$$u^i = u^i(m^i, q^i, b^i, g) \qquad i = 1, 2$$

where $u^i(\cdot)$ is a social welfare function, m is a numeraire good not related to rainforest products, q is a private good derived from the rainforest, for instance timber, b is a local public good and g is a global public good. Production is based on a unit of forest preservation, q, and is represented by the author as a Leontief technology. Thus timber output is derived from the forest as:

$$q^i = \alpha a^i$$

where q^1 is interpreted as the private goods derived from the forest preserved by the developed nation's resources, a^1. Local public goods are given by:

$$b^1 = b^{11} + b^{12} = \alpha^{11}a^1 + \alpha^{12}a^2$$

that is, the developed countries benefit from local public goods from the forest preserved by their own resources and those preserved by the tropical nations. Global public goods are given by:

$$g = g^1 + g^2 = \gamma(a^1 + a^2)$$

Each country faces an income constraint

$$M^i = m^i + pa^i$$

where p is the price of forest conservation. From the perspective of the developed nations, the outcome is likely to emerge as a suboptimal Nash equilibrium where it must maximise utility with a^2 fixed. If the two utility functions were to be maximised jointly the problem would be one of sharing the benefits between the two groups of countries.

The other aspect of this problem is that the total area is diminishing through time. If the developed nations benefit most from an early agreement, they are in a weak bargaining position relative to the tropical nations who place a relatively low value on the forest. This is equivalent to a game where two players must decide to share a cake which is shrinking in size through time (see Rubinstein, 1982).

■ *11.5* **Forest policies**

Standing forests provide positive externalities which benefit society; however, if forests are privately owned, no incentive exists in a free market to ensure that forests follow a socially optimal rotation. In particular, maximising private timber values takes no account of the value society places upon the non-timber values of a standing forest. To counteract this market failure, the government can tax private forest owners to induce them to follow socially optimal forest rotations. This policy is similar, in principle, to the use of a Pigouvian tax to reduce pollutants to a socially optimal level.

Five forms of tax commonly apply to forests: (1) a yield tax, δ, levied on the forest revenue, (2) a site-value tax on the value of trees and the land, (3) an unmodified property tax which applies to the value of the land, α, (4) a profit tax ϕ, and (5) a severance tax on the area of trees cut, γ. These can be incorporated into the private timber owner's maximisation problem for a forest:

$$J = \frac{e^{-rT}[pf(T)(1-\delta) - c - \gamma](1-\phi)}{1 - e^{-rT}} - \frac{\int_0^T e^{-rt}\alpha(pf(t))\,dt}{1 - e^{-rt}} - c \qquad (11.16)$$

This is a modified version of Faustmann's formula given in (11.3). The second term on the right-hand side is there to account for the property tax deducted as a percentage of the current stumpage value. If all taxes are set to zero (11.16) becomes Faustmann's formula.

The effect of taxation upon the length of the optimal rotation is determined by differentiating (11.16) with respect to T, setting equal to zero for a maximum and then differentiating the resulting function by the implicit function rule to find the derivative with respect to the tax rate in question and its sign.

Further results are reported in detail in Englin and Klan (1990). A profit tax has no effect upon the length of the rotation. A severance tax lengthens the rotation and would favour externalities which depend on old trees, whilst a yield tax has a similar effect. The affect of an unmodified property tax is ambiguous and depends upon the rate of forest growth: it lengthens the rotation for fast-growing trees and shortens it for slow-growing trees.

We consider the derivation of the result for a yield tax in more detail. From (11.16) a yield tax gives the private forestry owner the objective function

$$J = \frac{e^{-rT}[pf(T)(1 - \delta) - c]}{1 - e^{-rT}} - c$$

Differentiating wrt T to determine the optimal rotation and rearranging

$$\frac{r}{1 - e^{-rT}} = \frac{pf'(T)}{\dfrac{-c}{1 - \delta} + pf(T)} \tag{11.17}$$

This result indicates that the effect of a yield tax depends upon the cost of replanting since, if $c = 0$, the tax has no effect on the optimal rotation. It acts to increase the right-hand side of (11.17) by increasing the rate of return for any T. An example is given in Figure 11.5, based upon $p - 1$, $c = 1$ and the growth function (11.6). The tax invariably increases the length of the rotation but the effect depends upon the discount rate. In the figure there is a marked reduction in the optimal rotation when $r = 0.2$, but a negligible reduction when the discount rate is 0.04. The effect this tax has is analogous to that of a change in the cost–price ratio discussed in section 11.2 above.

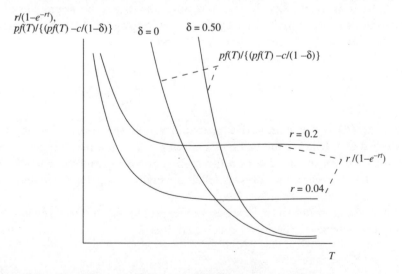

Figure 11.5 *The effect of a yield tax on the Faustmann rotation*

Setting the optimal yield tax involves finding the socially optimal rotation length, determining the timber growth rate at that age, $pf'(T^{**})/(pf(T^{**}) - c$ and adjusting the yield tax rate until the private optimal growth rate equals the socially optimal growth rate.

11.6 The optimal forest rotation under uncertainty

The forest manager faces uncertainty over timber prices, the rate of forest growth and the occurrence of forest fires and other natural disasters which could destroy the forest. The importance of uncertainty is increased by the long time horizon which is considered in forest management: in most situations uncertainty increases with the number of years into the future considered. The issue is whether the presence of uncertainty affects the optimal rotation length. Unfortunately, in the general case (Reed and Clarke, 1990; Reed, 1993), the application of Itô's lemma to optimal stopping problems is mathematically complex. For this reason we assess the problem for the case where uncertainty relates to forest fire alone. The model presented here is due to Reed (1984).

A forest is destroyed either by fire or by clear-felling. Assume fires occur according to a Poisson process, $\rho e^{-\rho t}$ at an average rate ρ. This implies that the probability of a forest fire is independent of the age of trees. The value of burnt trees is zero. Let $\tau_1, \tau_2, \ldots$ denote the times between successive destructions of the stand either by fire or by logging. If the policy is to cut the stand at an age T, the τ's are distributed

$$F(\tau(t)) = \text{pr}\{\tau_n \leq t\} = \int_0^t \rho e^{-\rho \tau} \, d\tau = 1 - e^{-\rho t}, \quad t < T$$

$$= 1 \qquad\qquad\qquad t \geq T$$

where $F(\tau(t))$ is the cumulative probability that the forest has not been destroyed at t. It takes the value of 1 when $t = T$ as the forest is felled. The economic return in the case of a fire is the cost of replanting, $\pi = -c_2$ and $\pi = pf(T) - c_1$ when the forest is felled normally at T; that is, revenue less felling costs c_1.

An optimal rotation maximises the expected discounted revenue, by harvesting whenever the forest reaches an age T

$$J = E\left\{ \sum_{n=1}^{\infty} e^{-r(\tau_1 + \tau_2 + \cdots + \tau_n)} \pi_n \right\} \tag{11.18}$$

That is, J equals the expected sum of the discounted economic return in each rotation where the discount factor is given by a series of rotations of random length. This term can be simplified as

$$J = \sum_{n=1}^{\infty} \prod_{i=1}^{n-1} E[e^{-r\tau_i}]E[e^{-r\tau_n}\pi_n] \tag{11.19}$$

This employs the product operator to simplify the discount factor and separates out the last profit term. Equation (11.19) can now be represented as the sum of a geometric progression:

$$J = E[e^{-r\tau}\pi]/(1 - E[e^{-r\tau}]) \tag{11.20}$$

It is now a matter of eliminating the expectations terms. The expected discount rate is

$$E[e^{-r\tau}] = \int_0^{\infty} e^{-r\tau} \, dF_\tau(t) = (\rho + re^{-(\rho+r)T})/(\rho + r) \tag{11.21}$$

and the expected present value of profit

$$E[e^{-r\tau}\pi] = \int_0^T (-c_2)e^{-r\tau}\rho e^{-\rho\tau} \, d\tau + e^{-rT}\rho e^{-\rho T}(V(T) - c_1)$$

$$= (V(T) - c_1)e^{-(\rho+r)T} - \rho c(1 - e^{-(\rho+r)T})/(\rho + r) \tag{11.22}$$

where $V(T) = pf(T)$. From (11.20), (11.21) and (11.22) J can be rewritten as

$$J = \frac{(\rho + r)(V(T) - c_1)e^{-(\rho+r)T}}{r(1 - e^{-(\rho+r)T})} - \frac{\rho}{r}c_2$$

If this is differentiated with respect to T and set equal to zero

$$\frac{V'(T)}{(V(T) - c_1)} = \frac{(\rho + r)}{1 - e^{-(\rho+r)T}}$$

which is a modified version of Faustmann's first-order condition (11.4). The risk of fire adds a risk premium to the discount rate by an amount equal to the average rate at which fire occurs.

Thus the presence of a fire risk reduces the length of the forest rotation. This might have implications if the non-timber value of the forest depends upon the presence of old growth trees. It also allows an evaluation of fire protection measures which reduce the probability of a fire occurring. The present value of fire protection, which reduces the instantaneous probability of fire from ρ_1 to ρ_2, is the difference between the maximum present value with protection, $J(\rho_2, r)$ and that without $J(\rho_1, r)$.

■ *11.7* Summary

This chapter considers forests as a natural resource. It starts with the economics of purely commercial forestry and establishes the main result, which is Faustmann's formula, for an optimal forest rotation. It then extends this basic model to the case where the forest has a non-timber value in the form of positive externalities derived by society from a standing forest. Next the relationship between agriculture and forestry is considered where there is competition for land. This is then extended to include the specific problems of tropical rainforests which are viewed as a non-renewable resource. The next section considers forest policy in the form of taxation, which may be used to provide private forest owners with an incentive to manage forests in a socially optimal way. The last section considers uncertainty relating to the occurrence of fire in the forest. In common with other resource problems, this tends to make private forest owners less conservationist in the sense that the forest rotation is reduced in length where there is uncertainty about future returns.

■ References

Bowes, M.D. and J.V. Krutilla (1985) 'Multiple Use Management of Public Forest Lands', in A.V. Kneese and J.L. Sweeny (eds), *Handbook of Natural Resource and Energy Economics*, Vol. II, Amsterdam: North-Holland.

Comolli, P.M. (1981) 'Principles and Policy in Forestry Economics', *Bell Journal of Economics*, 12, 300–305.

Crabbe, P.J. and N.V. Long (1989) 'Optimal Forest Rotation under Monopoly and Competition', *Journal of Environmental Economics and Management*, 17, 54–65.

Ehui, S.K. and T.W. Hertel (1989) 'Deforestation and Agricultural Productivity in the Côte d'Ivoire', *American Journal of Agricultural Economics*, 71, 703–11.

Ehui, S.K., T.W. Hertel and P.V. Preckel (1990) 'Forest Resource Depletion, Soil Dynamics, and Agricultural Productivity in the Tropics', *Journal of Environmental Economics and Management*, 18, 136–54.

Englin, J.E. and M.S. Klan (1990) 'Optimal Taxation: Timber and Externalities', *Journal of Environmental Economics and Management*, 18, 263–75.

Faustmann, M. (1849) 'On the Determination of the Value which Forest Land and Immature Stands Pose for Forestry', in M. Gane (ed.), *Martin Faustmann and the Evolution of Discounted Cash Flow*, Oxford: Oxford Institute.

Hartman, R. (1976) 'The Harvesting Decision When a Standing Forest Has Value', *Economic Inquiry*, 14, 52–8.

Heaps, T. (1984) 'The Forestry Maximum Principle', *Journal of Economic Dynamics and Control*, 7, 131–51.

Mitra, T. and H.Y. Wan (1985) 'Some Theoretical Results on the Economics of Forestry', *Review of Economic Studies*, 52, 263–82.

Reed, W.J. (1984) 'The Effects of the Risk of Fire on the Optimal Rotation of a Forest', *Journal of Environmental Economics and Management*, 11, 180–90.

Reed, W.J. (1993). 'The Decision to Conserve or Harvest Old-growth Forest', *Ecological Economics*, 8, 45–69.

Reed, W.J. and H.R. Clarke (1990) 'Harvest Decisions and Asset Valuation For Biological Resources Exhibiting Size-Dependent Stochastic Growth', *International Economics Review*, 31, 147–69.

Repetto, R. (1988) 'Overview', in R. Repetto and M. Gillis (eds), *Public Policies and the Misuse of Forest Resources*, New York: Cambridge University Press.

Rubinstein, A. (1982) 'Perfect Equilibrium in a Bargaining Model', *Econometrica*, 50, 97–109.

Samuelson, P.A. (1976) 'Economics of Forestry in an Evolving Society', *Economic Inquiry*, 14, 409–92.

Sandler, T. (1993) 'Tropical Deforestation: Markets and Market Failure', *Land Economics*, 69, 225–33.

Swallow, S.K, P.J. Parks and D.N. Wear (1990) 'Policy-relevant Nonconvexities in the Production of Multiple Forest Benefits', *Journal of Environmental Economics and Management*, 19, 264–80.

■ *Chapter 12* ■

The Theory of Non-Market Valuation

12.1 Introduction
12.2 Measures of economic value
12.3 Valuing risk and ex ante measures of value

12.4 Issues in non-market valuation
12.5 Concluding comments

■ *12.1* Introduction

Environmental resources supply a flow of direct and indirect services to society. The services provided by these ecosystems and their corresponding levels of biological diversity are numerous, ranging from basic life-support to the filtration of nonpoint source pollution from urban and rural run-off. But while these resources provide a nearly limitless set of valuable attributes, many of their services remain unpriced by the market. The services are rarely bought and sold by the pound on the auction block, and therefore never enter into private markets and remain unpriced by the public sector (see Chapter 2). For example, the market price of land does not generally account for the nutrient filtration and wildlife habitat services provided by a Minnesota wetland or a Scottish moor. The market undervalues wetland services because the associated costs and benefits accrue to more than just the owner of the land. Water filtration benefits all those downstream; wildlife does not stay within the confines of one landowner's property. This inability to exclude others from enjoying benefits or suffering costs prevents the market price from sending the correct signal about the true economic value of the wetland.

Recognition that environmental resources such as ecosystem and biodiversity services are systematically mispriced by the market has forced policy makers to consider other means to assess the value of these resources. Within a neoclassical, utilitarian framework, non-market valuation uses the implicit and explicit trade-offs between conservation and development to assess the value of unpriced environmental resources. The trade-off between development and conservation that performs such services as nutrient filtration reflects an economic value of a wetland, and the economist's job is to estimate its monetary value as accurately as possible. If an economist captures these trade-offs within a reasonable range of error, non-market valuation provides data to aid policy makers in their choices on how best to manage our natural resources.

This chapter examines some theoretical issues underlying the non-market valuation of environmental and natural resource services. Fuelled in the USA by court cases over natural resource damage assessment of Superfund waste sites (under the Comprehensive Environmental Response, Compensation and Liability Act of 1980) and the 1988 Exxon Valdez oil spill in Alaska, the past decade has witnessed an explosion in non-market valuation research. Probably as much collective intellectual energy has been spent on valuing environmental resources as on any other topic in natural resources and environmental economics. Section 2 defines two measures of economic value – the willingness to pay for improved ecosystem and biodiversity services and the willingness to accept compensation for decreased services. Section 3 considers non-market valuation under risk and uncertainty. Section 4 explores two analytical issues in non-market valuation – total value and warm glows and unfamiliarity and learning. The reader should also explore Braden and Kolstad (1991) and Freeman (1993), the most complete discussions of the ins and outs of non-market valuation.

■ *12.2* **Measures of economic value**

☐ *12.2.1 Environmental goods: preferences, utility and consumer surplus*

Economists have a distinct definition of value based on the ideals of rationality and consumer sovereignty – an individual consistently knows what he or she wants and needs (rationality) and is best able to make choices that affect his or her own welfare (consumer sovereignty). However odd the choices may appear to the outsider, a rational individual's consumption decisions are consistent with his or her purposes. If a person prefers grapes to bananas, rationality requires her to consistently select grapes (if both are free) and consumer sovereignty allows her to make that choice. The same logic applies to environmental goods and services – if the individual prefers improved wetland quality to a new truck, rationality requires her to consistently rank wetland quality over the truck.

Based on this foundation of rational choice, individuals are assumed to be able to value changes in environmental services despite their absence from the market. If a change occurs such that the person believes she is better off in some way, she may be willing to pay money to secure this improvement.

This willingness to pay reflects her economic valuation of improved environmental services. Alternatively, if the change makes her worse off, she might be willing to accept compensation to allow this deterioration. This willingness to pay (WTP) and willingness to accept (WTA) represent the two general measures of economic value for an environmental service. These measures of value are what economists would like to estimate so that environmental services and other non-market goods can be included in policy decisions on how to prioritize and allocate public monies. The WTP and WTA measures of economic value can be used as restrictions to guide policy or can be included, with caution, in the bottom-line cost–benefit analysis used to support public policy.

To get a better understanding of the way economists think about valuing non-market goods, consider Figure 12.1, which illustrates the three logical constructs that are used to derive a theory of economic value based on rational choice: the preference set, utility function, and consumer surplus. An individual is assumed to have a set of preferences over goods and services that can be ordered in a logical and consistent manner. The preference ordering restricts how an individual chooses between different consumption bundles. Axiomatic restrictions are usually imposed to define a consistent preference ordering, and guarantee the existence of a utility function that serves as an index for the preference ordering. The most important axioms are set out below (see Kreps, 1990, for more details). The utility function is an ordinal representation of preferences that allows us to express the most preferred consumption bundles by the highest level of utility. Utility is an unobservable, continuous index of preferences. If we impose a policy that changes the consumption bundle so that utility increases, then economists measure this change as consumer surplus – the money metric of the unobservable utility function. Consumer surplus can be either a willingness to pay or a willingness to accept compensation measure. To recap, we have preferences that are indexed by a utility function, and changes in utility are captured by consumer surplus measures. With the appropriate restrictions, an individual's willingness to pay for a change in environmental quality is based on a theory of rational choice, and is therefore a consistent estimate of preferences.

We now turn to the four axiomatic restrictions on preferences in more detail. Consider an individual choosing between alternative consumption bundles defined by n levels of environmental quality, $Q_1, Q_2, \ldots, Q_n$. If we

Figure 12.1 *Preferences, utility and consumer surplus*

write $Q_1 \succeq Q_2$ it implies that the level Q_1 is preferred to or indifferent to the level Q_2; $Q_1 \succ Q_2$ implies Q_1 is strictly preferred to Q_2; and $Q_1 \sim Q_2$ implies indifference between Q_1 and Q_2.

The following four axioms provide a basic mathematical foundation on which economists can model rational choice. Although debate continues today as to the relative importance of each axiom, they remain the cornerstone that allows one to assume an individual's choices will be consistent and acyclical, and therefore somewhat predictable.

1. *Reflexivity*. Each level of a good or service such as environmental quality is as good as itself; that is, for all $Q_i, Q_i \succeq Q_i$.
2. *Completeness*. For any two levels of environmental quality, Q_i and Q_j, either $Q_i \succeq Q_j$ or $Q_j \succeq Q_i$. The individual can always compare and rank all levels of environmental quality.
3. *Transitivity*. If $Q_i \succeq Q_j$ and $Q_j \succeq Q_k$, then $Q_i \succeq Q_k$. Preferences are acyclical.
4. *Continuity*. For any level of environmental quality Q_i, define $A(Q_i)$ as the 'at least as good set' and $B(Q_i)$ as the 'no better than set', then $A(Q_i)$ and $B(Q_i)$ are closed (that is, they contain their own boundary points). This implies that no level of environmental quality is absolutely necessary and that quality can be traded off at the margin for another good or income.

These four axioms allow the representation of preferences by a utility function, $U(Q_i)$. This implies that, if the individual prefers Q_1 to Q_2, then the utility associated with Q_1 is greater than the utility of Q_2, $U(Q_1) > U(Q_2)$. Let $U(Q_0)$ represent the utility received from a preassigned level of the environment good, Q_0. Economists generally assume that an individual's utility increases at a decreasing rate as Q_0 increases, that is, the law of diminishing returns – the more we have the less we value an additional unit of the good. Formally, we represent this as

$$U_Q \equiv \frac{dU}{dQ_0} > 0 \qquad U_{QQ} \equiv \frac{d^2U}{dQ_0^2} < 0$$

We now want to consider the individual's economic problem. We assume the individual derives utility from both environmental quality, Q_0, and all other market goods and services, $x = (x_1, x_2, \ldots, x_n)$, such that $U = U(x, Q_0)$. For simplicity, assume that all other market goods lead to positive utility, and utility increases at a decreasing rate; for example,

$$U_{x_i} \equiv \partial U / \partial x_i > 0 \qquad \text{and} \qquad U_{x_i x_i} \equiv \partial^2 U / \partial x_i^2 < 0, \quad \text{for all } i$$

The individual's choice of all market goods and services is constrained by fixed monetary income, M, and the prices of these goods and services, $p = (p_1, p_2, \ldots, p_n)$. We now have all the elements necessary to formally define the individual's economic problem. The individual's problem then is to maximise his or her utility by selecting a level of consumption of all market goods, $x = (x_1, x_2, \ldots, x_n)$ given that he or she is subject to a fixed income, M and vector of prices for all other goods and services, $p = (p_1, p_2, \ldots, p_n)$ and the exogenously determined level of the environmental good, Q_0. Formally, we write the individual's problem as

$$\text{Max}_{x} [U(x, Q_0) \,|\, M \geq px; Q_0 \text{ is preassigned}] \qquad (12.1)$$

One can read equation (12.1) as follows.

$\displaystyle\text{Max}_{x} [\cdot]$ The individual selects a level of consumption of all other market goods and services, x, to maximise utility, subject to the budget constraint and the fixed level of the environmental good.

$U(x, Q_0)$ The utility function, where we assume that

$$U_x \equiv \partial U/\partial x > 0 \qquad U_{xx} \equiv \partial^2 U/\partial x^2 < 0$$

$$U_Q \equiv \partial U/\partial Q > 0 \qquad U_{QQ} \equiv \partial^2 U/\partial Q^2 < 0$$

$M \geq px$ The budget constraint which implies that the individual spends less than or all of her income on the consumption good, x.

Q_0 The fixed level of the environmental good.

Given the individual's economic problem, the problem that now concerns us is formally defining the economic value of an increase in the level of the environmental good to Q_1 from Q_0. Since differences in utility are not measurable, economists have introduced the concept of consumer surplus – the money metric of changes in utility.

Since the economic value of environmental services is usually not reflected by direct market prices, consumer surplus measures are used to capture the value of changes in these services. Figure 12.2 illustrates the basic idea of consumer's surplus for quantity changes in an environmental service. Point A represents the utility level, U_0, given the fixed level of the environmental service, Q_0, and the composite market good, $\bar{x}$. If we increase the level of environmental services to Q_1 from Q_0 keeping $\bar{x}$ fixed, the individual's utility increases to U_1 from U_0 – more of Q gives the individual more utility. Now the first of two questions is, what is the maximum he or she is willing to pay (WTP) to secure this change to Q_1 from Q_0? The answer is the individual would give up the composite market good until he or she reached his or her original utility level, that is, the move to point C from point B. He would not give up more because then he would be worse off than when he started; if he gave up less that would not be the maximum he was willing to pay. Given an increase in the level of the environmental service, the maximum WTP is just the amount that would return him to his original level of utility – no more,

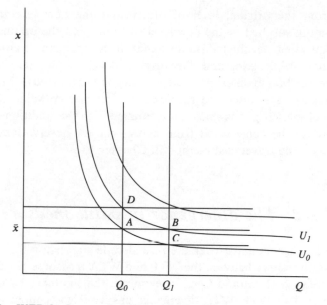

Figure 12.2 *WTP for improved environmental services*

no less. This maximum willingness to pay is called the Hicksian compensating surplus, named after Sir John Hicks. A value measure is a compensating surplus measure if two conditions hold – the original level of utility, U_0, and the new level of environmental quality, Q_1. In section 12.2.3 we will define consumer surplus as the difference between levels of expenditures, often an easier way to obtain the economic value of interest.

The second question then is, what is the minimum compensation the individual is willing to accept (WTA) to forgo the increase in the environmental good? The answer is, the individual would require an increase in the level of the composite consumption good such that he or she achieves the new level of utility, U_1, that would have been reached if the environmental good had increased to Q_1 from Q_0. This is represented by the differences between points A and D. If the individual asked for less, he would not reach the new utility level; the individual could ask for more, but this would not be the minimum WTA. This minimum WTA is called the Hicksian equivalent surplus. Two conditions must hold for the value measure to be an equivalent surplus: the new utility, U_1, and the original level of the environmental good, Q_0.

Note that for a decrease in environmental services the maximum WTP is a Hicksian equivalent surplus measure, while the minimum WTA is a Hicksian compensating surplus measure of value. The key to understanding which measure is which is not the direction of change in the level of the environmental service, but rather whether the individual is evaluating the change from the original level of utility and the new level of service (compensating surplus) or the new level of utility and the original level of service (equivalent surplus). Also note that, if the change is evaluated from the original utility level and the original level of the service, this is considered a Marshallian measure of consumer surplus. Marshallian consumer surplus is often the surplus measure used to value changes in the prices of market goods since it is estimated with the traditional demand curve that can be constructed from actual market observations. See the discussion on the travel cost method in Chapter 13.

☐ *12.2.2 The divergence in value measures*

Evidence has accumulated over the past decade suggesting that there is a significant divergence between the WTP and WTA measures of value. Often WTA exceeds WTP tenfold (see, for example, the summary by Cummings *et al.*, 1986). This WTP–WTA divergence has troubled economists, since it implies that the individual is not as rational as theory requires. Standard value theory predicts that WTP and WTA should be equivalent, or within a tight bound given small income effects (see Willig, 1976; Randall and Stoll, 1980). Therefore, since these value measures are used to help guide public policy decisions, the divergence raises questions about which measure to use in actual practice. If the decision is to conserve some environmental amenity, using a WTA measure could likely generate a significantly greater economic value for conservation than would a WTP measure – perhaps enough of a difference to tip the balance towards conservation. However, if this WTA measure is based on irrational behaviour, then it is of questionable use for the policy debate.

The question therefore is whether or not this divergence in value measures really implies irrational behaviour by individuals. The answer is that it does not – we should only expect convergence of WTP and WTA measures of value when the environmental good or service has a very close or perfect substitute (see Hanemann, 1991; Shogren *et al.*, 1994). The divergence in WTP and WTA depends on both income and substitution effects for discrete changes in the quantity of the good or service. The WTP–WTA divergence can range from zero to infinity, depending on the degree of substitution between an environmental good and other market or non-market goods. The fewer available substitutes the greater the divergence, since there are fewer possibilities to make up for this loss.

Figure 12.3 illustrates how substitution effects can influence the WTP–WTA divergence for discrete changes in quantity of an environmental service. Figure 12.3a shows the case where the environment service, Q, and

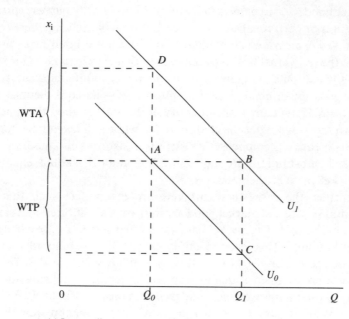

(a) Intermediate monetary adjustments

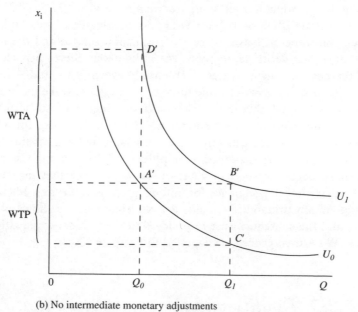

(b) No intermediate monetary adjustments

Figure 12.3 *WTP and WTA given perfect and imperfect substitutability (adapted from Shogren et al., 1994).*

some market good, x_i, are perfect substitutes. Linear utility curves represent the assumption of perfect substitutes – the frictionless exchange between x_i and Q. The WTA measure is the quantity of the market good necessary to compensate the individual to forgo a change in Q from Q_0 to Q_1. This is the amount AD which puts the individual on the higher indifference curve, but which maintains the original Q_0 consumption level – an equivalent surplus measure. The WTP measure is the quantity of the market good that one can take from an individual after the change to Q_1, while still leaving him or her as well off as before – a compensating surplus measure. This amount is BC. Given perfect substitution, BC equals AD, and both should equal the average market price of the good.

Now consider the case where markets are incomplete such that the environmental service and market good are imperfect substitutes, and cannot be perfectly exchanged. The market has friction that restricts the exchange of commodity holdings. This leads to utility curves of the standard shape – strictly convex to the origin. Now in this case, WTA will exceed WTP. The assumption of environmental quality and wealth as imperfect substitutes is reflected by the curvature of the indifference curves in Figure 12.3b. The individual's WTP to secure the new level of environmental quality, Q_1, keeping him at his original utility level, U_0, is $B'C'$. In contrast, the compensation (WTA) required to reach the new level of utility, U_1, while remaining at his original level of environmental service, Q_0, is $A'D'$. Note that $A'D'$ exceeds $B'C'$, or WTA > WTP. As the degree of substitutability decreases, the trade-off between the environmental service and the market good becomes less desirable, implying the indifference curves become more curved, thereby creating a greater divergence between WTA and WTP. The WTP–WTA divergence is not some form of cognitive mistake by irrational consumers, but is systematically related to the degree of substitutability between the environmental good and the good it is being traded for. Unique environmental assets may generate a relatively large WTA measure of value that probably should be accounted for in public policy questions. One cannot dismiss these larger measures of value out of hand since they may well be legitimate measures of preference for unique goods and services. Identifying the degree of substitutability remains a key element in the choice of value measure, and the subsequent use in policy decisions. Other explanations of the WTP–WTA divergence are suggested in Chapter 13.

☐ *12.2.3 Duality and the expenditure function*

Another useful way to illustrate the WTP and WTA value measures is to rewrite the problem as a cost minimisation problem. Cost minimisation is the 'dual' to the individual's problem of utility maximisation. Now the expenditure function plays the key role in defining the measures of economic value. The individual's cost minimisation problem is considered the dual to utility maximisation since we are reversing what the individual is optimising and the constraint. Recall that the utility maximisation problem in Section 12.2.1 selected levels of the market goods to maximise utility, subject to a fixed level of income and the environmental good or service. Cost minimisation flips this around by selecting levels of the market goods to minimise expenditures, subject to a fixed level of utility and the environmental good or service. The reason economists are interested in this dual approach is that it is often easier to collect data on expenditures, given that utility is held constant. There is no need to measure unobservable utility functions (see Freeman, 1993). Formally, we can write the individual's cost minimisation problem as

$$e(p, Q_0, \bar{U}) = \underset{x}{\text{Min}} \, [\, px \mid \bar{U} \geq U(x, Q_0); Q_0 \text{ is preassigned}] \tag{12.2}$$

where $e(p, Q_0, \bar{U})$ is the expenditure function – the minimum expenditure necessary to achieve the fixed level of utility, $\bar{U}$, dependent on prices and the level of Q. The maximum willingness to pay (WTP) for an improvement to Q_i from Q_0 is

$$\text{WTP} = e(p, Q_0, \bar{U}) - e(p, Q_1, \bar{U})$$

the difference between the two levels of minimum expenditures to achieve the fixed utility $\bar{U}$.

12.2.4 *Environmental hazards: value measures and the indirect utility function*

Up to this point we have focused on environmental goods rather than environmental bads or hazards. Now consider the case of measuring the value to reduce an environmental hazard, R. The hazard might be measured in the same manner as ambient concentration of some pollutants. Assume that an increase in the hazard decreases utility, $U(x, R)$, such that

$$U_R \equiv \partial U/\partial R < 0 \qquad U_{RR} \equiv \partial^2 U/\partial R^2 > 0$$

We can now rewrite the individual's problem as

$$V(M, p, R_0) \equiv \underset{x}{\text{Max}} \, [U(x, R_0) \mid M \geq px; R_0 \text{ is preassigned}] \tag{12.3}$$

where $V(M, p, R)$ is the indirect utility function. The indirect utility function represents the maximum attainable utility, given the budget constraint and the level of the hazard, and is a function of the exogenous parameters, income, prices and the level of the hazard. Note that one can use this indirect utility approach to measure the value for environmental goods too.

Figure 12.4 illustrates the relationship between the WTP and WTA measures of value, given an environmental hazard. The vertical axis represents the level of the environmental hazard measured, say, in an ambient concentration level of a pollutant. The horizontal axis reflects an individual's level of income, M. The set of curved lines that originate from the horizontal axis reflect the individual's preferences for income and for avoiding the hazard – the set of indirect utility functions. Each point on an indirect utility function represents different combinations of hazard and income which leave the individual at the same level of satisfaction. The slope of the indirect utility curve shows the willingness of the individual to trade between income and hazard while maintaining the same level of utility. The slope of the utility function is called the marginal rate of substitution – the willingness to trade the hazard for income holding utility constant. The flatter the slope the less effective is income as a substitute for the hazard, and more income is necessary to compensate the individual for an increase in the hazard. A steep slope implies the opposite:

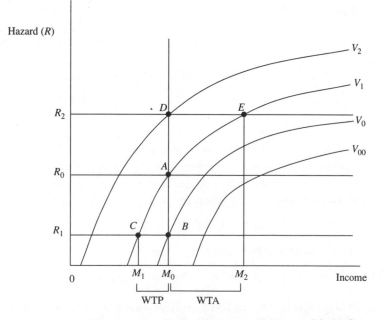

Figure 12.4   *WTP–WTA measure of value given an environmental hazard*

less income is needed to compensate the individual for an increase in the hazard. Note that utility increases as one moves to the right, $V_{00} > V_0 > V_1 > V_2$ for a given level of the hazard R. If the individual has more income and less of the hazard, the more satisfaction he receives. Also note that, although there are an infinite number of utility functions, only four are drawn on Figure 12.4.

Consider point A – the initial condition of hazard level, R_0, and income level, M_0, and utility level, V_1. If the level of the hazard decreased to R_1 from R_0, then, given the original wealth level, W_0, the individual's utility would increase to V_0, point B. Therefore, the maximum the individual would be willing to pay for this decrease in the hazard is the amount of wealth that would bring him back to his original utility function, V_1, WTP $= M_0 - M_1$, point C. The individual would pay no more than this because to pay more would lead to a lower level of utility than he possessed at the initial condition, V_1. The individual would surely pay less than this if he could, but this lower value is not the accurate economic value of a decreased hazard. The accurate value is the maximum WTP.

If the level of the hazard increased to R_2 from R_0, then, given M_0, the individual's utility level decreases to V_2, point D. The minimum amount of income that the individual would be willing to accept in compensation for the increase in the hazard equals WTA $= M_2 - M_0$, point E. This compensation restores the individual to his initial utility level, given the increased hazard. The individual would not accept less because this too would lead to a lower level of utility than he possessed at the initial condition, V_1. Again the individual would gladly accept more than the minimum WTA, but this higher value does not reflect the accurate economic value to accept an increase in the hazard. The accurate value is the minimum WTA.

Formally, the economic measures of value are defined as follows. The compensating surplus measure for a decrease in the level of the hazard is

$$V_0(M_0 - \text{WTP}, p, R_1) = V_0(M_0, p, R_0) \tag{12.4}$$

and the equivalent surplus measure is

$$V_1(M_0 + \text{WTA}, p, R_0) = V_1(M_0, p, R_1) \tag{12.5}$$

For an increase in the level of the hazard, the corresponding compensating and equivalent surplus measures are

$$V_0(M_0 + \text{WTA}, p, R_2) = V_0(M_0, p, R_0) \tag{12.6}$$

and

$$V_{00}(M_0 - \text{WTP}, p, R_0) = V_0(M_0, p, R_2) \tag{12.7}$$

12.3 Valuing risk and ex ante measures of value

12.3.1 Exogenous risk

So far, we have assumed that the individual confronts a certain change in the level of environmental good or hazard. But it is unlikely that the individual knows the exact change in environmental services with absolute certainty. Rather the individual probably has a set of beliefs or probabilities about the likely outcomes that could occur. Together these beliefs and outcomes define risk. For now, assume that these beliefs and outcomes are independent of his or her actions – the risk is exogenous, outside his or her control.

Recall the examples of the changes in the level of the environmental hazard, R_1 and R_2. Suppose the individual is uncertain as to which of these two levels of the hazard will actually be realised, but that his choice of consumption of all market goods does not have to be made until after uncertainty is resolved. This implies that there are two mutually exclusive and jointly exhaustive states of the world. A state of the world is defined by the outcome that is realised once the uncertainty is resolved. The individual assigns a belief to the likelihood that each state will occur. Let π_1 and π_2 represent the beliefs that hazard levels R_1 and R_2 will occur, such that $0 \leq \pi_i \leq 1$ $(i = 1, 2)$ and $\pi_1 + \pi_2 = 1$.

If the individual's indirect utility function is independent of the state that actually occurs, then the individual's economic problem, given exogenous risk, is written as

$$EV = \pi_1 V(M, p, R_1) + \pi_2 V(M, p, R_2) \tag{12.8}$$

where EV represents the individual's expected utility, the weighted average of the indirect utility functions that can occur depending on which outcome is realised. Note that we use the indirect utility function rather than the direct utility function, $U(x, R_i)$, since we have assumed that consumption choices can be made after the outcome is realised. If consumption decisions could not be postponed, then the direct utility function would be used.

Expected utility is the most popular theory of choice under risk and uncertainty. There are several additional axioms necessary to construct a theory of rational choice under uncertainty, the most controversial being the independence axiom (see Machina, 1987). The independence axiom requires that, if a person prefers lottery A to lottery B, and if a third lottery, C, is added to both A and B, the person will still prefer A to B. The fact that this axiom has been violated in numerous experimental studies should make the reader cautious as to the broad applicability of expected utility theory to all decisions under risk. For our current purposes, we proceed with expected utility theory, and send the reader to Machina (1987) or Camerer (1995) for alternative models of choice under exogenous risk.

The individual would prefer that state 1 occur since $V(M, p, R_1) > V(M, p, R_2)$, given $R_2 > R_1$ (recall R lowers utility). One measure of this individual's preference for increasing the likelihood that state 1 will be observed, either by measuring his ex ante willingness to pay, or option price (OP), to increase the likelihood of state 1 or by measuring his ex ante willingness to accept compensation (C) for a decrease in the likelihood of state 1. Both OP and C are the risky counterpart of the non-risk measure of value WTP and WTA defined earlier. The biggest difference is that option price (OP) and compensation demand (C) account for risk preferences; that is, is the individual risk-averse, risk-neutral, or risk-seeking? Risk aversion implies the individual is willing to pay an extra premium to avoid a risk; risk neutrality implies he will not pay a premium; and a risk seeker will need to be given a premium not to have the risk (see Hey, 1979, Cook and Graham, 1979 and Graham, 1981).

Formally, the option price (OP) that an individual would pay to increase the likelihood that state 1 occurs to $\hat{\pi}_1$ from π_1 due to some form of collective action is

$$\hat{\pi}_1 V(M - OP, p, R_1) + \hat{\pi}_2 V(M - OP, p, R_2)$$

$$= \pi_1 V(M, p, R_1) + \pi_2 V(M, p, R_2) \tag{12.9}$$

The individual pays OP to secure the increase to $\hat{\pi}_1$ from π_1 – his ex ante willingness to pay for a change in exogenous risk. The ex ante compensation demand (C) for a decrease in the likelihood that state 1 will occur, $\bar{\pi}_1 < \pi_1$, is written as

$$\bar{\pi}_1 V(M + C, p, R_1) + \bar{\pi}_2 V(M + C, p, R_2)$$

$$= \pi_1 V(M, p, R_1) + \pi_2 V(M, p, R_2) \tag{12.10}$$

The individual receives C in compensation for the decrease to $\bar{\pi}_1$ from π_1 – his ex ante willingness to accept compensation for a change in exogenous risk.

☐ 12.3.2 Endogenous risk

As we begin to understand the nature of valuing risk, an increasing number of economists have become uncomfortable with the maintained hypothesis that risk is exogenous – beyond the private actions of individuals. Not all risk reduction is derived from some collective action based on public policy.

Rather individuals often substitute private action to reduce risk for collectively supplied programmes. Examples include private water filtration, higher strength building material, improved nutrition and exercise regimens, and personal protective equipment. These private actions can reduce the likelihood that a bad state will occur or the severity of the state if realised, or both. By complementing or substituting for collective action, individual strategies to reduce risk influence both the probability and the magnitude of harm. Neglect of these private–collective interactions can imply unintended consequences of well-intended policy.

Some economists have argued it is always possible to redefine a problem so that the state of nature is independent of human action. This position allows one to continue working within the highly tractable framework of exogenous risk. Consider, however, a situation in which bacterial groundwater contamination threatens a household's drinking water. The probability of illness among household members can be altered if they boil the water. An analyst might define the situation as independent of the household's actions by focusing solely on groundwater contamination, over which the household likely has no control. But this definition is economically irrelevant if the question is the household's response to and damages from groundwater contamination. The household is concerned about the probability of being made ill and the severity of any realised illness, and it is able to exercise some control over those events. The household's risk is endogenous because by expending its valuable resources it can influence probability and severity.

Ehrlich and Becker (1972) define ex ante efforts to reduce probability as self-protection, s, and ex ante efforts to reduce prospective severity as self-insurance, x. The individual's economic problem now becomes selecting s and x to maximise his expected utility,

$$\max_{s,x} EU = [\pi(s, R)U(M - s - x) + (1 - \pi(s, R))U(M - L(x) - s - x)] \qquad (12.11)$$

where $\pi = \pi(s, R)$ is the probability of no loss that depends on s and the level of the hazard, R; M is wealth, L is the money equivalent of realised severity, and s and x are expenditures on self-protection and self-insurance. Assume $\pi_s = d\pi/ds > 0$, $\pi_{ss} = d^2\pi/ds^2 < 0$, $\pi_R = d\pi/dR < 0$, $\pi_{RR} = d^2\pi/dR^2 > 0$, $L_x = dL/dx < 0$, and $L_{xx} = d^2L/dx^2 > 0$. The necessary conditions for the individual's optimal levels of self-protection and self-insurance are then

$$s: \pi_s \bar{U} - \pi U_w(M - s - x) - (1 - \pi)U_w(M - L(x) - s - x) = 0 \qquad (12.12)$$

$$x: \pi U_w(M - s - x) - (1 - \pi)U_w(M - L(x) - x - s)(1 + L_x) = 0 \qquad (12.13)$$

where $\bar{U} = U(M - s - x) - U(M - L(x) - s - x) > 0$, and $|L_x| > 1$. Equations (12.12) and (12.13) state the standard result that an individual maximises expected utility by equating the marginal cost of influencing probability or severity with the marginal benefit acquired. Self-protection and self-insurance activities will not be undertaken if doing so is not expected to increase net benefits. Within this framework economists have explored the theoretical underpinnings and the behavioural implications of endogenous risk.

Specifically, maintaining the assumption of exogenous risk can lead to the undervaluation of reduced risk and the misidentification of those who value risk reductions most highly. There are several reasons for undervaluation, all involving the inability of an exogenous risk perspective to disentangle the relative values of private and collective contributions to risk reductions. When risk is considered exogenous to the individual, protection must be supplied collectively. Nonetheless, self-protection is often a viable substitute for collectively supplied protection; it can also expand an individual's opportunities to exploit personal gains from collective provision.

The valuation literature for exogenous risk characteristically assumes that the value of risk reductions declines as risk decreases. Empirical evidence that this marginal value actually increases is held to be a lapse from rational economic behaviour. Shogren and Crocker (1991) show, however, that endogenous risk within the traditional expected utility framework can generate behaviour consistent with increasing marginal valuations of risk reductions. In particular, if the marginal productivity effects of self-protection on probability differ from the effects on severity, increasing marginal valuations can occur. This result challenges the standard view that those who are at greater risk and who have greater wealth must value a given risk reduction more highly. It also implies that the undervaluations caused by a singular focus on collective risk reductions could increase with the degree of success gained by these collective efforts. As the marginal effectiveness of successive collective provisions declines, the relative effectiveness and therefore the value of private provision increases.

When self-protection and collective protection are perfect substitutes – equally effective in producing risk reductions – Shogren (1990) observed in a series of controlled experiments that the upper bounds on the values participants attached to risk reductions were consistently associated with self-protection; collective protection always represented the lower bounds. This implies, all else equal, that individuals prefer self rather than collective provision. In these experiments, participants could substitute between a single mechanism for self-protection and a single collective protection mechanism.

In addition, when researchers employ the concept of the value of a statistical life or limb, benefit–cost analyses do not acknowledge the existence of multiple or even single private risk reduction mechanisms. The value of a statistical life is defined as the cost of an unidentified single death weighted by a probability of death that is uniform across individuals. But even if individuals have identical preferences, substantial differences exist in their opportunities for or costs of altering risk. The statistical life or limb approach fails to address the differences in individual risks induced by self-protection. An individual who has ready access to private risk reduction mechanisms will value collective mechanisms less than otherwise. A complete assessment of this individual's value for a given risk reduction thus requires considering willingness to pay for self-provision as well as for collective provision. In essence, by virtue of its exclusive focus on collective provision, the statistical life or limb approach undervalues environmental threats to human health and endorses economically excessive levels of environmental degradation. The undervaluation problem can be resolved by assessing the individual's preference for alternative risk reduction strategies, by allowing the individual to reveal whether he or she would prefer to reduce risk privately or collectively or both, or by reducing the probability or severity or both.

■ *12.4* Issues in non-market valuation

The theory of non-market valuation has made significant advances over the past three decades, both in intensity and scope as economists attempt to value an increasing number of environmental goods from around the world. Increasing sophistication, both in analytical structures and estimation procedures, has increased the optimism of economists about using non-market valuation as a viable tool to assist decision making. But as non-market valuation advances, so do new controversies and debates. Below we consider two topics that play an important part in non-market valuation – total value and warm glows; and value formation and preference learning.

□ *12.4.1 Total value and warm glows*

The most difficult policy question to confront policy makers is the management and valuation of regional or global environmental services. This question involves open-access commons and public goods that are not controlled or managed by any one county, state or region. Therefore, given the dimensions of environmental services, the practice of non-market valuation faces a significant challenge in understanding how citizens perceive these services and how they value changes on the genetic, species, regional and global scale. One reason for difficulties is assigning economic value to goods that most people will never directly use. How can we attach an economic value to the mere existence of an environmental good that we may never use directly or even visit?

Following Krutilla (1967), economists have answered this question by proposing the concept of total value. Total value is the idea that consumers have both use and non-use values for environmental resources. Use value is straightforward – the economic value of current use. But a non-use value is more problematic and controversial. Existence value is the value of the mere existence of a resource, given that the individual has no plans ever to use it. As academicians debated the theoretical justification, the United States District of Columbia Court of Appeals ruled in 1989 that non-use value constitutes a valid representation of economic value. In *Ohio* v. *US Department of the Interior*, 800f.2d 432, the court stated that 'option and existence values may represent "passive use" but they nonetheless reflect utility derived by humans from a resource and thus *prima facie* ought to be included in a damage assessment'. Option value is the value to preserve the resource for potential future use. The view that non-use values are legitimate economic values is supported by the recently convened 'blue ribbon' panel (including two Nobel Prize-winners) evaluating contingent valuation (Arrow *et al.*, 1993).

We can illustrate the nature of non-use values by introducing a set of 'contingent claims' that specify the conditions under which access to an environmental service will be available. These contingent claims are defined over the physical, stochastic, spatial and intertemporal properties of access. For example, a contingent claim might specify access to the state of nature (good or poor quality), the time (now or in 10 years) and a site (Grand Canyon or Hell's Half-acre). The idea behind this contingent claim is to construct a market to allow exchange over a broad set of conditions that define access to a resource. These claims expand the dimensionality of the resource and allow the research to set the access parameters to the conditions one wants to value (see Smith, 1987). Non-use value can be captured by altering the contingent claim to restrict access to a future date or prevent access entirely.

Let Z_{ijk} represent a freely exchanged and fully enforceable contingent claim that defines access to a state of nature, Q_i $(i = 1, \ldots, n)$, at a time j $(j = 1, 2, \ldots, t)$, and at a site k $(k = 1, 2, \ldots, l)$. Let β_{ijk} be the price for this contingent claim. If we assume that the level of the environmental service, Q_i, is uncertain, then π_i represents the subjective probability of state i occurring.

With the planned expenditure function of Helms (1985) and Smith (1987), the individual chooses an expenditure-minimising quantity of a contingent claim subject to a fixed ex ante level of expected utility, $\bar{U}$:

$$\bar{e}(\beta_{ijk}; p; \bar{U}; \pi_1, \ldots, \pi_n; Q_1, \ldots, Q_n) = \min_{Z_{ijk}} \sum_i \sum_j \sum_k \beta_{ijk} Z_{ijk} + px$$

$$\text{subject to} \quad \bar{U} = \sum_i \pi_i U_i(x, Q_i, Z_{ijk}) \tag{12.14}$$

where $e(\cdot)$ is the expenditure function for a given level of expected utility. An alternative configuration to the expenditure function in Equation (12.14) is the distance function. A distance function is the dual of the expenditure function (Deaton, 1979). Crocker and Shogren (1991a) define the distance function, $d(\cdot)$ as

$$d(Z_{ikj}; p; \bar{U}; \pi_1, \ldots, \pi_n; Q_1, \ldots, Q_n) = \min_{\beta_{ijk}} \sum_i \sum_j \sum_k \beta_{ijk} Z_{ijk} + px$$

subject to $\displaystyle\sum_i \sum_j \sum_k c(\beta_{ijk}; x; p; \bar{U}; \pi_i; Q_i) = 1$ (12.15)

With either equation (12.14) or (12.15), one can examine the ex ante measures of value for alternative contingent claims defining conditions of access to Q_i: (a) the value (implicit marginal time preference) when an already secured access claim to Q_i is delayed until the tth time period; (b) the value that remains (existence value) after removing an already secured access claim from the choice set; and (c) the value added (locational value) when an already secured access claim is extended from one site to a set of k sites.

For a specific site and time the individual's option price, OP_i, for a change from π_i^0 to π_i^1 in the probability of securing an access claim to the ith environmental state is

$$OP_i = e(\beta_{ijk}; p; \bar{U}; \pi_i^0; Q_1) - e(\beta_{ijk}; p; \bar{U}; \pi_i^1; Q_i)$$ (12.16)

OP_i is thus the change in planned expenditures on Z_{ijk} to be allowed the individual if he is to be indifferent between π_i^0 and π_i^1. If the individual's expected utility function is concave in the Q_i, Jensen's inequality implies that OP_i will be greater than the income change required to recover the individual's expected utility level after the realisation of what was the average of the visibility states. The difference represents a risk premium which incorporates risk attitudes and risk beliefs or perceptions.

The outcomes of a programme to alter access to an environmental good are not immediately realised and abandoned, nor are the changes necessarily permanent. At a specific site, the individual values a delay from $j = 1$ to $j = n$, $n > 1$, in securing an access claim to a particular subjective probability, π_i^0, of the ith environmental state as

$$DV_i = e(\beta_{ilk}; p; \bar{U}; \pi_i^0; Q_i) - e(\beta_{ink}; p; \bar{U}; \pi_i^0; Q_i)$$ (12.17)

Estimation of DV_i allows the individual's marginal rate of time preference to be directly inferred using the appropriate present value and discounting formula.

Within this framework, existence value implies that the individual would value some particular probability of provision of Q_i at a specific site and time even though any claim of access to this Q_i is completely removed from his choice set. Thus existence value, XV_i, is

$$XV_i = e(\beta_{ijk}; p; \bar{U}; \pi_i^0; Q_i) - e(p; \bar{U}; \pi_i^0; Q_i) \tag{12.18}$$

Finally, we examine how ex ante valuations of a contingent claim to Q_i vary with the spatial coverage of the claim. Thus location value, LV_i, is

$$LV_i = e(\beta_{ijL}; p; \bar{U}; \pi_i^0; Q_i) - e(\beta_{ijk}; p; \bar{U}; \pi_i^0; Q_i) \tag{12.19}$$

where L is the union of locations, $k = 1, \ldots, m$. A small or zero magnitude for LV_i would be consistent with Kahneman's (1986) conjecture that site-specific value statements may well really represent surrogates for attitudes about environmental quality, broadly conceived – a 'warm glow' effect. Eliciting non-use values provides the opportunity for a respondent to state his or her general preference towards the environment rather than for the specific ecosystem or biodiversity service in question. The value revealed may reflect the 'warm glow' of contributing to save the general environment rather than the specific service in question. For example, Crocker and Shogren (1991a) find mixed evidence of surrogate bidding for atmospheric visibility in Oregon. They observed no significant difference in values for improved visibility in one specific mountain location as compared to the value for state-wide improvements. In addition, Arrow *et al.* (1993) note that the bimodal distribution of value estimates in many CVM studies – zero or a positive value around $30 to $50 – suggests that these values may serve a function similar to charitable contributions. Not only does the respondent want to support a worthy cause, but he or she also receives a 'warm glow' from donating to the cause.

The recent exchange between Kahneman and Knetsch (1992) and Smith (1992) further defines the debate. Kahneman and Knetsch observed that on average the willingness to pay to clean up one lake in Ontario was not significantly greater than the willingness to pay to clean up all the lakes in the province. They cite this as evidence that individuals are not responding to the good, but rather to the idea of contributing to environmental preservation in general – the warm glow. Smith questioned this view, arguing that incremental willingness to pay should decline with the amount of the good already available, and as such the evidence is consistent with economic theory. But other reports such as Desvousges *et al.* (1992) support the warm glow argument, finding evidence that the average willingness to pay to prevent 2000 birds from dying in oil-filled ponds was not significantly different from the value to prevent 20 000 or 200 000 birds from dying. While accepting the argument that willingness to pay for additional protection probably does decline, Arrow *et al.* (1993, p. 11) note that the drop to zero 'is hard to explain as the expression of a consistent, rational set of choices'. This discussion is extended to cover the concept of 'embedding' in Chapter 13.

Separating total value from surrogate bidding presents a challenge to the comprehensive monetary evaluation of regional or global environmental resources. Total values are more accurately estimated for well-defined areas and well-specified resources. But a piecemeal resource-by-resource approach will overestimate economic value because it does not address substitution possibilities across the set of resources. For example, if we value ten resources across a region, the summed values of ten unique studies over each resource most likely will exceed the value of one study over the ten resources. Hoehn and Loomis (1993) find that independent aggregation of the benefits of only two programmes overstates their total benefits by 27 per cent; the overstatement with three programmes is 54 per cent. But as we move towards one comprehensive non-market valuation study so as to account for substitutions and complementarities we increase the likelihood of surrogate values as the resources become less tangible and more symbolic. The sheer size of regional and global resources with their numerous ecosystem and biodiversity services requires a non-market valuation strategy that includes well-defined substitution possibilities and checks of internal consistency.

☐ 12.4.2 Unfamiliarity and learning

Even if we get beyond warm glows and elicit meaningful values for environmental services, we must still appreciate that many individuals are simply unfamiliar with most of the services and functions that ecosystems and biodiversity provide. As an example, a survey of Scottish citizens revealed that over 70 per cent of the respondents were completely unfamiliar with the meaning of biodiversity (Hanley and Spash, 1993). Such levels of unfamiliarity are of concern if consumer sovereignty is to command respect in resource policy questions.

The question of unfamiliarity is central to understanding the values estimated with non-market valuation. Standard guidelines suggest that non-market valuation is more reliable if the respondent is familiar with the good. The person who is familiar with the good will be better able to value changes in its provision. For example, most US respondents would be familiar with the bald eagle, and may be able to provide dollar values for increased levels of the species. But for many other environmental assets, such as wetland filtration, most respondents may be unfamiliar with the asset she is being asked to value. Consider two aspects to this problem – value formation and preference learning.

Hoehn and Randall (1987) define value formation as the process by which an individual assigns a dollar value to a good, given that she completely understands her ranking of the good relative to other goods. That is, a person knows that she prefers improved environmental quality to a new toaster, but has not attached a monetary value to that preference. The formation of this monetary value is affected by the time and resource constraints inherent in any decision to allocate wealth. Time and resource constraints inhibit the individual's ability to comprehend the complex services provided by the good, thereby making the service appear unfamiliar. Hoehn and Randall examine how values are formed by comparing the values obtained under the ideal consumer problem with the values obtained given time and resource constraints. They argue that imperfect communication can cause an individual to undervalue the service relative to the same measure of value formed under ideal circumstances. This undervaluation problem can be alleviated if more time and decision resources are devoted to the value formation process.

Figure 12.5 illustrates the value formation issue. The revealed value is presented on the vertical axis, while time taken to learn is represented on the horizontal axis. Note that, as time taken to learn about the good is constrained, the individual's valuation is low relative to her 'true' value. The individual did not have enough time to translate her preferences accurately into a monetary value. But as the time to form a value is increased, she has more opportunity to translate preferences into a monetary manifestation, and therefore revealed value will approach true value from below.

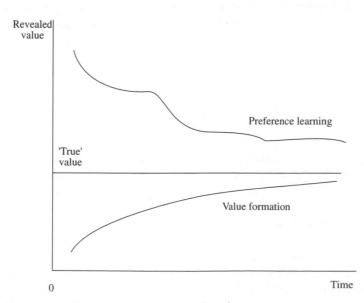

Figure 12.5 *Value formation and preference learning*

For example, suppose a policy increases the level of water quality such that there is a 50 per cent reduction in the ambient concentration of agrichemicals such as herbicides and fertiliser. If an individual could formulate a value from his preferences for this change without time or decision resource constraints, then we can write his Hicksian compensating measure as

$$HC(Q_0, Q_1, \bar{U}) = M - e(p, Q_1, \bar{U}) \qquad (12.20)$$

where

$$e(p, Q_1, \bar{U}) = \operatorname*{Min}_{x} [px \mid \bar{U} \geq U(x, Q_1)]$$

Note that HC is the economic value that accurately reflects the intensity of the individual's preferences for the increase in water quality.

Now if the individual cannot costlessly translate preferences into value because of time or decision resource constraints, it is likely that he or she will not be able to identify the minimum expenditure bundle, px^*, for the identified feasible bundles. If instead the individual settles for px^0 that satisfies the fixed utility constraint but, where $px^0 > px^*$ after some time-constrained search or decision, then

$$e(p, Q_1, t, \bar{U}^*) \geq e(p, Q_1, \bar{U}) \qquad (12.21)$$

and

$$fHC(Q_0, Q_1, t) = M - e(p, Q_1, t, \bar{U}) \leq HC(Q_0, Q_1, \bar{U})$$

where fHC is the time-constrained Hicksian compensating measure. Note that the net result of the constrained value formation process is that the value measure is not greater than the measure formed under ideal circumstances, $fHC \leq HC$. Incomplete value formation suggests that, if individuals know their preference ordering for all consumption bundles but are constrained by time or decision resources when translating this preference into a money metric, the revealed value will underestimate the true value of the increase in water quality.

However, the value formation argument presumes the individual understands her initial preferences for resources, and suffers no doubt about her preference for any additional outcome. This follows the standard view that preferences for goods are fixed and that changes in demand for an environmental service must occur because of changes in shadow prices, household technology or resource constraints. Demand changes cannot arise because the individual does not understand how an unfamiliar service affects his overall satisfaction or because of changes in preferences.

But there are numerous environmental goods and services with which individuals are unfamiliar. Frequently, the person has little day-to-day contact with the service, and has devoted little effort to understanding how these services affect her well-being. The individual, therefore, may well need to form conjectures and accumulate experience with the resource to assess more accurately her relative preference for the resource. If this is the case, then her revealed value will be greater than when she knows her preferences. The individual is willing to pay extra to acquire information about the potential value the resource may provide in the future. In contrast to value formation, this result suggests that a person will initially overvalue an unfamiliar environmental resource. Overvaluation should decrease, however, as the individual becomes more familiar with the service. Figure 12.5 illustrates this preference learning argument: as time increases, the revealed value approaches the true value from above.

More formally, consider Crocker and Shogren's (1991b) framework that describes the process of learning one's utility function in a multi-period world. Initially, the individual has some expectation of the utility he will derive from a particular environmental service – he does not know the exact utility that he will receive because he has not yet established the intensity of his preference for it. Given that each round of experience with the good constitutes a test of his conjectures about his preference for the commodity, the individual need not initially choose the commodity amount that will maximise his first-period utility. Instead, he may choose an amount that initially has smaller expected utility but which yields information about preferences that enables him to attain a greater utility level in subsequent periods. As he invests resources to gain more experience with the environmental service, his consumption horizon unfolds and his uncertainty about his utility function declines. The greater the initial investment, the more quickly can he determine this utility function. He deliberately invests in suboptimal commodity bundles to learn whether his currently conjectured preferences are true or in error.

Assume the individual chooses between two goods, x_1 and Q, to maximise his total expected utility – the sum of current utility $U(x_1, Q)$ and future utility $EU(x_1, Q)$, such that $U(\cdot) + EU(\cdot)$. He knows the utility he will derive from x_1 but does not know how, if at all, Q will offer utility. For example, x_1 might be electricity and Q might be rarely experienced, visibility-impairing levels of air pollution. For any particular value of x_1, the information the individual collects about his utility function is a non-decreasing concave function of the amount of Q that he consumes in the first period. This information allows him to increase his expected utility, $EU(x_1, Q)$, in future periods. Assume that $EU(\cdot)$ is non-decreasing in Q, implying that more valuable information is generated by greater consumption of Q – the individual can obtain a higher level of expected utility if beliefs are formed from a more informative experiment.

Given the two goods, one can select the appropriate measurement units so that $M = p_1 = q = 1$, where q is the shadow price of the environmental resource. Then $d_x = x_1$ and $d_Q = 1 - x_1$ represent the proportions of M spent on each good. In a single-period setting, the individual chooses x_1 and Q such that $\partial U/\partial x_1 = \partial U/\partial Q$. Let $(\hat{d}_x, \hat{d}_Q)$ be the solution to the one-period problem. It then follows from the concavity of the utility function that

$$\left.\begin{array}{l} d_x < \hat{d}_x \\ d_Q > \hat{d}_Q \end{array}\right\} \quad \text{if } \partial U/\partial x_1 > \partial U/\partial Q \tag{12.22}$$

and

$$\left.\begin{array}{l} d_x > \hat{d}_x \\ d_Q < \hat{d}_Q \end{array}\right\} \quad \text{if } \partial U/\partial x_1 < \partial U/\partial Q \tag{12.23}$$

In a multi-period programme, the individual will choose x_1 and Q in the first period such that $\partial U/\partial x_1 + \partial EU/\partial x_1 = \partial U/\partial Q + \partial EU/\partial Q$. Let $(\bar{d}_x, \bar{d}_Q)$ be this solution to the multi-period problem. By previous assumption, $\partial EU/\partial x_1 = 0$ and $\partial EU/\partial Q > 0$, which implies that $\partial U/\partial x_1 > \partial U/\partial Q$ if $(\hat{d}_x, \hat{d}_Q)$ is to be attained. It then follows that $\bar{d}_x < \hat{d}_x$ and $\bar{d}_Q > \hat{d}_Q$: the individual will be willing to pay relatively less for the commodity with the unambiguous utility impact, x_1, and relatively more for the service with the ambiguous utility impact, Q, than he would in a single-period problem or in a problem where he knows his utility function. Because $\bar{d}_x < \hat{d}_x$ and $\bar{d}_Q > \hat{d}_Q$ in the first period of the multi-period problem, $U(\hat{d}_x, \hat{d}_Q) - U(\bar{d}_x, \bar{d}_Q) > 0$: the individual sacrifices consumption utility in the first period to acquire information about the future utility that the environmental service might offer.

In addition, the greater the discrepancy between the expected and the realised utility of an environmental service, the greater the value of any information garnered by consuming the service in the initial period. If the individual has accumulated information about preferences, then $U(\hat{d}_x, \hat{d}_Q) - U(\bar{d}_x, \bar{d}_Q)$ must approach zero from above as time passes. The individual's expected and realised utilities will eventually coincide and he will no longer have an incentive to overconsume to acquire utility information. The individual's consumption of an unfamiliar environmental service will converge from above towards the level of consumption that would occur in a single-period problem or in a problem where he knows his utility function.

In summary, we have identified two effects of unfamiliarity and learning that work in opposite directions – value formation implies undervaluation, while preference learning implies overvaluation. This suggests that non-market valuation efforts should define explicit criteria which accurately specify the degree of value formation and preference learning. If such criteria can be defined, we can compare an individual's values when his situation, time and resource decision constraints, and his preference learning change simultaneously or sequentially. Otherwise, estimates of value for resources may well be misspecified.

■ *12.5* Concluding comments

This chapter has reviewed some theory of individual valuation for non-market goods such as environmental aesthetics or reduced risk. We have restricted our attention to measures of value, risk, and informational constraints. We have not addressed aggregation and temporal issues, nor have we considered how all forms anomalous behaviour due to cognitive illusions influence non-market valuation. These additional topics can be found in detailed discussions in Braden and Kolstad (1991) and Freeman (1993).

■ References

Arrow, K., R. Solow, P. Portney, E. Leamer, R. Radner and H. Schuman (1993) 'Report of the NOAA Panel on Contingent Valuation', mimeo, Washington, D.C.: Resources for the Future.

Braden, J. and C. Kolstad (eds) (1991) *Measuring the Demand for Environmental Quality*, Amsterdam: North-Holland.

Camerer, C. (1995) 'Individual Choice Theory', in J. Kagel and A. Roth (eds), *Handbook of Experimental Economics*, Princeton, Princeton University Press.

Cook, P. and D. Graham (1979) 'The Demand for Insurance and Protection: The Case of Irreplaceable Commodities', *Quarterly Journal of Economics*, 91, 143–56.

Crocker, T. and J. Shogren (1991a). 'Ex Ante Valuation of Atmospheric Visibility', *Applied Economics*, 23, 143–51.

Crocker, T. and J. Shogren (1991b) 'Preference Learning and Contingent Valuation Methods', in F. Dietz, R. van der Ploeg and J. van der Straaten (eds), *Environmental Policy and the Economy*, Amsterdam: North-Holland, 77–93.

Cummings, R., D. Brookshire and W. Schulze (1986) *Valuing Environmental Goods: An Assessment of the Contingent Valuation Method*, Totowa, NJ: Rowman and Allanheld.

Deaton, A.S. (1979). 'The Distance Function in Consumer Behavior with Application to Index Numbers and Optimal Taxation', *Review of Economic Studies*, 46, 391–405.

Desvousges, W., F.R. Johnson, R. Dunford, K. Boyle, S. Hudson and K. Wilson (1992) *Measuring Natural Resource Damages with Contingent Valuation: Tests of Validity and Reliability*, Research Triangle Park, NC: Research Triangle Institute.

Ehrlich, I. and G. Becker (1972) 'Market Insurance, Self-Insurance, and Self-Protection', *Journal of Political Economy*, 80, 623–48.

Freeman, A.M. (1993) *The Measurement of Environmental and Resource Values: Theory and Methods*, Washington, D.C.: Resources for the Future.

Graham, D. (1981) 'Cost-Benefit Analysis Under Uncertainty', *American Economic Review*, 71, 715–25.

Hanemann, M. (1991) 'Willingness to Pay and Willingness to Accept: How Much Can They Differ?', *American Economic Review*, 81, 635–47.

Hanley, N. and C. Spash (1993) *The Value of Biodiversity in British Forests*, Report to the Scottish Forestry Commission, University of Stirling, Scotland.

Helms, L.J. (1985) 'Expected Consumer Surplus and the Welfare Effects of Price Stabilization', *International Economic Review*, 26, 603–17.

Hey, J. (1979) Uncertainty in Microeconomics, New York: New York University Press.

Hoehn, J. and J. Loomis (1993) 'Substitution Effects in the Valuation of Multiple Environmental Programs', *Journal of Environmental Economics and Management*, 25, 56–75.

Hoehn, J. and A. Randall (1987) 'A Satisfactory Benefit Cost Indicator from Contingent Valuation', *Journal of Environmental Economics and Management*, 14, 226–47.

Kahneman, D. (1986) 'Comments', in R.G. Cummings, D. Brookshire and W. Schulze (eds), *Valuing Environmental Goods: An Assessment of the Contingent Valuation Method*, Totowa, NJ: Rowman & Allenheld, 185–94.

Kahneman, D. and J. Knetsch (1992) 'Valuing Public Goods: The Purchase of Moral Satisfaction', *Journal of Environmental Economics and Management*, 22, 57–70.

Kreps, D. (1990) *A Course in Microeconomic Theory*, Princeton: Princeton University Press.

Krutilla, J. (1967) 'Conservation Reconsidered', *American Economic Review*, 57, 787–96.

Machina, M. (1987) 'Choice Under Uncertainty: Problems Solved and Unsolved', *Journal of Economic Perspectives*, 1, 121–54.

Randall, A. and J. Stoll (1980) 'Consumer's Surplus in Commodity Space', *American Economic Review*, 71, 449–57.

Shogren, J. (1990) 'The Impact of Self-Protection and Self-Insurance on Individual Response to Risk', *Journal of Risk and Uncertainty*, 3, 191–204.

Shogren, J. and T. Crocker (1991) 'Risk, Self-Protection, and Ex Ante Economic Value', *Journal of Environmental Economics and Management*, 20, 1–15.

Shogren, J., S. Shin, D. Hayes and J. Kliebenstein (1994) 'Resolving Differences in Willingness to Pay and Willingness to Accept', *American Economic Review*, 84, 255–70.

Smith, V.K. (1987) 'Nonuse Values in Benefit Cost Analysis', *Southern Economic Journal*, 54, 19–26.

Smith, V.K. (1992) 'Arbitrary Values, Good Causes, and Premature Verdicts', *Journal of Environmental Economics and Management*, 22, 71–89.

Willig, R. (1976) 'Consumer's Surplus Without Apology', *American Economic Review*, 66, 589–97.

■ *Chapter 13* ■

Methods for Valuing Environmental Costs and Benefits

13.1 Introduction

13.2 Direct methods of valuation

13.3 Indirect methods of valuation

■ *13.1* **Introduction**

The previous chapter was concerned with an analysis of the theory behind the non-market economic value of the environment. This chapter, in contrast, is concerned with an analysis of methods for obtaining empirical estimates of environmental values, such as the benefits of improved river water quality, or the costs of losing an area of wilderness to development. By necessity, this chapter can only discuss briefly the many issues involved in what is now a vast literature. Excellent surveys of this literature can be found in Braden and Kolstad (1991) and Smith (1993).

Valuation methods are usually divided into two approaches: direct methods and indirect methods. Direct methods seek to infer individuals' preferences for environmental quality directly, by asking them to state their preferences for the environment. In contingent valuation surveys, for example, this might consist of asking people for either their maximum willingness to pay (WTP) for an increase in environmental quality or their minimum willingness to accept compensation (WTAC) to forgo such an increase. Respondents might instead be asked about their maximum WTP to avoid a decrease in environmental quality, or their minimum WTAC to accept this reduction. Because the level of environmental quality is usually chosen by a third party (such as the government requiring a certain level of air quality to be achieved) and not by the individual being questioned, these measures correspond to either Hicksian equivalent or compensating surplus (rather than equivalent or compensating variation, where quality/quantity is chosen by the individual). More general stated preference methods are also discussed in this chapter.

Indirect methods seek to recover estimates of individuals' WTP for environmental quality by observing their behaviour in related markets. In the hedonic pricing model, for example, the related market for urban air quality is the housing market, and economists seek to infer individuals' valuation of air quality improvements by considering their behaviour in this market. In the travel cost model, the analyst tries to infer the value people place on an outdoor recreational site through their expenditure on travel to the site.

■ *13.2*   **Direct methods of valuation**

☐ *13.2.1*   *The contingent valuation method*

The contingent valuation method (CVM) for the valuation of environmental goods was first used by Davis (1963) in a study of hunters in Maine. However, it was not until that mid-1970s that the method's development began in earnest (Brookshire *et al.*, 1976; Randall *et al.*, 1974). Since then, the method has become the most widely used and most controversial of all environmental valuation techniques. Comprehensive accounts of the method may be found in Mitchell and Carson (1989), Hanley and Spash (1993) and Bateman and Willis (1995). In what follows, we first run through the stages of a CVM, then review some major current controversies over the method. Finally, evidence on the reliability of CVM is considered.

Any CVM exercise can be split into five stages: (1) setting up the hypothetical market, (2) obtaining bids, (3) estimating mean WTP and/or WTAC, (4) estimating bid curves, and (5) aggregating the data.

Stage one: the hypothetical market

The first step is to set up a hypothetical market for the environmental service flow in question. For example, take a policy to restore old civic buildings in a city centre. Respondents might be told that the local government could engage in such restoration activities, describe what these would consist of and their effects, and explain that the operation could only go ahead if extra funds are generated. This sets up a *reason for payment* for services (the aesthetic quality of the built environment in this example), where no direct payment is currently exacted. How funds will be raised also needs to be described: the *bid vehicle* must be decided upon: for example, property taxes, income tax, utility bills, trust fund payments or entry fees. In this example, the bid vehicle could be higher property taxes or contributions to a civic trust fund. The survey instrument (questionnaire) should also describe whether all consumers will pay a fee if the change goes ahead, and how this fee will be set. How the decision on whether to proceed with the project (the *provision rule*) should also be explained. The questionnaire should be pre-tested before the main survey occurs: this is often done using small focus groups assembled to discuss their reactions to a questionnaire prior to a pilot study. The information given to respondents about all aspects of the hypothetical market, together with such information as is provided on the good being valued, constitute the 'framing' of the good.

Stage two: obtaining bids

Once the survey instrument is set up, the survey is administered. This can be done either by face-to-face interviewing, telephone interviewing or mail. Telephone interviews are probably the least-preferred method since conveying information about the good may be difficult over the telephone, partly owing to a limited attention time span. Mail surveys are frequently used, but suffer from potential non-response bias and often from low response rates. Interviews offer the most scope for detailed questions and answers, but interviewer bias may be a problem. The NOAA panel came out strongly in favour of face-to-face interviews in its appraisal of CVM (see Box 13.1).

Box 13.1   *The Exxon Valdez incident and CVM guidelines from the NOAA*

The wrecking of the oil tanker the *Exxon Valdez* off the coast of Alaska in 1989 was the somewhat unforeseen cause of a major spur to the development of CVM in terms of a legally acceptable method of valuing environmental damages in the USA. US law had gradually seen the introduction of damage claims for environmental losses, principally under the Comprehensive Environmental Response, Compensation and Liability Act regulations of 1986 and the Oil Pollution Act of 1990. Following a famous judgement by the DC Court of Appeals (*State of Ohio* v. *Department of the Interior*), non-use values (or more strictly, what has been termed 'passive use' values, including the values derived from watching wildlife on television, for example) were deemed relevant under this body of legislation, in that persons could sue responsible parties for lost passive use values. This clearly had an enormous implication for Exxon, since many of the environmental damages resulting from the Valdez spill (damage to wildlife and a pristine, fragile ecosystem) were likely to be passive use, as opposed to actual, active use, values, as actual active use of the area was relatively modest.

   As a counter to the possibly large size of damage claims being made against Exxon, the company funded a series of studies which basically tried to discredit CVM as a method for valuing losses in passive use values

(Cambridge Economics, 1992). The government body responsible for issuing regulations on the assessment of damages from oil spills, the National Oceanic and Atmospheric Administration (NOAA), convened a panel of distinguished economists thought to have no vested interest in the CVM method to conduct hearings on the validity of the CVM method in 1992. Members of the panel were Robert Solow, Kenneth Arrow, Edward Leamer, Paul Portney, Roy Radnor and Howard Schuman. The panel's report on their findings was published in January 1993 (*Federal Register*, 1993) and was basically a cautious acceptance of CVM for valuing environmental damages including lost passive use values. These findings have recently been developed as a set of proposed guidelines for future legally admissible CVM studies, which seem bound to at least influence the future development of the method (*Federal Register*, 1994).

The principal recommendations are as follows:

1. A dichotomous choice format should be used.
2. A minimum response rate from the target sample of 70 per cent should be achieved.
3. In-person interviews should be employed (not mail shots), with some role for telephone interviews in the piloting stages.
4. WTP, not WTAC, measures should be sought.
5. After excluding protest bids, a test should be made of whether WTP is sensitive to the level of environmental damage.
6. CVM results should be calibrated against experimental findings, otherwise a 50 per cent discount should be applied to CVM results.
7. Respondents should be reminded of their budget constraints.

These measures are, at the very least, a rather strange mixture of theoretically based recommendation and crude rules of thumb. It would be unfortunate if all CVM practitioners felt constrained to stick to these guidelines in future research, since the guidelines pose some awkward questions. These include the following:

1. Are all 'protest' bids giving the same signals? How should these signals be interpreted and utilised in any case?
2. Can the 50 per cent discount rule be justified empirically?
3. How can the weaknesses of the DC design format be overcome?
4. How do we decide what the relevant population should be from which to sample?

Individuals are asked to state their maximum WTP and/or minimum WTAC for the increase or decrease in environmental quality which is the subject of the survey. Taking WTP as an example, this figure may be derived in several ways:

1   As a bidding game: higher and higher amounts are suggested to the respondents until their maximum WTP is reached.

2. As a payment card. A range of values is presented on a card which may also indicate the typical expenditure by respondents in a given income group on other publicly provided services. This helps respondents to calibrate their replies.
3. As an open-ended question. Individuals are asked for their maximum WTP with no value being suggested to them. Respondents have often found it relatively difficult to answer such questions, especially where they have no prior experience of trading with the commodity in question.
4. As a closed-ended referendum: a single payment is suggested, to which respondents either agree or disagree (yes/no reply). Such responses are often known as dichotomous choice (DC) responses. Their analysis is more complicated than alternatives (1) to (3) above, since all that is revealed to the researcher is whether the respondent is willing to pay a particular sum (known as the offer price). A development of this method is known as 'trichotomous choice' valuation. Here, respondents who are indifferent to the offer price are explicitly modelled, along with those who reply 'yes' or 'no' (Svento, 1993). This state of indifference may be produced by vagueness on the part of respondents about the environmental change in question. Finally, double-bounded referendum models present those respondents who say 'no' to the first amount with a lower amount and those respondents who say 'yes' to the first amount with a higher amount (see, for example, Carson *et al.*, 1994).

Stage three: estimating average WTP/WTAC

If open-ended, bidding game or payment card approaches have been used, then the calculation of sample mean and/or median WTP or WTAC is straightforward. It is usual in CVM to find that mean WTP exceeds median WTP, since the former is influenced by a relatively small number of relatively high bids (that is, the distribution of sample WTP is skewed). If a dichotomous choice (DC) method has been used, then the calculation of average WTP/WTAC is more difficult, as we now explain.

In the DC framework, the researcher makes use of random utility theory (Hanemann, 1984). In particular, it is assumed that, whilst the representative individual knows their own preferences, these are not completely observable by the researcher. In particular, it is assumed that the utility function the individual has, $U = U(Q_j, y, x)$, where Q is the level of environmental quality, y is income (and all other goods, by implication) and x is a vector of socioeconomic characteristics, is only partly observable by the researcher. Suppose environmental quality improves from $j = 0$ to $j = 1$. The reseacher acts as though the utility function is:

$$v = (Q_j, y, x) + \varepsilon_j \qquad\qquad (13.1)$$

where ε_j is an identically and randomly distributed error with zero mean. Suppose now that the individual is asked if they would pay an amount A for the environmental improvement. The probability that they will accept this offer (that is, say 'yes') is:

$$Pr[\text{yes}] = Pr[v(Q_1, y - A, x) + \varepsilon_1) \geq v(Q_0, y, x) + \varepsilon_0] \qquad (13.2)$$

and the probability of saying 'no' is $\{1 - (Pr[\text{yes}])\}$. Equation (13.2) can be estimated statistically by first rewriting it as:

$$Pr[\varepsilon_0 - \varepsilon_1] \leq [v(Q_1, y - A, x)] - v(Q_0, y, x)] \qquad (13.3)$$

Define Δv as the change in the observable part of the utility function, and η as $(\varepsilon_1 - \varepsilon_0)$, and F_η as the cumulative distribution function of the error. We can then write that:

$$Pr[\eta \leq \Delta v] = F_\eta(\Delta v)$$

which, if $F_\eta(\Delta v)$ is assumed to have a logistic cumulative density function (as is often the case in empirical work), is equal to $(1 + e^{-\Delta v})^{-1}$. In order to proceed, a specific functional form for $v(\cdot)$ must be adopted; v may be simplified into the form $v = (\alpha + \beta y)$, with the change in utility determined by the change in this over the two states, and the offer price A. Supressing x in this case we have:

$$\Delta v = (\alpha_1 - \alpha_0) - \beta A$$

(where the α and β terms will depend on x), and the probability of a yes response is:

$$Pr(\text{yes}) = F_\eta[(\alpha_1 - \alpha_0) - \beta A]$$

Alternatively, if $v = \alpha + \beta \log y$, then the Δv is roughly equal to $(\alpha_0 - \alpha_1) - \beta(A/Y)$.

Utility-theoretic WTP measures are calculated by Hanemann from these models. Let W be true WTP (which is unobservable in the random utility framework). W is distributed according to the function G_w. Mean WTP is given by the integral:

$$\text{mean} \quad \text{WTP} = \int_0^T [1 - G_w] \, dA \qquad (13.4)$$

where T is some upper limit, infinite for a true mean or some upper value for a truncated mean. Median WTP is given by:

$$Pr[u(Q_1, y - W, x) \geq u(Q_0, y, x)] = 0.5 \qquad (13.5)$$

in other words, the WTP value at which exactly half of the population would say 'no', which is that value of A to which exactly half the population would say 'yes', since it is equal to or less than their true WTP). Hanemann gives formulae for the calculation of these values from the models for $v(\cdot)$. As Duffield and Patterson (1991a) point out, many CVM researchers use an alternative form for $v(\cdot)$ which, although (as Hanemann showed) does not give exact utility-theoretic measures of compensating or equivalent surplus, is thought to provide reasonable approximations. This involves specifying the probability that a respondent will say 'yes' to the offer price A as:

$$Pr[\text{yes}] = [1 + e^{-\alpha - \beta \log A}]^{-1} \qquad (13.6)$$

where the α term is the $(\alpha_1 - \alpha_0)$ term above. This is the model that Bishop and Heberlein (1979) used, and implies that WTP has a log-logistic distribution, which is everywhere positive and positively skewed. Median WTP can be calculated as $\exp - (\alpha/\beta)$; mean WTP must be evaluated by numerically integrating under the logistic function (13.6) between specified upper and lower bounds. Cameron (1988) gives an alternative approach to calculating welfare measures from DC data.

DC formats have a number of advantages over open-ended, payment card or bidding games:

1. They are incentive compatible, in that it is possible to show that the optimal strategy for a respondent is to reply truthfully to the CVM question, and not engage in strategic behaviour (Hoehn and Randall, 1987). In open-ended questions, the respondent may be attracted to either free-ride or overbid. (We briefly consider strategic behaviour later in this chapter.)
2. The payment/provision scenario under DC is more realistic, in the sense that individuals are usually faced with fixed prices for goods and services (and decide whether to buy or not at this fixed price). However, one might object that, since environmental goods are not usually traded in markets, this is a bogus claim.
3. It may be easier to convey the provision rule to respondents under DC ('If more than 50 per cent of respondents say "yes", then the project would go ahead.'); while the amount of environmental improvement that respondents are 'buying' may be easier to make clear.
4. In the USA, respondents may be familiar with voting on the supply of certain public goods.

However, against these advantages, certain disadvantages must be set:

1. There appears to be a tendency to say 'yes' to environmental improvements at higher stated offer prices than respondents would actually be willing to pay. This 'yea-saying' phenomenon might be linked with a reluctance on the part of respondents to signal a disapproval of environmental improvements, or a reluctance to trade off income/other goods against environmental quality. It is thus important to legitimise saying 'no' in the eyes of respondents. 'Don't know'

responses present a problem: should they be excluded, or interpreted as 'yes' or 'no' to the offer price? And does yea-saying negate the claim of incentive compatibility?

2. The estimates of mean and/or median WTP are sensitive to survey design and econometric practice. For example, the number of offer prices in a survey and their value are important. Cooper and Loomis (1992) showed that omitting or adding offer amounts in the upper end of the distribution (that is, at high prices) can significantly affect WTP estimates, although Kristrom (1990) found that WTP was more sensitive (by a factor of 50 per cent) to omitting the lowest offer price). A debate between these authors may be found in Kanninen and Kristrom (1993) and Cooper and Loomis (1992). Suggestions have been made for 'optimal' designs of DC formats in this respect: for example, Cooper (1993). Cooper's method involves basing offer amounts on the distribution of open-ended responses in a pilot survey, in order to minimise the mean square error of the welfare measure, given some finite sample size.

3. DC formats require larger sample sizes than open-ended, bidding game or payment card formats.

Stage four: estimating bid curves

Investigating the determinants of WTP/WTAC bids is useful in aggregating results (stage 5) and for assessing the validity of the CVM exercise. A bid curve can be estimated for open-ended CVM formats (which we now interpret as encompassing methods (1), (2) or (3) above), using WTP/WTAC amounts as the dependent variable and a range of independent variables. For instance, in an open-ended CVM survey, WTP bids might be regressed against income (Y), education (E) and age (A), as well as against some variable measuring the 'quantity' of environmental quality being bid for (Q), if this varies across respondents:

$$\mathrm{WTP}_i = f(Y_i, E_i, A_i, Q_i)$$

Dependent variables should clearly be chosen with regard to those variables which from a theoretical perspective might be expected to explain WTP. Bid curves are also useful to predict the valuation of changes in Q other than those suggested in the survey, and to test the sensitivity of WTP amounts to variations in Q. They also open up the possibility of predicting WTP amounts for changes in the level of some environmental variable Z, where Z and Q are both members of some set R, if stable and significant relationships can be found between Q and Y, A, E and other socioeconomic variables, and where the characteristics of Q can be mapped into those of Z. In DC frameworks, bid curves are the logit functions which predict the probability of a 'yes' response to a particular offer price. The explanatory power of bid curves (measured by adjusted R^2 or its maximum likelihood equivalent) might be considered a test of the success or failure of a CVM survey, in that a poor explanatory power indicates a poor survey. The reverse does not hold, however, in that high explanatory power does not necessarily mean reliable CVM results.

Stage five: aggregating data

Aggregation refers to the process whereby the mean bid or bids are converted to a population total value figure. This figure should include all those components of value found to be relevant (see below), such as existence value and use value, if a measurement of the total economic value for the environmental change/site in question is desired. Decisions over aggregation revolve around three issues.

First is the choice of the relevant population. This should have been decided when constructing the sampling frame from which the sample was drawn. The aim is to identify either (a) all those whose utility will be significantly affected by the action or (b) (which is the same or a smaller group) all those within a relevant political boundary who will be affected by the action. A decision must be made over the criteria to be used in deciding on who counts in (a) or (b). This group might be the local population, the regional population, the population of Scotland, or the population of the UK, or the whole of Europe.

Second is moving from the sample mean to a mean for the total population. Several alternatives have been proposed. The sample mean could be multiplied by the number of households in the population, N. However, the sample might be a biased reflection of the relevant population; for instance, it might have higher income levels or show a lower level of educational achievement. If these variables have been included in the bid curve, an estimated population mean bid, μ, can be derived by inserting population values for the relevant variables in the bid curve. This number could then be multiplied by N.

Third is the choice of the time period over which benefits should be aggregated. This will depend on the setting within which the CVM exercise is being performed. If the present value of environmental benefit flows over time is of interest, then benefits are normally discounted. Where an irreversible environmental loss is involved, then the present value is calculated by taking a perpetuity (that is, by dividing the constant real benefit flow by the discount rate). In all cases of benefit or cost flows over time where the time period is sufficiently long, society is confronted by the necessity of using current preferences to measure future preferences, as well as with the equity implications of discounting.

Problem areas in CVM may be listed as follows: (1) biases, (2) embedding, (3) WTP/WTAC differences, (4) information effects and (5) the transferability of benefit estimates.

Bias

Many early papers and books on CVM were very concerned with the large number of biases that could result from using the method. (Mitchell and Carson, 1989, give a compreshensive account of biases in CVM.) By 'bias', we mean a systematic over- or understatement of true WTP (or WTAC). Possible sources of such bias included the starting-point in bidding games (Boyle *et al.*, 1986; Thayer, 1981); the choice of bid vehicle (Rowe *et al.*, 1980) and hypothetical market bias (Bishop and Heberlein, 1979). Bishop and Heberlein found that actual WTP was overstated by WTP, as revealed in a CVM survey, since in the CVM process bids are not actually collected.

Another area of concern is strategic bias. If respondents believe that bids will be collected, they may understate their WTP for a welfare-improving change because environmental goods are typically non-excludable in consumption (the free-rider problem). For example, consider ten households living around a lake which is being polluted by a sewage works. Water quality can only improve if the works are upgraded, but this means higher sewerage bills for the households. Each household has an incentive to understate its maximum WTP to have the works upgraded (through higher bills), since they know that any improvement in water quality will benefit them as much as it benefits the other households, since the benefits of water quality are non-excludable in consumption. So by paying nothing, the free rider enjoys some benefits from improvements so long as someone states a willingness to pay higher bills, which is then translated into positive and better water quality.

The incentive to behave in this fashion could be reduced by stating that all will pay the average bid, or by stressing the hypothetical nature of the exercise and urging respondents to provide a true value, if they are able to formulate one. Alternatively, if respondents believe that their bids are purely hypothetical, they may overstate WTP for an environmental benefit, as this increases the probability of the improvement going ahead. Such behaviour can be reduced by suggesting that the survey results may indeed influence policy; they are therefore not purely hypothetical and might be collected (on the basis of average WTP) in order to provide the environmental gain in question. One suggestion may be to get respondents first to understate and then to overstate their true bid (using appropriate incentives) and then using the resultant interval of bids as guidance for policy makers. This essentially implies the acceptance of strategic behaviour within CVM.

Besides trying to reduce the likelihood of strategic bias, economists have been keen to test for its presence. With respect to the latter intent, two approaches are possible. First, one can examine the distribution of received bids and compare this with the hypothesised distribution of true bids (for example, Brookshire *et al.*, 1976). Strategic behaviour is assumed to flatten the distribution as relatively more high and low bids are made (over- and understatement). Negative bids are excluded, so that negative valuations accumulate as zeros. This tends to skew the distribution. Brookshire *et al.* assume that the true distribution is normal, concluding from this that there is no strategic bias in their sample, but the true distribution might equally be bimodal. However, even if one observed a concentration of very high and very low bids, this could be caused by other factors such as undetected protest bidding. Very high values may in any case cancel out very low values.

The second approach is to include questions to test for bias in the survey. This was done by Rowe *et al.* (1980): respondents were offered the chance to revise their bids following information on the mean bid recorded in the sample. Thus an individual who did not believe that her bid would actually be collected, but who wanted the environmental improvement to go ahead, might drastically increase her stated WTP in order to raise the mean bid, if she also thought that the actual decision over whether or not the environmental improvement would be provided would be based on this sample mean. Only one respondent revised their bid (an economics professor!).

Hoehn and Randall (1987) have argued that strategic bias can be eliminated by using a referendum format (yes/no responses) to parametrically increasing amounts. They show that truthful responses are always optimal in such a setting. Also, free-riding is a risky strategy if the supply of the public good is uncertain, but demand is certain: respondents may thus believe that they risk forgoing the environmental improvement by understating its true value, even though, if the good were provided, they might be able to free-ride. Milon (1989) and Bergstrom *et al.* (1989) find no statistically significant evidence of strategic behaviour occurring. Mitchell and Carson (1989) argue that strategic behaviour is more likely in mail surveys than in telephone or interview surveys, as respondents have more time for 'strategising' in the first case. They conclude that, on balance, strategic bias is of minor importance in well-designed CVM studies, especially as informational requirements for strategic behaviour are high. Recent findings from game theory and from experimental economics indicate that truth-telling may be optimal in revealing preferences over public goods in many circumstances (Evans and Harris, 1982).

The available evidence suggests that CVM studies are less prone to strategic behaviour than was once believed. However, this may apply less to

WTAC formats: asking individuals to state minimum compensation sums is clearly different from asking about maximum WTP. As discussed later, WTAC measures are problematic for other reasons as well.

A more recently recognised form of bias is mental account bias. The economic theory of consumer choice that lies behind demand curves (and thus consumers surplus) is based on the maximisation of utility subject to a budget constraint. In a hypothetical market, this constraint is not binding. Mental account bias (Hoevenagel, 1990) is possible where individuals have some 'mental account' for environmental protection, which is most easily envisaged as part of their total planned expenditure in a year. Imagine that Rose has decided that this year she is setting aside £100 of her income (which we will assume is equal to her annual expenditure) for spending on the environment. (Ecotec, 1993, report that average environmental spending in the UK was closer to £20 per person/year.) A CVM researcher asks her in January what she is willing to pay to protect rainforest in Borneo; Rose bids £50/year. In June, another CVM study estimates her WTP to clean up UK rivers at £35/year. In November, Rose is asked her maximum WTP to protect lowland heaths and bids £25/year, but now she has broken her mental account for the environment. The correct interpretation of her WTP bids is thus uncertain, since they cannot all be effective demands unless we permit Rose to revise her mental account as the year passes. Clearly the problem arises because (1) Rose does not know in January that she will be asked for other contributions; and (2) no actual expenditure is necessary on her part in any case. Given this possibility, many CVM surveys now ask respondents to state what existing expenditure they would reduce to free resources to cover their bid, but this is only a partial solution to this problem.

This phenomenon has also been discussed by Bishop and Welsh (1992), who refer to it as an adding-up problem, which they view as being synonymous with the path-dependency issue in standard welfare economics. Bishop and Welsh ask: if the citizens of Wisconsin reveal in a CVM exercise that, in aggregate, they are willing to pay $12 million to save an obscure fish (the striped shiner), would they be willing to pay $12 000 million to save 100 similar endangered but also obscure species? The answer must be no, since, if Wisconsin citizens view these endangered species as close substitutes for each other, the value placed on each one will depend on the order in which they are asked about the value of each. What is more, CVM studies which value, say, saving two species separately cannot be combined subsequently to show the value of an action which saves both species.

Embedding

Embedding occurs when the value placed on a good in a CVM study depends on the extent to which it is embedded in other goods. For example, a study could involve asking one sub-sample of respondents their maximum WTP to improve water quality in a particular loch in Scotland, Loch Tummel. A second sub-sample could be asked their maximum WTP to improve water quality in *all* Scottish lochs, and then asked their maximum WTP to improve quality at Loch Tummel alone. The embedding hypothesis is that the first response in each sub-sample is identical, in which case WTP for Loch Tummel = WTP for all lochs. Evidence to support the embedding hypothesis has been presented by Kahneman and Knetsch (1992), Diamond *et al.* (1992) and Desvouges *et al.* (1992).

Why might embedding occur? Most explanations revolve around a 'warm glow'/good cause argument. What people are doing in CVM studies is offering an amount of money that makes them feel good about their attitude to the environment. They therefore dump this 'warm glow' amount in the first commodity/scenario they are asked about in a CM study. Supporters of the warm glow view argue that this invalidates CVM. However, Carson *et al.* (1992) show that, according to the neoclassical model, we should expect embedding to occur, in that 'WTP for (an environmental good) will be greatest when valued first in a sequence (of environmental goods) and smallest when valued last'. This occurs as the result of substitution effects under imperfect information. In the same paper, the authors also review several empirical studies which test for but reject the existence of embedding. We note that some authors (such as Carson *et al.*) have sought to distinguish embedding from the related concept of nesting.

Differences between WTP and WTAC

In neoclassical welfare theory, WTP and WTAC are viewed as two equivalent ways of measuring either a decrease or an increase in welfare. Willig's famous 1976 paper showed that the difference between the two was in almost all cases very small, and due entirely to income effects, as was discussed in Chapter 12. However, many CVM researchers found that WTP measures were much less than WTAC measures for the same change in environmental quality (Rowe *et al.*, 1980; Hammack and Brown, 1974; Hanley, 1988). Initially, it was thought that this problem was unique to CVM, possible owing to the hypothetical nature of the exercise. However, an increasing body of evidence from the experimental economics literature also showed considerable divergences between the two measures (Knetsch and Sinden, 1984; Knetsch, 1989; Kahneman *et al.*, 1991). Moreover, this difference seemed to exist independently of income effects, transactions costs or how often the good was traded. This evidence suggests that people systematically value losses more highly than equivalent gains, and reductions in losses more highly than forgone gains (Knetsch, 1993).

Two, possibly competing, arguments have been put forward to explain this disparity. The first, associated with Knetsch and co-authors, and Kahneman and Tversky (1979) is loss aversion. This states that individuals judge all gains and losses from a reference point, which is their existing entitlement to resources (such as the existing level of air quality). Any decrease in the resource below this level causes a greater loss in welfare than the increase in welfare caused by an equivalent increase in the good. The implication is that we should expect WTAC to exceed WTP; and that, where a loss in welfare below the reference point is concerned, this should always be evaluated using a WTAC measure since WTP would understate the loss. Similarly, WTP measures should be used for environmental gains. This need for WTAC measures for losses is in direct conflict with the draft NOAA guidelines (see Box 13.1) which insist on WTP measures for losses.

The second explanation for WTP being less than WTAC revolves around substitution effects: this is the argument put forward in the preceding chapter.

Information effects

In most models of preference formation, information is crucial. For example, what people know about the hole in the stratospheric ozone layer and the cancer risks associated with it will influence the value they place on a programme to reduce emissions of ozone-depleting substances such as CFCs. Changing the information set that people hold will change their valuations of environmental goods, expressed in CVM studies as WTP or WTAC. Initial studies which found that changes in the information set held by individuals altered their WTP in CVM studies took the view that this constituted an undesirable bias. However, it may be argued that certain changes in the information set held by respondents should change their WTP and that, if CVM did not register these changes, it would be failing as a valuation method. A comprehensive review of CVM studies on information effects is given in Hanley and Munro (1994); here a brief account only is presented.

It is useful here to adopt Hoehn and Randall's two-stage conceptualisation of the process which individuals go through in forming responses to CVM surveys. This is that individuals first consider the proposed change in the environmental good, along with their preferences, income and the availability of substitutes and or complements for the good. This enables them to form a 'true WTP'. Individuals then decide whether to honestly reveal this value to the CVM researcher, as their 'stated WTP'. Stated WTP may differ from true WTP for reasons of strategic behaviour. True WTP may be affected by the researcher providing new information to respondents in the following categories:

- information about the characteristics of the good;
- information about substitutes/complements;
- information on relative expenditures.

In addition, stated WTP may be affected by:

- information on the behaviour of others;
- the provision rule.

Hanley and Munro (1994) report the results of a CVM survey of the protection of lowland heaths in southern England. Respondents were split into four groups, according to the type of information they were provided with in the CVM survey. Respondents then presumably combined this information with their priors in formulating their WTP for a policy to protect a specific heathland site (Avon Forest) and a different policy to protect all lowland heaths. The information sets were:

A. Information on the operation of the hypothetical market only (reasons for payment, bid vehicle).
B. Information on the declining level of heathland in the UK (that is, information on scarcity), plus that at A above.
C. Information on the animals and plants that could be found at Avon Forest, plus that at A above.
D. Information sets A, B and C.

As may be seen from Table 13.1, increases in information can produce big increases in estimates of WTP. This raises the awkward question as to how much information to provide in CVM surveys. This in turn raises the question as to how much information the average respondent (member of the general public) can absorb and understand. The Arrow–Solow panel (see Box 13.1) recommended that 'full, unbiased information' be supplied to respondents, with researchers seeking to test how well respondents have understood the information provided. This raises an awkward aggregation problem: can the WTP of individuals who have had their information sets added to in a CVM survey tell us anything about the WTP of the less-informed general public? (We are indebted to Colin Price for raising this question.)

Table 13.1 *Effects of more information on WTP to preserve heaths*

Scenario	Basic information (A)	Relative scarcity (B)	Characteristics (C)	Full information (D)
WTPs	6.77	11.49	10.39	10.32
WTPg	21.54	20.64	21.52	38.49

Notes: WTPs = site specific; WTPg = all heaths.

Benefits transfer

CVM surveys are expensive to carry out. It would therefore be an advantage if CVM results from one study could be generalised to other cases. For example, a CVM estimate of WTP for a given water quality improvement in a particular river (river A) might be capable of being 'transferred' to the measurement of the benefits of a similar improvement of water quality in a different river (river B), other things being equal. Such a straightforward transfer of benefits is not likely to be possible, however, since other things are typically not equal. For example, river A might support a wider range of uses than river B, or have different landscape qualities. River A might be the only one within 100 miles of the target population, whilst river B might be one of ten within a similar area. The population of beneficiaries for improvements to river A might be more wealthy and have a higher concern for water quality than those for river B. In a different context, Willis and Garrod report CVM estimates for recreation values for different forests in the UK varying by some 67 per cent, which is unsurprising, since both the forests and recreational populations differ greatly; Hanley and Ruffell (1993a) attempt to explain these differences econometrically (see Box 13.3 for details).

It is likely, therefore, that value estimates will have to be adjusted if transfers are to be made. This implies an empirical knowledge of the determinants of WTP. If, for example, we have been able to obtain WTP estimates for water quality improvements in 20 rivers across a country, it may be possible to relate these statistically to the socioeconomic characteristics using bid curves. Then it would be possible to predict WTP for a twenty-first river, using the estimated parameter values. However, given that many CVM studies result in bid curves where less than 50 per cent of the variation in WTP is explained, this procedure is open to criticism. Less rigorously, Willis (1995) surveyed UK estimates of CVM values for natural habitats, and found that values were higher where few substitutes exist than where many exist, and were higher when irreversible changes were in prospect. However, while such work can yield information on whether the CVM value in a given case should be higher or lower than some average, it does not tell us what that value will be in absolute terms, which is the sense in which values are used in cost–benefit analysis. Further discussion of benefits transfer in CVM may be found in Walsh *et al.* (1989).

Assessing the reliability of the CVM method

Two means of ascertaining the reliability of CVM results are test–retest procedures and convergent validity checks. Test–retest procedures involve conducting a CVM survey on a particular resource change and population of gainers/losers, then repeating the same CVM survey on a different sample from the same population some time (a few months, in most cases) later.

Results from the two samples are then compared for statistically significant differences. Jones-Lee *et al.* (1985) found statistically insignificant differences in mean bids for the same sample of people tested and then retested one month later. More recently, Loomis (1989) found no significant difference in CVM estimates of WTP to improve water quality in Mono Lake, in the Sierra Nevada mountains, when he resurveyed the original sample after a lapse of nine months. Loomis (1989, p. 83) concluded that 'the test–retest results... support the contention that the contingent valuation method provides reliable estimates of total willingness to pay for both visitors and [the] general [public]'. Test–retest correlations were higher for open-ended questions than for DC questions. Test–retest results for CVM were also reported by Laughland *et al.* (1991).

Convergent validity checks compare CVM estimates for a particular environmental good with estimates gained from other valuation methods such as the travel cost or hedonic price models. If a CVM study gives a result similar to a hedonic price or travel cost study, then at least the analysis is converging on one answer. Whether this is the correct answer may be unknowable but, without a reason to believe that the two methods should be converging on some other magnitude, it is reasonable to take the convergence of any two methods on the value of a given good as a desirable sign. However, defining convergence can itself be difficult. Many decisions must be made in the course of implementing any one of the methods, and the fact that there are cases where the correct choice is unknown means that more than one estimate is available from each technique. This makes comparisons vague. For example, Sellar *et al.* (1985) and Smith and Desvouges (1986) both produce more than one value estimate from each technique being compared (in these cases, TCM and CVM). Sampling, data analysis and survey instrument design all introduce possible bias and error into the calculation of a WTP amount. Authors engaged in convergent validity studies have therefore sought to find estimates which come within some specified or implicit bounds of other estimates. Cummings *et al.* (1986), in an early critical review of such work for CVM, use a ±50 per cent criterion (in terms of the acceptable overlap in consumers' surplus estimates). A comprehensive review of convergent validity results is given by Hanley and Spash (1993).

Enhancing reliability in CVM

Given the increased use of CVM, and the importance attached to CVM estimates of natural resource damages in US law, it is important to find ways of increasing the reliability of CVM. Guidelines for best practice in CVM have been proposed by several authors, such as Cummings *et al.* (1986) and Mitchell and Carson (1989); while the draft NOAA guidelines (see Box 13.1) seem likely to have a major influence in this respect. Increased use of focus groups, of the de-briefing of CVM respondents to see how well they have understood the survey, and why they gave the particular answers recorded, and further analysis of the human valuation process for environmental resources all seem likely to improve reliability. The CVM-X method (see Box 13.2) is another promising way of increasing reliability. While the jury is still out on the merits of CVM, the method has made much progress since its inception, and has yielded sufficiently encouraging results so far, in our view, to warrant further attention from both policy makers and environmental economists.

Box 13.2   *The CVM-X method*

Do people actually do what they say they will do in theory? This remains the central question in the debate over the contingent valuation (CVM) of non-market goods. If people do what they say, then economic values elicited from hypothetical questions can provide useful information. If they do not, then there are problems. Existing data suggest that hypothetical bids tend to overstate 'real' values obtained in actual markets (see Bishop and Heberlien (1979); Dickey *et al.* (1987); Duffield and Patterson (1991); Seip and Strand (1990)). Consequently, in its proposed regulations for natural resource damage assessment, the US National Oceanic and Atmospheric Administration (NOAA) has recommended that CVM values be deflated by a default factor of 50 per cent, unless they can be calibrated to actual market data. This arbitrary default factor will serve as a straw man until it can be determined if there is a systematic bias in hypothetical behaviour that can be statistically measured and corrected for with a calibration function.

Shogren (1993) introduced the idea of CVM-X into the calibration debate. The idea behind CVM-X is that it could be a cost-effective tool that combines the advantages of CVM and experimental auction markets by increasing the validity and accuracy of surveys while broadening the scope of non-market valuation in the lab. CVM-X consists of four basic steps. First, researchers run a CVM survey and elicit hypothetical values for the good in question. Second, the researchers bring sub-samples of the CVM respondents into the lab and elicit real bids for the actual good in an incentive-compatible auction that employs real goods, real money and repeated market experience. Experimental markets provide people with a well-defined incentive structure that enables the researcher to elicit more accurately the value of a non-market good, product or process. Third, estimate a calibration function relating the auction market bids of the sub-sample to their hypothetical bids (and other factors if appropriate). Fourth, use the estimated calibration function to adjust the values of CVM respondents who did not participate in the laboratory auction. Implicit in CVM-X is a test of validity since we can directly compare hypothetical bids with those elicited under non-hypothetical conditions in the laboratory.

Fox *et al.* (1994) provide the first application of the CVM-X method to value food safety, given that risk of illness is reduced by irradiation. They have demonstrated how the CVM-X method can verify and calibrate survey responses using experimental auction markets. Respondents were asked to value upgrades from typical to irradiated pork and vice versa. On average, respondents bid more in the hypothetical survey than in a non-hypothetical laboratory auction with real monetary incentives. The upward bias in hypothetical bids was greater in the sample bidding to avoid the irradiated pork. Fox *et al.*'s calibration procedure estimated that the hypothetical median bid for irradiated pork was overstated by about 9 per cent ($0.46 v. $0.50) and the median bid for non-irradiated pork overstated by 48 per cent ($0.27 v. $0.40). These results suggest that CVM-X can work, at least for private goods such as food safety. More application will be needed, especially with private proxies for public goods in laboratory markets, to understand the robustness of CVM-X.

□ 13.2.2 Stated preference methods

While it is true that CVM is a stated preference method, in that individuals state their preferences (in terms of WTP or WTAC) for environmental goods, it is only one example of this more general approach. Stated preference can be considerably generalised to encompass situations where individuals are asked either to rank a list of environmental options (contingent ranking: see Lareau and Rae, 1987) or else to choose between pairs of choices. These choices typically include attributes of the environmental good, and the cost of provision/access. These more general stated preference approaches have been pioneered by Adamowicz, Louviere and Williams (1994) with respect to environmental valuation, and in the general economics field by McFadden (1974, 1986). We illustrate the method using procedure and results from a stated preference study of recreational moose hunting in Alberta (Adamowicz *et al.*, 1994). In stated preference (SP) analysis, all possible attributes of the good in question are first identified, and ways found of measuring these attributes. Then, from the set of all attributes and all possible values these attributes could take, a much smaller sub-set is chosen using statistical design techniques. Interaction terms between attributes are usually ignored, in order to keep the design problem manageable. Alternative scenarios, between which respondents must choose, are selected so that the attributes of interest are not colinear (are 'orthogonal'); this assists subsequent econometric analysis of choices. In the moose hunting study, focus groups were used to identify those attributes of the hunting experience which were important to participants. These included moose population, crowding, ease of access, evidence of recent forestry activity, road quality and distance from home to site. Respondents were shown 16 choice sets, and in each case asked to choose one of three alternatives (site A, site B, or stay at home).

The means of obtaining welfare measures in SP analysis is similar to that used in the random utility model of dichotomous choice CVM, as discussed earlier, and the random utility version of the travel cost approach, discussed later on in this chapter. Each choice the respondent makes (for example, visit site A) generates utility for that site, U_i, according to a conditional indirect utility function:

$$U_i = V_i + \varepsilon_i \tag{13.7}$$

where V is an objective component and ε is an error term. The probability of choosing site i over site j is given by:

$$\Pi_i = Pr[V_i + \varepsilon_i > V_j + \varepsilon_j] \tag{13.8}$$

By making an assumption about the distribution of the error term, the parameters of the objective component V can be estimated.

In the moose hunting study, results from 266 hunters showed that utility increased as fewer other hunters are seen on a trip, and as moose populations increase. Increasing travel costs decrease utility. The value of increasing moose populations at one site was predicted from the SP model as $3.46 per trip. SP data can be combined with travel cost data (that is, based on actual rather than stated behaviour) and results from this exercise are given in Adamowicz *et al.* (1994).

The principal attraction of the SP approach, relative to CVM, is that it allows for the more direct valuation of the characteristics of environmental goods, which in turn is essential to benefits transfer. Stated Preference methods also avoid the 'yea-saying' phenomenon of DC CVM. However, the optimal design of SP experiments is an as yet to be settled research issue.

Box 13.3   *Contingent valuation of forest characteristics*

For some time now, environmental economists have been interested in how to explain estimates of consumer's surplus values for open-air, recreational resources. These resources have included rivers, forests and beaches. For example, an analysis of consumer's surplus estimates for the value of a day trip to a UK forest would show these to vary widely: the travel cost figures reported in Willis and Garrod (1991) range from £1.44 for Lorne (in Western Scotland) to £2.60 in the Brecon Beacons. Why should this be so? Clearly, a commonsense explanation would rely on a number of factors, including the attractiveness of any forest to the visitor. 'Attractiveness', however, is a difficult thing to measure empirically, although a number of proxy measures might be suggested. These might include the percentage of the forest accounted for by broadleaved trees, the extent of conifer diversity, and the presence or absence of marked paths and other interpretive facilities.

In a study reported in the *Journal of Agricultural Economics* in 1993, Hanley and Ruffell tried to explain the variation in consumer surplus amounts gained across UK public forests by variations in measurable characteristic levels (Hanley and Ruffell, 1993a). These characteristic measurements were taken both from Forestry Commission sources and from rankings by the forest visitors who were surveyed. For example, respondents were asked to score the quality of walking facilities, on a scale of one (poor) to five (excellent). This produced an average score for each forest for every characteristic so valued. Two CVM-based approaches were tried:

1. *A contingent valuation 'photograph pairs' approach.* Here, forest visitors were shown three pairs of photographs. In each pair, one characteristic varied significantly. For example, pair 'A' showed forests with and without a water feature. Respondents were asked to indicate their preference in each pair. Then they were asked to imagine that the preferred forest in each pair was more expensive for them to visit (in terms of travel costs) than the alternative, and to state the most extra travel costs they would be willing to incur to visit the preferred forest rather than the alternative. This gives an estimate for the marginal willingness to pay (WTP) for the increase in characteristic level for each pair. We found that 678 out of 899 respondents preferred a forest with greater height diversity, and were willing to pay an average of £0.33 extra in travel costs to gain access to this higher level of diversity (this compares to an average consumer's surplus for an individual's day visit to the forest, across the 60 forests in our study, of £0.93). Similarly, a majority of respondents preferred greater species diversity to less (with a mean incremental WTP of £0.49) and a water feature to no water feature (mean incremental WTP = £0.69). However, this approach suffers from a major weakness: it was not possible to measure how much of an increase in the characteristic levels respondents were 'buying' in each case.

2. *A contingent valuation bid curve approach.* Here, we statistically explained WTP bids for access to the forest where respondents were questioned, using bid curves. Explanatory variables in the bid curves included forest characteristic levels (11 characteristics were included); the main purpose of the respondents' visit (birdwatching, picnicking) and socioeconomic data on each respondent (age, income). We found that WTP for access to the forest increased as the level of many characteristics changed. Examples of this included increases in height diversity, the percentage of broadleaved trees, visitor's rating of views and the percentage of the forest as open space. In only a minority of cases, however, were these increases statistically significant, although with only one exception the direction of change of WTP was intuitively correct. The main weakness of this approach was the very large number of variables to be included in the bid curve, especially given the large

number of possible interactions between these variables: for example, height diversity might be more highly valued in a conifer-only forest than in a beech wood.

What conclusions can be drawn from this work, and from other similar studies? First, that it is possible to value changes in the levels of characteristics for outdoor recreational resources. This is important, since often management decisions will be taken which can change characteristic levels. Examples include decisions over the age structure and amount of open space in a forest, investments in water pollution treatment for public beaches, and restocking decisions in fishing rivers. Second, that variations in consumer's surplus estimates across different sites for a particular recreational resource can be explained. Third, however, that in many cases these two tasks may be difficult to implement in practice. For example, there are stark contrasts in the decisions a committed fisherman makes about which river to visit to fish for trout and the decision of a family about whether to visit a forest for informal recreation (and, if so, which forest to choose). In such 'informal' recreation settings, measuring the economic value of characteristics for resources such as forests can be a more difficult task.

■ *3.3* Indirect methods of valuation

An alternative to contingent valuation, and more general stated preference approaches, is to infer the value that individuals place on the environment from their behaviour in related markets. For example, the value an individual places on the opportunity to walk in a mountain area may be revealed by what that individual spends to get to the area. There are several such *indirect or revealed preference* approaches to environmental valuation, which are discussed at length in Braden and Kolstad (1991) and Hanley and Spash (1993). Here the major features of each are set down, and some examples of their use are given. The methods are the travel cost model and related random utility models; hedonic pricing; dose-response approaches; and averting expenditure/avoided cost approaches.

□ *3.3.1 The travel cost model and its variants*

This is one of the oldest approaches to environmental valuation, proposed in a letter from Harold Hotelling to the US Forest Service in the 1930s, first used by Wood and Trice in 1958, and popularised by Clawson and Knetsch (1966). The method involves using travel costs as a proxy for the price of visiting outdoor recreational sites. A statistical relationship between observed visits and the cost of visiting is derived and used as a surrogate demand curve from which consumer's surplus per visit-day can be measured (by integrating under this curve). The method has been widely used in both the USA and the UK for valuing the non-market benefits of outdoor recreation, especially recreation associated with national parks and public forests (Bowes and Krutilla, 1989). Recent developments of the technique allow the welfare effects of changing the characteristics of a site to be analysed. An excellent recent survey of the method may be found in Fletcher *et al.* (1990).

The travel cost method (TCM) assumes *weak complementarity* between the environmental asset and consumption expenditure. This implies that, when consumption expenditure is zero, the marginal utility of the public good is also zero. So if travelling to a forest becomes so expensive that no one goes any more, the marginal social cost of a decrease in the quality of that forest is also zero. The TCM cannot therefore estimate non-user values (although see Larson, 1992, for a contrary argument). An implicit assumption made in most travel cost studies is that the representative visitor's utility function is 'separable' in the recreation activity being modelled. This means that, if the activity of interest is fishing, then the utility function is such that demand for fishing trips can be estimated independently of demand, say, for cinema trips (alternative leisure activities) or for heating oil (alternative marketed non-leisure goods).

The simplest version of the TCM involves collecting data on visits to a site (V) from different parts of the surrounding country (zones, i) and explaining the visit rate per capita (V_i/P_i) as a function of travel costs, C_i. These costs are assumed to be some function of both distance and time spent travelling (travelling time is usually allocated a positive value to reflect the scarcity of leisure time) and of socioeconomic variables S_i.

$$V_i/P_i = f(C_i, S_i) \tag{13.10}$$

By predicting how visits per capita will fall as travel costs rise, a demand curve can be traced out for each zone, up to the cost at which visits become equal to zero (although in some functional forms of (13.9) visits will only approach zero asymptotically). Alternatively, visits per time period by a given individual j to a site ($VPAj$) may be used as the dependent variable, with the C and S terms becoming specific to that individual.

Many problems exist with such a simple model of the benefits of a single site. Most notably, the effect of other substitute sites is not included (Hof and King, 1982). This could be corrected by estimating, instead of (13.9):

$$V_i/P_i = f(C_i, S_i, X_i) \tag{13.10}$$

where X_i is a vector of 'prices' (that is, visiting costs) for other, substitute sites (Caulkins *et al.*, 1986). Alternatively, equation (13.10) may be estimated simultaneously for a group of sites (for example, all public forests within a region) (Burt and Brewer, 1974). Again, VPA may be the dependent variable rather than V/P.

Further problems exist with the model. These include, first, the value of travel/leisure time. Some authors (Chevas *et al.*, 1989) have argued that a distinction should be made between the commodity value of time, time that generates utility and the opportunity cost of time, which may be in terms of forgone earnings (in a minority of cases) or forgone recreational opportunities. They find the commodity value of time to be positive but small and call for this to be netted out from the opportunity cost of time in calculating consumer's surplus. Wilman (1980) argued that the distinction should be between on-site time and travel time. While the latter should be valued using the opportunity cost of recreation time (which, if labour market conditions permit, might be the hourly wage), the former should be valued in terms of travel time saved. The choice of a value for the cost of travel time can cause significant changes in consumer's surplus estimates. Such changes can also be caused by the choice of dependent variable (V/P or VPA): Willis and Garrod obtain estimates of consumer's surplus for UK forests which range from £1.44–£2.60 for V/P, and £0.12–£0.96 for VPA. In informal recreation settings, recall errors may be a problem in VPA data. Changes in consumer's surplus can also be brought about by the selection of functional form for the visit–travel cost equation: Hanley (1989) reports a variation from £0.32/visit (quadratic), £0.56 (semi-log independent), £1.70 (semi-log dependent) and £15.13 (log-log) for visits to Achray Forest in Central Scotland.

A final problem with the simple travel cost model considered here is that of multi-purpose trips. It may be necessary to distinguish 'meanderers' from 'purposeful visitors' in a sample of visitors to a site. The former describes those for whom a visit to the site in question is only part of the purpose of their journey. The latter term describes those for whom a visit to the site is the sole purpose of their trip. Consider people visiting a lake in a national park, who are also going on to visit a forest in the same national park. Clearly, some of the travel cost for such meanderers should be excluded from the minimum value they place on a visit to the lake, because they are also going to visit the forest during the same trip. Some of their travel costs should be apportioned to the lake, but how much? There are three options. The first is to ask people to score the relative importance of a visit to the lake; that is, relative to their enjoyment of the entire trip. This score, expressed as a number between 0 and 1, can be used to weight their total travel cost (for example, Hanley and Ruffell, 1993b). Second, meanderers may be excluded from the TCM analysis and a per visit consumer's surplus figure, based on these functions, computed. This average visitor consumer's surplus can then be aggregated across all visitors. This assumes, however, that meanderers, on average, value the site no less highly than purposeful visitors. Finally, separate demand functions could be estimated for each group.

On many occasions, policy makers are more interested in the value of changing the characteristics of a site rather than in the value of the site in toto. The travel cost model can be used for such calculations. A good example relates to changes in fishing quality at freshwater fishing sites. Two approaches may be distinguished: first, a 'varying parameter' model, whereby travel costs equations are initially estimated across a group of fishing sites. The travel cost coefficients from these equations are then regressed on the site characteristics (such as water quality, catch rates) across the sites in the sample. (These two steps can, in fact, be combined by specifying interaction terms between characteristics and travel costs in the initial equation: see Hanley and Ruffell, 1993b.) This enables the welfare gain associated with changing one of these characteristics to be estimated (Vaughn and Russell, 1982; Smith *et al.*, 1983). In the second approach, characteristics are used as shift variables in the visit–travel cost relationship. This was the approach taken by Loomis *et al.* (1986) to measure recreational fishing losses due to hydroelectric developments.

The hedonic travel cost model also attempts to place values on the characteristics of recreational resources. The hedonic travel cost model (HTC) was first proposed by Brown and Mendelsohn (1984), and has been applied recently to forest characteristics by Englin and Mendelsohn (1991) and to coastal water quality by Bockstael *et al.* (1987). The method is implemented as follows. First, respondents to a number of sites (for example, forests) are sampled to determine their zone of origin. The levels of physical characteristics (such as broadleaved/conifer areas and the percentage of forest as open space) are recorded for each site. Next a travel cost function is estimated for each zone:

$$C(Z) = c_0 + c_1 z_1 + c_2 z_2 + \cdots c_m z_m \tag{13.11}$$

where $C(Z)$ are travel costs, z_1 is distance to site, $z_2 \ldots z_m$ are characteristics and $c_0 \ldots c_m$ are coefficients to be estimated. A separate regression is performed for each zone of origin, so that each will have a vector of coefficients $\{c_0 \ldots c_m\}$ associated with it. For a given characteristic m, the utility maximising individual will choose visits such that the marginal cost of the characteristic (the coefficient c_m) is just equal to the marginal benefit to him or her. These marginal costs will vary, for a given characteristic, across zones of origin. As the forest is assumed to be a public good (and thus consumption of its recreational opportunities is non-rival), the marginal social value is the sum of all individual (zonal) marginal values. In Englin and Mendelsohn (1991), some of these marginal values are negative, implying that the individual would drive further to have less of the good. This is explained by Englin and Mendelsohn as being related to either undesirable characteristics (such as clear-cut or total felling) or cases where the individual is oversatiated with a desirable characteristic. In Bockstael *et al.* (1987) most of the marginal values which were thought a priori to be positive turned out to be negative in the estimation.

The second stage of the Brown–Mendelsohn approach is to estimate a demand curve for each characteristic. This is done by regressing site characteristic levels (the dependent variable) against the predicted marginal cost of that characteristic (which is implicitly the marginal value as explained above) and socioeconomic variables for each zone of origin. A separate regression is run for each characteristic. The expectation is that the coefficient on the marginal cost variable will be negative, so that, as the level of a characteristic rises, people are unwilling to pay as much for each further increment. Englin and Mendelsohn find this to be so for ten out of 11 characteristics modelled.

However, the HTC method has dropped somewhat out of favour with environmental economists owing to a number of problems, highlighted in papers by Bockstael *et al.* (1991) and Smith and Kaoru (1987). First, the marginal value of a characteristic in the HTC method is given by the extra costs individuals are prepared to spend to enjoy, for example, a river with a higher amenity value than a less visited, lower amenity site closer to home. Yet these relative values (that the clean river costs more to visit than the dirty river) are an accident of nature, in that the clean river just happens to be further away. Bockstael *et al.* give the example of the valuation of two characteristics of lakes, namely scenic beauty and fish catch. If fish catch increases with distance from a major population centre but scenic beauty simultaneously declines, then a positive price (value) for scenic beauty will not be found. Many authors have in fact found negative prices for characteristics which would be expected to have positive marginal values (see above). These difficulties have led some researchers to seek an alternative method of valuing site characteristics, with current research interest being centred on the random utility model of recreation demand.

The random utility model of recreation demand (Bockstael *et al.*, 1987; Coyne and Adamowicz, 1992; Adamowicz, Louviere and Williams, 1994) shares a theoretical foundation with the stated preference approach described in section 13.2 and the dichotomous choice variant of CVM. This is that utility is assumed to be composed of an observable, deterministic component and a random error term. Travel cost and characteristics data are collected for a number of substitute sites in an area. The probability that a given individual will visit site *i* rather than site *j* can then be calculated, depending on the costs of visiting each site and their characteristics, relative to the characteristics of all sites in the individual's choice set. In turn, estimates of the welfare effects of changing a characteristic can be arrived at. Bockstael *et al.* (1987) estimate a random utility model for choice of saltwater beach sites in the Boston area, and show that sites with higher pollution levels, higher noise levels and more crowding are less likely to be chosen. They also estimate a 'count' model which predicts how many trips will be made in total to all beaches in the area. Combining these models they are able to calculate the money value of benefits associated with reducing oil, chemical oxygen and faecal coliform pollution levels at all sites in the study area. A random utility model of hunting is described in Box 13.4.

Box 13.4 *A Random Utility model of Bighorn sheep hunting*

The random utility model is an extension of the travel cost model of recreation demand. Coyne and Adamowicz (1992) applied the method to the valuation of the site characteristics for alternative bighorn sheep (Ovis canadensis) hunting sites. Data came from a mail survey of registered hunters in Alberta. This survey gave information on socioeconomic characteristics, home location of hunter, number of hunting trips and choice of site. This gave 423 'choice occasions' when particular sites were chosen by particular hunters. A multinomial logit model (Madalla, 1983; Greene, 1990) showed that hunters' choice of site depended mainly on travel costs, total sheep population and crowding (number of hunters per unit area). This model also enabled the welfare effects of changes in these characteristics to be calculated: hunters would suffer a $7254 decrease in welfare per season if the resident sheep population fell by 10 per cent. Complete closure of any site was also valued; these values ranged from around $25000 to $4000 per season.

The reliability and validity of travel cost models has been addressed in a number of ways, including the use of the convergent validity criterion, whereby travel cost estimates for one site are compared with contingent valuation estimates for the same site (for example, Sellar, *et al.*, 1985; Smith and Desvouges, 1986). Another interesting approach has been the use of meta analysis. This involves trying to explain statistically the variation in consumer's surplus per visit across a large number of travel cost studies, according to the manner in which each was carried out (Smith and Kaoru, 1990). Results from one version of the models they estimate econometrically are given in Tables 13.2 and 13.3. The dependent variable is consumer's surplus per visit. As may be seen, this is statistically related to the treatment of substitute sites, the treatment of the opportunity cost of time, the type of recreational activities being undertaken (for example, hunting, swimming), the type of site (for example, river, wetlands, forest) and the functional form

Table 13.2   *Description of variables for analysis*

Name	Mean	Definition of variables
(*CS/v*)	25.24	Marshallian consumer surplus estimated per unit of use, as measured by each study (i.e., per day or per trip) deflated by consumer price index (base = 1967).
Surtype	0.86	Qualitative variable for measure of site use = 1 for per trip measure, 0 for per day measure.
Type of recreation activities		Water-based recreation (swimming, boating, fishing), hunting, wilderness hiking and developed camping were identified as the primary activities. The first three are introduced as qualitative variables with developed camping as the omitted category.
Type of recreation site		Lake, river, coastal area and wetlands, forest or mountain area, developed or state park, national park with or without wilderness significance are the designations. Coastal area and wetlands was the omitted category. Variables are unity if satisfying designation, zero otherwise.
Substitute price	0.29	Qualitative variable = 1 if substitute price term was included in the demand specification, 0 otherwise.
Opportunity cost type 1	0.24	Qualitative variable for the measure used to estimate opportunity cost of travel time = 1 if an average wage rate was used.
Opportunity cost type 2	0.32	Qualitative variable for the second type of opportunity costs of travel time measure = 1 for use of income per hour; the omitted category was the use of individual-specific wage rates.
Fraction of wage	0.37	Fraction of wage rate used to estimate opportunity cost of travel time.
Specific site	0.24	Qualitative variable for use of a state or regional travel cost model describing demand for a set of sites = 1, 0 otherwise.
Demand specifications		Linear, log linear and semilog (dep) are qualitative variables describing the specification of functional form for demand (semilog in logs of independent variables was the omitted category).
Year		The year of the data used in each study.
Estimators used[*]		OLS, GLS and ML-TRUNC are qualitative variables for estimators used; omitted categoris correspond to estimators with limited representations in studies – the simultaneous equation estimators.

[*] ML-TRUNC refers to maximum likelihood estimators adjusting for truncation and tobit estimators. GLS includes both single equation generalised least squares and seemingly unrelated regressions.
Source: Smith and Kaorn (1990).

Table 13.3 *Determinants of real consumer surplus per unit of use*

Intercept	−25.20
Surtype	19.18
(X_A) Type of recreation, Water based activities	45.39
Hunting	13.78
Wilderness	0.60
(X_s) Type of site, Lake	−21.19
River	−19.80
Forest	6.84
State park	22.18
National park	41.13
(X_B) Model assumption Substitution price	−14.39
Opportunity cost type 1	−14.28
Opportunity cost type 2	−15.89
Fraction of wage	48.59
Specific site/regional TC model	23.54
(X_D) model specification, Linear	−2.94
Loglinear	24.65
Semilog (dep)	18.61
(X_F) estimator OLS	−16.21
GLS	−8.58
ML-TRUNC	−68.98
R^2	0.43
n	399

Source: Smith and Kaorn (1990).

of the travel cost equation(s). Smith and Kaoru were able to explain 43 per cent of the variation in consumer's surplus figures across the studies and also to predict the effect on consumer's surplus of, for example, employing a particular functional form or treatment of travel time. Thus the consumer's surplus figures from travel cost studies are unlikely to be random numbers with no link to the value of a site: this is reckoned to be of some comfort to policy makers wishing to use such figures.

☐ *13.3.2 Hedonic pricing*

The hedonic pricing approach derives from the characteristics theory of value first proposed by Lancaster (1966) and Rosen (1974). This seeks to explain the value of a commodity as a bundle of valuable characteristics. One or more of these characteristics may be environmental. For example, the value of a particular house may depend on the number of rooms, whether it has a garden, and how close it is to the shops, but also on the noise level in the neighbourhood and/or air quality levels. Other possible environmental variables include pleasant views, distance from toxic waste dumps, or offensive smells from factories or farms. The hedonic price (HP) approach was first applied to environmental valuation by Ridker and Henning (1967) and proceeds through three stages. First, a hedonic price function is estimated; second, implicit prices are calculated for the environmental variable of interest; third, a demand curve for this variable may be estimated. The HP approach utilises the same weak complementarity assumption as does the travel cost method, and can thus only measure use (as opposed to non-use) values.

In order to estimate a hedonic price function, it is necessary to gather data on house sale prices and all characteristics of those houses thought relevant to their value. For example, the analyst might estimate:

$$Ph = f[S_i \ldots S_m; N_i \ldots N_n, Q_i \ldots Q_p] \tag{13.12}$$

where $S_i \ldots S_m$ are site characteristics (such as number of rooms, presence/absence of central heating), $N_i \ldots N_n$ are neighbourhood characteristics (crime rate, distance from city centre, quality of local schools) and $Q_i \ldots Q_p$ are environmental characteristics, such as air quality and noise levels. Partially differentiating with respect to any characteristic gives its implicit price. Unless (13.12) is linear, then these implicit prices will vary with the level of the characteristic. In Figure 13.1, we show the implicit

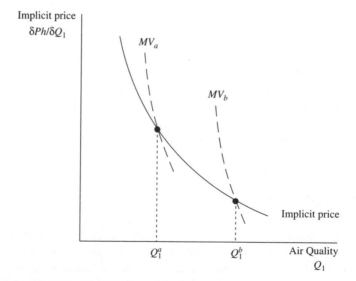

Figure 13.1 *Hedonic price measures of value*

price (the marginal cost) of environmental characteristic Q_1, which might be air quality, falling as Q_1 rises (although since the implicit price is everywhere positive, house prices are an increasing function of air quality levels).

So far, however, the analyst has only discovered the marginal cost for an individual of improving their personal level of environmental quality. To interpret this as a measure of the marginal benefit of improving environmental quality, the assumption must be made that each individual is in equilibrium in the housing market, in the sense that, for every characteristic, they have purchased exactly that amount which equates the marginal cost with their marginal valuation (MV). This is shown for two individuals in Figure 13.1, individuals a and b, who purchase levels Q_1^a and Q_1^b, respectively. If individuals are not in equilibrium in this sense (because, for example, they are poorly informed about how the level of air quality varies across a city), then implicit prices (marginal costs) cannot be interpreted as marginal benefits.

An optional third stage of a HP study pursued by authors such as Garrod and Willis, 1992 and Brookshire *et al.*, 1981, is to estimate an inverse demand curve for the environmental quality variable. This involves regressing calculated values of implicit prices against levels of the environmental variable and socioeconomic parameters. In the Brookshire *et al.* case, the authors had implicit price and quality observations for 14 neighbourhoods in the South Coast Air Basin of the western USA; community income was also included as an independent variable. Integrating under this function between two levels of environmental quality gives the total use benefits of an improvement from the lower to the upper level; the Brookshire *et al.* study found that improving air quality from 'poor' to 'fair' gave benefits of \$5800 per home per year.

Besides the assumption about equilibrium in the housing market discussed above, a number of other problems are associated with HP. These are discussed in detail in Hanley and Spash (1993) and Palmquist (1991). Briefly listed, they include the following.

1. Omitted variable bias: if some variable that significantly affects house prices is omitted from the HP equation, and is in addition correlated with one of the included variables, then the coefficient on this included variable will be biased.
2. Multi-collinearity: some environmental variables (such as alternative air pollution indicators) may be highly colinear. This means that separate equations for each may need to be estimated, otherwise the implicit prices will be difficult to disentangle.
3. Choice of functional form for the HP function. Economic theory does not specify which non-linear function should be used for the HP equation.

Choice of which form to use will thus depend on econometric considerations, although forms that give the best fit (such as flexible forms) may not have terms that are capable of economic interpretation (Cropper *et al.*, 1988). The choice of functional form will influence the value that implicit prices take.

4. Expected versus actual characteristic levels: house sales may be a function of expected future environmental conditions in addition to current observed conditions.

5. Attitudes to risk: Kask and Maani (1992) have pointed out that HP applications to the value of changes in risky environmental events (such as the Brookshire *et al.*, 1985, study of earthquake risks in California) are likely to produce biased estimates of consumer benefits of avoiding or reducing such risk. In choosing whether or not to buy a home in a safe area of San Francisco people are engaging in self-protection. When paying a premium for such a house, they reduce the probability of being located in an earthquake zone and thus reduce the expected loss from an earthquake. A problem arises in that individuals' subjective values of such losses are likely to be either less than or greater than the scientific (or endowed) probability of such events. This occurs for two reasons. First, studies have shown that people consistently overvalue very low probability events and consistently undervalue high probability events (Lichtenstein *et al.*, 1978; Viscusi and Magat, 1987). Second, people may have too little information, or information of too low a quality, to arrive at 'correct' probabilities. The implication, as Kask and Maani show, is that hedonic prices may either overestimate or underestimate welfare changes (according to whether a low or high objective probability event is being considered, and to the amount and quality of information available to individuals).

Examples of the application of HP to valuing the environment are Murdoch and Thayer (1988), Graves *et al.* (1988) and O'Byrne *et al.* (1985). The study by Garrod and Willis is briefly described in Box 13.5.

How reliable are hedonic price estimates of environmental benefits? Smith and Huang (1993) have recently conducted a meta analysis of 37 HP studies, to see how well they could detect the influence of air pollution on house prices. The authors report that 74 per cent of the studies found a negative and significant relationship between measures of air quality and house prices. They find that, overall, 'there is a systematic relationship between the modelling decisions, the descriptions used to characterise air pollution, the condition of local housing markets, and the conclusions reached about the relationship between air quality and house prices'. The pseudo-R^2 measure suggested that nearly 60 per cent of the variation in whether a significant relationship between air quality and house prices existed or not could be explained by the independent variables used.

Box 13.5 *A hedonic price study of forest amenity*

Many HP studies are concerned with air quality impacts on house prices. In contrast, Garrod and Willis consider the effects of proximity to woodland on house prices in Great Britain. If woods are a source of amenity, then being close to a wood should increase house prices, *ceteris paribus*. Garrod and Willis combined databases on house sales and structural characteristics with a Forestry Commission database, which showed the amount of woodland of three different types (all broadleaved; larch, Scots and Corsican pine; and all other conifers) in every kilometre grid square in Great Britain. Additional data, on regional unemployment, population density and age structure came from the Department of Employment's Manpower Information System. A hedonic price equation was estimated for all of Great Britain, treating it as one housing market. Results showed that house prices were positively related to the proximity of broadleaved woodland, but negatively and significantly to 'other conifers' (planted after 1940). House prices rose with proximity to larch, Scots or Corsican pine woods, but not significantly.

Owing to the functional form specified, implicit prices for each of these three types of woodland varied with the amount purchased, but holding all variables at their mean values gave implicit prices of £42.81 (per ha of broadleaved woods) and −£141 per ha of other conifers. People do not like living near to sitka spruce plantations on this evidence!

Garrod and Willis go on to estimate a demand curve for broadleaved woods. This is shown in Table 13.4 below. The price elasticity of demand for broadleaved woods is thus −1.76, and the income elasticity +0.82. Finally, the authors calculate an aggregate amenity value for all Forestry Commission woodlands in Great Britain using the implicit prices mentioned above; this gives a value of £353 323 per annum.

Table 13.4 *Demand curve for broadleaved woods*

Independent variable	Coefficient	t-ratio
lnIncome	0.8197	9.47
lnKids	0.4687	4.90
lnCon	−0.2763	−10.45
lnLarp	0.2013	5.34
lnMeanage	0.3214	2.89
lnPrice	−1.7600	−17.07

Notes:
$R^{2(adj.)} = 0.3114$ $n = 1031$

'lNnincome' is the log of current household income; 'lnKids' is the log of the number of children in the household; 'lnCon' is the log of the proportion of land

> in the kilometre grid square accounted for by conifers planted before 1940; 'lnLarp' is the proportion of larch, Scots and Corsican pine in the kilometre grid square; 'lnMeanage' is the average age of the adult members of the household; 'lnPrice' is the marginal implicit price from the hedonic price equation.

13.3.3 Dose response, averting expenditure and avoided cost methods

The dose-response method involves finding a link between environmental change and production conditions for some marketed good. Depending on the behavioural assumptions made and the statistical techniques employed, welfare estimates are then calculated using changes in, for example, profits from production of the marketed good. Two examples may be used to illustrate this approach. Ellis and Fisher (1987) estimate the contribution that wetlands protection makes to the production of shellfish. They estimate a production function for Florida blue crab off the Florida Gulf Coast which includes wetland acreage as an input, along with labour and capital. Wetland protection provides for increases in welfare through a rise in the total catch and a fall in the amount of effort that must be used to harvest a given catch. This increases producer's surplus. For example, the implied value of an increase in wetland acreage from 25 000 acres to 100 000 acres, calculated by this method, is $192 658 (in 1981$). A second example is the study by Kahn and Kemp (reported in Kahn, 1991). The authors carried out a very detailed dose-response analysis of the impacts of atrazine run-off from farmland on recreational and commercial fishing in Chesapeake Bay, owing to the loss of submerged aquatic vegetation (SAV). Increased atrazine levels in the water meant reduced habitat for striped bass, an important recreational and commercial fishing species. This in turn implied a lower carrying capacity and lower growth rates for the fishery. Marginal and total damage as a function of the percentage reduction in SAV due to atrazine leakage were calculated, using as a basis two equations relating (1) farm use of atrazine to atrazine concentrations in water; and (2) atrazine concentrations in water to the abundance of SAV. The former was specified (for a wet spring) as:

$$H = 20.7(A * CROP/3.36) \tag{13.13}$$

where H is the concentration of atrazine in parts per billion, CROP is the area planted, and A is the number of applications. The latter equation was specified as:

$$P = e^{-0.009H^{0.563}} \tag{13.14}$$

where P is the amount of SAV relative to what it would be in the no-pollution situation.

Many applications of the dose-response method have been made, especially with regard to air pollution damages to farm crops. Estimates tend to be sensitive to the modelling approach used (for example, linear programming versus a duality-based input demand approach) and to assumptions of the behavioural responses to environmental quality changes of consumers, producers and markets. For a fuller discussion of dose-response studies, see Hanley and Spash (1993).

The averting expenditure/avoided cost approach (like the travel cost model) employs the notion of a household production function. Households can be viewed as 'producing' certain service flows or goods, such as drinking water, by combining various inputs, one of which is environmental quality. Thus a rural household might combine water taken from its well with purification equipment to produce water fit to drink. If water quality in the well declines (owing, perhaps, to changes in farming practices) then the household must increase its expenditure on other inputs to maintain constant the quality of its drinking water. Courant and Porter (1981) showed that, under certain circumstances, this increase in 'averting expenditure' measured the welfare loss to the household of the decline in environmental quality. Box 13.6 gives an example of an application of the technique to drinking water quality. Other applications have been made to, for example, the value of reduced risks of car accidents (Blomquist 1979); the value of reduced risk of death as the result of fitting smoke alarms (Dardin, 1980) and noise nuisance from airports (Layard, 1972).

What are the conditions under which changes in averting expenditure (AE) produce exact welfare measures? First, the AE must not be a joint product (that is, must not generate other benefits apart from offsetting the change in environmental quality). Second, the AE must be a perfect substitute for the change in environmental quality. Third, the change in AE must be entirely due to the change in environmental quality. Fourth, none of the inputs (well water quality, water purification equipment) must enter directly into the person's utility function, only that which they produce (drinking water quality). Finally, expenditure must not yield benefits outliving the pollution incident.

These conditions could be summarised by saying that:

$$V(WQ^1, Y) = V(WQ^2, Y - AE) \qquad (13.15)$$

where V is indirect utility, WQ is well water quality, Y is income, AE measures averting expenditure and $WQ^1 > WQ^2$. In other words, utility with the higher level of well water quality and no averting expenditure is equal to utility with a lower level of well water quality and AE.

For more discussion of the *AE* approach, see Bartik (1988) and Harrington and Portney (1987).

Box 13.6   *Averting expenditure measures of groundwater quality*

Groundwater is an important source of drinking water supply in many parts of the United States, yet is threatened by numerous pollution inputs. Between 1985 and 1990, 33 states had enacted groundwater protection legislation in response to these threats (US Environmental Protection Agency, 1990). Abdulla *et al.* (1992) studied a groundwater contamination incident in southeastern Pennsylvania. In 1987, levels of trichloroethylele (TCE) seven times higher than the EPA's guidance limit were detected in wells owned by the municipality of Perkasie. A postal survey of 1733 households yielded 761 responses. This gave information on actions taken by the household to offset the possible presence of TCE in their water: these actions included buying bottled water, buying water treatment equipment, and boiling water. Time and money costs were included, yielding estimates of aggregate *AE* of between $61 313 and $131 334 over a 21-month period, depending on the household's valuation of their own time. Abdulla *et al.* also attempted to explain statistically the decision on whether or not to undertake averting expenditure, and how much *AE* to engage in. In the former case, respondents' rating of the cancer risk associated with TCE, the degree of information they had on the contamination incident and the presence of children in the household all significantly increased the probability of engaging in *AE*.

■ *13.4* Summary

In this chapter, we have looked at two classes of method for valuing the non-market aspects of the environment. Direct valuation methods, such as contingent valuation and stated preferences, can elicit both use and non-use values. Indirect methods, such as the travel cost and hedonic pricing methods, can only estimate use values, owing to the assumption of weak complementarity. All of the valuation techniques discussed here have been shown to suffer from numerous problems in their application, while it should be remembered that only utilitarian values for the environment are 'picked up' in all cases. Finally, we note that increasing use is being made of valuation techniques in policy making and litigation over the environment. Refining valuation methods is thus an important task for economists, in conjunction with other social and natural scientists, in the future.

■ References

Abdulla, C., B. Roach and D. Epp (1992) 'Valuing environmental quality changes using averting expenditures', *Land Economics*, 68, 163–9.

Adamowicz, W., J. Louviere and M. Williams (1994) 'Combining stated and revealed preference methods for valuing environmental amenities', *Journal of Environmental Economics and Management*, 26, 271–92

Adamowicz, W., P. Boxall, J. Louviere, J. Swait and M. Williams (1994) 'Stated preference methods for valuing environmental amenities', mimeo, Department of Rural Economy, University of Alberta.

Bartik, T. (1988) 'Evaluating the benefits of non-marginal reductions in pollution using information on defensive expenditures', *Journal of Environmental Economics and Management*, 15, 111–27.

Bateman, I. and K. Willis (eds) (1995) *Valuing Environmental Preferences: Theory and Practice of the Contingent Valuation Method*, Oxford: Oxford University Press.

Bergstrom, J., J. Stoll and A. Randall (1989) 'Information effects in contingent markets', *American Journal of Agricultural Economics*, 71, 685–91.

Bishop, R. and T. Heberlein (1979) 'Measuring values of extra market goods: Are indirect measures biased?', *American Journal of Agricultural Economics*, 61(5), 926–30.

Bishop, R. and M. Welsh (1992) 'Existence values in benefit–cost analysis', *Land Economics*, 68, 405–17.

Blomquist, G. (1979) 'Value of life saving: Implications of consumption activity', *Journal of Political Economy*, 87, 540–88.

Bockstael, N., M. Hanemann and C. Kling (1987) 'Estimating the value of water quality improvements', *Water Resources Research*, 23, 951–60.

Bockstael, N, K. McConnell and I. Strand (1991) 'Recreation', in J. Braden and C. Kolstad (eds), *Measuring the Demand for Environmental Quality*, Amsterdam: Elsevier.

Bowes, M. and J. Krutilla (1989) *Multiple Use Management: the Economics of Public Forestlands*, Washington, D.C.: Resources for the Future.

Boyle, K, R. Bishop and M. Welsh (1986) 'Starting point bias in contingent valuation surveys', *Land Economics*, 61, 188–94.

Braden, J. and C. Kolstad (1991) *Measuring the Demand for Environmental Quality*, Amsterdam: Elsevier.

Brookshire, D., B. Ives and W. Schulze (1976) 'The valuation of aesthetic preferences', *Journal of Environmental Economics and Management*, 3(4), 325–46.

Brookshire, D., R. d'Arge, W. Schulze and M. Thayer (1981) 'Experiments in valuing public goods', in V.K. Smith (ed.), *Advances in Applied Microeconomics*, (Vol. 1), Greenwich, CT: JAI Press.

Brookshire, D.S., M.A. Thayer, J. Tschirhart and W. Schulze (1985) 'A test of the expected utility model: Evidence from earthquake risk', *Journal of Political Economy*, 93, 369–89.

Brown G, and R. Mendelsohn (1984) 'The hedonic travel cost model', *Review of Economics and Statistics*, 66, 427–33.

Burt, O. and D. Brewer (1974) 'Estimation of net social benefits from outdoor recreation', *Econometrica*, 39, 813–27.

Cambridge Economics (1992) *Contingent Valuation: A Critical Assessment*, Cambridge, MA: Cambridge Economics.

Cameron, T. (1988) 'A new paradigm for valuing non-market goods using referendum data', *Journal of Environmental Economics and Management*, 15, 355–79.

Carson, R., N. Flores and M. Hanemann (1992) 'On the nature of compensable value in a natural resource damage assessment', paper to ASSA conference, New Orleans.

Carson, R., L. Wilks and D. Imber (1994) 'Valuing the preservation of Australia's Kakadu Conservation Zone', *Oxford Economic Papers*, 46, 725–49.

Caulkins, P., R. Bishop, and N. Bouwes (1986) 'The travel cost model for lake recreation: a comparison of two methods for incorporating site quality and substitution effects', *American Journal of Agricultural Economics*, May, 291–7.

Chevas, J.P., J. Stoll and C. Sellar (1989) 'On the commodity value of travel time in recreational activities', *Applied Economics*, 21, 711–22.

Clawson, M. and J. Knetsch (1966) *Economics of Outdoor Recreation*, Baltimore: Johns Hopkins University Press.

Cooper, J. (1993) 'Optimal bid selection for dichotomous choice contingent valuation', *Journal of Environmental Economics and Management*, 24(1), 25–40.

Cooper, J. and J. Loomis (1992) 'Sensitivity of WTP estimates to bid design in dichotomous choice contingent valuation', *Land Economics*, 68(2), 211–24.

Courant, P. and R. Porter (1981) 'Averting expenditures and the cost of pollution', *Journal of Environmental Economics and Management*, 8, 321–9.

Coyne, A. and W. Adamowicz (1992) 'Modelling choice of site for hunting bighorn sheep', *Wildlife Society Bulletin*, 20, 26–33.

Cropper, M., L. Deck and K. McConnell (1988) 'On the choice of functional form for hedonic price functions', *Review of Economics and Statistics*, 70, 668–75.

Cummings, R., D. Brookshire and W. Schulze (1986) *Valuing Environmental Goods: An Assessment of the Contingent Valuation Method*, Totowa, NJ: Rowman & Allenheld.

Dardin, R. (1980) 'The value of life: new evidence from the marketplace', *American Economic Review*, 70, 1077–82.

Davis, R. (1963) 'Recreation planning as an economic problem', *Natural Resources Journal*, 3(2), 239–49.

Desvouges, W., F. Johnson, R. Dunford, K. Boyle, S. Hudson and K. Wilson (1992) 'Measuring natural resource damages with contingent valuation: Tests of validity and reliability', in *Contingent Valuation: A Critical Assessment*, Cambridge, Mass.: Cambridge Economics.

Diamond, P., J. Hausman, G. Leonard and M. Denning (1992) 'Does contingent valuation measure preferences? Experimental evidence', in *Contingent Valuation: A Critical Assessment*, Cambridge, Mass.: Cambridge Economics.

Dickie, M., A. Fisher and S. Gerking (1987) 'Market transactions and hypothetical demand data: a comparative study', *Journal of the American Statistical Association*, 82, 69–75.

Duffield, J. and D. Patterson (1991a) 'Inference and optimal design for a wildlife measure in dichotomous choice contingent valuation', *Land Economics*, 67(2), 225–39.

Duffield, J. and D. Patterson (1991b) 'Field testing existence values: an instream flow trust fund for Montana rivers', paper presented to American Economics Association Conference, New Orleans, Jan.

Ecotec (1993) *A Cost-Benefit Analysis of Reduced Acid Deposition: A Contingent Valuation Study of the Aquatic Ecosystems*, Working Paper 5, Birmingham: Ecotec.

Ellis, G. and A. Fisher (1987) 'Valuing the environment as input', *Journal of Environmental Management*, 25, 149–56.

Englin, J. and R. Mendelsohn (1991) 'A hedonic travel costs analysis for the valuation of multiple components of site quality: the recreation value of forest management', *Journal of Environmental Economics and Management*, 21, 275–90.

Evans, R. and F. Harris (1982) 'A Bayesian analysis of the free rider meta-game', *Southern Economic Journal*, 49, 137–49.

Federal Register (1933) 'Report of the NOAA panel on Contingent Valuation', Washington, D.C.: US Govt., 58(10), 4601–14.

Federal Register (1994) 'Natural resource damage assessment: proposed rules', 59(5), 1062–91. Washington, D.C.: US Govt.

Fletcher, J., W. Adamowicz and T. Graham-Tomasi (1990) 'The travel cost model of recreation demand', *Leisure Sciences*, 12, 119–47.

Fox, J., J. Shogren, D. Hayes and J. Kliebenstein (1994) 'Calibrating contingent values with experimental auction markets', mimeo, Dept. of Economics and Finance, University of Wyoming.

Garrod, G. and K. Willis (1992) 'The amenity value of woodland in Great Britain', *Environmental and Resource Economics*, 2(4), 415–34.

Graves, P., J. Murdoch, M. Thayer and D. Waldman (1988) 'The robustness of hedonic price estimation: urban air quality', *Land Economics*, 64(3), 220–33.

Greene, W. (1990) *Econometric Analysis*, New York: Macmillan.

Hammack, J. and G. Brown (1974) *Waterfowl and Wetlands: Towards Bioeconomic Analysis*, Baltimore: Johns Hopkins University Press.

Hanemann, M. (1984) 'Welfare evaluations in contingent valuation experiments with discrete responses', *American Journal of Agricultural Economics*, 66, 332–41.

Hanley, N. (1988) 'Using contingent valuation to value environmental improvements', *Applied Economics*, 20, 541–9.

Hanley, N. (1989) 'Valuing rural recreation benefits: An empirical comparison of two approaches', *Journal of Agricultural Economics*, 40(3), 361–74.

Hanley, N. and A. Munro (1994) 'The effects of information in contingent markets for environmental goods', *Discussion Papers in Ecological Economics*, no. 94/5, University of Stirling.

Hanley, N. and R. Ruffell (1993a) 'The contingent valuation of forest characteristics: two experiments', *Journal of Agricultural Economics*, 44, 218–29.

Hanley, N. and R. Ruffell (1993b) 'The valuation of forest characteristics', in W. Adamowicz and W. White (eds), *Forestry and the Environment: Economic Perspectives*, Oxford: CAB International.

Hanley, N. and C. Spash (1993) *Cost–Benefit Analysis and the Environment*, Aldershot: Edward Elgar.

Harrington, W. and P. Portney (1987) 'Valuing the benefits of health and safety regulation', *Journal of Urban Economics*, 22: 101–12.

Hoehn, J. and A. Randall (1987) 'A satisfactory benefit cost indicator from contingent valuation', *Journal of Environmental Economics and Management*, 14(3), 226–47.

Hoevenagel, R. (1990) 'The validity of the contingent valuation method: Some aspects on the basis of three Dutch studies', paper to the European Association of Environmental and Resource Economists conference, Venice.

Hof, J. and D. King (1982) 'On the necessity of simultaneous recreation demand equation estimation', *Land Economics*, 58, 547–52.

Jones-Lee, M., M. Hammerton and P. Philips (1985) 'The value of safety: results from a national sample survey', *Economic Journal*, 95: 49–72.

Kahn, J. (1991) 'Atrazine pollution and Chesapeake fisheries', in N. Hanley (ed.), *Farming and the Countryside: an economic analysis of external costs and benefits*, Oxford: CAB International.

Kahneman, D. and J. Knetsch (1992) 'The purchase of moral satisfaction', *Journal of Environmental Economics and Management*, 22(1), 57–70.

Kahneman, D. and A. Tversky (1979) 'Prospect theory: an analysis of decision taking under risk', *Econometrica*, 47(2), 263–91.

Kahneman, D., J. Knetsch and R. Thaler (1991) 'The endowement effect, loss aversion and status quo bias', *Journal of Economic Perspectives*, 5, 193–206.

Kanninen, B. and B. Kristrom (1993) 'Sensitivity of WTP estimates to bid design in dichotomous choice valuation models: comment', *Land Economics*, 69(2), 199–202.

Kask, S. and S. Maani (1992) 'Uncertainty, information and hedonic pricing', *Land Economics*, 68(2), 170–84.

Knetsch, J. (1989) 'The endowment effect and evidence of nonreversible indifference curves', *American Economic Review*, December 1277–84.

Knetsch, J. (1993) 'The reference point and measures of welfare change', paper to Canadian Conference on Environmental and Resource Economics, Ottawa.

Knetsch, J. and J. Sinden (1984) 'Willingness to pay and compensation demanded: Experimental evidence of an unexpected disparity', *Quarterly Journal of Economics*, 94(3), 507–21.

Kristrom, B. (1990) 'A non-parametric approach to the estimation of welfare measures in discrete response valuation studies', *Land Economics*, 66, 135–9.

Lancaster, K. (1966) 'A new approach to consumer theory', *Journal of Political Economy*, 74, 132–57.

Lareau, T. and D. Rae (1987) 'Valuing willingnes to pay for diesel reduction odours', *Southern Economic Journal*, 728–42.

Larson, D. (1992) 'Further results on willingness to pay for nonmarket goods', *Journal of Environmental Economics and Management*, 23(2), 101–22.

Laughland, A., W. Musser and L. Musser (1991) 'An experiment on the reliability of contingent valuation', Staff Paper 202, Department of Agricultural Economics, Penn State University.

Layard, R. (1972) *Cost-Benefit Analysis*, Harmondsworth: Penguin.

Lichtenstein, S., P. Slovic, B. Fischoff, M. Layman, and B. Combs (1978) 'Judged frequency of lethal events', *Journal of Experimental Psychology*, 4(6), 551–78.

Loomis, J. (1989) 'Test–retest reliability of the contingent valuation method: a comparison of general population and visitor responses', *American Journal of Agricultural Economics*, February, 77–84.

Loomis, J., C. Sorg and D. Donnelly (1986) 'Economic losses to recreational fisheries due to small head hydro development', *Journal of Environmental Management*, 22, 85–94.

Madalla, F. (1983) *Limited-dependent and qualitative variables in economic analysis*, New York: Cambridge University Press.

McFadden, D. (1974) 'Conditional logit analysis of qualitative choice behaviour', in P. Zarembka (ed.), *Frontiers in Econometrics*, New York: Academic Press.

McFadden, D. (1986) 'The choice theory approach to market research', *Marketing Science*, 5, 275–97.

Milon, J. (1989) 'Contingent valuation experiments for strategic behaviour', *Journal of Environmental Economics and Management*, 17, 293–308.

Mitchell, R. and R. Carson (1989) *Using Surveys to Value Public Goods: the Contingent Valuation Method*, Washington, D.C.: Resources for the Future.

Murdoch, J. and M. Thayer (1988) 'Hedonic price estimation of variable urban air quality', *Journal of Environmental Economics and Management*, 15, 143–6.

O'Byrne, P, J. Nelson and J. Seneca (1985) 'Housing values, census estimates, disequilibrium and the environmental cost of airport noise', *Journal of Environmental Economics and Management*, 12, 169–78.

Palmquist, R. (1991) 'Hedonic methods', in J. Braden and C. Kolstad (eds), *Measuring the Demand for Environmental Quality*, Amsterdam: Elsevier.

Randall, A., B. Ives and C. Eastman (1974) 'Bidding games for the valuation of aesthetic environmental improvements', *Journal of Environmental Economics and Management*. 1, 132–49.

Ridker, R.G. and J.A. Henning (1967) 'The determinants of residential property values with special reference to air pollution', *Review of Economics and Statistics*, 49, 246–57.

Rosen, S. (1974) 'Hedonistic prices and implicit markets: product differentiation in pure competition', *Journal of Political Economy*, 82, 34–55.

Rowe, R., R. d'Arge and D. Brookshire (1980) 'An experiment on the economic value of visibility', *Journal of Environmental Economics and Management*, 7, 1–19.

Seip, K. and J. Strand (1990) 'Willingness to pay for environmental goods in Norway: A contingent valuation study with real payment', Memorandum 12, Department of Economics, University of Oslo.

Sellar, C., J. Stoll and J.P. Chevas (1985) 'Validation of empirical measures of welfare change', *Land Economics*, 61(2), 156–75.

Shogren, J. (1993) 'Experimental markets and environmental policy', *Agricultural and Resource Economics Review*, 22, 117–29.

Smith, V.K. (1993) 'Non-market valuation of environmental resources' *Land Economics*, 69, 1-26.

Smith, V.K. and W. Desvouges (1986) *Measuring Water Quality Benefits*, Boston: Kluwer Nijhoff.

Smith, V.K. and JiChin Huang (1993) 'Hedonic models and air quality; 25 years and counting', *Environmental and Natural Resource Economics*, 3(4), 381–94

Smith, V.K. and Y. Kaoru (1987) 'The hedonic travel cost model: A view from the trenches', *Land Economics*, 63(2), 179–92.

Smith, V.K. and Y. Kaoru (1990) 'Signals or noise? Explaining the variation in recreation benefit estimates', *American Journal of Agricultural Economics*, May, 419–33.

Smith, V.K., W. Desvouges and M. McGivney (1983) 'Estimating water quality benefits: an econometric analysis', *Southern Economic Journal*, 50, 422–37.

Svento, R. (1993) 'Some notes on trichotomous choice valuation', *Environmental and Resource Economics*, 3(6), 533–44.

Thayer, M. (1981) 'Contingent valuation techniques for assessing environmental impacts: further evidence', *Journal of Environmental Economics and Management*, 8, 27–44.

US Environmental Protection Agency (1990) *Progress in Groundwater Protection and Restoration*, EPA 440/6-90-001, Washington, D.C.: Office of Water.

Vaughn, W. and C. Russell (1982) 'The value of a fishing day: an application of the varying parameter model', *Land Economics*, 58(4), 450–63.

Viscusi, W. and W. Magat (1987) *Learning about Risk: consumer and worker responses to hazard information*, Cambridge, Mass.: Harvard University Press.

Walsh, R.G., D.M. Johnson and J.R. McKean (1989) 'Issues in non-market valuation: a retrospective glance', *Western Journal of Agricultural Economics*, 14, 178–88.

Willis, K. (1995) 'Benefits transfer', in K. Willis and J. Corkindale (eds), *Environmental Valuation: New Directions*, Oxford: CAB International.

Willis, K. and G. Garrod (1991) 'An individual travel cost method for evaluating forest recreation', *Journal of Agricultural Economics*, 42, 33–42.

Wilman, E. (1980) 'The value of time in recreation benefit studies', *Journal of Environmental Economics and Management*, 7, 272–86.

Wood, S. and A. Trice (1958) 'Measurement of recreation benefits', *Land Economics*, 34, 195–207.

■ *Chapter 14* ■

The Economics of Sustainable Development

14.1 Introduction

14.2 Possible sustainability rules

14.3 Indicators of sustainability

14.4 The Common–Perrings model
of sustainable development

■ *14.1* Introduction

Within the field of environmental economics, it is now widely recognised that the goal of sustainable development is principally an equity, rather than an efficiency, issue (Howarth and Norgaard, 1993). This is not to say that economic efficiency is irrelevant to sustainable development, as reducing the quantity of natural resources used up per unit of human satisfaction will clearly help reduce demands on the environment. However, as will be shown, economic efficiency is *not* a sufficient condition for sustainable development. Thus removing government policies or market failures which encourage inefficient use of environmental resources may improve the prospects for sustainable development, but will not guarantee it. Achieving sustainable development (SD) involves achieving equity both within generations (intragenerational equity) and across generations (intergenerational equity). As Asheim puts it: 'Sustainable development is a requirement to our generation to manage the resource base such that the average quality of life we ensure ourselves can potentially be shared by all future generations' (Asheim, 1991).

In this chapter our stress will be very much on equity between generations, rather than equity across a given generation. This is not to suggest that the latter is less important than the former, indeed the influential report by the World Commission on the Environment and Development (the Brundtland Report) in 1987 was keen to stress that these two aspects of equity were equally important, spelling out as it did the links between poverty and environmental degradation in developing countries. However, the large volume of literature on intragenerational equity is impossible to do justice to in this book; thus we leave readers to explore this area on their own (for an excellent introduction, see Dasgupta,

1988). Neither do we touch on the awkward question of whether the developed nations of the world should be allowed to restrict development in poorer parts of the world on the grounds that such development is environmentally damaging and unsustainable (an example here would be export-led growth through the felling of tropical rainforest), since the developed world attained its present state by engaging in comparable environmental degradation in the past. The industrial revolution of the eighteenth and nineteenth centuries was in many ways fed by the running down of environmental capital in the now developed world. However, identifying the appropriate trade-offs between intra- and intergenerational equity is an awkward issue.

Early work in neoclassical growth theory which incorporated natural resource contstraints on economic activity (Solow, 1974; Hartwick, 1977) implicitly modelled SD as non-declining consumption over time, and was concerned with intergenerational efficiency rather than equity. This literature led to the development of the Hartwick rule, explained below. However, given that individuals derive utility directly from the environment, and not just from the consumption goods that are produced partly with natural resources, non-declining consumption has been replaced by non-declining utility as a goal of policy in economic models (Pezzey, 1992). An alternative way of considering SD has been to concentrate on means rather than ends: since resources are necessary to produce utility, some constraint on the amount of resources passed forward to future generations might be an appropriate way of achieving SD.

In this chapter we shall set out certain approaches to operationalising SD (these approaches will be called 'rules'). Once possible rules for achieving SD have been identified, it is possible to discuss a range of indicators which might show whether an economy was becoming more or less sustainable. A variety of indicators are thus discussed, along with data requirements for implementing these indicators. Finally, we outline one important model of sustainable development, that of Common and Perrings (1992).

■ *14.2* **Possible sustainability rules**

□ *14.2.1　The Hartwick–Solow approach*

In an influential paper in 1977, John Hartwick proposed a rule for ensuring non-declining consumption through time, in the case where an economy made use of a non-renewable resource (such as oil) in its economic process. Hartwick showed that, so long as the stock of capital did not decline over time, non-declining consumption was also possible. The stock of capital could be held constant by *reinvesting all Hotelling rents from non-renewable resource extraction in man-made capital.* These rents are those resulting from the intertemperally efficient extraction programme for the non-renewable resource; although the price vector used to calculate these rents must be 'sustainability prices', prices from an inter-temporal model that includes a sustainability constraint (Toman *et al.*, 1994). Thus, as the stock of oil (a type of 'natural' capital) runs down, the stock of man-made capital is built up in replacement. This result has been very important for the development of the economics of SD. It arises in the Hartwick model owing to the assumptions employed therein: crucially, that the aggregate production function for consumption goods is a Cobb–Douglas one. This implies that, as the amount remaining of the non-renewable resource goes to zero, its average product goes to infinity (so that, even though the natural resource is technically essential for the production of consumption goods, it does not act as a constraint to growth). What is more, man-made and natural capital in this model are assumed to be perfect substitutes for each other (the elasticity of substitution is equal to one).

Criticisms of the Hartwick rule follow three lines. First, that individuals derive utility directly from the environment, and do not view it merely as an input to production. If this is the case, non-declining consumption is not equivalent to non-declining welfare over time. Second, that the rule depends on the particular functional form chosen for the aggregate production function. Hartwick was able to restate his rule for a CES (Constant Elasticity of Substitution) production function (Hartwick, 1978), but this function had the property that the elasticity of substitution between the natural resource and man-made capital was greater than one, so that the fixity in supply of the natural resource is actually irrelevant (Common and Perrings, 1992).

The third criticism of the Hartwick rule is that natural resources and man-made capital are not nearly so substitutable as the Hartwick–Solow approach suggests. In what follows, it will be useful to compare 'natural' capital with man-made capital. Natural capital may be defined to comprise all gifts of nature: land, animals, fish, plants, non-renewable and renewable energy and mineral resources. Natural capital can be exploited by man, but cannot be created by man (although management might increase breeding rates, for example). According to what might be termed the 'thermodynamic' school (Christensen, 1989), natural capital and man-made capital are in most cases complements rather than substitutes. Christensen terms the various elements of the natural capital stock 'primary inputs', and man-made capital and labour the 'agents of transformation'. While substitution possibilities are possibly high within each of the two groups (for example, wood for leather, plastics for copper, or machines for labour), substitution possibilities between the two are very low. Increasing output thus means increasing use of both types of input in most cases.

14.2.2 Non-declining natural capital stock approaches

Rather a different approach to the limited degree of substitutability between natural capital (*Kn*, from now on) and man-made capital (*Km*) is that of the London school (Pearce *et al.*, 1990; Klaasen and Opschoor, 1991; Pearce and Turner, 1990). Here the view is taken that, whilst some substitution is possible between certain elements of *Kn* and *Km* (for example, better machinery, meaning that less raw materials are used to produce certain products), many elements of *Kn* provide non-substitutable services ('keystone processes') to the economy. Examples of such 'critical' natural capital are the processes responsible for regulation of atmospheric composition, the spiritual values provided by wildlife, and nutrient cycles. If humans need the services of ecosystems, it is important to maintain these ecosystems in a functioning state. This in turn means protecting their natural resilience (ability to withstand shocks), which may be achieved by ensuring that certain species ('keystone species') are preserved (Turner, 1993). This concept of a critical component of the natural capital stock is taken up again in the model we present in the fourth section of this chapter.

If it is necessary to maintain some amount of the natural capital stock constant in order to allow future generations to reach the same level of utility as the average held by this generation, this holding constant of the natural capital stock becomes a rule for SD. The important question here, however, is: how much of *Kn* should be held constant? Three possible views would be (1) the existing level, (2) the level consistent with maintaining the critical element of *Kn*, and (3) some amount in between these two. All three of these alternatives, however, assume that we can measure the value of *Kn* at any point in time; in other words, that the different elements of *Kn* can be aggregated together in comparable units. For example, should natural capital be measured in physical or monetary units? Physical units confound addition since an oak forest cannot be added to a blue whale. Only if the two types of natural assets are expressed in a common numeraire can they be aggregated, the most obvious unit being money. However, this may be seen as objectionable, since one whale worth £10 million is then equivalent to 1000 whales worth £10 000 each. If natural assets are held constant in physical terms, the level at which the category is defined will become all-important. Consider the maintenance of woodlands in Britain by constant total area. This woodland stock definition might raise the objection that a hectare of sitka spruce is less valuable than a hectare of native Scots pine or of ancient oak. The category could be disaggregated to hold constant the stock of deciduous trees and the stock of conifers. However, some might wish to go further and distinguish between different types of deciduous woodland (oak forests, birch scrub and so on). Van Pelt (1993) identifies another problem with the constant natural capital stock concept. This is the problem of spatial aggregation: within which geographic area should we hold stocks constant?

If the natural capital stock cannot be fully aggregated, it may be necessary to compartmentalise it by sector, and keep each compartment constant. Van Pelt (1993) suggests pollution, renewable resources, biodiversity, pollution assimilation capacity (including, for example, the pollution assimilation capacity of wetlands) and non-renewable resources as possible categories. To these might be added the integrity of nutrient cycles. However, non-renewable resources, such as oil, are by definition fixed finite stocks which must decline with use. The only ways to maintain a constant economic reserve are for new discoveries to equal extraction and/or for costs per unit extracted to decrease with technological progress as quickly as they rise as the result of cumulative extraction. More strictly, given a finite total crustal abundance (see Chapter 8) of each non-renewable resource, only a zero extraction rate is consistent with a constant natural capital stock unless trade-offs are permitted between renewable and non-renewable resources.

Supposing that the aggregation problem for natural capital can somehow be overcome (perhaps by extensive disaggregation into separate classes and physical quantification), a rule for SD suggested by the London school is *to prevent reductions in the level of Kn below some constraint value* (or series of values for the separate classes). This might appear a heavy restriction on development if the current level of *Kn* is chosen as the constraint, since it would involve all projects/policies having a deleterious effect on *Kn* to be banned. The alternative to this suggested by Pearce *et al.* involves the use of 'shadow projects'. These are projects/policies designed to produce environmental benefits, in terms of additions to *Kn*, to exactly offset reductions in *Kn* resulting from a specified collection ('portfolio') of projects or policies. For example, such a portfolio could be all public sector investment projects in Scotland in 1992, or the sum total of a company's activities. Neglecting for the present the tremendous data requirements involved in fully operationalising this procedure, the idea is to impose either a 'weak' or a 'strong' sustainability constraint as a rule for SD.

The weak constraint might be stated as follows. Assume that B_t represent the benefits from the investment portfolio, C_t represent the non-environmental costs, E_t the environmental costs (such as habitat loss), and δ_t is the discount factor. Assume also that *Kn* is measured in monetary units. The normal cost–benefit analysis criterion is that, over the discrete time period $t = 1 \ldots T$,

$$\sum_{t=1}^{T} B_t \delta_t - \sum_{t=1}^{T} C_t \delta_t - \sum_{t=1}^{T} E_t \delta_t > 0 \qquad (14.1)$$

that is, that the sum of discounted net benefits is positive. The weak sustainability constraint is that:

$$\sum_{t=1}^{T} \sum_{i=1}^{n} E_{it}\delta_t \leq \sum_{t=1}^{T} \sum_{j=1}^{m} a_{jt}\delta_t \tag{14.2}$$

where there are $i = 1 \ldots n$ projects/policies in the portfolio and $j = 1 \ldots m$ shadow projects, and where a represents the environmental benefits associated with each shadow project a_{jt}. The strong sustainability constraint is:

$$\sum_{i=1}^{n} E_i \leq \sum_{j=1}^{m} a_j \qquad \forall t = 1 \ldots T \tag{14.3}$$

Thus, in the weak form, the discounted sum of environmental costs must be no greater than the discounted sum of offsetting benefits over the time period in question. In the strong form, however, we require that environmental costs are no greater than environmental benefits in *each time period*. This is clearly a more restrictive condition. Note that application of these shadow project rules requires a monetary evaluation of *all* environmental impacts. For a detailed criticism of the shadow project concept, see Hanley and Spash (1993). Note also that the natural capital stock level which becomes the constraint level need not include all species, so that this rule does not justify all nature conservation actions (Holland and Rawles, 1993).

☐ 14.2.3 The safe minimum standards approach

Closely linked to the non-declining natural capital stock approach is that of safe minimum standards (SMS), identified primarily with Ciriacy-Wantrup (1952) and Bishop (1978, 1993). The SMS approach originates from decision making under uncertainty. Society is deemed to be unsure about the future costs of current environmental degradation. Broadly, two classes of action may be taken: conserve environmental resources (such as a wilderness area) or do not conserve. Deciding not to conserve a resource is usually referred to as a decision to 'develop' (although this form of words has some unfortunuate internal inconsistencies!). Deciding to conserve today is shown to be the risk-minimising way to proceed if we are unsure about the consequences of environmental degradation, in that conservation can minimise the maximum possible loss to society (see Tisdell, 1990). As Randall and Farmer (1995) have pointed out, an SMS approach shifts the burden of proof from those who wish to conserve to those who wish to develop. The SMS rule is: prevent reductions in the natural capital stock below the safe minimum standard identified for each component of this stock unless the social opportunity costs of doing so are 'unacceptably' large.

How are these SMS levels identified? This has only really been worked out for flora and fauna, and corresponds to their minimum viable population levels in an area. An example would be the minimum viable population of spotted owls in the Pacific North-West, or minimum number of red kites in Wales, to ensure the survival of these species in these areas. Hanley *et al.* (1991) suggested that the current stock of Sites of Special Scientific Interest (SSSI), or possibly some higher number of sites, could be treated as an SMS for nature conservation sites in the UK. How should 'unacceptably large' opportunity costs of preservation be identified? By social consensus and the democratic process (although note that it is still only the preferences of the current generation that counts here). Perhaps for smaller scale potential losses, government agencies could be relied on to take such decisions. For larger losses, public referenda would be necessary. Economists would be charged with identifying the opportunity costs of conservation and with designing cost-minimising policies to protect the SMS; but not with estimating the non-market values of conserving wildlife, for example, since the economic benefits of conservation do not enter the SMS rule directly.

The key difference between the SMS approach and the critical natural capital approach is that, under the former, the SMS for any resource type is allowed to be breached if society deems the opportunity costs of preserving the SMS to be unacceptably high. Under the latter, however, no consideration is given to the costs of protecting the critical natural capital stock, which is to be preserved regardless of any cost consideration.

□ 14.2.4 Daly's 'operational principles'

In a 1990 paper in Ecological Economics, Daly identified what he termed 'operational principles' for SD. If these principles were followed, then nations could move towards a SD position. The principles are as follows:

OP1.   Renewable resources (fish, forests, game). Set all harvest levels at less than or equal to the population growth rate for some predetermined population size (remember that density-dependent growth is the rule for such resources).

OP2.   Pollution. For degradable pollutants, establish assimilative capacities for receiving ecosystems and maintain waste discharges below these levels. Daly proposes no rule for cumulative pollutants, but the implication is that their discharge should be set close to zero.

OP3.   Non-renewable resources. Receipts from non-renewable extraction should be divided into an income stream and an investment stream. The investment stream should be invested in renewable substitutes (for example, biomass for oil) such that, by the time period when the non-renewable resource reaches the end of its economic extraction, an identical level of consumption is available from the renewable substitute to what was available from the non-renewable resource at the start of the depletion programme. Only the income stream should be available for consumption. The proportion of funds which it is necessary to divert to the renewable substitute will depend on its growth rate, the rate of technical progress, the discount rate and the size of the non-renewable resource (El-Serafy, 1989). OP4.   Controls on macroeconomic scale. Daly believes that it is vital to minimise matter/energy throughput in the economy. This is a question of 'scale'. Such controls must be quantitative, and aimed at population levels and resource use.

What is not clear, however, is the extent to which Daly's rules are actually operational. For example, much scientific uncertainty exists over the assimilative capacities of ecosystems for many pollutants, while the calculation of the investment stream for non-renewables would be exceedingly difficult. Finally, the identification of the maximum (or optimal?) scale of the world economy, and the designing of policies to ensure these scales are realised, are both tasks which are fraught with difficulty.

☐ *14.2.5   Other possible rules*

One misconception which it is important to correct here is concerned with the valuation of non-market environmental goods. It might be thought that, if all environmental externalities are correctly valued (using methods such as contingent valuation and hedonic pricing), and if these values are properly incorporated in decision making by both private individuals/firms and governments, then the economy will move towards a sustainable development path. This is incorrect. While the correct valuation of non-market environmental goods is essential for an economy to be (intertemporally) efficient in its use of resources, it does *not* guarantee that the economy will develop sustainably. This is easily seen from equation (14.1) above: environmental costs (E_t) may be outweighed by net developement benefits ($B_t - C_t$), so that the cost–benefit analysis rule is consistent with a declining level of environmental quality and thus unsustainable development on natural capital stock grounds. This will be so unless shadow project constraints are implemented.

   That valuation of the environment will not necessarily result in SD has also been shown by Howarth and Norgaard (1992). In Figure 14.1, we show a utility possibility frontier, defined on given tastes, technology and resource endowments, across two generations. If environmental goods are incorrectly

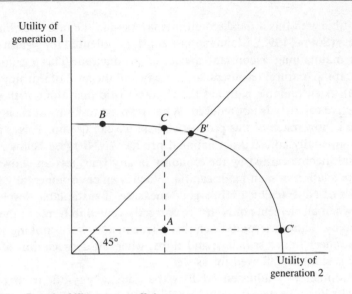

Figure 14.1 *Sustainability versus efficiency*

valued, then the economy must be at some point inside this frontier (for example, at point *A*). Correct valuation makes the economy efficient (we assume no other distortions), which might move the economy to point *B*. However, the move from *A* to *B*, whilst efficient, is not consistent with SD since the utility (welfare) of generation 2 has been reduced below that of generation 1. This will be so unless costless transfer mechanisms enable us to redistribute utility from *B* to, say, *B'*. Points along the line segment *B'C* can only be chosen if we know what the intertemporal social welfare function looks like.

We conclude this section by noting that, irrespective of the definition adopted for sustainability, there may be many paths that are sustainable over time: choosing amongst these paths is not an issue which we have addressed here (Pezzey, 1994).

■ *14.3* Indicators of sustainability

14.3.1 The Solow/Hartwick approach to sustainability and 'green' GNP

Methodological basis

The general definition of SD adopted here is that every future generation must have the option of being as well off as its predecessor. Discounting is compatible with this if the discount rate is less than the rate of technological progress (Solow, 1992). Maintaining a constant potential for wealth creation means maintaining a constant means of production. This includes man-made capital, natural resources, technology and the level of learning (human capital). A sustainable path has the characteristic that along it this overall productive capacity is not reduced. What we need to know at each moment in time is how much of this productive base we can use up. This is given by environmentally adjusted net national product (NNP) (see below). NNP is the total income earned by the economy in any year, less an allowance for the depreciation of man-made capital. When is an environmentally adjusted measure of NNP (call it ENP) a good measure of sustainable development? First, when all elements of NNP are correctly valued in terms of the current economic situation; second, when this is true in a forward-looking sense too (prices reflect future scarcity); and third, when all depreciation of natural capital is similarly allowed for as well.

Environmentally adjusted NNP is the annual 'pay-off' from our total (natural plus man-made) capital stock. ENP can rise through time if this total capital stock rises, and/or as technology improves. How can the total stock of capital be maintained? By following the Hartwick rule: each year, reinvest the Hotelling rents (price minus marginal cost) from an optimal non-renewable resource extraction plan in new natural or man-made capital. So the indicator is: is ENP rising or falling? If ENP is falling, then society's sustainable level of income is falling too.

Correct adjustments to GNP

The topic of adjusting the system of national accounts to incorporate SD considerations has been widely debated in the literature. Important references include Hartwick (1990a, 1990b), Maler (1991), Weitzman (1976), Solow (1986, 1992), Ahmad *et al.* (1989) and Lutz (1993). The analysis presented below is adapted from Hartwick (1990a) and treats each broad class of the natural capital stock separately. Net national product clearly fails as a measure of SD owing to many aspects of natural resource depletion being ignored by the system of national accounts (SNA); whilst expenditure on pollution clean-up actually adds to NNP, with any loss in welfare due to the pollution itself being ignored. Box 14.1 makes this clear with regard to several examples.

Box 14.1   *Natural resource accounting*

A country can fell its forests, erode its soils, exhaust its minerals, pollute its aquifers and erase its wildlife, without adversely affecting its measured income. By failing to recognise the asset value of natural resources, the UN

System of National Accounts (SNA) misrepresents the policy options which nations face. Although the model balance sheet in the SNA recognises land, minerals, timber and other environmental resources as economic assets to be included in a nation's capital stock, the SNA's income and product accounts do not. This mismatch can hide permanent losses of wealth beneath an illusion of gains in income.

In Costa Rica increases in the rates of deforestation, soil erosion and the consequent impacts on inshore fisheries and coral reefs, compounded by overexploitation, have had major socioeconomic impacts. Natural resource accounts compiled for the 1970s and 1980s using remotely sensed data on land use change, field data on forest productivity, GIS (geographic information system) studies of soil erosion and sample studies of fish populations reveal only part of the problem. The studies together suggested that Costa Rica had been depleting its forest, soil and fishery capital by at least 5 per cent average GDP per year since 1970. The asset value and sustainable profits of the principal fish species in the major fishing area in the Gulf of Nicoya dropped to zero as fishermen's earnings fell below the level of welfare payments to the destitute. Leaving aside the unquantified service value of Costa Rica's forests (as wildlife habitat, tourist attractions, ecosystem regulators and suppliers of non-timber products), the forestry sector generated substantially negative net national income throughout the 1980s and overall deforestation estimates from 1966 to 1989 were 28.2 per cent. Ignoring declines in soil fertility due to losses of micronutrient, biological activity and desirable soil structure, and restricting off-site concerns to siltation effects on hydroelectric systems, economic losses, primarily through the cost of replacing lost macronutrients, accounted for 8–9 per cent of all agricultural production (13 per cent for livestock and 17 per cent for annual crops). Using these conservative figures it can be shown that natural resource depreciation rose from 26 per cent of gross capital formation in 1970 to 39 per cent in 1989. Thus the conventional accounting framework overstated actual net capital formation by 70 per cent in 1989 (Repetto, 1990, 1992, 1993).

Using oil and forestry data for 1970–84 from Indonesia and a Javanese soil erosion study in 1985, Repetto *et al.* (1987, 1989) presented national accounts which incorporate measures of natural resource depletion, yielding environmentally adjusted 'net' domestic product (NDP). Indonesia's national income and economic growth have been overstated by conventional GDP which increased at an annual rate of 7.1 per cent from 1971 to 1984. Revenues from oil and gas production, hard mineral extraction, and the harvesting of timber and other forest products were used to finance government development and routine expenditures. However, the losses of oil reserves, topsoil and forest cover have resulted in a depleted natural resource base which will restrict future development opportunities. The annual rate of increase of NDP was 4.0 per cent. The raw data used for the soil erosion study are being debated and recent data give reason to doubt the assumed magnitude of soil erosion and the importance of human influences on the process (Arntzen and Gilbert, 1991). Nevertheless, a more complete accounting system which estimates the depreciation in future productive potential for other environmental resources such as fisheries, non-timber forest products, natural gas, coal, copper, tin and nickel would probably reveal even more unsustainable trends.

Similar natural resource accounting studies are currently being undertaken in Mexico, El Salvador, Bolivia, Brazil, Chile, the Philippines, China, India and Malaysia. Economists are also constructing such accounts in Norway, France, Germany, the Netherlands, Australia, the USA and Canada. The UN Statistical Commission and Statistical Office are in the process of revising SNA (for the first time in 20 years), including methodological guidelines for natural resource accounts complementary to the revised SNA (Repetto, 1993).

Hartwick's optimal adjustments to the national accounts can be summarized as follows.

Non-renewable resource. Each period, we should deduct the Hotelling rents of natural resource extraction from NNP, assuming all inputs/outputs are valued at their correct shadow prices. Formally: let C = aggregate consumption, K = stock of man-made capital, S = stock of non-renewable resources, R = current extraction from S, L = labour (allowed to grow at some rate n), U = utility, ρ = discount rate.

The economic problem is to maximise discounted utility from consumption:

$$\text{Max} \int U(C)\,e^{-\rho t} \tag{14.4}$$

subject to: $\dot{K} = F(K, L, R) - C - f(R, S)$ and $\dot{S} = -R$ $\hfill$ (14.5)

Here a dot represents a rate of change; $F(\cdot)$ is the aggregate production function, and $f(\cdot)$ is the cost of extracting non-renewables. Thus, the first equation in (14.5) says that the rate of change in the man-made capital stock K depends on production less consumption less the costs of extracting resources; whilst the second equation in (14.5) states that the rate of change in the non-renewable resource stock S is equal to annual production R (since there is no growth, and implicitly no new discoveries). Then we find (Hartwick, 1990a) that ENP is given by:

$$\text{ENP} = C + \dot{K} - [F_R - f_R]R = \text{NNP} - [F_R - f_R]R \tag{14.6}$$

where F_R is the marginal product (= price) of R and f_R is the marginal extraction cost. The expression in square brackets is the 'Hotelling rent' and is the *correct* way of calculating the amount of deduction from conventional NNP, as Hartwick shows. If published average costs are used instead (marginal costs are typically not recorded), then, given that we expect mining companies to be operating where $MC > AC$, this overstates the correct deduction and understates ENP. If new discoveries are made, so that $-R$ overstates the actual loss of the non-renewable resource, then this should be netted out before the conversion to ENP is made.

Renewable resources. Renewable resources differ from non-renewables in that positive growth can occur, subject to the population size and the rate of harvesting (see Chapter 10). Hartwick models the introduction of renewables into the system by including a term in the utility function to represent fish catch (E), so that we have a utility function, $U = U(C, E)$, where the cost function for fishing (say) is $f(E, Z)$, where Z is the stock of fish. Then we have:

$$\dot{K} = F(K, L) - C - f(E, Z) \quad \text{and} \tag{14.7}$$

$$\dot{Z} = g(Z) - E, \quad \text{where } g(Z) \text{ is the natural growth function} \tag{14.8}$$

as constraints in the model. When harvesting exceeds the growth rate, $\dot{Z}$ will be negative; when the reverse is true, $\dot{Z}$ will be positive, while $\dot{Z}$ will be zero if harvesting is equal to the growth rate. Hartwick derives the optimal deduction from NNP to allow for depreciation of the renewable resource (fish) as:

$$\text{ENP} = \text{NNP} - (U_E/U_C - f_E)\dot{Z} \tag{14.9}$$

in other words, the change in the stock Z valued by the term in parentheses: this is the ratio of marginal utilities ($=$ price in a competitive market) minus marginal fishing costs. When the harvest rate is less than the growth rate, this adjusment adds to NNP; when harvesting exceeds the growth rate, the adjustment reduces NNP.

A problem recognised by Hartwick is that all the variables in equation (14.9) are calculated at their socially optimal levels, but with open access to renewable resources, these values will not be optimal (recall from Chapter 10 that the growth rate, for example, varies with population size, which in turn depends on costs and prices). In general, we would expect the marginal cost to be too high and the price to be too low, as too much effort will be expended in the fishery, for example, under the open access conditions which describe many of the world's fisheries. If this is the case, we will need to regulate effort levels to their optimal amounts and use the prices/marginal costs that then result; or else calculate these optimal prices/costs and use them to value existing reductions in the stock. Notice that, if fish catches remain within the annual growth rate, no adjustment to NNP is necessary (since $\dot{Z} = 0$).

Pollution/environmental amenity effects. Pollution (X) is modelled as a stock which exerts negative effects on production. Production itself adds to this stock:

$$\dot{X} = -bX + \gamma F(K, L, X) \tag{14.10}$$

Here pollution dissipates at a natural rate b (this could be set equal to zero if the economy generates pollutants for which no assimilative capacity exists, when making ENP adjustments for such pollutants); and is added to by production according to some constant proportion γ. If the only way to reduce pollution is to cut output (an unlikely case in reality), the correct adjustment to NNP is:

$$ENP = NNP - V \cdot \dot{X} \tag{14.11}$$

where V is equal to:

$$\frac{-\dot{U}_c/U_c + \rho - F_k}{\gamma F_k} = V \tag{14.12}$$

The expression in (14.12) represents the value of the return on pollution in terms of the return on capital in the economy. As such, it would be difficult to calculate. If in addition we allow for direct pollution abatement activities (represented using a cost function $f(b)$), we get a simpler adjustment (since now pollution can be controlled directly). In this case, then, ENP is:

$$ENP = NNP - \delta(f_b)/\delta X \cdot \dot{X} \tag{14.13}$$

which is the change in the stock of pollution (the amount of pollution abatement) multiplied by the marginal cost of pollution control. Since, in most empirical studies, many opportunities exist beside output reduction to cut emissions, (14.13) is more likely to be relevant than (14.11).

Finally, consider the case of pollution entering directly into the utility function, as well as exerting a depressing effect on production. Hartwick actually models *changes* in the stock of pollution so that $U = U(C, \dot{X})$. This gives the adjustment:

$$ENP = NNP - [((-U_{\dot{x}}/U_c)\dot{X}) - (\delta f/\delta X \dot{X})] \tag{14.14}$$

The first term in square brackets is the ratio of marginal (dis)utilities of changes in the pollution stock and consumption (the price of reducing pollution in terms of the value of forgone consumption), multiplied by the change in the pollution stock. This is equal to willingness to pay for pollution reductions times the amount of pollution reduced. The second term in square brackets is the term found in equation (14.13), that is the marginal cost of pollution control times the reduction in the stock. Re-writing equation (14.14) makes the nature of the required adjustment clearer:

$$ENP = NNP - [U_{\dot{x}}/U_c + f_b/X] \cdot \dot{X} \tag{14.15}$$

The term in square brackets is positive, but for increases in the stock of pollution ($\dot{X} > 0$), the 'rent' here is negative (since we make negative the expression in square brackets). Thus an increase in pollution (a bad) is treated exactly the same way as a reduction in the stocks of either non-renewable or renewable resources (goods). Increases in the stock of pollution should lead us to reduce NNP (which is as expected!). Decreases in environmental amenity for reasons other than pollution should be allowed for in the national accounts in a manner analogous to the treatment of the 'amenity' effect of pollution, as shown in equation (14.14).

Summing up, we can derive optimal adjustments to NNP. These give us ENP, which shows the level of sustainable income in the economy. However, all the values in the equations above must be valued at their socially optimal levels (correct shadow prices). Since this is almost impossible, making adjustments along these principles yields an indicator (approximate ENP, AENP – Approximate Environmentally Adjusted National Product) which might be a reliable proxy indicator of sustainability, if we remain aware of the general limitations of NNP itself.

Box 14.2   *Adjusting national accounts for environmental degradation: the case of Zimbabwe*

Zimbabwe's pattern of resource dependency changed between 1974 and 1987 such that mining's contribution to GDP dropped from 7.6 per cent to 5.5 per cent (Adger, 1993). Although the contribution of agriculture declined to 10.9 per cent, more agricultural produce was exported. It is apparent that the biophysical basis of agriculture is being degraded by soil erosion and deforestation, but data on annual changes have not been collated.

In 1987 an estimated 9.47 million tonnes (mt) of fuelwood was harvested from Zimbabwe's forests which were reckoned to hold 654 mt of dry matter equivalent. The mean annual increment (MAI) added only 6.81 mt, leaving a shortfall of 2.66 mt. Using an average market price of ZM$68 per tonne, and an average (not marginal) cost of extraction based upon minimum agricultural wages, this fuelwood depletion represents a 9 per cent reduction in Zimbabwe's agricultural net product.

In contrast to the World Resources Institute (WRI)'s Costa Rica study (see Box 14.1) which calculated replacement costs of nutrients using the universal soil loss equation, initial estimates for the value of arable production lost through soil erosion were derived from land use data, soil erosion rates and estimates of productivity loss rates (3 per cent yield lost per cm topsoil lost). However, the absence of a large database of land use and observed soil erosion rates limits the accuracy of these estimates. Because of the extrapolation assumptions used, and since soil losses from grasslands and off-site soil erosion costs are excluded, the value put on lost production is likely to be an underestimate. Nevertheless, soil erosion resulted in an annual income loss of at least ZM$14 million, representing a 1 per cent reduction in the net product of Zimbabwe's agricultural sector.

In 1987 deforestation and soil erosion reduced Zimbabwe's net agricultural product by at least 10 per cent. Further improvements in the collation of existing data, together with the development of location-specific soil erosion models, will contribute to more accurate natural resource accounting. More

> accurate accounts will not only assist planning but should contribute to improved management for sustainable development. Ultimately, however, operationalising the concept of sustainable development will depend upon more equitable access to land and other natural resources.

However, the use of environmentally-adjusted national accounts has been criticised by several authors. Norgaard (1989) makes three criticisms of such procedures, First, that the SNA which is now used worldwide is not consistent with a consensus view of conventional macroeconomics, since no such consensus view exists (see, for example, Klamer, 1984). This may not be viewed as a serious problem, however, since the need for consensus remains to be demonstrated. (Indeed, in other papers Norgaard has argued against the desirability of a consensus, and in favour of methodological pluralism.) Second, that a 'value aggregation dilemma' exists, in that, for many environmental impacts to be entered in the SNA, they must have money values put on them. For non-market environmental effects, this necessitates the use of techniques such as contingent valuation. But if the willingness of individuals to pay for environmental goods (what the environment is worth in neoclassical economics) depends on preferences and income distribution in currently unsustainable economies, what use can such values be in guiding society towards sustainablility? This is especially true, Norgaard argues, given the large changes in economic behaviour and organisation needed to move us to a sustainable development path. Marginal changes are not enough, yet according to Norgaard valuation techniques only work well for such marginal changes: 'we are faced with the problem that economic techniques are more appropriate the less significant the problem' (Norgaard, 1989, p. 309).

The third problem for Norgaard with environmental adjustments to the SNA is that we currently possess inadequate models of the way the economy interacts with the environment. It is thus impossible to predict with sufficient accuracy the impact of economic events on the environment, and vice versa. Many competing models exist; until consensus is reached, however, no universally agreed upon adjustment process for the SNA is possible.

Critics of environmental adjustments to the national accounts have argued in favour of new and extended environmental accounts in physical units to be presented alongside conventional SNA accounts, and for wider measures of welfare which include environmental effects in physical units to be used (Daly and Cobb, 1990; Common and Perrings, 1992; Opschoor and Reijinders, 1991). Daly and Cobb show, for example, that, while real GNP per capita in the USA has risen more or less consistently over the period 1950–90, their preferred indicator of welfare (the Index of Sustainable

Economic Welfare, ISEW) has been on a slight downward path since the late 1970s. This is because the ISEW picks up many measures of social well-being (such as pollution, income inequality and the costs of future decommissioning of nuclear power plants in current use) which GNP does not (see Daly and Cobb for more details).

☐ *14.3.2 Natural capital stock approaches*

In order to develop an indicator of SD based on the natural capital stock approach, it is first necessary to answer some of the questions raised above in section 14.2. These are: (1) what units should the natural capital stock, Kn, be measured in (physical, energy or monetary units) and (2) what level of Kn should be chosen as the constraint level?

Once these questions have been answered, the development of an indicator is conceptually straightforward. For example, suppose Kn is to be measured in physical units, disaggregated into separate classes (area of forests, area of wetlands, numbers of breeding birds), and that the existing level of each is taken as the constraint. Then the indicator of SD is: are measured levels of natural capital in each class remaining above constraint levels? The data requirements for such an indicator are large, in that physical accounts (records) must be kept for each resource class and updated annually. This, of course, has large monitoring implications. However, the administration costs of implementing this form of indicator must be less than for the Hartwick/Solow type, since the latter requires the establishment of physical accounts *plus* the valuation of all changes in the stocks in monetary units to be fully implemented. For non-market resources, this would be an enormous task.

☐ *14.3.3 The SMS approach*

As will be recalled from section 14.2, the safe minimum standard approach to environmental policy assumes that:

1. quantifying environmental benefits and costs in money terms is too difficult; and
2. given uncertainty about the risks of environmental damage, and the irreversible nature of some environmental damages, rational (risk-averse) society will choose not to allow environmental resources (such as pollution assimilative capacity, the area of wetlands or rainforest, the population of a particular species) to fall below some safe minimum

standard (SMS). Going below the SMS should only be allowed if society believes the opportunity cost of maintaining the standard to be unreasonably large.

The indicator of SD arising here is thus: is the safe minimum standard being breached for any resource class? As noted earlier, this is not the same as allowing no decline in the level of resources. The information requirements for the SMS measure are as for the natural capital stock measure, namely physical accounts for all resource classes. In addition, it is necessary to have identified the SMS in each case. A major problem here, though, involves interdependencies. Suppose that the minimum viable population level for a bird species has been identified. This SMS is presumably defined on a given level of environmental quality: for example, given habitat areas, food availability, pollution levels, weather patterns and predation levels. If any of these givens changes, however, the minimum viable population size may rise or fall. Thus it will be necessary (1) to understand what determines the SMS for all relevant classes of resources, and (2) to review continually the SMS for each class in the light of changes in these explanatory variables. This introduces the possibility of a dynamic inconsistency: suppose that, in period 1, we identify the SMS as ten pairs of a species in an island region. Protecting the species is very expensive, so we allow the population to decline to exactly ten pairs. However, in period 2 a habitat change means that ten pairs are no longer a viable number; the SMS rises to 20 pairs, but we have already allowed a decline to ten (on cost–benefit grounds). Thus the SMS rule for sustainability is violated in period 2, owing to our enforcement of the rule in period 1. This might have been so even if a safety margin above ten pairs had been enforced in period 1, if the margin was less than 100 per cent.

Box 14.3　*Another economic measure of sustainability: the Pearce–Atkinson measure*

Pearce and Atkinson (1993) have proposed an indicator of weak sustainability based on the neoclassical assumptions inherent in the Hartwick/Solow approach, in that man-made and natural capital are assumed to be perfect substitutes for each other. This is rather different from what we referred to as the weak sustainability criterion when shadow projects are available, so we will refer to the case where there is assumption of perfect substitutability as the Pearce–Atkinson measure (PAM). The PAM is defined as:

$$\text{PAM} = \left(\frac{S}{Y}\right) - \left(\frac{\delta_M}{Y}\right) - \left(\frac{\delta_N}{Y}\right) \tag{14.16}$$

where, if $\text{PAM} > 0$, the economy is judged sustainable. Equation (14.16) states that PAM will be positive if savings exceed the sum of depreciation on man-made (δ_M) and natural (δ_N) capital. Pearce and Atkinson argue that this is a useful rule, in that, if countries fail even this weak test of sustainability, they are unlikely to pass a stronger test. Unfortunately, estimating δ_N is difficult; Pearce and Atkinson are able to uncover very partial estimates for 18 countries, however. They find that Costa Rica, Czechoslovakia, Germany, Hungary, Japan, the Netherlands, Poland and the USA all pass the weak test (PAM > 0); Mexico and the Philippines are classed as 'marginal' (PAM $\cong$ 0), while Burkina Faso, Ethiopia, Indonesia, Madagascar, Malawi, Mali, Nigeria and Papua New Guinea are unsustainable (PAM < 0).

In a more recent paper, Atkinson and Proops (unpublished) adopt the PAM measure to include imports and exports. They find that the USA becomes less sustainable when trade is included, but that global sustainability is positive. The Middle East becomes more sustainable with trade than without. The high savings rate in Japan makes a large contribution to world sustainability.

However, two criticisms may be made of the PAM measure: (1) it assumes perfect substitutability between natural and man-made capital; (2) in practice, very incomplete estimates of natural capital depreciation are available.

14.4 The Common–Perrings model of sustainable development

Modelling interactions between the economy and the environment has become a popular exercise in environmental economics (see, for example, Barbier, 1990; Pezzey, 1992). In this final section we review a recent model due to Common and Perrings (1992). This model has the feature that it tries to combine ecological concepts of stability with economic efficiency. Ecological stability is argued to be a prerequisite for the sustainability of the economic–ecological system as a whole. Such stability in turn requires ecosystem resilience, namely the capacity of the overall ecosystem to withstand external shocks without losing its 'self-organisation'. Protecting ecological sustainability is achieved by protecting ecosystem resilience. The concept of economic sustainability used is represented by the Hartwick rule. Common and Perrings show that 'while it is not necessary to sacrifice ... intertemporal efficiency ..., intertemporal price efficiency is not a necessary condition for ecological sustainability ... [and that] intertemporal efficiency ... may well be inconsistent with ecological sustainability' (p. 8).

Ecological sustainability is characterised formally using the approach of Holling (1973, 1986), where in general the resilience of an ecosystem is an increasing function of the diversity of that system. 'Holling resilience' is characterised in the model by the condition that the rate of change of the natural parameters of the ecosystem, z_t, with respect to economic activity be non-positive. These natural parameters include, for example, the rate of net primary production in the system, or population growth rates. Complex dynamic feedbacks between ecosystems and the economy typify the problem of 'environmental control' and that of achieving SD.

Common and Perrings argue that the main distinguishing feature of their model is the incorporation of a pair of constraints that are sufficient for ecological and economic sustainablity. These constraints are endogenous, in the sense that they are dynamically interdependent, reflecting the co-evolution of the overall system (Norgaard, 1984). The objective function is dependent on discounted welfare.

☐ 14.4.1 The model

Let $X_t(X = 1 \ldots n)$ be the resources available to the economic system at time t. These include natural capital, man-made capital and consumption goods. U_t are a sub-set of these resources that have private property rights attached to them and are economically exploitable. The distribution of the parameters of the ecosystems which make up the natural environment (as described above) are represented by Z_t, defined by a probability density function $z_t = \mathrm{pr}\,[Z_t]$. At any point in time, the system parameters z_t are a function h of the amount of disturbance to the ecosystem, indicated by $\hat{X}_t$. This disturbance is assumed equal to the level of economic resources, U_t. Undisturbed values of X_t are shown as $\bar{X}_t$. If we define $z_t = h(\hat{X}_t, \bar{X}_t)$ then the 'equation of motion' for the system is

$$\delta X_t/\delta t \equiv \dot{x} = f(\bar{X}_t, U_t, z_t, t) \tag{14.17}$$

Thus the growth in resources depends on natural growth $\bar{X}_t$ and economic use of the resources, U_t. Use itself depends on relative prices P_t, so that $U_t = U[P_t, t]$. The objective function in this model is given as follows:

$$J = W(T)[X_T, z_T, T]\,e^{-rT} + \int_0^T Y_t[\bar{X}_t, U_t, z_t, t]\,e^{-rt}\,dt \tag{14.18}$$

This is a conventional neoclassical expression, showing that, over the time period ending in period T, we add up economic benefits Y_t, which depend on consumption (contained in U_t), on the natural state of the ecosystem, and on the system parameters of the ecosystem (z_t) at any point in time, discounted at a rate r (assumed equal to the marginal efficiency of capital); plus a term expressing welfare W in the final period $T(W(T))$, which depends on the level of remaining resources X_t, and also on the system parameters of the ecosystem, discounted again at the rate r. The constraints on this optimisation problem are given in the equation of motion of the ecosystem (equation 14.17), the initial level of resource stocks and prices:

$$X(0) = X_0 \quad \text{and} \quad P(0) = P_0 \tag{14.19}$$

and an ecological sustainability constraint. The ecological sustainability constraint requires that the economic process does not have a destabilising effect on the ecosystem, represented in the constraint:

$$\delta z/\delta t = \dot{z}_t \leq 0 \tag{14.20}$$

Given that W and Y are also a function of z_t, then W and Y will themselves only be stable (that is, $\delta W/\delta t = \delta Y/\delta t = 0$) if $\dot{z}_t = 0$. This in turn implies a constant structure of preferences, for which Holling sustainability is both a necessary and a sufficient condition. Thus (14.20) is better written as a strict equality:

$$\dot{z}_t = 0 \tag{14.21}$$

This condition, as Common and Perrings show, is sufficient for ecosystem sustainability (what they term 'Holling resilience'). What is more, this is guaranteed by $\dot{U}_t = 0$, constant consumption and capital stocks over time (a zero rate of economic growth). Finally, an intertemporal efficiency constraint is imposed. This is basically a Hartwick rule requiring resource rents to be equal to net investment, both evaluated at their socially optimal values. Full results are given in Common and Perrings (1992, p. 27). However, we can summarise them as follows:

1. Along an optimal yet sustainable path, the marginal benefit for a reduction in the value of the resource base X_t should grow at a rate equal to the discount rate (the Hotelling rule).
2. Ecological sustainability reduces the desirability of economic growth, in that, along an optimal, sustainable path, any undesirable effects on ecosystem resilience must be deducted from pure economic benefits.
3. An intertemporally efficient price path is not necessary or sufficient for ecological sustainability. Such a price path may in some cases be compatible with sustainability, which can be shown as follows. Holling resilience of the system can be described as

$$\dot{z}(t) = h'_u \dot{U}(t) \leq 0 \tag{14.22}$$

where h'_u is the derivative of the $h(\ )$ function mentioned above with respect to U, and $\dot{U}$ is the rate of change of economic resources. The value of U is given by:

$$U_t = U([P_t, t] \tag{14.23}$$

so that $\dot{z}_t = 0$ is consistent with $\dot{p}_t = 0$. However, this is unlikely since this would imply over time that changes in the economic resource base have no effect on real prices, so that what is required is either $\dot{U}_t = 0$ or $h'_u = 0$. In the first case we have what Daly has referred to as a steady-state or stationary economy, which maintains constant its matter–energy throughput (see Chapter 1). In the second case, we have no effect on ecosystem parameters of changes in u.

4. From (3) it follows that to preserve or attain ecological stability which is consistent with intertemporal efficiency requires that we manage economic–environmental interactions in a way which does not interfere with system resilience: which keeps systems within their natural resilience boundaries. On the other hand, even an intertemporally efficient development path will not be ecologically sustainable if system resilience is adversely affected, and there is nothing about a purely economically efficient time path which guarantees that systems' resilience will be kept intact.

5. While the Solow/Hartwick notion of sustainability allows for a sustainability indicator which is value-based (such as environmentally adjusted GNP), Holling sustainability requires a set of physical indicators which measure the resilience of ecosystems. Since resilience is an increasing function of diversity, preserving biodiversity is vital for ecological sustainability.

The concept of ecological sustainability is, as Common and Perrings note, possibly at odds with the long-held belief in consumer sovereignty. For if consumers hold preferences which imply unsustainable consumption paths, government will have to overrule these preferences if they wish to achieve sustainability. As no markets exist for many environmental goods, increasing environmental scarcity cannot be picked up by rising relative prices, so that even given a set of preferences consumers may not alter their behaviour in a sustainable direction. Yet the message of this model is that, even if all environmental resources were 'correctly' valued, this would not guarantee sustainability. As Common and Perrings say:

> An ecological economics approach (to sustainability) requires that resources be allocated in such a way that they do not threaten the stability either of the system as a whole or of key components of the system . . . an ecological economics approach privileges the requirements of the system above those of the individual. Consumer sovereignty in such an approach is an acceptable principle only in so far as consumer interests do not threaten the general system – and through this, the welfare of future generations.

■ References

Adger, N. (1993) 'Sustainable national income and natural resource degradation in Zimbabwe', *Sustainable Environmental Economics and Management*, London: Belhaven Press.

Ahmad, Y., S. El Serafy and E. Lutz (eds) (1989) *Environmental Accounting for Sustainable Development: A UNDP–World Bank Symposium*, Washington, D.C.: World Bank.

Arntzen, J. and A. Gilbert (1991) 'Natural resource accounting: state of the art and perspectives for the assessment of trends in sustainable development', in O. Kuik and H. Verbruggen (eds), *In Search of Indicators of Sustainable Development*, Dordrecht: Kluwer.

Asheim, G.B. (1991) 'Defining sustainability when resource management does not have deterministic consequences', mimeo, Department of Economics, University of Oslo.

Barbier, E.B. (1990) 'Alternative approaches to economic–environment interactions', *Ecological Economics*, 2, 7–26.

Bishop, R.C. (1978) 'Endangered species and uncertainty: The economics of a safe minimum standard', *American Journal of Agricultural Economics*, 60, 10–18.

Bishop, R.C. (1993). 'Economic-efficiency, sustainability, and biodiversity', *Ambio*, 22(2–3), 69–73.

Christensen, P.P. (1989) 'Historical roots for ecological economics – biophysical versus allocative approaches', *Ecological Economics*, 1(1), 17–36.

Ciriacy-Wantrup, S. (1952) *Resource Conservation: Economics and Policy*, Berkeley: University of California Press.

Common, M. and C. Perrings (1992) 'Towards an ecological economics of sustainability', *Ecological Economics*, 6(1), 7–34.

Daly, H. (1990). 'Toward some operational principles of sustainable development', *Ecological Economics*, 2, 1–7.

Daly, H. and J. Cobb (1990) *For the Common Good*, London: Green Print.

Dasgupta, A. (1988) *Growth, Development and Welfare: An Essay on Levels of Living*, Oxford: Basil Blackwell.

El-Serafy, S. (1989) 'The proper calculation of income from depletable natural resources', in Y. Ahmad, S. El Serafy and E. Lutz (eds), *Environmental Accounting for Sustainable Development: A UNDP–World Bank Symposium*, Washington, D.C.: World Bank.

Hanley, N. and C. Spash (1993) *Cost–Benefit Analysis and the Environment*, Aldershot: Edward Elgar.

Hanley, N., A. Munro, D. Jamieson and D. Ghosh (1991) *Environmental Economics and Sustainable Development in Nature Conservation*, Peterborough: NCC.

Hartwick, J.M. (1977). 'Intergenerational equity and the investing of rents from exhaustible resources', *American Economic Review*, 67(5), 972–4.

Hartwick, J.M. (1978) 'Substitution among exhaustible resources and intergenerational equity', *Review of Economic Studies*, 45, 347–54.

Hartwick, J.M. (1990a) *Pollution and National Accounting*, Institute for Economic Research, Queens University, Kingston, Ontario.

Hartwick, J.M. (1990b) 'Natural resources, national accounting and economic depreciation', *Journal of Public Economics*, 43, 291–304.

Holland, A. and K. Rawles (1993) 'Values in conservation', *ECOS*, 14(1), 14–19.

Holling, C.S. (1973) 'Resilience and stability of ecological systems', *Annual Review of Ecology and Systematics*, 4, 1–23.

Holling, C.S. (1986) 'The resilience of terrestrial ecosystems', in W.C. Clark and R.E. Munn (eds), *Sustainable Development of the Biosphere*, Cambridge: Cambridge University Press.

Howarth, R.B. and R.B. Norgaard (1992) 'Environmental valuation under sustainable development', *American Economic Review*, 82(2), 473–7.

Howarth, R.B. and R.B. Norgaard (1993) 'Intergenerational transfers and the social discount rate', *Environmental and Natural Resource Economics*, 3(4), August, 337–58.

Klaasen, G. and H. Opschoor (1991) 'Economics of sustainablity or the sustainability of economics', *Ecological Economics*, 4, 83–92.

Klamer, A. (1984) *The New Classical Macroeconomics*, Hemel Hempstead: Harvester–Wheatsheaf.

Lutz, E. (1993) *Towards Improved Accounting for the Environment*, Washington, D.C.: World Bank.

Maler, K.G. (1991) 'National accounts and environmental resources', *Environmental Resource Economics*, 1(1), 1–16.

Norgaard, R.B. (1984) 'Co-evolutionary development potential', *Land Economics*, 60, 160–73.

Norgaard, R.B. (1989) 'Three dilemmas of environmental accounting', *Ecological Economics*, 1, 303–14.

Opschoor, J.B. and L. Reijinders (1991) 'Towards sustainable development indicators', *In Search of Sustainable Development Indicators*, Dordrecht: Kluwer Academic Publishers.

Pearce, D. and G. Atkinson (1993) 'Capital theory and the measurement of weak sustainability', *Ecological Economics*, 8, 103–8.

Pearce, D.W. and R.K. Turner (1990) *Economics of Natural Resources and the Environment*, Hemel Hempstead, Harvester–Wheatsheaf.

Pearce, D.W., E. Barbier and A. Markandya (1990) *Sustainable Development: Economics and Environment in the Third World*, Aldershot: Edward Elgar.

Pezzey, J. (1992) *Sustainable Development Concepts: An Economic Analysis*, Environment Paper No. 2, Washington, D.C.: World Bank.

Pezzey, J. (1994) 'The optimal sustainable depletion of non-renewable resources', paper to EAERE conference, Dublin.

Randall, A. and M. Farmer (1995) 'Benefits, costs and the safe minimum standard of conservation', in D. Bromley (ed.), *The Handbook of Environmental Economics*, Oxford: Blackwell.

Repetto, R. (1990) *Wasting Assets: the Need for National Resource Accounting*, Washington, D.C.: World Resources Institute.

Repetto, R. (1992) 'Accounting for environmental assets', *Scientific American*, 266(6), 94–100.

Repetto, R. (1993) 'How to account for environmental degradation', *Forestry and the Environment: Economic Perspectives*, Wallingford: CAB International.

Repetto, R., M. Wells, C. Beer and F. Rossini (1987) *Natural Resource Accounting for Indonesia*, Washington: World Resources Institute.

Repetto, R., W. McGrath, M. Wells, C. Beer and F. Rossini (1989) *Wasting Assets: Natural Resources in the National Income Accounts*, Washington: World Resources Institute.

Solow, R.M. (1974) 'The economics of resources or the resources of economics', *American Economic Review*, 64, 1–14.

Solow, R.M. (1986) 'On the intertemporal allocation of natural resources', *Scandinavian Journal of Economics*, 88, 141–9.

Solow, R. (1992) 'An almost practical step toward sustainability', *Resources Policy*, 19, 162–72.

Tisdell, C. (1990) 'Economics and the debate about preservation of species, crop varieties and genetic diversity', *Ecological Economics*, 2, 77–90.

Toman, M., J. Pezzey and J. Krautkraemer (1994) 'Economic theory and sustainability', paper to EAERE conference, Dublin.

Turner, R.K. (1993) 'Sustainability: Principles and Practice', in R.K. Turner (ed.), *Sustainable Environmental Economics and Management*, London: Belhaven Press.

Van Pelt, M.J.F. (1993) 'Ecologically sustainable development and project appraisal in developing countries', *Ecological Economics*, 7(1), 19–42.

Weitzman, M. (1976) 'On the welfare significance of national product in a dynamic economy', *Quarterly Journal of Economics*, 90, 156–62.

Index

abatement costs   108, 141
  see also marginal
Abdulla, C.B.   418
abundances of selected materials   220
acid rain   161, 162–3, 171–3
Adamowicz, W.   401, 402, 408, 409
adaptive expectation hypothesis   262–3
Adger, N.   439
Adriano, D.C.   162
adverse selection   49, 54–6
AENP   439
Africa   335
Agbeyegbe, T.D.   263
Agee, M.   165
Ahmad, Y.   434
air quality   117–18
Alkali Act 1874   6
aluminium   216, 220, 223
ambient charge   66–71
ambient permit system   139, 140, 141,
  152
ammonia   110, 115, 151, 162
Anderson, F.   218, 219, 223
Anderson, T.   29
Andrews, R.   136
Antarctic   165
APS   *see* ambient permit system
Arctic   165
Arnason, R.   291, 292, 298
Arnold, S.F.   329
Arnott, R.   51
Arntzen, J.   435
Arrow, K.   29, 373, 375, 386, 397
Arrow–Enthoven sufficiency
  theorem   102–3, 200
Asheim, G.B.   425
El Ashry, M.   162
Asia 60, 335
asymmetric information   *see* market
  failure
Atkinson, G.   442, 443
Atkinson, S.   140, 148–9, 150, 163
auctions   146–7

Australia 38, 84, 313, 436
Austria 39

Baker, C.K.   162
Barbier, E.B.   443
Barnett, H.J.   221, 222, 255
Barrett, S.   167–8, 169
Barrow, M.M.   263
Bartik, T.   418
Bateman, I.   384
Baumol, W.   29, 31, 64, 145
  pollution taxes   107, 112–13, 115,
  120, 126
bauxite   243
Beavis, B.   98, 99, 152, 183, 195, 198
Becker, G.   370
Beckerman, W.   154
Bell, F.W.   284, 285, 286
Bellman, R.E.   204, 212, 308
Berck, P.   295
Bergen Declaration 1990   6
Bergman, L.   108
Bergstrom, J.   393
Beverton, R.J.H.   275, 286
Bielorussia 39
Binmore, K.   316
biological oxygen demand   106, 109,
  111, 115, 139, 140, 142
Bishop, R.   389, 392, 394, 400, 430
Bjørndal, T.   304
Black Sea   39, 40
Bliss, C.J.   178
Blomquist, G.   417
Bockstael, N.   407, 408, 409
Bohm, P.   84, 85
Bolivia   436
Boulding, K.   11
Bovenberg, A.   127–8
Bowes, M.   338, 405
Boyle, K.   392
Braden, J.   357, 381, 383, 404
Brazil   163, 164, 436
Brewer, D.   406

Brock, W.A.   207
Brookshire, D.   384, 393, 413, 414
Brown, G.   395, 407, 408
Brownian motion   208, 210
Brundtland Commission/Report   6, 425
Bucharest Declaration 1989   40
Buckland, S.   163
Bulgaria   39
Burkina Faso   443
Burt, O.   406
Bush, G.   137

Cabe, R.   69–70
cadmium   3, 84
Camerer, C.   369
Cameron, T.   389
Canada   7
  environmental protection   84
  market failure   33, 39
  renewable resources   304–7, 319
  sustainable development   436
  transboundary pollution
    problems   160, 161, 162, 163
capital theory   179–82
Caputo, M.R.   201
carbon
  dioxide 1, 6, 131; pollution taxes 121,
    122, 123, 127, 128; transboundary
    pollution problems 160, 161, 164
  monoxide   5
  tax   127–8
  tetrachloride   171
Carson, R.   384, 393, 395, 399
cartels   *see* imperfect competition
Casson, T.   137, 147
Caulkins, P.   406
CES production function   427
Cesar, H.S.J.   170
CH₄   *see* methane
Chernobyl   40
Chevas, J.P.   406
Chiang, A.C.   98, 100, 183, 186, 194, 200
Chicago Board of Trade   137
Chile   436
China   161, 169, 170, 171, 436
chlorofluorocarbons   121, 122, 123,
    126, 396
  transboundary pollution problems
    160, 161, 165, 166, 169, 170, 171
Christensen, P.P.   12, 427
chromium   40
Ciborowski, P.   161
Ciriacy-Wantrup, S.   430

Clark, C.W.   178, 191, 196, 202, 225
Clarke, H.R.   352
Clawson, M.   404
Clean Air Act 1970   87, 136, 137, 141
Clean Air Act Amendments 1990   106,
    147, 171
cleaner technology   151
Cline, W.   121, 161
CO   *see* carbon monoxide
cooperation   167, 315–17, 322–4
co-ordination game   42
coal   223, 227
Coase, R.   25–7, 64
Cobb, J.   440, 441
Cobb–Douglas   285, 427
Common, M.   126, 145, 426, 427, 440,
    443–6
commons   37–42, 348
Comoli, P.M.   344
comparative dynamic models   288–98
  competitive fishery and social
    optimum with costs   291–5
  equilibrium shadow price against
    number of firms   294
  equilibrium stock and number of firms
    294
  fishery exploitation with endogenous
    prices   295–8
  monopoly fishery   289–91
  phase-plane representation of sole-
    ownership with endogenous price
    297
  sole ownership of competitive fishery
    and social optimum   288–9
compensation   277, 278
competition   96–7, 232–5, 248–50
Comprehensive Environmental
    Response, Compensation and
    Liability Act 1980   357, 385
Conrad, J.M.   125–6, 196, 202, 225,
    304
Conrad, R.F.   265
constant elasticity demand curve   235–6
contingent valuation method   384–401,
    402, 403, 408
  benefits transfer   308
  bias   392–4
  bid curves estimation   390–1
  CVM-X method   400–1
  data aggregation   391–2
  embedding   394–5
  forest characteristics 402–4
  hypothetical market 384–5

contingent valuation method (*continued*)
  information effects 396–7
  non-market valuation 375
  obtaining bids 385–7
  reliability assessment 398–9
  reliability enhancement 399–401
  willingness to accept compensation
    387–90, 395–6
  willingness to pay 387–90, 395–6,
    397
Cook, P. 369
Cooke, A.S. 162
Cooper, J. 390
copper 40, 218, 219, 220, 223, 225, 243
Cornes, R. 43
Costa Rica 435, 439, 443
costs *see* marginal
Courant, P. 417
Cournot *see* Nash–Cournot
Coyne, A. 408, 409
Crabbe, P.J. 339–40
Croatia 39
Crocker, T. 31, 36, 60, 78, 87, 130, 371,
  374, 375, 379
Crofting Reform Act 1883 38
Cropper, M. 414
crustal abundance 218–19
Cumberland, J. 154
Cummings, R. 362, 399
cyanide 110
Cyprus 84
Czech Republic 39, 443

Dales, J. 87, 130
Daly, H. 8, 431–2, 440, 441, 445
damage functions, possible 4
damages, uniformity of 159–61
Dardin, R. 417
Dasgupta, A. 425
Dasgupta, P. 180, 232
Davis, R. 384
DC *see* dichotomous choice
Deacon, R.T. 265
Deadman, D. 222
Deaton, A.S. 374
Declaration of the Third Ministerial
  Conference on the North Sea 5–6
Denmark 9, 84, 160, 171
depensation 277, 278
deposit refund systems 84
Desvouges, W. 375, 395, 399, 409
Devarajan, S. 224, 255

Diamond, P. 395
dichloro-diphenyl-trichloroethane
  (DDT) 3, 31, 40
dichotomous choice 386, 387, 389, 390,
  399, 402
Dickie, M. 165, 400
discrete-time model 202–3, 303–8,
  330–2
dissolved oxygen 109, 110, 115, 116,
  140, 141, 142
Dixit, A.K. 180, 207, 210, 212–13, 329
Dobbs, I.M. 98, 99, 183, 195, 198
Dobson units 165
Dorfman, R. 178, 183
Downing, P.B. 151
dry weather flow 116
duality and expenditure function
  364–5
Duffield, J. 398, 400
Dunn, J. 61
dynamic games 317–19
dynamic programming 203–6

Eagan, V. 263
Earth Summit Rio 1992 171, 348
Eckbo, P.L. 242
economic rent 224–5
Egypt 84
Eheart, J. 144
Ehrlich, I. 370
Ehui, S.K. 345, 347
eigenvalues 194, 195, 196, 197, 198,
  199, 298
eigenvectors 195, 198
El Salvador 436
Elder, H. 143, 144
Ellis, G. 416
EMEP *see* Monitoring and Evaluation
  Programme *under* Europe
emission
  charges 61–6
  permit system 135, 139, 140
  reductions 14, 15, 141
  tax differentiated by source category
    117–18
'end-of-pipe' technology 108
energy use, rising 9–10
England, R.A. 126
Englin, J.E. 351, 407, 408
English, R. 146
ENO 434
ENP 436–9

Enthoven   *see* Arrow–Enthoven
entropy law   12–13
environmental costs and benefits
    valuation   383–418
    direct methods 384–404; stated
        preference 401–4; *see also*
        contingent valuation
    indirect methods 404–18; dose
        response, averting expenditure and
        avoided cost 416–18; hedonic
        pricing 411–16; random utility
        model of Bighorn sheep hunting
        409; real consumer surplus per unit
        of use 411; travel cost model and
        variants 404–11
Environmental Defense Fund   137
environmental degradation   439–40
environmental goods   357–62
environmental hazards   365–7
environmental protection
    EMB curve   66
    EMC curve   64, 65, 89, 90, 91
    marginal benefit   59, 60, 63, 64, 65,
        66, 89, 90, 91
    marginal cost   59, 60, 63, 64, 65, 66,
        89, 90, 91
Environmental Protection Agency   6,
    136, 137, 147, 148, 149, 418
environmental quality standards   106,
    141, 142
environmental shirking   50
environmental subsidy   77
EPIC model   145
EPS   *see* emission permit system
Ethiopia 443
Europe
    environmental protection   60, 61, 62
    European Monitoring and Evaluation
        Programme   163, 172
    forestry exploitation   340
    tradeable pollution permits   150
    transboundary pollution problems
        162, 172; *see also* European
        Community; western
European Community   2, 7
    Large Plant Combustion
        Directive   162
    pollution taxes   127, 128
    renewable resources   301, 304, 307,
        313, 319
    transboundary pollution problems
        163, 171
Evans, R.   393

extraction   244–8, 266–70
    see also production technology
Exxon Valdez   357, 385–6

Faber, M.   224
Fankhauser, S.   173
Farman, J.   165
Farmer, M.   430
Farrow, S.   264
Farzin, Y.H.   254, 255, 258
Faustmann, M.   338, 339, 340, 341,
    342, 344, 345, 350, 351, 353–4
Finland   84, 168, 169, 172
Fisher, A.C.   113, 114, 220, 222, 224,
    255, 258, 266, 416
fisheries
    fishing effort   281–2
    grounds   39–40
    investment under uncertainty   213
    market failure   40–1
    open-access   286–7, 298
    see also natural resource exploitation;
        renewable resources
Fletcher, J.   405
Folk Theorem   173
Folmer, H.   169
forestry   402–4, 415–16
    see also forestry exploitation
forestry exploitation   335–54
    commercial economics 336–40;
        Faustmann rotation 339; model,
        extensions of and market structure
        339–40; tree growth function 336
    Faustmann rotation, effect of yield tax
        on 351
    fire risk   353
    land use and agriculture 343–50;
        deforestation in Ivory Coast 347–8;
        managed forests 343–4; natural
        forests 344–8; rainforest destruction
        348–50
    multi-use and socially optimal
        rotation 340–3; grazing benefit
        function 342; Hartmann rotation
        343
    optimal rotation under uncertainty
        352–3
former Soviet Union   168, 169
Forsund, F.   149–50
Fox, J.   401
France   9, 10, 84, 153, 319, 436
Fraser, G.A.   301
free-riding   43

Freeman, A.M. 357, 365, 381
Friends of the Earth 16–17
Fry, G.L.A. 162
Fudenberg, D. 14, 313, 318

Gaia hypothesis 1
game theory 14–20
  game emission reductions 17
  lobbying over policies 16–17
  pay-offs and emission reductions 14,
    15
  sequential games 17–20
  see also transboundary pollution
    control
Garrod, G. 398, 402, 406, 413, 414, 415
General Accounting Office 138
General Agreement on Tariffs and Trade
  128
general equilibrium model 31
geographic information system 435
Georgescu-Roegen, N. 13
Georgia 39
Gerking, S. 165
Germany 436
  energy use to gross domestic product
    ratios 9, 10
  environmental protection 72, 84
  market failure 39
  sustainable development 443
  tradeable pollution permits 153, 155
Gibbons, R. 14, 15, 17, 18
Gilbert, A. 435
Gilbert, C.L. 244
Global Environment Facility 170–1
global warming 160–1
  see also greenhouse gases
gold 219
Gomoiu, M.-T. 39
Gordon, H.S. 37, 286, 288, 298
government policy and taxation 264–5
Govindasamy, R. 82
Graham, D. 369
Graham, G. 171
Grant, I.F. 38
Graves, P. 414
Green, J. 147
Greene, W. 409
greenhouse gases 121–2, 123, 161
  see also carbon dioxide;
    chlorofluorocarbons; methane;
    nitrous oxide
Greenland 319
Groot, F. 237, 238, 241

gross domestic product 9, 9–10, 23,
  435, 439
gross national product 10, 440, 446
  see also Solow–Hartwick
groundwater quality 418
Groves mechanism 147

Hahn, R. 88, 137, 143, 144, 152, 154
Haigh, N. 6
Hall, D. 222–3, 224, 284, 285
Hall, J. 222–3, 224
Hallett, S. 106
Halvorsen, R. 255
Hamiltonian
  current-value: forestry exploitation
    346; natural resource exploitation
    188–9; non-renewable natural
    resources 230, 231, 246, 249, 253,
    256, 265; renewable resources 292,
    293
  expected value 260
  natural resource exploitation 185,
    186, 190, 191, 200, 203
  non-renewable natural resources 238
  present-value; natural resource
    exploitation 188; non-renewable
    natural resources 235; renewable
    resources 303; renewable resources
    288, 290, 296, 308, 309, 323
Hammack, J. 395
Hanemann, M. 362, 387–8, 389
Hanley, N. 376, 430, 431
environmental costs and benefits,
    valuation of 384, 395–9 *passim*,
    403–4, 406–7, 413, 417
  pollution taxes 107, 110–11
  tradeable pollution permits 141–2,
    145, 150, 154
Hardin, G. 37, 39
Hardin's 'Tragedy of the Commons' 17
harp seal 304–7
Harriman, R. 162
Harrington, W. 418
Harris, D. 218
Harris, F. 393
Harrison, G. 28
Hartman, R. 340, 343
Hartwick, J.M. 426–7, 445, 446
  see also Solow
HCFCs 126
Heal, G.M. 180, 263
Heaps, T. 339

Heberlein, T.   389, 392, 400
hedonic travel cost model   407–8
Hefindahl, O.   222
Heimlich, R.E.   2
Helms, L.J.   373
Henning, J.A.   412
Herriges, J.   69–70, 80, 82
heterogeneous reserve with exploration
    250–4
Hey, J.D.   207, 369
Hicks, Sir J.   361, 383
Hicksian compensating surplus   361,
    378
Hirshleifer, J.   207
Hodge, I.   146
Hoehn, J.   376–7, 389, 393, 396
Hoel, M.   17–20
Hoevenagel, R.   394
Hof, J.   405
Hoffman, E.   28
Holland, A.   430
Holling, C.S.   194, 443, 445
Holmström, B.   66, 80
Holt, S.J.   275, 286
Hool, B.   265
Hotelling, H.
    environmental costs and benefits
        valuation   404
    forestry exploitation   338
    natural resource exploitation   178,
        181, 182
    natural resources   222
    non-renewable natural resources
        227–32 *passim*, 236, 237, 245, 250,
        254, 258–63, 264, 270
    renewable resources   295, 296
    sustainable development   427, 434,
        436, 445
Howarth, R.B.   225, 425, 433
HTC   *see* hedonic travel cost model
Huang, JiChin   414
Hungary   443

Iceland   319
imperfect competition   236–44
    cartel stability   243–4
    gains to producers from cartelisation
        of exhaustible resources   242–3
    Nash–Cournot equilibrium   239–41
    non-renewable resource cartel   236–9
    Von Stackleberg leader–follower
        equilibrium   241–3

incentives for protection   58–103
    Arrow–Enthoven sufficiency theorem
        102–3
    competitive markets   96–7
    deposit refund systems   84
    evaluative criteria   91–5; effectiveness
        92; efficiency 92–3; equity 93–4;
        flexibility to achieve objectives 94–5
    information base and administrative
        capacity   95–6
    Kuhn–Tucker conditions   98–100
    legal structure   96
    linear programming   100–2
    non-compliance fees   79–84
    performance bonds   85–7
    political feasibility   97
    pollution control   59
    see also price rationing; quantity
        rationing
Index of Sustainable Economic Welfare
    440–1
India   84, 170, 171, 436
Indonesia   435, 443
Institute of Hydrology   145
insurance   51–4
International Development Association
    171
international environmental agreements
    170–1
Ireland   162
iron   216–17, 219, 220, 223
Italy   72, 172
Itô's lemma   206–14, 269, 325–30,
    347–8, 352
Ivory Coast   347–8

Jacobian matrix   194, 199, 298
Jamieson, D.   161
Japan   9, 10, 171, 313, 443
Jensen's inequality   374
Jevons, W.S.   221
Johansson, P.O.   7
Johnson, A.H.   162
Johnson, M.   221
Jones-Lee, M.   399

Kahn, J.   416
Kahneman, D.   375, 395, 396
Kamien, M.I.   186, 200, 206
Kanninen, B.   390
Kaoru, Y.   408, 409, 411
Karp, L.   237
Kask, S.   28, 414

Kaufman, R.K. 9–10
Kelman, S. 154
Kennedy, J.O.S. 206
Khalil, E.L. 12, 13
King, D. 95, 405
Kirkwood, G.P. 330
Klaasen, G. 149–50, 428
Klamer, A. 440
Klan, M.S. 351
Klarer, J. 60
Klieve, H. 313
Kling, C. 132
Kneese, A.V. 120
Knetsch, J. 375, 395, 396, 404
Kolmogrov forward equation 329
Kolstad, C. 357, 381, 383, 404
Koopmans, T.C. 266
Krautkraemer, J.A. 265
Kreps, D. 358
Kristrom, B. 390
Krupnick, A. 140, 147
Krutilla, J.V. 338, 373, 405
Kuhn–Tucker conditions 98–103, 135, 139, 187, 200, 238, 253
Kverndokk, S. 173

Laffont, J.-J. 78, 147
Lagrangean
  economic incentives 99, 100, 101, 102
  market failure 45
  natural resource exploitation 186, 202–3
  pollution taxes 113–14, 116, 122
  renewable resources 306
  tradeable pollution permits 135
Lancaster, K. 411
land use and agriculture *see* forestry exploitation
Lareau, T. 401
Larson, D. 405
Lasserre, P. 258
Laughland, A. 399
Layard, R. 417
lead 3, 40, 219, 220
Leal, D. 29
Leamer, E. 386
Lebanon 84
Ledyard, J. 24
Leivestad, H. 162
Leonard, D. 186, 349
Levhari, D. 313, 319, 322
Lewis, T.R. 75, 77, 267

L'Hopital's rule 256–7
Lichtenstein, S. 414
linear demand curve 232–5, 246–8
linear programming 100–2, 145
Liroff, R. 137
lobbying over policies 16–17
logistic growth curve 181
Long, N.V. 339–40
Loomis, J. 376, 390, 399, 407
Loury, G.C. 244, 245, 247–8, 266
Louviere, J. 401, 402, 408
Lovelock 1
Lozada, G.A. 13
Lutz, E. 434
Lyon, R. 147

Maani, S. 414
MAC *see* marginal abatement costs
MacAulay, T.G. 313
McFadden, D. 401
McGartland, A. 140
Machina, M. 368–9
McKee, M. 28
MacKenzie, J. 162
McLusky, D. 3
Macmillan, D. 163
McMullen, L.D. 34
Madagascar 22–3
Madalla, F. 409
Magat, W. 414
Malawi 443
Malaysia 436
Maler, K.-G. 163, 166, 171–3, 434
Mali 443
Malliaris, A.G. 207
Maloney, M. 144
Malthus, T. 223
Malueg, D.A. 151
marginal abatement costs 108–9, 111, 113–15, 118–21, 123
marginal benefit of delay 342, 343
marginal costs, non-convex 47
marginal damage cost 123–4, 167
marginal opportunity cost 342, 343
market failure 22–56
  asymmetric information 49–56; adverse selection 54–6; environmental shirking 50; moral hazard 50–4
  Coase theorem 28–9
  externalities 29–37; pollution, socially and privately optimal level of 30; self-protection 35, 36

market failure (*continued*)
incomplete markets 24–9; pollution, socially optimal level of 26, 27
non-convexities 46–9; multi-peaked net benefit curve 49; non-convex marginal costs 47; pollution, optimal level of 48; single-peaked net benefit curve 47
non-exclusion and the commons 37–42; co-ordination game 42; open access and prisoners' dilemma 41; property rights and resource use, efficiency of 37–9
non-rivalry and public goods   42–6
market structure and exploitation 228–48
competitive and monopoly extraction with linear demand curve   232–5
competitive structure and socially optimal extraction   229–30
constant elasticity demand curve 235–6
monopoly   230–2
see also imperfect competition
Marshallian consumer surplus   362
materials balance principle   11–12, 13
maximum principle application to fishery management   189–202
comparative dynamics   201–2
eigenvalues and eigenvectors   195
linear fishery problem   190–1
non-linear fishery problem   191–2
phase-plane diagram   193, 198
stability   193–9
sufficiency conditions   199–200
trajectory types   197
maximum principle of optimal control theory   182–9
current-value Hamiltonian   188–9
necessary conditions   182–6
transversality conditions   186–8
Mayflower problem   221, 224
MBD   *see* marginal benefit of delay
MDC   *see* marginal damage cost
mean annual increment   439
Mee, L.   39
Mendelsohn, R.   252, 407, 408
mercury   40, 84, 219, 220
methane   5, 121, 123, 160
Mexico   436, 443
Michaelis, P.   121–3
Middle East   443
Mill, J.S.   221

Miller, M.H.   264
Milliman, S.R.   119, 151
Milon, J.   393
mineralogical threshold   219
Mintzis, M.   165
Mirman, L.J.   313, 319, 322
Misiolek, W.   143, 144
Missfeldt, F.   159, 166
Mitchell, R.   384, 393, 399
Mitra, T.   340
mixing, uniformity of   161–3
Moazzami, B.   223
MOC   *see* marginal opportunity cost
Moffatt, I.   110–11, 141–2
Mohr, E.   170
Moldova   39
monopoly   230–5
Montgomery, W.   134, 136
Montreal protocol   6, 170–1
moral hazard   49, 50–4
Morse, C.   221, 222, 255
Moucher, P.   169
Moxey, A.   145–6
multiple pollutants   151–5
Muniz, I.P.   162
Munro, A.   144, 150, 396   –7
Murdoch, J.   414
Myers, N.   43

N₂O   *see* nitrous oxide
Nash, J.F./equilibrium
forestry exploitation   350
game theory   15–17, 19, 20
market failure   41–2
non-renewable natural resources   245
renewable resource economics 314–15, 317, 319, 320, 321, 322, 324
sequential games   18
transboundary pollution problems 167, 168, 169, 172, 173
Nash–Cournot equilibrium   237, 238–9, 239–41, 243, 244, 293
National Farmers Union   16–17
National Oceanic and Atmospheric Administration   385–6, 396, 399, 400
natural capital stock   428–30, 441
natural gas   223
natural resource exploitation   177–214
discrete-time maximum principle 202–3
dynamic programming   203–6

natural resource exploitation (*continued*)
  elementary capital theory 179–82;
    logistic growth curve 181;
    non-renewable 180–1;
    renewable 181–2
  Wiener processes, Itô's processes and
    stochastic calculus 206–14; Itô's
    lemma application 210–14;
    mathematical introduction 207–10;
    see also maximum principle
    application
natural resources 216–25
  accounting 434–6
  scarcity, measurement of 217–25;
    abundances of selected materials
    220; basics 217–20; economic rent
    224–5; mineralogical threshold 219;
    real prices 222–4; reserves 218, 220;
    unit cost measures 221–2
  types and classification 216–17; *see
    also* natural resource exploitation;
    non-renewable; renewable
Navrud, S. 163
Ncher, P.A. 185, 265
Nelson, R. 136, 154
net benefit curve 47, 49
net domestic product 435
net national product 434, 436–9
net present value 213–14
Netherlands 62, 71, 72, 127–8, 153,
  162, 436, 443
New Zealand 161
Newberry, D.M.G. 237, 241
Newton's method 232
NH₃ *see* ammonia
Nigeria 443
Nisbet, E.G. 1, 3, 165
nitrate pollution 34, 145–6
nitrogen 115, 118, 151, 162
  dioxide 161
  fertilizer 126
  oxide 117
nitrous oxide 5, 121, 123, 160
NO *see* nitrous oxide
NO₂ *see* nitrogen oxide
NOAA *see* National Oceanographic
  and Atmospheric Administration
Noll, R. 88
non-cooperation 167, 314–15
non-compliance fees 79–84
non-convexities 46–9
non-exclusion 37–42
non-linear cost 248–50

non-market valuation theory 356–81
  divergence in value measures 362–4
  duality and expenditure function
    364–5
  environmental goods 357–62
  environmental hazards: value
    measures and indirect utility
    function 365–7
  total value and warm glows 372–6
  unfamiliarity and learning 376–81
  value formation and preference
    learning 377
  valuing risk and *ex ante* measures of
    value 368–72
  willingness to pay-willingness to
    accept 363, 366
non-point pollution 145–6
non-renewable natural resources 227–70
  government policy towards taxation
    264–5
  oligopolistic extraction 244–8; with
    linear demand curve 246–8; Loury's
    theory 247–8
  theory application 258–64; Hotelling's
    theorem 258–63; output equation
    262
  uncertainty and rate of extraction
    266–70; *see also* market structure
    and exploitation; production
    technology and extraction costs
non-renewable resources 180–1
  cartel 236–9
non-rivalry 42–6
non-uniformly mixed pollutants 138–9
  see also pollution taxes
Nordhaus, W.D. 160, 166, 255
Norgaard, R.B. 221, 225, 425, 433,
  440, 444
North America 38, 228, 284–6, 340
  see also Canada; United States
North Sea 106, 159, 160, 218, 259
Norway 72, 84, 127, 172, 436
NOx *see* nitrogen

O₃ *see* ozone
Oates, W. 64, 140, 145
  pollution taxes 107, 112–13, 115,
    120, 126
O'Byrne, P. 414
O'Connor, D. 60
oil 40, 218, 223–4, 227, 228, 243,
  247–8, 259
Oil Pollution Act 1990 385

oligopolistic extraction   244–8
Olson, L.J.   125–6
Olson, M.   43
O'Neil, W.   116, 144
Oniki, H.   201
open access   41, 348
Opschoor, H.   428
Opschoor, J.B.   153, 440
optimal control   *see* maximum principle
Organisation for Economic Cooperation
    and Development
    environmental protection   60
    natural resources   217, 223
    non-renewable natural resources   228
    pollution taxes   107, 124
    tradeable pollution permits   153–4
    transboundary pollution problems
        163
Organisation of Petroleum Exporting
    Countries   236, 242, 243, 244
Ostrom, E.   41–2
Ouellette, P.   258
output equation   262
output, rising   9–10
overfishing   287
oxygen   *see* biological oxygen demand;
    dissolved oxygen
ozone   160, 165–6

Palmquist, R.   413
Pan, J.H.   146
Papua New Guinea   443
Pareto
    market failure   24, 25, 28, 29, 31–3,
        43
    renewable resource economics .314,
        315
    transboundary pollution problems
        167, 168, 172
Patterson, D.   398, 400
pay-offs   14, 15, 314, 315, 316
Pearce, D.W.   127, 428, 442
performance bonds   85–7
permits   *see* tradeable pollution permits
Perrings, C.   85–6, 426, 427, 440, 443–6
Pesaran, M.H.   258, 259, 262–3, 264
Pezzey, J.   107, 123–4, 426, 443
Philippines   436, 443
Pigou, A.C.   60, 61, 299, 350
Pimental, D.   10
Pindyck, R.S.   207, 210, 212–13, 242,
    251, 254, 267, 325, 328, 329, 330

Plourde, C.G.   125
Poisson process   352
Poland   39, 94, 443
Polasky, S.   244–5, 247
polluter pays principle   93, 107, 123–4
pollution   30
    market failure   26–8, 29, 30, 31, 33,
        36, 40, 48
    multiple pollutants   151–5
    non-point   145–6
    non-uniformly mixed   138–9; *see also*
        under pollution taxes
    optimal level   48
    production function   126
    socially optimal level   26, 27, 59
    socially and privately optimal level
        30
    subsidy   75; *see also* pollution taxes;
        tradeable pollution permits;
        transboundary
pollution taxes   74, 106–28
    efficiency properties 107–15; marginal
        abatement costs for a firm 109;
        pollution control in Tees estuary
        109–11
    non-uniformly mixed pollutants
        115–28; air quality 117–18; carbon
        tax in Netherlands 127–8; financial
        burden 124; greenhouse gases 123;
        multiple pollutants 121–3; savings
        under innovation 119, 120; stock
        pollutants 125–6
polychlorinated biphenyls (PCBs)   3
population growth models   276–80
Porter, R.   417
Portney, P.   136, 386, 418
precautionary principle   5–6
President's Council of Economic
    Advisors   137
Price, C.   397
price rationing   61–78
    ambient charge   66–71
    asymmetric information and
        environmental subsidy   77
    changes given uncertainty   65
    emission charges   61–6
    output   63, 70
    pollution tax   74
    product charges   71–2
    subsidies   72–8, 79
Prince, R.   119, 151
prisoners' dilemma   41
product charges   71–2

production technology and extraction
    costs 248–58
competitive industry with non-linear
    cost 248–50
heterogeneous reserve with
    exploration 250–4
resource scarcity 254–8
Proops, J. 224, 443
property rights 24–7, 29, 37–9, 348
public goods 42–6

quantity rationing 87–91
    mixed incentive system 91
    under uncertainty 89
quasiconcave programming *see* Arrow–
    Enthoven sufficiency theorem
quota system 299–300

Radnor, R. 386
Rae, D. 401
rainforests 335–6, 344–5
    see also foresty exploitation
RAINS model 150
Randall, A. 362, 376–7, 384, 389, 393,
    396, 430
rational expectation hypothesis 262
rationing *see* price; quantity
Rawles, K. 430
real prices 222–4
'Red List' substances 106
Reed, W.J. 330, 352
Reijinders, L. 440
renewable natural resources 181–2
renewable resource economics 275,
    278, 280, 290, 301, 309, 311–12, 319,
    325, 330
renewable resources 274–333
    fisheries policy 298–302; individual
        transferable quota system 299–300;
        taxes 299; traditional bioeconomic
        theory 301–2
    fishing under uncertainty 325–32;
        discrete-time model 330–2; Itô's
        lemma, application of 325–30;
        stochastic stock recruitment 331
    optimal investment in harvesting
        308–13
    population growth models 276–80;
        growth curve showing depensation
        278; logistic growth curve 277;
        Ricker curves 280; simple
        population cycle 279; stock growth

in continuous time 276–8; stock
    growth in discrete time 278–80
static models of fishery exploitation in
    continuous time 281–7; equilibrium
    between fishing effort and catch
    283; equilibrium between fishing
    effort and catch with critical
    depensation 284; equilibrium
    between fishing effort and stock
    283; equilibrium between fishing
    effort and stock with critical
    depensation 283; harvesting effect
    on population change 281; North
    American lobster fishery 284–6
theory application and discrete-time
    model 303–8; discrete-time
    maximum principle 303–4; dynamic
    programming 308; North West
    Atlantic harp seal 304–7; *see also*
    comparative dynamic models;
    strategic behaviour
Repetto, R. 348, 435, 436
reserves 218, 220, 250–4
resource use, efficiency of 37–9
Ricardo, D. 221, 223
Ricker, W.E. 279–80, 320
Ridker, R.G. 412
Riley, J.G. 207
rising output and rising energy use
    9–10
risk valuation 368–72
Roberts, M. 90
Romania 39
Rosen, S. 411
Rosenberg, N. 121
Rowe, R. 392, 393, 395
Rowley, C. 108, 109–10
Royal Commission on Environmental
    Pollution 109, 153
Rubinstein, A. 350
Ruffell, R. 398, 403, 406–7
Ruitenbeek, H. 164
Russell, C. 61, 72, 85, 145, 407
Russian Republic 39

safe minimum standards 430–1, 441–3
Salant, S.W. 237, 244
Samuelson, P.A. 43, 167, 344
Sandler, T. 17, 43, 349
Saudi Arabia 244
Scandinavia 161, 162
    see also Denmark; Finland; Norway;
    Sweden

scarcity 8, 254–8
  see also natural resources
Schaefer, M.B. 282, 285, 286, 288, 293, 296, 300, 309, 391
Schuman, H. 386
Schwartz, N.L. 186, 200, 206
Scottish River Purification Boards 106
scrap-value function 187
seals 304–7
Segerson, K. 66–7
Seip, K. 400
self-protection 35, 36
Sellar, C. 399, 409
separatrices 197–8, 199
El-Serafy, S. 432
Serbia 39
Seskin, E.P. 117, 118
sewage treatment works 109–10
sheep 409
Shogren, J. 28, 36, 61, 86, 87, 362, 371, 374, 375, 379, 400
Shortle, J. 61
Shultze, C.L. 120
side-payments 167–8
silicon 216
Sinden, J. 395
sites of special scientific interests 431
Skinner, B. 218, 219
Slade, M.E. 222, 223, 255
Slovakia 39
Slovenia 39
Small, G. 284
Smith, A. 22
Smith, J.B. 284, 285
Smith, T.R. 255
Smith, V.K. 373, 375, 383, 399, 407, 408, 409, 411, 414
SMS *see* safe minimum standards
SNA *see* system of national accounts
Soil Conservation Service 125
Solow, R.M. 251–2, 386, 397, 426–7, 446
Solow–Hartwick 433–41
  gross national product 434–41;
    adjustment for environmental degradation: Zimbabwe 439–40;
    natural resource accounting 434–6
  methodological basis 433–4
South America 335
SP model 402
Spain 39, 172, 319
Spash, C. 161, 164, 376, 384, 399, 404, 413, 417, 430

Spence, M. 90
Spitzer, M. 28
state implementation plan 117–18, 136, 141
steady-state equilibrium 182
Stiglitz, J.E. 49, 51, 232, 235
Stoll, J. 362
Storey, D. 115, 120
Strand, J. 400
strategic behaviour in fishery management 313–24
  cooperation 315–17, 322–4
  dynamic games 317–19
  fish wars 319–22, 324
  Nash bargaining solution 317
  non-cooperation 314–15
  pay-offs 314, 315, 316
  steady-state equilibria in fish war 324
STWs *see* sewage treatment works
submerged acquatic vegetation 416–17
subsidies 72–8, 79
sulphur dioxide 1, 2, 106, 108, 115, 126
  tradeable pollution permits 137, 138, 140, 147, 151, 152
  transboundary pollution problems 161, 162, 163, 168, 172
Superfund waste sites 357
sustainable development 425–46
  Common–Perrings model 443–6
  Daly's operational principles 431–2
  Hartwick–Solow approach 426–7
  natural capital stock 428–30, 441
  Pearce–Atkinson measure 442–3
  safe minimum standards approach 430–1, 441–3
  sustainability versus efficiency 433
  see also Solow–Hartwick approach
Swallow, S.K. 338, 341, 342
Sweden 72, 84, 172
Swierzbinski, J.E. 252
Switzerland 84
Syria 84
system of national accounts 434–5, 436, 440

Tahvonen, O. 168–9
taxation 117–18, 264–5, 299, 350–1
Taylor, C. 145
Taylor, R.E. 5, 6
Taylor series expansion, first-order 194
TCM *see* travel cost method
Thailand 2

Thayer, M. 392, 414
Tietenberg, T. 117–18, 134, 135, 136,
    137, 140, 147, 148–9, 150, 171, 223
tin 223
Tirole, J. 14, 313, 318
Tisdell, C. 430
Titus, J. 161
Townsend, R.E. 284, 286
tradeable pollution permits 87–91,
    130–55
  ambient 139, 140, 141, 152
  auctions 146–7
  economic instruments 153–5
  imperfectly competitive permit
    markets 143–6
  innovation 150–1, 152
  marketable 87–91
  multiple pollutants 151–5
  non-uniformly mixed pollutants
    138–9
  sequencing of trades 147–50
  trading rules and design of permit
    systems 139–43; uniformly mixed
    pollutants 130–8; firm's optimal
    response 131; revenues and
    expenditures 133; supply and
    demand 132; United States
    environmental policy 136–8
traditional bioeconomic theory 301–2
transboundary pollution control 159–73
  and game theory 166–73;
    international environmental
    agreements 170–1; Maler's acid rain
    game 171–3; non-cooperative and
    full cooperative outcomes 167
  as problem of international
    externalities 163–6
  uniformity of damages 159–61
  uniformity of mixing 161–3
travel cost method 399, 405, 406
  hedonic 407–8
Trice, A. 404
Tschirhart, J. 31
Tucker *see* Kuhn–Tucker
Turkey 39
Turner, R.K. 222, 428
Tversky, A. 396

Ukraine 39
Ulph, A. 241
ultra-violet light 165, 166
uncertainty 5–6, 65, 89, 266–70
  see also renewable resources

uniform emissions tax 117–18
uniformly mixed pollutants *see* tradeable
    pollution permits
unit cost measures 221–2
United Kingdom 2, 37–9, 111
  energy use to gross domestic product
    ratios 9, 10
  environmental costs and benefits
    valuation 394, 395, 397, 402, 403,
    405, 406, 415
  forestry exploitation 335, 344
  natural resources 223
  non-renewable natural resources 259
  pollution taxes 106, 107, 109–11
  renewable resources 319
  sustainable development 428, 429,
    431
  tradeable pollution permits 141–3,
    145, 150, 153, 154
  transboundary pollution problems
    160, 161, 162, 164, 171, 172
United Nations 163, 164, 171, 434, 436
United States 2
  Development Association 145
  energy use 10
  environmental costs and benefits
    valuation 384, 385, 389, 394, 399,
    401, 404–5, 409, 413–14, 416, 418
  environmental policy and tradeable
    permits 136–8
  environmental protection 60, 62, 73,
    84, 87–8, 93
  forestry exploitation 335, 341–3, 348
  market failure 31, 33, 34
  natural resources 221, 223, 224
  non-market valuation 357, 373, 375,
    376
  non-renewable natural resources 265
  pollution control 125–6
  pollution taxes 106, 117, 125, 128
  sustainable development 436, 440,
    443
  tradeable pollution permits 132,
    138, 140–1, 144, 147, 148, 153,
    154
  transboundary pollution problems
    161, 162, 163, 165, 166, 171
Upton, C.W. 264

valuation theory *see* non-market
Van Ierland, E. 162, 163
Van Long, N. 186
Van Pelt, M.J.F. 429

Varian, H.R.　178
Vaughn, W.　407
Vickrey second price auction　147
Viscusi, W.　414
volatile organic compounds　111
Von Stackelberg equilibrium　18, 20, 237, 238–9, 241–3
Vos, H.　153

Walker, M.　115, 120, 152
Walsh, R.G.　398
Wan, F.　251–2
Wan, H.Y.　340
warm glows　372–6
water quality　*see* groundwater; biological oxygen demand
Webb, A.H.　162
Weinstein, M.C.　266
Weitzman, M.　64, 434
Welsh, H.　163
Welsh, M.　394
western Europe　71–2, 93
Whalley, J.　169
White, B.　145–6
White, L.J.　151
White Paper 1990　6
Wiener processes　206–14
Williams, M.　401, 402, 408
Willig, R.　362, 395
willingness to accept　358, 361–4, 366–7, 369
willingness to accept compensation　383, 384
    environmental costs and benefits valuation　386–90, 392, 394–6, 401

willingness to pay
    environmental costs and benefits valuation　383–4, 386–90, 392–9 *passim*, 401, 403
    non-market valuation　358, 360–7 *passim*, 369
    tradeable pollution permits　147, 148
    transboundary pollution problems　164, 165–6
Willis, K.　384, 398, 402, 406, 413, 414, 415
Wilman, E.　406
Wilson, J.A.　301–2
Wood, S.　404
World Bank　171
World Resources Institute　439
Wright, R.F.　162
WTA　*see* willingness to accept
WTAC　*see* willingness to accept compensation
WTP　*see* willingness to pay

Xepapadeas, A.　79–80

Yandle, B.　144

Zeckhauser, R.J.　266
Zimbabwe　439–40
zinc　40, 220
Zwartendyk, J.　217–18
Zylicz, T.　94, 152